D1366038

Effects of Information Capitalism and Globalization on Teaching and Learning

Blessing F. Adeoye
University of Lagos, Nigeria

Lawrence Tomei
Robert Morris University, USA

A volume in the Advances in Educational
Technologies and Instructional Design (AETID)
Book Series

An Imprint of IGI Global

Managing Director:	Lindsay Johnston
Production Editor:	Jennifer Yoder
Development Editor:	Erin O'Dea
Acquisitions Editor:	Kayla Wolfe
Typesetter:	John Crodian
Cover Design:	Jason Mull

Published in the United States of America by
Information Science Reference (an imprint of IGI Global)
701 E. Chocolate Avenue
Hershey PA, USA 17033
Tel: 717-533-8845
Fax: 717-533-8661
E-mail: cust@igi-global.com
Web site: http://www.igi-global.com

Copyright © 2014 by IGI Global. All rights reserved. No part of this publication may be reproduced, stored or distributed in any form or by any means, electronic or mechanical, including photocopying, without written permission from the publisher. Product or company names used in this set are for identification purposes only. Inclusion of the names of the products or companies does not indicate a claim of ownership by IGI Global of the trademark or registered trademark.

Library of Congress Cataloging-in-Publication Data

Effects of information capitalism and globalization on teaching and learning /
Blessing F. Adeoye and Lawrence Tomei, editors.
     pages cm
Includes bibliographical references and index.
   ISBN 978-1-4666-6162-2 (hardcover) -- ISBN 978-1-4666-6163-9 (ebook) --
ISBN 978-1-4666-6165-3 (print & perpetual access) 1. Educational technology.
2. Information technology. 3. Education--Effect of technological innovations
on. I. Adeoye, Blessing F., 1957- II. Tomei, Lawrence A.
 LB1028.3.E4239 2014
 371.33--dc23
                              2014013855

This book is published in the IGI Global book series Advances in Educational Technologies and Instructional Design (AE-TID) (ISSN: 2326-8905; eISSN: 2326-8913)

British Cataloguing in Publication Data
A Cataloguing in Publication record for this book is available from the British Library.

All work contributed to this book is new, previously-unpublished material. The views expressed in this book are those of the authors, but not necessarily of the publisher.

For electronic access to this publication, please contact: eresources@igi-global.com.

Advances in Educational Technologies and Instructional Design (AETID) Book Series

Lawrence A. Tomei
Robert Morris University, USA

ISSN: 2326-8905
EISSN: 2326-8913

Mission

Education has undergone, and continues to undergo, immense changes in the way it is enacted and distributed to both child and adult learners. From distance education, Massive-Open-Online-Courses (MOOCs), and electronic tablets in the classroom, technology is now an integral part of the educational experience and is also affecting the way educators communicate information to students.

The **Advances in Educational Technologies & Instructional Design (AETID) Book Series** is a resource where researchers, students, administrators, and educators alike can find the most updated research and theories regarding technology's integration within education and its effect on teaching as a practice.

Coverage

- Instructional Design
- Educational Telecommunications
- Social Media Effects on Education
- Higher Education Technologies
- Virtual School Environments
- Adaptive Learning
- Bring-Your-Own-Device
- Game-Based Learning
- Hybrid Learning
- Curriculum Development

IGI Global is currently accepting manuscripts for publication within this series. To submit a proposal for a volume in this series, please contact our Acquisition Editors at Acquisitions@igi-global.com or visit: http://www.igi-global.com/publish/.

The Advances in Educational Technologies and Instructional Design (AETID) Book Series (ISSN 2326-8905) is published by IGI Global, 701 E. Chocolate Avenue, Hershey, PA 17033-1240, USA, www.igi-global.com. This series is composed of titles available for purchase individually; each title is edited to be contextually exclusive from any other title within the series. For pricing and ordering information please visit http://www.igi-global.com/book-series/advances-educational-technologies-instructional-design/73678. Postmaster: Send all address changes to above address. Copyright © 2014 IGI Global. All rights, including translation in other languages reserved by the publisher. No part of this series may be reproduced or used in any form or by any means – graphics, electronic, or mechanical, including photocopying, recording, taping, or information and retrieval systems – without written permission from the publisher, except for non commercial, educational use, including classroom teaching purposes. The views expressed in this series are those of the authors, but not necessarily of IGI Global.

Titles in this Series

For a list of additional titles in this series, please visit: www.igi-global.com

E-Learning as a Socio-Cultural System A Multidimensional Analysis
Vaiva Zuzevičiūtė (Mykolas Romeris University, Lithuania) Edita Butrimė (Lithuanian University of Health Sciences, Lithuania) Daiva Vitkutė-Adžgauskienė (Vytautas Magnus University, Lithuania) Vladislav Vladimirovich Fomin (Vytautas Magnus University, Lithuania) and Kathy Kikis-Papadakis (Foundation for Research and Technology, Greece)
Information Science Reference • copyright 2014 • 349pp • H/C (ISBN: 9781466661547) • US $195.00 (our price)

Engaging Language Learners through Technology Integration Theory, Applications, and Outcomes
Shuai Li (Georgia State University, USA) and Peter Swanson (Georgia State University, USA)
Information Science Reference • copyright 2014 • 388pp • H/C (ISBN: 9781466661745) • US $185.00 (our price)

Handbook of Research on Education and Technology in a Changing Society
Victor C.X. Wang (Florida Atlantic University, USA)
Information Science Reference • copyright 2014 • 1217pp • H/C (ISBN: 9781466660465) • US $495.00 (our price)

Educational Technology Use and Design for Improved Learning Opportunities
Mehdi Khosrow-Pour (Information Resources Management Association, USA)
Information Science Reference • copyright 2014 • 359pp • H/C (ISBN: 9781466661028) • US $215.00 (our price)

Handbook of Research on Digital Tools for Writing Instruction in K-12 Settings
Rebecca S. Anderson (University of Memphis, USA) and Clif Mims (University of Memphis, USA)
Information Science Reference • copyright 2014 • 684pp • H/C (ISBN: 9781466659827) • US $325.00 (our price)

Cases on Teaching Critical Thinking through Visual Representation Strategies
Leonard J. Shedletsky (University of Southern Maine, USA) and Jeffrey S. Beaudry (University of Southern Maine, USA)
Information Science Reference • copyright 2014 • 568pp • H/C (ISBN: 9781466658165) • US $215.00 (our price)

Online Tutor 2.0 Methodologies and Case Studies for Successful Learning
Francisco José García-Peñalvo (University of Salamanca, Spain) and Antonio Miguel Seoane Pardo (University of Salamanca, Spain)
Information Science Reference • copyright 2014 • 384pp • H/C (ISBN: 9781466658325) • US $195.00 (our price)

Andragogical and Pedagogical Methods for Curriculum and Program Development
Victor C. X. Wang (Florida Atlantic University, USA) and Valerie C. Bryan (Florida Atlantic University, USA)
Information Science Reference • copyright 2014 • 501pp • H/C (ISBN: 9781466658721) • US $205.00 (our price)

www.igi-global.com

701 E. Chocolate Ave., Hershey, PA 17033
Order online at www.igi-global.com or call 717-533-8845 x100
To place a standing order for titles released in this series, contact: cust@igi-global.com
Mon-Fri 8:00 am - 5:00 pm (est) or fax 24 hours a day 717-533-8661

Editorial Advisory Board

Abubakar Sadiq Bappah, *Abubakar Tafawa Balewa University, Nigeria*
Rex Crawley, *Robert Morris University, USA*
Florence Folami-Adeoye, *Millikin University, USA*
Robin Musson, *Independent Researcher, USA*
Anthony Robins, *Robert Morris University, USA*
Robert Loyal Siedenburg, *University of Illinois, USA*

Table of Contents

Section 1
Introduction

Chapter 1
    Blessing F. Adeoye, University of Lagos, Nigeria

Section 2
Cross-Cultural Communication and the Innovative Use of Digital Technology

Chapter 2
    Michele T. Cole, Robert Morris University, USA
    Daniel J. Shelley, Robert Morris University, USA
    Louis B. Swartz, Robert Morris University, USA
    Blessing F. Adeoye, University of Lagos, Nigeria

Chapter 3
    Blessing F. Adeoye, University of Lagos, Nigeria
    E. B. Anyikwa, University of Lagos, Nigeria

Chapter 4
    Ogunlade B. Olusola, Ekiti State University, Nigeria

Section 3
Technology Integration in the Classroom

Section 5
Globalization and Education

Detailed Table of Contents

Section 1
Introduction

Chapter 1

The author of this chapter explored informational capitalism, using a population of students and faculty
from and American university, and students and lecturers from an African university. The study explored
how digital technologies have transformed the productive forces of capitalism and enabled a global
economy. Interestingly, neither students nor faculty felt that cultural inclination had a significant impact
on their use of Web 2.0, but the majority of University of Lagos participants believed that adoption of
Web 2.0 supports cultural promotion.

Section 2
Cross-Cultural Communication and the Innovative Use of Digital Technology

Chapter 2

This chapter presents the results of a pilot study conducted in the summer of 2013, in which researchers
sought to discover how students and instructors at two universities were using selected digital technologies
in their coursework. To the extent that digital technologies were being used, did students find their use

to be helpful in learning course material? Researchers surveyed undergraduate students at an African university and an American university. There were significant differences in how helpful to learning the uses of certain technologies were, as perceived by the students. Another significant difference occurred in how soon new digital technologies would be adopted, with the American university lagging behind its African counterpart.

Chapter 3

Blessing F. Adeoye, University of Lagos, Nigeria
E. B. Anyikwa, University of Lagos, Nigeria

Especially in Africa, the increasing availability and use of technologies has amounted to a revolution that has brought immense change to teaching and learning at institutions of higher learning throughout the continent. This chapter surveys a wide range of technology devices and their application in different African Universities, showing the level of information capitalism, access to technology, and quality of higher education in Africa. The conclusion is that, given access to the proper technology, teaching and learning can be made available to thousands of additional students in Africa when Universities operate 24-7 online tutorials as a result of ICT and other technology infrastructure development.

Chapter 4

Ogunlade B. Olusola, Ekiti State University, Nigeria

This chapter focuses on the concept of instructional technology (IT) as a crucial element in education. Instructional technologies support curricula, promoting effectiveness and efficiency in academic performance at all levels of education in Nigerian schools. The chapter works toward a clearer definition of instructional technology, IT, as educational problem-solvers focus on emerging technologies for teaching and learning. The chapter also deals with some of the challenges of applying instructional technologies, the effective organization of instructional materials in schools, the usefulness of local instructional packages, and obstacles to using instructional technology in Nigerian schools.

Chapter 5

Ofomegbe Daniel Ekhareafo, University of Benin, Nigeria
Oroboh Ambrose Uchenunu, University of Benin, Nigeria

This chapter takes a look at the need for graduates in today's information age to be competitive in the marketplace upon graduation. It emphasizes that classroom ICT use has the potential to improve the capacity of the facilitators, but also the learning of students at all levels. Despite financial and other major challenges to integrating technology in learning, the chapter urges proactive steps to address the current, relatively low integration rate of ICT in African learning centers. It points out that graduates are competing with others with overseas qualifications, and with professionals already in the workplace, who already possess the requisite technological skills required today.

Section 3
Technology Integration in the Classroom

Chapter 6

Jerome Idiegbeyan-Ose, Covenant University, Nigeria
Mary Idahosa, Benson Idahosa University, Nigeria
Egbe Adewole-Odeshi, Covenant University, Nigeria

This chapter discusses the adoption and use of ICT in libraries and the implications of such adoption and use for the educational systems involved. It reports on a study to determine the present state of ICT in libraries throughout Nigeria, and lists some of the challenges faced in the adoption of ICT by libraries. It also documents some effective remedies to those challenges.

Chapter 7

Florence F. Folami, Millikin University, USA

This chapter explores the effectiveness of using Facebook to create a social network to improve community health improvement. It discusses social networking group reach rates and the effectiveness of a social network in delivering health messages and improving community health knowledge. A two-year study showed overall positive outcomes in reach, response time, and group engagement.

Chapter 8

Nwachukwu Prince Ololube, Ignatius Ajuru University of Education, Nigeria

The chapter explores the impact of the changing context of information technology (IT) and information systems (ISs) on teacher education (TE). The chapter uncovers a serious problem, as policy makers associated with educational programs look to market-based solutions without considering the challenges preventing effective integration and use of ITs and ISs in TE, particularly in developing economies. Using a theory-based method of analysis, the chapter gathers, reviews, and analyzes contemporary views and ideas about education and technology.

Chapter 9

Stephen Oyeyemi Adenle, University of Lagos, Nigeria
Jennifer N. L. Ughelu, University of Lagos, Nigeria

The chapter discusses the use of instructional media in teaching and learning basic sciences in primary and secondary schools. It concludes that these media are effective in driving home the lesson point of the subject being taught, and that they reduce stress for both teacher and student. The imaginative use of well-planned visual aids during classroom lessons are shown to boost student academic performance for physics, chemistry, biology, and mathematics. The chapter demonstrated that the use of instructional media had a positive impact on student learning outcomes.

This chapter covers e-portfolio teaching approaches and how andragogy and Bloom's Digital Taxonomy can be integrated into teaching and learning to provoke active learning through e-portfolio development. The chapter connects andragogy (the method and practice of teaching adult students) and integrates educational objectives into Bloom's cognitive domain as updated by Anderson and Krathwohl and aligned to the digital realm by Churches to serve as a model for teaching Web portfolio development in undergraduate courses.

As technology's presence in higher education rises, so does its cultural impact. Scholars have widely differing perspectives on the proper role of technology in higher education. This chapter works to reconcile such scholarly differences, using a constructive hermeneutic in our postmodern age to understand the limited and biased ground of one's own perspective. The chapter also presents a decision model for educators to evaluate uses of technology in higher education.

As the use of social networking sites and Web 2.0 tools are increases, research shows that education via Web 2.0 tools can increase student motivation and interest for learning. The chapter suggests that a positive teaching environment can be created using social networking sites in which Web 2.0 tools allow effective learning. It discusses a number of Web 2.0 tools available for creating an effective virtual learning environment and their positive effect on students.

The chapter reviews data showing that increased access to ICT tools and resources provides opportunities for learning technologies. The chapter focuses on classroom integration of social media among a group of Nigerian graduate students using asynchronous online discussion. The 33 participants engaged in a threaded discussion for 14 weeks at the College of Medicine, University of Ibadan. A major barrier to participation in AOD is limited access to computer and Internet facilities. The chapter recommends improvement of ICT infrastructure in on-campus residential environments for cheaper, unrestricted technology access.

Xiaobin Li, Brock University, Canada

Although China has the most Internet users of any nation (591 million users as of 2013), a lower percentage of the Chinese population (44%) has used the Internet than is the case in the United States (78%). The chapter discusses the effects ICT has on Chinese elementary and secondary education, and some continuing challenges in ICT applications. It also examines the use of ICT in Chinese higher education, particularly in distance learning, and issues that must still be resolved.

Zhonggen Yu, Zhejiang Yuexiu University of Foreign Languages, China
Qianqian Xu, Zhejiang Yuexiu University of Foreign Languages, China

Although clickers have gained popularity in the West, they are less commonly used in the East. This chapter reviews studies on the impact of the use of clickers on learning and cognitive loads. It points out the effectiveness and possible positive influence clickers can have on cognitive loads, suggesting that clickers might be more appropriate for use in large-enrollment classes, where they can permit quiet and anonymous student polling. Students have demonstrated feeling less nervous when answering questions anonymously.

Abubakar Sadiq Bappah, Abubakar Tafawa Balewa University, Nigeria

This chapter explores the infant state of studies about the adoption of digital technologies in educational administration, especially in the administration and management of technical and engineering education facilities. It examines opportunities to adopt digital technologies to the administration of general education and its implications on technical and engineering education.

Ayotunde Adebayo, University of Lagos, Nigeria

This chapter explores knowledge management as a discipline that makes maximum use of the knowledge available to an organization and, at the same time, creates new knowledge. Knowledge management is about understanding, appreciating, and making use of the knowledge of individuals, developing an organizational culture where knowledge sharing can flourish. This process permits the organization to create value from its intellectual and knowledge-based assets, with the goal of continual knowledge development, drawing on the knowledge base of employees (thus the concept of reverse mentoring).

Section 5
Globalization and Education

Chapter 18

    Jenna Copper, Slippery Rock Area High School, USA

This chapter champions the value of cross-cultural communication practices in schools with innovative Information and Communication Technology (ICT) support. A detailed theoretical foundation justifies the inclusion of global perspectives in the classroom through cross-cultural communication, made possible by ICT. This chapter details the perceptions of 80 pre-K to 12 teachers via a survey study, which shaped the author's suggestions for practical ICT cross-cultural communication opportunities in the classroom. Implementation strategies include classroom-to-classroom and classroom-to-world cross-cultural communication opportunities. This chapter suggests practical solutions supported by solid theoretical justifications for utilizing ICT to facilitate cross-cultural communication and to improve student global awareness.

Chapter 19

    A. O. K. Noah, Lagos State University, Nigeria
    Adesoji A. Oni, University of Lagos, Nigeria
    Simeon A. Dosunmu, Lagos State University, Nigeria

The chapter reviews several definitions of globalization, uses the working definition of the establishment of global markets for goods and capital, leading to multiple linkages and interconnections among places, events, ideas, issues, and things. A major limiting factor for globalization in a given nation is an educational system is not geared toward fostering meaningful and desirable change for that society. To achieve such an education system orientation, teacher education must be predicated on producing globalization-friendly teachers.

Chapter 20

    Oladiran Stephen Olabiyi, University of Lagos, Nigeria

This chapter emphasizes the relevance of Information and Communication Technologies (ICTs) in the field of Technical Vocational Education and Training (TVET). It points out that the workaday world is continuously changing, even as ICT itself is developing. These changes pose challenges to 21st century workers and the institutions responsible for preparing the next generation of workers. The chapter develops definitions, philosophy, and objectives for TVET, concepts and types of ICT, and the need for effective use of ICT in TVET.

Chapter 21

This chapter discusses mobile health (m-Health), the use of portable electronic devices to communicate health information via a wireless, electronic network of base stations. The chapter suggests that m-Health technology has the potential to provide long-term patient support via wireless networks, without requiring patients to sacrifice their autonomy, but sees the chief obstacle to a more rational development of such a network as the resistance of medical professionals.

Chapter 22

This chapter takes a look at the influence of globalization on teaching and learning. It finds a very low level of information literacy among students because of what the authors see as the neglect of information literacy programs in Nigerian tertiary institutions. It goes on to provide practical suggestions for incorporating information literacy programs in institutions of higher learning in Nigeria, and it discusses some of the challenges of doing that. It suggests that tertiary institutions administrators begin seeing information literacy as an academic issue, rather than just a "library thing."

Chapter 23

This chapter reviews various definitions of the concept of community and goes on to explore the raison d'etre of especially rural community organizations, which have the specific goal of improving living conditions for those concerned. It examines input from various scholars and from the United Nations about the organization and constitution of such organizations, emphasizing that they must be of the people (grassroots organizations) and for the good of the people.

Foreword

This book shares experiences from professionals who raise a number of significant issues regarding the use of technology in teaching, learning, and administration. It also shares challenges associated with cross-cultural interaction, such as culturally bound misunderstandings that often arise from the assumptions we unknowingly make about the use of technology. It is crucial to deal effectively with cross-cultural issues in the utilization of technology in teaching and learning, but the present struggles of addressing such cultural issues might actually help us to creatively reshape our own views about technologies and education itself.

In her book, *Digital Dead End* (2011), Virginia Eubanks tells us that the idea that technology would pave the road to prosperity has been promoted through both boom and bust. She goes on to say:

Today we are told that universal broadband access, high-tech jobs, and cutting edge science will pull us out of our current economic downturn and move us toward social and economic equality. That social equality can be linked to capitalism. Capitalism is an economic system that is based on private owner-ship of capital goods and the means of production, and the creation of goods and services for profit. (Jenks, 1998)

It refers to the increasing importance of information within capitalism under conditions of globalization and rapid technological development. The idea of "information capitalism" is closely related to similar concepts such as the knowledge economy, the postindustrial society, the information society, and the network society.

The development of capitalism has taken a new dimension and has today succeeded in conquering ev-erywhere and everything in the world. Today the world is seen as a global village, where everything and everybody can be reached from anywhere through the power of emerging technologies. Globalization has to do with processes by which different human communities and nations become integrated into one single system called [the] global village. Therefore, whether as a historical process or an ideological construct, globalization brings about greater interaction between countries and peoples all over the world. (Tomlinson, 1997)

The Tomlinson Committee's *Report on Inclusive Education* (1996) defines this phenomenon as "a rapidly developing process of complex interconnections between societies, cultures, institutions, and individuals worldwide." It goes on to say, "It is a social process [that] involves compression of time and space, shrinking distances through a dramatic reduction in time taken—either physically or representationally—to cross them, so making the world seem smaller and, in a certain sense, bringing human beings 'closer' to one another" (Tomlinson, 1997).

This book explores issues concerning *information capitalism* and *globalization* and the challenges and solutions we all face in applying these ever-emerging technologies to teaching and learning. It also illustrates the different challenges we face when we utilize technology for teaching and learning in various cultural settings, and it provides first-hand experience of how those challenges are being resolved in several parts of the world. The book presents carefully researched examples of how globalization affects learning, and of how educational organizations can find, create, and adapt technology for use in other cultures.

The editors have woven many threads into a single fabric to meet the needs of a multiplicity of readers. However, the book is designed above all to help readers chart their own paths through the various contributions from many researchers that make up this book. Even if a reader browses the contents for material he or she finds of immediate interest, that person can find much that relates to his or her field or to the challenges he or she is facing in implementing advanced technologies in a learning setting.

This book offers the reader a perspective on education as a critical factor in and as closely related to economic and social policies, the environment, culture, political systems, economic development, and human physical well-being in societies around the world. It shares some of the current thinking about education as a separate factor of production, discussing its impact on human capital and the reciprocal interaction of technology and economic conditions.

One cannot overstate the importance of education as a means of fostering globalization. We would be hard pressed to find a knowledgeable person in the industrialized or developing world who would deny the importance of education to the economic health of any country. The same importance would apply to the effects of information, cross-cultural communication, and digital technology. Citizens of all nations need to understand how globalization works and the policy choices (particularly technology-related policy choices) facing them and their societies. At its most fundamental and rudimentary level, globalization is affected by shrinking geographically defined borders in an attempt to encourage the flow of goods and services, along with the people and culture, of nations around the world. Today more than ever before, people around the world are connected socially through the media and telecommunications, culturally through movements of people, economically through trade, environmentally through sharing one small planet, and politically through international relations and systems of regulation. This book explores the interrelationships and interdependence of our fellow human beings, as we all experience globalization through the increasing ubiquity of applied technology.

Robert Loyal Siedenburg
University of Illinois, USA

Robert Loyal Siedenburg *earned a diploma in Russian Language from the Defense Language Institute. He earned a great books AB (Bachelor of Arts degree) in the humanities from Shimer College, a BA (Bachelor of Arts degree) and an MA in history from Western Illinois University, and he did extensive additional graduate work in geography and education. Siedenburg set up several computer training labs for the Department of Defense, designed and taught the technology literacy program at the Lincoln's Challenge Academy in Rantoul, Illinois, and also set up their computer labs. He later served as instructional technology consultant for projects at Publication Services, Inc., in Champaign, Illinois. He is the author of the Glossary of Publishing Terms. He teaches business writing and American culture at the Special Program for Administrators, China Executive Leadership Programs, University of Illinois, and is a special tutor at the English Center USA.*

REFERENCES

Eubanks, V. (2011). *Digital dead end—Fighting for social justice in the information age.* Cambridge, MA: The MIT Press.

Jenks, C. (1998). *Core sociological dichotomies.* London: Sage.

Tomlinson, J. (1997). Cultural globalization and cultural imperialism. In A. Mohammadi (Ed.), *International communication and globalization* (pp. 170–190). London: Sage.

Preface

OVERVIEW

Technology has become a sociopolitical force around the world. There are many reasons for this; the most obvious one is that technological change is the main source of new areas of profitable accumulation of wealth. Educational institutions play a role in helping to facilitate the complex maneuvers by which the accumulation cycle works.

OBJECTIVE OF THE BOOK

The goals of this book include exploring issues concerning informational capitalism and globalization, the challenges and solutions for teaching and learning, and illustrating the different challenges faced when utilizing technology for teaching and learning in various cultural settings and how they were resolved. They also include how globalization affects learning and how educational organizations can find, create, or adapt technology for use in other cultures.

DESCRIPTION OF THE TARGET AUDIENCE

The target audience includes those with a professional interest in educational technology and information technology, whether they use such technology as a tool in teaching, use technology to develop learning materials, or administer a department or institution that uses or needs to use such technology. These people include legislators, educators, researchers, instructional material designers, and students. They also include higher education administrators and government officials with the responsibility of implementing the use of ever-improving technology into the school systems of the world.

OVERVIEW OF THE CONTENT

This book consists of 23 chapters.

Chapter 1: Effects of Information Capitalism and Globalization on Teaching and Learning in a Developed and in a Developing Country – A Cross-Cultural Study of Robert Morris University in the United States and University of Lagos in Nigeria

Using a descriptive survey, the author of this chapter explored informational capitalism, using a population of students and faculty from an American university and students and lecturers from an African university. The study explored how digital technologies have transformed the productive forces of capitalism and enabled a global economy.

Interestingly, neither students nor faculty felt that cultural inclination had a significant impact on their use of Web 2.0, but the majority of University of Lagos participants believed that adoption of Web 2.0 supports cultural promotion. This chapter is of particular value to instructional faculty who are designing coursework around Web 2.0 or its introduction, and to administrators who are dealing with funding challenges and rationalization for updating IT equipment and access on their campuses.

Chapter 2: Using Digital Technologies to Aid E-Learning – A Pilot Study

This chapter presents the results of a pilot study conducted in the summer of 2013 in which researchers sought to discover how students and instructors at two universities were using selected digital technologies in their coursework. To the extent that digital technologies were being used, did students find their use to be helpful in learning course material? Researchers surveyed undergraduate students at an African university and an American university. There were significant differences in how helpful to learning the uses of certain technologies were, as perceived by the students. Another significant difference occurred in how soon new digital technologies would be adopted, with the African university lagging behind its American counterpart.

This chapter is of particular value to those weighing the options of online course delivery, especially in this day of strained budgets and limited ability to offer as many course as desired. Administrators, department heads, and instructional staff preparing online course material can profit from reading this information.

Chapter 3: The Era of Digital Technology in Teaching and Learning in African Universities

Especially in Africa, the increasing availability and use of technologies has amounted to a revolution that has brought immense change to teaching and learning at institutions of higher learning throughout the continent. This chapter surveys a wide range of technology devices and their application in different African universities, showing the level of information capitalism, access to technology, and quality of higher education in Africa. The conclusion is that, given access to the proper technology, teaching and learning can be made available to thousands of additional students in Africa when universities operate 24-7 online tutorials as a result of ICT and other technological developments.

This chapter is very useful not only to African educational policymakers but also to those in the West who are studying African systems of higher education or who are endeavoring to provide meaningful and effective support to higher education in Africa.

Chapter 4: Promoting Instructional Technology for Effective and Efficient Academic Performance in Nigerian Schools

This chapter focuses on the concept of Instructional Technology (IT) as a crucial element in education. Instructional technologies support curricula, promoting effectiveness and efficiency in academic performance at all levels of education in Nigerian schools. The chapter works toward a clearer definition of Instructional Technology (IT) as educational problem-solvers and focuses on emerging technologies for teaching and learning. The chapter also deals with some of the challenges of applying instructional technologies, the effective organization of instructional materials in schools, the usefulness of local instructional packages, and obstacles to using instructional technology in Nigerian schools.

The chapter is particularly helpful for educational policymakers from the national level down to the level of school administrators, and the content can provide guidance and encouragement for moving forward with the introduction of IT at every level of education.

Chapter 5: Cultural Factors Affecting Integration of Technology in Media Education in Nigeria

This chapter takes a look at the need for graduates in today's information age to be competitive in the marketplace upon graduation. It emphasizes that classroom ICT use has the potential to improve not only the capacity of the facilitators but also the learning of students at all levels. Despite financial and other major challenges to integrating technology in learning, the chapter urges proactive steps to address the current, relatively low integration rate of ICT in African learning centers. It points out that graduates are competing with others with overseas qualifications and with professionals already in the workplace, who already possess the requisite technological skills required today. This chapter is useful to educators and administrators, both in the West and in Africa.

Chapter 6: Adoption and Use of Information and Communication Technologies (ICTs) in Library and Information Centres – Implications on Teaching and Learning Process

This chapter discusses the adoption and use of ICT in libraries and the implications of such adoption and use for the educational systems involved. It reports on a study to determine the present state of ICT in libraries throughout Nigeria and lists some of the challenges faced in the adoption of ICT by libraries. It also documents some effective remedies to those challenges. The study is of particular interest to administrators, librarians, and educators in Nigeria, but is also useful for Nigerian government officials, who might have the ability to increase library funding as the chapter recommends.

Chapter 7: Efficiency of Technology in Creating Social Networks for Mobilizing and Improving the Health of a Community

This chapter explores the effectiveness of using Facebook to create a social network to improve community health improvement. It discusses social networking group reach rates and the effectiveness of a social network in delivering health messages and improving community health knowledge. A two-year study showed overall positive outcomes in reach, response time, and group engagement. The chapter should be of particular interest to community health workers and social networking scholars in all parts of the world.

Chapter 8: Managing and Planning Technology Usage and Integration in Teacher Education Programs in an Emergent Nation

The chapter explores the impact of the changing context of Information Technology (IT) and Information Systems (ISs) on Teacher Education (TE). The chapter uncovers a serious problem, policy makers associated with educational programs look to market-based solutions without considering the challenges preventing effective integration and use of ITs and ISs in TE, particularly in developing economies. Using a theory-based method of analysis, the chapter gathers, reviews, and analyzes contemporary views and ideas about education and technology. The chapter is useful to higher education administrators and to government policymakers who often drive the financing of such new technologies in education.

Chapter 9: Utilization of Instructional Media and Academic Performance of Students in Basic Science – A Case Study of Education District V1 of Lagos State

The chapter discusses the use of instructional media in teaching and learning basic sciences in primary and secondary schools. It concludes that these media are effective in driving home the lesson point of the subject being taught, and that they reduce stress for both teacher and student. The imaginative use of well-planned visual aids during classroom lessons are shown to boost student academic performance for physics, chemistry, biology, and mathematics. The chapter demonstrated that the use of instructional media had a positive impact on student learning outcomes. The chapter is of particular interest to classroom instructors and to administrators considering the use of IT in their schools' classrooms.

Chapter 10: Using Andragogy and Bloom's Digital Taxonomy to Guide E-Portfolio and Web Portfolio Development in Undergraduate Courses

This chapter covers e-portfolio teaching approaches and how andragogy and Bloom's Digital Taxonomy can be integrated into teaching and learning to provoke active learning through e-portfolio development. The chapter connects andragogy (the method and practice of teaching adult students) and integrates educational objectives into Bloom's cognitive domain as updated by Anderson and Krathwohl and aligned to the digital realm by Churches to serve as a model for teaching Web portfolio development in undergraduate courses. The chapter is useful for those teaching adult learners who wish to encourage their students to develop e-portfolios.

Chapter 11: Finding Common Ground – Uses of Technology in Higher Education

As technology's presence in higher education rises, so does its cultural impact. Scholars have widely differing perspectives on the proper role of technology in higher education. This chapter works to reconcile such scholarly differences, using a constructive hermeneutic in our postmodern age to understand the limited and biased ground of one's own perspective. The chapter also presents a decision model for educators to evaluate uses of technology in higher education. The chapter is of interest for those dealing with technology in higher education.

Chapter 12: Effective Virtual Learning Environment through the Use of Web 2.0 Tools

As the use of social networking sites and Web 2.0 tools are increases, research shows that education via Web 2.0 tools can increase student motivation and interest for learning. The chapter suggests that a positive teaching environment can be created using social networking sites in which Web 2.0 tools allow effective learning. It discusses a number of Web 2.0 tools available for creating an effective virtual learning environment and their positive effect on students. Anyone with interest in using Web 2.0 tools in the classroom can benefit from reading this chapter.

Chapter 13: Technology Integration in the Classroom – Report of an Asynchronous Online Discussion among a Group of Nigerian Graduate Students

The chapter reviews data showing that increased access to ICT tools and resources provides opportunities for learning technologies. The chapter focuses on classroom integration of social media among a group of Nigerian graduate students using asynchronous online discussion. The 33 participants engaged in a threaded discussion for 14 weeks at the College of Medicine, University of Ibadan. A major barrier to participation in AOD is limited access to computer and Internet facilities. The chapter recommends improvement of ICT infrastructure in on-campus residential environments for cheaper, unrestricted technology access. Those teaching students in African universities and university administrators should read this chapter.

Chapter 14: Information and Communication Technology in Teaching and Learning – Effects and Challenges in China

Although China has the most Internet users of any nation (591 million users as of 2013), a lower percentage of the Chinese population (44%) has used the Internet than is the case in the United States (78%). The chapter discusses the effects ICT has on Chinese elementary and secondary education, and some continuing challenges in ICT applications. It also examines the use of ICT in Chinese higher education, particularly in distance learning, and issues that must still be resolved. The chapter ends with practical recommendations for improving Chinese education using ICT.

Chapter 15: Adopting Digital Technologies in the Classroom – The Impact of Use of Clickers on Cognitive Loads and Learning in China

Although clickers have gained popularity in the West, they are less commonly used in the East. This chapter reviews studies on the impact of the use of clickers on learning and cognitive loads. It points out the effectiveness and possible positive influence clickers can have on cognitive loads, suggesting that clickers might be more appropriate for use in large-enrollment classes, where they can permit quiet and anonymous student polling. Students have demonstrated feeling less nervous when answering questions anonymously. Professors of large classes can benefit from reading this chapter, and Chinese school administrators in particular will find it of current interest.

Chapter 16: Adopting Digital Technologies in the Administration of Technical and Engineering Education

This chapter explores the infant state of studies about the adoption of digital technologies in educational administration, especially in the administration and management of technical and engineering education facilities. It examines opportunities to adopt digital technologies to the administration of general education and its implications on technical and engineering education. Facilities and laboratory managers, university administrators, and university security and administrative personnel can benefit from the information in this chapter.

Chapter 17: Knowledge Management and Reverse Mentoring in the Nigerian Tertiary Institutions

This chapter explores knowledge management as a discipline that makes maximum use of the knowledge available to an organization and, at the same time, creates new knowledge. Knowledge management is about understanding, appreciating, and making use of the knowledge of individuals, developing an organizational culture where knowledge sharing can flourish. This process permits the organization to create value from its intellectual and knowledge-based assets, with the goal of continual knowledge development, drawing on the knowledge base of employees (thus the concept of reverse mentoring). Leaders of any type of organization will benefit from reading this chapter, as will students of management.

Chapter 18: The Global School in the Local Classroom – ICT for Cross-Cultural Communication

This chapter champions the value of cross-cultural communication practices in schools with innovative Information and Communication Technology (ICT) support. A detailed theoretical foundation justifies the inclusion of global perspectives in the classroom through cross-cultural communication, made possible by ICT. This chapter details the perceptions of 80 pre-K to 12 teachers via a survey study, which shaped the author's suggestions for practical ICT cross-cultural communication opportunities in the classroom. Implementation strategies include classroom-to-classroom and classroom-to-world cross-cultural communication opportunities. This chapter suggests practical solutions supported by solid theoretical justifications for utilizing ICT to facilitate cross-cultural communication and to improve student global awareness. Primary and secondary teachers, school administrators, and legislators concerned with funding education can benefit from reading this chapter.

Chapter 19: Globalization and its Challenges for Teacher Education in Nigeria

The chapter reviews several definitions of *globalization*, uses the working definition of *the establishment of global markets for goods and capital*, leading to multiple linkages and interconnections among places, events, ideas, issues, and things. A major limiting factor for globalization in a given nation is an educational system is not geared toward fostering meaningful and desirable change for that society. To achieve such an education system orientation, teacher education must be predicated on producing globalization-friendly teachers. The chapter compares the concept of globalization with the goals of current teacher education in Nigeria.

Chapter 20: Challenges and Prospects of Information Communication Technology (ICT) in Teaching Technical Education towards Globalisation

This chapter emphasizes the relevance of Information and Communication Technologies (ICTs) in the field of Technical Vocational Education and Training (TVET). It points out that the workaday world is continuously changing, even as ICT itself is developing. These changes pose challenges to 21st century workers and the institutions responsible for preparing the next generation of workers. The chapter develops definitions, philosophy, and objectives for TVET, concepts and types of ICT, and the need for effective use of ICT in TVET. Those involved in the administration of or teaching in TVET departments will profit from reading this chapter.

Chapter 21: M-Health Technology as a Transforming Force for Population Health

This chapter discusses mobile health (m-Health), the use of portable electronic devices to communicate health information via a wireless, electronic network of base stations. The chapter suggests that m-Health technology has the potential to provide long-term patient support via wireless networks, without requiring patients to sacrifice their autonomy, but sees the chief obstacle to a more rational development of such a network as the resistance of medical professionals. Healthcare providers and administrators can benefit from this chapter.

Chapter 22: Influence of Globalisation on Teaching and Learning – What is the Stance of Information Literacy in Nigerian Tertiary Institutions?

This chapter takes a look at the influence of globalization on teaching and learning. It finds a very low level of information literacy among students because of what the authors see as the neglect of information literacy programs in Nigerian primary schools. It goes on to provide practical suggestions for incorporating information literacy programs in institutions of higher learning in Nigeria, and it discusses some of the challenges of doing that. It suggests that primary school administrators begin seeing information literacy as an academic issue, rather than just a "library thing." Those in higher education and (particularly) Nigerian primary school administrators can profit from reading this chapter.

Chapter 23: Re-Branding Community Organizations for the Actualization of Development Goals in the Rural Communities in Nigeria

This chapter reviews various definitions of the concept of *community* and goes on to explore the *raison d'etre* of especially rural community organizations, which have the specific goal of improving living conditions for those concerned. It examines input from various scholars and from the United Nations about the organization and constitution of such organizations, emphasizing that they must be of the people (grassroots organizations) and for the good of the people. Community organizers everywhere can benefit from reading this chapter.

CONCLUSION

Technology tools are becoming widely available in schools and classrooms. They can be used in many different ways, and how they are integrated into educational settings depends largely on teachers' instructional goals and strategies. Computer networks are also the technological foundation that has allowed the emergence of global network capitalism, that is, regimes of accumulation, regulation, and discipline that are increasingly helping to base the accumulation of economic, political, and cultural capital on transnational network organizations that make use of cyberspace and other new technologies for global coordination and communication.

Blessing F. Adeoye
University of Lagos, Nigeria

Acknowledgment

I would like to express my gratitude to the many people who saw me through this book, all those who provided support, talked things over, read, wrote, offered comments, allowed me to quote their remarks, and assisted in the editing, proofreading, and design.

I would like to thank Prof. Lawrence Tomei for encouraging me to publish this book. Above all, I want to thank my wife, Florence, and the rest of my family, who supported and encouraged me in spite of all the time it took me away from them. It was a long and difficult journey for them.

Throughout the process of writing this book, many colleagues from various universities have taken time out to contribute chapters and review some chapters. I would like to give a special thanks to them for their contributions to this book.

Thanks to the management at the University of Lagos, Nigeria and Robert Morris University, PA, USA. These two institutions supported me in carrying out this project.

We appreciate the Publisher (IGI) and the Editorial Advisory Board from various institutions around the world for helping in the process of selection and editing.

Last and not least, I apologize for all those who have been with me over the course of the years and whose names I have failed to mention.

Blessing F. Adeoye
University of Lagos, Nigeria

Introduction

Technology has become a sociopolitical force around the world. There are many reasons for this; the obvious one is that technological change is the main source of new areas of profitable accumulation of wealth. The educational institutions play roles in helping to facilitate the complex maneuvers by which the accumulation circuit works. Also, computers and Internet connections are becoming widely available in schools and classrooms. Information Communication Technology can be used in many different ways, and how it is integrated into educational settings depends largely on teachers' instructional goals and strategies. Computer networks are also the technological foundation that has allowed the emergence of global network capitalism, that is, regimes of accumulation, regulation, and discipline that are helping to increasingly base the accumulation of economic, political, and cultural capital on transnational network organizations that make use of cyberspace and other new technologies for global coordination and communication.

It is important to share experiences from various issues regarding the use of technology in teaching and learning. Challenges associated with any cross-cultural interaction, such as the misunderstandings that arise from the assumptions we unknowingly make (Hall, 1976), also influence teaching and learning. Dewey (1916) observed almost a century ago that deep and sustainable learning is dependent on the relevance of the curriculum to one's life-situation. The editor of this book believes that it is critical not only to effectively deal with cross-cultural issues in the utilization of technology to teach and learn, but also that the struggle of addressing cultural issues might even help creatively reshape our view of technologies and of education itself.

OBJECTIVE OF THE BOOK

The goal of this book is to explore issues concerning Informational Capitalism and Globalization and the challenges and solutions for teaching and learning, and to illustrate the different challenges faced when utilizing technology for teaching and learning in various cultural settings and how they were resolved. It also included how globalization affects learning and how educational organizations can find, create, or adapt technology for use in other cultures.

Blessing F. Adeoye
University of Lagos, Nigeria

Lawrence Tomei
Robert Morris University, USA

Section 1
Introduction

Chapter 1
Effects of Information Capitalism and Globalization on Teaching and Learning in a Developed and in a Developing Country:
A Cross-Cultural Study of Robert Morris University in the United States and University of Lagos in Nigeria

Blessing F. Adeoye
University of Lagos, Nigeria

ABSTRACT

Education is undergoing constant changes under the effects of globalization and information generation, processing, and transmission, which is termed "informational capitalism." The aims of this chapter are to explore how digital technologies have transformed the productive forces of capitalism and have enabled a globalized economy. The research design adopted for this study is the descriptive survey. The population for the study consists of students and faculty from Robert Morris University in Pennsylvania and students and lecturers from the University of Lagos, Lagos, Nigeria. The data collected are compared. The findings show that perceptions vary in the magnitude with which participants responded to the use of Web 2.0 for teaching and learning. Based on the responses from all participants, both students and faculty, cultural inclination has no significant impact on their use of Web 2.0 for learning. However, the majority of the participants from the University of Lagos, both students and lecturers, believe that adoption of Web 2.0 supports cultural promotion.

DOI: 10.4018/978-1-4666-6162-2.ch001

Copyright © 2014, IGI Global. Copying or distributing in print or electronic forms without written permission of IGI Global is prohibited.

INTRODUCTION

Education is undergoing constant changes under the effects of globalization and information generation, processing, and transmission, which is termed, "informational capitalism." The core of society consists of three subsystems: the economic system, in which values and property that satisfy human needs are produced, the political systems, in which power is distributed in a certain way, and collective decisions are taken, and the cultural system in which skills, meaning, and competencies are acquired, produced, and enacted in ways of life (Fuchs &Horak, 2006). All these systems are affected by Information Communication Technology (ICT), and they impact the effectiveness of teaching and learning. It is in this context that the concepts of information capitalism and globalization are introduced. Changes in the production forces generally encourage changes in the relations of production, the chief among them being technology. Technology enables human practices. Their main dimensions are the material access to them (in modern society, mainly with the help of money, as technologies are sold as commodities), the capability to use them in such a way that benefits oneself and others, and embedding them within institutions (Fuchs &Horak, 2006). Transformation through technology is an important ingredient for industrial growth, and so globalization and the information age are currently giving dynamism to capitalism. Technology thus becomes not merely a lever of material change, but a sociopolitical force within capitalism.

According to Fuchs (2008), the need to find new strategies for executing corporate and political domination has resulted in a restructuring of capitalism that is characterized by the emergence of transnational, networked spaces in the economic, political, and cultural system and has been mediated by cyberspace as a tool of global coordination and communication. Hence, these cyber tools are critical in transforming learning in this digital age. Around the world, educators and learners hope

that digital technologies will lead to increased knowledge, productivity, collaboration, social freedoms, and healthier lives. Students study and conduct research using computers, multimedia, and networks, whereas teachers access unlimited materials online, improve teaching methodologies, network, and conduct research efficiently.

Some scholars have described informational capitalism in different ways. For instance, Castells (2000) describes informationalism as a new technological paradigm characterized by "information generation, processing, and transmission," that have become "the fundamental sources of productivity and power." Fitzpatrick (2002) focused on computer as a guiding technology that has transformed the productive forces of capitalism and has enabled a globalized economy.

Perhaps the economic sector most affected by technology is education. According to Hooker (1997), education is in the midst of changing from an energy-based to a knowledge-based economy, which will alter the rules of international economic competition, thrusting universities into roles they have not traditionally played. Two of the greatest challenges educational institutions face are those of harnessing the power of digital technology and responding to the information revolution" (Hooker, 1997). As a result, most educational institutions, especially in the developed world, are undergoing major structural changes through transformation in digital technologies. The way an organization responds to structural change can determine its future. For educational institutions, structural change is the result of the confluence of two forces; the information revolution and the management revolution. The information revolution drives the shift from an energy-based to a knowledge-based economy, and the management revolution is driven partly by changes in the capacity to use information.

Technology is changing more rapidly than ever before, causing more confusion about the best way to use it in schools (Bailey, 1997). Glenn (1997) stated that public support for technology in schools is strong and vocal, and there is an expectation that no school can prepare students for tomorrow's society if new technologies are not available to students. Glenn indicated that teacher training has focused on word processing, test construction, automated transparency creation, and grading, rather than on creating a different learning environment. However, the vast array of digital technologies with the potential to impact the teaching and learning process includes learning-management systems, personal response system technologies, discussion boards, blogs, wikis, social networking sites, podcasts, and a plethora of Web-based tools. The pervasiveness of information technology in today's world complicates the multiple demands on lecturers by adding expectations of technological proficiency that far exceed the days of traditional tools that more lecturers experienced as undergraduates.

Nigeria started implementing ICT policy in April 2001 after the Federal Executive Council approved it by establishing the National Information Technology Development Agency (NITDA) as the implementing body (Agyeman, 2007). The policy empowers NITDA to enter into strategic alliances and joint ventures and collaborate with the private sector to realize the specifics of the country's vision of, "making Nigeria an IT capable country in Africa and a key player in the information society by the year 2005 through using IT as an engine for sustainable development and global competitiveness" (Agyeman, 2007). This vision is yet to be fully fulfilled due to challenges such as the lack of electric power and telecommunications infrastructure in a substantial part of the country. Mobile telecommunication currently covers 60% of the national territory, but mobile telephone companies generally power their base stations using electric power generators because the Power Holding Company of Nigeria (PHCN) is unable to supply them with a consistently available power source. This phenomenon is prevalent nationwide, and it creates a bottleneck to effective countrywide deployment of ICT in education.

Over the last several decades, the development of the ICT industry has made a positive impact on nearly every facet of the U.S. economy. The National Research Council found that the ICT industry accounted for 25 percent of U.S. economic growth from 1995 to 2007, measured as real change in GDP. Over the last two decades, the development and use of ICT has accounted for as high as 60% of annual U.S. labor productivity gains (Jorgenson, Ho &Stiroh, 2007). Also, from 1995 to 2005, use of ICT technologies was largely responsible for productivity in the U.S. growing by more than 3 percent per year (essentially twice the rate of the preceding 20 years), persisting through the recession of the early 2000's, when "productivity grew at the impressive—and counterintuitive—rate of 4.8 percent" (NRC, 2009).

The effects of globalization on education bring rapid developments in technology and communications that presaging changes within learning systems across the world, as ideas, values, and knowledge, changing the roles of students and teachers, and producing a shift in society from industrialization toward an information-based society. It reflects the effect on culture and brings about a new form of cultural imperialism (Chinnamma, 2005). Levin (2001) contends that open capitalism and global multinational corporations project a perception that the world is becoming a shared social place through technological and economic advances. The world has become so interlinked that there is a common consensus among educationists and policy makers that it is having a lasting impact on our educational missions and goals. In his own words, Levin indicated that, "It may be that consciousness of a global society, culture, and economy and global interdependence are the cornerstones of globalization, and these consciousness and interdependency have saliency in knowledge-based enterprises. There is certain inevitability that higher education institutions, because of their cultural, social, and economic roles, are caught up in and affected by globalization" (Levin, 2001, p. 9).

Statement of the Problem

In Nigeria, much of the discourse on using ICTs in teaching and learning, however, seems to focus on access to technology; that is, on the availability of computers, the Internet, and bandwidth, rather than on the way ICTs are being used in support of teaching and learning. However, in the United States, the focus has been on integration of technology in the classrooms (Christensen, 2002). In many contexts the focus on access has resulted in pedagogically poor applications of technology where ICTs are only used in transmission modes of teaching and learning. Following some spectacular failings of e-learning projects globally, (Latchem, 2005) there now seems to be a growing concern about the application of those technologies in teaching and learning to investigate how they can be and are being used to support teaching and learning (Czerniewicz& Brown, 2006).

Purpose

The aims of this study are to explore how digital technologies have transformed the productive forces of capitalism and have enabled a globalized economy. It will also compare the effects of cultural distance and country characteristics on the diffusion process and the penetration level that digital tools such as blogs, wikis, and podcast technologies reach in support of teaching and learning.

For this purpose, this study proposes to consider the utilization of educational tools such as blogs, wikis, and podcast technologies in teaching and learning. The educational tools indicated above are the latest in a series of continuing technological revolutions and are having significant influence on educational growth in many industrialized countries. Given the amazing speed at which these tools have been transforming teaching and learning, it is interesting to look into factors that may play a determining role in their diffusion across countries, especially North America and African countries.

Research Questions

1. What is the role of cultural factors in determining the adoption of digital technologies across countries?
2. Do cultural differences between countries have a significant impact on students' adoption of digital technologies for learning?
3. Do cultural differences between countries have a significant impact on lecturers' adoption of digital technologies for learning?
4. In what ways has technology transformed the productive forces of capitalism and enabled a globalized economy in the United States?

REVIEW OF LITERATURE

The advent of information and communication technology (ICT) in teaching and learning has witnessed a proliferation of study at all levels of education. Some researchers have focused on availability, accessibility of ICT (e.g., Olatokun, 2007; Jude &Dankaro, 2012). Some have focused on integration in teaching and learning (e.g., Christensen, 2002) while many have focused on cultural implications (e.g., Marcus & Gould, 2000). Regardless of their research focuses, the level of barrier differs from country to country; for instance, a study has shown that, in the developing countries, teachers' lack of technological competence is a main barrier to their acceptance and adoption of ICT (Pelgrum, 2001). According to Yelland (2001), traditional educational environments do not seem to be suitable for preparing learners to function or be productive in the workplaces of today's society. Yelland claimed that organizations that do not incorporate the use of new technologies in schools cannot prepare their students for life in the twenty-first century.

Most studies that look into the impact of culture are concerned with economic growth in general (e.g., Johnson &Lenartowicz, 1998). This study will also examine the role of cultural factors in determining ICT adoption across countries. The values and attitudes an individual has and the reaction he or she expects from the larger group play an important role in the innovation process. Naturally there would be variation in individual needs as well as in the behavior of individual, team, and organizations within any given national culture. Nevertheless, all individuals live and work within a cultural environment in which certain values, norms, attitudes, and practices are more or less dominant and serve as shared sources of socialization and social control (Erubam& Jong, 2003).

A study conducted at Illinois States University identified several factors that affected adoption of instructional technology by faculty especially the Internet and Web technologies (Butler &Sellbom, 2002). The majority of the faculty agreed or strongly agreed that three factors imposed barriers to adoption: lack of instructional support, lack of financial support, and lack of time to learn new technologies.

Theoretical Framework

This research is positioned within a theoretical perspective on teaching and learning that relates to sociocultural theories of learning (Vygotsky, 1978) and Hofstede's cultural dimensions (1980).

Sociocultural Theories of Learning

In his theory, Vygotsky (1978) stressed the interaction between developing people and the culture in which they live. He also described learning as a social process and the origination of human intelligence in society or culture, and stated that learning takes places, not at the individual level, but at the social level (Vygotsky, 1978). For a learning theory to be sociocultural, first, it should understand that mental action is situated in cultural, historical, and institutional settings, and that learning should be understood at the social level first. The basic premise of a sociocultural approach to learning is to believe that the social

dimension of consciousness is primary in time. Therefore, the individual dimension of consciousness is derivative and secondary (Vygotsky 1978). Although the learning process itself is considered to be highly individualistic, a sociocultural theory of learning looks at the social dimension of learning in the first place.

The main focus of Vygotsky's theoretical framework is that social interaction plays a fundamental role in the development of cognition. He believed everything is learned on two levels. First, through interaction with others, and then integrated into the individual's mental structure (Vygotsky, 1978). An important aspect of sociocultural theory is the claim that all human action is mediated by tools. In this study, the researcher interprets the idea of a tool to incorporate a wide range of artefacts (for example, blog, wiki, computer, and the Internet) and semiotic systems (for example, language, cultures, and graphics). Within this framework the idea of a person-acting-with-mediational-means (Wertsch, 1991) both expands the view of what a person can do and also suggests that a person might be constrained by his or her situated and mediated action.

According to Armstrong, Barnesa, Sutherland, Curranb, Mills and Thompson, (2005) sociocultural theory foregrounds the cultural aspects of human action. They indicated several aspects of culture that are important to take into account. First, the teacher and students work within a local classroom culture, which is influenced by local, national culture and globalization factors. Within this context, the teacher and students bring to the classroom a history of experiences that relate to their previous cultures of learning and the tools they use. So, when faced with a new technology, a teacher or a student is likely to make sense of it in terms of previous experiences of older technologies. This suggests that many teachers are likely to use digital tools as an extension of non digital tools. Students also draw on their out-of-school uses of ICT, and this has an impact on learning in the classroom (Facer, Furlong, Furlong, &

Sutherland, 2001; Kent & Facer, 2004). Another relevant framework used in this study is that of Hofstede's cultural dimensions.

Hofstede's Cultural Dimensions

Geert Hofstede's theory of cultural dimensions describes the effects of a society's culture on the values of its members, and how these values relate to behavior, using a structure derived from factor analysis (Hofstede, 1980). These national cultural dimensions are power-distance, individualism versus collectivism, masculinity versus femininity, and uncertainty avoidance. The fifth dimension was not used in this study because it was not one of the original four cultural dimensions that have been widely tested. The earlier Hofstede's model has been used and tested by many researchers (e.g., Bernard, 2000; Dunbar, 1991; Marcus & Gould, 2000) to explore the influence of culture on technology.

Power Distance - Power Distance (PD) refers to the degree to which people accept and expect that power is distributed unevenly within a group or society. In other words, people in high power-distance cultures are much more comfortable with a larger status differential than those in low-power distance cultures. The following countries are considered by Hoftede to be collectivist and large power-distance: India, Japan, Malaysia, Portugal, Singapore, South Korea, and Nigeria. Learners in this group expect to learn through a group activity. Therefore, e-learning should not be presented as a "personalized" solution (for example, as an individual learning portal) but as a collaborative solution (with blended online and classroom collaboration). Hofstede pointed out that finding the right solutions is difficult because this group has a large power-distance, which in a learning situation translates into heavy dependence on a teacher or expert mentor to guide the learning process, and reliance on structured curriculums. Learners will likely seek the approval of their group and the mentor before contributing ideas.

This culture responds easily to blended learning, prescribed curriculums, and virtual classrooms.

Individualism versus Collectivism - Individualism is the degree to which taking responsibility for oneself is more valued than belonging to a group, who will look after their people in exchange for loyalty. According to Hofstede (1980), many of Asian and African cultures are collectivistic, whereas Anglo cultures tend to be individualistic. In individualistic cultures, however, individual uniqueness and self-determination are valued (Hofstede, 1980; 1991). The following countries are considered by Hoftede to have low power-distance and individualistic cultures: Canada, Great Britain, Germany, Finland, Norway, Sweden, Ireland, and the United States. This culture can easily be familiar with learner-centered materials, personalized learning portals, collaborative learning, and knowledge management. They have limited dependence on teachers in learning situations and are used to taking the initiative.

Also, the following countries are considered by Hoftede to be large power-distance and individualistic culture: Belgium, France, Italy, South Africa, and Spain. The cultural expectation of these countries and their response to technology include easy familiarity with personalized learning portals, prescribed curriculums, and mentoring. Although personalized e-learning has appeal in these countries, learners are highly dependent on tutors and prescribed curriculum. One-on-one mentoring via e-mail or Web-based communication is highly suitable for this group (Hofstede, 1980).

Masculinity versus Femininity. Masculinity is the degree to which people value performance and status deriving from themselves, rather than quality of life and care for others. The cultures considered masculine tend to have very distinct expectations of male and female roles in society. Those with feminine cultures have a greater ambiguity in what is expected of each gender. Hofstede focuses on the traditional assignment to masculine roles of assertiveness, competition, and toughness, and to feminine roles of orientation to home and children, people, and tenderness.

Uncertainty Avoidance. Uncertainty Avoidance is the degree to which people develop a mechanism to avoid uncertainty. It also involves how cultures vary in the magnitude with which people vary in the extent that they feel anxiety about uncertain or unknown matters. This idea does not involve the most universal feelings of fear caused by known or understood threats, but rather the fear of potential difficulties, situations, or events. Cultures vary in their avoidance of uncertainty, creating different rituals and having different values regarding formality, punctuality, legal-religious-social requirements, and tolerance for ambiguity (Hofstede, 1997; Marcus & Gould, 2000). These cultures tend to be expressive. Teachers are expected to be experts who know the answers and may speak in cryptic language that excludes novices. In high uncertainty–avoidance culture, what is different may be viewed as a threat. By contrast, low uncertainty–avoidance cultures tend to be less expressive and less openly anxious. In these cultures, what is different may be viewed as simply curious, or perhaps ridiculous.

Significance

The outcome of this study will enhance successful deployment of digital technologies in education, which will in turn contribute to the development of knowledge societies in all nations, bridging the digital divide in Nigeria and stabilizing connectivity in the United States.

Higher education in both Nigeria and the United States cannot afford to miss the chance to participate in this revolution if it hopes to improve the quality of its academic development and management, and to alleviate the widespread poverty that seriously undermines human development. The successful utilization of digital technologies in teaching and learning can contribute to the development of knowledge in societies in both Nigeria and the United States.

This study will enable the researcher to critically and analytically understand and integrate theory and practice from Nigeria and the United States, and also bring together knowledge from both countries. It will help to identify differences and neuro-diversity to improve technological integration in education in both countries. The researcher will be able to understand multisensory classroom teaching practice to support a whole-institutional, inclusive approach and also to engage in collaborative learning through peer learning, discursive assessment, and online discussion activities.

Limitations

One of the limitations for this study was the time it took for the institutional review board (IRB) application to be processed. An institutional review board (IRB), also known as an independent ethics committee, or ethical review board, is a committee that has been formally designated to approve, monitor, and review biomedical and behavioral research involving humans. The IRB's intention is not to hinder research, but to ensure that human subjects' rights are protected and that the project complies with federal standards. However, it took three weeks before the application was approved.

It is important to be aware that Hofstede cultural dimensions are not 100% valid in every place in the world.

RESEARCH METHODOLOGY

Design

The research design adopted for this study is the descriptive survey. The population for the study consists of students and faculty from Robert Morris University, Pennsylvania, and of students and lecturers from the University of Lagos, Lagos, Nigeria. The sampled schools were purposefully selected based on the fact that they have technology-related programs in their schools. Descriptive statistical tools were used for data analysis and interpretation.

Instrument

Two surveys were developed (one for students and one for the faculty/lecturers). The aim of the surveys was to collect data from both students and faculty/lecturers on their perceptions of the use of digital technologies. Another purpose is to determine how their national cultural dimensions could have affected the usage. The study will also investigate the effects of cultural distance and country characteristics on the diffusion process and the penetration level that digital tools such as blog, wiki, and podcast technologies reach in support of learning.

The faculty/lecturers survey is very similar to the students' survey. The different is that the instructor survey focused on teaching, whereas the students' survey focused on learning. Faculty teaching at the Department of Science and Technology at the University of Lagos and those at the School of Communications and Information Systems at Robert Morris University were targeted for this study.

A Web-based survey was developed using Vovici, a survey software program offered online. The program offered many features, including an unlimited number of survey questions, custom redirects, result filtering, and the capability to export data for statistical analysis. The program provided a list of management tools where responses could be tracked by participant e-mail addresses, which proved to be useful for follow-up e-mails. The program also provided data protection and security to turn on SSL (Secure Sockets Layers) to utilize data encryption. The survey contained 20 closed-ended items and four open-ended questions that focused on the objectives of this study. The items were developed by the researcher. Participation was voluntary, and participants had the freedom

to participate or to withdraw from the survey at any time. The survey took about 20 minutes to complete.

Data Collection

An informal pilot study was conducted with a small group of lecturers at the researcher's home institution (University of Lagos). Conducting a local pilot study allowed the researcher to ask participants for suggestive feedback on the survey and also helped eliminate author bias. Once the pilot survey had been modified as per the educational expert's feedback, the survey was administered online to participants who were purposively selected.

The researcher created a survey invitation and sent it to all students and faculty in the School of Communications and Information Systems at Robert Morris University (RMU) in Pennsylvania in the United States, and to all the students and lecturers at the Department of Science and Technology Education at the University of Lagos, Nigeria. Study participants were contacted by e-mail, explaining the research objectives and asking them to participate. The e-mail also contained a link to the Web-based survey. Responses to the survey were recorded, exported in a spreadsheet, and transferred to a statistical software package (SPSS) for in-depth analysis. Descriptive statistics were conducted, and data relationships were examined.

DATA ANALYSIS

Data was analyzed using descriptive analysis such as frequency, mean, and standard deviation, on the closed-ended questions, and other questions were analyzed using content analysis. Content analysis is the process of identifying, coding, and categorizing the primary pattern in the data (Patton, 1990). This method was used to analyze the

Table 1. Participants' institution or university (n = 440)

Institution	F	%
Robert Morris University	140	31.8
University of Lagos	300	68.2
Total	440	100

Table 2. Participants' gender (n = 440)

Gender	Nigeria %	USA %
Female	44.7	50
Male	55.3	50
Total	100	100

content from messages, instructor anecdotes, and student response to open-ended survey items. Data collected from Robert Morris University and the University of Lagos was compared (see Table 1).

Survey Demographics for Students

A total of 440 students participated in this study; 31.8% from Robert Morris University and 68.2% from the University of Lagos. The participants from Robert Morris University consisted of 50% male and 50% female; however, participants from the University of Lagos consisted of 55.3% male and 44.7% female (see Table 2).

When participants were asked how often they typically used digital tools such as blog, wiki, and podcast technologies during the last 12 months, Table 3 shows various levels of usage based on daily, weekly, monthly, and occasionally. The

majority of the participants also indicated the use of smart phones and portable computers to access the Internet.

In order to further simplify the survey data, the response categories (e.g., strongly agree, agree, disagree, strongly disagree) were combined into two nominal categories, with neutral in the middle, such as agree/strongly agree, neutral, disagree/strongly disagree, etc.) (Tables 4-8).

Content Analysis

A conceptual analysis was conducted with the data collected from both the students and faculty. The responses are presented based on repeating ideas that lead to major themes that, in turn, inform conclusions and implications for this study. Total participants, both students and faculty are 440. The phrases that recurred more than five times are presented in this content analysis.

1. What are the impacts of Web 2.0 (blogs, wikis, and podcast technologies) on your culture (e.g., religion, family, language, socialization)?
   a. Enriches my faith through e-books and other information.
   b. Encourages socialization but paradoxically also turns people into loners.
   c. Helps to disseminate information for better awareness among different religion groups, family members, and social groups and within ethnic groups with different languages.

Table 3. Students' frequency of use of Web 2.0

	%	%	%	%	%	%
	Daily	Weekly	Monthly	Occasionally	Never	Total
Robert Morris University	52.8	22.1	2.85	19.4	2.85	100
University of Lagos	35.1	37.8	4.6	18.9	4.0	100

Table 4. Students perceptions of the use of web 2.0 applications

Item	Agree (%)		Neutral (%)		Disagree (%)	
Level of agreement/disagreement (%)	RMU	UNILAG	RMU	UNILAG	RMU	UNILAG
1. Cultural inclinations make me not to adopt Web 2.0 for learning.	5.7	10.4	11.2	12.8	82.7	77
2. Adoption of Web 2.0 supports cultural promotion.	42.2	81.6	58	9	21.7	19.3
3. Web 2.0 adoption has great impact on national relationship between countries.	59.6	85.1	12.8	3.4	27	1.2
4. Information Communication Technology adoption helps to boost my country's economy.	55.9	82.2	19.3	15	25	2.4
5. Instructors/Lecturers being afraid of using digital technology impacts its adoption during teaching.	39.9	40	8.5	24	24.3	35.2
6. Adoption of digital technology is influenced by my being afraid (technophobia) of using them during learning.	5.7	18	5.7	12.3	88.4	69.4
7. Western cultural imposition impacts the adoption of Web 2.0 by some countries	15.2	62	15.8	27	21.7	10.4
8. Social inequality hinders digital technology adoption in my country.	33	49	13.6	9	52.6	42
9. A country's welfare influences its adoption of Web 2.0.	42	76	41	7.3	16.5	16.7
10. Technology adoption promotes cultural identity imperialism.	27.8	72.7	33.6	19.8	38.3	6.6
11. Capitalism increases the adoption of Web 2.0 in my country.	44.3	63	34	22.5	19.9	13.8
12. Increased reliance on ICT is a threat to the globalization of our cultural heritage.	44.2	62.3	35.7	26	20	12.9
13. Increased reliance on ICT is an opportunity for the globalization of our cultural heritage.	12.9	31.4	16	12	26.3	55
14. I prefer formal instructor-led models of learning	58.8	89	32	6.3	8.5	4.2
15. I prefer clear learning path or syllabus and like to know all the expected achievements in advance.	39.2	50.5	32.8	29	25.4	20.5
16. I can be described as learner centered and I mostly prefer collaborative learning.	67.3	76	16.4	14.6	16.3	9
17. I prefer blended learning and prescribed curriculum.	43.8	73	33.6	18.8	19.3	8
18. I prefer personalized learning portal and prescribed learning curriculum. 19.	33.5	72.8	52	18	13	10.4

d. The Internet gives many people the false sense of anonymity. While it is possible for more people to have voices and share information if they can access the Internet and server space, it is also possible for hate speech, racism, and sexism to flourish sometimes.

e. Web 2.0 technologies have impacted a paradigm shift. It allows the vast majority of people in America, to have the same capabilities of access to knowledge as the privileged.

f. Students from all around the world can attend classes online—it can be presented fairly close to a face-to-face class with a podcast, and the blogs keep the information flow going, although these are all asynchronous.

g. The impacts of Web 2.0 are significant as the availability of information expands exponentially. The challenge is in having the consumers of the information learn how to make the best use of the technology and also how to discern the validity of information.

Table 5. Data comparison research question 1. This table sought to compare the findings across culture, faculty, and students.

Research Question 1. What is the role of cultural factors in determining digital technologies adoption across countries?	
Students	**Faculty/Lecturers**
When participants were asked if cultural inclinations make them likely not to adopt Web 2.0 for learning, out of the RMU students that participated in this study, 5.7% agreed, 11.2% were neutral and 82.7% disagreed that cultural inclinations make them not likely to adopt Web 2.0 for learning. Among students from the University of Lagos, 10.4% agreed, 12.8% were neutral, and 77.7% disagreed that cultural inclinations make them not likely to adopt Web 2.0 for learning.	When faculty/lecturers were asked if cultural inclinations make them not likely to adopt Web 2.0 for learning, 4.5% of the RMU faculty that participated in this study agreed, 20.7% were neutral and 76.8% disagreed that cultural inclinations make them not likely to adopt Web 2.0 for learning. Among the faculty from the University of Lagos, 100% disagreed that cultural inclinations make them not likely to adopt Web 2.0 for learning.
Forty-two percent of Robert Morris University students who participated in this study indicated that adoption of Web 2.0 supports cultural promotion, 58% of them were neutral in their opinions, and 21.7% of them disagreed. Also, 81.6% of the University of Lagos students who participated in this study indicated that adoption of Web 2.0 supports cultural promotion, 9% of them were neural in their opinions, and 19.3% of them disagreed.	About forty-five percent of Robert Morris University faculty who participated in this study indicated that adoption of Web 2.0 supports cultural promotion, 41.2% of them were neutral in their opinions, and 13.8% of them disagreed. Also, 58% of the University of Lagos lecturers who participated in this study indicated that adoption of Web 2.0 supports cultural promotion, and 41.6% of them disagreed.
When asked if social inequality hinders digital technology adoption in their country, 33% of RMU students who participated in this study agreed that it does, 13.6% were neutral, and 52.6% disagreed. Also, 49% of University of Lagos students who participated in this study agreed that it does, 9% are neutral, and 42% did not believe it does. Almost half of the participants from both universities disagreed that social inequality hinders digital technology adoption in their countries.	When asked if social inequality hinders digital technology adoption in their country, 38% of RMU faculty who participated in this study agreed that it does, 6.7% were neutral, and 55% disagreed. Also, 60% of University of Lagos lecturers who participated in this study agreed that it does, and 30% did not believe it does.

2. What would you consider the role of culture in determining Web 2.0 (blogs, wikis, and podcast technologies) adoption in your school?
   a. The role of indigenous culture is dwindling, paving the way for Western culture
   b. Culture would obviously affect the rate of adoption of technologies in schools.
   c. Although many programs are now available in languages other than English, the Internet itself (meaning the code behind it) is hegemonic.
   d. It is not culture, but pedagogical integrity and the students' lack of participation. In online learning environments, best practices suggest high dependence on discussion forums, yet most of the participation I've seen has been detectably disengaged.
   e. I think culture has a significant impact on the adoption of Web 2.0; by culture, however, I mean the culture of the institution and culture within the geographical region and country.
   f. In adopting technology in schools, culture should be flexible in imbibing, accommodating, and also in helping to create awareness about technology.
   g. It is beneficial because students can always learn at their convenience and from any location and time in which they find themselves using any of the following means: audio, video, document files, etc.
   h. Some professors may prefer tradition rather than the adoption of technology information sources, but most have realized the advantages blogs and wikis bring.

Table 6. Data comparison research question 2

Research Question 2. Do cultural differences between countries have a significant impact on students' adoption of digital technologies for learning?	
Students	**Faculty/Lecturers**
When asked if Web 2.0 adoption has great impact on national relationship between countries, 42.2% of Robert Morris University students who participated in this study agreed that it does, 11.4% are neutral, while 21.7% did not believe it does. However, 81.6% of University of Lagos students who participated in this study agreed that it does, 9% are neutral, while 19.3% did not believe it does. The majority of the participants from the University of Lagos (81.6%) believe that Web 2.0 adoption has great impact on national relationship between countries.	When asked if Web 2.0 adoption has great impact on national relationship between countries, 63% of Robert Morris University faculty who participated in this study agreed that it does, 30% were neutral, and 6.7% did not believe it does. However, 91.7% of University of Lagos lecturers who participated in this study agreed that it does, and 8.3% are neutral. The majority of the participant from the University of Lagos (91.7%) and RMU participants (63%) believe that Web 2.0 adoption has great impact on national relationship between countries.
Participants were asked if the Western cultural imposition impacts the adoption of Web 2.0 by some countries, 15.2% of RMU students who participated in this study agreed that it does, 8.5% were neutral, and 21.7% disagreed. Also, 62% of University of Lagos students who participated in this study agreed that it does, 27% are neutral, and 10.4% did not believe it does. The majority of University of Lagos students who participated in this study agreed that Western cultural imposition impacts the adoption of Web 2.0 by some countries.	Faculty/Lecturers were asked if the Western cultural imposition impacts the adoption of Web 2.0 by some countries: 40% of RMU faculty who participated in this study agreed that it does, 50% were neutral, and 10.2% disagreed. Also, 66.6% of University of Lagos lecturers who participated in this study agreed that it does, and 30.4% did not believe it does. More University of Lagos lecturers who participated in this study believe that Western cultural imposition impacts the adoption of Web 2.0 by some countries.
When asked if a country's social welfare influences its adoption of Web 2.0, 42% of RMU students who participated in this study agreed that it does, 41% were neutral, and 16.5% disagreed. Also, 76% of University of Lagos students who participated in this study agreed that it does, 7.3% are neutral, and 16.7% did not believe it does.	When asked if a country's social welfare influences its adoption of Web 2.0, 66.6% of RMU faculty who participated in this study agreed that it does, 26.6% were neutral, and 6.6% disagreed. Also, 66.6% of University of Lagos lecturers who participated in this study agreed that it does, 10% are neutral, and 25% did not believe it does. Faculty from both universities agreed that a country's social welfare influences its adoption of Web 2.0.
About thirteen percent of RMU students who participated in this study agreed that increased reliance on ICT is an opportunity for the globalization of their cultural heritage, 16% were neutral about this statement, and 26.3% disagreed. Likewise, 31.4% of University of Lagos students' participants agreed that increased reliance on ICT is a threat to the globalization of their cultural heritage, 12% were neutral about this statement, and 55% disagreed.	Forty-three percent of RMU faculty who participated in this study agreed that increased reliance on ICT is an opportunity for the globalization of their cultural heritage, 36.7% were neutral about this statement, and 20.4% disagreed. Likewise, 58% of University of Lagos lecturers' participants agreed that increased reliance on ICT is a threat to the globalization of their cultural heritage, 10% were neutral about this statement, and 7% disagreed.

Table 7. Data comparison research question 3

Research Question 3. Do cultural differences between countries have a significant impact on lecturers' adoption of digital technologies for learning?	
When asked if Instructors/Lecturers being afraid of using digital technology impacts its adoption during teaching, 39.9% of Robert Morris University students who participated in this study agreed that it does, 15.8% were neutral, and 24.3% disagreed. However, 40% of University of Lagos students who participated in this study agreed that it does, 24% are neutral, and 35.2% did not believe it does.	When asked if Instructors/Lecturers being afraid of using digital technology impacts its adoption during teaching, 83% of Robert Morris University faculty who participated in this study agreed that it does, 13.3% were neutral, and 3.3% disagreed. However, 50.3% of University of Lagos lecturers who participated in this study agreed that it does, 10% are neutral, and 30% did not believe it does.
About twenty-eight percent of RMU students who participated in this study agreed that technology adoption promotes cultural identity imperialism, 33.6% were neutral, and 38.3% disagreed. Also, 72.7% of University of Lagos students who participated in this study agreed that technology adoption promotes cultural identity imperialism, 19.8% were neutral, and 6.6% disagreed. A large percentage of University of Lagos students (72.7%) agreed that technology adoption promotes cultural identity imperialism.	About twenty-four percent of RMU faculty who participated in this study agreed that technology adoption promotes cultural identity imperialism, 44.8% were neutral, and 31.2% disagreed. Also, 33% of University of Lagos lecturers who participated in this study agreed that technology adoption promotes cultural identity imperialism, 20% were neutral, and 50% disagreed.

Table 8. Data comparison research question 4

Research Question 4. In what ways has technology transformed the productive forces of capitalism and enabled a globalized economy in the USA?	
About fifty-six percent of Robert Morris University students who participated in this study indicated that ICT adoption helps to boost their country's economy, 19.3% of them were neutral in their opinions, and 25% of them disagreed. Also, 82.2% of the University of Lagos students who participated in this study indicated Information Communication Technology adoption helps to boost their country's economy, 15% of them were neutral in their opinions, and 2.4% of them disagreed. The majority of the participants from the University of Lagos (82.2%) believe that adoption of Web 2.0 supports cultural promotion.	Seventy percent of Robert Morris University faculty who participated in this study indicated that ICT adoption helps to boost their country's economy, 26.6% of them were neutral in their opinions, and 3.3% of them disagreed. Also, 91.6% of the University of Lagos lecturers who participated in this study indicated ICT adoption helps to boost their country's economy, and 8.3% of them were neutral in their opinions. The majority of faculty who participated in this study from both universities agreed that ICT helps to boost their country's economy.
When asked if capitalism increases the adoption of Web 2.0 in their country, 44.3% of RMU students who participated in this study agreed that it does, 34% were neutral, and 19.9% disagreed. Also, 63% of University of Lagos students who participated in this study agreed that it does, 22.5% are neutral, and 13.8% did not believe it does. The perceptions of participants from both universities are almost the same on this issue.	When asked if capitalism increases the adoption of Web 2.0 in their country, 66.6% of RMU faculty who participated in this study agreed that it does, 23% were neutral, and 10.2% disagreed. Also, 60.3% of University of Lagos lecturers who participated in this study agreed that it does, and 30% did not believe it does. The perceptions of participants from both universities are almost the same on this issue.
Forty-four percent of RMU students who participated in this study agreed that increased reliance on ICT is a threat to the globalization of their cultural heritage, 35.7% were neutral about this statement, and 20% disagreed. Likewise, 62.3% of University of Lagos students' participants agreed that increased reliance on ICT is a threat to the globalization of their cultural heritage, 26% were neutral about this statement, and 12.9% disagreed.	Twenty -four percent of RMU faculty who participated in this study agreed that increased reliance on ICT is a threat to the globalization of their cultural heritage, 44.8% were neutral about this statement, and 43.3% disagreed. Likewise, 33% of University of Lagos lecturers' participants agreed that increased reliance on ICT is a threat to the globalization of their cultural heritage, 10% were neutral about this statement, and 58% disagreed.

3. In what ways has technology transformed the productive forces of capitalism in your country?

  a. Technology has transformed the capitalism productive forces in my country by making almost all the inhabitants be motivated in using the technology in one way or the other.

  b. It has turned the entire world into a global village.

  c. It has generally enhanced and democratized ways of doing things.

  d. Although giving our country a boost 20 years ago, I think technology has also shifted financial power to developing nations.

  e. Everyone has to do more and more work and important services like bookkeeping, filing, and secretarial support. These services have been completely devalued, and the labor dumped on people already doing other things.

  f. It has facilitated constant monitoring and collaboration from different locations; it's also eroded leisure.

  g. Technology effectively supplanted manufacturing in the USA. Technology plays a huge role in our economy beyond the scope of manufacturing as well.

  h. Through technology, many investors had invested immensely in the sustainability of the Nigerian economy. Examples are abounding in the telecommunication system especially.

  i. In a capitalist system like Nigeria, small businesses drive the economy and create jobs. Technology has really transformed the work force by providing small businesses.

  j. It has transformed the productive forces of capitalism in my country by keeping adequate records, and being able to determine inferior products.

k.   The productive forces of capitalism used to be a unilateral decision in the past governed by the desires of the supplier, but with the advent and proliferation of ICT, the decision has gradually moved toward the consumer end because there are several options.

4.   What do you think can hinder the prospect of ICT as a means of interaction today?

a.   There is less emphasis on the teaching and learning of my language because the new generations are more interested in "globalized" language—English language for international and even national interaction.

b.   Technology makes the professor a 24-hour a day job. Regardless of when or what time, I feel compelled to answer students' e-mails immediately from my phone. It is that immediate gratification that helps champion the idea of these new technologies.

c.   Culture has influenced the use of blogs negatively because of poor knowledge about ICTs.

d.   Lack of encouragement of citizens to imbibe the knowledge of technology and create an impact in the society.

e.   Technology has reduced barriers to information access among members of the communities.

Descriptive Analyses of Data Collected from the Faculty

A total of 126 faculty/lecturers participated in this study. The participants from Robert Morris University consist of 53.3% male and 46.7% female; however, lecturers from the University of Lagos consist of 41.7% male and 58.3% female (see Table 9).

Faculty were asked, how often did they typically use digital tools such as blogs, wikis, and podcast technologies during the last 12 months.

Table 9. Faculty's institution and gender

	Female	Male	Total
Robert Morris University	46.7	53.3	100
University of Lagos	58.3	41.7	100

Table 10 shows various levels of usage based on daily, weekly, monthly, occasionally, and those who never use them (see also Table 11).

DISCUSSION

It can be said that every technology operates in a cultural field and is under the effect of its component influences. That is, each and every one of the components of a technology (i.e., blog, wiki, media, etc.) exists within an environment that is dominated by: social-psychological factors like language, values, customs, traditions, management style; political factors such as bureaucracy, legal structure, degree of nationalism; and economic factors like markets, inflation, taxation, distribution systems tariffs, and so on.

Perceptions vary in the magnitude with which participants responded to the use of Web 2.0 for teaching and learning. Based on the responses from all the participants, both the students and faculty, cultural inclination has no significant influence on their use of Web 2.0 for learning. However, the majority of the participants from the University of Lagos, both the students and lecturers, believe that adoption of Web 2.0 supports cultural promotion.

The findings in this study also revealed that the majority of students who participated in this study from both universities disagreed that adoption of digital technology is influenced by their being afraid (technophobia) of using them for learning.

Students from the University of Lagos preferred formal instructor-led models of learning and can be described as learner centered, and they mostly prefer collaborative learning. This finding does not support Hofstede (1980), who indicated that

Table 10. Faculty's frequency of use of technology

	%	%	%	%	%	%
	Daily	Weekly	Monthly	Occasionally	Never	Total
Robert Morris University	26.6	16.7	10	30	16.7	100
University of Lagos	36.6	36.4	0	27.2	0	100

Table 11. Faculty/lecturers' perceptions of the use of Web 2.0 applications

Item	Agree (%)		Neutral (%)		Disagree (%)	
Level of agreement/disagreement (%)	RMU	UNILAG	RMU	UNILAG	RMU	UNILAG
1. Cultural inclinations make me not adopt Web 2.0 for learning.	4.5	0	18.7	0	76.8	100
2. Adoption of Web 2.0 supports cultural promotion	44.8	58	41.2	0	13.8	41.6
3. Web 2.0 adoption has great impact on national relationship between countries.	63	91.7	30	8.3	6.7	0
4. Information Communication Technology adoption helps to boost my country's economy.	70	91.6	26.6	8.3	3.3	0
5. Instructors/Lecturers being afraid of using digital technology impacts its adoption during teaching.	83	50.3	13.3	10	3.3	30
6. Adoption of digital technology is influenced by my being afraid (technophobia) of using it for teaching.	16.6	8.3	13.3	20	67	75
7. Western cultural imposition impacts the adoption of Web 2.0 by some countries.	40	66.6	50	0	10.2	30
8. Social inequality hinders digital technology adoption in my country.	38	60	6.7	0	55	30
9. A country's welfare influences its adoption of Web 2.0.	66.6	66.3	26.6	10	6.6	25
10. Technology adoption promotes cultural identity imperialism.	24	33	44.8	20		50
11. Capitalism increases the adoption of Web 2.0 in my country.	66.6	60.3	23	0	10.2	30
12. Increased reliance on ICT is a threat to the globalization of our cultural heritage	24	33	44.8	10	43.3	58
13. Increased reliance on ICT is an opportunity for the globalization of our cultural heritage.	43	83	36.7	10	20.4	58
14. I prefer formal instructor-led models of teaching.	43	33	33	0	23	60
15. My students prefer a clear learning path or syllabus and like to know all the expected achievements in advance.	93	100	6.6	0	11	60
16. My students can be described as learner centered, and I mostly prefer collaborative learning	40	75	30	0	30.6	25
17. My students prefer blended learning and prescribed curriculum.	70	66	20	10	10.2	25
18. My students prefer personalized learning portal and prescribed learning curriculum.	33.3	60	46.6	10	20.1	41.6

people from collectivistic culture such as Nigeria's cultural expectations include easy familiarity with personalized learning portal, prescribed curricula, and mentoring. However, the finding that forty-four percent of RMU students' participants' preferred blended learning and prescribed curriculum confirmed Hofstede's assertion that the cultural expectations of people from individualistic culture such as the United States include easy familiarity with personalized learning portal, prescribed curricula, and mentoring.

Another significant finding of this study was that the majority of the RMU faculty's' participants and University of Lagos lecturers agreed that their students preferred clear learning path or syllabus and like to know all the expected achievements. This finding is relevant to the students of the digital age and can be attributed to the implications of Vygotsky theory which indicated that learners should be provided with socially rich environments in which to explore knowledge domains with their fellow students, teachers and outside experts. Web 2.0 can be used to support learning by providing tools for discourse, communication, collaborating, problem-solving, and providing online support systems to scaffold students' evolving understanding and cognitive growth. When students are using Web 2.0 as a learning or communicating tool, they are in an active role rather than the passive role of the recipient of information transmitted by a teacher, textbook, or broadcast.

Fifty-eight percent of University of Lagos lecturers' participants agreed that increased reliance on ICT is a threat to the globalization of their cultural heritage; this result differs from other similar studies. According to Lau (2011), staff were increasingly using mobile technologies in tutorials and saw them as a valuable addition to the classroom. Further, mobile technology has the potential to become a critical tool for teaching (Bond 2010). This difference suggests that the technology does not have to be a threat, but can be used effectively if it is integral to the learning

process. However, if it is used as a distracting social tool in a tutorial, control of its use is justified.

CONCLUSION

Capitalism generally refers to an economic system in which the means of production are all or mostly privately owned and operated for profit, and in which investments, distribution, income, production and pricing of goods and services are determined through the operation of a market economy. Most capitalist states operate a market economy driven globally by technology, which presently has gone digital for improved performance. The emerging educational technology tools on the whole, have given impetus to developments in various fields and improved the quality of human life, especially in education. Students thus need to develop not only in this economic system but also to possess the skills of effective communication, collaboration, and social interaction in order to interact with people from a different culture (Chen, Hsu, &Caropreso, 2006).

Educational technology use allows students to be actively thinking about information sharing, making choices, and utilizing skills more than is typical in teacher-led lessons. When Web 2.0 is used as a tool to support learning, the students are in the position of defining their goals, making decisions, and evaluating their progress. The teacher's role has changed as well from teacher-centered to student-centered, setting project goals and providing guidelines and resources, suggestions, and support for student activity.

Globally and most especially in developing countries, the advent of ICT and other digital technologies has brought great changes to teaching and learning. For higher education institutions, especially in developing countries, there has been the introduction of various types of digital tools and the implementation of policies to facilitate their integration in teaching and administration of new curricula.

ACKNOWLEDGMENT

Appreciation is extended to the group of researchers and Faculty at Robert Morris University who supported all my efforts to complete this work. This study was funded through the Rooney Program at the Robert Morris University and the University of Lagos, Nigeria. I am very grateful to all my colleagues at Robert Morris University, especially Prof. Lawrence Tomei, Babara Levine, and Jim Vincent for their support with this study.

REFERENCES

Agyeman, O. T. (2007). *Survey of ICT and education in Africa: Nigeria country report.* Retrieved from www.infodev.org

Armstrong, V., Barnesa, S., Sutherland, R., Curran, S., Mills, S., & Thompson, I. (2005). *Collaborative research methodology for investigating teaching and learning: The use of interactive whiteboard technology.* Retrieved from http://smartboards.typepad.com/smartboard/files/article1.pdf

Bailey, G. D. (1997). What technology leaders need to know: The essential top 10 concepts for technology integration in the 21st century. *Learning and Leading with Technology, 25*(1), 57–62.

Bernard, M. (2000). Constructing user-centered websites: The early design phases of small to medium sites. *Usability News 2*(1).

Butler, D., & Sellbom, M. (2002). *Barriers to adopting technology for teaching and learning.* Retrieved from http://cmapspublic3.ihmc.us/rid=1KC10V38V-C21PMV-GG/Barriers%20To%20Technology.pdf

Chen, S. J., Hsu, C. L., & Caropreso, E. J. (2006). Cross-cultural collaborative online learning: When the west meets the east. *International Journal of Technology in Teaching and Learning, 2*(1), 17–35.

Chinnamma, S. (2005). Effects of globalisation on education and culture. In *Proceeding ICDE International Conference.* ICDE.

Christensen, R. (2002). *Effects of Technology Integration Education on the Attitudes of Teachers and Students.* Retrieved from http://mytechtips.pbworks.com/f/Effects%20of%20Technology%20Integration%20Education%20on%20the%20Attitudes%20of%20Teachers%20and%20Students%20(1).pdf

Creswell, J. W. (2008). *Educational research: Planning, conducting, and evaluating quantitative and qualitative research* (3rd ed.). Upper Saddle River, NJ: Pearson Education.

Czerniewicz & Brown. (2006). Paper. In *Proceedings of Scan ICT 20005: Economic commission for Africa: Fourth Meeting of the Committee on Development Information.* Addis Ababa, Ethiopia: Scan ICT.

Dunbar, R. (1991). Adapting distance education for Indonesians: Problems with learner heteronomy and a strong oral tradition. *Distance Education, 12*(2), 163–174. doi:10.1080/0158791910120203

Erumban, A. A., & Jong, S. B. (2003). *Cross-country differences in ICT adoption - A consequence of culture?* Retrieved from http://som.rug.nl

Facer, K., Furlong, J., Furlong, R., & Sutherland, R. (2001). *Screenplay: Children and computing in the home.* London: RoutledgeFalmer.

Fuchs, C., & Horak, E. (2006). *Informational capitalism and the digital divide in Africa.* Retrieved from http://storage02.video.muni.cz/prf/mujlt/storage/1205244869_sb_s02-fuchs.pdf

Gay, L., Mills, G., & Gall, J. (2006). *Educational research: Competencies for analysis and application* (9th ed.). Upper Saddle River, NJ: Prentice Hall.

Glenn, A. D. (1997). Technology and the continuing education of classroom teachers. *Peabody Journal of Education*, 72(1), 122–128. doi:10.1207/s15327930pje7201_6

Hooker, M. (1997). The transformation of higher education. In D. Oblinger, & S. C. Rush (Eds.), *The Learning Revolution*. Bolton, MA: Anker Publishing Company, Inc.

Johnson, J. P., & Lenartowicz, T. (1998). Culture, freedom and economic growth: Do cultural values explain economic growth? *Journal of World Business*, *33*, 332–356. doi:10.1016/S1090-9516(99)80079-0

Jorgenson, Ho, &Stiroh. (2007). *A retrospective look at the U.S. productivity growth resurgence.* Retrieved from http://www.newyorkfed.org/research/staff_reports/sr277.pdf

Jude, W. I., & Dankaro, J T. (2012). ICT resource utilization, availability and accessibility by teacher educators for instructional development in college of education Katsina-Ala. *New Media and Mass Communication, 3.*

Kent, N., & Facer, K. (2004). Different worlds? A comparison of young people's home and school ICT use. *Journal of Computer Assisted Learning*, *20*(6), 440–455. doi:10.1111/j.1365-2729.2004.00102.x

Latchem. (2005). Article. In *Proceedings of Scan ICT 20005: Economic commission for Africa: Fourth Meeting of the Committee on Development Information*. Addis Ababa. Ethiopia: Scan ICT.

Levin, J. S. (2001). *Globalizing the community college: Strategies for change in the 21st century*. New York: Palgrave Books. doi:10.1057/9780312292836

Marcus, A., & Gould, E. (2000). Cultural dimensions and global web user-interface design: What? So what? Now what? In *Proceedings of the 6th Conference on Human Factors and the Web* (pp. 1–15). Austin, TX: Academic Press.

NRC. (2009). *Assessing the impacts of changes in the information technology R&D ecosystem: Retaining Leadership in an Increasingly Global Environment.* Retrieved from www.nap.edu/catalog/12174.html

Olatokun, W. M. (2007). *Availability, accessibility and use of ICTs by Nigerian women academics.* Retrieved from http://majlis.fsktm.um.edu.my/document.aspx?FileName=564.pdf

Patton, M. Q. (1990). *Qualitative evaluation and research Methods* (2nd ed.). Newbury Park, CA: Sage Publications.

Pelgrum, W. J. (2001). Obstacles to the integration of Information Communication Technology (ICT) in education: Results from worldwide educational assessments. *Computers & Education*, *37*, 163–178. doi:10.1016/S0360-1315(01)00045-8

Vygotsky, L. S. (1978). *Mind in society*. Cambridge, MA: Harvard.

Wertsch, J. (1991). *Voices of the mind: a socio cultural approach to mediated action*. London: Harvester.

Yelland, N. (2001). *Teaching and learning with ICT for numeracy in the early childhood and the primary years of schooling*. Canberra, Australia: Department of Education, Training and Youth Affairs.

ADDITIONAL READING

Adeoye, B. F. (2004), The relationship between national culture and usability of an e-Learning system. Unpublished PhD. Dissertation, University of Illinois.

Adeoye, B. F. (2009). Usability of Internet among academics: Gender differences in Internet competencies among lecturers at University of Lagos, Nigeria. 11th Annual Conference on World Wide Web Applications Conference Proceedings. Port Elizabeth, South Africa. pp. 4-14.

Adeoye, B. F. (2011). Culturally different learning styles in online learning environments among a selected Nigeria university students. *International Journal of Information and Communication Technology Education*, *7*(2), 1–12. doi:10.4018/jicte.2011040101

Adeoye, B. F., Adeoye-Folami, F., & Houston, D. M. (2010). Adoption and Utilization of Information Communication Technologies among Families in Lagos, Nigeria. *International Journal on Computer Science and Engineering.*, *2*(7), 2302–2308.

Borgmann, A. (1984). *Technology and the Character of Contemporary Life*. Chicago: University of Chicago Press.

Branch, R. M. (1997). Educational technology frameworks that facilitate culturally pluralistic instruction. *Educational Technology*, *37*(2), 38–41.

Evers, V., & Day, D. (1997). The role of culture in interface acceptance. In S. Howard, J. Hammond, & G. Lindegaard (Eds.), *Human computer interaction INTERACT'97*. London: Chapman and Hall. doi:10.1007/978-0-387-35175-9_44

Fernandez, T. (1995). *Global interface design*. London: Academic Press.

Fuchs, C. (2009, July). A Contribution to the critique of the political economy of transnational informational capitalism. *Rethinking Marxism*, *21*(3), 387–402. doi:10.1080/08935690902955104

Fulcher, J. (2004). *Capitalism - A very Short Introduction* (p. 41). Oxford University Press. doi:10.1093/actrade/9780192802187.001.0001

Giddens, A. (1973). *Capitalism and Modern Social Theory. An Analysis of the Writings of Marx, Durkheim and Weber*. Cambridge: Cambridge University Press.

Hall, E. T. (1990). *Understanding cultural differences*. Yarmouth, ME: Intercultural Press.

Henderson, L. (1996). Instructional design of interactive multimedia: A cultural critique. *Educational Technology Research and Development*, *44*(4), 85–105. doi:10.1007/BF02299823

Hites, J. M. (1996). Design and delivery of training for international trainees: A case study. *Performance Improvement Quarterly*, *9*(2), 57–74. doi:10.1111/j.1937-8327.1996.tb00720.x

Hofstede, G. (1980). *Culture's consequences: International differences in work-related values*. Beverly Hills, CA: Sage.

MacKenzie, D. (1984). Marx and the Machine. *Technology and Culture*, *25*, 473–502. doi:10.2307/3104202

Marcel, C. LaFollette and Jeffrey K. Stine (1991). Technology and Choice: Readings from Technology and Culture, Edited by is published by University of Chicago Press.

Yonary, Y. P. (1998). *The Struggle Over the Soul of Economics* (p. 29). Princeton University Press.

KEY TERMS AND DEFINITIONS

Capitalism: "Social formation," to borrow Marx's useful term, with three historically unique features: an all-important dependency on the successful accumulation of capital; a wide-ranging use of a market mechanism; and a unique bifurcation of power into two sectors, one public, one private. Together these institutional features serve both to guide the system in its daily workings as well as to maintain or change its long-term historical thrust.

Globalization: The intensification of world wide social relations which link distant localities in such a way that local happenings are shaped by events occurring many miles away and vice versa.

Information Capitalism: An information generation, processing, and transmission, that have become the fundamental sources of productivity and power.

Technology: A sociopolitical force within capitalism, not merely a lever of material change. The reason, of course, is that technological change is the chief source of new areas of profitable accumulation. Here the market plays two roles, first in helping to facilitate the complex maneuvers by which the accumulation circuit works; later in bringing about the competition that will eat away at the profitability of these circuits.

Section 2
Cross-Cultural Communication and the Innovative Use of Digital Technology

Chapter 2
Using Digital Technologies to Aid E-Learning:
A Pilot Study

Michele T. Cole
Robert Morris University, USA

Daniel J. Shelley
Robert Morris University, USA

Louis B. Swartz
Robert Morris University, USA

Blessing F. Adeoye
University of Lagos, Nigeria

ABSTRACT

This chapter presents the results of a pilot study conducted in the summer of 2013 in which researchers sought to discover how students and instructors at two universities were using selected digital technologies in their coursework. To the extent that digital technologies were being used, did students find their use to be helpful in learning course material? Researchers surveyed undergraduate students at the University of Lagos, Nigeria, and undergraduate, masters, and doctoral students at Robert Morris University in Western Pennsylvania. For the most part, comparing responses from both universities demonstrated similarities in how and what digital technologies were used in coursework. However, there were significant differences found when the uses of certain technologies were examined at each institution and how helpful to learning they were for students. There was also a significant difference found in determining how soon new digital technologies would be adopted.

DOI: 10.4018/978-1-4666-6162-2.ch002

Copyright © 2014, IGI Global. Copying or distributing in print or electronic forms without written permission of IGI Global is prohibited.

INTRODUCTION

In their ten-year study of the nature and extent of online education in the United States, Allen and Seaman (2013) found that online education continues to expand at a rate faster than traditional campus-based programs. The authors reported the number of students enrolled in at least one online course to be at an all-time high of 32% of all enrollments in participating institutions. This represents an increase of 570,000 students from the previous year.

Increasingly, institutions are examining their online delivery models, particularly with regard to how online courses are designed to maximize student learning. The arrival of Massive Open Online Courses (MOOCs) has intensified the pressure on traditional institutions of higher education to find better ways to reach a changing student body. In their 2010 report, Allen and Seaman noted that 63% of the universities and colleges in their study reported that providing effective online instruction was a critical element of their institution's strategic plans. As more institutions of higher education, both public and private, are partnering with commercial educational technology companies, such as Coursera, to offer courses online world-wide, including offering some for credit, there is a rising concern about the ability of the institution to control both the quality and the effectiveness of these courses.

What role do digital technologies play in instructional development for e-learning? Discussing the benefits and risks to student learning provided by the use of simulations, digital libraries, and computer-based tutorial programs, Dubose (2011) suggests that while integrating social media into the virtual classroom is attractive on several levels including student satisfaction and success with e-learning, as well as institutional benefits such as lower overall instructional cost, firm conclusions as to the role digital technologies, particularly social media, can play in instructional design are premature.

Five courses at two universities were chosen for the pilot study. These consisted of two undergraduate courses, two master's level courses and one doctoral level course. This study focused on which digital technologies students and instructors were using in their courses in order to better understand how these technologies could be incorporated in coursework to enhance e-learning. Results from the pilot study provide some data on the role digital technologies could continue to have in designing online courses. The study also examined how these digital technologies were currently in use and which technologies students found to have contributed positively to their learning in an online environment.

BACKGROUND

For online course design to be effective, instructors need to incorporate the "reality of the digital world" because the newest generation of learners is "hardwired" to use multiple types of Web-based media (Baird & Fisher, 2005-2006, p.10). For example, Huang and Nakazawa (2010) found that different Web 2.0 technologies, such as wikis, positively impact student learning by opening access to the instructor and to the other students in the course. In another example, this one focusing on students' use of social media in a business communications course, Kelm (2011) found the students' use of specific social media proved to be crucial in understanding the material.

Focusing on how Facebook was being used for instruction, Bosch (2009) looked at how students and instructors might use other digital technologies to enhance instruction and maximize learning. Others have looked at the use of digital technologies in course design. Greenhow, Robelia and Hughes (2009) reported on the potential of using interactive technologies in teaching and learning.

Otte, Gold, Gorges, Smith and Stein (2012) described the impact of academic social networks in building community and facilitating resource sharing, resulting in a growing adoption of technology for academic purposes. In another study of how students were using digital technologies in their coursework, Baggett and Williams (2012) found the ones most often cited as useful to learning were Facebook, Google+ and Tumblr. Huang and Nakazawa (2010) also found that digital technologies, specifically wikis, affected learning in a positive way in that their use provided broader access to others in the course as well as to the teacher. Referring to social media, Goatman (2011) pointed to its usefulness in accessing both course material and the instructor.

Silius, Kailanto and Tervakari (2011) found that the use of digital technologies, e.g., Facebook, YouTube and blogs, in an educational context to enhance learning presented an upward trend. Yet the challenge for instructors and their institutions remains: how do they supportively link the students' needs with emerging technologies and translate that into effective pedagogy? Parker, Maor, and Herrington (2013) propose that the three together, student needs, emerging technologies and effective pedagogy, are necessary "…to construct more interactive, engaging and student-centered environments that promote 21st century skills and encourage self-directed learning" (p. 227).

Remarking on the evolution of digital technologies and their incorporation into teaching and learning practices, Hedberg (2011) reinforced the perception that today's student is experienced in the use of digital tools-- is a "digital native," as it were. His argument was that course design needed to focus on the technology-enablement student to achieve desired learning outcomes. In his study, he found that students performed at higher levels than before because they were more engaged in their learning. All participants, he reported, were using digital technologies at a higher level than they had been when the study began.

A study by Reynol (2012) reported that instructors are becoming increasingly more comfortable incorporating digital technologies such as social media into the classroom. In this study, results indicated that Facebook was used more for teaching purposes than Twitter. Reynol's study also indicated that "concerns about privacy," primarily related to Facebook and Twitter as they tend to be more public, were a barrier to using social media in the classroom.

Issues

Today, there is a clear and heightened awareness of social media among those in higher education. According to Moran, Seaman, and Tinti-Kane (2011), faculty members are very familiar with social media. More than 90% report that they are aware of such sites as MySpace, Facebook, Twitter, YouTube, and blogs. The awareness level drops to approximately 80% for other sites, such as wikis, LinkedIn, Flickr, and SlideShare.

In looking at how students and instructors were currently using digital technologies in their online courses, the researchers in this study were exploring whether incorporating interactive, collaborative tools such as Facebook, YouTube, Twitter, Wikipedia, LinkedIn, blogs and wikis enhanced student learning. The researchers were also interested in learning whether students' use of digital technologies in their daily activities might transfer and support their use in the online classroom.

To determine whether and how digital technologies were being used in the classroom, researchers framed three research questions:

1. Do students use digital technologies to help them learn course material?
2. Do instructors use digital technologies to present course material?

3. Do students find digital technologies to be helpful in learning course material?

Study Methodology

Researchers used a Web-based survey created in QuestionPro, an online survey software package used by both the U.S. and the Nigerian universities. Students in two undergraduate courses, two masters' level courses and one doctoral level course were asked to participate in the study via an e-mail solicitation from the instructor. The survey was anonymous. Survey results were transferred from QuestionPro to SPSS for analysis of selected responses. Cross tabulations of the selected questions were conducted in QuestionPro.

Sample

The sample population included undergraduate business majors, MBA students. MS in Instructional Technology, and doctoral students in education at Robert Morris University and at the University of Lagos, undergraduate students.

Sixty-four students participated in the survey in summer, 2013. Of these, 22 were undergraduate students at the University of Lagos, 44% of the sample. Forty-two students (graduate and undergraduate) from Robert Morris University participated, 65.6% of the sample. The response rate for students at the University of Lagos was 44%. The response rate from students at Robert Morris University was 72%.

Researchers compared responses to selected survey questions from the student samples at both universities. Responses were broken down by gender, age group and level of study.

Males represented 51.56% of the respondents, females, 48.44%. Thirty-three males (21 from RMU and 12 from the University of Lagos) and thirty-one females (21 from RMU and 10 from the University of Lagos) participated in the study.

Respondents self-identified as belonging to one of four age groups:

- Traditional Workers (born before 1946)
- Baby Boomers (born between 1946 and 1960),
- Generation X (born between 1961 and 1979) and,
- Generation Y (born after 1979) (Recursos Humanos, 2010)

Forty-four students, 71% of the sample, self-identified as belonging to Generation Y. Twenty-three of these were males, 21 respondents were females. Thirty-two, 74%, were students at RMU. Twelve, 63%, were U. of Lagos students.

Nine students, 14.5% of the sample, self-identified as being members of Generation X. Five of these were females; four were males. Four of these students were from RMU; five were students at the U. of Lagos.

Six students, 9.68% of the sample self-identified as members of the Baby Boomer category. Four were males, two were females. Five of the six were students at RMU. One student in this category was from the U. of Lagos. Three students, one male and two females classified themselves as "Other." Two students were from RMU. One student was from the U. of Lagos. Note that not all students responded to the question on age. Table 1 presents the generational profile of the two samples.

Twenty-one undergraduate students participated (32.8%). Eleven of these were students at RMU; ten were students from the U. of Lagos. Thirty-eight graduate students participated (59.3%). Five students (7.8%) chose "Other" when asked where they were in their course of study. All five were students from RMU. Of the 21 undergraduate students participating, 12 were males and nine were females. Of the 38 graduate students who responded, 19 were males and 19 were females. Two males and three females responded as "Other."

With regard to their respective age groups, 14 of the 21 undergraduates responded that they were members of Generation Y. Three said that they

Table 1. Generational breakdown by university

Generation	Total N=62 100%	RMU n=43 69% of total	U. of Lagos n=19 30% of total
Traditional (Before 1946)	0 0	0 0	0 0
Baby Boomer (1946-1960)	6 9.7%	5 8%	1 1.6%
Generation X (1961-1979)	9 14.5%	4 6%	5 8%
Generation Y (After 1979)	44 71. %	32 52%	12 19%
Other	3 4.8%	2 3%	1 1.6%

were members of Generation X. (Two respondents chose "Other.") Of the 38 graduate students, 27 were members of Generation Y. Six said they were members of Generation X. (Four students self-identified as belonging to the Baby Boomer generation.) In the "Doctoral/Other" category, three were members of Generation Y and two were members of the Baby Boomer Generation. Because not all students responded to each question, totals may differ among the tables. Table 2 presents the participant breakdown by level of study, comparing responses by university, gender, and generation.

Thirty-six students were enrolled full-time, 25 at RMU and 11 at the University of Lagos. Twenty-two of these were males, 14 were females. Twenty-two were members of Generation Y, eight were members of Generation X. (Five full-time students replied that they were members of the Baby Boomer generation. One person chose "Other.") Twenty-five respondents were enrolled as part-time students (16 at RMU and nine at the U. of Lagos). Ten of the part-time students were males, 15 were females. Twenty-one were members of Generation Y, one student responded as a member of Generation X. (Two people chose "Other.") Not all students responded to each

Table 2. Participant breakdown by level of study compared by university, gender, age

Level	Total N= 64	RMU n= 54	U. of Lagos n= 10	Male n=33	Female n=31	Gen. X n=9	Gen. Y n= 44
Undergrad.	21 33%	11	10	12	9	3	14
Graduate- MS.	38 59%	38	0	19	19	6	27
Doctoral/Other	5 8%	5	0	2	3	2 *	3

*Baby Boomers

Table 3. Participant enrollment status by university, gender, age

Status	Total n= 61	RMU n= 41	U. of Lagos n= 20	Male n=32	Female n=29	Gen. X n=9	Gen. Y n= 45
Full Time	36	25	11	22	14	8	22
Part-Time	25	16	9	10	15	1	21

Table 4. Experience with online/partially online courses by university, gender

# Courses	Total N= 64	RMU n= 42	U. of Lagos n= 22	Male n=33	Female n=31
One	15 23.4%	4	11	5	10
Two - Four	24 37.5%	18	6	16	8
Five-Ten	14 21.7%	13	1	5	9
Ten +	7 10.9%	7	0	4	3
Other/None	4 6.3%		4	3	1

question, particularly on age. As a result, the totals differ. Table 3 presents the participants' enrollment status compared by university, gender and generation.

To determine how familiar participants were with e-learning, researchers asked the participants how many online courses they had taken. Fifteen or 23.44% reported having taken one course (four from RMU and 11 from the University of Lagos). Five were males and ten were females. Twenty-four or 37.5% reported having taken between two and four courses (18 from RMU, six from U. of Lagos). Sixteen were males and eight were females. Fourteen or 21.68% had taken between five and ten fully or partially online courses 13 from RMU, one from the University of Lagos). Five were males, nine were females. Seven or 10.94% had taken ten or more online or partially online courses (all seven were from RMU). Four were males, three were females. Four students or 6.25% said that they not taken any online courses. These students were from the University of Lagos. Three were males and one was female. Table 4 presents the respondents' experience level with online or partially online courses compared by university, and gender.

Of those who self- identified as belonging to a particular age group, members of the Baby Boomer generation reported the most experience with online learning, followed by members of Generation Y. The nine members of Generation X who responded reported the least experience with online learning. Table 5 presents the mean scores.

Procedure

A 19-question survey was developed to assess how frequently students were using digital technologies in their daily activities as well as in their coursework. Researchers also wanted to know whether instructors had used digital technologies in the courses these students had taken and if so, which ones were used. To the extent that digital technologies were being used in e-learning, how effective did students think specific technologies were in helping them to learn course material? Finally, researchers asked how soon after release would students be likely to adopt new technology.

The initial question asked students which university they were attending, the University of Lagos or Robert Morris University. Students could choose "Other."

Questions two through five asked for demographic information, age group, gender, level of study and enrollment status. To determine the level of experience that participants had with e-learning, the sixth question asked how many

Table 5. Experience with online/partially online courses by age group

Generation	n =59	M
Baby Boomer (1946- 1960)	6	2.83
Generation X (1961-1979)	9	1.67
Generation Y (after 1979)	44	2.48

online or partially online courses the respondent had taken.

Questions seven through 14 sought information on the types of digital technology students were using and with what frequency. Question seven focused on students' use of selected digital technologies in daily activities. Question eight asked if other digital technologies were used and if so, with what frequency. Question nine asked if the same digital technologies listed in question seven were used in learning course material. Both questions seven and nine asked how frequently the specific technology was used. Question ten asked if other digital technologies were used to learn course material and if so, with what frequency.

Questions 11 through 14 shifted the focus to the student's impression of the instructor's use of technology in courses they had taken. If instructors were using digital technologies in their courses, researchers asked which technologies were being used and how often. Question 15 asked participants to rate the digital technologies they or their instructors had used with regard to how helpful the specific technology had been in learning course material. Question 16 asked about other technologies that might have been helpful in e-learning. Questions 17 and 18 were open-ended, asking what made digital technologies helpful in learning and what recommendations respondents could give to instructors regarding the adoption of additional or different technologies in coursework.

The final question asked how quickly students in either environment, the University of Lagos or Robert Morris University, would typically adopt new technology.

Following approval from the University's Institutional Review Board, instructors in each of the five courses solicited their students' participation in the study. Students were provided with the link to the survey in QuestionPro. Masters students in instructional technology and doctoral students

in education were the first to respond, followed by the undergraduate students at the University of Lagos. The final classes to respond were the undergraduate business law students and the MBA students. Between May 21, 2013 and July 6, 2013, 89 students began the survey in QuestionPro. Sixty-four students and one instructor completed the survey. The instructor's responses were not included in the analysis.

Seventy-seven percent of the respondents used a personal computer to take the survey, 71% of those used Windows. Twenty-two percent used their Smartphones to respond, 32% of those used Blackberry, 16%, the iPhone, and 53% used something else which was not identified. One percent used an iPad to respond to the survey.

Selected data from the completed surveys were transferred from QuestionPro into SPSS. Independent samples t-tests were run on questions asking how frequently respondents used certain digital technologies in daily activities (seventh), and in coursework (ninth). T-tests were also conducted on the questions concerning the instructors' use of selected digital technologies (13th and 15th) and on the final question on how quickly new technologies would typically be adopted to determine if there were any statistically significant differences based on which university the student attended.

The cross tab function in QuestionPro was used to break out responses by university on the demographic questions, age, gender, level of study, and enrollment status. The cross tab function was also used to review which students had what level of experience with e-learning.

Results

There were statistically significant differences on responses to the question on students' use of digital technologies in daily activities and on the question regarding students' use of digital technologies in coursework.

Daily Activities

On the question asking how frequently selected digital technologies were used in daily activities, respondents rated Facebook as most used (mean score of 4.64, 64 students responding), followed by YouTube (mean score of 3.15, 59 students responding) and Twitter (mean score of 3.08, 61 students responding). The mean scores for Wikipedia, Blogs, LinkedIn and Wikis were 3.05 (60 students responding), 2.35 (60 students responding), 2.03 (59 students responding) and 2.03 (58 students responding) respectively. The scale measuring frequency was 1-"Never" to 6 –"Multiple times during a day." Respondents noted e-books, Skype and Instagram under other digital technologies used for daily activities.

When asked how frequently selected digital technologies were employed for coursework, respondents rated Wikipedia most used with a mean score of 2.93, 56 students responding. Wikipedia was followed by You Tube (mean score, 2.80, 56 students responding) and Facebook (mean score, 2.44, 63 students responding). The mean scores for Blogs, Twitter, Wikis and LinkedIn were 2.05 (56 students responding), 2.02 (58 students responding), 1.84 (55 students responding), and 1.53 (57 students responding) respectively. The scale measuring frequency was 1-"Never" to 6 –"Several times/day." Smart Board and e-books were noted under other digital tools used for learning course material.

There was a statistically significant difference at the .01 level (.006, equal variances assumed) for students' use of Wikipedia in daily activities. The mean score was 3.05, 60 students responding. The mean score for students at the University of Lagos was 3.71. For students at Robert Morris University, the mean score was 2.71.

There were statistically significant differences at the .01 level (.013 and .000, equal variances as-sumed) for students' use of Twitter and YouTube in daily activities based on gender. The mean score for males responding (32) to the frequency of use for Twitter was 3.69. The mean score for females (29) was 2.41. With regard to frequency of use for YouTube, the mean score for males (32) was 3.69. The mean score for females responding (27) was 2.52.

There was a statistically significant difference at the .01 level (.012, equal variances assumed) based on level of study for students' use of Wikipedia in daily activities. The mean score for master's students (28) was 3.39. The mean score for doctoral students (10) was 2.20. There were no statistically significant differences among the undergraduate levels or between the undergraduate and graduate level students.

There were no statistically significant differences based on age in the responses to the question on students' use of digital technologies in daily activities.

Coursework

There was a statistically significant difference at the .01 level (.002, equal variances assumed) for students' use of wikis in coursework. The mean score was 2.93, 56 students responding. The mean score for students at the University of Lagos was 3.08. For students at Robert Morris University, the mean score was 2.83.

There was a statistically significant difference at the .05 level (.015, equal variances assumed) for students' use of YouTube in coursework based on gender. The mean score for males responding (32) to the frequency of use for Twitter was 3.16. The mean score for females (24) was 2.33.

There was a statistically significant difference at the .05 level (.038, equal variances assumed) based on level of study for students' use of Blogs for coursework. The mean score for 4th year undergraduate students (3) was 3.67. The mean score for doctoral students (10) was 2.00. There were no statistically significant differences among the undergraduate levels or between the undergraduate and master's level students.

There were no statistically significant differences based on age in the responses to the question on students' use of digital technologies in coursework.

Instructors' Use

Sixty-three students answered the question asking if their instructors used digital technologies. Forty-eight responded "yes" (29 from RMU, 19 from U. of Lagos). Seventeen respondents had taken one course in which the instructor had used digital technologies. Twenty-five students had taken two to four courses in which the instructor had used digital technologies. Four respondents had taken five to ten courses and two students had taken more than ten courses in which the instructor had used digital technologies.

Respondents cited Facebook most (51) when asked which technologies were used by instructors, followed by Blogs (49), YouTube (48), Wikis (46), and Twitter (43). YouTube was ranked strongest in terms of integration into the course design with a mean score of 3.33. On a score of one to six ranking how often the technology was used in the course, one represented "All the time (Integral to the course)" and six represented "Never." After YouTube, Facebook was second (mean score of 3.71), followed by Blogs (mean score of 3.82), Wikis (mean score of 4.09) and Twitter (mean score of 4.51). Skype was listed as used occasionally under other technologies used by the instructor.

There were statistically significant differences in the mean scores for the University of Lagos and Robert Morris University for Facebook, YouTube, and Blogs at the .01 level (.000, .039, and .000 respectively, equal variances assumed). Mean scores for Facebook were 1.71-University of Lagos (17 students responding); 4.71-RMU (34 students responding). Mean scores for YouTube were 4.00–U. of Lagos (11 students responding);

3.14-RMU (37 students responding). The mean scores for Blogs were 2.57-U. of Lagos (14 students responding); 4.31-RMU (35 students responding).

Helpfulness for Learning

When asked how helpful each of the selected technologies used were for learning course material on a scale of one (not helpful) to five (very helpful), students rated YouTube highest at 3.14 (RMU-3.20, U.Lagos-2.67), followed by Wikipedia at 2.59 (RMU-2.45, U.Lagos-3.00), Facebook at 2.38 (RMU-1.52, U.Lagos-3.86), Blogs at 2.02 (RMU-1.73, U.Lagos-2.89), Wikis at 1.95 (RMU-1.77, U.Lagos-2.50), Twitter at 1.89 (RMU-1.37, U.Lagos-3.25), and LinkedIn at 1.41 (RMU-1.30, U. Lagos- 2.25). Facebook blogs, Annotated lecture series and YouTube and Skype were listed under recommendations for adoption by instructors.

There were statistically significant differences in the mean scores for Robert Morris University and the University of Lagos at the .01 level, equal variances assumed with regard to the ratings for Facebook (.000), Twitter (.000), LinkedIn (.017), and Blogs (.019). Table 6 illustrates the results.

On the final question, "Could you tell us when you are most likely to begin exploring or using a new digital tool?," 43% (27 respondents) answered, "As soon as it becomes available." One third (21 respondents) said, "After it becomes widely used and less expensive." Six students (9.5%) said "Once my friends begin using it." Five students (8%) answered, "Only if my university or instructor requires its use." Four students (6%) chose "Other," but did not elaborate on the response.

There was a statistically significant difference between the mean scores (RMU-2.60, 42 students responding, and U. of Lagos-1.60, 20 students responding) at the .01 level (.003, equal variances assumed.) Table 7 illustrates the results.

Table 6. Usefulness of digital technology to online learning by university

			t- test for Equality of Means
	n	*M*	Sig. (2-tailed)
Facebook	42	2.38	.000
Twitter	36	1.89	.000
LinkedIn	32	1.41	.017
Blogs	40	2.02	.019

Table 7. Adoption of new digital technology by university

			t- test for Equality of Means
	N	*M*	Sig. (2-tailed)
RMU	42	2.60	.003
U of Lagos	20	1.60	

Recommendations

There were ten areas of statistically significant difference in the use of digital technologies by students at the two universities. These were: use of Wikipedia in daily activities; use of wikis in coursework; instructors' use of Facebook; instructors' use of YouTube; instructors' use of Blogs; helpfulness of Facebook for learning; helpfulness of Twitter for learning; helpfulness of LinkedIn for learning; helpfulness of Blogs for learning; and on adoption of new technologies. In all cases, students from the University of Lagos responded more positively than students at Robert Morris University.

There were three areas of statistically significant difference on the use of digital technologies based on gender and two areas of statistically significant difference on the use of digital technologies based on level of study. In the first instance, regarding the use of Twitter, and of YouTube in daily activities and the use of YouTube in coursework, males were more likely than females to use those technologies. With regard to the differences expressed based on level of study, master's stu-

dents were more likely than doctoral students to use Wikipedia in daily activities. Undergraduate students (4th year) were more likely than doctoral students to use Blogs in coursework.

Philip and Garcia (2013) argued that just because students' use of digital technologies in everyday activities was ubiquitous, it could not be assumed that students' ability to use and interest in those digital technologies would transfer to the learning environment. Their position was that the emphasis on technology in course design was misplaced. That instead, the focus needed to remain on effective teaching that is, on a teacher-focused perspective.

This study's results were interesting with regard to students' use of digital technologies in coursework as well as in daily activities. The relevance to instructional design in online course delivery is present if not overwhelming. Still, the recommendation to those teaching in an online forum would be to recognize the potential that digital technologies such as Facebook, YouTube, and LinkedIn offer for enhancing learning. It might also be argued that incorporating digital technologies into their courses would give instructors another set of tools to increase student engagement in the learning process.

Study Limitations

This was a pilot study with a limited sample. The courses taught at RMU used Blackboard as its online platform. The course taught at the University of Lagos used Facebook as well as Skype to deliver course material.

FUTURE RESEARCH DIRECTIONS

Although the use and application of the various forms of social media were apparent throughout the pilot study, it seems clear that these digital technologies in particular will assume an ever-increasing level of importance in university coursework as well as in students' daily activities. This study did provide direction for future research designed to answer the question concerning how both students and instructors are using digital technologies in online course design and instruction. Ongoing research is necessary to determine what place digital technologies will have in future instructional design and pedagogy.

Subsequent research may need to focus on the relationship, if any, between students' use of digital technologies in their everyday lives and their use of the same technologies in e-learning. Perhaps even more important, would be additional studies on the impact that the use of digital technologies in coursework has on student learning.

CONCLUSION

In this initial study, researchers sought to discover how students and instructors at two universities were using selected digital technologies in their coursework. The questions posed were:

1. Do students use digital technologies to help them learn course material?
2. Do instructors use digital technologies to present course material?
3. Do students find digital technologies to be helpful in learning course material?

In short, the answer to each of the three was "yes."

The study did demonstrate that both students and instructors were using digital technologies in the online learning environment. With regard to how useful students found the various forms of digital technology in learning course material online, this study did demonstrate that students felt that the use of certain tools, such as YouTube and Wikipedia was helpful for learning.

The results from this initial study indicate that there are significant differences in the adoption of new technology and the use of certain digital

technologies between students at the University of Lagos and Robert Morris University. However, additional studies are necessary before those differences could be attributed to cultural differences.

REFERENCES

Allen, E., & Seaman, J. (2010). Class differences: Online education in the United States, 2010. *BABSON Survey Research Group, Sloan Consortium.* Retrieved from http://sloanconsortium.org/publications/survey/survey05.asp

Allen, I. E., & Seaman, J. (2013). *Changing course: Ten years of tracking online education in the United States.* Babson Survey Research Group and Quahog Research Group. Retrieved from http://www.onlinelearningsurvey.com/reports/changingcourse.pdf

Baggett, S.B., & Williams, M. (2012, January-March). Student behaviors and opinions regarding the use of social media, mobile technologies, and library research. *Virginia Libraries*, 19-22.

Baird, D. E., & Fisher, M. (2005-2006). Neomillennial user experience design strategies: Utilizing social networking media to support always on learning styles. *Journal of Educational Technology Systems*, *34*(1), 5–32. doi:10.2190/6WMW-47L0-M81Q-12G1

Bosch, T. E. (2009). Using online social networking for teaching and learning: Facebook use at the University of Cape Town. *Communicatio*, *35*(2), 185–200. doi:10.1080/02500160903250648

Dubose, C. (2011). The social media revolution. *Radiologic Technology*, *83*(2), 112–119. PMID:22106386

Goatman, C. (2011, September 26). *How using social media can help you with your online college classes*. Retrieved from http://soshable.com/how-using-social-media-can-help-you-with-your-online-college-classes

Greenhow, C., Robelia, B., & Hughes, J. E. (2009). Learning, teaching, and scholarship in a digital age: Web 2.0 and classroom research: What path should we take now? *Educational Researcher*, *38*(4), 246–259. doi:10.3102/0013189X09336671

Hedberg, J. G. (2011). Towards a disruptive pedagogy: Changing classroom practice with technologies and digital content. *Educational Media International*, *48*(1), 1–16. doi:10.1080/09523987.2011.549673

Huang, W. D., & Nakazawa, K. (2010). An empirical analysis of how learners interact in wiki in a graduate level online course. *Interactive Learning Environments*, *18*(3), 233–244. doi:10.1080/10494820.2010.500520

Kelm, O. R. (2011). Social media: It's what students do. *Business Communication Quarterly*, *74*(4), 505–520. doi:10.1177/1080569911423960

Moran, M., Seaman, J., & Tinti-Kane, H. (2011). *Teaching, learning, and sharing: How today's higher education faculty use social media*. Pearson. Retrieved from www.pearsonlearningsolutions.com

Otte, G., Gold, M., Gorges, B., Smith, M., & Stein, C. (2012). *The CUNY academic commons: Social network as hatchery*. Sloan-C. Retrieved from http://sloanconsortium.org/effective_practices/cuny-academic-commons

Parker, J., Maor, D., & Herrington, J. (2013). Authentic online learning: Aligning learner needs, pedagogy and technology. *Issues in Educational Research*, *23*(2), 227–241.

Philip, T. M., & Garcia, A. D. (2013). The importance of still teaching the igeneration: New technologies and the centrality of pedagogy. *Harvard Educational Review*, *83*(2), 300–319.

Recursos Humanos. (2010). Dueling age groups in today's workforce: From Baby Boomers to Generations X and Y. *Universia Knowledge @ Wharton*. Retrieved from http://www.wharton.universia.net/

Reynol, J. (2012). The relationship between frequency of Facebook use, participation in Facebook activities, and student engagement. *Computers & Education*, *58*, 162–171. doi:10.1016/j.compedu.2011.08.004

Silius, K., Kailanto, M., & Tervakari, A.-M. (2011). Evaluating the quality of social media in an educational context. *International Journal of Emerging Technologies in Learning*, *6*(3), 21–27.

ADDITIONAL READING

Adeoye, B., & Wentling, R. M. (2007). The relationship between national culture and the usability of an e-learning system. *International Journal on E-Learning*, *6*(1), 119-146. Chesapeake, VA: AACE. Retrieved from http://www.editlib.org/p/6226

Anderson, T., & Dron, J. (2012). Learning technology through three generations of technology enhanced distance education pedagogy. *European Journal of Open, Distance and E-Learning 2*. Retrieved from http://ehis.ebscohost.com/eds/delivery?sid

Aviram, A., & Esher-Alkalai, Y. (2010). *Towards a theory of digital literacy: Three scenarios for the next steps*. Retrieved from www.eurodl.org/materials/contrib/2006/Aharon_Aviram.htm

Bates, A. W., & Poole, G. (2003). *Effective teaching with technology in higher education: foundations for success*. Indianapolis, In Jossey Bass.

Bullas, J. (2011*). 20 stunning social media statistics plus infographic*. Retrieved from www.jeffbullas.com/2011/09/20-stunning-social-media-statistics

Chen, H. (2009). The perspectives of higher education faculty on Wikipedia. *The Electronic Library*, *28*(3), 361–373. doi:10.1108/02640471011051954

Collins, A., & Halverson, R. (2009). *Rethinking education in the age of technology: The digital revolution and schooling in America*. New York: Teachers College Press.

Duhaney, D. C. (2012). Blended learning and teacher preparation programs. *International Journal of Instructional Media*, *39*(3), 197.

Gutnick, A. L., Robb, M., Takeuchi, L., & Kotler, J. (2010). *Always connected: The new digital media habits of young children*. New York: The Joan Ganz Cooney Center at Sesame workshop.

Head, A. J., & Eisenberg, M. B. (2009). *Lessons learned: How college students seek information in the digital age*. The Information School, University of Washington.

Howland, J. L., Jonassen, D., & Marra, R. M. (2012). *Meaningful learning with technology* (4th ed.). Boston, MA: Pearson Education, Inc.

Hutchings, M., Hadfield, M., Howarth, G., & Lewarne, S. (2007, August). Meeting the challenges of active learning in Web-based case studies for sustainable development. *Innovations in Education and Teaching International*, *44*(3), 331–343. doi:10.1080/14703290701486779

Jaffer, S. (2010). Educational technology pedagogy: A looseness of fit between learning theories and pedagogy. *Education As Change*, *14*(2), 273–287. doi:10.1080/16823206.2010.522066

Johnson, S. (2011). *Digital tools for teaching: 30 e-tools for collaborating, creating, and publishing across the curriculum*. Gainesville, FL: Maupin House Publishing, Inc.

Joosten, T. (2012). *Social media for educators: Strategies and best practices*. San Francisco, CA: Jossey Bass.

Junco, R., Heiberger, G., & Loken, E. (2011). The effect of Twitter on college student engagement and grades. *Journal of Computer Assisted Learning*, *27*(2), 119–132. doi:10.1111/j.1365-2729.2010.00387.x

Lever-Duffy, J., & McDonald, J. (2010). *Teaching and learning with technology* (4th ed.). New York, NY: Pearson Education, Inc.

Lwoga, E. (2012). Making learning and Web 2.0 technologies work for higher learning institutions in Africa. *Campus-Wide Information Systems*, *29*(2), 90–107. doi:10.1108/10650741211212359

Manning, S. (2011). *The technology toolbelt for teaching*. San Francisco, CA: Jossey Bass.

McEachron, D. L., Bach, C., & Sualp, M. (2012). Digital Socrates: A system for disseminating and evaluating best practices in education. *Campus-Wide Information Systems*, *29*(4), 226–237. doi:10.1108/10650741211253822

Nielsen. (2011). *The mobile media report: State of the media Q3 2011*. Retrieved from www.nielsen.com/content/dam/corporate/us/en/reports-downloads/2011-Reports/state-of-mobile-Q3-2011.pdf

Pitler, H., Hubbell, E. R., & Kuhn, M. (2012). Using technology with classroom instruction that works, (2nd ed.). Denver, CO: Mid-Continent Research for Education and Learning (McRel).

Roblyer, M. D., McDaniel, M., Webb, M., Herman, J., & Witty, J. V. (2013). Findings on Facebook in higher education: A comparison of college faculty and student uses and perceptions of social networking sites. *The Internet and Higher Education*, *13*(3), 134–140. doi:10.1016/j.iheduc.2010.03.002

Rogers, M. (2013) *Wired for teaching*. Retrieved from http://www.insidehighered.com/news/2013/10/21/more-professors-using-social-media-teaching-tools

Saeed, N., Yang, Y., & Sinnappan, S. (2009). Emerging web technologies in higher education: A case of incorporating blogs, podcasts and social bookmarks in a web programming course based on students' learning styles and technology preferences. *Journal of Educational Technology & Society*, *12*(4), 98–109.

Saltman, D. (2011). Turning digital natives into digital citizens. *Harvard Education Letter*, 27(5). Retrieved from www.hepg.org/hel/article511

Selwyn, N. (2011). Social media in higher education. *The Europa World of Learning 2012 (62nd ed.)*. Retrieved from http://www.educationarena.com/pdf/sample/sample-essay-selwyn.pdf.

Ullman, E. (2013). School CIO: Using social media as a professional learning tool. *Tech 7 Learning*, *34* (3), 32-38.

Watkins, S. (2009). *The young and the digital: What the migration to social-network sites, games, and anytime, anywhere media means for our future*. Boston, MA: Beacon Press.

KEY TERMS AND DEFINITIONS

Digital Technology: Technology that uses a discrete method to convey information, such as letters or numbers.

Generation X: People born between 1961 and 1979.

Generation Y: People born after 1979.

Online Education: Web-based instruction.

Online Learning: Knowledge gained through electronically supported instruction.

Partially Online: Hybrid or blended learning delivery models.

Social Media: An online channel for user-generated content and interaction.

Chapter 3
The Era of Digital Technology in Teaching and Learning in African Universities

Blessing F. Adeoye
University of Lagos, Nigeria

E. B. Anyikwa
University of Lagos, Nigeria

ABSTRACT

Technology for teaching and learning has transformed from its crudest form of communicating with stones, pebbles, and skin to modern day technology devices such as filmstrips, projected media, m-learning, and e-learning. This has brought immense change into higher institutions of learning in Africa. This change has brought a revolution in teaching and learning and the roles of universities in producing lifelong learners. A wide range of technology devices and their applications are outlined, ranging from multimedia to radio broadcasting with policies related to ICT applications in different African universities, showing the level of information capitalism, access, and quality of higher education in Africa. Even though low teledensity, inadequate supply of electricity, low funding, and high level of poverty are some of the challenges generally faced by African universities, it is recommended that ICT policies across African universities need to be revitalized. In addition, there is a need to provide sufficient computing facilities and specialized facilities like multimedia laboratories to enable e-content generation. Finally, teaching and learning can be made available to thousands of students in Africa when universities are operating 24-7 online tutorials as a result of ICT and other technological developments. This is explored in this chapter.

INTRODUCTION

Dewey was criticizing the academies of his day in about a century ago, when he indicated that education needed to adopt new instructional approaches based on future societal needs. These words resound more strongly than ever today. Current societal needs are definitely different at this information age. The Information Age has been described as the Computer Age or Digital Age. This period in human history is characterized by the shift from traditional industry that the industrial

DOI: 10.4018/978-1-4666-6162-2.ch003

Copyright © 2014, IGI Global. Copying or distributing in print or electronic forms without written permission of IGI Global is prohibited.

revolution brought through industrialization, to an economy based on the information computerization. This age has impacted education in several ways. It has created a situation in which students can learn, communicate and share information at any time and at any location. The onset of the Information Age is associated with the digital revolution, just as the industrial revolution marked the onset of the Industrial Age.

During the Information Age, the digital industry creates a knowledge-based society surrounded by a high-tech global economy that spans over its influence on how the manufacturing throughput and the service sector operate in an efficient and convenient way. The information industry is able to allow individuals to explore their personalized needs, therefore simplifies the procedure of making decisions for transactions and significantly lowers costs for both the producers and buyers. Educational organizations have taken advantage of this by developing virtual learning tools and providing education across the globe.

Educational institutions have been bombarded with technological tools such as the Internet, Information Communication Technology (ICT), electronic resources, digital technologies, and interactive games. For students to compete effectively in this digital age, they must be familiar with digital tools. Students in the 21st century learn in a virtual environment and not only in the common traditional classrooms. They are more inclined to find information by using ICT tools. Also, many teachers are collaborating, monitoring and issuing assignments via the same ICT tools.

Overtime, technology in education went with the passage of time from its crudest form of communicating with stone, pebbles, skin to modern days technology devices such as films strips, projected media, non-projected media, smart boards, the Internet, and to e-learning. All these together are interactive and collaborative tools that have transformed teaching and learning. The past decade has bought immense change to higher education. Technology such as course management

systems, learning management systems, portals, PDAs, wireless technology and Web services are being used to create virtual communities that provide interactive platforms for learning.

Educational institutions must understand this phenomenon of digital age and restructure themselves to take advantage of emerging technologies so that students can be prepared to be leaders who not only realize the benefits of using collaborative tools in virtual space, but also are competent in using the tools effectively. The development and proliferation of the Internet has contributed to a revolution in teaching and learning, it has also provided new opportunities for delivering instruction through various media. Information capitalism is the link in the expansion and use of new computer technologies for large-scale record keeping to a set of social practices. According to Kling and Jonathan (1993) it is a useful metaphor because it marries information with capitalism's dynamic and aggressive edge.

Educational systems have been affected by technology all over the world. Education is now seen as a crucial factor in ensuring economic productivity and competitiveness in the context of informational capitalism (Ball, 2008). The continued economic success in an ever-changing and technologically advanced economy requires those things both within and outside the labour market to engage in a constant updating of their employability profile through a process of constant re-engagement in education and training. This need for a flexible labour force has opened challenges of constant up-skilling and retraining of the workforce; hence universities have a big role to play in order to produce lifelong learners. Capitalism as an institutional system also depends upon structure that facilitate reinvesting profit into a development organization since information capitalism refers to a different, but contemporary, shift in the ways that information is managed (Mcfarland, 1984; Ives & Learmonth, 1984); therefore, the era of information age in teaching and learning in African Universities started with the introduction of ICTs.

Barker (2002) indicated that ICT has proving to be a very powerful tool in educational reforms. Based on this assertion, higher institutions in African countries in the last few years have been reviewing their mission, goals strategies and operations in order to position themselves more effectively to meet the challenges of the Universities through the understanding of ICT, as regards when, how, what technology to use and where to use it. Challenges affecting ICT penetration in Africa include language, level of illiteracy, internal digital divide within the African continent, restrictive regulatory framework, poverty and the lack of infrastructure. Also, provisions of sufficient computing facilities and specialized facilities like multimedia laboratories to enable e-content generation are a problem in some areas. Bandwidth problem is a common challenge for almost all African Universities. The high cost of bandwidth, inadequate and unreliable telecommunication services and applications still remains a major challenge (Mmugenda, 2006). Information Communication Technology applications could be deployed in modes of e-learning, blended learning and mobile learning.

ICT initiatives in Africa have opened a new understanding of technology that is applicable in Africa educational institutions at all levels. Most Universities in Africa have integrated variety of media devices and technology applications into their teaching and learning.

Table 1 is a summary of technology deliveries and devices used.

ADVANTAGES AND DISADVANTAGES OF DIGITAL TECHNOLOGY FOR TEACHING AND LEARNING

There are many advantages that have come since the introduction of digital technology within classrooms at all education levels. Each advantage and disadvantage can be argued and debated over whether or not they are accepted. However, a common consensus is that the quality of education is not dependant on the technology in the classroom but rather on the teacher who is able to take the needs and abilities of their students into account integrating any form of technology in the classroom.

- **Advantages:**
  - Enables learning in distant or disadvantaged locations
  - Reduces long term education expenses by shifting learning to the Web
  - Utilizes online tools such as online calendars, search engines and online help guides.
  - Assessment consists of standard tools such as online grading books, exams and quizzes.
  - Utilizes communication tools such as emails, instant messaging, chat rooms, discussion boards and file transfers.
  - Ability to reach the world instantaneously with the latest news and technologies
  - Enables teacher to be up-to-date; enhancing the quality of work by both teachers and students
  - Increases student engagement and motivation and accelerates learning
  - Reduces costs associated with instructional materials, program delivery.
- **Disadvantages:**
  - Quality education received by only a few, leading to low penetration
  - Large gap in terms of digital divide
  - Changing technology may create barriers to accessing learning environments
  - Limited understanding of effective online teaching methods

Table 1. Summary of technology deliveries and devices used for teaching and learning

Media/Devices/Tools	Technology Applications
Multimedia	Traditional teaching methods, seminars, tutorials, classes, workshops, conferences and lectures. One-to-one interaction, either between educator and learner, learner and learner, e-learning, and group work.
Visual /Print Media	Books, booklets, and pamphlets (either already published or written specifically for a course). Study guides, written either as stand-alone material or as 'wrap-around' guides to already published material. Workbooks, newspapers, journals, periodicals, newsletters, magazines, maps, charts, photographs and posters.
Computers applications	Electronic publishing which include: Study guides, written either as stand-alone material or as wrap-around guides to already published materials. Instructional material ended for use in conjunction with other technologies (for example, audio or video cassettes or printed materials. Newspapers, journals, periodicals, newsletters, and magazines. Also, learner support material (for example, self-tests, project guides, notes on accreditation requirements, or other aspects of courses, bibliographies, and materials or comments passed between learner and educator).
Audio Cassettes and Audio compact disc	Audio programmes (music, talk radio, documentary, lecture, panel discussion, news, current affairs, debate, drama etc.).
Television	Broadcasting (terrestrial, satellite or cable, digital or analogue transmission, including narrowcast educational television).
Video Cassettes/Discs	Video programmes (music, talk shows, documentary, literature review, lecture, panel discussions, news, current affairs, debates, game shows, drama, films etc). Lectures/simulations of procedures and processes.
Video Conferencing Equipment	Video conferences (with two-way audio and video or one-way video and two-way audio). Also, point-to-multi-point classes with interactive video and audio.
Internet/e-learning	Electronically delivered learning (e-Learning) has become one of the most important and potentially significant and efficient instructional methods to improve teaching and learning. Its greatest advantages include flexibility and convenience for the learners. It transcends the boundaries of traditional classroom instruction. Apart from creating virtual schools, it promotes equity by providing students with access to qualitative educational materials.
Networking/Linking Computer-based workstation	Presentation and sharing of materials and resources integrating text, audio and video and possible applications of e-learning and simulations.
Communication tools	Telephone allows for one-to-one contact between the students and lecturers. The use of teleconferencing becomes reasonable when the communicators and communicants are widely dispersed and separated by difficult terrains. Where-communication is efficient; it may replace, substitute or supplement the face-to-face technique.
Radio	Programmes can be designed and disseminated to organized audiences, either in schools, or community learning centers based on prescribed curriculum content. It can pace students through logical presentation of instructional materials, provide feedback so that students have a sense of belonging and make corrections in the existing materials (Asogwa, 2006). By incorporating an audio bridge, learners in remote places can call in for synchronous conversation. Like the teleconferencing teaching and learning instruction, the radio broadcasting as a medium of teaching and learning has a positive implication which is basically on effective instruction and learning activity carried out through the radio broadcast.

- ◦ Course content and teaching methodology is rigid and cannot be experimented with.
- ◦ High cost of computer hardware and software, weak infrastructure, lack of human skills, knowledge in ICT, lack of appropriate and culturally suitable software for African continent.

INFORMATION CAPITALISM AND EFFECTIVE TEACHING AND LEARNING PROCESS

Students must have access to education and training if they are to be empowered to shape the destinies, meet the social, economic and personal challenges of the global knowledge-based economy. To achieve this, there is a need to look beyond the conventional mode of providing education.

It is not only ICT that is transforming the way students learn; e-learning is also becoming popular in transforming education. E-learning is seen as one of the promising options that can successfully cope with the ever-growing need for access, equity and quality higher education in African countries. Hoffler (2000) described e-learning as a specific learning technology that covers a wide array of applications and processes, including computer-based learning, virtual classrooms, and digital collaboration. E-learning and most of the digital technologies are facilitated and supported through the use of ICT. They include the delivery of content via the Internet, Intranet, Extranet (LAN/WAN), audio and videotape, satellite, interactive TV and CD-ROM (Kaplan-Leiserson, 2000). E-learning can benefit any student irrespective of their backgrounds, as a result of enhanced learning opportunities provided by ICT. A key issue in pedagogy is individualization that is, adapting the teaching to the needs of various learners. E-learning, thus, provides accelerated and required courses which eventually lead to increased graduation rates and highly reduced drop-out rates of students (Olorundare, 2010). It promotes equity by providing students with access to courses which may not ordinarily be available.

STATUS OF ICT AND RELATED POLICIES IN EDUCATION IN AFRICAN UNIVERSITIES

The advent of the information age and its acceleration effect on globalization are leading the world to a new economic order driven by information and knowledge based economies. Also, the ICT initiatives going on in Africa continent today have opened a new understanding of technology that is applicable in their educational institutions at all level. Most universities in Africa have their ICT policies that drive their activities. And these policies can tell about the efforts of various Universities in national development and in being ICT compliant. Below is a summary of policies related to ICT application in African Universities:

University of Ibadan- Nigeria: Their ICT policy is to help some decision-makers keep long-term strategic issues in perspective and give a clear basis for decision-making thereby reducing ad-hoc decisions and minimizing the potential for crisis management. It also provides a framework for operating in a uniform, predictable manner and to ensure that ICT truly reflects priorities. All these must be in consonance with the dreams and aspirations of the University.

University of Ghana- Ghana: The university provides a sound theoretical and empirically informed basis for informing policy on the teaching and learning using ICT. It provides a basis for communication between the educational research community and the commercial sector on the subject of the usage of ICT in teaching and learning. They provide a template to assist school communities to develop agreements with students as to what constitutes an acceptable use of the Internet, intranet, ultranet, netbooks and other online and digital technologies in their country.

Obafemi Awolowo University- Nigeria: The goal of ICT is to promote the training of computer science, engineers and professionals. It actively encourages research in the advancement of computer science and technology. It is also to cooperate with similar professional organisations throughout the world, and to develop the competence, and encourage integrity in individual that engage in the computing profession.

Ogun State University- Nigeria: The goal of ICT in Ogun State University is to promote the interchange of information about science and art of processing information among specialist and the public. It is also to determine the academic standard in computing computer science, computer engineering and so on.

University of Winneba- Ghana: The goal of the university's ICT policy is to become a Centre of

Excellence where the potential of ICT is harnessed to serve as a catalyst for effective teaching, research and learning which is aimed at the promotion of innovation in educational technology and transformation of academic excellence. The mission is also to support the successful achievement of her vision and mission statement through the effective use of ICT resources.

University of Nairobi- Kenya: The university's ICT Centre was established in the late 2002 with the aim of assisting the university to realize its mandate to provide university computer network services, analyze, develop and maintain management information systems application to support as well as help in meeting the academic and administrative needs of university. Their ICT goal is to ensure that staff and students of the University have guaranteed access to ICT facilities that helps in learning, teaching and research. Among the services rendered by their ICT department include; Management Information System (MIS) services, network, communications services, and e-learning.

University of Hargeisa- Somalia: The objective of Somalia information communication technology strategy is to develop a well teaching structure that will last for many years, establish linkage and collaboration that will facilitate lifelong learning and enhance individual institutional capacity in higher institution. In order to achieve this, the University expressed strong interest in development of ICT and access to well equipped digital tools. Currently, the University is working on the needs for an electronic linking universities, government and research institution in Somaliland and giving high speed access to the internal and development of the regulatory framework in the telecom sector and for long-distance teaching system in using the electronic networks.

The University of Kenya- Kenya: The development of ICT both mobile telephone and computer technology had started gaining upward momentum in the rural and urban centers in Kenya. The objective of University of Kenya's ICT programme

is to increase the use of ICT in teaching and learning, in sharing information, subscribing to academic journals, use of social media and other e-learning tools. Also to achieve this, the university has focused on investing more heavily on ICT to enhance quality university education.

National University of Rwanda- Rwanda: The mission of the National University of Rwanda's ICT centre is to promote research and teaching by maintaining and managing the entire University Campus Area Network and centralized database systems with computer and electronic equipment. Their main objective is to set standards for classroom, set the standard for grades and progression to the next stage of education, monitoring the standards on system performance indicators, inspects and advises on standards adherence and compliance.

Virtual University of Tunis, Tunisa: It was established as a government initiative in 2003 and provides 20% of courses through e-learning. It provides interactive tutored courses, training and development of content. There are 207 modules, representing more than 8,000 hours that are ready for use. There are another 56 modules in progress and 110 in the evaluation phase. Another 51 are to be added within the framework of the co-operation and the partnership with the Sun and Nettuno.

Makerere University- Uganda: It is University policy to promote ubiquitous and equitable access to ICT resources for students and staff to the network through the establishment of network infrastructure in all work areas of students and staff. It is also to provide adequate computing time for each student and staff through the provision of sufficient computing facilities and access times. It is the University policy to acquire, deploy, use and dispose of ICT facilities in ways that ensure environmental sustainability. The university is to provide access to ICT services located both within the University network and on the Internet through Common Network Services. Such access will at all times be governed by the University Network acceptable use policy. They are to provide each student and member of staff with an e-mail address under the official university domain name structure, and Internet access to all its students and staff for use for the purposes of facilitating research and learning.

African University- Zimbabwe: The Information and Communication Technology Department is a key service department in the University and its mission is to promote the development of Information and Communication Technology (ICT) at Africa University. It also aims at improving the efficiency, effectiveness and responsiveness of the University administrative and academic departments, improve teaching and learning and research so that the institution may be recognized as a leading teaching/learning and research centre.

Kigali Institute of Science, Technology and Management- Rwanda: The policy of this institution is to become a Regional Centre of Excellence in delivering hands on vocational and professional courses in ICT and technology related fields, carry out extensive research activities and knowledge dissemination by being a link between academia and Industry in order to provide absorption capacity to the Industry and to provide technical assistance to all sections of the community. The ICT centre is also involved in capacity building in a bid to rapidly increase the stock of Rwandan technicians trained to maintain computing hardware, software and networks.

University of Lagos- Nigeria: The University created a Centre for Information Technology and Systems (CITS) in 2007. The centre took over from the former computer centre. Initially it has 2 subnet - the citsnet and the senate subnet. But gradually it took the building of backbone infrastructure with fibre laid all over the campus. The network spans the entire campus with about 32km of fibre optics Web. This delivers services that range from the Internet, mail, intranet and all kind of services. The CITS runs 24-hours non-stop computer and network services to support the ICT needs of the University. The CITS has also developed a Web-based Information system

accessible via their Website, to provide staffs and students with comprehensive management information. The Web-based system support a wide range of administrative applications including human resources, student records, and finance while students can register courses, view examination results, hostel accommodation, and to change personnel information. This system ensures up-to-date information which helps both the staffs and students in the daily teaching and learning environment. Currently the CITS is building a network 'eko-konnect' that will connect the University of Lagos, Federal college of Education Akoka, Yaba College of Technology, Lagos University Teaching Hospital for a start and eventually be able to connect 31 institutions in Lagos area.

University of Port Harcourt- Nigeria: The Director of the University's Information and Communication Technology Centre (ICTC) had a vision to advocate the use of modern instructional technology in the teaching/learning process amongst the academic staff of the University of Port Harcourt. The institution has conceived the idea of designing and developing the classroom of the 21st century in the university. The purpose was to envision an education system that impacts what/how the University of Port Harcourt teaches, taking cognizance of latest trends and technologies, flexible classrooms, innovative teaching/learning plans and flexible teaching/learning environments in order to implement best practices in teaching with modern instructional technology.

University of Johannesburg, South Africa: The University of Johannesburg is recognised in South Africa as an institution that meets the needs of industry and business. The University's vision and mission is demonstrated in the recent introduction of specialisations in Software Development, Web and Application Development, Information and Technology Management as well as Support Services. These specialisations include traditional aspects of IT such as software development, secure systems, network management and information systems all geared towards the university's readiness for ICT.

Botswana university, Botswana: Botswana University in August 2007 entered into a memorandum of understanding with Helsinki University Finland with the intension of integrating/infusing ICT across the curriculum in their various departments/schools, the application, adaptation and development of the Cultural Historical Activity Theory (CHAT) and other methodologies in the context of school and community transformation in Botswana as well as planning, developing and implementing training to support educational transformation. All of these are hinged on the fact that the University takes important child centred learning which is one of the key features of its ICT programme (Masalela, 2012).

INFORMATIONAL CAPITALISM'S ACCESS, EQUITY, AND QUALITY HIGHER EDUCATION IN NIGERIA/AFRICA

In an increasingly globalized world, where information technology has become one of the key determinants of growth, many African countries are facing new challenges as a result of the emerging information technologies. For instance, in 2006, six-hundred thousand candidates sat for the University Matriculation Examination (UME); that is the common entrance examinations to Nigeria universities. The Joint Admissions and Matriculation Board (JAMB) could not offer admission to one-tenth of the applicants due to lack of resources. The increase in human population and the ever-growing need for further education are beyond the capacity of formal system of education in African countries.

The enabling role that ICT can play in facilitating and accelerating socio-economic development is now being recognized by most African governments. Also, the continuous increase in the demand for formal higher education in Africa has forced the existing universities to admit beyond their carrying capacities, with attendant effects on quality. Even at that, the number denied, access to higher education still remains quite high. Equally, with upward increase in the cost of education, the intelligent children of the poor families will not find their ways into any higher institution.

ICT has opened many doors to learning; students are exposed to greater varieties and depths of information in the digital areas, than in the traditional classroom situation. Besides, they can become responsible for their learning. Furthermore, students can access current information and development in their area of specialization specifically through online via the Internet or Offline using CD-ROMs and other software's. However, the issues of availability and accessibility are the leading problems in Africa countries.

Accessibility

Universities should provide a vision, strategy and an enabling environment that promotes the use of information and communication technologies (ICTs) in particular and society in general. Through access to information and freedom of expression, students are able to gain civic competence, collaborate with other students around the world, and engage in discussions and deliberations with their peers, all of which provides the citizen with an enlightened understanding of life (Mmugenda, 2006). By facilitating access to diverse curricular materials, higher institutions with Internet access provide a broad range of possible education options to learners at no great cost in terms of space and personnel. Through such open programming, gender parity and multi-cultural tolerance would become institutionalized (Menchik, 2004). Providing educational equality opportunity which is defined by Levesque (1979) as equality of access, equality of treatment and equality of results irrespective of sex, race, religion or social class- ideals propounded at World Summit on the Information Society (WSIS) might be realized through e-education. Accessibility of ICT in African universities is still a challenge today. There are several factors that have contributed to the issue of accessibility, and these include the following:

- **Inadequate supply of electricity:** Almost all the e-tools depend on electrical power to function. At the moment, the power supply in many African countries general is very low, unstable and not available in some rural areas where majority of students reside. The implication of this situation on education is negative.

- **Low teledensity:** Access to unhindered utilization of ICT tools such as telephone and Internet has been very low in many areas. Though, the recent introduction and infusion of GSM telecommunication technology in Nigeria has improved access greatly, it is still far below what is needed to boost the actual utilization of ICT resources for educational purposes. According to Joseph (2006), Nigeria has the second largest telecom in Africa (behind South Africa) with a subscriber base of 20 million, but with teledensity of less than 15%. It is equally sad to note that Nigeria's IT rating is 90 out of 115 counties in the world and ranked 13th in Africa behind the Gambia, Namibia, Uganda, Tunisia, South Africa and Mauritius which occupy 1st, 2nd, and 3rd place ranking in IT respectively. Also, Gambia, Namibia and Uganda occupy 8th 10th, and 12th position in IT world rating.

- **Skills in designing course wares/software:** There is currently dearth of skills possessed by lecturers to design and-deliver their courses in electronic format. Many are still not ICT-compliant; therefore, are not enthusiastic about its use in education.

- **Funding:** The Government investment on ICT for education purposes in Nigeria and Africa is very low, as can be observed by

the ratio of students per computer and the level of Internet connectivity. In Nigeria and Africa in general, these are still very low funding.

- **High level of poverty:** The cost of computers and other ICT resources are still far beyond the reach of common man in Nigeria and Africa. There is a low level of computer literacy among African students and lecturers.

CONCLUSION

Educational systems around the world are being redesigned to rely on electronic delivery methods. No conventional higher institution can successfully cope with the ever-growing demand for admission into higher institutions without utilizing some king of online program. Digital tools with its provision of learning opportunities at any time, any place convenient to the users will adequately provide access, equality and quality higher education in Africa. As the Internet is leveling barriers in social relations around education, students, through the use of digital tools, are more individually and actively involved in the learning process, more independent in their learning and able to make more choices about how, what, and where they learn. Of the seventeen 17 policy summaries for major countries in African universities, there are common and related policies in the areas of national development, collaboration, communication, supporting teaching and learning.

Recommendations

ICT policy across African universities needs to be revitalized in three areas - telecommunications (especially telephone communications); broadcasting (radio and TV) and the Internet. ICT policy in education cannot be formulated without addressing national ICT policy and cover issues such as infrastructure, adequate information systems and services. All these require good knowledge of environment, and consideration of other sectoral policies (e.g., education, welfare, health, industry, etc.). Baryamureeba. (2007) indicates that governance is the way power is exercised in managing a country's economic and social resources for development. ICTs present opportunities for African countries to implement e-governance/egovernment. The Internet, distance-learning opportunities, online (electronic) learning, computerized library packages and strategic databases must be brought nearer to the isolated and poor African nations unable to integrate their economies and intellects with the powerful and respected community of states (Baryamureeba, 2007).

According to Mmugenda (2006), local content development is critical for ICT development. The area of generation of local content in most African countries is still untapped. There is a need to generate local content that can be put on the Web and also used in e-learning. Mmugenda also indicated that ICT should enable universities to operate 24-7 via online tutors who could operate from any location. Many universities across the global provide education to thousands of students off campus (online) for several awards ranging from certificates to degrees in different disciplines. ICTs will present opportunities for lifelong learning in Africa.

REFERENCES

Asogwa, U. D. (2006). *Integration of information and communication (ICT) for quality distance education*. Paper presented on the occasion of 2006 Annual Conference of Institute of Education. Nsukka, Nigeria.

Ball, S. (2008). *The education debate*. Bristol, UK: Policy Press.

Barker, C. (2002). *The role of ICT in Higher Education: ICT as a change agent for education*. Academic Press.

Baryamureeba, V. (2007). *ICT as an Engine for Uganda's Economic Growth: The role of and opportunities for Makerere university*. Retrieved from http://www.cit.mak.ac.ug/iccir/downloads/SREC_07/Venansius%20Baryamureeba,_07.pdf

Hoffler, E. (2000). *Equity research*. WR Hambrecht & Co. Retrieved from http://www.wr-hambrecht.com/research/coverage/elearning/ir/ir_explore.pdf

Ives, B., & Learmonth, G. (1984). The information system as a competitive weapon. *Communications of the ACM*, 27(12), 1193–1201. doi:10.1145/2135.2137

Joseph, A. (2006, April 21). Nigeria places 90th of 115th Countries in IT ratings. *The Punch*, 3.

Kaplan-Leiserson, E. (2000). *Glossary*. Alexandria, VA: American Society for Training and Development. Retrieved from http://www.learningcircuits.org/glossary.html

Kling, R., & Jonathan, P. (1993). *How the marriage of management and computing intensifies the struggle for personal privacy*. Retrieved from http://glotta.ntua.gr/IS-Social/KlingInfoCapitalism.html

Levesque, C. (1979). *Learning: The paradigm shift*. Paris: UNESCO.

Masalela, R. K. (2012). *Implementing e-Learning at the University of Botswana: The practioner's perspective*. Retrieved from www.westga.edu/.../Masalela_142.html

McFarland, F. W. (1984). Information technology changes the way you compete. *Harvard Business Review*, 62(3), 98–103.

Menchik, D. (2004). *Educational equality through technology*. Paper presented at the World Summit on the Information Society and Schooling in Development. New York, NY.

Mmugenda, O. M. (2006). *University roles in meeting aspirations for ICT and economic development*. Retrieved from http://www.foundation-partnership.org/pubs/leaders/assets/papers/mugendasession4paper.pdf

Olorundare, S. (2010). *Utilization of Information and communication Technology (ICT) in curriculum development, implementation and evaluation*. Paper presented at the 1st International Conference on Higher Education: Collaboration of Education Faculties in West Africa (CEFWA). New York, NY.

ADDITIONAL READING

Adeoye, B. F., Udeani, U., & Oni, S. (2009). Virtual Construction of Social Reality through the Internet and Its Applications among Nigerian University Students. 4th International Conference on ICT for Development, Education and Training, Dakar, Senegal from May 27-29, 2009.

Busari, O., Maduekwe, A., & Adeoye, B. F. (2007). The implementation of e-learning in the 3 tiers of the Nigeria educational system. 10th Annual Conference on World Wide Web Applications Conference Proceedings. Cape Town, South Africa. pp. 4-10.

Campbell-Kelly, M., & Aspray, W. (1996). *Computer: A History of the Information Machine*. New York: Basic Books.

Castells, M. (1989). *The Informational City: Information Technology, Economic Restructuring, and the Urban Regional Process*. Cambridge: Blackwell.

Clements, D. H., & Sarama, J. (2003). Strip mining for gold: Research and policy in educational technology—A response to Fool's Gold. Educational Technology Review, 11(1), 7–69. Retrieved September 21, 2005, from http://www.aace.org/pubs/etr/issue4/clements2.pdf

Coppola, E. M. (2004). *Powering up: Learning to teach well with technology*. New York: Teachers College Press.

Hooker, M. (1997). The transformation of higher education. In Diane Oblinger and Sean C. Rush (Eds.) (1997). The Learning Revolution. Bolton, MA: Anker Publishing Company, Inc

Karanja, D. (n.d). Types of digital technology. Available from http://www.ehow.com/list_7457479_types-digital-technology.html.

Lee, K. (2000). English teachers' barriers to the use of computer-assisted language learning. The Internet TESL Journal, 6(12). Retrieved September 21, 2005, from http://iteslj.org/Articles/Lee-CALLbarriers.html

Levin, D., & Arafeh, S. (2002). The digital disconnect: The widening gap between Internet-savvy students and their schools. Washington, DC: American Institutes for Research. Retrieved September 21, 2005, from http://www.pewinternet.org/pdfs/PIP_Schools_Internet_Report.pdf

Luckett, K. (2001). A proposal for an epistemically diverse curriculum for South African higher education in the 21st century. *South African Journal of Higher Education*, 15(2), 49–61. doi:10.4314/sajhe.v15i2.25354

Madiope, M., et al. (2005) The implementation of mobile communication at the University of South Africa. Poster presentation at the 4th World Conference on mLearning, Cape Town, October.

Mafanga, S., & Pretorius, B. (2003). *Shared vision for ICT skills development in South Africa. A public private partnership contributing to an integrated learning delivery model. Unpublished mimeo, Central Johannesburg FET College*. Troyeville Campus.

Mhlanga, E. (2005) University transformation and ICT: The case of Wits University. Paper presented at the Lifelong E-Learning, European Distance and E-Learning Network (EDEN) Annual Conference, Helsinki University of Technology, 20–23 June.

MOC (Ministry of Communication). (2003). *Presidential national commission, e-schooling strategies for networking African schools: Focus on South Africa*. Pretoria: MOC.

Moll, I., & Matshana, J. (2006) An overview of the pedagogical integration of ICTs in South Africa. Presentation to the Project Development Workshop, Pan African Research Agenda on the Pedagogical Uses of ICTs, Dakar, Senegal, September.

Morrow, W. (1993) Epistemological access in the university. AD Issues, 1(3/4).

Mphahlele, M. L., & Mashamaite, K. (2005) An appraisal of the use of the cellphones and the short message service (SMS) language as a teaching and learning aid in a tertiary learning environment. Paper presented at the 4th World Conference on mLearning, Cape Town, October.

Roberts, L. (1996). A Transformation of learning: Use of the NII for education and lifelong learning. In D. P. Ely, & B. B. Minor (Eds.), *Educational Media and Technology year hook 1995/1996* (pp. 50–66). Englewood, CO: Libraries Unlimited.

KEY TERMS AND DEFINITIONS

Digital Technology: Primarily used with new physical communications media, such as satellite and fiber optic transmission.

ICT Policy: Sets out the school's aims, principles and strategies for the delivery of Information and Communication Technology.

Information Capitalism: Information Capitalism, It is an information generation, processing, and transmission, that have become the fundamental sources of productivity and power.

Information Technology: The collection of technologies that deal specifically with processing, storing, and communicating information, including all types of computer and communications systems as well as reprographics methodologies.

Chapter 4

Promoting Instructional Technology for Effective and Efficient Academic Performance in Nigerian Schools

Ogunlade B. Olusola
Ekiti State University, Nigeria

ABSTRACT

The concept of Instructional Technology (IT) has become recognized as a crucial element in the educational field. Instructional technologies are now supporting curricula that promote effectiveness and efficiency in academic performance of all levels of education in Nigerian schools. The objectives of bringing all the instructional tools together are to engage students and have the best potential that enhances learning outcomes. The concern of this chapter, therefore, is to address the agreeable definition of instructional technology, IT as educational problem solver focused on emerging technologies for teaching and learning. Areas of consideration are instructional technologies and its challenges, effective organization of instructional materials in schools, usefulness of local instructional packages, and obstacles in using instructional technology in Nigerian schools. The chapter concludes and recommends that schools should create enabling environments for the use of Instructional Technology (IT), which would enhance efficiency in teaching and learning.

INTRODUCTION

Instructional technology has the potential for enhancing students learning effectiveness in education so as to motivate and energize teachers for better teaching and learning. According to Armstrong and McDaniel (1993), in developed economies, education at all levels has instructional technologies as a force that drives curriculum enhancement. Consequently, the developing countries including Nigeria have become aware of the invaluable role of instructional technologies for effective and efficient teaching and learning. Nigeria has been able to make significant progress

DOI: 10.4018/978-1-4666-6162-2.ch004

Copyright © 2014, IGI Global. Copying or distributing in print or electronic forms without written permission of IGI Global is prohibited.

in improving education through this medium. Also, concerted efforts have been made by successive governments in Nigeria to initiate Internet connectivity and technology training programmes but the efforts have not been yielding expected results. Such programmes are expected to link schools and libraries around the world to improve education, enhance cultural understanding, and develop vital skills of creativity; problem-solving and independent thinking which learners need for academic performance in global world. As used in this write-up, the term instructional technology includes hardware such as personal computers, smaller peripherals such as Global Positioning Systems (GPSs) and Personal Digital Assistants (PDAs) that interface with computers, and other equipment such as video cameras, VCRs and other educational resources. Also included is the software that runs on these devices and networks that allow them to send and share information concerning teaching and learning.

Research on how instructional technology can promote effective academic performance was conducted by Duffy, Brown, and Cunningham, (1996) and concluded that technology can enhance teaching and learning by facilitating the incorporation of real-world problems into the curriculum. Instructional technology can help make a learning environment more learner-centered by providing a greater variety of resources that allows students to follow their own interests and build upon their strengths. It can also help teachers motivate students to work toward deep understanding or transfer by illustrating how what is under study in the classroom relates to the world beyond it by accessing real-time data on current events.

Technology therefore can help teachers meet students' differentiated needs, by serving as a tool for enrichment or review, or for presenting information in additional formats Berson (1996); Ehman and Glenn, (1991). However, conventional

teaching has emphasized content in almost all the subjects without much reference to instructional technology to be used. For many years courses or subject have been written around textbooks, teachers have taught through lectures and presentation interspersed with tutorials and learning activities designed to consolidate and rehearse the content (Abanikanda 2011).

In summary, Instructional technologies are now favouring curricular that promote effectiveness and efficiency in academic performance, at all levels of education in Nigerian schools (Ogunseye 2001). There is an urgent need for the teacher to be creative through application of instructional strategies appropriate to the students of 21st century.

There is no consensus definition for the term, "Instructional Technology" but according to Richey (2008), instructional technology is the theory and practice of design, development, utilization, management and evaluation of processes and resources for learning. The words Instructional Technology in the definition mean a discipline devoted to techniques or ways to make learning more efficient based on theory; but theory in its broadest sense, not just scientific theory. In this sense, theory consists of concepts, constructs, principles, and propositions that serve as the body of knowledge. Practice on the other hand is the application of that knowledge to solve problems. Practice can also contribute to the knowledge base through information gained from experience. "Design, development, utilization, management, and evaluation" refer to both areas of the knowledge base and to functions performed by professionals in the field. "Processes" are a series of operations or activities directed towards particular results. "Resources" are sources of support for learning, including support systems and instructional materials and environments. The purpose of instructional technology therefore, is to affect and effect learning" (Seels & Richey, 1994a, pp. 1-9). Instructional technology is often referred to as a subset of educational technology. It also covers the processes and systems of learning and instruction, educational technology includes other system used in the process of developing human capability.

According to Randy (2003), the uses of instructional technology cannot be attributed to a specific person or time. In addition to instructional technology utilization, access to technology has become a major area of concern in the education community. In President Clinton's 1998 State of the Union Address in the United States, he stated that, "the day is not far off that every child will be able to stretch a hand over a keyboard and reach every book ever written, every painting ever painted, and every Symphony ever composed" (Clinton, 1998). In Nigeria today, access to instructional technology is a major concern of educators and administrators nationwide.

Instructional technology is a growing field of study which used technologies as a means to solve educational challenges, both in the classroom and in distance learning. More (1989), argues that learner –content interaction should be the major focus of instruction. Instructional technology is of two parts; one is teaching technology and other is learning technology. It is however a field concerned with improving the efficiency and effectiveness of instruction, which involves:

- Designing instruction (including all phases of activity from needs assessment to evaluation)
- Applying learning theory to instructional design.
- Selecting delivery systems and designing techniques for a given delivery system
- Assessing human characteristics.
- Integrating instruction with other factors that influence human performance.
- Implementing delivery to reach learner when they need it.
- Using technology in support of the development and delivery of instruction.

INSTRUCTIONAL TECHNOLOGY AS PROBLEM SOLVER

Problem solving and product design experience can empower student by presenting unique learning opportunities (Foster, 1994), as technology becomes more transparent to the end user, the user is required to be interested in the technicality of the technology. A few decades ago, computer programming was a challenge in the schools, now the emphasis is more on the use of instructional technology. Problem solving is one of the basic 21st century skills in instructional technology, which enables every student and teacher to be able to integrate skills so as to develop maximally. By implication, problems solving in relation to Instructional Technology inherently involves decisions-making which is another important skill not only for academic performance but for success in life in general.

Instructional Technology encourages class room teachers, librarians, media specialists and technology facilitators to collaboratively design instruction that can intentionally create challenging and exciting learning experiences. Students learn to use technology, easily and creatively as part of the information problem solving process to achieve greater success in the classroom. Problem solving activities require the learners to apply what have been learned to develop a viable solution or solution path to a complex, real-world problem. It helps students connect theories and take responsibility for knowledge. Problem solving requires deductive powers, inferential reasoning, testing assumptions, and decision making skills (Jonassen, 2011). Although, the only legitimate cognitive goal of education (formal, informal, or others) in every education context (public and private schools, universities and (especially) corporate training is problem solving. Research has shown that knowledge constructed in the context of solving problems is better comprehended, retained, and therefore more transferable (Jonasses, 2011).

Perhaps this was what motivated Jonasses (2011) to share the opinion that the best practices for instructional technology problems solving activities require intentional learning where human behaviour is goal-driven. According to her, goals for solution should be made clear for meaningful learning. Instructional design suggests authentic problems-solving tasks which apply to students' lives, current or future jobs. Students will be more likely to retain knowledge learned from solving authentic and real educational problems. Instructional technology will therefore help learner to:

- Verify, define, in detail the problem;
- Establish evaluation criteria
- Identify alternative solution paths
- Evaluate alternative solution
- Display and distinguish among alternatives solutions (Jonases 2011).

All the aforementioned solutions to instructional technology require learners to make decision at critical junctures in a real project, provide learners with an online journal update as regards learning technology or require a blog where they can collect decisions and reflection into an ongoing document that they can be reviewed and taken away at the end of the course. However, targeting the problem solving strategies at the activities that are self-directed, where students individually and collaboratively assume responsibility for generating learning issues and processes is very germane. This way, students can accomplish problem solving through self-assessment, peer assessment, as well as accessing their own learning materials. It is essential to include self-reflective components where learners monitor their understanding and learn to adjust strategies for learning. Teachers that understand the use of Instructional Technology can enrich learning environments and enable students to achieve considerable performance in academics. It is critical that educators accept the potential benefits of technology for learning in solving educational problems. Most problem-solving tools for effective and efficient performance in instructional technology are games and simulation.

Game and simulation increase student's attention and motivation. Games offer the opportunity to exercise a skill that closely matches thinking, planning, learning, and technical skills that are highly demanded by employers of labour.

In the area of planning, the fast-paced simulation game helps learner improve strategic planning, decision-making, and increase collaboration within teams and groups. Games have proven to be a powerful planning tool for use in teaching and learning situation. There are opportunities in games. Virtual games are sophisticated and can be adapted in explaining complex systems. Meanwhile, games are also, structured to require application of contents knowledge and skill in order to "win" the game. These games offer second by-second decision making that allow the students to go through processes that require them to make decisions, show action, give feedback, and reflect on their decisions. This is the basic for all learning (Morrison-Lowther, 2010).

Instructional software can be used to solve problem through drill and practice, tutorials, and integrated learning system. Drill and practice software offers the students the opportunity to engage in interactive basic skill practice that provides immediate individual interactivity to teach students basic skills and new information. According to Morrsion-Lowther (2010), while, integrating learning system provides instructional content, feedback, mastery –type practice and assessment there has been an increase in students performance in math and reading by using integrated learning system.

EMERGING CATEGORIES OF INSTRUCTIONAL TECHNOLOGY

Walsh (2012) observed that today technology is emerging from the seemingly endless array of tools and concepts that are out with different application and ideals to best position learning to its normal place in enhancing, engaging and impacting knowledge. Also, pointedly focused on emerging technologies, it should not come as a surprise that there are a lot of new entries that remain prevalent and potent, but are more established than emerging. The objectives of bringing all the instructional tools together are to engage students and to have the best potential to enhance learning outcomes. Top emerging instructional technologies are discussed as follows:

- **The Flipped Classroom:** This is not a technology per se but a facility that enables teaching techniques. This is a response to growing interest and unique regarding flipping the iPods equipped classroom. The flipped classroom doesn't necessarily require any special technology in the classroom but it does required students to be able to consume digital learning content outside of class.
- **The Emergence of Virtual High School:** This is a form of school whose instruction is Internet-based. It is designed for special needs of students with limited English proficiency. Students learning virtually have as much, if not interaction with teachers and other students. Therefore, most people have not heard about Virtual High School, it is an outline college and students earn certificates as learners.
- **Remote Teacher Online Instruction:** It is common in Brazil and Russia. This is online learning with no regular face-to-face instruction or facilitation, though it may include some occasional interaction with human teachers and facilitators.
- **Mobile Learning via Tablets and Smart Phone:** With the explosion of the tablet niche in the last few years launched by Apple's ipad and the ever increasing computing power in our pockets, this is an opportunity to learn anywhere, anytime without any difficulty.

- **One to one and BYOD (Bring Your Own Device) initiative**: This is an initiative of Casey (2012) if students have the device in their hand or available at a moment notice, they are going to be more inclined to use them and better acquire the 21st century skills that we know they will need to succeed. Teachers have to be provided with the development that will enable them to help students leverage the device, and administrators have to work with faculty to develop carefully thought out plans regarding how to use them. Poorly planned or inadequate supported 1 to 1 and BYOD programs are a waste of tax and tuition (do it right, or don't do it at all).
- **Open Education Resources (OER):** Are teaching and learning materials that are freely available online for everyone to use, whether you are instructor, student or self-learner. Examples are full courses, modules, syllabi, lectures, homework assignments, quizzes, lab and classroom activities, pedagogical materials, games, simulations and many more resources contained in digital media collections around the world. Consequently, possibilities for lowering textbooks costs have never been better or commons and many other organizations are leading the march towards unlock free resources that can beat back the burden of ridiculous text books costs.
- **The Wealth of Online Learning Resource:** Self-directed learning has never been easier. Options for learning about a subject from different angles and different experts have never been more numerous. Therefore, learning resources are texts, videos, software, and other materials that teachers use to assist students to meet their expectations for learning as defined by state or local curricula. Before a learning resource is used in a classroom, it must be evaluated and approved at either state or

local level. Evaluation criteria may include curriculum fit, social considerations, and age or developmental appropriateness.

- **Collaborative and Social Learning:** The ability for students to work together in and out of classroom with tools that enable collaboration and social learning is being further embraced everyday. Collaborative tools like Goggle drive go hand in hand with social learning, and the need to work in collaborative team with tools like these is something students are highly likely to encounter in the workplace.

- **Web Pages for Every Class**: Are a Web document that is suitable for the World Wide Web and the Web browser. A Web browser displays a Web page on a monitor or mobile device. Web, these tools are not expensive (there are even good free options like Wikis and Google Application for Education) they are not hard to use.

- **Adaptive Learning:** Adaptive learning tools are still maturing, their potential remains tremendous. This is the educational method which uses computer as interactive teaching devices. Computer adapts the presentation of educational material according to students' learning needs, as indicated by their responses to questions and tasks (Adaptive learning System, 2008).

- **Professional Development (In technology integration):** All the technologies are rendered meaningless if the teachers that are working with these tools aren't given adequate training in how to use them in the instruction setting

INSTRUCTIONAL TECHNOLOGIES AND ITS CHALLENGES

Today education is faced with enormous challenges of how to learn and to effectively solve learning difficulty and at the same time design

and apply appropriate instructional tool, and have a high level of expertise with a variety of technologies. However, students are at the centre stage where teachers play the role of facilitators and guides. This time, emphasis is on students as active agents in the process of findings, organizing, analyzing and applying information to solve problems. In consequence, activities such as "think –pair –share and Jigsaw" techniques as a means of placing students in the centre of learning process is very relevant to contemporary Instructional Technology. This method did not consider the needs of receptive, analytic, linear learners who may be disadvantaged by active approach (Karen, 1997). At every point in time, teacher should constantly recreate the instructional process and offer a variety of choice for approaching information and tasks in order to meet learners' ever changing, needs.

In order words, high ability learners may invest more on instructional technology in a challenging task, such as reading a book, than in a task perceived to be easy, such as learning from television. Low ability students may invest more in instructional technologies they believe to be attainable than one they perceive to be challenging.

Effective Organization of Instructional Materials in Schools

For maximum effectiveness of the use of instructional technology in schools, many authorities have agreed that these tools should be properly organized. Weaver *et al.,* (1968) in Ogunsheye (2001) suggested that a visual programme must be properly organized and managed if it will efficiently function. They emphasised the importance of the provision of sufficient fund, proper equipment, adequate space and competent management, they advised that schools should start with whatever she has to organize its learning resources. They confirmed that not all schools that have enough resources at an advantage. Organizations are to plan visual aids program commensurate to their responsibilities and curriculum demands.

Beswick (1972) believes that the organization of instructional materials for use will improve communication about learning resource among teachers. He observes that at the heart of our schools there is a communication problem. School possess equipment, knowledge resources, expertise and creative abilities, yet their presence is not always known to these who may need them and is all too frequently under employed. He stresses that all equipment and materials in the secondary schools must be catalogued and indexed so that all members of the school, teachers, pupils, newcomers can know what is already available to them. He therefore recommends a resources centre which he defines as an agency for stimulating the active creation and use of a resource collection. Such a resource centre must have the following five elements:

1. Production of home made resource.
2. Selection and acquisition of other resources.
3. Classification and indexing for retrieval storage.
4. Use, including guidance, lending etc and
5. Evaluation.

Agun (1982) sees the library as a traditional way of planning and organizing educational resources with regards to instructional materials, especially the print materials. He says the library is no more adequate. He contends that; now, the library, as a way of organizing and using educational materials are considered inadequate.

Many educators seem to share the view (Agun, 1982) that the library as it is traditionally conceived, organized and run cannot adequately meet the information needs of both the teachers and the learners. He therefore advocates for educational resource centre apart from the provision of a wide range and variety of instructional materials to stimulate and support teaching and learning activities. Interactive Television, Radio

and Video Disc in the Classroom. Friend (1989), opined that lessons should be planned as a 'conversation' between the children and the radio, scripts are written as half of a dialogue with pause carefully timed so that students can be active in the learning process.

He recounted that the USAID funded the development of a new methodology for educational radio for young children through the introduction of three projects; the Radio Mathematics Project of Nicaragua, the Radio Language Arts Project of Kenya and the Radio Science Project of Papua New Guinea. According to Imhoof, (1988) interactive instructional radio and Television programming is an innovative, inexpensive and highly effective educational tool. In interactive radio and Television programming, lesson are provided by a radio and television instructor prompts responses from the radio and television audience, provides pauses for audience responses and then supplies the correct response to the prompt.

The lessons are generally supervised by a classroom teacher and the students respond to the radio prompts either orally or in writing. The lessons encourage student participation and the programs frequently require more than hundred audience responses for each half hour.

He noted that the technique is especially appropriate for use in primary schools and in non-formal adult education programs and that the tool is especially useful for teaching mathematics and second language. He recommended that educators in developing countries should develop interactive instructional television and radio programs, evaluate these programs and then integrate the approach in the school curriculum. The participants noted that the technique can serve to upgrade the quality of in-service training. He further recommended that administrator and parents should be provided with information about the technique and its advantage and that effort should be made to immediately promote its uses. Magarick and Galbracth (1988) viewed that interactive videodiscs have the potentials to enhance the efficiency of training by allowing teaching of geographically scattered students, substituting for live teachers and supplementing classroom work, especially on an individual basis. Many video discs teach through practice and duplicate patience situation. The interactive videodisc will be advantageous because poorer nation do not have money to build new classroom or hire additional teacher. The developing countries have to improve their educational system and training before they can be able to make adequate economic and social progress in the use of interactive videodiscs. The last group of audio-visual aids is graphic materials which are made up of posters, charts, graphs, photographs, maps and globes that can be displayed to students in class to view the pictures physically so as to feed the students imaginative power.

According to Ogundare (2003) realia is part of instructional technology resource that can be valuable for effective teaching in the classroom. Realia is the introduction of actual or real articles for examination and study in the classroom which have powerful impact on students' interest and motivation to the study of the subjects. The examples of realia are: weapons, machines, musical instruments, implements, regalia, etc; they transform ordinary discussion into meaningful focused exchange by bringing the real outer world into classroom which automatically makes learning interesting, important and permanent to students. Osokoya (1996) stressed that the history teacher's success in carrying out classroom instruction depends on his or her creative efforts, sustained by a spit of inquiry and exploration to bring into harmony the dynamic and unique relationship between students, teachers and the subject. Teachers find it more challenging and productive to be the creator and the manager of a stimulating environment rather than being a dispenser of facts and retriever of information that is tailored along the child-centered approach to the teaching-learning process. He also opined that for teacher to really create and manage simulation

teaching-learning environment the importance of instructional technology for teaching-learning process cannot be over-emphasized. He classified instructional resources into three namely: display boards, electronic materials and graphic materials.

This *display board* used in schools is of different types and purpose. Boards are very common in schools: all the classrooms have chalk-boards which is the oldest, cheapest and probably the most used of visual aids. *Chalk-board* is used to write out the summary of the lesson and other vital information about the lesson for the students. *Flannel board* is another type of display board; it is also known as felt board which is aboard covered with a hair surfaced cloth, flannel or felt board is used o display graphic materials.

Magnetic board is another type of display board which is similar to flannel board. Magnetic board is made up of a steel sheet to which magnet is attracted. It is used to display cardboard cut outs. *Bulletin boards* is also one of the types of display board which is use to display reports, projects or information. The *electronic materials* are the second group of instructional resource. This include: *overhead projector* which is the most popular and versatile visual aid and it can be used in a chalkboard. *Films* are audio-visual which enable student to view events they might not have been opportune to experience. *Slides* are individual picture which are projected on a screen for students to view. It can be used with or without sound. *Film strips* are usually between twelve and fifty frames in length. It is an elaboration of the slide. *Tape recorder* is another versatile teaching aid which can be used to pre-record the lesson and played later in the class. *Video cassettes* can also perform the same functions as films in the classroom instruction. It is very easy to use and less expensive than film.

Fadeiye (2001) suggested some guidelines that teacher should bear in mind when selecting the instructional material to be used for teaching-learning process. They are:

- It must be conspicuous.
- It must be relevant to their subject.
- It must have clear and audible sound
- It must be concrete.
- It must be current i.e. up-to-date. Teachers must consider the suitability and appropriateness of the resources.
- It must be simple and understandable as to enable the student to derive maximum benefit from them.

Beck (2008) said instructional technology, usually digital and Web-based, that can be used and re-used to support learning. It also offers a new conceptualization learning course need to include video, mathematical equation using mathematics, chemistry equations using CML and other complex structures the issue becomes very complex, especially if the systems needs to understand and validate each structure and then place it correctly in a database.

The following is a list of some of the types of information that may be included in an instructional technology:

- General course descriptive data; course identifiers language of content (English, Spanish, etc) subject area (Math, Reading etc) descriptive text, descriptive keywords.
- Life cycle, including: version, status.
- Instructional content, including: text, Web pages, image, sound, video.
- Glossary of terms, including terms definition, acronyms.
- Quizzes and assessments, including: questions, answer.
- Rights, including: cost, copyrights, restrictions on use.
- Relationships to other courses, including prerequisite courses.
- Educational level, including: grade level, age range, typical learning time, and difficulty Nagy. (2005).

According to Karrer, (2007) the key issues in using instructional tools is their identification by search engines. This is usually facilitated by assigning descriptive instruction, metadata just as a book in a library has a record in the card catalogue. Michael (2003) observes that the proliferation of definition for term instructional object or resources makes communication confusing and difficult. Most generally, the Institute of Electrical and Electronics Engineers (IEEE) defines an instructional object as any entity, digital or non- digital, that may be used for learning, education or training. More specifically and pointing out the extreme breadth of the IEEE's definition.

According to Michael (2003) "learning object" as an instructional object that has been 're-purposed and or re-engineered, changed or simply re-used in some way different from its original intended design' produces the term 'contextual instructional object', to describe an instructional object that has been designed to have specific meaning and purpose to an intended learner'.

Effective technology-based teaching is more likely the result of teacher's abilities to design lessons based upon robust instructional principle than technologies per se (Saveny, Davidson, & Smith, 1991), consequently; guidance for designing effective technology- based classroom should be grounded on effective pedagogy in general. Most real world task are ill – structured. Problems that are "well structured" generally occur with two principles to be considered in using instructional technology classroom.

Principle 1: Effective Learners Actively Process Lesson Content

During the past 30years the shift from behaviorism to cognitivistism has modified our conceptions of effective and efficient learning and instruction. By this, it means that effective learning requires students to do more than simply respond to stimuli. Instead, learners must actively seek and generate relationship between lesson content and instructional technology. One common myth is that instructional technology increase interactivity and thereby improves learning. The source of this perception is not difficult to trace, the result of a research on students attitudes towards working with instructional technologies especially computers, are generally positive (Martin, Heller, & Mahmoul, 1991). Furthermore, research contends that instructional use of technology involves more than simply using a computer to deliver an electronic presentation or browse the Internet for technology-supported activities (Dockstader, 1999). Dockstader (1999) and Bouie (1998) suggest enabling factors which lead to effective technology integration into teaching and learning environments. These factors include: knowledge of technology-enhanced curriculum development; access to instructional technology materials, support, and training; time and interest in developing technology-enhanced curriculum; institutional support in experimenting with new technology interventions; familiarity with standards-correlated technology in the content area; awareness of successful technology use in subject areas; reward structure for developing/implementing technology-enhanced curriculum; technology literacy of the instructor (Bouie, 1998; Byrom & Bingham, 1999; Dockstader, 1999; OTA, 1995)

Principle 2: Effective Use of Instructional Technology Should be Built around Students Knowledge and Experiences and be Grounded in Meaningful Contexts

One of the roles of technology is to bridge personal experience and formal instruction. It should also be sufficiently flexible to adapt to students ongoing instructional needs. One of the hallmarks of a master teacher is the ability to recognize and repair students misunderstanding and misconception. When learning difficulties arise, therefore, Technology –based instruction should be sufficiently flexible to bring about effective

learning outcome. However, instruction should be grounded in familiar contexts to stimulate and improve instructional efficiency (Merrill, 1991).

Usefulness of Local Instructional Package

The use of locally produced instructional package in the teaching and learning situation has many advantages. Some of them according to Abolade and Olumorin (2004) and Abolade (2009) are that:

- They can present objects and model because the raw materials are locally sourced.
- They can present objects and model in either 2 to 3 dimensional view.
- They can be used to teach large classes
- They encourage class participation since majority of the raw material are within the reach of the learner.

Obstacles in the Way of Instructional Technology in Nigerian Schools

Behind the challenges facing usability of Instructional Technology are also pervasive constrains that may hinder the effective and efficient use of Instructional Technology in teaching and learning for better academic performance.

- Lack of necessary human resources, and financial wherewithal to realize their ideas
- Classroom professionals should begin to realize that they are limiting their students by not helping them to develop and use digital media literacy skills across curriculum.
- Lack of formal training is being offset through professional development or informal learning.
- Inability to blend formal and informal learning with technology
- Traditional lectures and subsequent teaching are still dominant learning vehicles in schools.

- The demand for personalized learning is not adequately supported by current technology in Nigeria.
- Institutional barriers present formidable challenges to moving forward in a constructive way with emerging technology.
- Learning that incorporates real life experience is not given enough encouragement and is undervalued when it does take place.

CONCLUSION

In this chapter, the emergence of new technology to compliment instructions in classroom teaching and learning for effective and efficient academic performance is appreciated. It is expedient to note that teachers/instructors must not only familiarise with those technologies but have adequate knowledge of how to integrate technology to solve learning problems either individually or collectively. It is however in line with research findings from cognitive psychology and other related areas that teachers/instructors can create environments in which students actively engage in cognitive partnership with technology. Although, due to high cost of ready made instructional technologies, teachers should endeavour to produce or improvise materials for teaching from local resources.

Recommendations

The following are therefore recommended to promote instructional technology effectively and efficiently in Nigeria Schools.

1. Schools should create an enabling environment for the use of Instructional Technology (IT) which would enhance the active use Educational Technology tools such as, of social network, Facebook, you-tube, twitter by the student in order to boost competency.

2. More effort should be put into periodic workshops, seminars, symposia and training and re-training of teachers as professionals. Such trainings should be organized in schools to increase the awareness and knowledge required for students and instructors alike in the use of Instructional Technology to ensure efficiency in contemporary teaching and learning

3. The teaching profession should be properly professionalized, well remunerated and motivated so as to improve the prestige of teaching as a profession.

4. Adequate funding should be allocated to the procurement of Instructional Technology facilities. This fund should not be spent on other things under any guise than new teaching and learning tools that will translate Nigeria into a higher level in the comity of nations.

REFERENCES

Abanikanda, M. O. (2011). *Integrating Information and Communication Technology (ICT) in Teacher Education*. Higher Education & Globalization.

Abolade, A. O. (2009). Importance of Learning and Instructional Material in Nigerian Educational Industries. *Nigeria Journal of Curriculum Studies*, *12*(1), 22–108.

Adiwas, A., & Iyamu, E.O.S. (2004). Curriculum Implementation in Nigeria. *Journal of Technology Education*.

Agun, I. (1982). Strategies for developing resources centers in Nigerian secondary schools. *Nigeria Educational Forum*, *3*(1).

Angline, G. (1995). *Instructional technology: Past present and future* (2nd ed.). Englewood, CO: Libraries Unlimited, Inc.

Beck, R. J. (2008). *What are learning objects?* University of Wisconsin. Retrieved from http://www.uwm.Edu/Dept/CIE/AOP/LO

Berson, M. J. (1996). Effectiveness of computer technology in the social studies: A review of the literature. *Journal of Research on Computing in Education, 28,* 486–499.

Beswick, W. (1972). *School resources centers.* London Evans/Methuen Educational.

Bouie, E. L. (1998). Creating an information rich environment. *Technological Horizons in Education, 26*(2), 78–79.

Byrom, E., & Bingham, M. (1999). *Factors influencing the effective use of technology for teaching and learning: Lessons learned from the SEIR*TEC intensive site schools.* Southeast and Islands Regional Technology in Education Consortium (SEIR*TEC).

Casey, K. (2012). *Risks Your BYOD Policy Must Address.* Information Week.

Clinton, W. J. (1998, January 28). President Clinton's 1998 state of the union address. *The New York Times,* pp. A20-21.

Cognition and Technology Group at Vanderbilt. (1992). The Jasper experiment: An exploration of issues in learning and instructional design. *Educational Technology Research and Development, 40,* 65–80. doi:10.1007/BF02296707

Diame, Heller, & Mahmoud. (1991). American and Soviet Children's Attitude towards Computer. *Journal of Educational Computing Research, 8*(2), 155–185.

Dockstader, J. (1999). Teachers of the 21st century know the what, why, and how of technology integration. *Technological Horizons in Education, 26*(6), 73–74.

Duffy, T. M., & Cunningham, D. J. (1996). Constructivism: Implications for the design and delivery of instruction. In D. H. Jonassen (Ed.), *Handbook of research for educational communications and technology.* New York: Macmillan.

Fadeiye, J.O. (2001). *Social studies for NCE.* Oyo: Immaculate-City Publisher.

Friend, J. (1989). *Interactive radio instruction developing instructional methods.* Academic Press.

Garrison & Anderson. (2003). [*st* century: A framework for research and practice. Routledge.]. *E-learning,* 21.

Honebein, P. C. (1996). Seven goals for the design of constructivist learning environments. In B. G. Wilson (Ed.), *Constructivist learning environments: Case studies in instructional design.* Englewood Cliffs, NJ: Educational Technology Publications.

Imhoof, K. (1985). *Interactive radio in the classroom.* Academic Press.

James, Bangert, & Williams. (1983). Effect of Computer–Based Teaching on Secondary School Students. *Journal of Educational Psychology, 75,* 19–26. doi:10.1037/0022-0663.75.1.19

Jonassen, D. H. (2011). Learning to solve to solve troubleshoot problems. *Performance Improvement, 42*(4), 34–38. doi:10.1002/pfi.4930420408

Jonassen, D. H. (in press). *Problem solving: the enterprise.* Mahwah, NJ. *Lawrence Eribaun Associates.*

Karrer, T. (2007). *Understanding e-learning.* Retrieved from http://www learning circuit. org/2007/0707 karrer.html

Magarick, R. H., & Galbracth, C. (1988). *The teaching of production of materials by computer assisted learning system and interactive video disc technology.* Academic Press.

Mc Daniel, E., Melnerney, W., & Armstrong, P. (1993). Computer and School. *Reform Educational Technology Research and Development*, *4*(91), 73–78. doi:10.1007/BF02297093

Merrill, M. D. (1991). Constructivism and Instructional Design. *Educational Technology*, *3*(5), 45–53.

Miller, G. S., & Miller, W. W. (1999). Secondary agriculture instructor's opinion and usage of a telecommunications network for distance learning. In *Proceedings of the 53rd Annual AAAE Central Region Research Conference & Seminar in Agricultural Education*. St. Louis, MO: AAAE.

Morrison, G., & Lowther, D. (2010). *Integrating computer technology into the classroom, skills for the 21st century* (4th ed.). Boston, MA: Pearson Education.

Nagy, A. (2005). The impact of e learning. In E. Content (Ed.), *Technologies and perspective for the European Market*. Berlin: Springerverlag.

National Institute of Standards and Technology. (n.d.). Adaptive learning systems. *National Institute of Standards and Technology*.

Office of Technology Assessment (OTA). (1995). *Teachers and technology: Making the connection*. Washington, DC: U.S. Government Printing Office. Retrieved May 28, 2001, from http://www.wws.princeton.edu/~ota/disk1/1995/9541_n.html

Ogundare, S. E. (2003). *Fundamentals of teaching social studies. Oyo*. Immaculate Publishers.

Ogunsheye, F. A. (2001). *Syllabuses for library use*. Ibadan: University of Ibadan, Abadina Media Resources Centre.

Osokoya, I. O. (1996). *Writing and teaching history: A guide to advanced study*. Ibadan: Lawrel Educational Publishers.

Randy, D. G., & Terry, A. (2003). [*st century: A Framework for research and practice*. Routledge.]. *E-learning*, 21.

Reiser, R. (1987). Instructional Technology: A History. In R. Gagne (Ed.), *Instructional Technology: Foundation* (pp. 11–48). Hillsdale, NJ: Lawrence Associates.

Reiser, R. A., & Dempsey, J. V. (2002). *Trends and Issues in Instructional Design and Technology*. Upper Saddle River, NJ: Merrill Prentice Hall.

Richey, R. C. (2008). *Reflection on the 2008 AECT Definitions of the field Tech Trends*. Academic Press.

Riel, M. (2003, September). *Written testimony for the web-based education commission*. Retrieved from http://www.gse.uci.edu/mriel/e-testify/

Seels, B. B., & Richey, R. C. (1994a). *Instructional technology: The definitions and domains of the field*. Washington, DC: Association for Educational Communications and Technology.

Seels, B. B., & Richey, R. C. (1994b). Redefining the field: A collaborative effort. *TechTrends*, *2*(39), 36–38. doi:10.1007/BF02818746

Shaw. (2003). *Contextual and mutilated learning in the context of design, learning and (RE) use teaching and learning with technology*. Retrieved from http://www.shawmultimedia.com/edtechOct.B

Walsh. K. (2012). *Flipped class workshop in a book*. Retrieved from http://www.knewton.com/flip

ADDITIONAL READING

Abanikannda, M. O. (2009). problem and prospect integration of the ICT in secondary school curriculum in *Nigerian*. *Journal of Curriculum Studies*, *16*(3), 9–17.

Akude, I. (2004). *A handbook on educational technology. Owerri.* Bonaway publishers.

Akude, I. (2010). *New technologies and innovative technologies in education. Owerri.* Bonaway publisher.

Angling, G. (Ed.). (1995). *Instructional technology past, present and future* (2nd ed.). Eaglewood, Colorado: Libraries Unlimited, Inc.

Dick, W. Carey, L & Carey, J.O. (2008). The system designs of instruction. 7th Ed. Boston: Allyn & Bacon.

Dike, H. I. (2008). *A textbook of educational technology. Port-Harcourt.* Capiic publisher.

Duffy, T., & Cunningham, D. (1996). *Constructivism: implication for the design and delivery of instruction: handbook of research for Educational telecommunication and technology. N.* York: Macmillan.

Haddad, W. D. (2003). *Is instructional technology a must for learning?* Knowledge Enterprise Inc. Retrieved on 3rd October, 2008 from http://www.techknowledge.org

Heinich, R. M., Molenda, M., & Russell, J. D & Smaldon, S. F. (2001) Instructional Media and Technology for learning. (7th ed) New York: Macmillan Publishing Company

Ike, G. A. (2006). *Concept of educational technology. Owerri.* Peace publishers Ltd.

Jonassen, D. H. (1992). *What are the cognitive tools?* Berlin: Springer-verlag.

Lenhart, A (2009). Teens and social media: *An overview*, 22 New York: Pew Internet & American life project.

Lever-Duffy, Judy (2008), *Teaching and Learning with technology.* Pearson education, Inc.

Majed, A. (1996). Students' teacher use of instructional media and it implications. *International Journal of Instructional Media, 23*(1), 59–78.

McDaniel, E. Melnerney, W., & Armstrong, P. (1993). *Computer and school reform.* Educational Technology Research and Development 4(91).73-78

Onasanya, S. A., & Adegbija, M. V. (2007) Practical Handbook on Instructional Media 2nd Ed. Ilorin: Graphcom

Onasanya, S. A., & Ogunojemite, G. B. (2005). *Conceptual pedagogy for engaging in effective multimedia and instructional e-learning courseware design. Research in Curriculum Studies Journal, A publication of the Curriculum Studies Department.* University of Ado-Ekiti.

Peter, B. (2009). *Leadership in instructional technology and design*: an overview. *EDUCAUSE Quarterly, 28*(4), 12–17. http://wwweducause.edu/ir/library/pdf/egm0542pdf

Reiser, R. A., & Dempsey, J. V. (2002). *Trend and issue of instruction Design and Technology.* Upper Saddle River, NJ: Meric Prentice Hall.

Russell, A. L. (1996). Six stages in learning new technology. Retrieved from: http://www.fed.qut.edu.au./russel/stages.htm

Siemens, G. (2005). A learning theory for the Digital age. *Instructional Technology and Distance education,* 2(1), 3-10 http://wwwelearnspace.org/Articles/connectivism.htm

Svin-Kachala, J., & Bialo, E. R. (2006). Reports on the effectives of technology in schools software information. Information. In Technology and child development, part I: A ten- year Review pp. 20-22.

Wadi, T. (1994). *Managing an instructional development center with necessary information technology strategies.* Francisco Jossey Bass.

Walter, A. (1998). *Instructional Technology, it nature and use*. New York: Holiday Lithography Corporation.

Yusuf, M. O., & Onasanya, S. A. (2004). *ICT and teaching in tertiary institutions*. Faculty of Education University of Ilorin.

KEY TERMS AND DEFINITIONS

Academic Performance: This is the level of in-depth knowledge, fitness in a subject.

Effective: Some of the technological learning support based tools have abilities to produce intended result on the learners.

Efficient: Learners learn very fast when instructors teaches with technology.

Instructional Technology: Is a way of designing appropriate solution to teaching and learning problem with the help of technology.

Nigeria: Is a country in Western Africa. It has highest number of schools and learner, where technology needs to be used to solve learning problem.

Promoting: Making some technological tools known to some educational stake holders.

Chapter 5
Cultural Factors Affecting Integration of Technology in Media Education in Nigeria

Ofomegbe Daniel Ekhareafo
University of Benin, Nigeria

Oroboh Ambrose Uchenunu
University of Benin, Nigeria

ABSTRACT

Today's world is aptly described as an information age, driven primarily by Information and Communication Technologies. This chapter stresses the idea that ICT usage in media education will not only improve the capacity of the students to learn but also improve the capacity of the facilitators. Although there are a number of factors that affect the integration of technology in learning, the chapter advocates that against the benefit of ICT education proactive steps need to be taken to redress the low trend if the graduates must compete with others, particularly those with overseas qualifications and other professionals in today's globalised and evanescent technological world.

INTRODUCTION

Information and Communication Technologies have been described as drivers of modern societies. This chapter seeks to establish the value of Information and Communication Technologies (ICTs) in media education. It paints a picture of the state of ICTs knowledge and usage among academics and the low level of their usage in teaching and learning. The chapter draws on the different benefits of their usage in learning particularly in media education. It also x-ray practices which have become ingrained in the management of universities and the attitude of university academics have hindered the successful integration of ICTs into media education.

Essentially, this chapter:

- Explain Information and Communication Technology and media education.
- Highlight the benefits of media technology education.
- Describe the state of ICT usage in media education in Nigeria.

DOI: 10.4018/978-1-4666-6162-2.ch005

Copyright © 2014, IGI Global. Copying or distributing in print or electronic forms without written permission of IGI Global is prohibited.

- Explain the cultural trends that hindered the effective integration of ICT in media education and learning in general.

BACKGROUND

There is no doubt that vicarious changes have taken place in the world over as a result of ICT. The obvious impact of ICTs manifest in the use of e-payment, e-learning, e-banking, and e-trading, to mention a few, in the area of education, ICTs have challenged the old method of teaching and even raised a serious concern for curriculum development experts. These serious concerns for curriculum developers are developing online database for students, online examination, course material development, online assessment, student-teacher interaction amongst others. This is because teaching in the digital age, especially media educators must incorporate sound knowledge of ICTs, such as digital editing, multi-media application, online journalism creations, and computer based presentation methods amongst others.

The present level of communication development in the society has not always being digital centred. Society has transited from oral culture to the written culture and then to the present electronic era, the era of technologies and globalization. Faniran (2010) observes that, in human history, society has evolved different means of storing and distributing information from spoken word to the written/printed word, to the broadcast-image word and now to the emerging digital multimedia word. The introduction of ICT has provided us with new ways of reading, learning and understanding the world around us. Today, quite a number of people learn one or two skills as a result of their exposure to media content. The new media in particular, presents diverse ways of learning. For instance, security experts attribute the ability of terrorist groups to assemble explosives and share the procedures on the Internet. It is therefore safe to say that the media serves as a potent instrument in

media education. Scarratt (2007) posit that "Media education is the process of teaching and learning the whole range of modern communications, and the issues and debates about them."

Media Literacy Week (online not dated) contends that "Media education is the process through which individuals become media literate - able to critically understand the nature, techniques and impacts of media messages and productions." The magazine states that, "In the digital age, the principles of media education are the same as they've always been, but the existence of cyberspace is adding new and challenging questions." In other word new technologies are challenging the new ways of acquiring skills in media knowledge and use.

Agba (2005) asserts that "there is a dawn of a new technological era in which better pieces of communication equipment are increasingly replacing and complementing traditional communication media as tools of transmitting disseminating distance educational materials.

Inspite of the benefits of ICTs knowledge in media education, quite a number of academics are yet to be abreast with their use. This perhaps, can be inferred from Okebukola in Abubakar (2003) assertion that many university lecturers settle for lecture method of instructional delivery. He noted that they merely stand in front of the class, read lecture notes in drab monotone with students busy copying notes, which they regurgitate for examination. Okebukola further stated that while the lecture method is useful in a meaningful setting, it is contradictory in a setting where creativity, innovativeness and meaningful learning are being promoted. Consequently, the National Universities Commission (NUC) organized training programme for stakeholders, which focused on methods of teaching (Abubakar, 2003).Thus, it is clear that the intention of the NUC in organizing training programmes for academics in higher institutions is to make available new methods for better empowerment in teaching.

In the recent past, various government/institutions have supported the introduction of computer technology in all aspect of instruction and administration (Collins, Hammond and Wellington (1997), Anao, (1999-2000). The introduction of computer may challenge or has challenged existing educational philosophy and practices in unexpected ways-some positive and some not so positive (Brown & Mclntre 1982; Richardson, 1991, Katz, Dalton & Giaquinta, 1994). For instance in some e-books, students are made to propose alternative ending for stories. They are required to be more than passive readers. They become part of the unfolding process, control of which has shifted away from the teacher, ironically (Miler & Olson, 1998).

The level of ICT knowledge amongst academic has not become common place. Some are yet to know the different softwares use in editing, data presentation and analysis, desktop publishing and Web application. In some instances, those having poor knowledge and use of ICTs shy away from conferences and seminar that task their abilities to use them. There are cases where some become offensive when serious questioning from students may bruise their ego. For some academics that are already vast in ICTs usage, some of their approaches to learning tend to be questioned by non-literate member of staff. For instance, a lecturer who insists that his supervisees should forward their undergraduate project works to him online is largely seen by his colleague as promoting a new culture which is alien to the system.

The implication of these scenarios is that there is a yawning gap in ICTs knowledge and usage amongst Academics in some universities in Nigeria. Where majority of the non-literate in ICTs hold sway, they become adverse to curriculum change meant to promote current trends in media education.

The beauty of enhancing media education through ICTs according to (National grid for learning undated) is that "Learning through ICT not only offers the chance to become proficient in the skills needed in the world of work. It enhances and enriches the curriculum, raising standard and making learning more attractive. The best educational software is not alternative to books or class teachers. It is rather a new chapter of opportunity." It highlights the following benefits:

- Teachers will be able to share and discuss best practice with each other and with experts while remaining in their schools;
- Materials and advice will be available online when learners want them – to help develop their literacy and numeracy skills. including in their own time;
- Children in isolated school will be able to link up with their counterparts' curriculum, to help them work together and gain the stimulus they need;
- Language learners will be able to communicate directly with speakers of the target language;
- Learners at home or in libraries will be able to access a wider range of quality learning programme, materials and software.
- All learning on the Grid will be able to be tailored to the interest and abilities of the individual"

Students are expected to become active in the midst of a multi-media package-as in the classroom situation in which a video-tape "the voyage of the Mimi": (a documentary that showed the experiences of the Mimi with graphic and visual illustrations that helped relate their experiences better) was exhibited (Black & Atkin, 1996: 152-154, cited in Olson 2000: 1-2) while the teacher remains passive.

The disposition for adopting an innovation depends on teachers' attitude toward receptivity to that curriculum novelty. Nevertheless, Morris (1995, cited in Lee, 2000) reasons that positive attitude toward a curriculum innovation may not be an accurate predictor of implementation of an innovation, since teachers' attitude can be crucial in determining the success and failure of an innovation (Brown & Mclntyre, 1982; Richardson, 1991, in Lee, 2000). Age, sex and experience are also factors affecting teacher receptivity to change (Bridges &Reynolds, 1968).

Anao (2003) observes that in the universities, the inclination and zeal to modernize and adopt the imperative of the emerging technology is not significantly demonstrated. Traditional chalk and duster approach still dominate in our teaching pedagogy. Scientific research and information transfer using ICT tools is minimal. This situation does not augur well for the teacher who needs to operate on the same wavelength with his or her counterpart in the developed world. This is because learning through technologies will serve as:

- "Techniques for monitoring and evaluating their own teaching.
- Their institution's mission and how it affects teaching and learning strategies.
- Implication of their quality assurance for practice.
- Regulation, policies and practices affecting their own work" (see Sir Ron Dearing report, 1997).

Against this backdrop, the National Grid for learning provides an insight of what ICT offers the educator who needs to have up-to-date information to improve his or her work in the curriculum. Learning through ICT not only offers the curriculum, raising standards and making learning more attractive. The best educational software is not an alternative to books or class-teachers-it, but a new chapter of opportunity. This is what the National Grid of learning emphasises when it states that:

- Teachers will be able to share and discuss best practice with each other and with experts while remaining in their schools.
- Materials and advice will be available online with their counterparts' curriculum,

to help them work together and gain the stimulus they need.

- Language learner will be able to communicate directly with speakers of target language.
- Learner at home or in libraries will be able to access a wider range of quality learning programmes, materials and software.
- All learning on the Grid will be able to be tailored to the interests and abilities of the individual.
- Recommendations provided by curriculum experts are in sharp contrast with the time honoured practices of the teacher where the normal distribution curve dominates learning outcomes.

The teacher expects only a minority of the students to perform either excellently well or poorly, but majority of the students fall within the average. Consequently, the essence of these old practices according to Badmus (1997) is to place students at a disadvantage as these are bringing about a self-fulfilling prophecy. Also, Abel (1979) explains that certain students are naturally endowed with a high IQs (Intelligence Quotient). This explanation gives credence to the traditional teaching style which does not give the less intelligent ones a chance to be productive.

The modern trend and the dynamism of the curriculum are contrary to the traditional practices of the old fashioned teacher. He or she does not take accountability, individual needs to encourage all the students to achieve at least 80% mastery of all tasks and skills taught. In this way, he or she ensures that the question of accountability greatly emphasized by curriculum experts is accommodated. High achievement in pedagogy can be enhanced tremendously with Information Communication Technology (ICT) in particular and other educational facilities. With the ICT, the process oriented goals of education will be actualized. Thus, teachers are asked increasingly to offer students more individualized and individualistic instruction with resources which require new skills- such as accessing the use of electronic media, as they implement rapidly changing educational policies (Olson, 2002; Feenberg, 1999; Chon & Tsai, 2002).

Traditionally, curriculum development is teacher – centred, and teachers themselves identify instructional goals and objectives. However, as Jones (1997) notes, since the nature of the Internet promote equal participation of all users, it nourishes a "participatory democracy." If we agree that this result of Internet use is a positive one, we need to reconsider the authorship of the curriculum shifting authority from teacher to student may further advance such democratic ideas and practices.

French, Hale, Johnson, and Farr, (1999) contend that the figure of 'teacher' has traditionally been regarded as the sage on the stage', the individual who primarily determines the instructional objectives and provides most of the learning materials. However, in an Internet-based learning environment and teacher is depicted more often as a guide on the side'. However, both the teacher and learner are simultaneously 'guides' and sages because they become continual learners and peer – teachers who adapt rapidly to set learning objectives in the light of changing information.

Relan and Gillian (1997) explored the differences between traditional instruction and Web-based instruction. They found that in a student centred Web-based curriculum the relative amount of time that student talk is equal to or greater than the amount of time that teachers talk. Students also help to choose the content to be organized and learned. French et al., (1999) also consider that Web-based learning is suitable for self-directed learning in which students have more choice of, or control over, not only their learning time and pace, but also the objectives or learning outcomes. As a result, Web-based curriculum designers and instructors must determine how to:

1. Include students, especially adult students of non-traditional age and students undergoing on the job training, in the process of identifying instructional objectives.

2. Balance both teachers' and students' authorship in developing Web-based curricula. For example, a forum in which both instructors and students discuss course direction and process may shape instructional objectives as the course progresses. A distinct, identifiable area in the Web-based curriculum can be allocated for students to contribute their learning materials (such as links to related Web-sites and new groups); teachers can screen students' contributions to determine which materials are suitable for the curriculum and the course.

BENEFITS OF ICTS IN MEDIA EDUCATION

Media scholars and educationist (e.g. Adeoye, 2010; Agba 2005, Landow 1997) have raised a number of benefits which have been tested and proved to enhance not only learning but also simplify the communication process between students and their course tutors. Against this backdrop, the following are suggested as possible benefits to media education:

To Encourage Learners

According to Agba (2005, p.25) "certain media are designed to be used by individual learners. These include slides, film-strips, video and audiocassettes. Another major aim of these media is to overcome one common shortcoming of radio and television-transiency of message. Thus, these personalized media, apart from incorporating the audio-visual elements, allow message recall in case the learner fails to understand something at first reading or listening." Where a member of an academic board is unable to attend a lecture, these can be deployed to serve the lecture purpose of that day. Students can take back the tape home and listen carefully to issues raised in the lecture. In this case, they are not only taught, but also learn at their own pace.

Makes Possible Multi-Media Platforms in Learning

The Web is basically a hypertext system. Landow (1997) contents that hypertext is basically an inter-textual system, open, non-fixed and boundless rather than closed, fixed and bounded. The inter-textual nature of hypertext makes it very different from page-bound text. In addition, Landow suggests that in producing and processing hypertext, we need to abandon the concepts of centre, margin, hierarchy and linearity upon which traditional text is based to replace them with concept of multi-linearity, nodes, links and networks, all of which are hallmarks of hypertext. Relan and Gillaini (1997) agree with this in their claim that the major sources of content in Web-based learning shifts from the textbook and the teacher to more varied sources of information and the nature of content becomes dynamics rather than static, limited to texts published on a certain date. Under the circumstances, teachers and designers must determine how to evolve Web curricula that are open, non – fixed and boundless and how to link Web resources in such a way that curriculum contents is enriched and students attention is both captured and maintained.

When teachers and designers attempt to enrich their curricula by harnessing the unlimited hypertext information on the Internet, they ought to review and screen a large amount of information from many Websites and make links on appropriate places during the 'course'. In the same light, Draves (2000) points to the necessity of providing some kinds of guidance for students' vis-à-vis these links. The simplest way is to split those links into three teachers – assigned categories: Critical' (must read), 'important' (should read), and

'Nice' (could read). With that, each student can determine what linked materials to read, and when, depending on their schedules and learning paces.

Gives Guidance

The use of ICTs in learning can facilitate students understanding of locations, and developments in history by using empirical analysis and visual based tools. Chou and Lins (1998) investigated navigational maps in a computer hypertext learning and discovered that the map-type had a significant effect on students' development of cognitive maps within the course structure. The study demonstrated that when students are presented global maps, in which the entire hierarchical knowledge structure for the course is provided, by means of a list of the concept names of all hypertext nodes, it enabled them to effectively and efficiently search for, locate and learn from curriculum content, and more.

Unlike traditional linear text, hypertext organizes information in sets of associative links (Conklin, 1987). For Landow (1997), hypertext also denotes text composed of blocks of texts and electronic links that join them. The concept of hypermedia simply extends the notion of the text in hypertext by including visual information, sound, animation and other forms of information. Hypertext grants learners freedom to navigate through cyberspace in a non-linear fashion – they can select, search, and browse in an infinite number of sequential, and often recursive, patterns.

When authoring learning materials in hypertext format, Woodhead (1991) suggests three basic rhetorical techniques: 1 Gradual Disclosure —— a smooth progression into finer, richer and more specific levels of detail. 2 Foreshadow——giving repeated sequences to forthcoming times to guide audience needs. 3 Recapitulation——prior topics are repeated for emphasis or to allow the audience to draw themes together.

Beer (2000) also offer some guidelines for organizing Web learning content, including providing a site overview, using consistent vocabulary across the whole learning content, including providing a site offers some consistent vocabulary across the whole learning site, explaining the content architecture, and using hyperlink sparingly and carefully. Chou and Sun (1996) have suggested providing 'next' buttons at the end of each instructional node to indicate the designer's recommendation for the next node to visit. The 'prerequisites' for moves can also be set in a Web curriculum. That is, students have to read one node before they jump to other, related nodes.

Offers Choices in Presentation

The Web is a multi-million system that incorporate text, graphics, audio, animation and video, and it provides teachers with more choices of presentation methods than are usual in traditional curricular. Indeed, the growing use of Internet technologies opens new possibilities that move well beyond the provision of more sophisticated delivery tools. In a study by Chou et al., (2001), a combined presentation of virtual reality modelling language, (VRML) and hypertext, marked up language (HTLM) was designed to demonstrate the human digestive system for university students who were not majoring in health or science. Three-dimensional graphics written in VRML allowed student not only to view the digestive system from any direction but also to enter the digestive organs themselves using navigation tools provide by VRML browsers. In addition, text and /or 2-D graphics are organized by HTML in order to offer detailed health science information.

Kearsley (2000) argues that most online curricula materials would benefit from graphics in the form of illustrations, diagnosis icons and backgrounds. Teachers or designers, however, may not have the graphics skills and knowledge of graphic software to corporate the elements into their curriculum and courses. Moreover, some degree of background knowledge, understanding of, and skill in multimedia production are necessary

to produce audio/or video elements in Web-based learning sites.

Similarly, the creation of animations or simulations requires special programming skills and experience, which teachers and designers may not have. Before, teachers and designers need to be adept at preparing and organizing content-appropriate presentations in digital multimedia form. If they do not have necessary knowledge or skill themselves, they need technical support personnel.

Help in Assessing Students Performances

Bear (2000) considers that the Internet in general and the Web in particular have unique contribution to make to a broader conception of assessment. He provides several new assessment ideas, such as inviting experts to evaluate online individual and collaborative work as well as the content of Web discussion, and argues for connection assessment of learning resources and using the Web for individual self-assessment, such as projects, seminar papers and assignments in film studies.

In response to such ideas, teachers and designs must be able to grasp the unique requirements and features of Web technology for implementing and maintain Web-based assessments, and to design effective Web-based tests and assignments that accurately assess students' learning and provide the useful data for further curriculum development. Cho (2000) contends that when analyzing the use of Web-based test, the dimensions of time and location of testing can help developers conceptualize the use of any testing system Nothing whether time and location are specific or fixed, i.e. specific time/filed location, flexible time/fixed location, specific time/non-fixed location, and flexible time/non-filed location testing types and situation can be characterized.

When designing online assignments, in particular, Harrison and Bergen (2000) suggest preparing a detailed list of weekly assignment. The list should include the pages to read, questions to be answered and problems to be solved. It should also cover the materials for online discussions. This will help to ensure progress in students' discussions, and allow students to follow that progress effortlessly.

Make Possible the Creation of Learning and Discussion Groups

Students get links to UseNet, which makes it possible for them to belong to discussion groups. Thus, students can access such discussions by experts and learn new ideas from them

Help in Formative Evaluation

Formative evaluation, a critical step in curriculum development, is the process of gathering information to advice design production and implementation decisions (Flagg, 1990 cited in Chou and Tsai, 2002). Kearsley, 2000 suggests that the biggest problem in developing online curricula may not be their initial creation but rather subsequent revisions and updating: even if the content of a course does not require much change, many small details, such as links to other sites, need to be updated on a regular basis.

Conducting a formative evaluation of Web-based curricula requires experts in course content, curricula, media and administration to work together to develop evaluative methodologies that take into account students and experts' presence at remote sites. Consequently, teachers and designers need to develop methods for conducting formative evaluations within complete technology – dependent learning environments and curricula, to set up a reasonable work schedule for continual updating and revision, and to work closely with formative evaluation team members.

In Chou (1998) a formative evaluation system was developed for Web-based distance learning. The Computer Logging of User Entries (CLUE) system combined computer logging techniques to collect commentary during users' interactions

with the learning materials, and was designed to be used to collect input from large numbers of users working in different remote locations. The inputs are automatically stored, calculated and then presented in format that can easily be interpreted by curriculum designers and instructors. Innovative formative evaluation methods and system such as CLUE are becoming increasingly necessary in order to guarantee that more Web-based learning materials can be effectively evaluated.

Note: Kindly read through this paper and correct all the grammatical errors.

CHALLENGES TO THE EFFECTIVE INTEGRATION OF ICTS IN MEDIA EDUCATION

The following are some of the factors which have hindered or vitiated the successful integration of technology in media education.

Poor funding: Successive administrations in Nigeria have shown poor attitude to educational funding thus creating multiple problems in the educational sector. For instance, in the 2013 strike embarked upon by the Academic Staff Union of Universities (ASUU), pictures of paraffin stoves serving as bunsen-burner where prominently displayed in the flyer to buttress why the educational system is in dire need of funding. In addition, some media studios still use the manual method of developing film negatives, because resources have not been provided to acquire digital printing machines. In the area of digitization, some media studios are still dominated by analogue systems. One unfortunate thing about this state of affairs is that society talks about digital switch over, whereas, the training received from students in higher institutions of learning who will work in digital environment are yet to fully grasp what the whole concept is. Learning remains more theoretical based than vocational thereby depriving the students of the capacity to actor compete with their counterparts from other parts of the world.

- **Empire Building:** Empire building is a cultural practice in Nigeria higher institutions where departments and faculties are created to favour the perceived political interest of associates and administrators. The import of this is that programmes are usually not well scrutinized before they are introduced. The interest of the promoters tends to dominate the long term benefit. Although, reasons are usually canvassed to justify such, the after effect is that the manpower, technology and resources needed may not be readily available. Where this is the case, students operate on abstract facilities for long, until help may come.

- **Traditional Values:** In Nigeria, respect for the seniors is a norm. This practice transcends the traditional society to higher institutions. Many of the older ones in the system stick to their age long practices in teaching and curricula development. Since, many of the younger ones are their products in some cases; they kept mum in order to protect the ego of their seniors. In a recent curriculum review in our department, a junior lecturer proposed courses which are more in line with ICTs usage and trends, but some of the older lecturers rejected the proposal, because they perceived that if such proposal scales through at the faculty board, they have very little contribution to make to the system. Thus, there is a sort of misunderstanding amongst the older group, leaving the junior ones to haggle over the relevance of the old curriculum in this digital age.

- **Aversion to Change:** One major problem that inhibits people from adopting ICT into their curricula is that generally, humans are known to have been averse to changes from the status quo. The reason is multifarious. Fear of failure to be able to adapt to the new system. Indolence to want to embark on such arduous task when there is a work-

ing alternative which they are comfortable in. The notion of safety. Information could get corrupted or altered by scrupulous individuals. Cost of hosting sites and designing sites are and could be enormous to the individual tutor if subvention is not kept aside for that by an authority. A case in point is a lecturer at the department of mass communication at the University of Benin, got frowned at by old colleagues for reading supervisee's work online rather than the traditional file submission.

- **Poor Training:** On the job training is a common practice in corporate organizations. The same cannot be said of higher institutions offering media education training. The best we have seen for the past four years at the University of Benin is mostly individual effort at self-development. Thus, issues about digital editing, online publishing, and trends in film making are programmes individual lecturers take advantage of at their own expense. Although, in federal institutions the creation of the Tertiary Education Trust Fund (TETFund) assisted some academics to travel for international conferences and seminars, only a handful of academic have benefited from the fund. The rigours associated with claiming approved funds sometimes discourage many from applying. Update or refreshing courses on the job ought to be the practice, especially now, where ICTs development and deployment have become common place.

- **Nepotism:** Ironically, the issues that are challenging Nigeria's quest for development are not remote from the university system. Where opportunities call for special training of ICTs personnel or the provision of such facilities in the schools, consideration is usually given to the ethnic group the authority belong or loyalists without a corresponding consideration for the human resource that will assist in the training of students. Thus, such projects end up as elephant projects. In our visits to schools with Petroleum Technology Development Fund ICTs grant centres, many of the centres were and are more in name. Blocks of classrooms with such label as PTDF-ICT CENTRE have no computers or broadband facilities to power the operations of the centres. This is because, in approving such projects, consideration was not given to broadband availability, power and other sundry considerations which are germane to the running of such a centre.

CONCLUSION

The potential and power of ICTs knowledge and applications in facilitating learning in modern society have been highlighted, although cultural factors continue to play down the roles in both adoption and usage of ICTs in relevant disciplines, however, creating the right environment for knowledge transfer and interaction will help in raising the standard of training. This paper emphasises the need for technology integration in learning, especially media education, to enable educators compete with their contemporaries and raise graduates well equipped enough to fit into the labour market of the digital age. This we believe can be done in an environment free of prejudice, where appointments are based on merits and competence, where the required funding necessary for technology education is provided and above all, where authorities are committed to adopting new technologies with the desire to train the trainers and end users.

Solutions and Recommendations

Incorporating ICTs in media education and breaking cultural barriers to technology integration to learning require a number of steps which at the present developmental level in Nigeria will find difficult to accomplish. However, we believe much can be done if:

1. Programmes are properly scrutinised with the necessary funding for technology and human capacity spelt out before they are introduced.
2. Emphasis should be placed on merit and potential for growth, when the need arises for ICT training for staff. Irrespective of a staff place of birth or state of origin, primary consideration should be the staff capacity to learn the skills, techniques and train others.
3. Appointments of departmental heads should flow from experience and what such individuals hope to bring into the system. In this way, would-be head with vast experience on IT can leverage on such platform to develop better ways of promoting IT in media education. Alternatively, the head should be someone ready for change and should encourage that in those who are willing.
4. The provision of adequate infrastructure such as power supply, well lit classrooms and the necessary IT infrastructure will make classroom learning much easier.
5. The National University Commission (NUC) should set the minimal bench mark for media education. Such benchmarks will encourage institutions to evolve ways of providing the needed equipment to run such programmes.
6. Regular training on new technologies and their applicability to media education should form the annual training and retraining programmes for academic staff and technologist.
7. At the entry level, knowledge and application of the fundamentals of ICTs should be part of the criteria for academic employment.
8. In order to challenge the poor attitude to ICT knowledge and usage, ability to use some ICTs relating to media education should form part of the criteria for promotion. This will in no doubt challenge those adverse to change.

9. Promotions should not be based on publication alone, but also on display of ICT knowledge. In this way, those aspiring to rise will be forced to take up training and practice it, thus phasing out the fears and lack of interest in those caught up midways by the technology.

10. In organizing training for academic staff, the most important consideration should be those who have flare and passion for ICTs in order to make adaptation faster. In this way, they can become better resource for retraining of other staff members.

11. A gradual integration of ICTs into the school master plan through yearly prioritization of projects that have immediate benefits for enhanced learning and research will help deepen the culture of ICT usage.

FUTURE RESEARCH DIRECTION

For Nigeria educational institutions to meet up to the challenges of 21st century learning, we advocate online handling of students' projects supervision in order to deepen the culture of ICTs knowledge and usage. Schools should develop portals for lecturers where lecture notes can be hosted, assignment given and discussion raised. Against this background, an evaluation can be made on student's competence. We propose that learning in an ICT environment breeds both academic and students competent in the specialised field of ICTs, we also hypothesize that a culture resistant to change will find ICT utilization a big dream.

REFERENCES

Abubakar, M. (2003). *Stewardship Report of Professor A.R. Anao: Information and Communication Technology Department, 1999-2004.* University of Benin.

Adeoye, B. F. (2010). The use of ICTs in education: A case study of lecturers from the University of Lagos, Nigeria. *Journal of Educational Review, 3*(4), 429–434.

Agba, P. C. (2005). Media Technology and the Enlarging World of Distance Education in Nigeria. *International Journal of Communication, 2,* 21–31.

Anao, A. (2003, November 11). Society, knowledge incubation and management. *The Guardian,* p. 75.

Anao, A. R. (2004). *Stewardship Report of Professor A.R. Anao: Information and Communication Technology Department, 1999-2004.* University of Benin.

Beer, V. (2000). *The Web Learning Fieldbook: using the World Wide Web to build workplace learning Environments.* San Francisco, CA: Jossey-Bass.

Black, P., & Atkin, J. M. (Eds.). (1996). *Changing the Subject: Innovations in Science, Mathematics and Technology Education.* London: Routledge.

Bridges, E. M., & Reynolds, L. B. (1968). Teachers' Receptivity to Change. *Administrator's Notebook, 16*(6), 1–4.

Brown, S., & McIntyre, D. (1982). Influences upon teachers' attitudes to different types of innovation: A study of Scottish integrated science. *Curriculum Inquiry, 12*(1), 35–51. doi:10.2307/1179745

Chou, C. (1998). Developing CLUE: A formative evaluation system for computer networks learning courseware. *Journal of Interactive Learning Research, 10*(2), 179–193.

Chou, C. (2000). Constructing a computer-assisted testing and evaluation system on the world wide web-The Cates experience. *IEEE Transactions on Education, 42*(1), 179–193.

Chou, C., & Lin, H. (1998). The Effect of Navigation Map Types and Cognitive Styles on Learners' Performance in a Computer-networked Hypertext Learning System. *Journal of Educational Multimedia and Hypermedia, 7*(2/3), 151–176.

Chou, C., & Sun, C. T. (1996). Constructing a Cooperative Distant Learning System: The CORAL experience. *Educational Technology Research and Development, 44*(4), 71–84. doi:10.1007/BF02299822

Chou, C., & Tsai, C. C. (2002). Developing web-based curricula: issues and challenges. *Journal of Curriculum Studies, 34*(6), 623–636. doi:10.1080/00220270210141909

Chou, C., & Tsal, H. F. (2001). Developing a networked VRML, learning system for health science education in Taiwan. *International Journal of Educational Development, 21*(4), 293–303. doi:10.1016/S0738-0593(00)00003-1

Collins, J., Hammond, M., & Wellington, J. (1997). *Teaching and Learning with Multimedia.* London: Academic Press.

Conklin, J. (1987). Hypertext: An introduction and survey. *Computer, 20*(9), 17–41. doi:10.1109/MC.1987.1663693

Dearing, R. (1997). *National Committee of Inquiring into Higher Education.* Retrieved from http://.www.leeds.ac.uk/educol/ncihe/

Draves, W. A. (2000). *Teaching Online.* River Falls, WI: LEARN Books.

Faniran, J. (2010). Paul's Communication Strategies: A challenge to Agents of Evangelisation in the Third Millennium. In CATHAN: A searchlight on Saint Paul (pp. 162-176). Makurdi: Aboki.

French, D., Hale, C., Johnson, C., & Farr, G. (Eds.). (1999). Internet Based Learning: An Introduction and Framework for Higher Education and Business. Sterling, VA: stylus.

Harrison, N., & Bergen, C. (2000). Some design strategies for developing an online course. *Educational Technology, 40*(91), 57–60.

JISC. (1950). *Explaining Information System in Higher Education.* Retrieved from http://info.mccuk/Nti/JISC-issues.htm

Jones, S. G. (1997). The Internet and its social Landscape. In S. G. Jones (Ed.), *Virtual culture: Identity and communication in Cyber Society* (pp. 7–35). London: Sage.

Katz, E. H., Dalton, S., & Giaquinta, J. B. (1994). Status risk taking and receptivity of home economics teachers to a state wide curriculum innovation. *Home Economics Research Journal, 22*(4), 401–421. doi:10.1177/0046777494224003

Kearsley, G. (2002). *Online Education: Learning and Teaching in Cyberspace.* Toronto, Canada: Wadsworth.

Laurilland, D. (2005). *How Can Learning Technologies Improve Learning?* Retrieved from http://www.law.warwick.ac.uk/ltj/3-2j.htm

Media Education. (n.d.). Retrieved from http://www.medialiteracyweek.ca/en/101

Miller, L., & Olson, J. (1998). Literacy research oriented to features of technology. In D. Reinking, M. Mckenna, L. Labbo, & D. Kieffer (Eds.), *Handbook of Literacy and Technology* (pp. 343–360). Mahwah, NJ: Erlbaum.

National Grid for Learning. (n.d.). *Connecting the Learning Society.* Retrieved from http/www.opwn.gov.uk/defee/grid/content.htm

Olson, J. (2002). Systemic change / teacher tradition: Legends of reform continue. *Journal of Curriculum Studies, 34*(2), 129–137. doi:10.1080/00220270110085697

Relan, A., & Gillani, B. B. (1997). Web-based instruction and the traditional classroom: Similarities and difference. In B. H. Khan (Ed.), *Web-based instruction* (pp. 41–46). Englewood Cliffs, NJ: Educational Technology Publications.

Richardson, V. (1991). How and why teachers change. In S. C. Conely, & B. S. Cooper (Eds.), *The School As a Work Environment, Implications for reform* (pp. 66–78). Boston, MA: Allyn and Bacon.

Scarratt, E. (2007). *Citizenship and Media Education: An Introduction*. Retrieved from www.citized.info/pdf/commarticles/Elaine%20Scarratt.doc

Woodhead, N. (1991). *Hypertext and Hypermedia: Theory and Application*. Winslow, UK: Sigma Press.

ADDITIONAL READING

Agba, P. C. (2001). *Electronic Reporting: Heart of the New Communication Age*. Enugu: Snaap press.

Asemah, S. E. (2011). Selected Mass Media Themes. Jos: University of Jos Press.

Baran, S. J. (2009). *Introduction to Mass Communication: Media Literacy and Culture*. Boston: McGraw-Hill.

Diment, G., & Goodlad, L. (1998). 'Virtual-Class Trend Alarms Professors, Chronicle of Higher Education, http://www.oucs.ox.ac.uk/ltg/projectsml,/itap/reports/teaching/ chapter 1.html (retrieved April 6,2013).

Eilers, F. (Ed.). (2003). *E-generation: The Communication of Young People in Asia- A Concern of the Church*. Manila: Logos.

Eze, C. I. (2007). Adaptation and Utilization of ICTs in Sub-Saharan Africa: Problems and Prospect. In Nwosu, I. E., & Soola, O.E. (Eds.) Communication in Global, ICTs & Ecosystem Perspectives: Insights from Nigeria. 171-180.

Kersley, G. (2002). *Online Education: Learning and Teaching in Cyberspace*. Toronto, ON: Wadsworth.

Malone, P. (2001). *On screen*. Philippines: Paulines.

McQuail, D. (1997). *The function served by the mass media in audience analysis*. London: Sage.

Miller, L., & Olson, J. (1994). Putting the Computer in its place: A Study of teaching with technology. *Journal of Curriculum Studies*, 26(2), 121–141. doi:10.1080/0022027940260201

Nordkvell, Y. (2004). Technology and Didactics: Historical Mediations of a Relation. *Journal of Curriculum Studies*, 36(4), 427–444. doi:10.1080/0022027032000159476

Obukoadata,O,P. (2008) The Challenges and Prospects of the Internet and Interactive Mediain Nigeria Advertising Scene. no 9. 397-412.

Okpoko, J. (2006) Prospects of Information and Communication Technology on Business Operations in Nigeria. *Journal of Nigerian Institute of Public Relations*.

Olosan, J. (2000). Trojan Horse of Teachers Pet? Computers and the Culture of the School. *Journal of Curriculum Studies*, 32(1), 1–8. doi:10.1080/002202700182817

Oriafo, S. O. (1998). Education and Perspectives of Quality in science and technology in Nigeria. *Benin Journal of Education Studies*, 142(7), 63–71.

Potter, J. (2001). *Media Literacy*. California: Sage.

Relan, A., & Gillani, B. B. (1997) Web-based instruction and the traditional classroom: similarities and difference. In B. H. Khan (Ed.) web-based instruction (Englewood Cliff's, NJ: Educational Technology Publications) 41-46.

Simpson, B. (2004). *Children and television*. New York: Continuum International Publishing Group.

Singer, D., & Singer, J. (2001). (Eds.) HandBook of children and the media. London: Sage.

Soukup, P. (1996). Communication Theology in Soukup, P. (1996). (Ed.) Media Culture and Catholicism. Kansas City: Sheed and Ward.

Straubhear, J., & LaRose, R. (2000). *Media now: Communications media in the information age* (3rd ed.). New York: Wadsworth.

Topic, M. (2002). Streaming Media, New York: McGraw Hill.

Tsal, C. C. (2001). The Interpretation Design Model for Teaching Science and its Application to Internet-based Instruction in Taiwan. *International Journal of Educational Development, 21*(5), 401–414. doi:10.1016/S0738-0593(00)00038-9

Tsal, C. C. (2002). Developing Web-based Curriculum: issues and Challenges. *Journal of Curriculum Studies, 34*(6), 623–636. doi:10.1080/00220270210141909

Uwakwe, O. (2010). Introduction to Mass Communication in the Digital Age. Onitsha: Base 5 Publishers Ltd.

Wister, R. (1996). The use of media in the teaching of Church history in Soukup, P. (1996). (Ed.) Media Culture and Catholicism. Kansas City: Sheed and Ward.

KEY TERMS AND DEFINITIONS

Cultural Factors: They are practices and attitudes which affect the deployment of ICTs and their integration to learning in public tertiary institutions in Nigeria.

Information Culture: A society or system with high demand for information relevant to the daily lives of the people.

ICTs: Concerned with the storage, retrieval, manipulation, transmission of digital data through electronic means.

Media Education: The knowledge of media literacy.

Media Literacy: The ability to effectively use, understand and apply media technologies in learning and other purposes.

Technology Integration: The idea that electronic gadgets can be fused into the classroom environment to stimulate learning in a seamless manner.

Virtual Learning: A cyber sphere in which learning takes place outside the four walls of a classroom.

Section 3
Technology Integration in the Classroom

Chapter 6

Adoption and Use of Information and Communication Technologies (ICTs) in Library and Information Centres:
Implications on Teaching and Learning Process

Jerome Idiegbeyan-Ose
Covenant University, Nigeria

Mary Idahosa
Benson Idahosa University, Nigeria

Egbe Adewole-Odeshi
Covenant University, Nigeria

ABSTRACT

This chapter discusses ICTs adoption and use in libraries and its implication on the educational systems. The survey method is used; data is collected with the aid of questionnaires. The purpose of the study is to find out the present state of ICTs in libraries in Nigeria, the areas where ICTs have impacted the library and educational system, opportunities of ICTs adoption and use in libraries, challenges of ICTs adoption and use in libraries, and remedies to the challenges for effective ICTs adoption and use in libraries. Five universities, each from South-South and South-West Nigeria, are used for the study. The findings reveal that the libraries have adopted and are using ICT facilities for their functions and services. It also reveals that ICT facilities in libraries have impacted the educational systems in several ways. The chapter recommends that government should fund libraries adequately for effective and efficient service delivery.

DOI: 10.4018/978-1-4666-6162-2.ch006

Copyright © 2014, IGI Global. Copying or distributing in print or electronic forms without written permission of IGI Global is prohibited.

INTRODUCTION

Information and Communication Technologies (ICTs) adoption and use in libraries and information centres simply put implies the application of computers and others communication technologies such as scanners, printers, mobile phones, Internet and so on in libraries and information centres to assist in performing routine activities and render services to users. The routine activities may include selection of materials, acquisition, processing, dissemination and preservation of information materials. The adoption and use of ICTs in libraries and information centres has imparted positively in several ways on service delivery to the users. Academic libraries are established in institutions of higher learning. Their main objective is to support the curriculum of their parent institution, which is the teaching and learning process. The adoption and use of ICTs in libraries and information centres has imparted positively on the standard of teaching and learning in institutions.

Chisenga, (2004), stressed that the adoption and use of information and communication technologies (ICTs) has resulted in the globalization of information and knowledge resources. Bibliographic databases, full-text documents, and digital library collections are always available to users, thereby improving the quality of teaching and learning.

The problems contributing to the digital divide are currently being addressed via hundreds of projects implemented by a multitude of governmental and non-governmental organizations around the world (United Nations, 2003). Norris (2001) opines that the notion of the global digital divide relates to the disparities in ICT use between people living in different parts of the world. Information and Communication Technology (ICT) includes technologies such as desktop and laptop computers, software, peripherals and connections to the Internet that are intended to fulfill information processing and communications functions (Statistics Canada, 2008). In order to support the country's ICT master plan and in line with the country's drive to fulfill Vision 2020, the education system has to be transformed (Chan, 2002). One of the efforts that can be made for this transformation is by the full utilization of libraries and information centers. Students go to the libraries to study, to complete their homework and tasks, to find information, and also for leisure. The libraries provide information and services that are fundamental to function successfully in today's information and knowledge-based society, which equip students with information literacy skills and help them develop life-long learning habits, enabling them to be knowledgeable and responsible citizens (Fadzliaton & Kamarulzaman, 2010). It is evident that if libraries/information centers operate a system allowing student access on a need basis, and by providing the quality and variety of resources, including ICT provision, these significant factors will enhance teaching and learning process. (Islam & Islam 2006)

Maruthi and Nagaraja (2011). (ICT) is used in libraries for selection, acquisition, storage, processing and dissemination of information. They further explained that libraries and information centers have been using ICT based information resources and services to improve teaching and learning in our educational system. And that the use of information and communication technology has become increasingly important in teaching and learning process. ICT based resources and services enable the library and information centres to render services at accelerated pace. This is made possible through E-journals, CD-ROM databases, online databases, e-books, Web based resources and a variety of other electronic resources by complementing the traditional methods of librarianship that is characterized with prints collections and manual service delivery. To buttress this point, Akpoghome and Idiegbeyan-ose, (2010) explained that the establishment of digital libraries in institution of higher learning in Nigeria has made research work easier and interesting.

Information and Communication Technologies (ICT), enable the libraries and information centres to use different types of technologies to improve their services they render to clientele including the lecturers and the students thereby making their services more effective and efficient.

The impacts of new technologies are felt by libraries in every aspect from the point of selection of materials, acquisition, processing, dissemination and preservation. To compliment this, Maruthi, and Nagaraja (2011) further stated that technological development has reshaped the way that libraries access, retrieve, store, manipulate and disseminate information to users. The academic library has been an integral part of institutions of higher learning from the beginning, and new technologies are affecting libraries services delivery to their users positively.

Krubu, and Osawaru, (2011), cited Oyedun (2007),who explained that academic libraries are those libraries that are mainly found in tertiary institutions, they are established to support learning, teaching and research processes. Over the past twenty seven years, academic libraries have been affected by changes in information and communication technology. The rate of changes is still accelerating in this area. The introduction of various information technology (ICT) trends has led to reorganization, change in work patterns, and demand for new skills, job retraining and reclassification positions. Technological advancement of the past twenty five years, such as the electronic database, online services, CD-ROMs and introduction of Internet has radically transformed access to information. Rana (2009) opines that ICT holds the key to the success of modernizing information services. Applications of ICT are numerous but mainly it is used in converting the existing paper-print records to digital formats in the entire process of storage, retrieval and dissemination of information, preservation of knowledge for generations yet unborn.

Krubu, and Osawaru, (2011). citingSharifful and Nazmul (2006) stated that the component of ICT in the library is the computer for library automation and databases to add value to library holdings these are in electronic form. As many journals are being published in CD form, it becomes necessary to equip the libraries to optimize the use of information's-mail, online retrieval networking, multimedia and Internet, are the other important technologies, which can be used for faster access to information. The place of ICT in libraries cannot be overemphasized, it is used to capture, store, manipulate, and distribute information. ICT can be used to carry out library functions such as circulation, cataloguing, serials control, acquisition control, stock maintenance and other routine office works and developing in-house database that allow library users to access databases of other libraries through library networks.

BACKGROUND

It is worthy of note that the adoption and use of ICTs in libraries and information centres has added value to the routines activities and services the librarians render to the clientele.Islam and Islam, (2006). supported this assertion in their study on information and communication Technology (ICT) in libraries; they opined that information and communication technologies (ICTs) has assisted library professionals to provide value added quality information service and give more remote access to the internationally available information resources. A library no longer refers to physical building located in a specific geographic location, but electronic, digital or virtual libraries that can be accessed from anywhere. The adoption of ICT in the library has helped to facilitate the storage of huge amounts of data or information in a very compact space. It has also helped to revolutionize our concept of the functions of a traditional library and a modern information centre. It has changed the mode of library operations and services. Akpoghome and Idiegbeyan-ose (2010) further stressed that digital libraries facilities and resources has imparted positively on the teaching and learning process.

ONLINE PUBLIC ACCESS CATALOGUE AND USER SERVICES

Library catalogue is the key to the library holdings,it shows at a glance what is available in the library perhaps the most important tool for locating materials in the Library. The adoption of ICTs in library, has finally brought the library to the customer, wherever he or she may be located, in the form of Online Public Access Catalogue (OPAC), Web Public Access Catalogue. (Webpac). To buttress this fact, Chauham (2004) explained that OPAC provides access to the catalogue through a computer terminal to allow users to search the entire catalogue online, conveniently and quickly, using one or more search criteria. Such as author, title, subject, keywords, class number or as the case may be. The computerized catalogue shows the current status of a book, whether it is loaned out, available on the shelf or lying elsewhere.

The implication of this in educational systems is that it makes it fasters for Teachers/students to access library holdings at a glance, at their convenience. With modern library systems using WebPAC, it is also possible to provide access to the library catalogue from anywhere in the world via Internet. WebPAC enables the teachers/Learners to do the following, book reservations, loan requests for postal loan, loan renewals, membership application, address change, suggesting books etc,all these facilitates and enhance teaching and learning, users can access and use library resources anywhere, anytime with the aid of Internet enabled WebPAC

INFORMATION SERVICES AND DELIVERY

The adoption and use of ICTs in Libraries effective and efficient information service delivery to the Clientele.ICTs adoption in library has brought about e-references, e-SDI, e-current awareness services and so on.

Bibliography Service

Chauhan, (2004) revealed that Browsing through the manual indexes and abstracts is a tedious and time consuming work, and does not always produce up to date result. With the advent of ICTs in Libraries, users now have easy access to databases in electronic form on CDROM or online, It is convenient, efficient and cost effective retrieval of information. The implication on educational system is that students/ researchers, lecturers have various databases available for their research work. They are not limited to the physical collections in their libraries as in the case of traditional libraries. The adoption and use of ICTs in libraries and information centres has made the users have access to the virtual collections in form of databases, e-journals, e-books, C-Ds that their parent institution subscribe to, the researchers are not limited to time and space as the library e- resources are always available for access and use 24/7. The aspect of multiple access to document come to mind as well, as millions of users can access and use the same e-resources at the same time.

Current Awareness Service

The introduction of ICTs in libraries and information centres has imparted on the current awareness services. It has made it more effective and efficient. For instance the use of e- mail, mobile phones and others has imparted positively on current awareness services.

Chauham (2004) stressed that ICTs has impactedthe library in the area of Current Awareness Services as a means of keeping the users up to date in their areas of interest. A current awareness service may be as simple as copy of table of contents or a bulletin containing bibliographic records, of articles selected from the current issues of journals and other material, and usually organized by subjects

INTER-LIBRARY LOANS AND UNION CATALOGUES

The adoption of ICTs in the library has impacted the library in the area of inter-library loans and resource sharing. This system is adding value to the educational process. It makes it possible for an institutional library to have access to other library holdings, through resource sharing and thereby better satisfaction of the library users. And this in turn improves the teaching and learning process.

Statement of the Problem

Libraries of all types and sizes are integrating Information and Communication Technologies (ICTs) to improve their operations and services, these ICTs are at additional cost to the library and their parent organization, the issue at stake is that, is there any way these ICTs can contribute to the operations and services of the Library in particular and education system in general?

Research Questions

1. What is the present state of ICTs in libraries in Nigeria?
2. What are the areas ICTs has imparted the library and educational system?
3. What are the opportunities of ICTs adoption and use in libraries?
4. What are the challenges of ICTs adoption and use in libraries?

5. What are the remedies to the challenges for effective ICTs adoption and use in libraries?

Methodology

Survey research design was used for this study, the instrument for data collection was the questionnaire, the population of the study comprised of 5 randomly selected university libraries in south-south and south west Nigeria respectively. A total of 200 copies of the questionnaires were administered in all the universities, this represents 10 copies each of the university. 174 copies of the questionnaires were returned and used for analysis this represents 87% response rate. The data was analyzed using descriptive statistics.

Data Analysis and Interpretation

Table 1 shows the different universities used for the study, the number of questionnaires administered and the number returned and the percentage rate from various institution.

Table 2 reveals the sex of respondents. 68 (39.1%) are male, while 106 (60.9%) are female respondents.

Table 3 above represents the respondents view on whether their library is using ICTs for their library operations and services. It can be deduced that all the respondents 174 (100%) responded positively to the question. this implies that all the libraries used for the study are using ICTs in their operations and services. This is imparting positively on the teaching and learning process in their parent institutions.

Findings from Table 4 reveal the ICT facilities that are in use in these libraries. 174 (100%) that is all the respondents agreed that they have computers and they are using them in their libraries, in the same way, all the respondents 174 (100%) also stated that printers are in use in their libraries. 174 (100%) respondents agreed that scanners are available for usage in their libraries. 111 (63.4%) respondents stated that mobile phones

Table 1. Name of library

Name of Library	No of Questionnaires Administered	No of Questionnaires Returned	Percentage
Ambrose Alli University Library	20 (10%)	16	8
Benson Idahosa University Library	20 (10%)	20	10
Covenant University Library	20 (10%)	20	10
Delta State University Library	20 (10%)	18	9
Ekiti State University Library	20 (10%)	13	6.5
Lead City University Library	20 (10%)	15	7.5
Novena University Library	20 (10%)	17	8.5
Pan African University Library	20 (10%)	18	9
University of Benin Library	20 (10%)	20	10
University of Lagos Library	20 (10%)	17	8.5
TOTAL	200 (100%)	174	87%

are available for library operations and services delivery. Moreso, 67 (35.5%) of the respondents has intercoms in their libraries, Internet facilities and photocopiers are available in the libraries and 174 (100%) respondents attested to this. 78 (43.1%) of the respondents has electronic security systems in their libraries.

Table 5 shows the areas ICTs has imparted the library for effective service delivery. 121 (69.5%) of the respondents strongly agree that ICT has imparted the library in the area of selection of

Table 2. Sex of respondents

Sex of Respondents	Frequency	Percentage
Male	68	39.1%
Female	106	60.9%
TOTAL	174	100%

Table 3. ICTs adoption and usages in libraries

Is your library using ICTs for its operations and services to users	Frequency	Percentage
Yes	174	100
No	-	-
TOTAL	174	174

materials, in the same way, 53 (30.5%) of the respondents also agree. In the case of acquisition of materials, 99 (65.9%) of the respondents strongly agree that ICTs has imparted positively on library acquisition methods, 75 (43.1%) also agree with the statement. In the case of processing of library materials for patron usages, 144 (82.8%) strongly agree that ICTs has imparted on processing of library materials, that is cataloguing and classification, abstracting and indexing. Also, 30 (17.2%) respondents agree. In the case of dissemination of information to users that is service delivery, all the respondents 174(100%) strongly agree that ICTs has affected the library information dissemination positively. 127 (73.0%) respondents strongly agree that ICTs application and use in libraries has imparted on preservation of materials in the library in the same way, the remaining 47 (27.0%) respondents agree also. All the respondents 174(100%) strongly agree that ICTs in libraries has imparted on their communicating to the users and educating them.

Table 6 reveals the areas ICTs adoption and usage in library has imparted the educational systems. It shows that there is improvement on service delivery to the users as 118 (67.8%) of the respondents strongly agree that ICTs adoption

Table 4. ICT facilities available in libraries

Which of these ICTs Facilities are available for usage in your library	Frequency	Percentage
Computers	174	100%
Printers	174	100%
Scanners	174	100%
Mobile Phones	111	63.4%
Intercoms	67	38.5%
Internet	174	100%
Photocopiers	174	100%
Electronic security system	75	43.1%

and use in library has led to effective and efficient service delivery. Also, 56 (32.2%) respondents agree with the statement. 165 (94.8%) of the respondents strongly agree while 9 95.2%) agree that ICTs usage in libraries has led to faster service delivery to users. In the case of multiple access of materials at the same time, all the respondents 174(100%) strongly agree that ICTs adoption and use in libraries has imparted the educational systems in this regard very positively. The adoption and use of ICTs in libraries has imparted on the

educational systems in the area of 24/7 access to libraries resources. All the respondents 174 (100%) attested to this.

Table 7 shows the challenges that are hindering the libraries from effective adoption and use of ICT facilities. 166 (95.4%) strongly agree that high cost of ICTs infrastructures constitute a major challenge . in the same way, 8 (4.6%) of the respondents agree also. All the respondents 174 (100%) stated that power outage and lack of government support are serious challenges that libraries are facing. 98 (56.3%) of the respondents strongly agree that lack of fund to implement ICTs in libraries is a challenge and 76 (43.7%) of the respondents agree with that. Another challenge that libraries face in the implementation of ICTs is a lack of cooperation from some parent institutions. As shows in the above table, 45 (25.9%) of the respondents strong agree, 23 (13.2%) respondents agree while 106 (60.9%) of the respondents are undecided.

Table 8 above reveals the remedies to the challenges. All the respondents 174 (100%) strongly agree that government should fund libraries adequately, 143 (82.2%) of the respondents strongly aree that there should be alternative power supply for libraries, 23 (13.2%) respondents also agree.

Table 5. Areas ICTs has imparted the library

Areas ICTs has imparted the library and educational systems	Strongly Agree (SA)	Agree (A)	Undecided (UD)	Disagree (DA)	Strongly Disagree (SDA)	Percentage
Selection of materials	121 (69.5%)	53 (30.5%)	-	-	-	100%
Acquisition of materials	99 (56.9%)	75 (43.1%)	-	-	-	100%
Processing of materials	144 (82.8%)	30 (17.2%)	-	-	-	100%
Dissemination of information	174 (100%)	-	-	-	-	100%
Preservation of information materials	127 (73.0%)	47 (27.0%)	-	-	-	100%
Communicating and educating the users	174 (100%)					100%

Table 6. Areas ICTs adoption and use in libraries has imparted the educational systems

ICTs application in libraries has imparted the educational systems in these areas.	Strongly Agree (SA)	Agree (A)	Undecided (UD)	Disagree (DA)	Strongly Disagree (SDA)	Percentage
Effective and efficient service delivery	118 (67.8%)	56 (32.2%)	-	-	-	100%
Faster services to use the clientele	165 (94.8%)	9 (5.2%)	-	-	-	100%
Multiple access to resources	174	-	-	-	-	100%
24/7 access to resources	174		-	-	-	100%

43 (24.7% of the respondents strongly agree that ICTs competent staff should be recruited, 85 (48.9%) agree also, while 40 (23.0%) are undecided and 6 (3.4% disagree. In the case of parent institution to support libraries adequately, all the respondents 174 (100%) strongly agree that it is necessary for the parent institutions to support libraries adequately for them to render effective and efficient services to the clientele.

Solutions and Recommendations

- Libraries of all types should adopt and use ICTs for effective and efficient service delivery this will improve the quality of teaching and learning process.

- Government at all levels should fund libraries adequately, so that they will be able to adopt and use ICTs facilities to improve the educational systems.

- Librarians should be encouraged to train and retrain themselves in order to acquire the needed ICTs skills. This can be possible through attendance at conferences, workshop/seminars, short courses, both local and international; the parent institutions should sponsor them to acquire these modern days library skills.

Table 7. Challenges to ICTs adoption and use in libraries

The Challenges to ICTs adoption and use in libraries are	Strongly Agree (SA)	Agree (A)	Undecided (UD)	Disagree (DA)	Strongly Disagree (SDA)	Percentage
High cost of ICTs infrastructures	166 (95.4%)	8 (4.6%)	-	-	-	100%
Power outage	174	-	-	-	-	100%
Lack of government support	174	-	-	-	-	100%
Lack of fund to implement ICTs	98 (56.3%)	76 (43.7%)				100%
Lack of ICTs competent staff in libraries	-	34 (19.5%)	112 (64.4%)	28 (16.1%)	-	100%
Lack of cooperation from the parent institution	45 (25.9%)	23 (13.2%)	106 (60.9%)	-	-	
Vendors instability	118 (67.8%)	56 (32.2%)				

Table 8. Remedies to the challenges

Remedies to the Challenges	Strongly Agree (SA)	Agree (A)	Undecided (UD)	Disagree (DA)	Strongly Disagree (SDA)	Percentage
Government should fund libraries adequately	174 (100%)	-	-	-	-	100%
There should be alternative power supply for libraries	143 (82.2%)	23 (13.2%)	8 (4.6%)	-	-	100%
Libraries should recruit ICTs competent staff	43 (24.7%)	85 (48.9%)	40 (23.0%)	6 (3.4)	-	100%
Parent institution should support libraries.	174 (100%)	-	-	-	-	100%

- Alternative power supply should be provided for libraries, because ICT facilities require electricity to function effectively.
- Library schools should introduce more ICTs related courses in their curriculum so that their graduates will be more equipped with ICTs skills.

FUTURE RESEARCH DIRECTIONS

There is need to carry our research to find out whether attitude of library staff toward the learners and the teachers affect the use of library and thereby imparting on the standard of education.

CONCLUSION

There is no gainsaying that library is the hub in which academic activities revolves, education lead to development. The application and use of ICTs in libraries and information centres has imparted positively on the educational systems. The establishment of the virtual library which is a product of ICTs in libraries has made teaching and learning more rewarding. Therefore, government at all levels including owners of private schools should make sure that libraries are funded adequately to perform maximally. This in turn will lead to improve quality of education and thereby lead to national development. No nation can developed without quality education, quality education can only be achieved through improved educational facilities, libraries inclusive.

REFERENCES

Akpoghome, T. U., & Idiegbeyan-Ose, J. (2010). The role of digital library in law research. *International Journal of Library and Information Science, 2*(6).

Chan, F. M. (2002). *ICT in Malaysian schools: Policy and strategies.* Retrieved from http://unpan1.un.org/intradoc/groups/public/documents/apcity/unpan011288.pdf

Chauhan, P. (2004). *ICT enabled library and information service journal of winter school on ICT enabled.* Academic Press.

Chisenga, I. (2004). *ICT in libraries: An overview and general information to ICT in libraries in Africa.* Paper presented at INASO ICT Workshop. Johannesburg, South Africa.

Fadzliaton, Z., & Kamarulzaman, I. (2010). *Measuring Malaysia school resource centers standards through IQ-PSS: An online management information system.* Academic Press.

Islam, M. S., & Islam, M. N. (2006). Information and Communication Technology in Libraries: A New Dimension in Librarianship. *Asian Journal of Information Technology*, 5(8), 609–617.

Krubu, D., & Osawaru, K. (2011). *The impact of information communication Technology (ICT) in Nigeria library and information services*. Tietpatiala.

Norris, P. (2001). *Digital divide: Civic engagement, information poverty, and the internet worldwide*. Cambridge, UK: Cambridge University Press. doi:10.1017/CBO9781139164887

Rana, H. K. (2009). *Impact of information and communication technology on academic libraries inpunjab*. Retrieved from http/www.goarticles.com/cgi-bin/showa/cgi

Sharma, P., Singh, M., & Kumar, P. (2009). Approach to ICT in library Training education and technology issuess and challenges. In *Proceedings of ICAL*. ICAL.

Statistics Canada. (2008). *Information and communications technologies (ICTS)*. Retrieved from http://www.statcan.gc.ca/pub/81-004-x/def/4068723-eng.htm

United Nations. (2003). *Youth information and communication technologies (ICT)*. Retrieved from http://www.un.org/esa/socdev/unyin/documents/ch12.pdf

KEY TERMS AND DEFINITIONS

Adoption of ICTs: This implies the process of inculcating ICTs part of Library facilities.

ICTs: Meaning Information and Communication Technologies.

Learning: The act, experience of gaining knowledge that will modify the learner behavior.

Library and Information Centres: Collection of information materials in different formats properly organized for effective use and easy retrieval.

Teaching and Learning Process: This has to do with the teacher and the learner, the teacher imparting knowledge and learner acquiring knowledge.

Teaching: The act, practice or profession of teachers. It is also the act of imparting knowledge to someone.

Use of ICTs: Means to put ICTs facilities into use, apply them or employ them for functions and services.

WebPAC: Web Public Access Catalogue (WebPAC) computerized form of library catalogue that enable users to access the library catalogue any where any time with internet access.

Chapter 7

Efficiency of Technology in Creating Social Networks for Mobilizing and Improving the Health of a Community

Florence F. Folami
Millikin University, USA

ABSTRACT

A great deal of focus has been placed upon improving population health and providing for the well-being of communities across the nation. The advances of new media skills are vital to creating social networks for mobilizing and improving the health of a community. The purpose of this chapter is to explore the efficiency of Facebook in creating social networks to mobilize community improvement. This chapter discusses social networking group reach rates and the effectiveness of social networking in delivering health messages and improving community health knowledge. An Internet scan of a Facebook Support Group using quantitative outcomes is done. The group was followed for 2 years to track the following metric: weekly frequency of posting, the average number of followers, response time, and group engagement. Overall, this study shows positive outcomes in terms of reach, response time, and group engagement.

INTRODUCTION TO THE STUDY

A great deal of focus has been placed upon improving population health and providing for well-being of communities across the nation. Major advances in the health of the American people have resulted from public health involvements designed to reduce significant forces to the health of communities (Abroms & Maibach, 2008). Zilberberg (2011) defines a social media

as any Website that allows social collaboration. Social media is essentially defined by its ability to offer an collaborating environment for users, where discussion flows in multiple directions, and users are encouraged to contribute. A growing literature is emphasizing the role social networks play in health and how the appearance of social media provides new ways to form and involve networks (Cain & Policastri, 2011; Bennett & Glasgow, 2010). While effectiveness and profi-

DOI: 10.4018/978-1-4666-6162-2.ch007

Copyright © 2014, IGI Global. Copying or distributing in print or electronic forms without written permission of IGI Global is prohibited.

ciency of media campaigns are well documented in the literature (Cain & Policastri, 2011; Bennett & Glasgow, 2010), social technology use such as Facebook use in health messaging remains an inexplicable topic with little evidence. For this reason, this paper is devoted on the efficiency of technology in creating social network for mobilizing and improving health of a community.

The advances of new media skills are vital in creating social network for mobilizing and improving health of a community. Social networking services foster learning through what Noar (2006) describes as a participating culture which is a culture that consists of a space that allows engagement, sharing, mentoring, and an opportunity for social interaction. The need for critical evaluation of efficiency of technology for poupulation health intervention is needed therefore this study evaluated efficiency of technology in creating social network for mobilizing and improving health of a community.

The expansion of social media has changed how individuals network in the community. Social technology has palyed major roles in informing multiple aspects of individuals' lives, including their access to health information (Schein, Wilson, & Keelan, 2010). Social technology like Facebook allows individuals to instantly connect with large networks of friends and colleagues. Facebook offers accessible sites to create social network to mobilize community improvement. The purpose of this study is to explore the efficiency of facebook in creating social network to mobilize community improvement. This paper will discuss social networking group reach rates and effectiveness of a social networking in delivering health messages and improving community health knowledge.

REVIEW OF THE LITERATURE

A systematic review of the literature was conducted using an appropriate search approach and inclusion criteria of public health communications and the use of social media delivering health messages. Tian, Brimmer, Lin, Tumpey, and Reeves (2009) conducted a study on information seeking and social support in online health communities. They concluded that it is the information seeking effectiveness rather than the social support which affects patient's perceived empathy in online health communities. The online health information need to focus more on developing tools that will make information seeking more effective and efficient.

Social media have given social communications the speed and people around the world constantly use social-media platforms to seek and share information. Reports suggest that social media is an option that can be used to promote public health messages (Bennett& Glasgow, 2009; Bramlett & Harrison, 2012). Several explanations have been offered in the literatures that suggest that educating people through social media has been shown to be effective (Bennett & Glasgow, 2009; Schein, Wilson, & Keelan, 2010; Bramlett & Harrison, 2012). Vance, Howe, and Dellavalle (2009) examined how social media can be effectively used as a component of public health interventions focused on decreasing sexual risk taking among Latino youth. They found that 90.8% (355/391) of respondents had access to a mobile phone either through having their own or through borrowing or sharing one. Of those who had access to a mobile phone, 94.1% (334/355) used SMS, with 41.1% (113/275) sending and receiving more than 100 text messages per day. The authors perceived these as credible and essential methods of communication in the context of public health programs.

Bramlett and Harrison (2012) evaluated the use of social media for food safety education. Participants who spent more time on the Facebook page had greater improvements in food safety attitudes and practices. Results from the study revealed improvements in food safety attitudes, practices, and knowledge among the participants. Social media cater to the needs of the community who are engaged and desire to be more involved in their health. The developments of new media skills are paramount in helping mobilizing and improving health of a community. Public health interventions must continue to innovate and maximize new ways to reach people to reinforce public health messages and education.

Conceptual Framework

Transtheoretical Model was used to examine individual readiness to act on a new behavior and to measure the outcomes of the change. It is also used to assess the development of social media and how it has changed individual's interaction in the community. Many studies used Transtheoretical Model to examine behavior change. Some of the studies that used Transtheoretical Model showed some form of improved behavior, including improved eating habits, increased preventative behaviors towards abuse and improved smoking quit rates (Avery, Lariscy, Amador, Ickowitz, Primm, & Taylor, A, 2010).

RESEARCH METHOD

The aim of this study was to discuss efficiency of technology in creating social network for the mobilization and improving health of community. The recent proliferation of online social networking sites such as Facebook, Twitter and MySpace, has provided researchers with developer platforms and services to develop their own research tool for carrying out academic research (Bramlett & Harrison, 2012). This research shifts the emphasis from research about online social networking sites to research through online social networking sites. An Internet scan of a FacebooK Support Group using quantitative outcomes was done. The FacebooK Support Group is monitored for usage over two years period. Support group bodies can sign up for a page through Facebook. The Facebook Support Group was started in January, 2010. This FacebooK Support Group allows for

most of the features of social network group (a wall for posts, photo and video uploads, discussion boards, etc.). The group allows users to like the facebook group Web. When users click to like the Facebook page, they automatically receive updates and posts through their page. The group contains 350 members at the time of this study. The group was followed for 2 years to track the following metric: weekly frequency of posting, the average number of followers, response time, and group engagement.

RESULTS

Frequency of Posting

Weekly frequencies of posting were assessed by counting the number of new post per week. New posts were made regularly, ranging from one to two times per day to a total of 10 to 12 times a week. The posting are tailored messages that are directly related to the support group audience. Tian, Brimmer, Lin, Tumpey, and Reeves (2009) acknowledged that the use of social media is growing exponentially, and extending into the health field. The authors identified that Facebook posting frequency needs to be understood in terms community members interest on site (Figure 1).

The average number of users following each post was measured by counting the average number of interactions (likes + comments + shares) per post. The interaction for each post ranged from 185-250. The average number of followers allows for sharing from the support goup (health consumers) themselves, facilitating two-way communication that is a unique and exhilarating concept in public health. This study showed a high interaction index which indicates a relative high amount of active fans and vice versa. The rate of interaction also shows how the social network reaches the target population and promotes public health messages. Vance, Howe, and Dellavalle (2009) found that reach can be expanded by tak-

Figure 1. Average number of followers

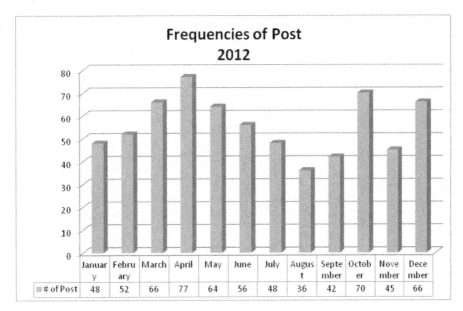

	Januar y	Febru ary	March	April	May	June	July	Augus t	Septe mber	Octob er	Nove mber	Dece mber
# of Post	48	52	66	77	64	56	48	36	42	70	45	66

ing advantage of the existing social networks of audience on social networking sites. Growing reach on social networking sites can create mobilization of public health messages and improving health of a Community. This study identified and demonstrated considerable reach associated with facebook support group. The support group can be used to effectively reach and engage high numbers of participants. The more people like the support group page, the more people will be exposed to the content because the content will appear in those people Facebook news-stream (Figure 2).

Timeliness is very important and it is measured by how recent the post and new comments can revive an old post. The purpose of measuring the response time is to monitor how quickly the participant questions are answered. Response time measurement of user questions is a sensitive issue and should be monitored as Facebook is becoming more and more a place for support. Responding quickly and specically on facebook is as important as listening to converstion on real life. The analysis of the response time for this study revealed average response times of less than 10 minutes. Vance, Howe, and Dellavalle (2009)

discussed testing the waters by posting messages on the site at a different time every day to identify the time postings performed the best in order to reach more people with the post.

Group Engagement

Group engagement measures the number of people who engaged with the page and it also measure participant clicks on any of the content for each post. The more engagement, the more likely the content reaches a larger audience. It is very important to get a quick focus group-like reaction and a better view on whether or not the content will be embraced by the larger community. An average of 250 people was engaged with each of the new post which shows facebook support group has ability to promote engagement in populations. Since engagement is well documented in this study, the prticipant of facebook support group should be encouraged to share the content with friends who might have a vested interest in the topic area. However, Glik (2007) identified that controlled studies are needed before social media's role in public health can be adequately defined.

Figure 2. Response time

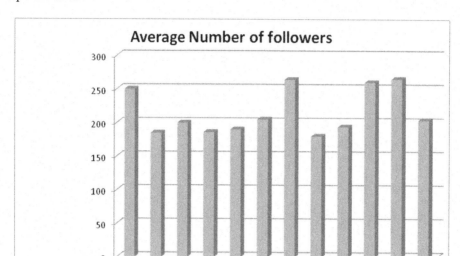

Overall, this study shows positive outcomes in terms of reach, response time, and group engagement. Data from this report, for example, could be used to explain relationships between health messages and social media use. The study shows opposite of what Cain and Policastri (2011) discussed as the typical interaction funnel where many users view the page's content (Page Total Reach), but less click on them (Page Engagement Users). The study demonstrates good reach and active group engagement.

SUMMARY, CONCLUSION, AND RECOMMENDATIONS

It is clear that public health messages adopting social media support groups can be effectivly delivered to the community with this study. This type of social media delivery of public health messages can improve population health and providing for well-being of communities across the nation. Based on the contents of this study the following recommendations are made. The first recommendation is the use of evidence based information to guide support group discussions on social media. This means that schorlarly research journals should be examined for creating public health messages for group discussions.

The second recommendation is to view support group as the foundation for community. Social media support group can be viewed in terms of social relationships that formed the foundation for community. In some instances, such relationships are great for moblizing and improving the health of a community. Group interaction should always be encouraged with each post because the more people who click the Like button on the post, the more people will see the message. It is very important to encourage group members to tell their friends to like the facebook group in order to get a multiplicative benefit from their interaction.

Lastly, the social network can be used to harness the power of peer pressure to get people to adopt healthy behaviors. Support group members are more likely to hear and personalize messages, and thus change their attitudes and behaviors, if they believe the messenger is similar to them.

REFERENCES

Abroms, L., & Maibach, E. (2008). The effectiveness of mass communication to change public behavior. *Annual Review of Public Health, 29*, 219–234. doi:10.1146/annurev.publhealth.29.020907.090824 PMID:18173391

Avery, E., Lariscy, R., Amador, E., Ickowitz, T., Primm, C., & Taylor, A. (2010). Diffusion of social media among public relations practitioners in health departments across various community population sizes. *Journal of Public Relations Research, 22*(3), 336–358. doi:10.1080/10627261003614427

Barton, A. (2011). Big pharma wants to 'friend' you. *Globe and Mail, 25.*

Bennett, G., & Glasgow, R. (2009). The delivery of public health interventions via the internet: Actualizing their potential. *Annual Review of Public Health, 30*, 273–292. doi:10.1146/annurev.publhealth.031308.100235 PMID:19296777

Cain, J., & Policastri, A. (2011). Using Facebook as an informal learning environment. *American Journal of Pharmaceutical Education, 75*(10), 207. doi:10.5688/ajpe7510207 PMID:22345726

Glik, D. (2007). Risk communication for public health emergencies. *Annual Review of Public Health, 28*, 33–54. doi:10.1146/annurev.publhealth.28.021406.144123 PMID:17222081

Noar, S. (2006). A 10-year retrospective of research in health mass media campaigns: Where do we go from here? *Journal of Health Communication, 11*(1), 21–42. doi:10.1080/10810730500461059 PMID:16546917

Schein, R., Wilson, K., & Keelan, J. (2010). *Literature review on the effectiveness of the use of social media: A report for peel public health.* Academic Press.

Tian, H., Brimmer, D., Lin, J., Tumpey, A., & Reeves, W. (2009). Web usage data as a means of evaluating public health messaging and outreach. *Journal of Medical Internet Research, 11*(4), e52. doi:10.2196/jmir.1278 PMID:20026451

Vance, K., Howe, W., & Dellavalle, P. (2009). Social internet sites as a source of public health information. *Dermatologic Clinics, 27*(2), 133–136. doi:10.1016/j.det.2008.11.010 PMID:19254656

Zilberberg, M. (2011). The clinical research enterprise: time to change course? *Journal of the American Medical Association, 305*(6), 604–605. doi:10.1001/jama.2011.104 PMID:21304086

ADDITIONAL READING

Anria, S. (2009). The impact of Social Networking 2.0 on organisations. *The Electronic Library, 27*(6), 906–918. doi:10.1108/02640470911004020

Bacon, J. (2009). *The art of community: building the new age of participation (theory in practice).* Sebastopol, CA: O'Reilly Media.

Cattell, V. (2001). Poor people, poor places, and poor health: the mediating role of social networks and social capital. *Social Science & Medicine, 52*, 1501–1516. doi:10.1016/S0277-9536(00)00259-8 PMID:11314847

Connor, A. (2009). *18 rules of community engagement: a guide for building relationships and connecting with customers online.* Silicon Valley, CA: Happy About.

Fine, A. (2006). *Igniting social change and the connected age.* San Francisco: Jossey-Bass.

Free, M. (2004). Achieving appropriate design and widespread use of health care technologies in the developing world. *International Journal of Gynaecology and Obstetrics: the Official Organ of the International Federation of Gynaecology and Obstetrics, 85*(1), S3–S12. doi:10.1016/j.ijgo.2004.01.009 PMID:15147849

Gabbert, T., Metze, B., Bührer, C., & Garten, L. (2013). Use of social networking sites by parents of very low birth weight infants: experiences and the potential of a dedicated site. *European Journal of Pediatrics, 172*(12), 1671–1677. doi:10.1007/s00431-013-2067-7 PMID:23913310

Hawn, C. (2009). Take Two Aspirin And Tweet Me In The Morning: How Twitter, Facebook, And Other Social Media Are Reshaping Health Care. *Health Affairs, 28*, 361–368. doi:10.1377/hlthaff.28.2.361 PMID:19275991

Hsiu-Sen, C. (2013). Continuous usage of social networking sites: The effect of innovation and gratification attributes. *Online Information Review, 37*(6), 851–871. doi:10.1108/OIR-08-2012-0133

Jain, H. (2009). Practicing Medicine in the Age of Facebook. *The New England Journal of Medicine, 361*, 649–651. doi:10.1056/NEJMp0901277 PMID:19675328

Lobb, A., Mock, N., & Hutchinson, P (2012). Traditional and Social Media Coverage and Charitable Giving Following the 2010 Earthquake in Haiti Prehospital and Disaster Medicine, 4, 319-24.

Pachucki, M., & Breiger, R. (2010). Cultural holes: beyond relationality in social networks and culture. *Annual Review of Sociology, 36*, 205–222. doi:10.1146/annurev.soc.012809.102615

Park, B., & Calamaro, C. (2013). A Systematic Review of Social Networking Sites: Innovative Platforms for Health Research Targeting Adolescents and Young Adults. *Journal of Nursing Scholarship, 45*(3), 256–264. PMID:23676115

Pittenger, L. (2013). The Use of Social Networking to Improve the Quality of Interprofessional Education. *American Journal of Pharmaceutical Education, 77*(8), 1–9. doi:10.5688/ajpe778174 PMID:23460753

Royo-Vela, M., & Casamassima, P. (2011). The influence of belonging to virtual brand communities on consumers' affective commitment, satisfaction and word-of-mouth advertising. Online Information Review, 35, 517-542. Stempniak, M (2012). Is this health care's Facebook? *Hospitals & Health Networks, 86*, 22.

Weinstein, D. (2012). Using Facebook to influence health. *Medical Marketing & Media, 47*, 26.

Woolford, S., Esperanza, M., Alicia, D., Sami, A., & Blake, N. (2013). Let's Face It. *Patient and Parent Perspectives on Incorporating a Facebook Group into a Multidisciplinary Weight Management Program Childhood Obesity, 9*, 305–310. PMID:23869854

World Health Organization. (2010). *Medical Devices: Managing the Mismatch.* Geneva: WHO Press.

Yan, H., & Dan, S. (2013). Facebook as a Platform for Health Information and Communication: A Case Study of a Diabetes Group. *Journal of Medical Systems, 37*(3), 1–12.

Yang, C., & Brown, B. (2013). Motives for Using Facebook, Patterns of Facebook Activities, and Late Adolescents' Social Adjustment to College. *Journal of Youth and Adolescence, 42*(3), 403–416. doi:10.1007/s10964-012-9836-x PMID:23076768

Yu, J., Zo, H., Choi, M., Kee, C., & Andrew, P. (2013). User acceptance of location-based social networking services: An extended perspective of perceived value. *Online Information Review, 37*(5), 711–730. doi:10.1108/OIR-12-2011-0202

KEY TERMS AND DEFINITIONS

Community: Community is A a locality-based entity, composed of systems of formal organization reflecting society's institutions, informal groups, and aggregates.

Evidence Based: A descriptor that is used to describe medically-related reference resources.

Peer Pressure: Influence that a peer group, observers or individual exerts that encourages others to change their attitudes, values, or behaviors to conform the group norms.

Social Media: Interaction among people in which they generate and interchange evidences and ideas in virtual groups and networks.

Social Network: An online community, such as Facebook.

Support Group: A group of people who are available to support one another emotionally and socially.

Technology: Technology can also be defined as the scientific methods and materials used to achieve industrial objectives.

Chapter 8

Managing and Planning Technology Usage and Integration in Teacher Education Programs in an Emergent Nation

Nwachukwu Prince Ololube
Ignatius Ajuru University of Education, Nigeria

ABSTRACT

This chapter explores the impact of the changing context of Information Technologies (ITs) and Information Systems (ISs) on Teacher Education (TE). ITs and ISs have influenced educational philosophy and classroom practices all over the world. Significant technological innovations over the last three decades have altered the environment in which educators operate and profoundly changed the experience of both formal and informal education. The impact and pervasiveness of ITs and ISs have forced traditional Colleges of Education and University Faculties of Education into a period of transition and transformation. Colleges and Faculties of Education have, for example, become sites of branding and rebranding. The policy makers associated with these programs reflexively look to market-based solutions without first giving serious thought to the challenges preventing the effective integration and use of ITs and ISs in TE, particularly in developing economies. Using a theory-based method of analysis, this chapter gathers and analyzes contemporary views and ideas on education and technology. This chapter finds that the impact of ITs and ISs on TE programs in Nigeria has shortchanged these programs. As a result, education consumers and stakeholders are dissatisfied with the slow integration and use of ITs and ISs in government-owned institutions of higher education in general and in TE programs in particular.

DOI: 10.4018/978-1-4666-6162-2.ch008

Copyright © 2014, IGI Global. Copying or distributing in print or electronic forms without written permission of IGI Global is prohibited.

INTRODUCTION

The globalization of the education sector and impacts of globalization on the workforce require a different kind of education; one that enhances the ability of learners to access, assess, adopt, and apply knowledge, to think independently, to exercise appropriate judgment, and to collaborate with others to make sense of new circumstances. Much like globalization, emerging technologies have impacted all aspects of national economies and societies. Teacher education has been highly affected by global trends in technology, particularly its economics and business content (Singh & Papa, 2010). Among UNESCO's recent strategic objectives for improving the quality of higher education are the diversification of content and methods, the promotion of experimentation and innovation, and the diffusion and sharing of information, best practices and policy dialogues (UNESCO, 2002, 2003). Many of these objectives relate directly to information technologies (ITs) and information systems (ISs) which have become critical personal and social tools and have had a revolutionary impact on how we see and love in the world (Ololube, Kpolovie, Amaele, Amanchukwu, & Briggs, 2013). In the context of teacher education, ITs and ISs involve the gathering, processing, storing, distributing and use of information in a range of strategy, management and operational activities with the aim of improving the effectiveness and efficiency of teachers.

Information capitalism and globalization have likewise impacted the ways in which teaching and learning are carried out in education programs around the world (Singh & Papa, 2010). Innovations in educational technologies are revolutionizing educational design and methodology (Miniaoui & Kaur, 2014). These trends, however, are not widespread and must be further strengthened if they are to reach a large percentage of the population, especially in the third world. In a complex society like Nigeria, many factors affect the use and integration of technologies in the teaching and learning process. As a result, a proactive, interdisciplinary and integrated approach is required to ensure the successful development of teacher education and, in turn, the successful future development of the national economy (Ololube, 2014).

The global academic landscape includes research, teaching and learning. It includes educational programs and courses, the pedagogy or methodology of teaching, the research process (including dissemination and publication), library information systems and services, and administration and management. The integration of IT and ISs in teacher education programs has been the topic of a great deal of debate throughout this landscape. In Nigeria, the relationship between the development of ITs and ISs for teacher education programs and their diffusion into programs in Colleges of Education and university Faculties of Education is dependent upon governmental policies (Ololube, 2011).

Information technologies and systems are indispensable and have been accepted as part of the contemporary world especially in industrialized societies. In fact, many have already begun considerable adjustments to meet the challenges and opportunities of the knowledge age. The pervasiveness of ITs/ ISs has brought about rapid changes in technology and attendant social, political, and economic transformations (Ololube, 2006a). The field of education has not gone untouched. Without a doubt, ITs and ISs have impacted the quality and quantity of teaching, learning, and research in teacher education programs globally and to some extent in Nigeria. ITs and ISs provides opportunities for student teachers, and academic and non-academic staff to communicate with one another more effectively during formal and informal teaching and learning (Yusuf, 2005). Consequently, student teachers and academic and non-academic staff now require training not just in basic computer literacy, but also in the use of various communication and educational software packages and applications (Ololube, 2006b).

Teachers today must begin to learn at the outset of their teacher training programs about how to effectively integrate ITs/ISs into their classroom activities and school structure. Given that the quality of faculty is known to be a key predictor of student learning (Ololube, 2011), teacher education faculty training in ITs/ISs use is thus critical. Both ITs and ISs can facilitate student teacher training and help student teachers to take full advantage of the potential of technology to enhance quality and student learning in their own future classrooms. ITs/ISs have also introduced a new era in traditional face-to-face (f2f) methods of teaching and learning and in blended learning (BL). It is therefore pertinent that Nigerian education settings open themselves to the benefits that these new trends have offer in terms of building capacity and improving access to information.

The ability to effectively manage and plan for ITS/ISs enhances the proactivity of authorities with respect to information relevant to teaching services, in line with global best practices. When properly approached, ITs/ISs management can provide some of the essential information needed to manage education systems in an efficient and productive manner. This management effort must involve teachers and students as well as administrators and policymakers (Figure 1).

PURPOSE OF THE STUDY

In a complex society like Nigeria, we recognize that a number of prominent factors affect the successful development of teacher education programs. As such, it is quite impossible to consider all such factors at present. The purpose of this study is thus to address, exclusively, ITs and ISs in relation to teacher education and the sustainable development of education in Nigeria. This paper asserts that the effective use of ITs/ISs in teacher education addresses both the problem and solution to technology-based learning. ITs/ISs enable synergistic results that benefit pre-service teachers as they graduate and carry out their duties as teachers. Nonetheless there remains a need to better design teacher education curriculum and programs so that pre-service teachers can better plan for unanticipated and unintended results that confront them in the classroom in terms of ITs/ISs. At the societal level, ITs/ISs help us to better manage complex information flows and to integrate these flows in effective policy formulation and planning towards the maximization of human capital and potential.

It is more important now than ever that teacher education programs recognize these and other positive ramifications of ITs/ISs and ensure their graduates are equipped with effective and integrated tools and training modules to lead the next generation of students in the dynamic and innovative use and further development of these tools. Despite efforts by both the federal and state government, however, to establish effective teacher education programs in Nigeria, an ongoing lack of adequate ITs/ISs infrastructure on university and college campuses has reduced access to ITs/ISs instructional material for both faculty and students. Consequently, most teachers and student teachers rarely, if ever, come into contact with ITs/ISs aided instructional materials (Ololube, Umunadi & Kpolovie, 2014).

The desire to carry out this research arose from the need to examine the effectiveness of teacher education programs in Nigeria in relation to the role and usage of ITs/ISs. Theoretically, this paper aims to ascertain the degree to which ITs/ISs has impacted the development of teacher education. In general, the purpose of this study is to verify the research hypothesis as a basis for encouraging Nigerian institutions of higher education to maintain or improve the quality of their teacher education programs. This paper hopes to provide education administrators, planners and policymakers with the empirical models that will help them to better come to terms with the reality on ground in terms of the effective application of ITs/ISs in teacher education programs.

Figure 1. Image for information systems management. Source: (http://www.leadership-idn.com/definition-of-information-system-management/).

TEACHER EDUCATION PROGRAMS IN NIGERIA

Nigerian Colleges of Education and Faculties of Education in universities are openly committed to excellence in teacher education programs. Excellence in teacher education can be taken to mean effectively providing teaching and learning experiences that prepare student teachers for the challenges of today's multifaceted, ever varying, and varied workplace (Ololube, 2006). The guiding philosophy of teacher education is to produce student teachers with sharp intellectual minds capable of further critical intellectual inquiry (Ololube, 2011). Colleges and Faculties of Education are among several institutions in Nigeria that offer teacher education services to students who wish to specialize in subjects including agricultural science, arts, environmental sciences, health education, humanities, information and communication, management and social sciences, and the natural and applied sciences.

Colleges of Education offer post-secondary National Certificate in Education (NCE) training programs. The NCE is the qualification required to teach in junior secondary schools and technical colleges. In addition to training junior secondary school teachers, Colleges of Education now also train primary school teachers. The NCE has become the minimum qualification for primary school teaching as of 1998. Some of the Colleges also offer NCE pre-primary courses to produce qualified teaching personnel for the pre-primary level (Moja, 2000). Universities in Nigeria offer Bachelor of Education degree programs to both senior secondary school graduates and senior secondary school teachers who already have NCE qualifications. They also offer Masters and Doctorate degree programs in education.

Introduction to Computer Science is a fundamental course for student teachers in Nigeria either as part of their program or as a part of a previously completed major. Computer science is ideally taught in a general and applied fashion and produces graduates who are scientifically and technically skilled in information processing, data collection and analyses, and communication. All of this should be set in a problem-solving context where students learn about the planning and management processes involved in using computers. Introduction to Computer Science should also involve teaching and learning about the information needs of computers, the design of information management systems, and the principles and practices of system usage.

The successful completion of an introductory course in computer science is a critical accomplishment for undergraduate students who may one day be at the helm of decision making in their workplace and looking to keep pace with the demands of a globalized economy. This course is equally important for students who are planning to further their studies in the future and who, as graduates, will need to make informed professional development decisions using ITs/ISs. Introduction to computer science courses are challenging classes to teach because the technical complexity of the course material is quite high while student interest in this material can, unfortunately, be quite low. In most cases, take home assignments are given to students with basic instructions and sources for materials on the Internet. In some cases, assignments are submitted to faculty members via e-mail and feedback is provided to students days after the submission also via e-mail.

In Nigeria, the need for well qualified teachers cannot be underemphasized. Teacher education is a means of providing teachers with the skills and knowledge needed to carry out their teaching responsibilities (Osunde & Omoruyi, 2004). Teacher education is concerned with the art of acquiring professional competencies and professional growth. It is designed to produce highly motivated, sensitive, conscientious and successful classroom teachers who will handle students effectively and professionally towards better educational achievement (Ololube, 2005a, b). According to Amedeker (2005), inadequate teacher preparation programs results in teachers' inability to demonstrate adequate knowledge and understanding of the structure, function and development of their disciplines. An effective

teacher education program is thus a prerequisite for a reliable and resilient education which leads to confidence among both teachers and students as a result of effectively and professionally co-ordinated learning (Lawal, 2003; Umunadi and Ololube, 2014).

Teacher education programs in Nigeria are under the supervision and control of governmental organizations. The National Commission for Colleges of Education (NCCE) (2013) has responsibility for teacher education in Nigeria delivered by Colleges of Education. At present there are 74 Colleges of Education, of which 22 are controlled and funded by the Federal Government, 47 are controlled and funded by state governments, and 3 are owned by private agencies. The NCCE was established in 1990 to set minimum standards for all teacher education programs and accredit their certificates and other academic awards after obtaining the prior approval of the Minister. The Commission has also been given responsibility for approving guidelines and establishing criteria for accreditation for Colleges of Education in Nigeria. Nigeria's 129 universities, in contrast, are under the direct supervision of the National Universities Commission (NUC) (2013). Polytechnics, of which 9 run Nigeria Certificate in Education (NCE) programs, fall under the National Board for Vocational Colleges and Technical Education (NBTE) (2013) (Table 1).

The National Teachers Institute (NTI) was established to provide refresher and upgrade courses to teaching personnel, to organize workshops, seminars and conferences, and to formulate policies and initiate programs that will lead to improvement in the quality and content of education in the country. In pursuit of this, the Institute has initiated training and retraining programs to help unqualified primary school teachers receive the qualifications now required. Recently, the Institute also embarked on an NCE program through a Distance Learning System (DLS). Lastly, the Institute provides training for the Pivotal Teachers Training Program (PTTP) also by means of a DLS.

Table 1. Status and list of institutions that offer teacher education programs in Nigeria

Institutions	Numbers
Federal Colleges of Education (Regular)	11
Federal Colleges of Education (Technical)	10
Federal Colleges of Education (Special)	1
State Colleges of Education	47
Private Colleges of Education	5
Polytechnics with NCE Programs	9
Universities with Teacher Education Programs	89

The PTTP was introduced in 2002 as a means of producing teachers to fill the gap in teacher supply for the Federal Government's newly introduced Universal Basic Education (UNBE) (Osunde & Omoruyi, 2004).

The requirements for admission to teacher training differ depending on the type of institution. Colleges of Education require prospective candidates to have at least three credits in senior school and two other passes. At the university level, prospective candidates must have five senior school credits that include the chosen major teaching subjects. Prospective College of Education and Polytechnic students are required to sit for and pass the Polytechnic/College of Education Matriculation Examination, while prospective university students are required to pass the Joint Admission and Matriculation Board Examination (Moja, 2000).

ITS/ISS AND TEACHER EDUCATION

Many Nigerian teachers have been unable to find effective ways to use technology in their classrooms or any other aspect of their teaching and learning life. In terms of an explanation, teachers often note that cite their use of technology in the classroom has not been encouraged and that they have not been well trained in the use of ITs/ISs as teaching tools and a means for educational sus-

tainability (Ololube, 2006), notwithstanding the specifications in the National Policy of Education (FRN, 2004). Nigeria as a nation has come late and slow to the use of ITs/ISs in all sectors, particularly education. This is a result of chronic limitations brought about by both economic disadvantages and government policies. These factors have a direct impact on the nation's educational development.

In a 2005-2006 study by Global Information Technology (2005), the Networked Readiness Index (NRI) was used to measure the degree of preparation of 115 economies for participating in and benefitting from ITs/ISs development. Nigeria ranked 90th out of the 115 countries surveyed. The United States of America topped the list, followed by Singapore, Denmark, Iceland, Finland, Canada, Taiwan, Sweden, Switzerland and the United Kingdom. In a similar study of 104 countries in 2004 Nigeria ranked 86th (Global Information Technology, 2004). Thus rather than showing improvement, Nigeria's readiness is declining. Slow or limited access to basic ITs/ISs equipment, low Internet connectivity, inadequate computers, and poor use of audiovisual materials and equipment (films, slides, transparencies, projectors, globes, charts, maps, bulletin boards, programmed materials, information retrieval systems, and instructional television) in teacher education programs are very real barriers to the effective and professional development of teachers in Nigeria (Ololube, 2006). Administrators and instructors must thus make educational technology an integral part of teaching and learning so as to provide a clear demonstration of how the use of instructional technology tools can address the personal and general objectives of teaching and learning in Nigeria.

In recent years the integration of ITs/ISs in university teaching, and particularly in teacher training programs, has been the topic of much discussion (Larose et al., 1999) as ITs/ISs has impacted the quality and quantity of teaching, learning, and research in traditional and distance education institutions around the world. In concrete terms, ITs/ISs literacy has enhanced teaching and learning through its dynamic, interactive, and engaging content, and has provided real opportunities for individualized instruction (Newhouse, 2002a). Information and communication technology has the potential to accelerate, enrich, and deepen skills, motivate and engage students in learning, help to relate school experiences to work practices, help to create economic viability for tomorrow's workers, contribute to radical changes in school, strengthen teaching, and provide opportunities for connection between institutions and the world. ITs/ISs can make education more *efficient and productive* by engendering a variety of tools to enhance and facilitate teachers' professional activities (Yusuf, 2005). To Newhouse (2002b), technology is further developed to solve problems, improve living standards and to increase productivity. It is reasonable to expect educational technology to be developed with similar objectives. That is, if a teacher selects the most appropriate educational technology, student learning can be optimized and an increase in the value of the outcome obtained (Ololube, 2014).

Newhouse (2002a) explains educational productivity as a concept most happily found in economics textbooks where the productivity of a worker or economic unit is defined by dividing the output (revenue) by the input (costs). This is generally more difficult to define for the education industry since the output is not easily measured, particularly in monetary terms, to enable its comparison with costs. Nonetheless, Newhouse offered a helpful definition of output as the quality and quantity of learning demonstrated by students, or learning outcomes.

The concept of teacher ITs/ISs literacy is theoretically unclear and changing in that the precision of the definition depends on whether it occurs at the level of operational abilities or at other levels. Most contemporary authors tend to center the definition of ITs/ISs literacy on a few core competencies or abilities, which might then

determine whether teachers know or do not know how to use ITs/ISs instructional material. Ideal definitions go beyond this to include the ability to prepare and use a selection of appropriate and operational ITs/ISs materials, and the ability to identify and efficiently affect specific student purposes in order to build knowledge and develop critical and creative thinking. Teachers committed to improving their competence in ITs/ISs are likely to contribute, directly or indirectly to the growth of student's achievement (Ololube, 2014).

Teacher education and training is a means for professional updating, which deals with all developmental functions, directed at the maintenance and enhancement of one's professional competence and literacy. Teacher education and training must support the idea that ITs/ISs is an important factor in teachers' job effectiveness and professional development. Studies concerning staff training and education clearly demonstrate the need to offer teachers better opportunities to develop their ITs/ISs based knowledge in order to support this effectiveness (Kautto-Koivula, 1993, 1996). Teachers need techniques, tools and assistance that will help them to develop ITs/ISs based projects and activities designed to elevate the level of teaching in required subjects and in turn improve student learning and academic achievement (Aduwa-Ogiegbaen & Iyamu, 2005).

Newhouse (2002b) has classified the educational impacts of the use of ITs/ISs along five dimensions. These are:

- Students Attributes [ITs/ISs Capability, Engagement, Achievement of Learning Outcomes]
- Learning Environments Attributes [Learner-centered, Knowledge-centered, Assessment-centered, Community-centered]
- Teacher Professional ITs/ISs Attributes [Vision and Contribution, Integration and Use, Capabilities and Feelings]

- School ITs/ISs Capacity Attributes [Hardware, Connectivity, Software, Technical Support, Digital Resource Materials]
- School Environment Attributes [Leadership and Planning, Curriculum Organization, Curriculum Support, Community Connections, Accountability]

In contrast to many of the studies citing the benefits of ITs/ISs teacher training, Larose et al., (1999) argue that regardless of the quality of ITs/ISs equipment available to teachers and independent of the quantity of courses they have taken in their undergraduate studies, the transfer of acquired competencies and learning into practice is poor. The major impact of education on the educated, in fact, remains at the level of the "private" use of these technologies and not in their integration into daily teaching practices. In their findings, many of the educated, no matter the level of education, are computer literate but do not use technologies in their teaching because of their fear that the rate of obsolescence of the hardware and/or software will make their task more complex and interminable.

Furthermore, a recent research study (Ololube et al., 2013) which focused on the perceived use, ease of understanding, self-efficacy, facilitating conditions, behavioural intentions, and attitudes and anxieties towards computer use among higher education students and faculty in a developing economy, found that IT/IS constitute an important force in efforts to build an information technology society and to join the international community in meeting the Millennium Development Goals. Higher education institutions are enduring entities that must ensure and create the diffusion of knowledge for national development. Society depends on these institutions for its growth and for the production of new knowledge, its transmission through education and training, and its dissemination through information communication technologies.

DISCUSSION

Theoretical and personal observation evidence suggests that teacher training programs provided by Nigerian institutions of higher education are hindered by their ineffective use and provision of ITs/ISs instructional materials. Although, based on observation, teacher preparation programs have slightly impacted the level of performance of Nigerian teachers this has not been to the extent needed to meet UNESCO's (2005) Millennium Development Goals (MDGs) for education. It might be deduced that there is a considerable relationship between ITs/ISs integration and usage and the poor standard of teacher education programs in general which invariably affect the student and in-service teachers' classroom performance. Yusuf's (2005) study, for example, found that most teachers in Nigeria do not have the needed experience and competence in the use of computers for educational or industrial purposes. Most, in fact, lack competence, skills and knowledge in basic computer and software operations. Yusuf found no significant difference between male and female teachers in their experience in using ITs/ISs materials, their levels of proficiency in computer operations, and their use of common software. Furthermore, the introduction of computer education into Nigerian secondary schools in 1988 has largely been unsuccessful as a result of teacher incompetence. Studies (e.g., Yusuf, 2005) have recognized that teachers' ability and willingness to use ITs/ISs materials and integrate these into their teaching is largely dependent on the quality of professional ITs/ISs development received.

Teachers trained in today's teacher education programs are not technologically equipped to meet the challenges of the 21st century and carry out their duties in line with global transformations in science and technologies. Existing curriculum designed for the training of student teachers in Nigeria does not include the practical usage of ITs/ISs materials such as computers, software, slides, and overhead projectors. In situations where computers are provided, training is based only on theoretical models. Student teachers rarely come into contact with ITs/ISs instructional materials, including those in the department of educational technology proper.

The institutions responsible for the provision of teacher education programs provide programs within the confines of the mandate given to them by federal and state governments through various bodies that coordinate their activities. Their ability to be effective is dependent, for the most part, on the policies set by these bodies and the availability of funds for the purchase and maintenance of much-needed ITs/ISs equipment. According to Osunde and Omoruyi (2004), the greatest problem faced by teacher education programs is inadequate funding coupled with a lack of library facilities and inadequate teaching/learning materials. This may account for much of the limited effectiveness of the teacher training programs. It is possible as well that some of the hardship faced by these institution, and their inability to develop an effective and proficient ITs/ISs literate teaching cadre, is as a result of corrupt practices by both federal and state government officials on the one hand, and the regulatory bodies and officials in teacher education institutions on the other.

CONCLUSION AND RECOMENDATIONS

Technological changes over the past three decades have rendered teacher education and training more important than ever. Teacher education programs around the world, however, are struggling to keep up with the new demands placed on them by the 21st century classroom. They are working, albeit slowly, towards providing their graduates with the knowledge and skills needed in evolving market-places and sophisticated learning environments,

and to prepare teachers for lifelong learning. In order to meet these challenges, many countries have begun to focus concurrently on expanding access, improving internal efficiency, promoting the quality of teacher teaching and learning, and improving system management (Haddad & Jurich, [n.d]).

Quality education is seen as the main instrument for social, political and economic development of a nation. Thus the strength, security and well-being of Nigeria rest squarely on the quality of education provided for its citizens. Education has enabled a steady supply of human resources for national economies, especially in the west where education is seen and accepted as an effective instrument for success. It is thus essential that we recognize that teachers are indispensable for successful learning about ITs/ISs, and learning and teaching through ITs/ISs s to improve the standard of education in Nigeria.

ITs/ISs is an important instrument in the development of quality teaching and learning in educational systems around the world, as well as a means for fundamentally transforming existing school principles and practices to better prepare students to meet innovations in the global arena. Achievements in ITs/ISs penetration and usage in Nigeria teacher education programs are dependent on the recognition, by federal and state governments and educational authorities, of the importance of ITs/ISs application to education for sustainable development. This recognition must manifest as useful policies and the provision of sufficient funds on the one hand and the implementation of policies by coordinating bodies and the institutions themselves on the other. It is clear that secondary school students in Nigeria are already far behind their peers in developed countries and that the digital divide continues to grow (Aduwa-Ogiegbaen & Iyamu 2005). Federal and state governments, through The National Universities Commission (NUC) and the National

Commission for Colleges of Education (NCCE), must thus invest heavily in the institutions that offer teacher education programs. Such an effort will create an enabling environment in which teacher education programs can to strive to produce highly qualified and ITs/ISs literate teachers that will help to make the integration and use of ITs/ISs in schools a success.

Teacher education institutions in Nigeria must assume leadership role in revolutionizing education or be left behind in the wake of rapid technological changes. Accordingly, for Nigerian education to reap the full benefits of ITs/ISs in learning, it is essential that student teachers and in-service teachers are able to effectively use ITs/ISs tools for learning. As noted by Newhouse (2002a, 2002b) and UNESCO's (2002) with emerging technologies, the teaching profession is evolving from emphasis on teacher-centered, lecture-centered instruction to student-centered interactive learning environments. Designing and implementing successful ITs/ISs enabled teacher education program is thus the key to fundamental, wide-ranging educational reforms.

Teacher education institutions and programs must provide leadership in new teacher education models, pedagogies and tools for learning through an effective strategic plan. That is, leadership in teacher education programs should be visionary about conceiving a desired future state, which includes the depiction of where and what the teacher education program should be in the future, without being constrained by such factors as funding and resources. It must then work backward to develop an action plan to bridge the gap between the current and desired state (Ololube, 2014).

This chapter sought to provide an understanding of the impact of ITs/ISs on teacher preparation so as to support the nurturing of a new caliber of teachers whose professional abilities are key to the development of a struggling economy. This is so because the purpose of teacher education is no longer simply to convey a body of knowledge, but

to teach how to learn, how to problem-solve and how to blend the old with the new. It is therefore imperative to establish innovative programs and curriculum that will address the challenges of teacher education in a globalized world.

This study proposes that Colleges and Faculties of Education undertake a strategic planning analysis to determine their strengths, weaknesses, opportunities and threats (SWOT). As part of this analysis, they should first determine the intellectual capabilities needed to cope with current complexities in teacher education programs. Second, they will need to set priorities for teacher education programs according to the present and future needs and demands of Nigeria's citizenry. Third, they must be on the lookout for opportunities to improve and guarantee the quality of education. Finally, Colleges and Faculties of Education must be creative and prepare themselves for the challenges of the 21st century in line with the MDGs for both education for sustainable development.

REFERENCES

Aduwa-Ogiegbaen, S. E., & Iyamu, E. O. S. (2005). Using Information and Communication Technology in Secondary Schools in Nigeria: Problems and Prospects. *Journal of Educational Technology & Society*, *8*(1), 104–112.

Amedeker, M. K. (2005). Reforming Ghanaian Teacher Education Towards Preparing an Effective Pre-service Teacher. *Journal of Education for Teaching*, *31*(2), 99–110. doi:10.1080/02607470500127194

Beebe, M. A. (2004). Impact of ICT Revolution on the African Academic Landscape. In *Proceedings of CODESRIA Conference on Electronic Publishing and Dissemination*. Retrieved September 20, 2013 from http://www.codesria.org/Links/conferences/el_publ/beebe.pdf

Federal Republic of Nigeria (FRN). (2004). National policy on education (4th Ed.). Lagos: NERDC Press.

Global Information Technology Report. (2004). *The Networked Readiness Index Rankings 2005.* Author.

Global Information Technology Report. (2005). *The Networked Readiness Index Rankings 2005.* Retrieved September 21, 2013 from http://www.weforum.org/pdf/Global_Competitiveness_Reports/Reports/gitr_2006/rankings.pdf

Haddad, W. D., & Jurich, S. (n.d.). *ICT for education: Potential and potency.* Retrieved September 20, 2013 from http://cbdd.wsu.edu/edev/Nigeria_ToT/tr510/documents/ICTforeducation_potential.pdf

JAMB. (2006/2007). *Joint Admissions and Matriculation Board: Polytechnics, and Colleges of Education and the programs / courses offered.* Retrieved September 20, 2013 from http://www.jambng.com/pce_institution1.php

Kautto-Koivula, K. (1993). *Degree-Oriented Professional Adult Education in the Work Environment: A Case Study of the Mian Determinants in the management of a Long-term Technology Education Process.* (Unpublished PhD Dissertation). University of Tampere, Tampere, Finland.

Kautto-Koivula, K. (1996). Degree-Oriented Adult Education in the Work Environment. In Professional Growth and Development: Direction, Delivery and Dilemmas. Career Education Books.

Larose, F., David, R., Dirand, J., Karsenti, T., Vincent Grenon, V., Lafrance, S., & Cantin, J. (1999). Information and Communication Technologies in University Teaching and in Teacher Education: Journey in a Major Québec University's Reality. *Electronic Journal of Sociology.* Retrieved September 20, 2013 from http://www.sociology.org/content/vol004.003/francois.html

Lawal, H. S. (2003). Teacher Education and the Professional Growth of the 21st Century Nigeria Teacher. *The African Symposium, 3*(2).

Mac-Ikemenjima, D. (2005). *e-Education in Nigeria: Challenges and Prospects.* Paper presentation at the 8th UN ICT Task Force Meeting. Dublin, Ireland.

Miniaoui, H., & Kaur, A. (2014). Introducing a Teaching Innovation to Enhance Students' Analytical and Research Skills: A Blended Learning Initiative. In N. Ololube (Ed.), *Advancing Technology and Educational Development through Blended Learning in Emerging Economies* (pp. 21–35). Hershey, PA: Information Science Reference.

Moja, T. (2000). *Nigeria Education Sector Analysis: An Analytical Synthesis of Performance and Main Issues.* World Bank.

National Board for Technical Education (NBTE). (2013). *List of institutions with contact addresses under the purview of NBTE.* Retrieved September 12, 2013 from http://www.nbte.gov.ng/institutions.html

National Commission for Colleges of Education (NCCE). (2013). *Welcome to NCCE.* Retrieved September 12, 2013, from http://ncceonline.org/about-us/

National University Commission (NUC). (2013). *List of Nigerian universities.* Retrieved September 12, 2013, from http://www.nuc.edu.ng/pages/universities.asp

Newhouse, C. P. (2002a). *The Impact of ICT on Learning and Teaching.* Perth, Australia: Special Educational Service.

Newhouse, C. P. (2002b). *A Framework to Articulate the Impact of ICT on Learning in Schools.* Perth, Australia: Special Educational Service.

Ololube, N. P. (2005a). Benchmarking the Motivational Competencies of Academically Qualified Teachers and Professionally Qualified Teachers in Nigerian Secondary Schools. *The African Symposium, 5*(3), 17-37.

Ololube, N. P. (2005b). School Effectiveness and Quality Improvement: Quality Teaching in Nigerian Secondary Schools. *The African Symposium, 5*(4), 17-31.

Ololube, N. P. (2006a). Teachers Instructional Material Utilization Competencies in Secondary Schools in Sub-Saharan Africa: Professional and non-professional teachers' perspective. In *Proceedings of the 6th International Educational Technology Conference EMU*. EMU.

Ololube, N. P. (2006b). Appraising the Relationship Between ICT Usage and Integration and the Standard of Teacher Education Programs in a Developing Economy. *International Journal of Education and Development Using ICT, 2*(3), 70–85.

Ololube, N. P. (2007). The Relationship between Funding, ICT, Selection Processes, Administration and Planning and the Standard of Science Teacher Education in Nigeria. *Asia-Pacific Forum on Science Learning and Teaching, 8*(1), 1–29.

Ololube, N. P. (2011). Blended learning in Nigeria: Determining students' readiness and faculty role in advancing technology in a globalized educational development. In A. Kitchenham (Ed.), *Blended learning across disciplines: Models for implementation* (pp. 190–207). Hershey, PA: Information Science Reference. doi:10.4018/978-1-60960-479-0.ch011

Ololube, N. P. (2014). Blended Learning Methods in Introduction to Teaching and Sociology of Education Courses at a University of Education. In N. P. Ololube (Ed.), *Advancing Technology and Educational Development through Blended Learning in Emerging Economies* (pp. 108–127). Hershey, PA: Information Science Reference.

Ololube, N. P., Kpolovie, P. J., Amaele, S., Amanchukwu, R. N., & Briggs, T. (2013). Digital Natives and Digital Immigrants: A study of Information Technology and Information Systems (IT/IS) Usage between Students and Faculty of Nigerian Universities. *International Journal of Information and Communication Technology Education, 9*(3), 42–64. doi:10.4018/jicte.2013070104

Ololube, N. P., Umunadi, K. E., & Kpolovie, P. J. (2014). Barriers to Blended Teaching and Learning in Sub-Saharan Africa: Challenges for the Next Decade and Beyond. In N. P. Ololube (Ed.), *Advancing Technology and Educational Development through Blended Learning in Emerging Economies* (pp. 232–247). Hershey, PA: Information Science Reference.

Osunde, A. U., & Omoruyi, F. E. O. (2004). An Evaluation of the National Teachers Institute's Manpower Training Program for Teaching Personnel in Mid-western Nigeria. *International Education Journal, 5*(3), 405–409.

Singh, N., & Papa, R. (2010). *The Impacts of Globalization in Higher Education*. Retrieved September 30, 2013 from http://cnx.org/content/m34497/1.1/

Umunadi, K. E., & Ololube, N. P. (2014). Blended Learning and Technological Development in Teaching and Learning. In N. P. Ololube (Ed.), *Advancing Technology and Educational Development through Blended Learning in Emerging Economies* (pp. 213–231). Hershey, PA: Information Science Reference.

UNESCO. (2002). *Information and Communication Technologies in Teacher education: A Planning Guide.* Paris: UNESCO.

UNESCO. (2003). *Manual for Pilot Testing the Use of Indicators to Assess Impact of ICT Use in Education.* Retrieved September 20, 2013 from http://www.unescobkk.org/education/ict/resource

UNESCO. (2005). *United Nations Decade of education for Sustainable development 2005-2014.* Retrieved September 20, 2013 from http://portal.unesco.org/education/en/ev.php-URL_ID=27234&URL_DO=DO_TOPIC&URL_SECTION=201.html

Yusuf, M. O. (2005). Information and Communication Technologies and Education: Analyzing the Nigerian National Policy for Information Technology. *International Education Journal, 6*(3), 316–321.

ADDITIONAL READING

Adekola, O. A. (2007). *Language, literacy, and learning in primary schools: Implications for teacher development programs in Nigeria.* Washington, DC: World Bank. doi:10.1596/978-0-8213-7048-3

Aremu, A., & Adediran, E. M. (2011). Teacher Readiness to Integrate Information Technology into Teaching and Learning Processes in Nigerian Secondary Schools: A Case Study. *African Research Review, 5*(4), 178–190. doi:10.4314/afrrev.v5i4.69275

Dania, P. O., & Enakrire, R. T. (). The Utilization of Information and Communication Technology (ICTs) for effective teaching of social studies in secondary schools in Delta State. *Prime Research on Education, 2*(10), 378-389.

Hlatshwayo, N. F. (2008). The readiness of teachers to integrate information and communication technology for learning in a selected school in the GautengOnline project. Retrieved on 24 April, 2009 from http://ujdigispace.uj.ac.za:8080/dspace/bitstream/10210/901/3/Title.pdf.

Jegede, O. P., & Owolabi, J. A. (2003). Computer education in Nigerian secondary schools: gaps between policy and practice. Meridian, 6(2), Retrieved October 10, 2013 from http://www.ncsu.edu/meridian/sum2003/nigeria/index.html.

Jung, I. (2005). ICT-Pedagogy Integration in Teacher Training: Application Cases Worldwide. *Journal of Educational Technology & Society, 8*(2), 94–101.

Jung, I. S. (2003). A comparative study on the cost-effectiveness of three approaches to ICT teacher training. *Journal of Korean Association of Educational Information and Broadcasting, 9*(2), 39–70.

Kenechukwu, S. A., & Oboko, U. (2013). Information and Communication Technology in Teacher Education in Nigeria. *International Journal of Educational Foundations and Management, 1*(1), 23–31.

Kleiner, B., Thomas, N., & Lewis, L. (2007). *Educational Technology in Teacher Education Programs for Initial Licensure (NCES 2008-040).* Washington, DC: National Center for Education Statistics, Institute of Education Sciences, US Department of Education.

Kpolovie, P. J., Iderima, C. E., & Ololube, N. P. (2014). Computer Literacy and Candidate Performance on Computer-Based Tests. In N. P. Ololube (Ed.). Advancing Technology and Educational Development through Blended Learning in Emerging Economies (pp. 80-106). Hershey, PA: Information Science Reference. doi: doi:10.4018/978-1-4666-4574-5.ch005.

Oguzor, N. S. (2011). Computer usage as instructional resources for vocational training in Nigeria. *Educational Research Review, 6*(5), 395–402.

Oguzor, N. S., Adebola, H. E., Opara, J. A., & Eziefula, J. F. (2010). Information and communication technology (ICT), Its role and value in adult education in Nigeria. Proceedings of the 10th International Educational Technology Conference and Exhibition.

Okewale, O., & Adetimirin, A. (2011). Information Use of Software Packages in Nigerian University Libraries. *Journal of Information Technology Impact, 11*(3), 211–224.

Pukkaew, C. (2013). Assessment of the Effectiveness of Internet-Based Distance Learning through the VClass e-Education Platform. *International Review of Research in Open and Distance Learning, 14*(4), 254–276.

Su, B. (2009).Effective technology integration: Old topic, new thoughts. *International Journal of Education and Development using Information and Communication Technology, 5*(2), 161-171.

Thakrar, J., Zinn, D., & Wolfenden, F. (2009). Harnessing Open Educational Resources to the Challenges of Teacher Education in Sub-Saharan Africa. *International Review of Research in Open and Distance Learning, 10*(4), 1–15.

UNECSO. (2008). *Education for all by 2015: Will we make it?* Paris. Retrieved September 24, 2013, from http://www.unesco.org/education/gmr2008.

Weber, E. (2007). Globalisation, glocal development, and teachers' work: A research agenda. *Review of Educational Research, 77*(3), 279–301. doi:10.3102/003465430303946

Wolfenden, F. (2008). The TESSA OER experience: Building sustainable models of production and user implementation. *Journal of Interactive Media in Education.* Retrieved September 18, 2013, from http://jime.open.ac.uk/2008/03/.

Zhou, G., Brouwer, W., Nocente, N., & Martin, B. (2005). Enhancing conceptual learning through computer-based applets: The effectiveness and implications. *Journal of Interactive Learning Research, 16*(1), 31–49.

KEY TERMS AND DEFINITIONS

Information Systems (ISs): An integrated set of components that collect, store, and process data for delivering information, knowledge, and digital products. Twenty-first century schools rely on information systems to carry out and manage their teaching and learning processes.

Information Technologies: (ITs): The application of computers and telecommunication materials that store, retrieve, transmit and manipulate data in diverse contexts. ITs are commonly referred to as computers and computer networks, which encompass other information distribution technologies such as projectors, the Internet, blended learning tools, televisions, mobile phones, etc.

ITs/ISs Infrastructures: ICT components and resources such as computers, Internet access, power supply, and telecommunication facilities as well as ITs/ISs libraries, personnel, and funds, among others.

ITs/ISs Knowledge: The knowledge, skills, experiences, and abilities needed to stay informed of current technological developments. It is a collective knowledge that is interested in contributing to further ITs/ISs knowledge that will, in turn, lead to individual, national and global development.

Teacher Education: The procedures designed to equip prospective teachers with the skills, attitudes, knowledge and behaviors required to perform tasks effectively in the school setting and community.

Teacher Training: Specialized training organized to promote and produce cutting edge professionals for high quality teaching. It helps teachers to develop subject matter command, skill, and ability combined with exceptional understanding of how to create positive student learning experiences.

Chapter 9
Utilization of Instructional Media and Academic Performance of Students in Basic Science:
A Case Study of Education District V1 of Lagos State

Stephen Oyeyemi Adenle
University of Lagos, Nigeria

Jennifer N. L. Ughelu
University of Lagos, Nigeria

ABSTRACT

The use of instructional media is of vital importance for the teaching and learning of the basic sciences in primary and secondary schools, as it drives home the lesson point of the subject being taught and reduces stress for both teacher and student. The imaginative use of well-planned visual aids during classroom lessons does boost academic performances of students learning physics, chemistry, biology, and mathematics. This chapter investigates the impact of instructional media or design usage on the learning outcomes of students in the basic sciences in Lagos, Nigeria. The research design is Quasi-Experimental. The sample population consists of an experimental and a control group. The experimental group is taught with instructional media for a fortnight. The findings show that the use of instructional media positively impacted the learning outcomes of the students, thus highlighting the vital essence of using instructional media during lessons for enhancement of students' learning.

DOI: 10.4018/978-1-4666-6162-2.ch009

Copyright © 2014, IGI Global. Copying or distributing in print or electronic forms without written permission of IGI Global is prohibited.

INTRODUCTION

The basic disciplines of physics, chemistry, biology, and mathematics constitute the foundation upon which science is built. The Basic Sciences disciplines of physics, chemistry, biology and mathematics are usually complex and abstract. Primary and secondary school students need experiences teacher to enable them understand the abstract subjects by getting through concrete ideas. However, the effective learning of the Basic Sciences in primary and secondary schools remain a daunting and difficult task in Nigeria. Majority of the literature have linked poor learning outcomes in the Basic Sciences to inadequate, inappropriate or poor instructional media or designs adopted during lessons in primary and secondary schools in Nigeria (Esiobu, 2005; Okonkwo, 2000; Familoni, 2013; NERDC, 2005). Instructional media is a broad term, which is often used interchangeable and synonymously with other terms such as educational design and educational technology to generally refer to the technological tools, such as computer programmes, films, video-editing programmes, word-processing equipment and calculating instruments used for teaching and enhancing learning outcomes in students or learners (Ask.com, 2013; Hodges, 2006). Media refer to channels of communication. They are carriers of information between a source and a receiver (Smaldino, Russell, Heinich & Molena, (2005). Media are very essential to good teaching and; to get the most from them, they must be selected properly and used effectively. Examples of media include power point, slides, videotapes, diagrams, printed materials, and computer software. These are considered as instructional media when they carry messages with an instructional purpose. Accordingly, the purpose of instructional media is to facilitate communication as well as to enhance learning. Instructional media serve a variety of roles in education. Their primary role is to help students learn. One way they do this is by providing an information-rich environment (Newby et al., 2006). Instructional media provide stimulated experiences. For example, visuals give added meaning to words, and as such students can see what a new invention looks like, not just hear or read a verbal description of it. Video or a series of pictures are used to demonstrate a process; and this gives learners the best opportunity to see skill demonstrated before being asked to practice it. Hence, instructional media are used to reflect colours, sound and motion that students' interest and motivate them to learn.

Instructional media that are commonly used in the primary and secondary schools in Nigeria include texts such as study guides, manuals, worksheets, textbooks and computer/Internet displays; visuals such as verbal (text or word) elements as well as graphic (picture or picture-like) elements, which can be presented in either printed or projected form; audio, such as audiotapes and compact discs; and real objects and models, such as coins, tools, plants, animals, three-dimensional representation of real objects, realia etc.

The use of instructional media by teachers to teach and drive home their subject points at the primary and secondary school levels of our education system is incontrovertibly a paramount important issue in practical classroom interaction and successful transfer of knowledge from the teacher to the learners. The fact is that these media used by teachers ally their teaching in the class tend to have a significant implication for pragmatic knowledge transfer toward attainment of individual subject objectives as well as achievement of academic excellence in the learners in the subject in-question. This is because the truth is that instructional media are channels, which assist teachers to make their lessons explicit to learners. They are also used to transmit information, ideas and notes to learner (Ijaduola, 1997). These media serve as supplement as well as lubricant to the normal instruction processes.

Also, the importance and technicality of the various subjects taught in the secondary schools make it necessary that relevant instructional media should be used to teach it to the learners. This fact is supported by scholars like Macaulay (1989) who asserted that visual aids makes lesson come alive and help students to learn better. He further stated that an adequate and appropriate utilization of visual and general teaching aids is an evidence of teachers' preparedness for the lesson. Ehizojie (1989) also summarized the importance of instructional media as one of the ways of relaxing in the classroom atmosphere, motivating the students and teaching a subject creatively and interactively.

Also, due to technological development, computer is used to aid teaching and learning. Nowadays, in the developed countries, the micro-computer is seen as powerful equipment because it appears to be capable of keeping track of individual students and responding to them, or, prescribing to them, in spite of independent variation ability, learning styles and learning rates (Scalon & O'Shea, 1987).

Computer Assisted Instruction (CAI), which is an automated instructional technique in which a computer is used to present an instructional programme to the learner through an interactive process on the computer; and applied when computer is being used on as teaching aid, or as a proxy for human tutor is used in conjunction with its software obtained in the form of a written package that is rich in graphics representations to teach and present subject materials on screen. Correct answers are also rewarded, usually by means of a comment on the screen such as "well done," incorrect respond triggers a beep or some other error signal. This type of programming is essentially a stimulus response sequence, providing fast positive reinforcement for the right answer. According to Smaldino, et al., (2005)

such immediate feedback is an important factor in motivating students to learn. A well written programme according to Smaldino, et al., should lead the students to select the correct answer ninety (90) percent of the time.

It is against this background that this study attempts to examine utilization of Instructional Media and Academic Performance of Students in Basic Science (case study: Education District (V1) of Lagos state).

Statement of Problem

The act of teaching is fundamentally concerned with passing ideas, skills and attitude from the teacher to the learner. In Nigeria, for example, experience has shown that spoken words alone in the communication of ideas rigorously ineffective and inefficient in producing desired learning outcomes. Every year, when the results of Junior Secondary Certificate Examination (JSCE) are released, there has always been mass failure of public junior secondary school students in Basic Science. The reason for this could be the fact that there are topics in Basic Science that pose serious problem of comprehension to students. Some topics cannot be taught effectively without the use of relevant instructional media to make the learning practical. On the foregoing, scholars like Mutebi and Matora (1994) have emphasized the effect of instructional media utilization on teaching and learning. According to them, we learn and remember 10% of what we hear; 40% of what we discuss with others; and as high as 80% of what we experience directly or practice. However, the questions here are: Would the use of instructional media influence JSS students' performance in Basic Science? Is teaching enhanced by the use of instructional media? Could students' learning be enhanced by the use of instructional media? Finding answers to these questions and more summarizes the entire problem of this study.

Purpose of Study

The purpose of this study is to examine the impact of instructional media utilization on the academic performance of JS-11 Basic Science Students. In this regard, the study specifically sought to:

1. Ascertain the adequacy of available instructional media in public junior secondary schools in Education District V1 of Lagos State;
2. Determine the influence of instructional media on the academic performance of public junior secondary school students in basic science.

Research Questions

The following research questions were raised to guide the study.

1. How adequate is the availability of instructional media in public junior secondary schools in Education District V1 of Lagos State?
2. How do instructional media influence the academic performance of public junior secondary schools students in basic science?

Research Hypothesis

There is no significant difference between the performance of students exposed with the use of instructional media and those who are not exposed.

Research Method

This chapter presents the methods adopted in conducting this study. These include the study design, study population, sample and sampling technique, the study instrument, validity of the instrument, data collection procedure and data analysis procedure.

The research design adopted for this study was the Quasi Experimental Design, which is pre-test and post test. The students were tested before administering treatment to ascertain their level of knowledge without instructional media usage.

Consequently, the names of all the students sampled for the study were written on separate pieces of papers, folded and put in a bowl. These names were drawn out, one by one, alternately putting them into piles. All the names of the students in the first pile was put in one group (A) called the experimental group, while all the names of students the second pile formed another group (B) called the control group. Instructional media were used to teach the experimental group in Basic Science II for two weeks, after which a test (post-test) on Basic Science was administered on both groups.

Nevertheless, this design was considered most appropriate for this study because it is one of the most relevant designs that would enable us determine the cause and effect relationships among the study's variables. Besides, the structure and rules of the design allows the isolation of single factors and examination of their associations and effects in a way that is difficult in cluttered real life situations.

Population of the Study

The researcher covers district (VI) of Lagos State Education Board for junior secondary section. This district was made up of three zones and they are Ikeja, Mushin, and Oshodi. Table 1 represents the district:

Sample and Sampling Technique

The sample size used for the study comprised of one hundred (100) respondents for the experimental group from one zone and six hundred (600) students from the three zones of the district and two hundred students from each zone. The experimental group was composed using the sample random

Table 1. Education District VI of Lagos State

Zones	No. of J.S Schools	No. of Teachers	No. of Students
Ikeja	13	591	12,944
Mushin	16	545	16,807
Oshodi	18	913	23,273
Total	47	2,049	53,024

Source: LED VI school Records, 2010

sampling technique. First and foremost, one public secondary school was randomly considered from the public secondary schools in District (VI). Out of the JS II students of this secondary school, one hundred (100) students were randomly composed and divided into two groups of fifty (50) students for the control group and fifty (50) students for the experimental group. This sample and sample technique is for question 2 only.

Research Instrument

Two research instruments were designed and used for collecting data for this study. These instruments included a questionnaire structured by the researcher for the students as well as forty-item objective achievement tests on Basic Science for the pre and post tests. The questionnaire had two sections, A and B respectively. The section 'A' of the questionnaire contained questions meant to generated data on the biographic characteristics of the respondents, while section 'B' contained questions meant to generate relevant data on the study's variables in line with the research questions raised in the study. Also, the forty-item objective achievement tests on Basic Science were administered to the sampled students before and after the experiment to the experimental group of students were taught with relevant instructional media such as audio visual (television and computer) in order to generate information on the academic performance of the two groups of students in Basic Science.

Validity of the Research Instruments

The samples of the instruments were shown to the researchers' supervisor, an expert in instructional media/measurement and evaluation, and an expert in Measurement and Evaluation from the department of Educational foundation.

The researcher visited the secondary school sampled for the study and sought the permission of the school authority. The sampled teachers and students were then organized as required by the study. The students constituting the experimental class in the school were taught for two weeks, using JSS II syllabus on Basic Science and relevant instructional media. The students in both the control and experimental groups were later merged and the forty-item objective achievement tests on Basic Science were administered on them. Also, the questionnaire copies were allowed enough time to respond to the questionnaire items before instant retrieval. All the research questionnaires were retrieved from on the respondents immediately.

Data Analysis

Data collected on the demographic features of the respondents were analyzed and presented in frequency tables and turned into means. Other data generated from the respondents' responses to the questionnaire items as well as from written test were used to analyze both the research questions and hypotheses raised in the study, chi-square and correlation.

The entire data generated for this study had been statistically analyzed in line with the research questions and hypotheses raised in the study. The results are presented below in three parts. The first part contains the summary of the respondents' demographic characteristics; the second part contains the descriptive analysis of the research questions raised in the study; while the third part contains the results of the statistical analysis of the hypotheses posited in the study.

BIO-DATA OF RESPONDENTS

Table 2 shows that 47% of the students that participated in the study are males, while 53% are females. Also, 56% of the students involved in the study are between the ages of 11 and 12; 31% are between the ages of 13 and 14; while 13% are above 14 years old.

Pre-Test Result: The students were tested to know their level of understanding of the different topics that poses challenges in learning of basic science in the junior secondary school in Lagos State. The result is represented in Table 3.

The scores of student were calculated using percentage, 40% of the student got 20marks, 25% scored 15marks and 45% scored 30 and above.

Answers to Research Questions

Note: In analyzing data to answer the research questions raised in the study, strongly agree responses and agree responses were grouped as agreed, while strongly disagree and disagree were grouped as disagreed.

Table 2. Sex and age distribution of respondents

Sex	Frequency	%
Male	47	47
Female	53	53
Total	100	100
Age	Frequency	%
11 – 12yrs	56	56
13 - 14	31	31
Above 14	13	13
Total	100	100

Table 3. Scores obtained from the achievement test given to students

20	15	30
40%	25%	45%

Research Question 1: How adequate is the availability of instructional media in public junior secondary schools in Education district VI of Lagos State?

The data collected in order to answer the question above is presented in the Table 4.

Table 4 showed that, out of the responses gathered from the students on their perception of whether there is adequate availability of instructional media for enhancing the teaching and learning of basic science public junior secondary school. Majority of the students with a mean rate 76.5 agreed that the availability of instructional media in the public junior secondary schools enhanced teaching and learning of basic science; while the remaining students with a mean rate 23.5 were on the contrary affirmed that there is no availability of instructional media therefore learning of Basic Science is not enhanced by the use instructional media.

Research Question 2: How does the use of instructional media influence the performance of Public Junior Secondary Schools students in basic science?

The data collected in order to answer the question is presented in Table 5.

Table 5 shows that out of the responses gathered from the students on their perception of whether the use of instructional media influences their academic performance, majority of the students with a mean response of 71.3 agreed that the use of instructional media influences their academic performance; while the remaining students with a mean response of 28.7 on the contrary asserted that the use of instructional media does not influence their academic performance.

Hypothesis: There is no significant difference between performances of students taught with instructional media and those who are taught without instructional media (see Table 6).

Table 4. Perception of students on whether there is adequate availability of instructional media for enhancing the teaching and learning of Basic sciences in public junior secondary school in Lagos state.

Items	Agree	Disagree	Remark
Does instructional media available in your school?	25	75	Disagreed
Do you enjoy learning with available instructional media in your school?	81	19	Agreed
Does your teacher involve the use of instructional media made available by the state Government?	83	17	Agreed
Do your teachers use available instructional media to facilitate teaching and learning of practical?	74	26	Agreed
I do not understand basic science any better when taught using instructional media?	67	33	Agreed
Using instructional media to teach basic science makes the subject more understanding.	79	21	Agreed
Total	459	141	
Mean Response	76.5	23.5	

X cal = 21.03

df= (r-1)(c-1)=4f

@ 0.05

X crt= 9.49

Table 7 shows the calculated chi-square value of 21.3 is greater than the chi-square tabulated of 9.49 at degree of freedom of 0.05 of significant level. The result supported that the use of instructional media has impact on teaching and learning of basic science in junior secondary schools of Lagos state Education Board.

Discussion of Finding

The hypothesis was the researcher's opinion that there is significant difference between the performances of students' taught with instructional media to those taught without. This showed that the use of instructional media will facilitate learning of basic science in junior secondary schools of

Table 5. Perception of student on whether the use of instructional media influences their performance in learning basic science Junior Secondary Schools or not.

Items	Agree	Disagree	Remark
I perform better whenever I am taught with instructional media.	69	21	Agreed
I do my home work well and make high scores in my subjects whenever I am taught the subjects with appropriate instructional media.	63	37	Agreed
Teachers use appropriate instructional media to teach their subjects in order to enhance their students' understanding and performance in the subjects.	78	22	Agreed
Use of instructional media in teaching enhances student's performance.	65	35	Agreed
Total	285	115	
Mean Response	71.3	28.7	

Lagos state if it is well utilized. This finding supports Ajelabi (2000) who noted that instructional media lend supports and authenticity to whatever the teacher says to the learner which the learner is able to confirm or refute the teacher's assertions.

Recommendations

In line with the findings of this study, the following recommendations were made for necessary remediation.

1. Secondary School Administrators should provide enough instructional media to enable teachers' clarity their lesson. Adequate infrastructural facilities and conclusive atmosphere are sine qua non for effective learning and retention of what is learnt.
2. Secondary School Administrators should send their Basic Science teachers to seminars

and workshops in order to up - date their knowledge and acquired new methods of using instructional media. They should be encouraged to produce new ones through creativity.

3. Basic Science teachers should conduct the teaching and learning of the subject effectively, efficiently and interestingly. They should be resourceful, knowledgeable and vary their teaching methods at all times. They should also ensure appropriate use of instructional media in teaching their lessons as well as try their possible best to improvise these instructional media where necessary to really enable the students learn the subject properly and profoundly.

4. Students should read extensively worthwhile publications, journals and recommended books in Basic Science as well as listen to radio and television analysis

Table 6. Questionnaire data

Zones in Districts Six of Lagos Education Board	No of Questionnaire Distributed	Collected Questionnaire	Not Collected
Ikeja	200	190	10
Oshodi	200	193 ·	7
Mushin	200	195	5
Total	600	578	22

Table 7. Result of chi-square analysis on the performance of students when taught with instructional media and they are not taught with them

Roll	Ikeja A	Oshodi B	Mushin C	TOTAL	RATIO	Oi-ei Ei
Agreed	200 0.105	200 0.073	200 0.051	600	0.347	0.229
Disagreed	15 24.7	20 9	10 1.9	45	0.054	52.7
Not agreed	5 39	3 65.7	7 55.1	15	0.24	159.8
Total	220	223	217	660		X^2=21.03

on economic issues. This will widen their knowledge in Basic Science and drastically reduce mass failure of secondary school students in Basic Science.

CONCLUSION

In conclusion, teachers are at the centre of educational instruction. They should strive hard to make their teaching very effective. Akande (1989) asserts that medical doctor buries his mistake, the engineer dies with his mistake but the whole society perishes with the mistake of a teacher. This showed how valuable a teacher is in the growth of an individual and the society at large. Then the teachers of Basic Science and that of all other subjects should make imperative the use of instructional media during teaching so that learning will be positively influenced for results in building the right type of human capital for the desired growth and development of the nation.

REFERENCES

Ajelabi, A. (2000). *Production and utilization of educational media.* Lagos: Reltel Communication.

Akande, M. O. (2002). *The theory and practice of professional teaching. Lagos.* Ekanag Publishers.

Ask.com. (2013). *What is instructional media?* Retrieved December 16, 2013 from www.ask.com/question/what-is-instrumental-media

Elizojie, P. O. (1989). The use of A-V and other aids in the teaching of English. In Handbook for junior secondary school language teachers. Lagos: NERDC.

Esiobu, G. O. (2005). Gender issues in science and technology educational development. In Science and technology education for development, (pp. 137-156). Lagos: NERDC.

Familoni, O. (2013). *Science education can solve our problems.* The Punch Newspaper.

Ijaduola, K. O. (1997). *Psychology of Learning Made Easy. Ijebu-Ode: Lucky Odoni, Nig.* Enterprise.

Maduekwe, A. N. (2007). *Principles and Practice of Teaching English as a Secondary Language.* Lagos: Vitamins Educational Books.

Mueller, G. (1980). Visual Contextual Clues and listening comprehension: An experiment. *Modern Language Journal, 64,* 335–340. doi:10.1111/j.1540-4781.1980.tb05202.x

Newby, T. J., Stepich, D. A., Lehman, J. D., & Russell, J. D. (2006). *Educational technology for teaching and learning.* Pearson Education, Inc.

Nigeria Educational Research and Development Council (NERDC). (2005). *Workship on difficult concepts: Physics group report.* Lagos: NERDC.

Okonkwo, S. C. (2000). Relationship between some school and teacher variables and students achievement in mathematics. *Journal of Science Association of Nigeria, 35,* 43–49.

Oremeji, C. J. (2002). *Strategies in educational administration and supervision.* Port Harcourt: High Class Publishers.

Smaldino, S. E., Russell, J. D., Heinich, R., & Molenda, M. (2005). *Instructional technology and media for learning* (8th ed.). Upper Saddle River, NJ: Pearson/Prentice Hall.

KEY TERMS AND DEFINITIONS

Academic Performance: Students achievements in assessment of tests done by them after a period of instruction or teaching on a subject matter; or the achievement level of learning a student attains of a subject matter taught him.

Basic Science: The subject disciplines of physics, Chemistry, Biology and Mathematics.

Biology: The branch of science concerned with the study of plants and animals characteristics and behavior within an environment; or the study of the structure, function and behavior of organisms or types of organisms in a particular area or region; or the study of all living matter or life.

Chemistry: The branch of science concerned with the study of the composition and constitution of substances and the changes that they undergo as a result of alterations in the constitution of their molecules; or the application of chemical theories and methods to substances.

Computer: A programmable electronic device for performing mathematical calculations and logical operations, as well as for the processing storage and retrieval of large amounts of data (information) very quickly, and; especially employed for the manipulation of texts, graphics accessing the Internet, and playing games or media.

Educational Technology: The technological tools used for teaching to enhance the acquisition of knowledge by students (Learning) and which includes computers, video tapes, Internet facility, computer software, etc.

Effective Learning: The permanent in change of behavior or thinking having the power to produce a required effect or effects, or capable of producing a decided or decisive effect; in other words learning that produces a required decisive effect or effects.

Instructional Media: Educational technology that carry messages with an instructional purpose which facilitate communication as well as enhance learning by reflecting colours, sound and motion that capture the students' interest and motivate them to learn.

Physics: The branch of science concerned with the study of properties and interactions of space, time, matter and energy; or concerned with or pertaining to the physical aspects of a phenomenon or a system, especially those studied in physics.

Science: The particular discipline or branch of learning that deals with measurable or systematic principles rather than intuition or natural ability; or the collective discipline of study or learning acquired through the scientific method, including the totality of knowledge acquired from such methods and discipline.

Chapter 10

Using Andragogy and Bloom's Digital Taxonomy to Guide E-Portfolio and Web Portfolio Development in Undergraduate Courses

John DiMarco
St. John's University, USA

ABSTRACT

This chapter offers suggestions and discussion on e-portfolio teaching approaches and how andragogy and Bloom's Digital Taxonomy can be weaved into teaching and learning to create active learning through e-portfolio development. The chapter connects andragogy (Knowles, 1980) and integrates the educational objectives in the cognitive domain put forth by Bloom in 1956 and then updated by Anderson and Krathwohl (2001) and eventually aligned to the digital realm by Churches (2009) to use as a model for teaching Web portfolio development in undergraduate courses. The Web portfolio has value for the student as a real-world tool for use in career advancement. It can be integrated into curriculum by faculty as a platform for assessment of higher-level cognitive objectives. This chapter includes a framework for a portfolio seminar course and how it implements Web portfolio (e-portfolio) components, which may provide a model for faculty developing future e-portfolio courses.

INTRODUCTION

The mission of this chapter is to identify and define the value of Web Portfolios for undergraduate courses using the lens of Bloom's Digital Taxonomy. The Web portfolio (also known as the e-portfolio -the terms are virtually interchange-

able today) is a critical platform for students and graduates to connect their skills, abilities, and accomplishments and present them to teachers, professors, potential employers, clients, and other assessment centric audiences. The objectives of this chapter are to offer a template for faculty who are investigating, managing, and developing Web

DOI: 10.4018/978-1-4666-6162-2.ch010

Copyright © 2014, IGI Global. Copying or distributing in print or electronic forms without written permission of IGI Global is prohibited.

portfolio (e-portfolio) initiatives in undergraduate communications courses for use as an active learning tool, not simply as a repository. The chapter will provide insight into problems, solutions, and challenges facing faculty with regards to integrating Web portfolio (e-portfolio) into curriculums as an active learning objective.

BACKGROUND

Goldsby and Fazal (2001) cited that student created portfolios are commonly "used in teacher preparation programs to demonstrate teaching skills and expertise. This practice was introduced as test scores alone lack the comprehensive scope needed for effective assessment and evaluation, portfolios can be implemented to interpret/make decisions regarding learning of teaching competencies" (2001, 607-608). The case for the student portfolio in any discipline can be made on the same basis; electronic portfolios provide a new level of assessment that cannot be measured by traditional methods such as standardized tests, applications, and resumes. Electronic portfolios and Web portfolios provide assessment of competency within a discipline.

The old models of professional and personal identity, skills assessment, and promotion are fading in what Dr. Stephen Covey (2004) describes as the age of the knowledge worker. In the knowledge worker age, the focus is on intellectual capital and exhibiting the skills of someone who is technologically savvy, but sensitive to the vision and voice of traditional values that enable people to thrive, such as mentoring. The Web portfolio feeds the emergence of intellectual capital by providing a platform for the knowledge worker to exhibit their personal and professional qualities. Mentoring will be increased as the Web portfolio becomes a standard learning tool within mainstream education at all levels. Teachers will need to teach students how to make Web portfolios. In turn, these students will later become mentors to others in their

lives who are creating Web portfolios. Electronic portfolios and Web portfolios feed the process of lifelong learning (DiMarco 2006).

Educators on all levels need to embrace the Web portfolio as a tool, regardless of their discipline. As a tool, it should be mastered by teachers and taught to students within the appropriate contexts of their disciplines. If a student creates an art portfolio, it has a structure and presentation style that will focus on the artwork and the skills of the artist. If the portfolio is for a student in the discipline of English, the portfolio should focus on the writings and literature aptitude of the creator. In his personal case study on Web-based portfolios for technology education, Professor Mark E. Sanders (2000, 11) stated that:

"These technologies should be prominent within our curriculum. Often, they are not. Web-based portfolios offer a meaningful way for technology students to gain a thorough understanding of these critical new technologies beyond mere Web research. Web-based portfolios provide benefits that can never be realized with conventional portfolios."

To follow up Professor Sander's statement, it is critical for all instructors and students to embrace Web portfolio exploration, creation, and development not only in technology and education driven disciplines, but also in all disciplines. The Web portfolio has been growing well beyond the boundaries of education and technology fields and is finding its way outside of educational institutions and into human resources and other corporate directions. This idea is supported by Moonen and Tulner (2004) and Conrad (2008) who describes interest in electronic portfolio is growing. Starting as early as 2004, EIfEL (European Institute for E-Learning) provided all of its members with an electronic portfolio, the most innovative and fastest growing technology in the field of education, training and human resource development. While most current e-Portfolio initiatives happen in primary, secondary, and higher education, the full potential of e-Portfolios will be demonstrated through lifelong learning. With this in mind, the Web portfolio should be viewed as a default medium for human persuasion, promotion, assessment, and communication and as such has a place in information and communications education.

Web Portfolios Have Learning Value to Students during and after the Process

Students in communications courses are frequently creating professional and artistic works that emulate the projects that they will encounter when moving into the professional world. This applied necessity requires a constructivist approach to learning, which means that students are actively engaging in the learning process as they create materials that will have function in their immediate lives. The development of an e-portfolio/ Web portfolio is an adult learning experience. This not a teacher leading student process, but a constructivist process that utilizes technology and active learning. Students must engage in analysis of works, visual design of a Web portfolio, development of a portfolio site, evaluation of the online vehicle and future editing and updating. The e-portfolio - Web portfolio lives beyond the undergraduate years. The platform becomes useful in future career searches and provides the creator to utilize the Website for job seeking and promotion, but also for freelance and entrepreneurship, depending on the platform used. The portfolio is updated as the person grows so life long learning and reflection is built into the process.

The Connection Between Andragogy, E-Portfolios, and Bloom's Digital Taxonomy

Teaching Web portfolio development on the undergraduate level requires motivation beyond a grade. The Web portfolio/e-portfolio is intimately connected to higher cause that extends past assessment to professional development and self

esteem. This idea must bring teachers closer into the expectations of their students, rather than the other way around. The motivation of students to do well in a portfolio course is not simply a grade, but an opportunity to use the work in the class to gain something of value outside of class, such as a prominent internship, a job, or a freelance opportunity. These possibilities are intriguing to students and provide a tangible benefit to remind them of when you are trying to foster strong work ethics and quality online portfolios.

Teaching the development of Web portfolios in an undergraduate communications course draws the professor toward adapting the coursework to allow students to learn and navigate the process while maintaining milestones for grading purposes. Instruction must take on an andragogical approach, rather than a pedagogical one. The adult version of pedagogy, andragogy, centers on engaging learners with the structure of a learning experience. Knowles (1980) put forth the idea that teaching adults, a term called andragogy, set out four key assumptions, which included: moving learners toward self directedness, adults have high levels of experience that drives learning, people want to learn in the context of real life tasks or problems, and learners see education benefit competence. Two additional assumptions were added in 1998 by Knowles, Holton, and Swanson (St. Clair 2002), which posited that adults need to know the reason for learning and that self esteem is the most potent motivator. This method of teaching has value for teaching young adult/ adult students in undergraduate portfolio courses in communication programs.

Stripping Knowles' andragogy into four distinctive areas with the goal of easy implementation into practice, DiMarco (2012) used the acronym NORF to clarify the main points of the Knowles andragogy theory:

- **Need to Know:** Adults need to know the reason for learning something;
- (objectives based) use: pretest

- **Orientation:** Adult learning is problem-oriented, rather than content-oriented; (solving problems should be key to content) use: simulation and case study
- **Readiness:** Adults are most interested in learning subjects having immediate relevance to their work and/or personal lives; (understanding the prerequisite learning experiences) use: learner analysis
- **Foundation:** Experience (including error) provides the basis for learning activities; (building a "learning spiral," where one experience leads to another)

Creating a Web portfolio brings adult learning to the apex because it is well suited to addressing an actual learning experience where reflection and collection of assets are key components. A learning spiral occurs that runs through the core of Bloom's revised taxonomy with a pathway from knowledge to application to evaluation to creativity. Complementing areas: are motivation and self-concept, which drive the learner to engage in the experience. The Web portfolio becomes a personal statement about ones self actualization in their career, which gives creating a Web portfolio distinct relevance to someone's life. The idea of NORF, a slim version of the adult learning theory of andragogy, put forth by Malcolm Knowles, can be coupled with the revised version of Bloom's Taxonomy, developed by Anderson and Krathwohl (2001), which has been appropriately updated and labeled Blooms Digital Taxonomy (Churches, 2009) to provide a framework for teaching and learning with Web portfolios. In the new digital taxonomy, "creating" has overtaken evaluation as the highest level of cognitive objective. One deliverable that has been identified with the highest level of Blooms Digital Taxonomy is creating Web portfolios and Web based media (blogs, slideshows, galleries, forums, and podcasts). All of these items can be presented in a Web portfolio. The act of teaching how to make a Web portfolio aligns well with Bloom's Digital Taxonomy and

Knowles andragogy because it engages the student in active learning and requires an approach to adult learning that directs the benefits and goals of the lessons to be directly related to the vision of the student.

DiMarco (2007) described the Web portfolio as a self directed; self developed Website that provides insight and evidence into the skills, experience, and accomplishments of a person. The creation of Web portfolios and teaching one how to do it leads to the integration of andragogy into practice. As well, the identification of high level cognitive objectives in Bloom's Digital Taxonomy (analyzing and creating) further connects with the creation of a Web portfolio (e-portfolio) as an activity for higher level learning. According to Churches (2009) designing, constructing, planning, producing, and making are at highest order thinking skills available. These skills are inherently used in developing a Web portfolio (e-portfolio).

Evaluating professional and academic credentials requires evidence, which can be effectively presented in a Web portfolio, also known as an e-portfolio, which is short for electronic portfolio. Online e-portfolios and Web portfolios have been widely used during the past several years along with the diffusion of electronic teaching-learning systems (Wang 2012). Scholars including Wang (2012), DiMarco (2007, 2012), and Greenberg (2004) have called for an increase in active learning when using e-portfolios. DiMarco (2012) and Barrett (2007) pointed out that e-portfolio systems have varying levels of creative possibilities. These levels of creativity relate to features, functions, and freedom allowed by the host institution. DiMarco identified differences in creative control of e-portfolio systems that were related to the needs of faculty and administrators, which highlighted control and assessment as critical. In addition, student's needs, which are grounded in creativity and freedom are sometimes not inline with the objectives of administration, which are assessment and control.

DiMarco (2012) stated

Each e-portfolio solution has different value based on student needs, faculty needs, and administrator needs. Students need a more robust environment, but with that come less control for administration and faculty. Faculty and administrators want assessment abilities and control over site content, which leads to a weaker platform for students to build the sites with.

Focusing on a student-centered approach that highlights active learning, Wang and Wang (2012) have suggested that "for the time being e-portfolio is viewed more as an assessment tool or a showcase tool, but less as an active learning tool." The authors point out that current generic e-portfolio systems store artifacts in the chronological order on the course basis, and seem to provide few facets for active thinking, which points to an interesting problem. How can active learning be integrated into curriculums using Web portfolios?

TEACHING WEB PORTFOLIO DESIGN AND DEVELOPMENT IN AN UNDERGRADUATE COMMUNICATION COURSE

Chapter Focus

Specifically, the main focus of this chapter will be to present a framework for Web portfolio development in an undergraduate communications courses. Discussion will provide a framework for teaching Web Portfolio development based on experience teaching this process for the past five years in undergraduate communications courses with students from advertising, public relations, and mass communications majors in a private 4-year university in New York City serving over 25,000 students. Examination of this short case will present the issues, controversies, and solutions that were gathered during the course from 2008-2013.

Issues

Several prominent issues have emerged each year since I begun teaching the undergraduate portfolio seminar in 2006. The first issue encountered was student's ability to conceptualize their portfolio and how it fit into their life and career plan. The second prominent issue was the ability of students to reflect and collect appropriate work to add to the portfolio. The third issue was the ability of students to create a Web portfolio using industry standard Web development tools.

The Question of Conceptualization and Focus

One problem that students face in this are and faculty should address is the time and effort spent by student when conceptualizing their personal brand and the main focus of the portfolio. Rough sketches to visualize page elements and flowcharts to envision potential content.

Students need to create Web portfolios (e-portfolios) that illustrate their strengths and provide tangible evidence that create a professional image for them and their personal brand. To do this, students must conceptualize their portfolios and answer one specific question:

This Web portfolio (e-portfolio) promotes me as a _____. (DiMarco 2013)

Then, it is critical for students to reflect on their own happiness and determine what careers will give them fulfillment and then what are those careers. Once they can identify what they are attempting to become, then they can cater the messages, images and content in the Web portfolio (e-portfolio) into a representative work that promotes and brands them as professionals in their field.

The Question of Reflection and Collection

Students need to provide a body of content, which needs subsequent updating in their e-portfolios. The issue that I have found that students typically face is the dilemma of not having enough or adequate work to fill the portfolio. The portfolio development process, whether it be for an analog or digital portfolio requires a tremendous amount of reflection. Students may realize that they have a deficit of work in an area that they are deeply interested in pursuing. This problem can be solved by suggesting ancillary projects for students to complete so that they can build their skills and fill out the sections of their portfolios. Volunteer work and homegrown events are widely available at most colleges. I encourage students to engage these opportunities and develop portfolio level work with an accompanying case study so that each experience can be document and capitalized on as nourishment for future experiences.

The process of reflection and collection is reliant upon student using organizational strategies such as creating outlines of categories of work and developing a simple flowchart that provides an outline of work to be included in the portfolio. These items are used as homework items and can be used as a platform for individual or group discussions on appropriate content and portraying professionalism and marketability.

The Question of Tools and Technologies

Originally, as the professor of an undergraduate course in portfolio development in 2006, I taught students how to create Web portfolios using professional grade WYSIWYG software, Adobe Dreamweaver, Flash, and Fireworks were the tools of choice. This was my method due to the fact that I was formerly a graphic design professor teaching art students how to make electronic portfolios. I moved into the domain of communications and realized that students in who had not had used Adobe Dreamweaver or the other Web design software products had difficulty learning how to create Websites. In addition, students needed to use FTP software and acquire server space and a domain, as our university did not offer such resources in 2006-2007.

In 2006, I changed my course outline for the undergraduate portfolio seminar course to include the use of PortfolioVillage.com, a site that utilizes DIY (Do it Yourself) tools to create sites rather than traditional design software and hosting. This enabled students to avoid steep learning curves and costly software and hosting and allowed them to concentrate on content and process. In addition, the site offers well designed templates that can be updated so students didn't have to wrestle with design considerations, which consequently supported the development of better looking portfolio sites. PortfolioVillage provides the software, hosting and sub domain for free for life. This allows students to keep and update their portfolios after they graduated, which is critical to success in career searches.

Controversies

A small controversy was evident in our institution regarding the use of online portfolio tools. Another e-portfolio application has also been adopted by the university that has a limited interface and extremely limited creative control, which is loathed by students, especially in the arts and communications. However, it provided assessment tools and control, which is highly desired by administrators. The university determined that the use of multiple systems would be appropriate and beneficial to students across curriculums. So in essence, the university uses multiple e-portfolio system and Web portfolio systems. Students can decide which one to use and they can also be guided by faculty to use one or the other depending on the course requirements or mentoring advice. Web portfolio sites can be used beyond portfolios for mock Website projects, event Websites, blog and photo sites, and academic research sites.

SOLUTIONS AND RECOMMENDATIONS

Using the E-Portfolio Technology Platform

The most evident obstacles in creating an e-portfolio is access to technology tools, Web hosting, and the skills needed to effectively create a Website that looks good and performs well. The Website, www.portfoliovillage.com helps users to create Websites and Web Portfolios that are output in HTML5 and are viewable on desktop, tablet, and mobile devices. The site provides a Flash-driven Web Sitemaker in addition to free hosting and sub domain, which provides each essential element for students to create an e-portfolio. The site purports to bridge the digital divide by providing easy to use Web development tools for free and without the need to know how to code using HTML or CSS. As a Web based tool that provides both software (Sitemaker) and hardware (server), PortfolioVillage allows students work independently on laptops or at home, without being required to use resources such as a campus computer lab. Using DIY Website tools such as PortfolioVillage.com for creating Web portfolios is applicable with the highest level of cognitive objective in Bloom's Digital Taxonomy, which is "creating." PortfolioVillage seems to address the technical and financial difficulties students and faculty face when trying to create and teach e-portfolio development.

Course Development

Initiation of a portfolio course can be processed through faculty channels if there is no course currently offered. Undergraduate departments that already have portfolio courses typically include art and design, IT and technology, education, business, communications, public relations and advertising, humanities, and others across disciplines. Whether developing a new course, updating an existing course, or a creating a workshop, the outline below provides a framework for teaching Web portfolio and e-portfolio development in undergraduate courses. This model can be modified and applied to an e-portfolio seminar course across disciplines. This framework is used in teaching undergraduate portfolio seminar courses in the Mass Communication Division at St. John's University.

Course Description

This course provides students with an opportunity to develop a digitally designed, multimedia-based e-portfolio. Instruction includes conceptualization through personal reflection, categorization of works, and production of a (subject/discipline/purpose here) portfolio for the Web. Final grading is assessed on completion of an effective portfolio that follows industry standards and the meets criteria listed in the course rubric.

Learning Objectives

After completing the course, students should be able to:

- Understand and explain why e-portfolios are important tools in academia, career, and lifelong learning
- Reflect, evaluate and execute content collection decisions and processes.
- Develop assets and thematic content based on industry research
- Conceptualize, plan, design, and output a Web based portfolio.
- Use DIY Website building site PortfolioVillage.com for Web authoring and multimedia design.
- Critically review and evaluate created portfolios to insure they meet specific disciplinary criteria, industry standards, and specific career goals.

Course Activities

Note to Instructor: Take an andragogical approach to teaching this course. Motivate students by explaining how portfolios validate their skills and can help them achieve their goals in the future with internships, getting jobs, freelance opportunities and even entrepreneurship.

Utilize NORF in Teaching Activities

- **Need to Know:** Explain to students why they need a Web portfolio
  - ○ **Teaching Activity:** Pretest students verbally or in writing to see what their knowledge and experience is with e-portfolios.
- **Orientation:** Explain to students that creating an e-portfolio is about solving a problem. The problem is how to present *you* in a persuasive, professional Website that achieves a goal oriented result.
  - ○ **Teaching Activity:** Orient students by using case studies of others who have used e-portfolios to get internships, jobs, and other rewards.
- **Readiness:** Explain to students that each person is different so every portfolio will be different, depending on the person.
  - ○ **Teaching Activity:** Ready students to prepare the portfolio by helping them analyze their goals and help them connect relevance the portfolio to their work and/or personal lives. Guide students on researching careers and quantify their skills and career directions using informational interviews, checklists of criteria, labor statistics from BLS.gov, and other industry information sources.
- **Foundation:** Explain to students that the portfolio development experience provides a foundation skill for life that can be used

over and over again as well as the fact that the portfolio can be constantly updated to present new value to your career and life.
  - ○ **Teaching Activity:** Provide several levels of critique during the portfolio development process so that errors can be found and designs can be polished and finalized. The portfolio should be updated as the author's career evolves.

Utilizing Bloom's Digital Taxonomy in Learning Objectives

The course activities for an e-portfolio or Web portfolio course should include the following active learning modules that support Bloom's Digital Taxonomy (Anderson and Krathwohl 2001, Churches 2009)

Bloom's Taxonomy Level 1

- **Anderson and Krathwohl's taxonomy definition – Remembering (lowest level of low order thinking):** "Remembering: Retrieving, recalling or recognizing knowledge from memory. Remembering is when memory is used to produce definitions, facts or lists, or recite or retrieve material."
- **Learning Objectives:**
  - ○ Defining the terms:
  - ○ Web portfolio and e-portfolio
  - ○ Reflect and collect
  - ○ Assets
  - ○ Thematic content
  - ○ Artifacts
  - ○ Lifelong learning
  - ○ Learning spiral
  - ○ Students will learn the terms and their meanings.

Bloom's Taxonomy Level 2

- **Anderson and Krathwohl's taxonomy definition – Understanding (low order thinking):** "Understanding: Constructing meaning from different types of function be they written or graphic."
- **Learning Objectives:**
  - Understanding what a Web portfolio/e-portfolio is and how it can benefit your career and life.
  - Students will review online portfolios to understand structure and content.

Bloom's Taxonomy Level 3

- **Anderson and Krathwohl's taxonomy definition - Applying (low order thinking):** "Applying: Carrying out or using a procedure through executing or implementing. Applying related and refers to situations where learned material is used through products like models, presentation, interviews and simulations."
- **Learning Objectives:**
  - Applying e-portfolio terms and strategies to use in your career plan and conceptualization of a Web portfolio.
  - Students will perform career research using BLS.gov to determine which skills are necessary for a particular job and then represent those abilities in a Web portfolio.

Bloom's Taxonomy Level 4

- **Anderson and Krathwohl's taxonomy definition – Analyzing (higher order thinking):** "Analyzing: Breaking material or concepts into parts, determining how the parts relate or interrelate to one another or to an overall structure or purpose. Mental actions include differentiating, organizing

and attributing as well as being able to distinguish between components."
- **Learning Objectives:**
  - Analyzing career opportunities and analyzing personal accomplishments, work samples, and career goals to determine overall focus.
  - Students will engage in class discussion on career goals and skills needed.

Bloom's Taxonomy Level 5 (was Synthesis in Bloom's Original Taxonomy from 1956)

- **Anderson and Krathwohl's taxonomy-Evaluating (higher order thinking):** "Evaluating: Making judgments based on criteria and standards through checking and critiquing."
- **Learning Objectives:**
  - Evaluating the work that will be used in the portfolio and evaluating the career path that the portfolio will reinforce.
  - Students will engage in evaluation of past work to determine value of assets for the portfolio.

Bloom's Taxonomy Level 6 (was Evaluating in Bloom's Original Taxonomy from 1956)

- **Anderson and Krathwohl's taxonomy-Creating (highest level of high order thinking):** Creating: Putting the elements together to form a coherent or functional whole; reorganizing elements into a new pattern or structure through generating, planning or producing.
- **Learning Objectives:**
  - Creating the e-portfolio from concept to final output on the Web.

○ Students will use PortfolioVillage. com to create their own online electronic Web portfolio.

Assessment of the E-Portfolio

Assessment of electronic portfolios can be done using rubrics, which provide a standardized set of criteria and a scaled rating system. Scholars including Diller and Phelps (2008), and Forawi and Liang, (2005), found that rubrics can be an effective, pragmatic vehicle for evaluating electronic portfolios in science and information literacy. Olele (2005) suggested that "the best ways of getting learners to exhibit what they can do with the knowledge, skills, and experience they have acquired is through performance - based assessment or authentic work." The approach to developing a rubric for portfolio evaluation should be catered to the discipline so that a focus on industry styles

and approaches can be cultivated throughout the portfolio development process.

E-portfolio assessment should consider four main areas: concept, design, content, execution. Each area has specific components that can be assessed (Table 1).

FUTURE RESEARCH DIRECTIONS

The use of e-portfolios in higher education has grown into an enigmatic subject that requires further research and approaches to teaching and learning with portfolios. There is a need for identification of new models and approaches that examine e-portfolios further under the various lens of inquiry across social science. The use of e-portfolios as a teaching and learning tool gives way to a world of applied research that can further the dialog and literature on active learning using portfolios. In addition, more research on student

Table 1. E-portfolio / Web Portfolio Rubric sample (Adapted from DiMarco 2013)

SCORING	Concept	Design	Content	Execution
1. Unacceptable	The portfolio has no clear visual concept and does not relate to the target industry or goals	The portfolio design is not acceptable or properly structured. Navigation, type, images, and flow need major improvement.	The portfolio does not present appropriate content for the target industry and does not present an adequate quantity of work samples and related content.	The portfolio contained many spelling errors, many image errors, navigation errors, and had broken/missing content.
2. Poor	The portfolio has somewhat of a clear visual concept but does not relate to the target industry and goals of the creator.	The portfolio is properly structured and presents a nearly acceptable design. Navigation, type, images, and flow need major improvement.	The portfolio provides somewhat appropriate content for the target industry but does not provide an adequate quantity of work samples and related content.	The portfolio contained many spelling errors and many image/text errors. (incorrect size or scale, typos, blurry or inappropriate images).
3. Good	The portfolio has a clear visual concept that relates to the target industry and goals of the creator.	The portfolio has an acceptable design. Navigation, type, images, and flow need minor improvement.	The portfolio has appropriate content for the target industry provides an adequate quantity of work samples and related content.	The portfolio contained very few spelling or image errors.
4. Excellent	The portfolio has a very strong, clear visual concept that relates to the target industry and goals of the creator.	The portfolio has a highly effective design and presents proper navigation, type and images.	The portfolio has highly effective content for the target industry and presents an adequate quantity of work samples and related content.	The portfolio contained no spelling errors, image errors, navigation errors, or broken/missing content.

attitudes and opinions toward Web portfolios is needed. Finally, future study of the use of e-portfolio/Web portfolio systems and the faculty and student challenges involved are warranted as these learning initiatives grow.

CONCLUSION

The notion of the e-portfolio/Web portfolio has value for teaching and learning in undergraduate courses in a wide variety of disciplines. The e-portfolio, also known as the Web portfolio can be a valuable tool in self promotion, adult learning, and assessment. Digital portfolios carry the promise of active learning for students and can illustrate a person's benefits to teachers, professors, potential client, and hiring managers who want clear evidence of the skills, abilities, and value a person may have on an organization. As well, companies and corporations will begin to embrace Web portfolios to evaluate candidates and employees alike as the trend in knowledge work continues.

Using Bloom's Digital Taxonomy combined with Knowles theory of Andragogy, instructors can provide students with an active learning approach for creating e-portfolios/Web portfolios. Each level of Bloom's taxonomy can be addressed in the Learning objectives in the course. Using a teaching style that emphasizes andragogy, an instructor can motivate students and make the portfolio development process relatable by delivering information on how the process of creating a Web portfolio will benefit them and how the Web portfolio will help them in the future.

REFERENCES

Anderson, L. W., & Krathwohl, D. (Eds.). (2001). *A taxonomy for learning, teaching, and assessing: A revision of Bloom's taxonomy of educational objectives*. New York: Longman.

Barrett, H. (2009). My Online Portfolio Adventure. *electronicportfolios.org*. Retrieved from http://electronicportfolios.org/myportfolio/versions.html#Overview

Bloom, B., Englehart, M., Furst, E., Hill, W., & Krathwohl, D. (1956). Taxonomy of educational objectives: The classification of educational goals. In I. Handbook (Ed.), *Cognitive domain*. New York: Longmans, Green.

Churches, A. (2009). Bloom's Digital Taxonomy v3.01. *Educational Origami*. Retrieved from http://edorigami.wikispaces.com/file/view/bloom%27s+Digital+taxonomy+v3.01.pdf

Conrad, D. (2008). Building Knowledge through portfolio learning in prior learning assessment and recognition. *Quarterly Review of Distance Education, 9*(2), 139-150, 219.

Covey, S. (2004). *The eighth habit*. New York, NY: Free Press.

Diller, K. R., & Phelps, S. F. (2008). Learning outcomes, portfolios, and rubrics, oh my! Authentic assessment of an information literacy program. *Portal: Libraries and the Academy, 8*(1), 75–89. doi:10.1353/pla.2008.0000

DiMarco, J. (2006). *Web Portfolio Design and Applications*. IGI Global.

DiMarco, J. (2007). Web Portfolio Design for Teachers and Professors. In *Proceedings of the 2007 Information resources management Association International Conference*. IGI Global.

DiMarco, J. (2012). Implementing a Website Portal using PortfolioVillage to evaluate Professional Credentials. In *Technology Integration and Foundations for effective Technology Leadership*. Hershey, PA: Idea Group. doi:10.4018/978-1-4666-2656-0.ch018

DiMarco, J. (2013). *Career Power Skills*. New York: Pearson.

Forawi, S. A., & Liang, X. (2005). Science electronic portfolios: Developing and validating the scoring rubric. *Journal of Science Education, 6*(2), 97–99.

Goldsby, D., & Fazal, M. (2001). Web-Based Portfolios for Technology Education: A Personal Case Study. *Journal of Technology and Teacher Education, 9*(4), 606–607.

Greenberg, G. (2004). The digital convergence: Extending the portfolio. *EDUCAUSE Review, 39*(4), 28.

Knowles, M. S. (1980). *The modern practice of adult education: From pedagogy to andragogy. Englewood Cliffs, NJ*. Cambridge: Prentice Hall.

Moonen, J., & Tulner, H. (2004). *E-Learning and electronic portfolio: Some new insights*. Retrieved from http://www.csun.edu/cod/conf/2004/proceedings/12.htm

Olele, C. N. (2012). Alternative assessment: Emerging trends of classroom assessment in digital era. *Academic Research International, 3*(1), 42–49.

Sanders, M. (2000). Web-Based Portfolios for Technology Education: A Personal Case Study. *The Journal of Technology Studies*. Retrieved from http://scholar.lib.vt.edu/ejournals/JOTS/Winter-Spring-2000/pdf/sanders.pdf

St. Clair, R. (2002). Andragogy revisited: Theory for the 21st century. *Cal-Pro Online*. Retrieved from www.calpro-online.org/eric/docs/mr00034.pdf

Wang, S., & Wang, H. (2012). Organizational schemata of e-portfolios for fostering higher-order thinking. *Information Systems Frontiers, 14*(2), 395–407. doi:10.1007/s10796-010-9262-0

ADDITIONAL READING

Anderson, J. (2007). *A conceptual framework of a study in preferred learning styles: Pedagogy or andragogy.* Spalding University). *ProQuest Dissertations and Theses,* 189 p. Retrieved from http://search.proquest.com/docview/304736724

Attia, M. (2010). Student teachers' perceptions about the E-portfolio as a performance assessment tool. Paper presented at the 6-X. Retrieved from http://search.proquest.com/docview/869619010

Bossu, C., & Tynan, B. (2011). OERs: New media on the learning landscape. *Horizon, 19*(4), 259–267. doi:10.1108/10748121111179385

Clark, T. (2008). *Exploring culturally responsive andragogy in a community college.* The University of North Carolina at Charlotte). *ProQuest Dissertations and Theses,* Retrieved from http://search.proquest.com/docview/304376869

Johnson, G., Hsieh, P., & Kidwai, K. (2007). Perceived value and persistence of Web publishing skills: Implications for e-portfolio systems. *International Journal on E-Learning, 6*(3), 379–394. Retrieved from http://search.proquest.com/docview/210328448

Norris, L. (2011). *The effects of pedagogy and andragogy instruction on critical thinking skills in higher education.* Walden University). *ProQuest Dissertations and Theses,* Retrieved from http://search.proquest.com/docview/861923130

Wilson, L. (2005). *A test of andragogy in a postsecondary educational setting.* Louisiana State University and Agricultural & Mechanical College). *ProQuest Dissertations and Theses,* 448 p. Retrieved from http://search.proquest.com/docview/304988305?accountid=14068

Zocco, D. (2011). A recursive process model for aacsb assurance of learning. *Academy of Educational Leadership Journal*, *15*(4), 67–91. Retrieved from http://search.proquest.com/docview/887042756

KEY TERMS AND DEFINITIONS

Andragogy: Known as "leading adults" it is a premise that adults learn differently than children. Malcolm Knowles was a pioneering researcher and advocate of the principles of andragogy.

E-Portfolio: A collection of artifacts that provide evidence of someone's professional skills and abilities in a multimedia format. Downloadable or executable.

Portfoliovillage: A Website that provides Web 2.0 tools for creating Web portfolios and Websites on the Internet. A social entrepreneurship project that aims to help people overcome financial and technical obstacles with creating a Website.

Web Portfolio: A collection of artifacts that provide evidence of someone's professional skills and abilities in a multimedia format on the Internet.

Chapter 11
Finding Common Ground:
Uses of Technology in Higher Education

Matthew D. Fazio
Robert Morris University, USA

ABSTRACT

As technology's presence in higher education rises, so does its impact on culture. Scholars with vastly different opinions have written on what they perceive as the place of technology in higher education. This chapter aims at reconciling those differences. Rather than agreeing with one side over the other, this chapter takes its stance using a constructive hermeneutic in a postmodern age: understanding the limited and biased ground of one's own perspective and learning, which is the pragmatic good in a time of difference. Finally, this chapter offers a decision model for educators to evaluate the uses of technology in higher education.

FINDING COMMON GROUND: USES OF TECHNOLOGY IN HIGHER EDUCATION

Technology is present in many higher education courses. With the advent of fully online schools and classes, hybrid courses, and the implementation of presentation technologies during lectures, a typical college student would be hard-pressed to receive a college degree without encountering some of these technologies. Educators, philosophers, and critical theorists have varied views on the subject, usually forming into two large camps: 1.) the people who believe that technological advances are good and we should embrace progress and 2.) the people who believe that technology is stifling education and deteriorating the learning process. This paper aims at reconciling the dichotomy between the two perspectives by providing an alternative view to the uses of technology in higher academics. I will begin with an overview of the debate on technology as an educational tool as it is understood in scholarly literature, focusing on the work of Neil Postman; I will then discuss the role of technology in education as it relates to distance and phenomenology; next, I will champion the concept of a constructive hermeneutic and explain how the philosophical perspective can be implemented in higher academics; and finally, the paper will conclude with a decision model for educators to evaluate the use of technology in higher education.

DOI: 10.4018/978-1-4666-6162-2.ch011

Copyright © 2014, IGI Global. Copying or distributing in print or electronic forms without written permission of IGI Global is prohibited.

THE ROLE OF TECHNOLOGY IN HIGHER EDUCATION

A study completed by Babson College estimated that over 6.1 million students, nearly one-third of all college students, took at least one online course during the fall semester of 2010; this was an increase of over 560,000 students from the previous year (Allen & Seaman, 2011, p. 4). As the number of students taking online-based courses continues to grow, so does the need to be cognizant of the effects of technology in education. The Babson College study also questions the comparable outcomes of face-to-face learning versus online learning. The first report of the study, completed in 2003, found that only fifty-seven percent of academic leaders rated the learning outcomes in online education as the same or superior to those in face-to-face courses. The numbers have slowly but surely increased each year, peaking at sixty-seven percent in 2011(Allen & Seaman, 2011, p. 5). Although the numbers have increased, roughly a third of all participants, based on the responses from more than 2,500 colleges and universities, still believe that online learning is inferior to face-to-face learning. Even as the numbers increase for those in favor of online learning, there are still many professionals who question online learning's legitimacy.

While concerns with online courses are coming to the forefront, concerns with technology in the classroom have been expressed for quite some time. In the early 1980s, Neil Postman saw education's biggest problem as a "rapid changeover to a culture based on the electronic image. He describes the competition between television and schools (a competition the schools are losing) and suggests ways in which educators might best preserve the values of a traditional education" (Postman, 1983, p. 310). Postman had apprehensions about technology and education over 30 years ago. One of Postman's strongest claims is that the "Age of the Electronic Image" brought with it a discontinuous and fragmented curriculum (1983, p. 313). The

technologically-infused classroom has many of the same problems. A 2008 study conducted by Vanhorn, Pearson, and Child identified the major communication challenges of online learning. Among the list of challenges are the transition from a face-to-face classroom to an online class room, technological difficulties, communication issues, and the lack of community.

The lack of student interactivity can also affect the feeling of 'community' in the classroom. Students often feel isolated, as if they are taking an online course by themselves, rather than being part of a learning community in which they can share ideas and experiences with each other. (2008, pp. 33-34)

Much like Postman's "Age of the Electronic Image," the online classroom is creating a fragmented curriculum as the traditional sense of community fades away. Communication is now being mediated by technology, which in turn changes the education process itself.

The future of higher education may be unknown, but online courses are now part of the landscape (The Sloan Consortium, 2007). The question is no longer *if* technology will be a part of higher education, but rather a question of what to do with technology now that it is a part of higher education. Postman attempts to reestablish his scope:

What we need to consider about the computer has nothing to do with its efficiency as a teaching tool. We need to know in what ways it is altering our conception of learning, and how, in conjunction with television, it undermines the old idea of school. (1992, p. 19)

Postman's statement marks a clear distinction between "the old idea of school" and the implied new, technological age. The use of the term "undermines" shows that Postman does not see this shift as a natural change, but rather an eroding of the foundation of education. In his book *Technopoly*,

Postman explains that "Technopoly is a state of culture…it is what happens to society when the defenses against information glut have broken down" (1992, pp. 71-72). Postman, a technological determinist, believes technology for technology's sake is a mistake. Postman's proposed solution to a culture with "rights without responsibilities" is to become a "technological resistance fighter" (1992, p. 185). In the final chapter of his book, Postman asserts that schools should be leading the resistance against the Technopoly:

I have no illusion that such an educational program can bring a halt to the thrust of a technological thought-world. But perhaps it will help to begin and sustain a serious conversation that will allow us to distance ourselves from the thought-world, and then criticize and modify it. (1992, p. 199)

Postman's call to action is a paradigm shift; he is proposing educational systems realize the detriment of technology and fight against its effects. But what are the effects of technology? And, more importantly, are these effects actually negative?

There are many scholars who believe that most of the effects of technology on higher academics have been positive. Specific to distance learning, two scholars of education, Lei and Govra, note that institutions benefit by maximizing their available resources; faculty members have more flexible schedules allowing them to publish essays, and students benefit by completing a degree on their own schedule (2010, pp. 618-620). The sheer convenience of technology is alluring to many potential students. There are many life events that prevent potential students from higher academics: some work full-time jobs, some have children to care for, and some have regular obligations on their time. These people can now choose an online program to attain their degree. Online courses are also taken by traditional students; they are perfect for student-athletes, students with internships, and those who would like to cut down on travel time to classes.

Using technology has become second nature for many people, making a college degree in an online format seem just as natural as a traditional classroom. But make no mistake, there is a difference. Although the degree may still carry the same emblem on the diploma, those who spend fifteen credit hours per week, every week, each semester for four years in a traditional classroom will receive a *different* learning experience than those who utilized distance education. There is an inherent difference in education when distance is involved.

The electronic age has ushered in a globalized world; people from different parts of the world can communicate with little difficulty. Just as the Internet has changed this generation, Johannes Gutenberg changed the world in 1450. Elizabeth L. Eisenstein claims that the printing press was the single most influential piece of technology (circa 1980). Eisenstein observes that the printing press caused a shift from a people assembled to a people dispersed (1980, p. 132). Prior to the printing press, people needed to engage in the community to receive information. People shared information by coming together in the town or other gathering places. Gutenberg's invention allowed for information to be widely accessible and transportable. Harold Innis, a media ecology scholar, makes the observation that space-biased media, media that is less durable but more portable in character, promotes wider reach and area in administration (1950, p. 7). As the media changes, so does the civilization and society around it.

Although they studied different eras, both Eisenstein and Innis came up with similar conclusions: the media and technology that a society uses will in turn shape the society itself. It is interesting to note that they both studied distance in their understanding of new technologies. Both scholars' emphasis on distance is not coincidental; distance is essential to technology's effect on the learning process.

THE ROLE OF DISTANCE IN TECHNOLOGY-BASED EDUCATION

From fully online programs to courses that use technology in the classroom, distance mediates education. The physical distance is important because it changes the perception of the learning. Learning styles have been studied and researched for years. Students' learning styles are known to affect their performance in higher academics (Marriott & Marriott, 2003). Positing that learning styles can affect the performance, the way in which the information is conveyed is then understood differently by each student. Some students may excel in independent reading whereas others are more successful when learning through group discussion.

It is widely accepted that the learning styles of students change the way information is processed and understood. Thus, it can be said that information that is mediated by technology has an effect on students, regardless of whether that effect is positive or negative. The experience of learning is conceptually different for students with different learning styles.

Distance in education, then, is more about how that distance is experienced than its physical nature. Distance is phenomenological. Phenomenology is the study of structures of experience, or consciousness. Literally speaking, phenomenology is the study of phenomena. The way in which education is experienced is just as important as the way in which the education is delivered. This is to say that a person could potentially feel closer in "distance" in a fully online classroom than in a traditional setting.

Education grounded in technology can be useful in many respects. The usefulness of technology is readily apparent. However, the question that continues to be asked remains the same: is distance education as effective as traditional education? It is my understanding that the question remains the problem. To compare traditional education with distance education is comparing proverbial apples and oranges. Education, when mediated by technology, is phenomenologically and fundamentally different. It is within that difference that one can better understand the role of technology in education.

THE CONSTRUCTIVE HERMENEUTIC

Technological determinists who reject technology for its power over society have valid claims, yet they miss the usefulness of technology. On the other hand, those who believe all new technological advances are good are driven by the outdated philosophical movement of modernity -- "modernity's demand for more efficiency, progress and individual autonomy" (Arnett, Fritz & Bell, 2009, 167). Rather than quibble over the two sides and choose which has more compelling claims, it would seem more beneficial to learn from both perspectives. Ronald C. Arnett speaks of something similar to this in Arneson's book, *Exploring Communication Ethics: Interviews with Influential Scholars in the Field*:

I think the primary thing that we need to do is to say as teachers, as educators, that my task is not to destroy someone's ground but to question with my own admitted limitations. That is why I made the move to a constructive hermeneutic that seeks implications; such a position is not naive but is reluctant to assume the modern premise that I can stand above human history and proclaim truth for the misinformed. (2007, p. 61)

Arnett critiques both modernity and deconstructionism. Using a constructive hermeneutic approach means to assess others' perspectives, to question those perspectives, and to provide a constructive implication to the work.

Neil Postman is one of the leading scholars on technology's effects on educational systems. He uses solid scholarly research to ground his claims, and he is an astute cultural critic. While Postman's methodology is sound, it is my understanding that he falls short on his conclusion. To critically question technology is thoughtful; to disregard technological advances is naive. Postman claims that technology "does not invite a close examination of its own consequences" (1992, p. xii). Postman's "resistance fight maintains an epistemological and psychic distance from any technology, so that it always appears somewhat strange, never inevitable, never natural" (p. 185). However, what is to be said for the technological advances that have endured over time? In Plato's *Phaedrus,* the character of Socrates, who has been seen by many as Socrates himself, explains the downfalls of the written word:

(Writing will) introduce forgetfulness into the soul of those who learn it: they will not practice using their memory because they will put their trust in writing, which is external and depends on signs that belong to others, instead of trying to remember from the inside, completely on their own. (1990, pp. 117-118)

It would be difficult for many modern day educators to imagine a world without writing. According to Postman, technology, which includes the written word, should never feel natural. Postman's "absolute" thinking makes it difficult to subscribe to his theoretical position.

Similarly, it seems that those who abide by the religion of technology are a part of a Modernist culture. Modernity is marked by its advantage given to the "new." "Postmodernity finds definition in difference and incommensurability of views of the good" (Arnett, Fritz & Bell, 2009, p. 211). Those who are overindulgent in technological advances are operating in an outdated, unreflective philosophical framework. In a time

difference, a la postmodernity, learning is the pragmatic good. By learning from the Other, we can begin to reconcile these differences. This is not a compromise – each side will not be given equal weight – instead this is an opportunity to become mindful and reflective, not leery and pessimistic.

IMPLICATIONS

So, what does this mean for the aim of this paper? A constructive hermeneutic can be used as a philosophical perspective to best view and understand new technologies. Postman's initial reaction to examine each new technology as it is introduced and then weigh its consequences against its benefits is very intelligent. However, to be critical of something before it is understood is just as illogical as accepting something before it is understood. Postman wages wars against those who believe what is new is automatically better, but his premise that everything that is new is *not* better has the same flawed perspective.

That is why it is necessary to understand the effects of a new technology prior to fully accepting it. There is no doubt that with new technologies come both tremendous advances as well as paralyzing deficiencies. It is the responsibility of educations to understand technology's effects on learning. From a phenomenological perspective, distance education and technology in the classroom are simply different types of learning than traditional classrooms; how that experience is understood can vary from person to person, but is undoubtedly different. The technological classroom is different than the traditional classroom. Instead of attempting to assess which is a more effective form of education, perhaps a constructive hermeneutic can be applied and educators can begin *learning* from both sides.

Having taught fully-online courses, hybrid-courses, and traditional courses, I believe that each use or non-use of technology is important.

Though one pedagogical style may be preferred over another, one cannot discredit the merits of the various styles of teaching.

If one were to stop and think of the evolution of technology in the last twenty years, it would be staggering. Computers, televisions, and cellular devices have changed our culture. With these ever present changes, educators must be aware of technology's implications on the human condition. Postman was a visionary in a number of respects: technology is power; technology has the power to change a society; and educators should take a stand against "rights without responsibilities." However, to disregard technology's advances is myopic.

Although my foundational research is grounded in the work of Neil Postman, I aim to also adopt a constructive hermeneutic to this project. It is our goal as educators to be thoughtful in our uses of technology in the classroom, weighing out the potential effects; we should learn from that which is different, never stagnant, but also hold on to our values and traditions grounded in our personal pedagogical perspectives.

IMPLEMENTATION

To theorize about pedagogy is important, but its implementation is essential. Prior to explaining the decision model, it should be noted that this is simply one way to evaluate the use of technology in the classroom. Again, the good is found in that which one "protects and promotes" (Arnett, Fritz & Bell, 2009, p. 4). This section will include a decision model for educators to evaluate the use of technology in higher education.

The first of the four criteria is proficiency. One recurring issue with technology in higher education is the lack of instructor familiarity with the technologies. Before choosing to implement any form of technology into the classroom, an instructor should first become proficient with the technology. One misnomer is that because an instructor feels confident with the content material of the

class, that person also feels confident explaining that material through technology. When instructors learn on the job with technology training, time is taken away from the actual course material and instead is spent with the instructor learning to work with the technology. Many schools have training programs to ensure the instructor is comfortable using the technology before teaching with the new tools. Instructors should first become proficient with technology prior to using it in the classroom.

After learning how to use a given technology, an instructor should analyze if there is an inherent benefit to using that particular technology in the classroom. Often times, instructors learn to use new tools and implement them into courses immediately without reflecting on the use value. There is no rationale or reflection in the Modernist idea of progress – in this case, that would be technology for technology's sake. To use a new tool simply because it is new is to discredit the old tool simply because it is old. The last few years have provided new technological tools that have been implemented into higher education with amazing benefits: electronic drop boxes are environmentally conscious and allow teachers to provide comments to students' papers directly on the computer; group video chatting enables the online classroom to break distance barriers; and online databases permit for more effective and comprehensive scholarly research. All of these technologies are useful in higher academics; however, that does not mean that all technologies are always useful in higher academics. It is imperative that instructors are mindful of the choices that they make and have clear rationales for implementing a new form of technology.

Just as instructors should be aware of the reasons for using technology in the classroom, they should also be aware of the negative aspects of embracing a new technology. The third criterion is to be mindful of what will be lost and/or changed when using a new tool. Just as Plato's character Socrates was apprehensive of writing for the fear that it would ruin our memory, so should the instructor be apprehensive prior to the implementation a new technological tool. Earlier in this essay, we reviewed Postman's claim that technology "does not invite a close examination of its own consequences" (1992, p. xii). Postman was right. If technology will not examine itself, it is the duty of the instructor, Postman's "resistance fighter," to be aware of the consequences of a new technology. When new technology is adopted and old practices are no longer used, undoubtedly something will be lost. The instructor must determine if the new technology's advances will outweigh what will be lost in the process. An example of this can be seen in word processing systems: now, students rely on word processing programs for spell check and grammar check. By using a word processer, many students will not use their own memory for spelling and proper grammar. However, the reproducibility of a document, the ease of changing mistakes, the ability to submit in an electronic format, and the readability of the writing are all examples of why the advances outweigh the losses. Technology has a way of touting its advances, but omitting its deficiencies. This is precisely why teachers should listen to Postman's call for "resistance fighters" and be mindful of the change technology has on education.

If the first three criteria all align, and an instructor deems the new technology worthy of use, there is still a final step. It is not enough to simply use technology, but rather to use the appropriate technology at the appropriate times. The final portion of the decision model is the appropriateness of technology in the specific situation. Subject matter, class size, complexity of the content, and the type of class are all factors in deciding what type of technology to use. A general education course on U.S. history in a room with 150 students will not call for the same teaching technologies as a doctoral level course on continental philosophy. The instructor must understand the audience prior to choosing the technology. Traditional courses are significantly different from fully online courses, and instructors

will have to change their technology accordingly. Part of this final step comes with experience. The main purpose of this assessment is to be aware that the audience and situation often dictate the use or non-use of technology.

Technology absolutely has a place in higher education; that much is clear. Higher education's landscape will likely continue to change with the advent of new technologies. When new technologies emerge, instructors should follow the decision model from this essay:

1. Instructors should be proficient in using any technology prior to implementing it in a course.
2. Instructors should have a clear rationale for the use of any given technology.
3. Instructors should be conscious of what could potentially be lost by using a new form of technology.
4. Instructors must choose appropriate technological tools for each individual situation.

By following this decision model, instructors will be better prepared to assess technology for higher education classrooms. There is no "correct" way of using technology in education. The use or non-use of technology is chosen on a case by case basis. Each time a new technology emerges, instructors should act as "resistance fighters" by learning and understanding the technology and assessing if it has a place in higher education.

REFERENCES

Allen, I. E., & Seaman, J. (2011). *Going the Distance: Online Education in the United States 2011*. Pearson.

Arneson, P. (2007). *Exploring communication ethics: Interviews with influential scholars in the field*. New York: P. Lang.

Arnett, R. C., Fritz, J. M., & Bell, L. M. (2009). *Communication ethics literacy: Dialogue and difference.* Los Angeles, CA: SAGE Publications.

Eisenstein, E. L. (1980). *The Printing Press as an Agent of Change.* Cambridge, UK: Cambridge University Press. doi:10.1017/CBO9781107049963

Innis, H. A. (2008). *The bias of communication* (2nd ed.). Toronto, Canada: University of Toronto Press.

Lei, S., & Govra, K. (2010). College Distance Education Courses: Evaluating Benefits and Cost from Institutional, Faculty and Students'. *Perspectives in Education, 130*(4), 616–631.

Marriott, N., & Marriott, P. (2003). Student learning style preferences and undergraduate academic performance at two UK universities. *International Journal of Management Education, 3*(1), 4–13.

Phenomenology. (2013). *Stanford Encyclopedia of Philosophy.* Retrieved April 5, 2013, from http://plato.stanford.edu/entries/phenomenology/

Plato, . (1990). Phaedrus. In *The Rhetorical tradition: Readings from classical times to the present.* Boston: Bedford Books of St. Martin's Press.

Postman, N. (1983). Engaging Students in the Great Conversation. *Phi Delta Kappan, 64*(5), 310–316.

Postman, N. (1992). *Technopoly: The surrender of culture of Technology.* New York: Alfred A. Knopf.

Sloan Consortium. (2007). *Making the grade: Online education in the U.S., 2006.* Retrieved April 1, 2013, from http://www.sloan-c.org/publications/survey/index.asp

Vanhorn, S., Pearson, J. C., & Child, J. T. (2008). The Online Communication Course: The Challenges. *Qualitative Research Reports in Communication, 9*(1), 29–36. doi:10.1080/17459430802400332

ADDITIONAL READING

Anderson, R., Cissna, K. N., & Arnett, R. C. (1994). *The reach of dialogue: confirmation, voice, and community.* Cresskill, N.J.: Hampton Press.

Arendt, H. (1958). *The human condition.* Chicago: University of Chicago Press.

Arendt, H. (1963). *Eichmann in Jerusalem, a report on the banality of evil.* New York: Viking Press.

Arnett, R. C., & Arneson, P. (1999). *Dialogic civility in a cynical age community, hope, and interpersonal relationships.* Albany, N.Y.: State University of New York Press.

Bakhtin, M. M. (1993). *Toward a philosophy of the act.* Austin: University of Texas Press.

Callahan, R. E. (1962). *Education and the cult of efficiency, a study of the social forces that have shaped the administration of the public schools.* Chicago: University of Chicago Press.

Ellul, J. (1964). *The technological society* (1st American ed.). New York: Knopf.

Hauser, G. A. (1999). *Vernacular voices: The rhetoric of publics and public spheres.* Columbia: University of South Carolina Press.

Innis, H. A. (2008). *The bias of communication* (2nd ed.). Toronto, Ontario: University of Toronto Press.

Isssroff, K., & Scanlon, E. (2002). Using technology in Higher Education: An Activity Theory perspective. *Journal of Computer Assisted Learning, 18*(1), 77–83. doi:10.1046/j.0266-4909.2001.00213.x

Little, C. A., & Housand, B. C. (2011). Avenues to Professional Learning Online: Technology Tips and Tools for Professional Development in Gifted Education. *Gifted Child Today, 34*(4), 18–27.

Lyotard, J. (1997). *The postmodern condition: a report on knowledge*. Minneapolis: University of Minnesota Press. (Original work published 1979)

McLuhan, M. (1962). *The Gutenberg galaxy: The making of typographic man*. Toronto: University of Toronto Press.

Mumford, L. (1955). *Sticks and stones, a study of American architecture and civilization* (2d rev. ed.). New York: Dover Publications.

Mumford, L. (1962). Technics and civilization (8. impr. ed.). London: Routlege & Kegan Paul.

Ong, W. J. (1982). *Orality and literacy: The technologizing of the word*. London: Methuen. doi:10.4324/9780203328064

Postman, N. (1985). *Amusing ourselves to death: public discourse in the age of show business*. New York: Viking.

Schrag, C. O. (1986). *Communicative praxis and the space of subjectivity*. Bloomington: Indiana University Press.

Veblen, T. (2009). *The theory of the leisure class. Waiheke Island*. Floating Press. (Original work published 1899)

Walters, P., & Kop, R. (2009). Heidegger Digital Technology, and Postmodern Education: From Being in Cyberspace to Meeting on MySpace. *Bulletin of Science, Technology & Society*, *29*(4), 278–286. doi:10.1177/0270467609336305

KEY TERMS AND DEFINITIONS

Constructive Hermeneutic: The method of interpretation that seeks implications through learning with others; this method admits one's own limitations and does not presume to "proclaim the truth for the misinformed" (Ronald Arnett).

Distance Education: Education that takes place away from the traditional classroom; often times related to online courses or hybrid courses.

Human Condition: That which is inherent and innate to human beings (Hannah Arendt and Thomas Hobbes).

Media Ecology: The study of technology in society and the ways in which all forms of media affect human perception, understanding, feeling, and value (Neil Postman, Harold Innis, and Marshall McLuhan).

Postmodernism: A philosophical movement which is a reaction to and reject of Modernism; incommensurability of views of the good (Jean-François Lyotard and Ronald Arnett).

Technological Determinism: The reductionist theory that is driven by the principle that technology influences society (Thorstein Veblen, Neil Postman, and Walter Ong).

Traditional Education: Education taking place in a face-to-face classroom without the use of modern technology.

Chapter 12
Effective Virtual Learning Environment through the Use of Web 2.0 Tools

Huseyin Bicen
Near East University, Cyprus

ABSTRACT

The use of social networking sites and Web 2.0 tools is increasing. Research shows that education via Web 2.0 tools increases students' motivation and their interest in the learning. Therefore, a teaching environment can be created using social networking sites in which Web 2.0 tools allow effective learning. In this chapter, some of the Web 2.0 tools available for effective virtual learning environment creation are examined. Suggestions are provided regarding possible uses of tools such as Classmint, Pinterest, Voki, Screenleap, Pageflip-flap, Youtube, Prezi, Secondlife, Animoto, Sketchfu, and Quizrevolution, and their positive effects on students.

INTRODUCTION

Tablets, smart phones, the Internet and other technologies are increasingly being used in the development of education. Historically, Distance Education has gone through similar periods of development with the use of a variety of communication tools. This development started with physical mailing methods and has continued through the Information Communication Technologies that are being used currently (Newby, Cutright, Barrios & Xu, 2006; Passarini & Granger, 2000). These modern tools include: printed materials, radio, voice tapes, video tapes, television, telephone, fax, video conference, teleconference, computer, the Internet, and e-mail (Koçer, 2001). As these technologies and communication tools have developed, intercontinental sound and video transfers have become simpler and more immediate. The first application of distance education appeared in the second half of 1800s (Tsinakos, 2003); however, the term was only catalogued by Wisconsin University in 1892. In 1906, it was used in a publication by William Lighty, the director of a university (Kaya, 2004).

Despite this extensive history, the term 'distance education' has many definitions. Aşkar (2003) defined distance education as "education

DOI: 10.4018/978-1-4666-6162-2.ch012

Copyright © 2014, IGI Global. Copying or distributing in print or electronic forms without written permission of IGI Global is prohibited.

that is created through some communication technology tools for student, teacher and materials in different places" (Moore & Kearsly, 1996). Briefly, distance education can be defined as teacher(s) and student(s)s in different locations practicing their planned teaching-learning activities through communication technologies (Almogbel, 2002; Scott, 2003; Genç, 2004). Examination of historical distance education programmes show that methods show initial use of mailing, then one-way sound transfer following the invention of radio. In the 1950s, one-way video transfer began to be used as a method after television became widespread in daily life. In 1968 the British Open University was developed as an alternative to traditional education paradigms, and has since served as a model for similar programmes. In 1970s and 1980s newly-developed cable television, closed-circuit television and video conferencing technologies were incorporated into distance education programmes.

Most recently, the rapid improvements in Web technologies have helped to develop Web 2.0 tools and increased their day–to-day use around the world. As a result, resources are required to inform teachers about the Web tools available to them and how they may be used. Many studies have shown that lessons conducted using Web 2.0 tools increase students' motivation and success (Bicen & Uzunboylu, 2013; Cochrane & Bateman, 2010; Hoffman, 2009). This section of this book, Web-based education and the development of Web 2.0 technologies are discussed.

Online Learning

According to Tapanes, Smith and White (2009), online learning technologies increase interpersonal communication and sharing applications through the Internet, irrespective of the distance between participants. 'Online learning' – also known as Web based, Internet based or online learning - is a teaching model that can be carried out over the Internet(Usta, 2007). In online learning, students are able to access educational materials on demand and can be informed about updates instantly.

Chuang and Tsai (2005) stated that online interaction had peaked in the preceding years. In particular, online learning environments have become indispensable for students. Internet usage in distance education provides more advantageous environments for implementing constructivist learning theory (Passerini & Granger, 2000). Allen et al., (2007) emphasized that four model can be used in education: traditional learning, Web based learning, blended learning and online learning.

WEB 1.0 AND WEB 2.0

Nowadays, rapid development and spreading of developments allow Web technologies to be used and improved rapidly and effectively. As a result, Internet users were first able to use Web 2.0 and associated tools in 2004 (O'Reilly Media, 2005). Garcia, Rey, Ferreira and Puerto (2007) have specified the differences between Web 1.0 and Web 2.0 (Table 1). During the era of Web 1.0, users could only read information, share personal information, consume information rather than producing it. Also, passively visiting only the pages they know, students keep information that they learned to themselves due to a lack of sharing opportunities, maintain to content based information and the use of one-way communication.

Web 2.0 users, in contrast, were able to experience a participative Internet environment. Internet users were suddenly able to access blogs, wikis and social networking sites. They had the opportunity to design pages within a site for themselves and to create their own profile pages. After only having a chance to read published pages in the period of Web 1.0, Web 2.0 users had the opportunity to read pages with Web 2.0, design profiles for themselves and share pages through these profiles (McLoughlin & Lee, 2007). As a

Table 1. Difference between Web 1.0 and Web 2.0 (Garcia, Rey, Ferreira & Puerto, 2007)

Web 1.0	Web 2.0
Limiting with group	Sharing with society
Reading	Writing
Sharing personal information	Sharing cooperative information
What did you learn?	How did you learn?
Consumption	Production
Transfer of information	Construction of information
Looking for meaning	Creating meaning
Passive	Active
One to one	Multiple to multiple
Interpersonal	Social Networking
Privacy	Openness
Competitive	Cooperative
Configuration	Social Constructivist
Content based	Tool based
One way communication	Multi way communication
Static pages	Dynamic pages

result of Web 2.0 becoming widespread, its extension into educational use was inevitable. Research was conducted to assess the results of blog, wiki and social networking site usage in education (Johnson, Levine & Smith, 2009).

The usage of Web 2.0 and its tools provides a cooperative Internet environment due to the inherent openness in information sharing, as well as both the reading and sharing of information and the ability to add comments. Multidimensional structures, openness of communication and researcher identity were key developments. Uzunboylu, Bicen and Cavus (2011) also pointed out that individuals can design quality teaching environments using Web 2.0 without having any knowledge of design and/or coding. It has become significantly easier to publish and share multi communication tools, written materials, voice recordings and video images using Web 2.0 tools. As a result, the usage of Web 2.0 and associated social interactions in education has gained importance.

Social Networking Sites

After Web 2.0 was developed, social networking sites emerged as a structure that gave users opportunities to be participative and create their own profile pages. Using these environments, Internet users can establish online friendships their real life friends. In this environment, the user can transfer a variety of multimedia tools using tools in these social networks, and can share Web 2.0 tools in this environment easily (Boyd & Ellison, 2007). Through social networking sites, the users can display events from their lives, show where they are using notifications, and make suggestions by taking photos of the locations they visit. Therefore, participators in Web 2.0 can create a virtual community. Internet users can give feedback by adding a variety of comments as well as 'liking' shared information. Nowadays, Facebook and Twitter are amongst the most used social networks (Alexa, 2013). As a result, a teaching environment can be created using social networking sites and a very effective learning environment can be formed through Web 2.0 tools. Through opening an education page or a group on Facebook, information can be given to students using Web 2.0 tools - and therefore students may be more willing to learn through effective material support. Similarly, by opening a Twitter account, a Web 2.0-based educational environment can be created. By following educators on Twitter, students can access course materials and make learning more entertaining.

Web 2.0 Tools that Can Be Used in Teaching

Along with the many tools developed since the advent of Web 2.0, many researchers show that education delivered through Web 2.0 increases students' motivation and their interest in the course(s). Students can become skilful both at self-expression and problem solving through the tools used in these environments (Uzunboylu, Bicen & Cavus, 2011; Leslie & Landon, 2008).

Web 2.0 tools currently used for educational purposes are as follows:

1. Classmint.com
2. Pinterest.com
3. Voki. com
4. Screenleap.com
5. Pageflip-flap.com
6. Youtube.com
7. Prezi.com
8. Secondlife.com
9. Animoto.com
10. Sketchfu.com
11. Quizrevolution

Classmint

Students can take audible and interactive notes using the Classmint site. Through these notes, an electronic mind map can be formed, meaning that students can learn information more easily and practically using their own methods. This tool can also be used easily by teachers to share information with students and to enable them to understand the delivered courses much better. Classmint notes are formed interactively, thereby facilitating a more fun and long-lasting learning environment. Study notes created through Classmint can further be segregated into separate files including Biology, Mathematics, Foreign Language and Chemistry. Both vocal and written explanations can also be annotated to a particular region of an uploaded picture. Finally, interactive notes created through Classmint can be shared by converting into Word, PDF and PowerPoint presentation formats; they can be used both via the Web and through a mobile application (Classmint, 2014).

Pinterest

With Pinterest students can create 'boards' according to their interests and 'pin' the information they have found. Pinterest can also be used both on the Internet and via a mobile application. Users can pin pictures, videos or documents they have found on the Internet and share their sphere of interest with other users. Thus, they can connect with people interested in the same areas and have a chance to expand their fields of interest. Pinterest is modelled on the board used in classrooms, meaning that boards can be designed about a course's contents and digital board support can be given to students. Furthermore, information drawn from diverse environments can be given in one environment, provided more sources on the course subject for students. Students can be asked to open a Pinterest account for themselves and provide their field of interest as it ties in with a course subject, thereby increasing the students' motivations and interests in the course (Pinterest, 2014).

Voki

Through the Voki site, a virtual teacher avatar can be created and a virtual learning agent established by adding a voice to this avatar. Courses uploaded to the Voki virtual environment can both increase students' motivation and also expand their interest in learning via the Web. Through the avatar - which is chosen according to clarifying - more creative courses can be created and students are encouraged to have more fun. Avatars created through Voki can easily be shared on blogs and social networking Webs.

Along with creating an avatar, Voki classrooms can also be designed. In Voki classrooms, location and character choices can be made, allowing the design of a more interactive and fun classroom environment. A variety of activities can be organized in this virtual classroom and be uploaded to the Voki environment (Voki, 2014).

Screenleap

Screenleap (www.screenlap.com) is a site that provides its users with an opportunity for screen sharing. The Screenleap site gives users the chance to share images on your screen instantly, without any membership. Therefore, any information found on the Internet can be shared with students easily; similarly, information concerning which sources they should use can be delivered instantly. The Screenleap site can be used through every media, and the display image can be shared using a tablet, PC or smart phone (Screenleap, 2014).

Pageflip-Flap

Pageflip-flap (www.pageflip-flap.com) is a site that converts PDF and Word documents into interactive flipbooks. Without requiring any membership, Pageflip-flap site sends user(s) an e-mail after uploading a file and then convert document into a kind of online journal. The Pageflip-flap file can be shared easily on social networking sites. The advantage of this site for courses is that converting course materials by this method allows students to read course notes as they read journals or newspapers, motivating students to read notes about the course (Pageflip-flap, 2014).

Youtube

Youtube is one of the most watched video uploading and sharing sites around the world. Users can create their own video channels which can be used on smart phones and tablets along with mobile applications. With its easy sharing and integration structure, Youtube.com now allows HD videos to be uploaded. Along with having the opportunity to make comments on videos, Youtube allows users to both follow video channels and state whether they liked the video or not. Youtube hosts official channels for several video companies, and is also used as an education tool - videos that were shot about courses can be shared in this environment very easily. Through creating a course video channel, videos can be uploaded to this online environment with the goal of encouraging students to comment on those videos. In addition to this, students can be encouraged to record and

share their own videos about subjects taught in the course(s). Watching of and commenting on these videos by the other students can allow the responsible student to improve the videos they created on the basis of the critical thinking of their peers. As a result, students can improve their critical thinking skills and have an opportunity to develop their creativity. Through their smart phones, teachers can record the course they have taught in a classroom and share using this environment at the end of the course. Therefore, students can repeat the parts that they did not understand in the classroom (Youtube, 2014).

Prezi

Prezi is a new generation method of creating presentations which provides the opportunity to prepare presentations online. It became easier and more fun to add new points of view to the various ideas created through Prezi. The main goal of Prezi is to be creative and facilitate easy addition of new ideas to the presentations prepared therein. When preparing presentations for a course, using Prezi can motivate students when they watch the presentations and, provided they have access to an Internet connection, can allow them to reach presentations created with Prezi wherever they are. Preparation of collaborative presentations can be expected from students when using Prezi in education. Due to the universal accessibility of Prezi, students can prepare presentations collaboratively. Finally, through the option of preparing more creative and idea-oriented presentations through an editor embedded in Prezi, students can develop techniques of preparing presentation more easily (Prezi, 2014).

Second Life

Secondlife (www.secondlife.com) is a site that provides game based learning and helps create a virtual world. In Secondlife.com, teachers and student have the opportunity to create their own avatars which they can bring together in the virtual worlds they have designed and share a variety of information. Designing their own school in this virtual world means that teachers can make students feel like they are in a school environment. In this virtual school the teacher can give a lecture as if they are in a real classroom; when the teacher asks a question, students can give answers in real time. In this virtual environment, which almost completely reflects real life, various documents and videos found on the Internet can be shared. By creating several study rooms, students can also be expected to develop projects in small groups and present these projects in the classroom environment. An approach such as this allows the students to learn while having fun, to increase their interest in the course and to develop their creativity due to feeling like they are in a game. As this environment helps students to communicate with each other and plan various events, it also helps them to work collaboratively and allows students to feel like they belong to the environment. Along with the opportunities for organization, planning and imagination development, Second Life is a tool that teachers can use to teach in a fun way through various multimedia supports on the Internet (Second Life, 2014).

Animoto

Animoto is a tool that allows creation of video animations from static pictures. Animoto is a tool through which stories can be told using a combination of pictures found on the Internet or images captured with smart phones. Animoto has can be used as a mobile application and a Web tool, especially in giving history lessons. Through this tool, teachers can easily share the animation they have created about a lesson they want to give either in the classroom or in a virtual learning environments. Animoto, which can be supported with various background images and sound files, can be used as an effective tool for teaching students (Animoto, 2014).

Sketchfu

Sketchfu (www.sketchfu.com) site is an online version of the whiteboard found in a traditional classroom environment. Through this whiteboard, which has drawing tools, students can develop electronic drawing skills and share their drawings with their friends. Moreover, teachers can use this board during giving a lecture (Sketchfu, 2014).

Quizrevolution

With Quizrevolution, multimedia based questions can be delivered to students. To ask questions, text, video and sound files can all be used simultaneously. In particular, the key concepts in a course can be delivered to students through various video supports and students can be expected to test themselves. Because of its multimedia basis, Quizrevolution can draw students' attention and increase their eagerness to learn. Students can also create their own questions and share them on social networking sites, thereby helping their friends to learn. In order to transfer cultural information and increase the skill of research, students can be expected to conduct research on a specific subject and share the questions they have developed on social networks that they have created about this subject. Therefore, student will be more knowledgeable about this issue and learn techniques of research and question development (Quizrevolution, 2014).

Recommendations

Technology is developing everyday; the result of educational Web 2.0 tool development is the need for relevant information. Therefore, this chapter discusses how we can use the various Web 2.0 tools for educational purposes. The use of Web 2.0 provides many educational teaching tools. It is hoped that this section has shown some of the most important ones that can be used effectively. Nowadays, the ubiquitous use of Facebook and

Twitter, the straightforward sharing of Web 2.0 tools in this environment and the accessibility of these tools via mobile technologies have removed many of the boundaries in education. For this reason, if Web 2.0 tools specified in this chapter are used as a support for courses of education, positive effects on students' learning can be achieved.

With a group on the Facebook social networking site, communication between students can be strengthened and their interest in courses can be increased. Through the Classmint.com Web 2.0 tool - which can be used within the Facebook group environment - students can understand and remember concepts more easily. Furthermore, with Pinterest.com site they can share things about their field of interest, thereby strengthening communication with other students in the same field of interest and inspiring their friends. Virtual agents created through Voki.com can increases students' interest in a course; in particular, students having difficulties in pronunciation in learning a language can find this tool to be a motivator for them. Screenleap.com, on the other hand, can be used particularly effectively in software teaching where teachers can guide students by capturing screen images. With written materials converted to journal format through Pageflip-flap, students can feel like they are reading a current magazine, increasing their interest in the course. Moreover, for the new generation accustomed to using tablets and smart phones, reading this type of written material will be more comfortable and familiar. Along with taking advantage of many videos in Youtube.com site, students can be expected to record new videos, and in the process learn how to create a product step by step. As a result of problems they face while producing a video, students will learn skills in problem solving. Presentations created with Prezi.com site will make students more focused on ideas, consequently providing students with opportunities to create new ideas and improve their self-critical skills. The fact that students can develop presentation collaboratively through Prezi is advantageous in that these presentations will be universally accessible. Therefore, students can learn how to distribute tasks and develop collaborative experience. With the design of virtual classrooms through Secondlife.com, students can have fun while learning, feel like they are in the real world and strengthen communication with their friends. Furthermore, as use of Secondlife is a game based learning method, students will feel like they are obliged to complete tasks in a computer game and will learn to compete with their friends. Through the tool that is offered by Animoto.com, students can create animations from the pictures they took for their research subject and develop their skills in writing a story. As a result, students will improve their skills in scenario development and storytelling. In addition to this, Sketchfu.com allows students to develop their drawing skills in a digital environment and to create ideas about the subjects they want to share with their friends using drawing tools. Finally, through multiple questioning techniques available on the Quizrevolution.com site and its use of multimedia, student can answer tests about the subject as if they were on a quiz show, increasing their eagerness to learn.

CONCLUSION AND FUTURE STUDIES

According to a number of recent studies, a positive effect on students can be seen when Web 2.0 tools and social networks are used together. (Bicen & Uzunboylu, 2013, Mokobane, 2011, Golder, Wilkinson, & Huberman, 2007, Stutzman, 2006, Educause, 2006). In this chapter, some of the Web 2.0 tools are described in order to inform the creation of the most effective virtual learning environments. These tools are described in the order in which they allow students to have fun and develop their creativeness. Given that modern students have either smartphones or tablets; students can use various tools with state-of-the-art technology. As a result, while teaching several fictionalized tasks should be given to students for developing their creativity, and tools should be used that will support collaborative learning studies. Classmint, Pinterest, Voki, Screenleap, Pageflip-flap, You-tube, Prezi, Secondlife, Animoto, Sketchfu and Quizrevolution are all Web 2.0 tools that can easily operate within social networking sites. Further studies will focus on how mobile applications can be used for educational purposes.

REFERENCES

Alexa. (2013). *Top 500 Global Sites*. Retrieved October 5, 2013 from http://www.alexa.com/topsites

Allen, V. G. Heitschmidt & Sollenberger. (2007). Grazing systems and strategies. Academic Press.

Almogbel, A. N. (2002). *Distance Education in Saudi Arabia: Attitudes and Perceived Contributions of Faculty, Students and Administrators in Technical Collage*. (Unpublished Ph.D. Thesis). University of Pittsburgh, Pittsburgh, PA.

Animoto. (2014). *Animoto Web Site*. Retrieved January 13, 2014, from http://animoto.com

Aşkar, P. (2003). *Uzaktan Eğitim Teknolojileri ve TCMB'de Teknoloji Destekli Bilgisayar Eğitimi Konferansı*. Ankara.

Bicen, H., & Uzunboylu, H. (2013). The Use of Social Networking Sites in Education: A Case Study of Facebook. *Journal of Universal Computer Science*, *19*(5), 658–671.

Boyd, D. M., & Ellison, N. B. (2007). Social network sites: Definition, history, and scholarship. *Journal of Computer-Mediated Communication*, *13*(1), 210–230. doi:10.1111/j.1083-6101.2007.00393.x

Chuang, S.-C., & Tsai, C.-C. (2005). Preferences toward the constructivist internet-based learning environments among high school students in Taiwan. *Computers in Human Behavior*, *21*(1), 255–272. doi:10.1016/j.chb.2004.02.015

Classmint. (2014). *Classmint Web Site*. Retrieved January 13, 2014, from http://classmint.com

Cochrane, T., & Bateman, R. (2010). Smartphones give you wings: Pedagogical affordances of mobile Web 2.0. *Australasian Journal of Educational Technology*, *26*(1), 1–14.

Educause (2006). Seven Things you should know about Facebook. *Educause learning initiative*. Retrieved September 22, 2013 from http://net.educause.edu/ir/library/pdf/ELI7017.pdf

García, M. R., Rey, I. G., Ferreira, P. B., & Puerto, G. D. (2007). *University 2.0 - How well are teachers and students prepared for Web 2.0 best practices*. Paper presented at MICTE 2009. Lisbon, Portugal.

Genç, Ö. (2004). *Uzaktan Eğitimde Alternatif Yaklaşımlar, Bilişim Teknolojileri Işığında Eğitim Kongresi ve Sergisi*. Bildiriler Kitabı.

Golder, S. A., Wilkinson, D., & Huberman, B. A. (2007). *Rhythms of social interaction: Messaging within a massive online network*. Paper presented at the 3rd International Conference on Communities and Technologies (CT2007). Academic Press.

Hoffman, E. (2009). Social media and learning environments: Shifting perspectives on the locus of control. *Education*, *15*(2).

Johnson, B., & McClure, R. (2004). Validity and Reliability of a Shortened, Revised Version of the Constructivist Learning Environment Survey (CLES). *Learning Environments Research*, *7*(1), 65–80. doi:10.1023/B:LERI.0000022279.89075.9f

Kaya, N. (2004). Sezgilerimiz ve Takıntılarımız. *Sistem Yayıncılık, 2*.

Koçer, H. E. (2001). *Web Tabanlı Uzaktan Eğitim, Yayınlanmış Yüksek lisans Tezi, Selçuk Üniversitesi, Fen bilimleri Enstitüsü*, Konya.

Leslie, S., & Landon, B. (2008). *Social software for learning: What is it, why use it?* The Observatory.

McLoughlin, C., & Lee, W. J. M. (2007). *Social software and participatory learning: Pedagogical choices with technology affordances in the web 2.0 era*. Academic Press.

Mokobane, S. (2011). The academic engagement of intellectually challenged learners in inclusive schools: A case study. *Cypriot Journal of Educational Sciences*, *6*(2), 83–90.

Moore, M. G., & Kearsley, G. (1996). *Distance education: A systems view*. Wadsworth Publishing Company.

Newby, B. M. Z., Cutright, T., Barrios, C. A., & Xu, Q. (2006). Zosteric acid-an effective antifoulant for reducing fresh water bacterial attachment on coatings. *Journal of Coatings Technology and Research*, *3*(1), 69–76. doi:10.1007/s11998-006-0007-4

O'Reilly. (2005). *What is web 2.0?* Retrieved April 23, 2013 from http://www.oreillynet.com/pub/a/oreilly/tim/news/2005/09/30/what-is-Web-20.html

Pageflip-Flap. (2014). *Pageflip-flap Web Site*. Retrieved January 13, 2014, from http://pageflip-flap.com

Passerini, K., & Granger, M. J. (2000). A Developmental Model For Distance Learning Using The Internet. *Computers & Education*, *34*(1), 1–15. doi:10.1016/S0360-1315(99)00024-X

Pinterest. (2014). *Pinterest Web Site*. Retrieved January 13, 2014, from http://pinterest.com

Prezi. (2014). *Prezi Web Site*. Retrieved January 13, 2014, from http://prezi.com

Quizrevolution. (2014). *Quizrevolution Web Site*. Retrieved January 13, 2014, from http://quizrevolution

Scott, B. G. (2003). *Faculty Attitudes Toward Residential and Distance Learning: A Case Study in Instructional Mode Prefences Among Theological Seminary Faculty*. (Unpublished Ph.D. Thesis). University of North Texas.

Screenleap. (2014). *Screenleap Web Site*. Retrieved January 13, 2014, from http://screenleap.com

Secondlife. (2014). *Secondlife Web Site*. Retrieved January 13, 2014, from http://secondlife.com

Sketchfu. (2014). *Sketchfu Web Site*. Retrieved January 13, 2014, from http://sketchfu.com

Stutzman, F. (2006). *An evaluation of identity-sharing behavior in social network communities*. Paper presented at the iDMAa and IMS Code Conference. Oxford, OH.

Tapanes, M. A., Smith, G. G., & White, J. A. (2009). Cultural diversity in online learning: A study of the perceived effects of dissonance in levels of individualism/collectivism and tolerance of ambiguity. *The Internet and Higher Education*, *12*(1), 26–34. doi:10.1016/j.iheduc.2008.12.001

Tsinakos, A.A. (2003). Asynchronous distance education: Teaching using case based reasoning. *Turkish Online Journal of Distance Education*, *4*(3).

Usta, E. (2007). *Harmanlanmış Öğrenme ve Çevrimiçi Öğrenme Ortamlarının Akademik Başarı ve Doyuma Etkisi*. Gazi Üniversitesi, Eğitim Bilimleri Enstitüsü.

Uzunboylu, H., Bicen, H., & Cavus, N. (2011). The efficient virtual learning environment: A case study of web 2.0 tools and windows live spaces. *Computers & Education*, *56*(3), 720–726. doi:10.1016/j.compedu.2010.10.014

Voki. (2014). *Voki Web Site*. Retrieved January 13, 2014, from http://voki.com

Youtube. (2014). *Youtube Web Site*. Retrieved January 13, 2014, from http://youtube.com

ADDITIONAL READING

Ajjan, H., & Hartshorne, R. (2008). Investigating faculty decisions to adopt Web 2.0 technologies: Theory and empirical tests. *The Internet and Higher Education*, *11*(2), 71–80. doi:10.1016/j.iheduc.2008.05.002

Alexander B. (2008), Web 2.0 and emergent multiliteracies. Theory Into Practice, 47(2), 150-160. Retrieved November 22, 2013, from10.1080/00405840801992371

Anderson, P. (2007) What is Web 2.0? Ideas, technologies and implications for education, Bristol: JISC, http://www.jisc.ac.uk/media/documents/techwatch/tsw0701b.pdf

Benson, V. (2008). Perceptions of trust and experience. Potential barriers to Web 2.0-based learning. *International Journal of Knowledge and Learning*, *4*(5), 427–437. doi:10.1504/IJKL.2008.022061

Bicen, H., & Uzunboylu, H. (2013). The Use of Social Networking Sites in Education: A Case Study of Facebook. *Journal of Universal Computer Science*, *19*(5), 658–671.

Boulos, M., & Wheeler, S. (2007). The emerging Web 2.0 social software: An enabling suite of sociable technologies in health and health care education. *Health Information and Libraries Journal*, *24*(1), 2–23. doi:10.1111/j.1471-1842.2007.00701.x PMID:17331140

Boulos, M. N. K., Maramba, I., & Wheeler, S. (2006). Wikis, blogs and podcasts: A new generation of Web-based tools for virtual collaborative clinical practice and education. *BMC Medical Education*, *6*(41). PMID:16911779

Bower, M., Hedberg, G. J., & Kuswara, A. (2010). A framework for Web 2.0 learning design. *Educational Media International*, *47*(3), 177–198. doi:10.1080/09523987.2010.518811

Boyd, D. M., & Ellison, N. B. (2007). Social network sites: Definition, history, and scholarship. *Journal of Computer-Mediated Communication*, *13*(1), 210–230. doi:10.1111/j.1083-6101.2007.00393.x

Cochrane, T., & Bateman, R. (2010). Smartphones give youwings: Pedagogical affordances of mobile Web 2.0. *Australasian Journal of Educational Technology*, *26*(1), 1–14.

Collis, B., & Moonenb, J. (2008). Web 2.0 tools and processes in higher education: quality perspectives. Educational Media International. 45(2). 93 106.

Ellison, N., & Wu, Y. (2008). Blogging in the classroom: A preliminary exploration of student attitudes and impact on comprehension. *Journal of Educational Multimedia and Hypermedia*, *17*(1), 99–122.

García, M. R., Rey, I. G., & Ferreira, P. B. ve Puerto, G. D (2007). University 2.0 - How well are teachers and students prepared for Web 2.0 best practices, MICTE 2009, Lisbon, Portugal.

Hew, K. F. (2011). Students' and teachers' use of Facebook. *Computers in Human Behavior*, *27*(2), 662–676. doi:10.1016/j.chb.2010.11.020

Hoffman, E. (2009). Social media and learning environments.Shifting perspectives on the locus of control.in education, *15*(2).

Hung, H., & Yuen, S. (2010). Educational use of social networking technology in higher education. *Teaching in Higher Education*, *15*(6), 703–714. doi:10.1080/13562517.2010.507307

Liaw, S. S., Chen, G. D., & Huang, H. M. (2008). Users' attitudes toward Web-based collaborative learning systems for knowledge management. *Computers & Education*, *50*(3), 950–961. doi:10.1016/j.compedu.2006.09.007

Maloney, E. (2007). What Web 2.0 can teach us about learning? *The Chronicle of Higher Education*, *25*(18).

Meyer, K. A. (2010). A comparison of Web 2.0 tools in a doctoral course. *The Internet and Higher Education*, *13*(4), 226–232. doi:10.1016/j.iheduc.2010.02.002

O'Reilly. (2005). What is web 2.0? Retrieved April 23, 2013 from http://www.oreillynet.com/pub/a/oreilly/tim/news/2005/09/30/what-is-Web-20.html

Santarosa, L., Conforto, D., & Machado, R. P. (2014). Whiteboard: Synchronism, accessibility, protagonism and collective authorship for human diversity on Web 2.0. *Computers in Human Behavior*, *31*(1), 91–601.

Shen, A., Lee, M., Cheung, C., & Chen, H. (2010). Gender differences in intentional social action: We-intention to engage in social network-facilitated team collaboration. *Journal of Information Technology*, *25*(2), 152–169. doi:10.1057/jit.2010.12

Su, A. Y. S., Yang, S. H., Hwang, W. Y., & Zhang, J. (2010). A Web 2.0-based collaborative annotation system for enhancing knowledge sharing in collaborative learning environments. *Computers & Education*, *55*(2), 752–766. doi:10.1016/j.compedu.2010.03.008

Sykes, J., Oskoz, A., & Thorne, S. L. (2008). Web 2.0, Synthetic Immersive Environments, and Mobile Resources for Language Education. *CALICO Journal*, *25*(3), 528–546.

Thompson, J. (2008). Don't be afraid to explore Web 2.0. *Education Digest*, *74*(4), 19–22.

Uzunboylu, H., Bicen, H., & Cavus, N. (2011). The efficient virtual learning environment: A case study of web 2.0 tools and windows live spaces. *Computers & Education*, *56*(3), 720–726. doi:10.1016/j.compedu.2010.10.014

KEY TERMS AND DEFINITIONS

Blended Learning: Face-to-face and online learning methods are conducted in courses.

Online Learning: Online media training performed in a synchronous format.

Social Networking Sites: Which occurs with Web 2.0 tools users, can communicate each other with profile page on the social networking site by creating a virtual network.

Virtual Classroom: A variety of online courses carried out with Web tools virtual classroom environment.

Web 2.0: People can communicate with one another to strengthen; photos, videos and documents without knowing any coding knowledge can share the new generation Web technology in different environments.

Chapter 13

Technology Integration in the Classroom:
Report of an Asynchronous Online Discussion among a Group of Nigerian Graduate Students

Adekunle Olusola Otunla
University of Ibadan, Nigeria

Joshua Odunayo Akinyemi
University of Ibadan, Nigeria

ABSTRACT

Increased access to ICT tools and resources has provided opportunities for learning technologies. This chapter focuses on classroom integration of social media among a group of Nigerian graduate students using asynchronous online discussion. The study involved an intact class of 33 participants who were engaged in a threaded discussion for a period of 14 weeks at the College of Medicine, University of Ibadan. A duly validated instrument with reliability co-efficient of 0.85 was used, and data collected were analysed using frequencies and percentages. Results revealed high competency level among the majority (84.8%) in checking, composing, and sending e-mail. Participants were actively engaged in AOD during the period, even though access to the Internet by the majority (63.6%) was through the commercial cyber cafes. The majority (66.7%) actively participated in the AOD, and their opinion was predominantly positive about the perceived impact of AOD. A major barrier to their participation in AOD is limited access to computer and Internet facilities. Therefore, the authors recommend provision of ICT infrastructure within the learning and on-campus residential environments by university administrators for cheaper and unrestricted technology access and that lecturers should become more proactive in technology-driven teaching.

DOI: 10.4018/978-1-4666-6162-2.ch013

Copyright © 2014, IGI Global. Copying or distributing in print or electronic forms without written permission of IGI Global is prohibited.

INTRODUCTION

Products and services provided by the telecommunication industry is making a lot of impact in the way and means by which people communicate and socialize using diverse social networking and media platform such as e-mail communications; listserves, mailing list, media such as Facebook, Twitter, among other emerging platforms. Uses of these ranges of platforms are found to be common among university students. These technologies are adaptable and applicable through curriculum integration especially, in form of blended learning delivery systems and or collaborative learning. It implies that online communication and social media platforms could be converted to instructional advantages and serves the purpose of supplementing classroom and teacher-students interactions.

Furthermore, computer-based interactions as become part of global trends in professional development programmes and recruitment for employment. Therefore, it is imperative for graduate students to become familiar with related skills that can prepare them for such technology-driven environment in preparation for work life. Arguably, modern day professional development depends more on computers and other forms of information technologies for appropriate integration in a variety of fields including law (Tebo, 2000), education (Moore, 2002) and even among government workers (Saunders, 2003).

Ruhleder and Michael (2000) state that benefits of online collaboration include reflection and peer feedback. Reflection according to Moon (1999) is 'a mental process with purpose and / or outcome in which manipulation of meaning is applied to relatively complicated or unstructured ideas in learning or to problems for which there is no obvious solution'. Peer feedback is closely related to peer learning which refers to getting responses from contemporaries of the same status in forms of feedback for cross fertilization of ides on issues relating to their learning. Online learning impacts

the learning process by improving socialization skills among students, as well as enhancing critical thinking; it also increases learners' motivation and engagement in learning and education and constitute a potent tool for effective delivery of quality higher education (Jegede, 2002; Mavers, 2005; Okebukola, 2005). Mobile technologies such as tablets, personal digital assistants (PDAs), mobile and smart phones, iPods and Androids are particularly motivating, and allow for greater flexibility in teaching, with teachers taking advantage of the mobility of the technology to move outside the classroom thereby, ensuring overall students' satisfaction and perceived learning which have a positive effect on the quantity and frequency of participation. (Starkey, 2006; Mellar, 2007)

Asynchronous online discussion (AOD) according to McInnerney and Robert (2004) is a form of collaborative or cooperative learning whereby learners or participants relates together using the electronic platform to communicate, consult and contribute. Asynchronicity connote 'non-real time' as against synchronicity meaning 'real time'. The terms 'collaborative' and 'cooperative' are often used interchangeably, the term collaborative learning is a learning method that implies "working in a group of two or more to achieve a common goal, while respecting each individual's contribution to the whole." It has been argued that incorporating well-planned collaborative activities into online learning benefits students, since higher order thinking skills are more likely to be generated (Schultz, 2003).

Hron and Friedrich (2003) postulates that online learning environments equipped with communicative technologies bring about improvement on collaboration in an asynchronous manner, but with a caution that computer-mediated communications puts other demands on participants or group members. Hron and Friedrich (2003) indicated that these demands require that participants or group members should;

- Have access to computer and the Internet resources,
- Possess some identifiable skills; such as social skills including emotional stability to work within the team,
- Possess effective use of communication skills, and
- Possess computer proficiency skills such as keyboarding, word processing, text formatting and editing skills using conventional software applications.

These set of skills are to ensure active participation of member's in the asynchronous online discussion group. More specifically, Mcmillan (1996) identified the following computer competencies or "operational" abilities which are identifiable as part of computer literacy. It includes the ability of individual to:

- Use word processing software, an e-mail and a browser for Internet navigation.
- Register or of download information on external saving unit, so as to recuperate and print it elsewhere.

Adoption refers to technology use by end-users or the decision to purchase technology. According to Rogers (1983), adoption is "a decision to make full use of an innovation as the best course of action available, while rejection is "a decision not to adopt an innovation." Innovativeness according to Rogers (1983) is the extent to which an individual or other unit of adoption is relatively more eager in adopting new ideas than the other members of a system. There is increased awareness and interest to integrate Internet - based and online courses into higher education teaching and instruction; such that universities and training organisations have adopted new technologies in an attempt to improve their performance and adapt to new teaching and technology-driven learning environments (Helmi, 2002; Damoense, 2003; Holahan, Aronson, Jurkat and Schoorman, 2004; Rosenberg, 2004).

STATEMENT OF PROBLEM

Traditional course delivery system is still prevalent in higher institutions in Nigeria; it suffices to conclude that face-to-face teaching is predominantly and widely practised among University teachers in Nigeria. Moreover, use of social media and online mobile networking services is a common practice among university students in Nigeria, but these services are used basically and mostly for socialization and non-academic communications within and among students. Therefore, this study examines graduate students' mode of accessibility to computer/Internet, students' computer skills and level of participation in an asynchronous online discussion (AOD) forum as a technology integration strategy in higher education in Nigeria.

PURPOSE OF THE STUDY

The purpose of the study is to; examines graduate students' mode of accessibility to computer/Internet, access graduate students' computer skills and determine graduate students' level of participation in an asynchronous online discussion (AOD) forum.

RESEARCH QUESTIONS

The followings are the research questions that will be answered in this study:

1. Do graduate students possess the required computer skills to actively participate in the asynchronous online discussion?

2. What is the mode of gaining access to use of computer and Internet resources by graduate students?

3. What is the level of participation of graduate students' in the asynchronous online discussion?

4. What is the opinion of graduate students' about the impact of asynchronous online discussion?

5. What is the major barrier to graduate students' participation in the asynchronous online discussion?

METHODOLOGY

Research Design

The study employs ex-post facto research design because; no variable will be manipulated as they have already taken place and inferences will be made from the data collected. Because of the need to create an online environment for electronic interaction during the period, an asynchronous online discussion group was created on the Yahoo! Groups. Yahoo! Groups is one of the world's largest collections of online discussion boards. The term 'Groups' refers to Internet communication which is a hybrid between an electronic mailing list and threaded Internet forum. In other words, group messages can be read and posted by e-mail or on the Groups Web page like a Web forum. Groups can be created with public or member-only access. Some groups are mainly announcement bulletin boards, to which only the Group moderators can post, while others are discussion forums.

The AOD was a member-only with the name 'hpe702avtec@yahoogroup.com'. The group e-mail was created with the combination of course code and the abbreviation of the course title i.e. 'Audiovisual Media Technology in Health Promotion' on the Yahoo Groups Home page. Yahoo group was adopted as the platform based on an initial baseline survey carried out within the targeted group and for ease of technology use in completing the asynchronous online group assignments. A moderator was appointed who invited class members to the forum and made initial postings through participants' e-mail addresses. The participants were engaged in a threaded discussion that was centred on the course content, assignment and emerging issues in media use in community health interventions in relation to health promotion and education. The discussion lasted for a period of approximately fourteen weeks (October, 012 – January, 2013) during the second semester of 2011 / 2012 academic session at the college of medicine, University of Ibadan.

Sample and Sampling Technique

The study employed purposive sampling technique with an intact class of thirty-three participants comprising of 16 males (48.5%) and 17 females (51.5%). Majority (69.7%) of the participants are below 30 years. The participants' academic first degrees cut across applied sciences, medical and health science and social sciences.

Instrument for Data Collection

A self-reported instrument designed by the first author was used to collect data. Apart from the participants' demographic data, the instrument consisted of closed and open-ended questions on computer / ICT competencies, mode of Internet access, as well as level of engagement in, and barrier to participation in the asynchronous online discussion. Participants' opinion about the impact of the AOD forum was also sampled. The pilot-tested instrument was validated and its consistency and reliability was tested using Cronbach Alpha which yielded reliability co-efficient of 0.85. The authors later reviewed the items on the instrument in line with the findings from the pilot testing. Furthermore, group activities and postings were tracked using online discussion transcripts.

Table 1. Graduate students' computer and ICT skills

Computer /ICT skills and competencies	Highly Competent No %	Slightly Competent No %	Not Competent No %
Typing and formatting documents on MS Word and MS Power Point.	25 (75.8)	6 (18.2)	2 (6.1)
Checking, composing and sending e-mail	28 (84.8)	4 (18.1)	1 (3.0)
Web browsing, downloading and saving document on any external storage devices	26 (78.8)	6 (18.1)	1 (3.0)

Data Collection

The first author taught the course 'Audiovisual Media Technology in Health' (HPE 702) to a total of thirty-three Masters in Public Health (MPH) class, during the 2011/2012 academic session. Face-to-face teaching and interaction was predominantly used during the previous sessions, but AOD was introduced as a form of blended learning approach. At the end of the semester, the pilot-tested questionnaire was administered to the students. The first author also provided guidance to the participants before responding to the instrument. Data collected from the participants were analysed and interpreted by the second author using frequency counts and percentages.

FINDINGS

Research Questions 1: Do graduate students possess the required computer and ICT skills to actively participate in the asynchronous online discussion?

Table 1 shows that high competency rating was recorded among the majority of the participants (84.8%) in checking, composing and sending e-mail communication. Web browsing, downloading and saving document on any external storage devices also recorded high competency level (78.8%) and typing and formatting documents (75.8%).

Research Questions 2: What is the mode of gaining access to use of computer and Internet resources by graduate students?

Table 2 shows that mode of access to computer and Internet use by the majority of the participants is mainly through the school or commercial cyber cafes (63.6%).

Research Questions 3: What is the level of participation of graduate students' in the asynchronous online discussion?

Surprisingly, Table 3 shows that majority (66.7%) of the graduate students (i.e. total percentages of participants with two, four and five postings) actively participated in the asynchronous online discussion. This findings is not in congruence with the high level of competencies (84.8%) recorded by participants in checking, composing and sending e-mail which is a pre-requisite skill for

Table 2. Graduate students' mode of access to computer and internet resources

Computer and Internet Resources	No	%
Gain access to Computer / Internet use via School /Public cyber café.	21	(63.6)
Gain access to Computer / Internet use via personal ownership and subscriptions	12	(36.4)

Table 3. Graduate students' Participation in the asynchronous online discussion

Frequencies of Participants' Posting During the Asynchronous Online Discussion	No %
Nil	9 (27.3)
Once	1 (3.0)
Two Postings	10 (30.3)
Three postings	0 (0)
Four postings	7 (21.2)
Five posting	5 (15.2)

the discussion forum (see Table 1). Therefore, to further answer research question three effectively on participants' level of engagement and participations. Group activities of members' postings were tracked using online discussion transcripts. Typical examples of the posting extracted from the participants' transcripts are presented as follows:

Posting on Multimedia Use Among Low Literate People

Subject: [hpe702avtec] Multimedia Equipment Use Among Low Literate People

Dear colleagues, let me share my little concern with you on the above subject, recently I was going to deliver a talk to a group of low literate people and I thought it would be good to make use of projector to deliver the talk: the idea is to show them some images but at a stage I realize pictures alone would not be enough because I may not have all the time to explain the message I intend to pass across that which prompted the use of a particular picture, the need to add some text, the issue here is that how effective and efficient do you consider the use of multimedia (precisely power point) among low literate audience? Remember that they are low literate and some could at least read while others could not read at all. They can get distracted easily because the technology is new to them. The messages have to be in local

language. There is the issue of culture and religion etc. Thanking you in advance for your comments.

The above transcript is one of the participants' contributions to the discussion on use of multimedia equipment among low literate people. Media intervention is a basic requirement for health promotion and education in the communities where the graduate students are expected to carry out some of their practicals. Similar transcripts were analysed to ascertain participants' involvement in the AOD.

Posting on Announcement to Participate in Health Certification Course

Subject: [hpe702avtec] Global health e learning Centre

Hello Colleagues,

This is to again remind us about the Global health e learning Centre that was shared with us some time ago. Try and log on and take some courses. I have done mine and I have my certificate now. I took a course on 'Data Quality'. You only need internet for like 3 to 4 hrs at most. The programme is being run by the United states Agency for International Development in collaboration with the John Hopkins University. That is to say I now have a certificate bearing John Hopkins too. You can have yours too.

Cheers!

The above transcript represents one other useful information on opportunities, resources, tools and announcements that was posted to participants on online during the threaded discussion.

Research Questions 4: What is the opinion of graduate students' about the impact of asynchronous online discussion?

Table 4. Graduate students' opinion about the impact of asynchronous online discussion

Opinion	High No %	Medium No %	Low No %
Opportunity for collaboration with my fellow Students Colleagues and Lecturers?	20 (60.6)	7 (21.2)	3 (9.1)

Majority of the participants (60.6%) rated the impact of asynchronous online discussion as high as platform tor collaboration among themselves and their lecturer (Table 4).

Research Questions 5: What is the major barrier to graduate students' participation in the asynchronous online discussion?

Table 5 reveals that major barrier to participants on asynchronous online discussion is limited access to computer and Internet facilities (42.4%) while lack of knowledge (42.4%) and time (39.4%) are rated as minor barriers by the graduate students. Majority (72.7%) are highly interested in the asynchronous online discussion forum and supplementary to face-to-face teaching.

DISCUSSION

Findings from this study revealed that participants in this study are capable of integrating asynchronous online discussion (AOD) as supplementary to face-to-face classroom interactions. They are equally interested in using the platform as a form of blended learning, this is in line with the reports

of Helmi (2002); Damoense (2003); Holahan, Aronson, Jurkat and Schoorman (2004); Rosenberg (2004) whose findings focussed on increased awareness, interest in Internet / online courses and adaptation to new teaching and learning environments in higher education; teaching and instruction. It also supports Mellar (2007) who postulated that mobile learning technologies is particularly motivating, and enable greater flexibility in teaching, with teachers taking advantage of the mobility of the technology to move outside the classroom. Thus, University lecturers should become innovative in integrating social media and mobile networking to their teaching activities.

CONCLUSION

Findings of this study have no doubt established the fact that electronic communication and other mobile media devices that are being used largely for non-academic purposes by graduate students could be integrated into the classroom as learning tools. It implies that online communication and social media platforms could be converted to instructional advantages and serves the purpose of supplementing teacher-students face-to-face

Table 5. Barrier to graduate students' participation in the asynchronous online discussion

Barriers	Not a Barrier No %	Minor Barrier No %	Major Barrier No %
None or limited access to computer and Internet facilities.	12 (36.4)	7 (21.2)	14 (42.4)
Lack of knowledge about ways to participate.	11 (33.3)	14 (42.4)	8 (24.2)
Not enough time to check mails	14 (42.4)	13 (39.4)	6 (18.2)
Lack of interest since the teacher is not available physically	24 (72.7)	5 (15.2)	4 (12. 1)

interactions and by extension broadens classroom-related activities beyond the school periods. More importantly, with the present situations in Nigeria where incessant lecturers' strike has become a common phenomenon; it means academic interactions could continue among students and colleagues during such strike period and students could gainfully engage themselves in worthwhile activities while the strike lasts.

Recommendation

As a result of our findings from this study, we recommend;

- Classroom integration and adoption of social networking media as supplementary to classroom interactions among University lecturers.
- Collaboration among teachers to provide assistance for cross-fertilization of ideas and experiences on integration of asynchronous online discussion (AOD).
- Orientation through seminars, workshops and teachings for University teachers and students on effective and active participation in asynchronous online discussion (AOD).
- Formation of online discussion forums or online collaborative groups for blended learning and cooperative learning among lecturers and students.
- Integration of asynchronous online discussion into conventional teaching methods by lecturers in form of blended learning and.
- Provision of computer and ICT infrastructure within the learning and students' residential environments by University authorities to ensure cheaper and unrestricted Internet access.

REFERENCES

Damoense, M. Y. (2003). Online learning for higher education in South Africa. *Australian Journal of Educational Technology, 19*(1), 25–45.

Helmi, A. (2002). An analysis on the impetus of online education Curtin University of Technology, Western Australia. *The Internet and Higher Education, 4*(3-4), 243–253. doi:10.1016/S1096-7516(01)00070-7

Holahan, P. J., Aronson, Z. H., Jurkat, M. P., & Schoorman, F. D. (2004). *Implementing Computer Technology: A multiorganizational test of Klein and Sorra's model.* Academic Press.

Hron, A., & Friedrich, H. F. (2003). A review of web-based collaborative learning: Factors beyond technology. *Journal of Computer Assisted Learning, 19*(1), 70–79. doi:10.1046/j.0266-4909.2002.00007.x

Jegede, O. J. (2002). Facilitating and sustaining interest through an on-line distance peer-tutoring system in a cooperative learning environment. *Virtual University Gazette,* 35-45.

Mavers, D. (2005). *ICT Test Bed Evaluation.* Retrieved from http://www.evaluation.icttestbed.org.uk/

McInnerney, J., & Robert, T. S. (2004). Collaborative or cooperative learning. In T. S. Roberts (Ed.), *Online collaborative learning: Theory and practice* (pp. 203–214). Hershey, PA: Information Science Publishing.

Mcmillan, S. (1996). Literacy and computer literacy: Definitions and comparisons. *Computers & Education, 27*(3-4), 161–170. doi:10.1016/S0360-1315(96)00026-7

Mellar, H. (2007). *A study of effective practice in ICT and adult literacy*. Retrieved from http://www. nrdc.org.uk/publications_details.asp?ID=87

Moon, J. A. (1999). *Reflection in learning and professional development: Theory and practice*. Sterling, VA: Kogan Page.

Moore, K. (2002). Professional development through distance learning. *Scholastic Early Childhood Today, 16*(6), 6–7.

Okebukola, P. A. O. (2005). *Quality Assurance in Teacher Education: The role of Faculties of Education in Nigerian Universities*. Paper presented at the Annual Meeting of the Committee of Deans of Education in Nigerian Universities. Ilorin, Nigeria.

Rogers, E. M. (1983). *The diffusion of innovations* (3rd ed.). New York: The Free Press.

Rosenberg, R. (2004). *The Social Impact of Computers* (3rd ed.). London: Elsevier Academic.

Ruhleder, K., & Michael, T. (2000). Reflective collaborative learning on the web: Drawing on the master class. *First Monday, 5*(5). doi:10.5210/fm.v5i5.742

Saunders, J. (2003). Campusdirect helps Government Employee Continue e-learning. *Technology in Government, 10* (9).

SchulzB. (2003). Collaborative learning in an online environment: Will it work for teacher training? In Proceedings of the 14th Annual Society for Information Technology and Teacher Education International Conference (pp. 503-504). Charlottesville, VA: Association for the Advancement of Computers in Education.

Starkey, H. (2006). *Designing online tasks for effective discussions*. Retrieved from http://www. cde.london.ac.uk/support/awards/generic2534.htm

Tebo, M. G. (2000). First Class Delivery. *ABA Journal, 86*(87), 1.

ADDITIONAL READING

Bates, A., & Sangrà, A. (2011) *Managing Technology in Higher Education: Strategies for Transforming Teaching and Learning San Francisco:* Jossey-Bass/John Wiley & Co. Brief information available at: http://www.tonybates.ca/2011/05/15/book-managing-technology-in-higher-education-now-available/#sthash.0oHDeAD1.dpuf

Camianne, D. (2010). *Open and distance learning terms and definitions*. Available at: http://e-articles.info/e/a/tittle/open

Carr, V. H. (2000). *Teaching adoption and Diffusion*. Available at: http://tlc.nlm.mih.gov/resources/publication

Januszewski, A. (2001). *Educational Technology: The Development of a Concept*. U.S.A.: Libraries Unlimited Inc.

Lee, S., Groves, P., Stephens, C., & Armitage, S. (1999) *On-line teaching: Tools and projects-* Available at: http://www.jtap.ac.uk

Lee, S., Groves, P., Stephens, C., & Armitage, S. (1999) *On-line teaching: Tools and projects*. Information available at: http://www.jtap.ac.uk

Mason. R., & Kaye, A. (1989) *Mindweave: Communication, Computers and Distance Education*. Oxford, UK: Pergamon Press. Information available at: http://www.tonybates.ca/2008/07/06/mindweave-communication-computers-and-distance-education/#sthash.xAf0D2EB.dpuf#

Moon, J. A. (1999) Reflection in learning and professional development: Theory and practice. London Sterling, VA: Kogan Page: Stylus Pub.

Owhotu, V. B. (Ed.). (2006). *An Introduction to Information Technologies in Education*. Lagos: Sibon Books Ltd.

Robert, T. S. (2004). *Online collaborative learning: Theory and practice*. Hershey, PA: Information Science Publishing.

Rogers, E. M. (2003). *Diffusion of Innovations* (5th ed.). New York: Free Press.

Rosenberg, R. (2004). *The Social Impact of Computers* (3rd ed.). London: Elsevier Academic.

Russell, A. L. (1996). *Six stages in learning new technology*. Available at: http://www.fed.qut.edu.au/russell/Stages.htm

Saettler, L. P. (1990). *The evolution of American Educational Technology*. Englewood: Libraries Unlimited Inc. Information available at: http://www.books.google.com/books

KEY TERMS AND DEFINITIONS

Adoption: Technology use by end-users or the decision to purchase technology. According to Rogers (1983), adoption is "a decision to make full use of an innovation as the best course of action available, while rejection is "a decision not to adopt an innovation."

Asynchronous Online Discussion (AOD): A form of collaborative or cooperative learning whereby learners or participants relates together using the electronic platform to communicate, consult and contribute. Asynchronicity connote 'non-real time' as against synchronicity meaning 'real time' (McInnerney & Robert, 2004).

Collaborative Learning: A learning method that implies "working in a group of two or more to achieve a common goal, while respecting each individual's contribution to the whole." The term 'collaborative' learning is often used interchangeably with the term 'cooperative' learning.

Ex-Post Facto: A methodology where no variable will be manipulated as they have already taken place and thereafter inferences are made from the data collected.

Groups: Internet communication which is a hybrid between an electronic mailing list and threaded Internet forum.

Reflection: 'A mental process with purpose and / or outcome in which manipulation of meaning is applied to relatively complicated or unstructured ideas in learning or to problems for which there is no obvious solution' (Moon, 1999).

Chapter 14

Information and Communication Technology in Teaching and Learning:
Effects and Challenges in China

Xiaobin Li
Brock University, Canada

ABSTRACT

This chapter provides an overview of the current development of Information and Communication Technology (ICT) utilized in teaching and learning in the People's Republic of China. Specifically, the chapter describes and discusses the effects contemporary ICT has on Chinese elementary and secondary education, as well as the existing challenges in ICT applications. The chapter also examines ICT's application in higher education, particularly in distance education, and the issues that have to be dealt with. The chapter discusses the potential for further developing education with ICT. In addition, it makes recommendations with regard to providing better education with ICT in China.

BACKGROUND

On July 17, 2013, China Internet Network Information Center reported that about 591 million Chinese had used the Internet regularly as of June 30, 2013. This places China as the country with the most Internet users in the world. About 44 percent of the Chinese population has used the Internet, which means today Chinese use information and communication technology (ICT) more extensively in their life, including in education. With increasingly sophisticated ICT, it is easier

for Chinese learners to receive distance education than before (Wang, 2010). However, when compared with the United States where about 78 percent of the population use the Internet regularly (Miniwatts Marketing Group, 2012), the gap is still great. There are also obvious gaps within China between different regions.

While proportionately Chinese lag behind developed countries in using the Internet, the increase in the number of users in the first half of 2013 is approximately 2 percent (China Internet Network Information Centre, 2013), higher than

DOI: 10.4018/978-1-4666-6162-2.ch014

Copyright © 2014, IGI Global. Copying or distributing in print or electronic forms without written permission of IGI Global is prohibited.

that in most developed countries. As more Chinese go online, the Internet has grown in importance as a venue for business, entertainment, as well as education. As Chinese are more involved in international affairs, Chinese educators' awareness of internationalization has also increased, and the interaction between Chinese educators and international colleagues has been increasing. China is the only country among Economic and Social Commission of Asia and Pacific members that has extended its commitments to liberalize access in all five subsectors of educational services (Raychaudhuri & De, 2007).

Chinese still spend a smaller percentage of their gross domestic product on education than the average level in the Organization of Economic Cooperation and Development countries (The World Bank, 2012). The Chinese economy is the second largest in the world, next only to that of the United States, but the Chinese population is four times that of the United States. The gap in education between China and the United States is obvious. In 2011 the Chinese expected years of schooling was 11.7, compared with 16.8 of the United States (United Nations Development Programme, 2013). The demand for education in China is huge and the potential of the education market is great (Wang, 2010). It is impossible for the traditional means of education to fulfill this important task on its own. Within China, because of income disparities, the gap in education attainment between densely populated eastern regions and sparsely populated western regions is wide with western regions lagging behind.

In China, formal education from grade 1 to grade 9 is compulsory, which is referred to as basic education. Education from grade 10 to grade 12 is not compulsory, but 85 percent of the relevant age group was enrolled in grades 10 to 12 in 2012 (Ministry of Education, August 16, 2013). Since China opened up in 1978, more youth receive higher education. However, in 2012 the Chinese higher education participation rate was 30 percent (Ministry of Education, August 16, 2013), still

lower than that in developed countries. Besides, many Chinese are not happy with the current provision of education, and many Chinese students are not interested in learning (Sang, 2010). To catch up economically with developed countries, Chinese have to catch up educationally, when utilizing contemporary information and communication technology (ICT) in teaching and learning will be helpful.

In November 2006 the Ministry of Science and Technology and the Ministry of Education launched the Public Service Demonstration Project for Digital Education, hoping to advance key information and communication technologies in providing education to the general public and to contribute toward the establishment of a life-long learning system. The national government invested substantial amounts of money to implement the "rural distance education project" and "connecting all villages project" to make ICT available across the country (Sang, 2010). ICT can and should play a greater role in meeting the huge demand for education. In addition, per student cost for distance education with ICT is lower than that for face to face programs (Zhou, 2007). By September 2012 China formed the largest network education system in the world (CIConsulting, 2012).

ICT IN ELEMENTARY AND SECONDARY EDUCATION

Rapid social development in China requires the continuous advancement of its education system, in which ICT application has been increasing. Progress in education ICT helps the Chinese education system deal with challenges brought by fast economic and social change and the increasing demand that education be available for all. It has been pointed out that there are problems in the Chinese elementary and secondary education system and it needs a comprehensive reform, particularly a reform in its curriculum. With the advancement of contemporary education ICT, the application of multi-media computers and the Internet is increasing in classrooms, which is conducive to a comprehensive curriculum reform.

Today Chinese are more aware of international competition, which ultimately is the competition of people, especially well-educated and creative people. Encouraging students to think critically and creatively is the most important task. ICT may facilitate the establishment of a learning environment where students can develop their acuteness of acquiring and using information on their own, which is a necessary quality of innovative people actively participating in the globalized knowledge economy. ICT breaks the constraints of time and space, helping develop students' ability in obtaining and using information outside school hours. ICT may facilitate the availability and understanding of knowledge, assisting students' self-exploration, self-discovery, and self-study. Developing the most advanced education ICT is one thing that must be accomplished to narrow the gap between Chinese education and education in developed countries.

The development of education in China is inequitable among different regions. With contemporary ICT teachers and students in less developed regions can share some of the same educational resources as students in more developed regions. With unbalanced regional income, inadequate financial resources, and a huge task of developing human capital, ICT should play a greater role in making the provision of education more equitable across the country.

There are 308,868 elementary and secondary schools in China with about 191 million students (Ministry of Education, August 16, 2013). Across the nation on average approximately there is one computer provided by school for every 13 students in grades 1-9 (Ministry of Education, 2013, February 28), and for every 9 students in grades 10-12. Usually urban schools have more computers than rural schools. About 16 percent of elementary schools (grades 1-6), 46 percent of junior secondary schools (grades 7-9), and

77 percent of senior secondary schools (grades 10-12) are connected to the Internet (Ministry of Education, November 14, 2011). Many western rural area schools still need to be connected. The demand for education hardware and software is the biggest in the world. ICT courses are available in all senior secondary schools, 95 percent of junior secondary schools, and 50 percent of elementary schools (Ministry of Education, February 28, 2013). In December 2012 the National Education Resource Platform was launched, utilizing cloud technology to gradually connect regional education resource platforms and business resource service platforms and establishing an exchange and sharing environment to serve resource suppliers and users at various levels of education. In 2013 the Ministry of Education started a national training program, collaborating with China Mobile and China Telecom to train 500,000 teachers in using ICT (Ministry of Education, February 28, 2013). Currently, connecting all schools and making ICT education available in all schools is the focus of the Ministry of Education.

Although many Chinese schools are connected with ICT, school networks face a variety of problems. There is a general lack of comprehensive understanding of these networks among teachers and administrators. It is estimated that most school networks are not functioning effectively in helping to provide better teaching and learning. Many teachers, particularly rural area teachers, are not familiar with ICT, do not have the competence to apply ICT, and there is a significant gap between reality and what is required for integrating ICT into teaching (Ministry of Education, November 19, 2013). The positive impact from ICT is far from what is expected. To improve the situation, the Ministry of Education launched a national project to enhance elementary and secondary teachers' ICT application competence, hoping to complete the training of more than 10 million teachers, particularly those in rural regions, by the end of 2017 and promote the application of

ICT in daily teaching (Ministry of Education, November 19, 2013).

ICT IN HIGHER EDUCATION

Chinese higher education participation rate has increased from around 3 percent in 1978 to 30 percent in 2012 with over 33 million students (Ministry of Education, August 16, 2013). In June 2013 approximately 9 million Chinese took the higher education entry examination (Lu, 2013), but only about 6.9 million would be admitted into various programs in the fall (CCTV, July 6, 2013). It seems that part of the demand for higher education is not met by the current supply.

To increase access to higher education, instructors in four universities started to use ICT in their distance education programs in 1999 with 2,900 students. The Ministry of Education approved 69 universities to provide degree programs over the Internet and through other distance education means. In 2009 these universities had over four million students registered in various distance education programs utilizing ICT, which was about 13 percent of all higher education students (Wei, 2011). Distance higher education through ICT is provided in all 31 provinces, ethnic autonomous regions, and municipalities directly under the national government. Besides the Internet, most distance education programs also use cable television networks and satellite technology. The admission rate for distance education programs is higher than that for face to face programs. Most students in distance education programs are people with a job, and their education is considered continuing education. A significant proportion of distance education program students are people who have not been successful in entering a face to face program because their higher education entry examination grades are not high enough (Xiong, Xie & Wu, 2010).

In addition to increasing access, ICT provides an important condition for student-centered learning. Through educational networks, students can individually obtain information on the most recent scientific development from institutions around the world. Without the constraints of time and space, distance education with ICT provides an ideal venue of learning for anyone who has access to ICT. As the open access movement increases its momentum, more educational resources are available on the Internet for anyone interested in learning. Some Chinese universities have produced open courseware and made it available online (Ministry of Education, June 26, 2013).

The vast majority of Chinese higher education students are frequent Internet users (China Internet Network Information Center, 2012), and they may expect their instructors to deliver courses in a variety of ways. In higher education institutions there is approximately 1 institutionally provided computer for every 5 students, and on average in every institution there are about 68 courses provided through contemporary ICT (Ministry of Education, November 14, 2011).

With China's huge educational needs and geographic dispersion, distance higher education with the use of ICT has great potential. It can provide opportunities to different people at various levels in different places if they have access to ICT. It should play a unique and increasingly important role in connecting the whole country for higher education. China has the largest radio and TV university system in the world providing distance education originally through radio and television broadcasting and now increasingly with contemporary ICT. In 2012 the Chinese State Council decided to transform the radio and TV universities in five provinces and municipalities directly under the national government to open universities, where more distance education with ICT, satellite technology, and TV broadcasting will be provided to increase access to higher education. In July 2012 China Central Radio and TV University became the Open University of China, indicating that it is more open for people interested in learning. One thing the Open University of China is doing is developing an education platform through ICT for all Chinese citizens. The intention of transforming radio and TV universities into open universities is to share educational resources, promote equity, satisfy increasingly diverse educational needs, and build a learning society. It was hoped that within 10 years open universities would become an important element of the higher education system in the country with their unique characteristics (Deng & Kong, 2011).

Another factor that influences ICT application in Chinese higher education is the increasing impact of internationalization. Like their American distance higher education colleagues who espouse internationalization (Boubsil, Carabajal & Vidal, 2011), Chinese educators also welcome internationalization (Liao, Tan & Zhu, 2008). Open courseware from well-known Western universities, particularly those in the United States, has been very popular in China and has been used to point out the shortcomings of Chinese open courseware (Wang, 2011). Chinese open universities may still need to understand how to operate in an international context, and Chinese have much to learn from their colleagues in developed countries (Li, Y., 2011).

In 2004 the Ministry of Education promulgated *the Regulation on Chinese-Foreign Collaboration in Education in the People's Republic of China*, which stated that the government encouraged the introduction into China of quality international education institutions to establish collaboration with Chinese institutions. Currently there are over 1,000 Chinese and foreign joint institutions and programs providing instruction to 450,000 students in China, who are about 1.4 percent of all Chinese higher education students. These joint institutions and programs have graduated 1.5 million students (Ministry of Education, September 5, 2013). Opening up the Chinese higher education services allows Chinese educators to learn from colleagues abroad. The National Medium and Long-Term Education Reform and Development Plan (2010-2020) stated that the Chinese education system would be more open to the world (Ministry of Education, July 15, 2011). In encouraging students to develop a strong international awareness, the Ministry of Education has also decided to promote English as a medium of instruction in higher education institutions. In addition, there are Chinese students studying in Western programs through the Internet while they remain in China, although these Western programs have not been approved by the Chinese government.

In 2012 almost 400,000 Chinese went overseas for further education, and it is estimated that in 2013 over 450,000 Chinese will go abroad for education (Ma, 2013). In 2012 there were 300,000 foreign students in China (Yuan, 2012). As more Chinese go abroad to receive further education, more international students are studying in China. Distance education with ICT should play a role in helping Chinese understand the world and helping the world understand China. The Chinese Language Center at the Open University of China (n. d.) offers a wide range of teaching materials on Chinese language and culture to learners throughout the world via the Internet, satellite TV, and traditional publication and distribution channels. Overall, however, most Chinese distance educators have yet to recognize the benefits and challenges of internationalizing distance higher education (Li, Y., 2011).

While Chinese distance higher education with ICT has developed significantly in the last decade, increasing access to education, there are problems. Distance higher education programs are still at the margin of the higher education system and they do not enjoy the same reputation as traditional face to face programs (Liu & Zhang, 2010; Li, Y., 2011). Since 2004 students studying some general courses through distance higher education have to take national standardized examinations, which is necessary to improve the quality of distance higher education programs.

CHALLENGES AND RECOMMENDATIONS

When compared with education utilizing ICT in developed countries, Chinese education with ICT lags behind and it is in need of continuous improvement. Although it develops rapidly, it is far from meeting people's expectations. Some of the challenges are described in the following paragraphs.

Over the years various Chinese information banks have been established; however, quality information banks are scarce. There is a lack of high quality education resources (Ministry of Education, March 13, 2012). A national distance education resource bank has to be established, where information can be shared. There is also the problem with standardization, and sharing is difficult (Deng & Kong, 2011). The online educational platform the Open University of China is building may meet the need of a national education information bank.

In distance higher education with ICT, teaching models are few. Most network courses stress content presentation and explanation, and instructors do not pay adequate attention to creating a favorable learning environment. The teaching model used most often is a mere transmission of information. A large part of education with ICT content is direct video broadcasting of instructors' lectures, with little or no interaction between instructors and students, or among students. In recent years there has been some improvement in these areas, but still, Chinese higher education with ICT so far is mainly a transmission of teaching resources and course content (Liang, Ran & Wan, 2013).

The graduation rate of distance higher education programs with ICT is significantly lower than that of face to face programs (Wei, 2011).

The main reasons for students withdrawing from distance education programs are job constraints, financial pressure, low independent study ability, and difficulties in study (Li, Chen & Han, 2010). In addition, it has been reported that there are unethical practices in some distance education programs, such as inaccurate advertisements, cheating in examinations, and admitting students without following the necessary rules (Peng, 2011). Although ICT is generally shared and there is an opportunity for cooperation, educators use it at their discretion. Institutions sometimes repeat what has already been done by others, which is a waste of resources (Feng, 2010). This problem is similar to what happened in Western Europe (Cartelli, Stanfield, Connolly, Jimoyiannis, Magalhaes & Maillet, 2008).

In Chinese higher education there is a shortage of instructors with teaching expertise utilizing ICT. Most instructors using ICT are regular instructors with little knowledge of ICT and little teaching experiences with ICT. They have heavy workloads of regular teaching and research, and when they use ICT in teaching they do not put enough time into meeting the needs of students. There is a lack of specialized quality assurance systems and quality standards (Li, B., 2011; Li, Y., 2011). When there are standards these standards are not sufficiently enforced (Liu, 2011). The quality of distance higher education programs is still an important issue that educators and administrators have to work on (Deng & Kong, 2011).

Since in distance higher education students and instructors do not meet in person, network support services are vital. However, students are not provided with sufficient guidance. Few of them receive feedback on their work from instructors, and there is little individualized teaching (Li, Y., 2011). When designing course materials and structures, instructors tend to emphasize content transmission over student support (Wang, 2011). Shortcomings in programs let students simply get by, not really interested in acquiring substantive knowledge (Xing, 2010). In addition, China's transition to a marketable social system has introduced new sources of inequality into the provision and availability of higher education (Ertl & Kai, 2010). Fees are sometimes too high, networks are not always stable, and people have misconceptions about distance higher education (Xing, 2010). Some distance education programs do not meet students' needs and do not enjoy the same reputation as face to face programs (Li, Y., 2011). Since most distance education programs are paid for mainly or exclusively by students, equity is a serious issue owing to income disparities among students. Chinese financial resources for distance higher education lag behind those in developed countries, and there are development gaps among different regions (Zhang, 2011).

To meet the requirements of economic and social change and build a country capable of innovation, Chinese educators and ICT professionals have much to do before China can catch up with developed countries. To provide quality education with ICT, I make several recommendations here, of which most have been developed from a review of the relevant literature.

Currently nine year compulsory education is available for almost every Chinese child in the relevant age group. However, only 85 percent of the youth in the relevant age group are enrolled in grades 10 to grade 12. In reaching the Ministry of Education's goal of making it available for 93 percent of the age group by 2015, ICT may play an important role. Chinese educators may learn from Indian colleagues, who have been using ICT to make secondary education available for more youth. In making the K-12 curriculum more engaging with ICT, Chinese educators may consider joining the International Association for K-12 Online Learning and learn from international colleagues.

There is an obvious digital divide between eastern regions and western regions in school ICT hardware and connection. Government officials need to provide more equitable distribution of educational resources, increase the sharing of resources, and encourage organizations and individuals to participate in providing education services (Hu & Bian, 2010).

Chinese education with ICT needs to aim at mainly providing higher education, continuing education, and life-long learning opportunities to the masses. Higher education institutions could consider what they may do to fully utilize their strengths to meet various people's needs and to contribute to developing education in western regions. In addition, institutions need to strengthen the quality of their distance education programs and increase the sharing of their resources (Zhang, 2011). Educators may consider applying the Sloan Consortium Quality Framework to improve the quality of online learning. Open universities need to think more freely, be innovative, transform their traditional model of serving students, and be flexible (Deng & Kong, 2011).

Chinese educators need to continue to learn from international colleagues' expertise, reflect on their own practices, and construct theories appropriate for distance education with ICT (Li, Y. 2011). Distance education instructors and administrators need to make their programs more effective and more student-centered (Peng, 2011). Universities that already provide distance education should promote research and train instructors for distance education. Chinese educators may consider attending the annual conference of Quality Matters to learn from their American colleagues.

For learning to occur, there needs to be dialogues, discussions and exchanges of ideas (Sang, 2010). Network platforms need to be designed to emphasize interactions between students and instructors. Ideally, students should have an environment where they can freely discuss ideas with instructors and receive support. For example, there is a need for a resource center that would help students select courses and complete assignments (Zhang, 2011).

The Chinese economy has changed from a planned economy to a mainly market economy, yet the education system is still quite isolated from the market. Some scholars argue that the Chinese government should allow market forces to play a greater role in providing education (Dahlman, Zeng & Wang, 2007). Further allowing international and domestic organizations and individuals to participate in education will help to meet people's expanding and increasingly diverse needs for education. In addition, there is an urgent need for laws and regulations that both facilitate and monitor the development and operation of distance higher education programs (Huang & Jiang, 2011). It is also useful to encourage the media to expose unethical practices and bring those who violate laws and regulations to justice. There is a need to promote ethical practices in distance higher education programs, and Chinese may learn from American colleagues, particularly the book *Educational Technology: A Definition with Commentary* published by the American Association for Educational Communications and Technology (Peng, 2011).

Finally, to develop more distance education with ICT programs, regulate them more effectively, increase higher education participation rate to 40 percent by 2020, and transform China into a country with human capital at the same level as developed countries, governments at all levels need to invest more in education with ICT. It is encouraging to see that the national spending on education reached 4 percent of GDP in 2012 (Ministry of Education, September 6, 2012).

In the National Medium and Long-Term Education Reform and Development Plan (2010-2020), the Chinese government (2010) stated that it would continue to build a national education resource network, introduce international digital teaching resources into China, develop Chinese courseware, and build digital libraries. The government hoped to have more innovative network teaching models and develop high quality distance education degree programs. It stated that it would continue to promote distance education for rural and remote schools so that teachers and students

there would be able to share quality education resources. It would continue to promote ICT application in education and help teachers raise their abilities in utilizing ICT so that their teaching will be more effective. It encouraged students to increase their abilities of using ICT in analyzing issues and solving problems. It hoped to develop education with ICT faster so that soon it would be available for all Chinese children.

The National Medium and Long-Term Education Reform and Development Plan (2010-2020) urged government officials at all levels to prioritize the development of educational ICT, hoping to connect all schools with ICT by 2020. In developing educational ICT networks, the Ministry of Education hoped policy makers would invest more in rural areas to reduce the digital divide between urban centers and rural areas. The Ministry planned to standardize education ICT and promote the connection among various networks (The Central People's Government of the People's Republic of China, 2010). The World Bank (2012) recommended that the Chinese government improve the productivity and quality of higher education with the help of information technology. The Ministry of Education (March 13, 2012) planned to strengthen the building of digital campuses and facilitate the sharing of resources, promote educators' ICT application competences, encourage innovation and interaction in teaching and learning, help students develop their self-study ability, strengthen the assistance to institutions in western regions, promote internationalization of Chinese education, and help to bring about a comprehensive improvement in the quality of higher education. The Ministry will continue to build a platform to provide continuing education, facilitate the transformation of open universities to serve citizens in a convenient, flexible and individualized learning environment, and build a life-long learning system for all Chinese.

The Open University of China launched a national digital education resource network center

(Ministry of Education, February 28, 2013). In June 2013 the first batch of 120 Chinese university open courses were uploaded (Ministry of Education, 2013, June 26). In addition, China Education and Research Network has become the largest national academic network in the world. Chinese have made significant progress in getting connected for learning, but there is still a long way to go before Chinese are at the same level as those in developed countries in their educational connectedness. Chinese will continue to make efforts to catch up. All indications are that more Chinese will be connected with contemporary ICT for the purpose of learning.

REFERENCES

Boubsil, O., Carabajal, K., & Vidal, M. (2011). Implications of globalization for distance education in the United States. *American Journal of Distance Education*, 25(1), 5–20. doi:10.1080/08923647.2011.544604

Cartelli, A., Stanfield, M., Connolly, T., Jimoyiannis, A., Magalhaes, H., & Maillet, K. (2008). Towards the development of a new model for best practice and knowledge construction in virtual campuses. *Journal of Information Technology Education*, 7, 121–134.

Central People's Government of the People's Republic of China. (2010). 国家中长期教育改革和发展规划纲要 *(2010-2020年)*. [The National Medium and Long-Term Education Reform and Development Plan (2010-2020)]. Retrieved from http://www.gov.cn/jrzg/2010-07/29/content_1667143.htm

China Internet Network Information Center. (2012). *CNNIC发布《第29次中国互联网络发展状况统计报告*. [CNNIC announces the 29th Chinese Internet development report]. Retrieved from http://www.cnnic.net.cn/dtygg/dtgg/201201/t20120116_23667.html

China Internet Network Information Center. (2013). *CNNIC发布《第32次中国互联网络发展状况统计报告》*.[CNNIC announces the 32th Chinese Internet development report]. Retrieved from http://www.cnnic.net.cn/hlwfzyj/hlwxzbg/hlwtjbg/201307/t20130717_40664.htm

CIConsulting. (2012). *2013-2017年中国网络教育行业投资分析及前景预测报告* [2013-2017 Chinese network education investment analysis and perspective report]. Retrieved from http://service.ocn.com.cn/rpts/fw/wangluojiaoyu.htm

Dahlman, C., Zeng, D., & Wang, S. (2007). *Enhancing China's Competitiveness through Lifelong Learning*. Retrieved from http://web.worldbank.org/WBSITE/EXTERNAL/WBI/WBIPROGRAMS/KFDLP/0,contentMDK:21387573~menuPK:1727232~pagePK:64156158~piPK:64152884~theSitePK:461198,00.html

Deng, X., & Kong, L. (2011). 广播电视大学的战略转型. [The strategic transformation of radio and TV universities]. *Distance Education in China, 8.*

Ertl, H., & Kai, Y. (2010). The discourse on equality and equity in Chinese higher education. *Chinese Education & Society*, 43(6), 3–14. doi:10.2753/CED1061-1932430600

Feng, L. (2010). 远程教育资源库资源共享服务研究. [A study of the sharing of information from distance education resource banks]. *Contemporary Distance. Education Research*, 2, 48–52.

Hu, X., & Bian, J. (2010). 信息化进程中教育资源配置的区域性差异研究. [A study of the regional differences in the distribution of educational information and communication technology resources]. *Journal of Distance Education*, 3, 64–68.

Huang, X., & Jiang, H. (2011). 论开放大学的法律地位及其办学自主权的法律保障.. [On judicially safeguarding open universities' legal status and their autonomy]. *Contemporary Distance. Education Research*, 2, 3–8.

Li, B. (2011). 我国远程高等教育质量保证活动执行主体研究. [A study of the implementers of Chinese distance higher education quality assurance policies]. *Contemporary Distance. Education Research, 3*, 30–34.

Li, Y. (2011). 开放大学国际合作模式探究. [An exploration of international cooperation among open universities]. *Distance Education in China, 11.*

Li, Y., Chen, H., & Han, Y. (2010). 为什么辍学. [Why do they withdraw from their programs?]. *Open. Education Research, 4*, 71–75.

Liang, Z., Ran, L., & Wan, S. (2013). 远程教育综合型网络课程开发.. [Development of combined network courses in distance education]. *Distance Education in China, 7.*

Liao, J., Tan, G., & Zhu, X. (2008). 我国大学教育国际化的路径选择.. [The approach we should adopt in internationalizing our higher education]. *Chinese. Higher Education, 1.*

Liu, C. (2011). 新一轮教育改革与远程开放教育的发展(五). [New education reform and the development of distance open education (5)]. *Distance Education in China, 3.*

Liu, H., & Zhang, X. (2010). 社会认可:远程教育质量外因分析. [Social recognition: An analysis of external quality factors in distance education]. *Contemporary. Distance Education, 6*, 22–24.

Lu, P. (2013, July 1). 高考:今年不再炒状元. [Higher education entry examination: No more fuss about the first place]. People's Daily Overseas Ed., p. 4.

Ma, H. (2013, September 13). *45* [It is estimated that this year over 450,000 will go overseas for education]. (p. 6). People's Daily Overseas Ed.

Ministry of Education. (2004). *The Regulation on Chinese-Foreign Cooperation in Education in the People's Republic of China.* Retrieved from http://www.moe.edu.cn/publicfiles/business/htmlfiles/moe/moe_621/201005/88508.html

Ministry of Education. (2011a, July 15). 教育部新闻发布会: 介绍《国家中长期教育改革和发展规划纲要（2010—2020年）》发布实施一年来贯彻落实有关情况. [Ministry of Education news conference: The implementation of the national medium and long-term education reform and development plan (2010-2020) one year after its promulgation]. Retrieved from http://www.moe.edu.cn/sofprogecslive/webcontroller.do?titleSeq=2657&gecsmessage=1

Ministry of Education. (2011b, November 14). 中国教育概况—*2010*年全国教育事业发展情况. [Chinese Education—2010 Chinese Education Development]. Retrieved from http://www.moe.edu.cn/publicfiles/business/htmlfiles/moe/s5990/201111/126550.html

Ministry of Education. (2012a, March 13). 教育部关于印发《教育信息化十年发展规划*(2011-2020*年*)*》的通知. [Ministry of Education Announcement: The 10 Year Development Plan for the Informationalization of Education (2011-2020)]. Retrieved from http://www.moe.gov.cn/publicfiles/business/htmlfiles/moe/s5892/201203/xxgk_133322.html

Ministry of Education. (2012b, September 6). 国新办就中长期教育改革和发展规划纲要颁布实施两年来介绍发展情况 [State Council News Office conference on the implementation of the National Medium and Long-Term Education Reform and Development Plan two years after its promulgation]. Retrieved from http://www.moe.edu.cn/publicfiles/business/htmlfiles/moe/s6819/201209/141694.html

Ministry of Education. (2013a, February 28). 教育信息化工作进展情况. [Development of education informationlization]. Retrieved from http://www.moe.gov.cn/publicfiles/business/htmlfiles/moe/s7204/201302/148023.html

Ministry of Education. (2013b, June 26). 首批中国大学资源共享课上线. [First batch of Chinese open university courses are uploaded]. Retrieved from http://www.moe.edu.cn/publicfiles/business/htmlfiles/moe/s7432/201306/153524.html

Ministry of Education. (2013c, August 16). *2012 年全国教育事业发展统计公报*. [2012 Chinese Education Development Statistics]. Retrieved from http://www.moe.edu.cn/publicfiles/business/htmlfiles/moe/moe_633/201308/155798.html

Ministry of Education. (2013d, September 5). 教育规划纲要实施三年来中外合作办学发展情况. [Development of Chinese and foreign collaboration in education three years after the National Medium and Long-Term Education Reform and Development Plan]. Retrieved from http://www.moe.gov.cn/publicfiles/business/ htmlfiles/moe/s7598/201309/156992.html

Ministry of Education. (2013e, November 19). 介绍教师队伍建设相关政策.[Recent policies on teacher development]. Retrieved from http://www.moe.edu.cn/publicfiles/business/htmlfiles/moe/s7731/201311/159548.html

Miniwatts Marketing Group. (2012). *Top 50 countries with the highest Internet penetration rate.* Retrieved from http://www.internetworldstats.com/top25.htm

Open University of China. (n.d.). *The Chinese Language Center.* Retrieved from http://en.crtvu.edu.cn/academics/clc

Peng, S. (2011). 论远程教育人员的道德建设. [On enhancing ethical practices of people working in distance education]. *Distance Education in China, 6.*

Raychaudhuri, P., & De, P. (2007). Barriers to trade in higher education services: Empirical evidence from Asia-Pacific countries. *Asia-Pacific Trade and Investment Review, 3*(2), 67–88.

Sang, X. (2010). 探究返璞归真的教育变革之道. [Exploring the way of educational change by returning to the nature of things]. *Journal of Distance Education, 5,* 3–9.

United Nations Development Programme. (2013). *Human Development Report 2013*. Retrieved from http://hdr.undp.org/en/media/HDR_2013_EN_complete.pdf

Wang, L. (2011). 开放教育资源的社会化分析. [A socialization analysis of open education resources]. *Distance Education in China, 7.*

Wang, Y. (2010). 进步与发展之路：开放远程教育与信息通讯技术在中国的应用.[Progress and development: The application of open distance education and information and communication technology in China]. *Open. Education Research, 16*(3), 56–61.

Wei, S. (2011). 网络高等教育学生毕业时间预测研究. [A study of graduation time of students in network higher education]. *Distance Education in China, 10.*

World Bank. (2012). *China 2030: building a modern, harmonious, and creative high-income society.* Retrieved from http://wwwwds.worldbank.org/external/default/WDSContentServer/WDSP/IB/2012/02/28/000356161_20120228001303/Rendered/PDF/671790WP0P127500China020300complete.pdf

Xing, X. (2010). 对开放教育学生惰学现象的思考. [Thoughts on the phenomenon of open education students' lack of interest in learning]. *Contemporary. Distance Education, 4,* 22–24.

Xiong, Y., Xie, B., & Wu, Y. (2010). 中国远程教育发展环境的SWOT分析. [An SWOT analysis of the Chinese distance education environment]. *Contemporary Distance Education, 6,* 18–21.

Yuan, G. (2012, September 6). *Responses to questions at the Ministry of Education news conference*. Retrieved from http://www.moe.gov.cn/sofprogecslive/webcontroller.do?titleSeq=4305&gecsmessage=1

Zhang, W. (2011). 我国开放大学的地位、理念和办学策略的探讨. [Positions, concepts and strategies of Chinese open universities]. *Distance Education in China, 6.*

Zhou, J. (2007). 现代远程教育—实现我国高等教育公平的砝码. [Contemporary distance education, a means to realize equity in Chinese higher education]. *Contemporary. Distance Education, 113,* 9–13.

KEY TERMS AND DEFINITIONS

China: The People's Republic of China. In the last three decades China's economy has been developing faster than that of the rest of the world.

Distance Education: Mainly higher education in China provided via the Internet, satellite technology, and television broadcasting.

Elementary Education: Formal education from grade one to grade six in China.

Equity: A belief that students must be treated equally regardless of family wealth and students with different needs must be treated differently so that they can reach similar mandated learning outcomes.

Higher Education: Any formal education one receives after one graduated from secondary education.

Information and Communication Technology: Any technology employed in distributing and transferring information for the purpose of communication.

Secondary Education: Formal education from grade nine to grade twelve.

Chapter 15
Adopting Digital Technologies in the Classroom:
The Impact of Use of Clickers on Cognitive Loads and Learning in China

Zhonggen Yu
Zhejiang Yuexiu University of Foreign Languages, China

Qianqian Xu
Zhejiang Yuexiu University of Foreign Languages, China

ABSTRACT

Clickers have been obtaining popularity in the West, although they are less popularized in the East. This chapter, by reviewing the studies on the impact of use of clickers on learning and cognitive loads, identifies the effectiveness of clickers, and the possible influence of the use of clickers on cognitive loads is also explored. This may pave a solid foundation for further popularization in the East. It is concluded that Clickers technology might be more suitable for large-enrollment classes in that it could provide students with opportunities of polling anonymously and quietly. Students might feel less nervous when answering questions anonymously.

INTRODUCTION

Technologies could be integrated into learning and teaching to improve the effectiveness. A number of researchers and institutions acknowledged the value of technology use in teaching and learning. For example, use of clickers showed large gains in learning outcomes (Caldwell, 2007 Mayer et al., 2009); Using clickers in the small-enrollment seminar-style biology courses was proved effective (Smith et al., 2011). Advanced technologies have been proved to provide learners and teachers with a convenient medium in learning and instruction. It has been widely acknowledged that technology is able to facilitate the process of learning, thus improving learning outcomes and releasing cognitive loads.

DOI: 10.4018/978-1-4666-6162-2.ch015

Copyright © 2014, IGI Global. Copying or distributing in print or electronic forms without written permission of IGI Global is prohibited.

Personal hand-held responders, often called "clickers," are one of the latest technologies used for teaching (Beatty, 2004; Duncan, 2005). Clickers are a kind of technology easily applied in education (Bruff, 2009). Clickers are also called a Classroom Communication System, Student Response System, or Audience Response Technology, referring to inquiry-based teaching strategies coupled with a clicker technology system, a computer technology that enables instructors to raise questions and has students respond using hand-held devices (clickers). The questions and answers summarizing student responses can be displayed simultaneously on the multimedia projector (Han & Finkelstein, 2013). Clickers with a long history are widely used in many educational institutions in the United States. For example, at the University of Colorado, 19 departments, 80 courses, and over 10,000 clickers were applied during the spring semester 2007 (Keller et al., 2007).

BACKGROUND

Although many studies claimed the benefits of the use of clickers in classes (e.g. Caldwell, 2007; Mayer et al., 2009; Smith et al., 2011; Heward, 1994; Berry, 2009), some studies still denied benefits of use of clicker in classes. Especially in small-scale classes, some lecturers tended to complain that use of clickers in small-scale classes produced nothing beneficial for learning and teaching but too much interaction in class. Teachers and students, with clickers, spent too much time on interaction which could have been avoided in traditional classes. Instead of too much interaction, students could focus more on self-learning and self-pondering, which was more helpful to memorize and understand the new conceptions.

Too much interaction might consume excessive time and students immerged in peer discussion might also diminish their self understandings and perceptions about the issues. Especially for introverted students, who were not good at communication and discussion, peer discussion might be a nuance for them to join. Therefore, they may prefer thinking and learning by themselves to discussing with peers.

In small-scale class, lecturers frequently indicated they felt convenient to interact with students directly which did not need any computer technology involvement including clickers. Experienced lecturers could exactly judge whether most students perceived the issue or not and determined whether to continue to the next issue or repeat it and further explain it. Clickers promoted peer participation in class through anonymous voting. However, this device meanwhile frustrated the students who were active learners and thinkers and were ready to respond to teachers' questions without anonymity. On the contrary, they enjoyed the attention drawn through their active performance. With anonymous voting, their activeness was possibly weakened. It was also assumed that learning through clickers might not be helpful for long memory in that students' memory might have been distracted by discussion and voting. The final argument needed to be clarified was that whether use of clickers among non students was as beneficial as students, since non students might not be so regulated by the device and less interested in technology if they were frequently faced with technologies when working.

Generally, the literature falls into three categories: case studies that aim to offer "best practice" advice drawing on actual classroom experience," statistical analyses that demonstrate how the use of clickers improves class attendance or test and examination results, and those that explore how clickers improve student engagement in the learning process. The theme of this study is to review literature on the use of clickers, and to discuss the impact of use of clickers on cognitive loads and learning outcomes.

MATERIAL AND METHODS

This review was conducted in order to extensively examine past studies on advantages and problem of clicker use. Its major objective was to provide an extensive and useful reference for any interested reader. To achieve this objective, the following methods were used to locate and select studies for the pillar of this review: First, online databases including Web of Science and Science Direct were searched ranging from the year 1950 to 2013 for relevant studies. The following key words guided the search: clicker(s), Classroom Communication System, Student Response System, and Audience Response Technology. Once an item was located via electronic search, the abstract was perused. If the abstract looked promising, then the item was obtained from the libraries of one distinguished University in China. For items that could not be located in the above libraries, it was loaned from other local, statewide, national, and international libraries. Another complementary method involved close examination of the references of the selected articles for citations of additional relevant studies.

The criteria of selecting previous studies as the pillar of this study were: 1) the paper included had to be published in a peer reviewed journal in edited collections; 2) master's or doctoral dissertations and short reports were excluded; 3) the paper had to focus explicitly or implicitly on blended learning; 4) the paper had to provide a sufficient description of data and data analysis from which the results were concluded.

It is worth mentioning that the included research resources are limited to the author's own ability. The author could only reach the resources within his own scope. It is assumed that there may be other publications out of the author's reach.

REVIEW OF LITERATURE

Engagement and Participation

Studies have considered it important to engage students in the class, and most successful college lecturers have made every effort to attract students in the process of instruction (e.g. Bain, 2004; Fang, 2009; Han & Finkelstein, 2013). Student responses in a data file accessed only by the instructor realized the anonymity and most instructors consider the display result as an important reference to activate peer discussion, evaluate student perception and reward active participation in the class activities.

It is hard to solicit student engagement, especially when they are away from the lecturing site. Domestically, a course is usually conducted through a lecture supported by PowerPoint slides, coupled with quizzes and case studies. Faculty note that students tend to be distracted from the topic at hand with the use of enhanced PowerPoint presentations. Lack of engagement and perception is evident on exams; students always find the contents on the slides difficult to follow, even though they think they are familiar with the information. Clickers have been proved to exert positive influence on class performance such as improving attendance and increasing participation. A sea of research related to use of clickers has been carried out, proving the functions of engaging students and encouraging them to join classroom activities.

General Use of Clickers in Learning

Furthermore, lecturers in universities and colleges in UK were challenged to figure out the impacts of updated technologies on education, especially the teaching and learning in the classroom (Kirkwood & Price, 2005). The way to impart lecturers' knowledge and enhance the communication among students in higher education in USA was put on an essential agenda (Bransford, Brophy & Williams, 2000).

Efforts were made to solicit students' viewpoints in the classroom using clickers technologies, which established a fundamental basis for teaching pedagogy aided with clickers (Heward, 1994). Unlike traditional pedagogy where students raise their hands to answer questions in class, clickers aided instruction realizes immediate feedback without revealing students' personal information. (Roschelle, Penuel & Abrahamson, 2004). It is therefore deemed necessary that clickers provide students with a satisfactory platform to answer questions or poll anonymously, which encourages students to respond to lecturers' questions and to keep pace with the lecturer. By immediate display of feedback on the screen through frequencies and percentages without identity disclosed, students could evaluate the matching degree of their responses compared with peer responses, from which students might think deeply about the reasons for matching and contradicting. In this way, mutual communication and inner pondering over questions would be established, paving a solid way for improvement on their performance. Proponents of clickers argued that clickers to a large extent changes students' way of learning and teachers' medium of lecturing (Beatty, 2004). Clickers' technologies have been widely accepted as a facilitator in the process of learning and teaching, where student performance as well as teacher instruction has been significantly improved and enhanced.

Use of Clickers in China

Some domestic studies showed that clickers system was used earlier in Taiwan (e.g. Chen, et al., 2010; Chi, et al., 1994). As early as 1995, National Central University had begun to study the issue how to integrate class feedback with technologies. In 2000, under the leadership of National Central

University there were 15 primary schools taking part in the study and started to promote clickers use in local government which was called "Using a clickers system in class." In 2002, clickers system was widely used among 1000 experimental classes in 150 primary schools in Taiwan. In 2004, Taiwan government set up more than 2000 experimental classes. In Mainland China, interactive teaching and learning was under investigation conducted by research departments assisted by Clickers system (Bojinova & Oigara, 2011).

In Mainland China there are a few studies on use of clickers system and application of clickers system, which mainly focus on primary and secondary schools. It is, however, still new in colleges and universities. The purchase and application of clickers in educational institutions remain an awkward issue to be addressed.

Use of Clickers Outside China

Although clickers system is relatively new in China, it has more than a decade history in USA. There have been more than 700 colleges including Harvard University, Northwestern University, Washington University and Ohio State University, together with some primary and secondary schools where clickers are use in class.

Clickers system can improve teaching quality. Some studies showed that clickers system was used in universities in USA as early as 1960s (Judson & Sawada, 2002). During that time, clickers system could not be widely used because of the limitation of technology of wired transference. Until the 1980s, there appeared a wireless clickers device, i.e. an infrared remote control, but the size is too large to hold in hand. After the 1990s, the online version of clickers system began to emerge aided with the popular Internet in Americans' daily life. There were no charges for the software whose cost was several thousand dollars a few years ago. Students could directly download software they needed from the Internet. Clickers technology stepped into a more mature and reliable stage. Clickers system could be used not only in traditional class but also on online learning environment. Other electronic devices were also used in clickers system such as PDA, mobile phone and so on (Fang, 2009). With the development of technology, clickers system has recently been widely used in USA and become one of the latest teaching technologies.

Satisfaction of Use of Clickers

Use of clickers, in both upper level class and lower level class, as well as average level, received increasing satisfaction. Studies on clickers use in terms of acceptance showed that most students were willing and voluntary to use clickers technology (e.g. Troy, et al., 2009; Berry, 2009; Chen, et al., 2010). The majority of students and lecturers highly valued the use of technology. Lecturers in psychology courses including both basic courses and advanced ones welcome the use of clickers in that the technology effectively incorporate clickers technology with student involvement and student satisfaction in the classroom (Troy, Beckert, Elizabeth & Kaelin, 2009). It was also found through survey items that clickers were fun to use and receiving credit merely for active response made students more likely to use clickers' technology (Berry, 2009).

Clickers' technology, despite the relatively new appearance and application in the classroom in higher education, continues the positive influence on learning and teaching. Numerous studies have obtained data indicating positive evaluation of clickers use among lecturers (e.g. Beatty, 2004; Caldwell, 2007; Duncan, 2005). However, students, as main group of consumers, should act as important evaluators to measure the psychological acceptance or rejection towards clickers use. Consequently, the degree of psychological satisfaction among students, together with lecturers' assessment should be taken into a serious consideration. Previous literature (e.g. Troy, et al., 2009; Chen, et al., 2010), however,

tended to study the satisfaction of clickers use in terms of involvement and performances, without considering students' inner psychological factors. It might be reasonable for future studies to shift from angles of student performances and lecturers' assessment to psychological measurement using experimental equipment in the field of psychology.

Participation and Peer Discussion

It was argued (McKeachie, 1990; Smith, 1977) that participation and peer discussion could result in higher-order learning activities. Clickers provide students with an effective way to encourage students to participate in classroom activities and group discussions. It is commonly acknowledged that sharing and discussing viewpoints and issues among peers enable students to develop mutual understanding and cooperating in learning. Additionally, the process where students poll and then view the whole class polling, followed by communication with each other and discussion on interesting topics and difficult questions provides students with a favorable opportunity of sharpening thinking and deepening understanding since they were exposed to a sea of both complementary and opposing opinions (Chickering & Gamson, 1991); new knowledge was therefore included into existing knowledge framework.

Lecturers should play a less active role in the classroom than commonly suggested (Fassinger, 1995). Instead, peer interaction among students should play a major important role in learning and teaching process. It was supported by describing the way clickers were used in a developmental biology class to activate peer discussion on key conceptions in the course (Knight and Wood, 2005). Clickers questions were designed to measure students' understanding about the fundamental conception through individual response. The results showed that obvious disagreements significantly existed among students' understandings. Then the lecturer grouped students into several subgroups to discuss the conceptions of those in disagreements again. Students were also divided into subgroups to discuss general conceptions about developmental biology prior to the instructor's soliciting clickers' responses. The findings indicated that in group discussion, students felt relaxed to meaningfully and actively debate the possible responses with their group members. This produced a generalized answer which was more reasonable than individual answers.

The powerful functions of clickers technology might be participation and discussion encouragement, coupled with attendance facilitation. Several studies show that using a clickers system increases attendance. For example, Homme, Asay, and Morgenstern (2004) revealed that students attendance increased by 5%, which lasted for around 2 years. Another study reported that students attendance increased to 80-90% when clickers test scores formed the final academic result (Caldwell, 2007).

Cooperative learning aided with clickers among peers can be stimulated and promoted. Meanwhile, clickers could also encourage shy students to voice their opinions without risking being mocked at because shy students prefer to answer questions through anonymously clicking the button rather than raising their hands in public. Shyness leads to students' drawing back from participation in classroom activities, which will exert negative influence on their academic performance. Young learners who were considered shy performed more poorly in vocabulary test than those who were not shy. Nevertheless, the difference in performance between shy and non-shy learners was not found when both shy and non-shy learners took the written test in groups where they could form peer discussion and poll anonymously compared with when they received the written test alone in the presence of invigilators (Crozier & Hostettler, 2003).

Several reasons why shyness could hinder student performance were explored (Mehrabian & Stefl, 1995). In the first place, responses realized by traditional hand-raising might be of less variety compared with keypad response. Keypad response might be able to enhance greater conformity to major opinions. Shyness might be eliminated when the opinion conformed to others. In the second place, clickers technology might enlarge the differences between shy and non-shy students, prompting shy students to be more subject to peer opinions. In the third place, anonymity attracted shy students more than non-shy ones because shy students would most likely feel easy in anonymous settings. Therefore, they might be more nervous when answering questions in public in the class. Clickers technology equipped with anonymous polling function might have compensated for this regret.

Immediate Feedback

Immediate feedback might be able to facilitate learning and teaching. It was reported that both faculty and students at the University of Wisconsin believed the immediate feedback produced by the clickers technology was beneficial to the process of learning (Kaleta & Joosten, 2007). Faculty especially favored clickers due to the function of immediate feedback because it enabled them to evaluate students' understanding immediately. If the feedback indicated that students commanded the conception perfectly, then faculty could continue to the next topic, needless to worry about students' keeping pace. If the feedback showed that students did not understand the teaching contents to some degree, then faculty could slow down the lecturing or repeat some necessary contents. Faculty could also balance the lecturing speed and difficulties according to feedbacks. Students also reported the effectiveness of immediate feedback as 75% students (n=2,013) reported that immediate feedback could enhance their knowledge and deepen their understanding about the course contents (Kaleta & Joosten, 2007).

Different Voices

Although there have been many studies advocating use of clickers technology in learning and teaching (e.g. Troy, et al., 2009; Berry, 2009; Chen, et al., 2010), some of the studies (e.g. Miller, Ashar & Getz, 2003; Salmon and Stahl, 2005) found negative effect of clickers. A comparative study related to the short-term knowledge retention of three groups of people in a workshop was conducted (Salmon and Stahl, 2005). Both groups participated in a posttest at the end of the workshop. Clickers were used for the posttest in one group, while pencils and paper were used for the posttest in the other. The third group did not join the posttest. No significant differences in the posttest scores between both groups were found. The group that used clickers did score a little higher, but it was not considered statistically significant. This study mainly examined the effectiveness of use of clickers in test taking. However, the benefits of clickers should be highlighted in the process of learning and teaching rather than in test taking. It is hard for clickers to contribute greatly to the test results after a short period of testing since this technology is mainly designed to be used in instruction and learning which might last for a much longer period.

Another study which examined the use of clickers in continuing education programs for physicians did not show effective use of clickers as well (Miller, Ashar & Getz, 2003). Participants from 42 continuing education programs across the country were surveyed and studied. The orators who used clickers to aid their lectures received significantly higher scores on the final evaluation than those who did not use. The participants in the workshop also showed their positive attitude toward use of clickers. They were especially satisfied with the anonymous mode of question answer and expressed that the clickers system kept them alert. The group which used clickers and the one which did not both joined a posttest after the session. No statistically significant differences, however, were found in the test scores.

This study failed to reveal any significant different scores although the clickers users highly valued the use of clickers. This negative finding seems contradictory with the users' positive attitudes. The random errors such the testing environment, the invigilating, the testing contents and other possible factors might have contributed to this paradoxical finding.

Cognitive Loads

In the theory of cognitive load it is claimed that there is a burden on the learner's brain processing when a task is under way (Sweller, 2010). According to previous studies (e.g. Homer, Plass & Blake, 2008), three types of cognitive load were theoretically defined: intrinsic load, extraneous load, and germane load. Intrinsic load refers to the difficulty of the content presented. It includes the difficulty of the material itself and learns' learning experience Intrinsic load is related to the complexity of the content required by a task. Extraneous load is caused by ineffective activities in learning. Germane load refers to individual differences and learning characteristics which can help build schema in learning. These three types are a whole. In order to improve learning effectiveness, both intrinsic and extraneous load should be decreased, while germane load should be increased.

Due to the complexity of content, intrinsic load is unchangeable to instructional manipulations (Sweller, 2010). Individuals are required to concentrate on the exposed information when learning. The learning outcomes tend to be largely influenced by the lecturing format and learners' individual abilities such as prior relevant knowledge and experience (Sweller, 2010). The harder the information is to be perceived by the learners, the higher the intrinsic load will become. A high germane load is needed to retrieve and process the information in the learning process (Sweller, 2010). The properly selected form of content presentation may reduce germane load and provide access to learned information (intrinsic load).

The Impact of Clickers Use on Cognitive Loads

The positive impact of use of clickers system on learning outcomes might contribute to the widespread use of clickers system. The use of clickers can enhance learning outcomes, which might make a difference in cognitive loads.

Cognitive load theory demonstrates that clickers system can provide a platform allowing students to build knowledge framework in their own mind. It is assumed that human cognitive structure is divided into working memory or short-term memory and long-term memory. The capacity of working memory is limited because it can't deal with too much information at the same time. However, knowledge can be stored in the form of schema. The main aim of teaching is to store information in the long-term memory. But before knowledge is stored in long-term memory, the brain must process in working memory inherent nature of the materials, the form of material presented and students' activities. When students perform a task, old and new knowledge interact in students' memory and thus loads on learners' mind are generated.

There have been many other reports describing the impact of use of clickers on learning outcomes, but there have been virtually few studies describing the effect of clickers use on cognitive loads. Futures study might focus on how to use the clickers technology to decrease intrinsic load and extraneous load, while to increase germane load, thus aiming to maximize the effectiveness of clickers use in learning and instruction.

Expense

Students on a tight budget tend to feel difficult to afford to purchase clickers system although it may be affordable for workers. Students kept complaining about the expense of clickers until they realized they could obtain a significantly higher score with the aid of clickers (Ribbens, 2007) Financial support in a research project could possibly afford clickers so that students could get the equipment in class free of charge. This is very helpful to strengthen the use of clickers and popularize the equipment across the world.

Cheating

Students were found worried about whether their polling had been correctly recorded and projected to the screen, so that some students might consider clickers an evaluation tool more than a learning system. What is worse, some students openly cheated by consulting their peers in class about the correct choice without the lecturer's permission. Students might directly follow peer option without any deep thinking by themselves, which possibly undermined the true value of clickers use (Brothen & Wambach, 2001; Daniel, 2006). However, if consulting peers about the answer could deepen students' insight into the question, could activate peer discussion or could promote cooperative learning; this consultation should be encouraged and correctly guided. Therefore, it is urgent for lecturers to work out an appropriate solution to address the cheating issue. Lecturers should also establish proper guidelines before requiring students to poll with clickers. Examples are: (1) any direct copy is forbidden; (2) students must think independently before and after discussion; and (3) students should make every effort to avoid following others' suggestion without their own thinking.

FUTURE RESEARCH DIRECTIONS

More studies on clickers and other new technologies are still needed to further push forward effectiveness of learning. Learning effectiveness will lag behind unless it can keep pace with development of technologies, without which learning and teaching will possibly fail to be effective. In a word, this study paved a solid foundation for future studies on educational technologies via reviewing studies on use of clickers in education. Future studies on use of clickers should also take into consideration cross-disciplinary theories, such as computer, learning, psychology, cognition and neurology. Clickers may not be the best choice as a technology used in education. More advanced and convenient technologies should be constantly developed to promote levels of education.

CONCLUSION

Clickers have been in use for more than ten years in western countries. They were most popular in educational institutions such as universities, high schools and primary schools. Comparatively speaking, Clickers system might be applicable in China as well, since it has obtained popularity in most institutions in the west. Traditional pedagogy might require students to raise their hands before orally answering questions in class, which is difficult to be realized in large-enrollment classes. Students might feel nervous when answering questions surrounded by a large number of peers and they might feel difficult to make them heard and understood by many students. This educational technology might be more suitable for large-enrollment classes in that it could provide students with opportunities of polling anonymously and quietly.

ACKNOWLEDGMENT

The author wishes to thank the people who helped this study and the projects which financially supported this study: 2011 Youth Fund of Humanities and Social Sciences of Ministry of Education of China "The Regression and Threshold Hypotheses of English Negative Sentences Attrition among English Learners in China," (Project No.: 11YJC740138); 2011 Teaching Innovation Project of Tongda College of Nanjing University of Posts & Telecommunications "The Regression and Threshold Hypotheses of Foreign languages and Teaching Innovation of College English in Civil Colleges" (Project No.: TD02011JG02); The Second Batch of Post-doctoral Research Fund of Jiangsu Province in 2012 "The Regression and Threshold Hypotheses of English Language Attrition among Students in China" (Project No.: 1202112C)," 2013 Philosophy and Social Science Guidance Research Project of Education Bureau of Jiangsu Province (Project No.: 2013SJD740005), Special Fundamental Research Fund for the Central Universities (Project No.: 2013B33914), 2013 Shaoxing Important Research Project of Higher Education Reform, and 2014 Research Project of Zhejiang Yuexiu University of Foreign Languages (Project No.: N2014013).

REFERENCES

Bain, K. (2004). *What the Best College Teachers Do?* Harvard University Press.

Beatty, I. (2004). Transforming student learning with classroom communication systems. *Educause Research Bulletin*, *3*, 1–13.

Berry, J. (2009). Technology support in nursing education: Clickers in the Classroom. *Nursing Education Perspectives*, *30*(5), 295–298. doi:10.1043/1536-5026-30.5.295 PMID:19824239

Bojinova, E. D., & Oigara, J. N. (2011). Teaching and Learning with Clickers: Are Clickers Good for Students? *Interdisciplinary Journal of E-Learning and Learning Objects*, *7*, 169–184.

Bransford, J., Brophy, S., & Williams, S. (2000). When computer technologies meet the learning sciences: Issues and opportunities. *Journal of Applied Developmental Psychology*, *21*(1), 59–84. doi:10.1016/S0193-3973(99)00051-9

Brothen, T., & Wambach, C. (2001). Effective student use of computerized quizzes. *Teaching of Psychology, 28*(4), 292–294. doi:10.1207/S15328023TOP2804_10

Bruff, D. (2009). *Teaching with Classroom Response Systems: Creating Active Learning Environments*. San Francisco, CA: Jossey-Bass.

Caldwell, J. E. (2007). Clickers in the large classroom: Current research and best-practice tips. *Life Sciences Education, 6*(1), 9–20. doi:10.1187/cbe.06-12-0205 PMID:17339389

Chen, J. C., Whittinghill, D. C., & Kadlowec, J. A. (2010). Classes that click: Fast, rich feedback to enhance students' learning and satisfaction. *Journal of Engineering Education, 99*(2), 158–169. doi:10.1002/j.2168-9830.2010.tb01052.x

Chi, M. T. H., De Leeuw, N., Chiu, M., & Lavancher, C. (1994). Eliciting self explanations improves understanding. *Cognitive Science, 18*, 439–477.

Chickering, A. W., & Gamson, Z. F. (Eds.). (1991). *Applying the seven principles for good practice in undergraduate education*. San Francisco, CA: Jossey-Bass.

Crozier, W. R., & Hostettler, K. (2003). The influence of shyness on children's test performance. *The British Journal of Educational Psychology, 73*(3), 317–328. doi:10.1348/000709903322275858 PMID:14672146

Daniel, D. B. (2006). *Do teachers still need to teach? Textbook-related pedagogy and student learning preferences*. Paper presented at the Teaching of Psychology Preconference of the Annual Convention of the Association for Psychological Science. New York, NY.

Duncan, D. (2005). *Clickers in the classroom: How to enhance science teaching using classroom response systems*. San Francisco, CA: Pearson Education/Addison-Wesley/Benjamin Cummings.

Fang, B. (2009). From Distraction to Engagement: Wireless Devices in the Classroom. *EDUCAUSE Quarterly, 32*(4), 12–18.

Fassinger, P. A. (1995). Professors' and students' perceptions of why students participate in class. *Teaching Sociology, 24*(1), 25–33. doi:10.2307/1318895

Han, J. H., & Finkelstein, A. (2013). Understanding the effects of instructors' pedagogical development with Clicker Assessment and Feedback technologies and the impact on students' engagement and learning in higher education. *Computers & Education, 65*, 64–76. doi:10.1016/j.compedu.2013.02.002

Heward, W. L. (1994). Three low-tech strategies for increasing the frequency of active student response during group instruction. In *Behavior analysis in education: Focus on measurably superior instruction*. Pacific Grove, CA: Brooks/Cole.

Homer, B., Plass, J., & Blake, L. (2008). The effects of video on cognitive load and social presence in multimedia learning. *Computers in Human Behavior, 24*(3), 786–797. http://doi.org/c45wb6 doi:10.1016/j.chb.2007.02.009

Homme, J., Asay, G., & Morgenstern, B. (2004). Utilisation of an audience response system. *Medical Education, 38*(5), 575. doi:10.1111/j.1365-2929.2004.01888.x PMID:15107128

Judson, E., & Sawada, D. (2002). Learning from past and present: Electronic response system in college lecture halls. *Journal of Computers in Mathematics and Science Teaching, 21*(2), 167–181.

Kaleta, R., & Joosten, T. (2007). Student response systems: A university of Wisconsin system study of clickers. *Educause Research Bulletin*, (10), 1-12.

Keller, C., et al. (2007). *Research-based Practices for Effective Clicker Use*. Paper presented at Physics Education Research Conference. New York, NY.

Kirkwood, A. (2009). E-learning: You don't always get what you hope for. *Technology, Pedagogy and Education, 18*(2), 107–121. doi:10.1080/14759390902992576

Knight, J. K., & Wood, W. B. (2005). Teaching more by lecturing less. *Cell Biology Education, 4*(4), 298–310. doi:10.1187/05-06-0082 PMID:16341257

Mayer, R. E., Stull, A., DeLeeuw, K., Almeroth, K., Bimber, B., & Chun, D. et al. (2009). Clickers in college classrooms: Fostering learning with questioning methods in large lecture classes. *Contemporary Educational Psychology, 34*(1), 51–57. doi:10.1016/j.cedpsych.2008.04.002

McKeachie, W. (1990). Research on college teaching: The historical background. *Journal of Educational Psychology, 82*(2), 190–200. doi:10.1037/0022-0663.82.2.189

Mehrabian, A., & Stefl, C. A. (1995). Basic temperament components of loneliness, shyness, and conformity. *Social Behavior and Personality, 23*(3), 253–264. doi:10.2224/sbp.1995.23.3.253

Miller, R. G., Ashar, B. H., & Getz, K. J. (2003). Evaluation of an audience response system for the continuing education of health professionals. *The Journal of Continuing Education in the Health Professions, 23*(2), 109–115. doi:10.1002/chp.1340230208 PMID:12866330

Ribbens, E. (2007). Why I like personal response systems. *Journal of College Science Teaching, 37*(2), 60–62.

Roschelle, J., Penuel, W. R., & Abrahamson, L. (2004). *Classroom response and communication systems: Research review and theory*. Paper presented at the 2004 Meeting for the American Educational Research Association. San Diego, CA.

Salmon, T. P., & Stahl, J. N. (2005). Wireless audience response system: Does it make a difference? *Journal of Extension, 43*(3), 26–31.

Smith, D. (1977). College classroom interactions and critical thinking. *Journal of Educational Psychology, 69*(2), 180–190. doi:10.1037/0022-0663.69.2.180

Sweller, J. (2010). Element interactivity and intrinsic, extraneous, and germane cognitive load. *Educational Psychology Review, 22*(2), 123–138. http://doi.org/dmvdm doi:10.1007/s10648-010-9128-5

Troy, B. E., Elizabeth, F., & Kaelin, O. (2009). Clicker satisfaction for students in human development: Differences for class type, prior exposure, and student talkativity. *North American Journal of Psychology, 11*(3), 19–32.

ADDITIONAL READING

Bruff, D. (2009). *Teaching with Classroom Response Systems: Creating Active Learning Environments*. San Francisco: Jossey-Bass.

Carpenter, C. R. (1950b). The film analyzer (rapid mass learning). Technical report. (pp. W. Office of Naval Research, NY. Special Devices Center, Trans.), Pennsylvania State Univ., University Park. College of Education.

Coleman, E. B. (1998). Using explanatory knowledge during collaborative problem solving in science. *Journal of the Learning Sciences, 7*(3-4), 387–427. doi:10.1080/10508406.1998.9672059

Coleman, E. B., Brown, A. L., & Rivkin, I. D. (1997). The effect of instructional explanations on learning from scientific texts. *Journal of the Learning Sciences, 6*(4), 347–365. doi:10.1207/s15327809jls0604_1

Collins, J. (2008). Audience response systems: Technology to engage learners. *Journal of the American College of Radiology, 5*(9), 993–1000. doi:10.1016/j.jacr.2008.04.008 PMID:18755440

Draper, S. W., & Brown, M. I. (2004). Increasing interactivity in lectures using an electronic voting system. *Journal of Computer Assisted Learning, 20*(2), 81–94. doi:10.1111/j.1365-2729.2004.00074.x

Emenike, M. E., & Holme, T. A. (2012). Classroom Response Systems Have Not Crossed the Chasm: Estimating Numbers of Chemistry Faculty Who Use Clickers. *Journal of Chemical Education, 89*(4), 465–469. doi:10.1021/ed200207p

Fagen, A. P., Crouch, C. H., & Mazur, E. (2002). Peer instruction: Results from a range of classrooms. *The Physics Teacher, 40*(4), 206–209. doi:10.1119/1.1474140

Fies, C., & Marshall, J. (2006). Classroom response systems: A review of the literature. *Journal of Science Education and Technology, 15*(1), 101–109. doi:10.1007/s10956-006-0360-1

Freeman, M., Bell, A., Comerton-Forder, C., Pickering, J., & Blayney, P. (2007). Factors affecting educational innovation with in class electronic response systems. *Australasian Journal of Educational Technology, 23*(2), 149–170.

Hoekstra, A. (2008). Vibrant student voices: Exploring effects of the use of clickers in large college courses. *Learning, Media and Technology, 33*(4), 329–341. doi:10.1080/17439880802497081

Johnson, T., & Meckelborg, A. (2008). *Student response systems: A cure for lecturalgia?* Paper presented at the World Conference on Educational Multimedia, Hypermedia and Telecommunications 2008, Vienna, Austria.

Kay, R. H., & LeSage, A. (2009). Examining the benefits and challenges of using audience response systems: A review of the literature. *Computers & Education, 53*(3), 819–827. doi:10.1016/j.compedu.2009.05.001

Kroma, M. M. (2006). Organic Farmer Networks?: Facilitating Learning and Innovation for Sustainable Agriculture. *Journal of Sustainable Agriculture, 28*(4), 5–29. doi:10.1300/J064v28n04_03

Kuo, H. V., Kohl, P. B., & Carr, L. D. (2011). Socratic dialogs and clicker use in an upper-division mechanics course. AIP Conference Proceedings Volume 1413, pp. 235-238, doi: doi:10.1063/1.3680038 (4 pages).

MacGeorge, E., Homan, S., Dunning, J. Jr, Elmore, D., Bodie, G., & Evans, E. et al. (2008). Student evaluation of audience response technology in large lecture classes. *Educational Technology Research and Development, 56*(2), 125–145. doi:10.1007/s11423-007-9053-6

Mayer, R. E., Stull, A., DeLeeuw, K., Almeroth, K., Bimber, B., & Chun, D. et al. (2009). Clickers in college classrooms: Fostering learning with questioning methods in large lecture classes. *Contemporary Educational Psychology, 34*(1), 51–57. doi:10.1016/j.cedpsych.2008.04.002

Miller, M., & Hartung, S. Q. (2012). Evidence-Based Clicker Use: Audience Response Systems for Rehabilitation Nurses. *Rehabilitation Nursing, 37*(3), 151–159. doi:10.1002/RNJ.00041 PMID:22549633

Nicol, D. J., & Boyle, J. T. (2003). Peer instruction versus class-wide discussion in large classes: A comparison of two interaction methods in the wired classroom. *Studies in Higher Education, 28*(4), 457–473. doi:10.1080/0307507032000122297

Offerdahl, E. G., & Tomanek, D. (2011). Changes in instructors' assessment thinking related to experimentation with new strategies. *Assessment & Evaluation in Higher Education, 36*(7), 781–795. doi:10.1080/02602938.2010.488794

Porter, L., Lee, C.B., Simon, B., & Zingaro, D. (2011). Peer Instruction: Do Students Really Learn from Peer Discussion in Computing? *International Computing Education Research*. 45-52.

Rao, S. P., & DiCarlo, S. E. (2000). Peer instruction improves performance on quizzes. *Advances in Physiology Education, 24*(1), 51–55. PMID:11209565

Russell, J. S., McWilliams, M., Chasen, L., & Farley, J. (2011). Using clickers for clinical reasoning and problem solving. *Nurse Educator*, *36*(1), 13–15. doi:10.1097/NNE.0b013e3182001e18 PMID:21135677

Siau, K., Sheng, H., & Nah, F. (2006). Use of classroom response system to enhance classroom interactivity. *IEEE Transactions on Education*, *49*(3), 398–403. doi:10.1109/TE.2006.879802

Simpson, V., & Oliver, M. (2007). Electronic voting systems for lectures then and now: A comparison of research and practice. *Australasian Journal of Educational Technology*, *23*(2), 187–208.

Smith, M. K., Wood, W. B., Adams, W. K., Wieman, C., Knight, J. K., Guild, N., & Su, T. T. (2009). Why peer discussion improves student performance on in-class concept questions. *Science*, *323*(5910), 122–124. doi:10.1126/science.1165919 PMID:19119232

Stowell, J. R., & Nelson, J. M. (2007). Benefits of electronic audience response systems on student participation, learning, and emotion. *Teaching of Psychology*, *34*(4), 253–258. doi:10.1080/00986280701700391

Tanner, K. D. (2009). Talking to learn: Why biology students should be talking in classrooms and how to make it happen. *CBE Life Sciences Education*, *8*(2), 89–94. doi:10.1187/cbe.09-03-0021 PMID:19487494

Trigwell, K. (2010). Teaching and learning: a relational view. In J. C. Hughes, & J. Mighty (Eds.), *Taking stock: Research on teaching and learning in higher education* (pp. 115–128). Montreal and Kingston, Canada: McGill-Queen's University Press.

Weimer, M., & Lenze, L. F. (1991). Instructional interventions: a review of the literature and interventions. In J. C. Smart (Ed.). Higher education: Handbook of theory and research, 7, 294-333). New York, NY: Agathon Press.

KEY TERMS AND DEFINITIONS

Anonymous Polling: this refers to Tthe response way when learners are receiving education especially assisted with clickers. They can poll with their identity keeping secret.

Clickers: This is a kind of technology mainly used in education, also called "Personal hand-held responders" This technology can realize instant anonymous feedback through projecting to the screen connected the computer.

Cognitive Loads: This is a term frequently used in psychology, which refers to the burden on brain when learning. They generally include intrinsic, extrinsic and germane loads.

Extraneous Load: It is caused by ineffective activities in learning and instruction.

Germane Load: It refers to individual differences and learning characteristics which can help build schema in learning.

Intrinsic Load: It refers to the difficulty of the content presented. It includes the difficulty of the material itself and learns' learning experience Intrinsic load is related to the complexity of the content required by a task.

Peer Discussion: This refers to the discussion among students in the same age, which can be stimulated by use of clickers.

Satisfaction: This is a psychological term, referring to the state when learners feel the learning style acceptable and desirable in this study.

Chapter 16
Adopting Digital Technologies in the Administration of Technical and Engineering Education

Abubakar Sadiq Bappah
Abubakar Tafawa Balewa University, Nigeria

ABSTRACT

Available literature on the use and integration of digital technologies in education place too much emphasis on variables at classroom level and neglect other areas of possible application. Traditionally, they are more concerned with the prospects and limitations of digital tools in transforming the present isolated, teacher-centered, and text-bound classrooms into rich and student-focused learning environments using mainly presentational software such as PowerPoint and interactive whiteboard software, revision software, and online content services. However, the level of studies in the area adoption of digital technologies in education administration is still in its infancy, especially that which focuses on administration and management of Technical and Engineering Education. In order to have a fairly distributed literature, this chapter presents an up-to-date technical review on the applicability of digital technologies in school administration. Specifically, it examines the vast opportunities for the adoption of digital technologies in the administration of general education and its implication on Technical and Engineering Education. These emerging technologies provide a diverse set of technological tools and resources for effective and efficient administration of Technical and Engineering Education appropriate to the changing world of work.

INTRODUCTION

Technical and Engineering Education is concerned with the acquisition of functional knowledge, positive attitudes, and hands-on skills appropriate to the dynamic world of work. Key to sustainable development in the contemporary knowledge based global community is a functional education that guarantees job creation, poverty alleviation, growth and social inclusion. Educational adminis-

DOI: 10.4018/978-1-4666-6162-2.ch016

Copyright © 2014, IGI Global. Copying or distributing in print or electronic forms without written permission of IGI Global is prohibited.

tration can be described as that force which directs human and material resources towards educational goals and standards. Management functions in education would reside with educational policy makers while administrative functions would refer to those day-to-day leadership roles of the school heads. Three main things are common in all forms of administration; policy formulation, resources allocation and policy execution (Musaazi, 1982). A major goal of every educational institution is changing the behavior of the students that spans from the levels of knowledge and skills acquisition to that of inculcation of right values and attitudes (F.R.N., 2004). Unfortunately, however these educational objectives are somewhat ambiguous and difficult to pursue. Surely difficulty of appraisal and goal immeasurability are unique characteristics of schools and other people processing organizations. These militate against meaningful and directive changes in school policies. Another peculiar feature of educational administration is the task of managing unlimited clientele system. The school is such a complex social system whose major functions seems to be delegated to it by the other systems, and to a degree, the effective functioning of the other systems depends on the effective functioning of the educational system. In Nigeria, recent increase in access to education at all levels brings about a corresponding expansion in terms of geographical distribution enrolment figures and subject offerings which explains why their problems increase not only in number but also in nature (Moja, 2000). No doubt, education is at the confluence of powerful and rapidly shifting educational, technological and political forces that will shape the structure of educational systems across the globe for the remainder of this century. The school is the only organization in which every member of the society considers himself as stakeholder. As a result, the school is vulnerable to much of public visibility and sensitivity so that the school is always being scrutinized even by those who know little or nothing about schooling. For schools to survive such pressures

they require proactive leaders with dynamic, sophisticated technical and managerial expertise. However, this does not imply subscribing to trait theory and the situational approach to leadership that were based on the organizational metaphor originating mainly in Taylorism and bureaucracy. Rather delineating an effective blend of certain leadership and managerial role skills right from routine classroom situation to high levels of decision-making. The trend is such that the more we appreciate the differences between leadership and management, the better we understand that they are inseparable.

In recent years there has been a groundswell of interest in the rapidly shifting paradigms that challenge traditional structure of educational systems across the globe as a response to a changing world of work. These changes are brought about by digital technologies which combine the traditional elements of hardware and complete software solutions to provide a wide range services. They provide diverse set of technological tools and resources for effective and efficient administration of technical and engineering education appropriate to the changing world of work. These tools comprise of a series of information and communication services used in many walks of life to collaborate at a distance with colleagues and implement cloud computing. Also available, is a series of technical and engineering solutions such as, industrial robots, Computer Aided Design tools, and modeling software that are ever increasing in flexibility and sophistication. Sequel to the unique nature of Technical and Engineering Education Programs, digital solutions and support services could differ slightly in the way and manner they are applied in general education administration. Areas of major differences such as special digital support services to help staff and students in workshop scheduling, tracking as well as retrieval of tools, equipments and machineries were comprehensively discussed. Novel approaches such as e-finance; facility management and automated energy optimization were all discussed as new tools applicable in financial, staff and students' administrative support services. Researchers and practitioners alike appraise the power of digital technology to achieve increased efficiency in managing a more dynamic, unpredictable, global, and competitive school system (Lai, 2011). These digital technologies could provide an array of powerful tools that may help in evolving a digitally-inspired administrative supports of technical and engineering education appropriate to the changing world of work. These emerging technologies are moving the leading economies forward and, at the same time, enabling the developing world to leapfrog from their current status straight into the forefront of development (Kumar, 2008). Hence, technology integration in education administration enables the development of knowledge intensive processes and services appropriate for the increasingly digital workplace, and raise educational relevance of its products at all levels technical and engineering education in Nigeria.

ELECTRONIC SOLUTIONS FOR ADMINISTRATIVE SUPPORT IN EDUCATION

In recent years there has been a wave of interest in the adoption of administrative e-solutions as a response to the intertwined trending processes of globalization and proliferation of the digital technologies. Many countries are engaged in a number of efforts to effect changes in the classroom processes of preparing students for information and technology based society (Clark-Wilson, Oldknow, & Sutherland, 2011). Thus, modern organizations recognize the need to maintain and manage information as an organizational asset for the survival of firms in this very competitive knowledge-based world. They also recognize the need for today's managers to be well versed in information resources management and competent in adapting to these global changes. A typical technical and engineering training institution requires

a comprehensive data and information management plan to support the effective management of training facilities, tools and equipments as well as to assist in external reporting and accountability. Such information would guide the government to plan and deliver its public resources effectively. The use of digital administrative support services are too numerous to mention in this era of globalization and information revolution. However, this chapter has captured them all under two successive but technically intertwined services as Content Management and Facility Management services. Pertinent outlets for technology integration under either of them were identified and exhaustively discussed with particular reference to technical and engineering education in Nigeria. The layout is embedded with at least one central database server to either include or support at least one permanent operator workstation connected directly or via Internet protocol to integrate a number of digital solutions into a common user interface as shown in Figure 1.

Content Management Services

Content management services are those paperless office procedures that are fast replacing the traditional hardcopy and often classified information format. The Web-based communications and information system offers consistent, current and readily accessible information to a range of internal and external stakeholders. Essentially, the system avails content and activity options that respond to the needs of the interested public, potential students, current students and staff. Comprehensive adoption of content management services in the administration of technical and engineering education will minimize unnecessary bureaucratic bottlenecks concerning staff matters, students' affairs, finance, and general administrative procedures. For the purpose of this chapter, the scope of content management services covered three distinct but technically intertwined support

Figure 1. Electronic administrative support services

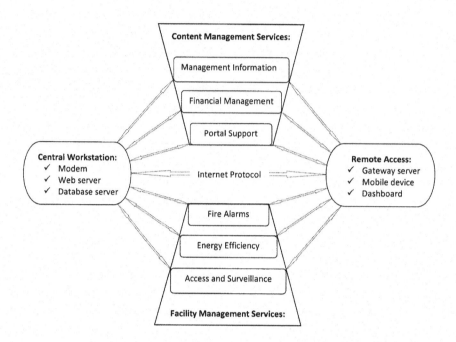

areas as; management information, financial management and portal support services. These application areas are well presented in Table 1.

1. **Management Information:** Management information describes the use of clearly defined electronic standards and procedures that generate, analyze, transmit, store and retrieve variety of information necessary to manage an institution effectively (Laudon, Laudon & Brabston, 2012). It therefore, provides an objective system of handling information and reduces expenses related to task-intensive manual activities. Academic boards and management committees in educational technical institutions would rely on such vital information in making strategic decisions and meeting important timeframes. Typical areas of application include establishment and service matters where digital solutions could be employed in assessing staffing needs, conducting staff recruitment, monitoring staff and students'

progression, and staff access to and engagement in training and development. There is also a very high feasibility of using smart card technology to aggregate a range of students' support services, including library borrowing, printing from network computers, access to workshop and laboratory facilities, class attendance, payment of fees, access to online systems, assessments and results, and so on. Some activities may be charged while others are considered part of the enrolment fee. In both cases, activity is tracked. Students pay into their smart card account, which is automatically debited when undertaking designated activities.

2. **Financial Management:** Records of budget preparation, financial reporting, grants administration and cash flow monitoring carried out by institutions need proper documentation for reference purposes. These records were kept in hardcopies before the advent of digital technologies. Fortunately, nowadays there is an increasing possibil-

Table 1. Content management services in technical and engineering institutions

Application Category	Services Rendered
(a) Management Information	✓ Establishment and service matters. Assessing staffing needs, staff recruitment, monitoring staff and students' progression, training and development. ✓ Internal and external memos. Staff and students' circulars, directives and communications to other offices. ✓ Monitoring the implementation of institutional strategic plan. ✓ Students' Support: using smart card technology to aggregate library borrowing, printing from network computers, access to workshop and laboratory facilities, class attendance, payment of fees, and so on.
(b) Financial Management	✓ e-Accounting. Supporting budget preparation; financial reporting in terms of year-to-date income and expenditures and variances; grants administration; cash flow monitoring; regular performance reporting; preparations for annual reporting and audits. ✓ e-Procurement. Monitoring of contract performance, equipment bookings, and ordering. ✓ Equipment inventory. Maintaining records of the capital infrastructure, including buildings, furniture, hardware, machinery used in training, classroom equipment and vehicles.
(c) Portal Support	✓ Institutional information. Academic calendar, course description, research support, faculty evaluations, statistical analyses. ✓ Yellow pages. Maintaining Website giving access to administrative units, faculties and departments; managing e-mail accounts for faculty staff and students.

ity of utilizing flexible financial software solutions over an institutional portal to capture, process, and report all transactions electronically. Financial administrators attest to the fact that Web-based electronic transactions the potential to promote operating efficiency and provide significant cost savings (Zwass, 2003). Corroborating to this fact, (Aboelmaged, 2010), opined that e-procurement has become one of the most successful applications of electronic commerce, having been implemented by many companies seeking better business processes. Assuredly, this process would facilitate the acquisition of right item at the right time with the right price devoid of any corruption practices and in misuse of power. The implication for education administration will be on the aspects of online purchase of goods and services (consumables and repairs) and resources record keeping. These records may also include cost, depreciation and a schedule for the maintenance and replacement of assets. The system should also include monitoring of contract performance, invoicing and payment. Invariably

therefore, successful integration of content management services in a technical and engineering institution will to a greater extent help educational administrators handle their job effectively and efficiently.

3. **Portal Support:** Portals are one of the emerging knowledge-based content management systems. They are essentially sites on the Internet that serve as search engines to facilitate users' browsing experience from the morass of sources. A prelude to sustainable integration of content management services is through institutional Websites by which teachers, students and parents can access a wide variety of information related to the institution. Portal support services relevant to technical and engineering educational institutions can be categorized into three; institutional, networking, and resource-based portal services. An Institutional Website would general information about itself, courses offered, staff profiles, subscription services, projects, and publications for both internal and external consumptions. The situation of administering educational institutions without these portal services

is such that data about teachers, salaries, student grades, the number of pupils per class, and statistical information in general are scattered and are not readily available in a single unit of database (Jhurree, 2005). Secondly, an institutional portal should serve as a networking anchor site or gateway from which to access various educational services such as World Wide Web, e-mail services, and chat rooms both online and offline. It would be responsible for maintaining various students' support services like course applications, course and examination registration, viewing of examination results, and access to timetables. Finally, an institutional portal incorporates a feature of resource-based portal that provides access to subject-specific educational resources online, subscription services, as well as links to other resource sites.

Facility Management Services

Facility management solution is a leading administrative support deployed to different sectors of the economy for the purposes of surveillance, facility booking, resource tracking, and efficient energy management in a building (Akpınar & Kaptan, 2010). Implication of facility management in technical and engineering education has to do with deployment of digital solutions that would integrate highly sophisticated Closed Circuit Television (CCTV) surveillance and access control facilities to help in monitoring day-to-day workshop operations and to reduce the risk of injuries due to congestion in the work spaces. Generally, facility management services in a typical technical and engineering institution can be classified under three distinct categories as presented in Table 2.

1. **Access and Surveillance**: Intrusion detection is more than ever an urgent need in Nigeria has had a long and unfortunate history of

communal conflicts and ethno-religious violence(Walker, 2012). Unsuspecting staff and students often become the soft targets for reprisal attacks, hostage taking for ransom or they are used as shied by criminals escaping arrest. A proactive answer to this ugly situation is in the integration of CCTV surveillance and access control facilities. Accordingly, an efficient facility management should help school administration to fast-track inventory management, personal records maintenance and workshop schedules. Radio Frequency Identification (RFID) system that finds applications in real time location tracking and monitoring the movement of objects or human beings in other organizations is a potential candidate for this task (Ayoade, 2007). This unit consists of RFID tags which are tiny computer chips connected to miniature antennas that can be affixed to physical objects or living creatures. RFID tags can also be embedded in objects or injected hypodermically under the skin of humans and animals. In this way, RFID numbers transmitted by RFID tags (transponders) are retrieved by RFID readers (interrogators) using either wireless sensor network or Internet protocol (Matrix-Controls, 2009). The RFID tag attached to a workshop facility, for instance, sends ID through RFID reader to the notebook or any mobile device. The notebook will request from the server the realtime data on the workshop. A mote senses environmental data as a means to detecting objects and locations. The mote gateway updates database server which in turn transmits the same to the Web server at user's request. Pertinent data being updated in the case of a workshop, for insatance, include workshop's name, eligible users, and schedules. Perceived benefits of adopting RFID technology in schools include improved visibility of assets, more effective access to school facilities and reduced

Table 2. Facility management services in technical and engineering institutions

Application Category	Services Rendered
(a) Access and Surveillance	✓ Workshop tools and equipment tracking through Radio Frequency Identification (RFID) ✓ Closed Circuit Television (CCTV) surveillance on school facilities ✓ Facility booking service ✓ Intrusion detection
(b) Energy Efficiency	✓ Heating, Ventilation and Air conditioning (HVAC) regulation ✓ Automated energy optimization ✓ Lighting control
(c) Fire Alarms	✓ Smoke detection ✓ Real-time fire alarm system ✓ Automated emergency exit

unattended assets loses. In other words, that user-friendly Web-based IT solution could allow technical and engineering staff and Students to book for certain limited resources such as seminar rooms, recreation rooms, lecture rooms, workshop space, library facilities, sports facilities, tools and machineries needed to carry out certain experiments. The benefits of facility booking cannot be over-emphasized as users can log on workstation to check facilities and time slots available for classes or meetings, and to book the facilities online. Modern booking systems incorporate additional flexibility features such as booking amendment, cancellation, extension and historical bookings.

2. **Energy Efficiency:** Energy efficiency is another integral part of modern designs which automates the optimization of building's energy needs (energy management) including heating, ventilation and air conditioning (HVAC), lighting control, security and access control, and fire alarm and safety (Wang & Ma, 2008). Once a facility is booked, the booking system, being connected to the energy efficiency service unit, will activate the air-conditioning, lighting system and the door to the facilities at the right time before the scheduled activity. The system will also turn off the utilities shortly after the completion of the activity. This way, not only is the

institute able to manage usage of resources effectively, it is also able to maximize the availability of facilities, save energy, and ensure that facilities are not booked by those unauthorized. This approach to resource utilization optimizes energy consumption efficiency by determining when systems are in demand and turning them off when there is no reason to have them operational.

3. **Fire Alarms:** Due to the improved fire, security and other emergency procedures that the technology offers, the workplace will be much safer. The technology can locate potential hazards within the workplace, notify emergency response teams, and inform personnel about the potential danger (Craighead, 2009). In the event of fire outbreak in a workshop space, for instance, the fire system could immediately signal the air flow system to close the dampers, immediately restricting air flow. At the same time, it could signal the building access system to release all door locks. Elevators could be instructed to return to the nearest floor, open and cease operating, and video cameras could be instructed to begin recording at specific locations. At the same time, IP phone calls could be automatically generated to the fire department as well as to all relevant departments, students, and staff. This could all occur within seconds,

helping to save lives and limit property destruction. Furthermore, teachers can incorporate their school's energy features into their curriculum, providing students with hands-on learning opportunities about energy and the environment. The ability for a building to monitor and self-regulate energy consumption offers enormous potentials to school administrative support in that it cuts energy bills, reduces annual maintenance costs and conserves finite resources.

CONCLUSION

Education is at the confluence of powerful and rapidly shifting educational, technological and political forces that will shape the structure of educational systems across the globe for the remainder of this century. Hence, the imminent need for administrators to keep date with new administrative techniques and trends associated with the specific features of technical and engineering education programs, such as flexible entry and re-entry patterns, continuous training in the workplace, and relevance to the needs of the world of work. To accomplish this goal there requires both a change in the traditional view of the administrative process and an understanding of how the new digital technologies can create unrivaled learning environments in which available resources are allocated in line with the objectives and priorities of the various programs to ensure their efficient utilization. Hence, applicability of digital technologies in meeting these needs cannot be overemphasized. Successful adoption of digital tools to support financial services, staff and students administrative support services would definitely make significant impact in the smooth running of educational sector. Due to the unique nature of technical and engineering training program, digital applications for the support of staff and students' administrative services could differ in with those applied in general education

administration. The differences observed in this chapter are digital deployments in the areas of workshop and laboratory scheduling, tracking and monitoring of tools, equipments and machineries. These complex services would require that timely, accurate and accessible information is available for effective decision-making and accountability mechanisms.

REFERENCES

Aboelmaged, M. G. (2010). Predicting e-procurement adoption in a developing country: An empirical integration of technology acceptance model and theory of planned behaviour. *Industrial Management & Data Systems*, *110*(3), 392–414. doi:10.1108/02635571011030042

Akpınar, S., & Kaptan, H. (2010). Computer aided school administration system using RFID technology. *Procedia: Social and Behavioral Sciences*, *2*(2), 4392–4397. doi:10.1016/j.sbspro.2010.03.699

Ayoade, J. (2007). Roadmap to solving security and privacy concerns in RFID systems. *Computer Law & Security Report*, *23*(6), 555–561. doi:10.1016/j.clsr.2007.09.005

Clark-Wilson, A., Oldknow, A., & Sutherland, R. (2011). *Digital technologies and mathematics education: A report from a working group of the Joint Mathematical Council of the United Kingdom*. London: Joint Mathematical Council.

Craighead, G. (2009). *High-rise security and fire life safety*. Burlington, MA: Butterworth-Heinemann.

F.R.N. (2004). *National Policy on Education* (4th ed.). Lagos: NERDC Press.

Jhurree, V. (2005). Technology integration in education in developing countries: Guidelines to policy makers. *International Education Journal*, *6*(4), 467–483.

Kumar, K. (2008). Virtual design studios: Solving learning problems in developing countries. In S. Hirtz, D. G. Harper & S. Mackenzie (Eds.), *Education for a Digital World: Advice, Guidelines, and Effective Practice From Around the Globe* (pp. 23 – 30). BCC and Commonwealth of Learning. Retrieved from http://creativecommons.org

Lai, K.-W. (2011). Digital technology and the culture of teaching and learning in higher education. *Australasian Journal of Educational Technology*, 27(8), 1263–1275.

Laudon, K. C., Laudon, J. P., & Brabston, M. E. (2012). *Management information systems: Managing the digital firm* (Vol. 12). Pearson.

Matrix-Controls. (2009). *Facility booking system (FBS)*. Retrieved from http://www.matrix-controls.com/cms/index.php?page=content/products

Moja, T. (2000). *Nigeria education sector analysis: An analytical synthesis of performance and main issues*. World Bank Report. Retrieved from http://siteresources.worldbank.org/NIGERI-AEXTN/Resources/ed_sec_analysis.pdf

Musaazi, J. C. S. (1982). *The theory and practice of educational administration*. London: Macmillan Nigeria.

Walker, A. (2012). *What Is Boko Haram?* (United States Institute of Peace Special Report). Washington, DC: US Institute of Peace. Retrieved from http://www.xtome.org/docs/groups/boko-haram/SR308.pdf

Wang, S., & Ma, Z. (2008). Supervisory and optimal control of building HVAC systems: A review. *HVAC&R Research, 14*(1), 3-32.

Zwass, V. (2003). Electronic commerce and organizational innovation: Aspects and opportunities. *International Journal of Electronic Commerce, 7*(3), 7–38.

ADDITIONAL READING

Annan, K. A. (2000). *We the Peoples: The Role of the United Nations in the 21st Century* [new Century-New Challenges]. New York: United Nations Publications.

Asiabaka, I. P. (2010). Access and Use of Information and Communication Technology (ICT) For Administrative Purposes by Principals of Government Secondary Schools in Nigeria. *The Researcher, 2*(1), 43–50.

Baillie, C., & Moore, I. (2004). *Effective learning and teaching in engineering*. New York: Routledge. doi:10.4324/9780203415986

Bardadym, V. A. (1996). *Computer-aided school and university timetabling: The new wave Practice and theory of automated timetabling* (pp. 22–45). Heidelberg: Springer-Berlin.

Bates, A. (2000). *Managing technology change: strategies for college and university leaders*. San Francisco: Jossey-Bass.

Beetham, H., & Sharpe, R. (Eds.). (2013). *Rethinking Pedagogy for a Digital Age: Designing for 21st Century Learning*. New York: Routledge.

Cheng, Y.-C. (2005). *New paradigm for re-engineering education: Globalization, localization and individualization* (Vol. 6). Dordrecht: Springer.

Cohen, E. (2002). *Challenges of information technology education in the 21st century*. Hershey: IGI Global.

Demir, K. (2006). School management information systems in primary schools. *The Turkish Online Journal of Educational Technology, 5 (2)*.

Hall, P. (1988). Cities of tomorrow Retrieved from https://www.gdfsuez.com/wp-content/uploads/2013/05/BD-plaquetteGDF-GB-V5.pdf

Hattangdi, A., & Ghosh, A. (2008). *Enhancing the quality and accessibility of higher education through the use of Information and Communication Technologies.* Paper presented at the International Conference on Emergent Missions, Resources, and the Geographic Locus in Strategy as a part of the 11th Annual Convention of the Strategic Management Forum (SMF), India 2008.

Heywood, J. (2005). *Engineering education: Research and development in curriculum and instruction.* New Jersey: Wiley-IEEE Press. doi:10.1002/0471744697

Jensen, D., & Draffan, G. (2004). *Welcome to the Machine: Science, Surveillance, and the Culture of Control.* Vermont: Chelsea Green Publishing Company.

Kalman, C. S. (2008). *Successful science and engineering teaching: Theoretical and learning perspectives* (Vol. 3). Bonn: Springer. doi:10.1007/978-1-4020-6910-9

Kelly, A., & Harris, M. J. (1978). *Management of industrial maintenance.* London: Newnes-Butterworths.

Lauglo, J., & Maclean, R. (2005). *Vocationalisation of secondary education revisited* (Vol. 1). Dordrecht: Springer. doi:10.1007/1-4020-3034-7_1

Levermore, G. (2002). Building Energy Management Systems: An Application to Heating, Natural Ventilation, Lighting and Occupant Satisfaction. (0203477340). from Taylor & Francis

Lowry, G. (2002). Factors affecting the success of building management system installations. *Building Services Engineering Research and Technology, 23*(1), 57–66. doi:10.1191/0143624402bt022oa

Maclean, R., & Wilson, D. N. (2009). International Handbook of Education for the Changing World of Work: Bridging Academic and Vocational Education (Vol. 1 - 6). Bonn: Springer.

Marginson, S. (1999). After globalization: Emerging politics of education. *Journal of Education Policy, 14*(1), 19–31. doi:10.1080/026809399286477

N.F.P.A. (2011). *NFPA 101: Life Safety Code 2012.* Quincy: National Fire Protection Association.

Niederman, F., Brancheau, J. C., & Wetherbe, J. C. (1991). Information systems management issues for the 1990s. *Management Information Systems Quarterly, 15*(4), 475–500. doi:10.2307/249452

Proulx, G. (1995). Evacuation time and movement in apartment buildings. *Fire Safety Journal, 24*(3), 229–246. doi:10.1016/0379-7112(95)00023-M

Seeley, I. H. (1987). *Building maintenance.* Macmillan Basingstoke.

Sriskanthan, N., Tan, F., & Karande, A. (2002). Bluetooth based home automation system. *Microprocessors and Microsystems, 26*(6), 281–289. doi:10.1016/S0141-9331(02)00039-X

Tien, F. F., & Fu, T.-T. (2008). The correlates of the digital divide and their impact on college student learning. *Computers & Education, 50*(1), 421–436. doi:10.1016/j.compedu.2006.07.005

Tinio, V. L. (2003). ICT in Education Retrieved from http://www.apdip.net/

Zain, M. Z., Atan, H., & Idrus, R. M. (2004). The impact of information and communication technology (ICT) on the management practices of Malaysian Smart Schools. *International Journal of Educational Development, 24*(2), 201–211. doi:10.1016/j.ijedudev.2003.10.010

Zajda, J. I. (Ed.). (2005). *International handbook on globalisation, education and policy research: Global pedagogies and policies.* Dordrecht: Springer. doi:10.1007/1-4020-2960-8

KEY TERMS AND DEFINITIONS

Adoption: Integration.

Digital Solution: A user dedicated application software package.

Educational Administration: A force which directs human and material resources towards educational goals and standards.

E-Finance: A digital solution through which financial transactions are captured, processed, stored, and reported on demand electronically.

E-Management: Utilization of technological tools and resources for effective and efficient attainment of organizational goals and objectives.

Energy Efficiency: A degree to which energy resources are optimized to bring about best results.

Technical and Engineering Education: That type of education which is geared towards acquisition of functional knowledge, positive attitudes, and hands-on skills appropriate to the dynamic world of work.

Technology: A systematic application of scientific knowledge for the production of goods or provision of services.

Chapter 17

Knowledge Management and Reverse Mentoring in the Nigerian Tertiary Institutions

Ayotunde Adebayo
University of Lagos, Nigeria

ABSTRACT

The effective management of knowledge is now believed to be the main core competence in order for an organization to survive within the competitive business environment in Nigeria. However, the current implementation of KM within the Nigerian tertiary institution is still in its developmental phase. The Nigerian tertiary institution is resource-oriented, and as such, the most important assets to the universities within the educational sector are their knowledge assets. Therefore, Nigerian tertiary institutions need to understand and appreciate that knowledge is a valuable asset that can help sustain their competitive advantage within this sector. This chapter, therefore, focuses on the relationship between knowledge management and reverse mentoring within the Nigerian tertiary sector. It also focuses on the challenges of reverse mentoring and how value can be derived when knowledge is shared as a result of the mentoring relationship being established between the participants involved (mentor and the mentee).

INTRODUCTION

The interests in knowledge management have grown due to the fact that there is an element of trust and certainty that knowledge creation and transfer is of significance to an organization's effectiveness on a long term basis (Hurley & Green, 2005). Knowledge management tries to make maximum use of the knowledge made available to an organization and at the same time creating new knowledge in the process. Knowledge management is about understanding, appreciating and making use of the knowledge of individuals and also developing an organizational culture where knowledge sharing can flourish. As a result of this process, the organization creates value from their intellectual and knowledge based assets; hence the organization would continually develop as a result from the knowledge of the employees throughout the organization. The implementation of Knowledge Management in the Nigerian edu-

DOI: 10.4018/978-1-4666-6162-2.ch017

Copyright © 2014, IGI Global. Copying or distributing in print or electronic forms without written permission of IGI Global is prohibited.

cational sector is still in its development phase, and as such it is an interesting area to focus on.

Reverse mentoring is a concept that is being used in organizations today as a tool for effective knowledge sharing. However, the challenge it poses sometimes outweighs its benefits. This paper therefore focuses on the relationship between knowledge management and reverse mentoring within the Nigerian tertiary sector. It also focuses on the challenges of reverse mentoring and how value can be derived when knowledge is shared as a result of the mentoring relationship being established between the participants involved (mentor and the mentee).

In the area of Knowledge Management, there have been several efforts carried out on how to define, categorize and classify knowledge; and some of these definitions have been changed, widened and have been subject to query. As such, there is not a particular definition of knowledge and as such many authors have their views and perception of the phenomenon. The definitions of knowledge are as follows:

- Webster dictionary describes knowledge as "the application to facts or ideas acquired by study, investigation, observation or experience"(Merriam-Webster, 2010). This definition stresses the fact that knowledge goes beyond information. It also involves facts and ideas that have been somehow got through experience.
- Knowledge can also be defined as "actionable information"(Tiwana, 2001).This also means information used for a purpose. The term actionable is a concept that signifies importance, and to be available at the right place at the right time so as to enable decision making (Tiwana, 2001).
- Davenport and Prusak (1998) describes Knowledge as a blend of values, experiences, contextual information, and grounded intuition that gives an environment for evaluation and a framework for incorpo-

rating new experiences and information. Knowledge is initiated and is functional in the minds of the people who possess the knowledge.
- Zand (1997) defines knowledge as "organised information applicable to problem solving."
- "Knowledge consists of truths and beliefs, perspectives and concepts, judgements and expectations, methodologies and know-how" (Wiig, 1997).
- Polanyi (1975) defines knowledge as "information that has been organised and analysed to make it understandable and applicable to problem solving and decision making."
- Gamble and Blackwell (2001) defines knowledge as "information connected in relationships."

For the purpose of this paper, knowledge would be defined as a blend of values, experiences, contextual information, and grounded intuition that gives an environment for evaluation and a framework for incorporating new experiences and information (Davenport & Prusak, 1998). This definition combines all the definitions of all the authors above in a systematic way. This definition shows that knowledge is initiated and is functional in the minds of the people who possess the knowledge. It also shows that knowledge emerges through conversation and exchange of ideas. This definition also stresses that fact that the path to knowledge is through people and relationships. According to Nonaka and Takeuchi (1995), there is a clear definition between information and knowledge. The Table 1 below shows the comparison between information and knowledge.

For better understanding, knowledge is described from the perspective of its hierarchical view which involves the data, information and knowledge (Gupter & Sharma, 2004). From this standpoint, data involves numbers or characters, information can imply clear and simple processed

Table 1. Comparison between information and knowledge

Information	Knowledge
It is easily expressed in written form	Hard to communicate, and difficult to express in words
Processed data	Actionable information
It simply gives us the facts	It allows the making of predictions and predictive decision.
It evolves from data, and formalized in databases, books, manuals and documents.	It is formed, established in and shared among collective minds. It also grows and changes with experience, success and failures.
It is simple, clear and structured.	It is partly unstructured and can be unclear or muddy.

Source (Nonaka & Takeuchi, 1995); Tiwana, 2001).

data while knowledge refers actionable information which can be influenced by experiences.

Bahra (2001) suggests that knowledge is the most important factor of production for many companies. Nevertheless, knowledge is not usually understood. But it is worth mentioning that knowledge is not to be overlooked. It is easy to confuse knowledge with information or data, and so Figure 1 depicts the relationship amongst the three parameters which is called the knowledge hierarchy. Each phase of the hierarchy builds on the one below. For instance, data is needed to produce information, but as suggested by Gupter and Sharma (2004), information involves more than just data. This is the same in the case for information being required to produce knowledge but knowledge involves more than just information.

CLASSIFICATION OF KNOWLEDGE

Tiwana (2001), and other authors such as Gamble and Black well (2001), Nonaka and Takeuchi (1995) all suggest that knowledge can be split into two broad categories which are the tacit and the explicit forms of knowledge. These two types of knowledge are explained in the sub-sections below.

Tacit Knowledge

Ruggles and Holtshouse (1999) describe tacit knowledge as one that is stored in the heads of people. Gamble and Blackwell (2001) also stress the fact that this type of knowledge is a context-specific knowledge which is hard to record, articulate and formalize. They also suggest that tacit knowledge includes individual beliefs, images and technical skills.

The characteristics of tacit knowledge are:

- It is personal and context-specific
- It is stored in heads of people
- It is difficult to manage and support with IT
- Through a process of trial and error in practice, tacit knowledge can be established and developed.

Explicit Knowledge

The other form of knowledge (explicit) is described by Ruggles and Holtshouse (1999) as knowledge that is put into a formal language including grammatical statements and mathematical expressions. Explicit knowledge is a type of knowledge that can be stored in a database and processed by a computer. It can also be electronically transmitted. This type of knowledge can be easily shared and expressed in document form. Tiwana (2001) explains the characteristics of explicit knowledge with regards to its nature, development process, formalization, location, conversion process, IT support and the medium needed. This is shown in Table 2.

Different perceptions of knowledge result into different views on Knowledge Management. Universities within Nigeria that view knowledge

Figure 1. Knowledge hierarchy
Source (Gupter and Sharma, 2004).

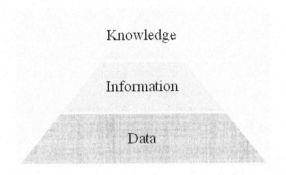

as either 'a state of mind', 'an object', 'a process' or 'capability' would have possible implications for KM been implemented within their respective universities. Knowledge should be viewed by the universities within the Nigerian tertiary institutions as a 'process'. This is because the possible implications for KM would be to focus on the KM process of the university which includes the creation of knowledge, knowledge sharing, knowledge storage, knowledge transfer and application. These KM processes are important as they can be supported by various KM tools and techniques such as intranets, communities of practice (CoP), and project teams (Gamble & Blackwell, 2001).

Knowledge management is significant as it is used to achieve business goals, and also to gain

Table 2. Characteristics of explicit knowledge

Characteristic	Explicit
Nature	It can be codified
Formalization	It can be codified and conveyed in a systematic and formal language
Development process	It is developed through the clarification of tacit understanding
Location	It is stored in databases, documents etc.
IT support	It is supported by existing IT
Medium	It can be transferred through usual electronic channels.

Source (Tiwana, 2001).

competitive advantage (Tiwana, 2001). This is done by controlling the core business competencies, improving and speeding up innovation, enhancing decision making, enhancing cycle-times, hence leading to the achievement of business goals. Davenport and Pursak (1998) suggest that KM helps to create, distribute and explore knowledge so as to establish and retain value from core business competencies. There are various ways in which the knowledge management concept appeals individuals and a result; there are various definitions of KM. The definitions of knowledge management are as follows:

- Knowledge Management is "getting the right knowledge to the right people at the right time so they can make the best decision"(Holzner & Marx, 1979).
- Knowledge Management "applies systematic approaches to find, understand, and use knowledge to create value" (Dretske, 1981). This simple definition of KM focuses on value creation through the production of knowledge.

For the purpose of this paper, Knowledge Management is defined as "the systematic, explicit, and deliberate building, renewal, and application of knowledge to maximize an enterprise knowledge-related effectiveness and returns from its assets" (Wiig, 1997). This definition incorporates the essence of knowledge management and also shows the necessity of having control of the knowledge possessed by the individual within an organisation so as to improve its competitiveness in a business context. This definition also hints that there is the creation of an atmosphere that encourages knowledge sharing; because in the world of business today, competitive advantage is fully dependent on the ability of an organisation to successfully arrange and position its organisational knowledge and intellectual capital.

KNOWLEDGE MANAGEMENT PROCESS

Wiig (1997) proposed a step knowledge management process which is outlined below:

- Creation and Sourcing
- Storage and Retrieval
- Transfer
- Application and Value realisation.

Knowledge Creation

According to Tiwana (2001), knowledge creation is initiated when knowledge is created and expanded through the interactions of tacit and explicit knowledge socially. Table 3 illustrates knowledge transformation.

Table 4 shows the form of interaction between the tacit and explicit knowledge, which interact between the individual and the organization

In order to understand the nature of knowledge creation, Nonaka and Takeuchi (1995) proposed a model of the knowledge creating process which is the SECI model. This model consists of three elements which are listed as follows:

- SECI
- Ba
- Knowledge Assets

The SECI, "Ba" and knowledge assets interact with each other in a dynamic form. Tiwana (2001) suggests that an organisation's knowledge assets are gathered together, organized and shared in "Ba." Nonaka and Takeuchi (1995), Tiwana (2001) and Sanchez (2001) all agree to the fact that the tacit knowledge possessed by people is converted by the spiral of knowledge through the SECI (Socialization – Externalization – Combination – Internalization). Figure 2 shows the SECI model.

Source (Nonaka and Takeuchi, 1995)

According to Wiig (1997), knowledge creation involves the continuous process of interaction between tacit and explicit knowledge. Therefore, the four various types of knowledge conversion relate in the knowledge creation spiral shown above in Figure 3. New spirals of knowledge creation can be triggered as it moves up through the organizational levels. According to Nonaka and Takeuchi (1995), the processes of knowledge conversion are as follows:

- **From tacit to tacit:** This is the situation where individuals acquire new knowledge directly from others. This is done by sharing experiences to form tacit knowledge such as technical skills.
- **From tacit to explicit:** This is the articulation of tacit knowledge into explicit concepts. This can be done through hypothesis, models, and concepts.
- **From explicit to explicit:** This is the blending of different forms of explicit knowledge. Examples of these are that of documents or databases. Individuals join and exchange knowledge through conversations, documents etc. The information gathered is re-organised by categorising and sorting. Numerous training programmes take place in this format.
- **From explicit to tacit:** This is the process in which individuals internalize knowledge from documents into their experience.

Table 3. Knowledge transformations

From / To	Tacit Knowledge	Explicit Knowledge
Tacit Knowledge	Socialization (Sympathized Knowledge)	Externalization (Conceptual Knowledge)
Explicit Knowledge	Internalization (Operational Knowledge)	Combination (Systematic Knowledge)

Source (Tiwana, 2001).

Figure 2. The SECI Model

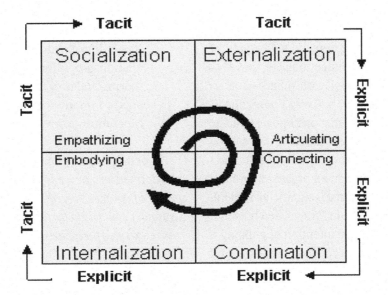

Internalization is the process of conversion of explicit to tacit. This form of transformation is said to be related to "learning by doing."

Knowledge Storage and Retrieval

According to Tiwana (2001), knowledge storage and its retrieval is a significant part in organisational knowledge management. Tiwana further argues that knowledge storage and its retrieval is linked with explicit knowledge which can be stored in documents, databases etc.

Gamble and Blackwell (2001) suggest the importance of the difference between individual and organisational memory for successful knowledge compilation.

- **Individual memory:** "This is a subjective experience in which memories belong to individuals, helping to build identity by differentiating this individual from others" (Lavenne, Renard & Tollet, 2005).
- **Organisational memory:** "This can be defined as the way an organisation ap-

plies past knowledge to present activities" (Morrison & Olfman, 1998).

Knowledge is acquired through learning by individuals or groups. This knowledge acquired is now fixed in the individual, group and organisational memory (Bencisk, Lore & Marosi, 2009).

Knowledge Transfer

Knowledge transfer is the passing across of knowledge from one person or place to another.

According to Carlile and Rebentisch (2003), knowledge transfer is an important area in knowledge management that is associated with the movement of knowledge across the boundaries created by specialized knowledge domains.

Knowledge transfer has been talked about together with the word knowledge sharing due to the fact that researchers and authors have not succeeded in providing a plain and clear definition for knowledge transfer. It is worth mentioning that these two concepts are different in some areas.

According to Ryu, Ho and Han (2003), knowledge sharing is a people-to-people process. This process can be described as a two-way process because individuals engage in the mutual or joint exchange of knowledge (Kucza, 2001). Knowledge sharing also involves the demand and supply of new knowledge. Knowledge transfer involves enthusiastically discussing with others so as to learn what they know or actively communicating to other individuals what one knows (Kucza, 2001). Knowledge transfer mechanisms can be used to acquire knowledge especially in a situation whereby employees within an organization have identified the knowledge that is significant to them. KM and knowledge transfer are viewed by some as a process solely for the intention of creating a culture associated with knowledge sharing, and communication so as to improve organizational innovation (Liebowitz, 2002).

DEFINITION REVERSE MENTORING

In the area of mentoring, there have been several efforts made to define and classify the techniques involved in mentoring and as such, there is no particular definition of the word mentoring majorly due to the fact that so many scholars who have attempted to define this phenomenon have different views and perception on the word mentoring. The definitions of the word are as follows:

- Davenport and Prusak (2002) define mentoring as "a process that involves communication and it is relationship based."
- Gamble and Blackwell (2001) define mentoring as "a personal relationship in which a more experienced and knowledgeable person helps to guide a less experienced and knowledgeable person." This definition focuses more on the objectives of mentoring which is knowledge transfer from one person to another.
- Barha (2001) defines Mentoring as "a process for the informal transmission of knowledge, that provides psychosocial

support which in turn is perceived by the recipient as relevant to their career or professional development." This definition shows that mentoring is more than just a relationship. It focuses more on knowledge sharing and how this knowledge can be applied to improve an individual's skills and capabilities for work.

For the purpose of this paper, Mentoring would be defined as *a process for the informal transmission of knowledge, that provides psychosocial support which is in turn perceived by the recipient as relevant to their career or professional development* (Barha 2001). This definition combines all other definitions listed above in a systematic way.

From the definitions above, it can be seen that mentoring involves informal communication, which can be face-to-face between an individual who has greater knowledge and a person who is perceived to have less knowledge.

Mentoring Techniques

Various techniques can be used by mentors depending on the psychological mindset of the mentee and also the present situation of the mentee. According to Barha (2001), mentors are advised to search for "teachable moments" so as to realize the potentials of the individuals in the organization they lead. These teachable moments help the mentees to acquire and apply the knowledge being transferred to them. However, quality mentoring should be recognized as a skill that needs to be developed so that the right knowledge can be transferred both efficiently and adequately to the mentee. The major mentoring techniques are listed below (Beijerse, 2000; Kaplan, 2007; Marling, 2004):

- **Accompanying:** This technique involves the mentor taking part side-by-side in the learning process with the mentee so as to deliver as much value in terms of knowledge transfer.

- **Sowing:** The major challenges mentors have is preparing the learner prior to the changing. Therefore, the concept of sowing is very important because a situation would arise where the mentor knows that what he says might not be accepted or understood by the mentee at first – however, it would eventually make sense and add value to the mentee when the situation arises.
- **Catalyzing:** This process involves changing the mentee's mindset. When this happens, learning escalates. This process involves the mentor re-ordering the values of the mentee and changing the mentee's identity.
- **Showing:** This process involves the mentor leading by example. This involves the mentor carrying out activities and demonstrating a skill by using his own example so as to ease understanding for the mentee.
- **Harvesting:** This process involves the creation of awareness by the mentor to the mentee on what was learned through the experience. Such questions that could be asked are "what have you learned or gained from this experience?"

Mentorship in Education

Mentorship programmes are offered in secondary and tertiary institutions in Nigeria with the sole aim of offering the following (Nonaka, 2001):

- Offer support to students in programme completion
- Enhance the students in building their confidence
- Help students transit to further education or workforce.
- Transfer valuable knowledge from the mentor to the mentee

It is a known fact that mentorship programmes are still in the development stages within the tertiary institutions in Nigeria. And as such, there should be peer mentoring programmes designed specifically to bring under-represented populations into science and engineering. However, the Internet has brought university alumni closer to students who are graduating. This is because graduate university alumni in the tertiary institutions in Nigeria are engaging students in career mentorship through the use of interview questions and answers.

Reverse Mentoring

Research has shown that mentoring is both beneficial to individuals and organizations (Leanard-Barton, 1995). With this established it is therefore important for the tertiary institutions in Nigeria to develop such cultures of mentoring with the sole aim of transferring knowledge from one person to another since there has being a paradigm shift from knowledge is power to knowledge sharing is power.

Traditional mentoring involves a senior colleague or an expert who is perceived to have valuable knowledge in a particular field to provide and counsel a young colleague who is perceived to be inexperienced. Reverse mentoring however turns this formula inside out.

Reverse Mentoring can be defined as a younger employee acting as a mentor by sharing expertise with the senior colleague being the mentee (Nonaka, 2001). Organizations such as Time Warner, Dell and Procter and Gamble have included reverse mentoring as a best practice within their company (Chen, 2007; Coogan, 2008). This shows that there is a clear cut benefit in adopting reverse mentoring whereby an organization taps into the expertise of the young employees.

According to Lin (2007), reverse mentoring is credited as a cost effective professional development tool that essentially focuses on building the bridges between generations (i.e. those born before

1978 and those born between 1978 and 1999). It is very apparent that reverse mentoring has a very clear application in the world of today; however, there is very little interest in the academic field and no empirical work on reverse mentoring for educational studies (Kaplan, 2007).

Characteristics of Reverse Mentoring

In the context of reverse mentoring, there are certain overlaps with the traditional mentoring and the alternative styled mentoring. This is because there are various emphases laid on its individual structures and purpose. Reverse mentoring relationships are characterized by various elements which include the following (Ruggles & Holtshouse, 1999; Robertson, 2004):

- Unequal status of the colleague with the mentee rather than the mentor, the senior member in the hierarchy of the organisation.
- Knowledge sharing with the mentee with a major focus on learning from the mentor's technical expertise.
- Focus on mentor's professional and leadership skills development
- Commitment to the shared goal of mutual learning and support.

It is important that institutions that want to practice reverse mentoring such as the Nigerian tertiary institutions must take notice of these structural feature so as to manage the reverse mentoring relationships effectively.

Unequal Status of Colleagues

Following the definition of reverse mentoring which comprises of a junior colleague acting as a mentor to a more senior colleague who is more experienced. The participants' unequal status is majorly reinforced by the difference in the hierarchical rank within the organization (Nonaka,

2001). This is characterized by a scenario whereby the mentee has a higher status and power in the organization relative to the mentee.

The basic structural role reversal poses a major challenge because the senior colleague (the mentee) has to give up his traditional role and some control of the process and show some willingness to learn from the junior colleague (the mentor). This in itself can pose a major challenge in the Nigerian tertiary industry due to the fact that the presence of the cultural background of the senior colleagues (Alvi "& Leidner, 2001) can prevent the willingness to learn thereby hindering the knowledge sharing process.

It is worth mentioning that this reverse mentoring arrangement builds relationships that foster knowledge sharing which is paramount to the growth of Nigerian tertiary institutions.

Emphases on Knowledge Sharing

In reverse mentoring relationship, the major focus for the mentee is to acquire knowledge and expertise from the mentor. It is important that both parties understand that this goal is essential due to the fact that senior level mentees would only require assistance by seeking information from the mentors when they think is appropriate and also when they perceive that the mentors are competent enough through the skills and capabilities they possess (Alvi & Leidner, 2001).

In traditional mentoring whereby the mentee acquires knowledge from the mentor, this knowledge is based on experience gained by the mentor over the years as opposed to the current technological expertise of the mentors (i.e. the junior colleague) based on recent educational experiences gained by the mentors.

In the establishment of mentoring relationships, learning occurs as a result of knowledge sharing. Gurteen (1999) however, defines three types of learning through knowledge being exchanged in mentoring relationships. These are:

- Cognitive learning,
- Skill based learning
- Affective based learning.

Focus on Leadership Skills

In reverse mentoring, there is an assumption that much of leadership development is personal development (Baumard, 1999). In traditional mentoring relationships, one of the most important outcomes for mentees is personal learning which includes the combination of interpersonal skills and relational learning while only relational learning is important for mentors (Baumard, 1999; Nonaka, 2001). However, in reverse mentoring relationship, it is important for mentors to carry out leadership development activities in form of personal learning so as to increase job satisfaction and reduce role ambiguity. Therefore it is worth mentioning that the development in relationships that foster leadership skills and cross-generational communication between mentor and mentee in the Nigerian tertiary industry will benefit both parties if they both have a shared goal.

Mutual Learning and Support

It is important that both participants (i.e. mentors and mentees) must have a major objective which is to have a shared goal of mutual learning and support. As this is important for any mentoring relationship, it is however critical for reverse mentoring relationship because of the unusual dynamics of this relationship which includes individual differences, cross generational differences and trust levels between the participants (Beijerse, 2000; Beckman, 1999). It is logical to conclude that in order to enhance reverse mentoring outcomes; both the mentors and mentees should be encouraged to do the following (Beckman, 1999):

- Share knowledge amongst each other
- Show a positive meaning approach towards mutual learning when sharing knowledge

- Create a positive connection that can help build relationships and increase the bond amongst participants.

In the Nigerian tertiary industry, mutual support for learning can only be fostered if both the mentor and the mentee establish and develop a close mentoring bond which is solely dependent on the high quality connection that depicts relational mentoring. In essence, by simply supporting each other's learning (Eftekharzadeh, 2008), both participants may experience positive meaning through the relationship they have built over time and therefore encourage the authentic expression of positive emotions to create opportunities for growth.

Key Challenges of Reverse Mentoring

It is a known fact that there are potential benefits to the reverse mentoring concept being applied in the Nigerian tertiary industry. However, it is important that both parties involved in this relationship must be aware of the challenges associated with this relationship being a success. Participants must be sensitive to both their individual differences especially in reverse mentoring relationships. These challenges are (Beckman 1999):

- **Individual Differences:** This involves differences such as gender, race, ethnicity and personality. All these pose a challenge to mentoring relationships. According to Liebowitz (2002), individuals tend to be attracted to those they see as similar to themselves – hence leading to a scenario whereby cross-race and cross-gender mentoring may pose individual challenges.
- **Role Reversal:** In this process, reverse mentoring gives the opportunity for employees in their early career to partake in a challenging professional developmental experience (Beijerse, 2000). When the

younger students take the role as mentors in the Nigerian tertiary industry, they get exposed to the senior colleagues such as lecturers and professors. However it is unlikely that they would be experienced in managing such relationships in the tertiary environment.

- **Trust and Interpersonal Comfort:** In reverse mentoring, building trust between the mentor and the mentee is very important due to the fact that knowledge can only be shared effectively if the trust is being established as a result of the high quality connection between the participants. According to Keskin (2005), trust is the complete willingness of a party to be vulnerable to the actions of another party. This gives the opportunity for either party to take risks by asking questions in the learning process most especially in relationships underpinned by trust.

CONCLUSION

The implementation of Knowledge Management within the Nigerian educational sector is still in its infancy stages. However, it can be seen without a doubt that KM delivers exceptional value when implemented correctly within an institution. The major objective of mentoring programmes is to share valuable knowledge and experience between participants. It can be deduced that for effective knowledge to be shared, quality bond must be established with trust being its focal point between the mentor and the mentee.

In conclusion, the aim of reverse mentoring programmes is to pair junior workers who act as mentors with senior workers who take the roles of mentees to share knowledge amongst them. Leadership development and learning is one of the major objectives of the relationship being built between the mentor and the mentee. It is however logical to deduce that since reverse mentoring

can only flourish if a strong relationship is being built between both parties, the strengths of these participants are being developed with the sole aim of adding exceptional value to one another especially when knowledge is being shared. Reverse mentoring can be categorized as a tool that can bring about innovation in an organisation and also the Nigerian tertiary institution. It can also be used as a tool for universities that choose to encourage cross-generational learning since this in itself is used to establish and develop the leaders of tomorrow.

REFERENCES

Alavi, M., & Leidner, D. E. (2001). Knowledge management and knowledge management systems. *Management Information Systems Quarterly*, 25(1), 107–137. doi:10.2307/3250961

Anantatmula, V. S. P. (2004). *Criteria for measuring knowledge management efforts in organizations.* Retrieved from http://proquest.umi.com/pqdweb?index=6&did=765360761&SrchMode=1&sid=2&Fmt=6&VInst=PROD&VType=PQD&RQT=309&VName=PQD&TS=1265786437&clientId=9678

Bahra, N. (2001). *Competitive Knowledge Management*. Palgrave Houndmills. doi:10.1057/9780230554610

Balasubramanian, S., & Manivannan, S. (2010). *Knowledge Management in Software Organisation*. Retrieved from http://www.indianmba.com/Faculty_Coloumn/FC1077/fc1077.html

Baumard, P. (1999). *Tacit Knowledge in Organisations*. Sage Publications Limited.

Beckman, T. (1998). *Designing Innovative Systems through Reengineering*. Paper presented at the 4th World Congress on Expert Systems. Mexico City, Mexico.

Beckman, T. J. (1999). The Current State of Knowledge Management. In *The Knowledge Management Handbook*. Boca Raton, FL: CRC Press.

Beijerse, R. P. (2000). Knowledge Management in Small and Medium-sized companies: Knowledge management for entrepreneurs. *Journal of Knowledge Management*, *4*(2), 162–182. doi:10.1108/13673270010372297

Bencisk, A., Lore, V., & Marosi, I. (2009). From Individual Memory to Organisational Memory: Intelligence of Organisations. *World Academy of Science. Engineering and Technology*, *56*, 1–6.

Biggam, J. (2008). *Succeeding With Your Masters Dissertation: A Step-by-Step Handbook*. The McGraw-Hill Companies.

Chen, C. (2007). Analysis of the knolwegde creation Process: An Organisational Change Perspective. *International Journal of Organization Theory and Behavior*, *10*(3), 287–313.

Davenport, T., & Prusak, L. (1998). *Working Knowledge: How Organizations Manage What They Know*. Harvard Business School Press.

Drestke, K. (1981). *Knowledge and the Flow of Information*. MIT Press.

Oxford Economics. (2010). *Nigeria*. ABI/INFORM Global.

Eftekharzadeh, R. (2008). *Knowledge Management Implementation in Developing Countries: An Experimental Study*. St John's University.

Gamble, P. R., & Blackwell, J. (2001). *Knowledge Management: A State of the Art Guide*. Biddles Ltd.

Gordon, J. R. (1993). *A Diagnostic Approach to Organisational Behaviour* (4th ed.). Simon & Schuster, Inc.

Gupter, J. N. D., & Sharma, S. K. (2004). *Creating Knowledge Based Organizations*. Idea Group Inc.

Gurteen, D. (1999). Creating a Knowledge Sharing Culture. *Knowledge Management Magazine, 2*(5).

Haggie, K., & Kingston, J. (2003). Choosing you Knowledge Management Strategy. *Journal of Knowledge Management Practice*.

Jones, J. (2009). *Research Methodology: Questionnaire Design and Interviewing Skills*. Warwick Manufacturing Group.

Jyothi, P., & Venkatesh, D. N. (2006). *Human Resource Management*. Oxford University Press.

Kaplan, B. (2007). *Creating Long-Term Value as Chief Knowledge Officer: Key Attributes, Messages and Ambitions for Success-Seeking CKOs*. KM Review.

Keskin, H. (2005). The relationships between explicit and tacit oriented KM strategy and firm performance. *Journal of American Academy of Business*, *7*(1), 169–173.

Kreie, J., & Cronan, T. P. (2000). Making Ethical Decisions: How Companies might influence the Choices one Makes. *Communications of the Association for Computing*, *43*(12), 66–71.

Lavenne, F., Renard, V., & Tollet, F. (2005). Fiction Between Inner Life and Collective Memory: A Methodological Reflection. *New Acardia Review*, *3*, 1–11.

Learsk, M., Lee, C., Milner, T., Norton, M., & Rathod, D. (2008). *Knowledge Management Tools and Techniques: Helping you Access the Right Knowledge at the Right Time*. Improvement and Development Agency for Local Government.

Leonard-Barton, D. (1995). *Wellsprings of Knowledge: Building and Sustaining the Sources of Innovation*. Boston, MA: Harvard Business School Press.

Leonard-Barton, D. (1995). *Wellsprings of Knowledge: Building and Sustaining the Sources of Innovation*. Boston, MA: Harvard Business School Press.

Liebowitz, J. (2002). Knowledge management and its link to artificial intelligence. *Expert Systems with Applications*, *20*(1), 1–6. doi:10.1016/S0957-4174(00)00044-0

Lin, H. (2007). Knowledge Sharing and Firm Innovation Capability: An Empirical Study. *International Journal of Manpower*, *28*(3/4), 315–332. doi:10.1108/01437720710755272

Liyanage, C., Elhag, T., Ballal, T., & Li, Q. (2009). Knowledge communication and translation - A knowledge transfer model. *Journal of Knowledge Management*, *13*(3), 118–131. doi:10.1108/13673270910962914

Maczewski, M. (2003). *Research Methodologies*. Retrieved from http://webhome.cs.uvic.ca/~mstorey/teaching/infovis/course_notes/researchmethods.pdf

Malhan, I. V., & Gulati, A. (2003). *Knowledge Management Problems of Developing Countries, with Special Reference to India*. SAGE Publications.

Manasco, B. (1996). Leading Firms Develop Knowledge Strategies. *Journal of Knowledge Management Practice*, *1*(6), 1–29.

Marling, L. (2004). *Knowledge Management: People, Process and Technology*. Retrieved from http://www.cutter.com/content/itjournal/fulltext/2004/12/itj0412b.html

McAdam, R., & McCreedy, S. (2000). A Critique of Knowledge Management: Using a Social Constructionist Model. *New Technology, Work and Employment*, *15*(2), 155–168. doi:10.1111/1468-005X.00071

McKellar, H. (2005). *KMWorld's 100 Companies that Matter in Knowledge Management*. Retrieved from http://www.kmworld.com/Articles/Editorial/Feature/KMWorld%27s-100-Companies-That-Matter-in-Knowledge-Management--9611.aspx

Meridith, L. (2007). *Knowledge Management and Solutions*. Retrieved from http://www.cio.com/article/40343/Knowledge_Management_Definition_and_Solutions?page=2&taxonomyId=3000

Morrison, J., & Olfman, L. (1998). *Organisational Memory*. Paper presented at 31st HICSS. Maui, HI.

News, B. B. C. (2010). *Nigeria Country Profile*. Retrieved from http://news.bbc.co.uk/1/hi/world/africa/country_profiles/1064557.stm

Nonaka, I., & Takeuchi, H. (1991). *The Knowledge Creating Company*. Oxford University Press.

Nonaka, I., & Takeuchi, H. (1995). *The Knowledge-Creating Company: How Japanese Companies create the Dynamics of Innovation*. Oxford University Press.

Nonaka, I., & Teece, D. (2001). *Managing Industrial knowledge creation, transfer and utilization*. SAGE Publications Ltd.

NSE. (2010). *The Nigerian Stock Exchange*. Retrieved from http://www.nigerianstockexchange.com/index.jsp

O'Dell, C., & Grayson, C. J. Jr. (1998). *If Only We Knew What We Know*. New York: The Free Press.

Odigie, H. A., & Li-Hua, R. (2009). *Unlocking the Channel of Tacit Knowledge Transfer*. Retrieved from http://motsc.org/unlocking_the_chennel_of_tacit_knowledge_transfer.pdf

Oketola, D. (2010). *Nigeria's Software Industry and the Journey Ahead*. Retrieved from http://www.punchng.com/Articl.aspx?theartic=Art2010061412141350

Okunoye, A., Innola, E., & Karsten, H. (2002). *Benchmarking Knowledge Management in Developing Countries: Case of Research Organisations in Nigeria*. The Gambia and India: University of Turku.

Pfeffer, J., & Sutton, R. I. (2000). *The Knowing-Doing Gap: How Smart Companies Turn Knowledge into Action*. Academic Press.

Polanyi, M. (1975). Personal Knowledge. In *Meaning*. University of Chicago Press.

Quintas, P., Lefrere, P., & Jones, G. (1997). Knowledge management: A strategic Approach. *Journal of Long Range Planning*, *30*(3), 385–391. doi:10.1016/S0024-6301(97)90252-1

Remenyi, D., Williams, B., Money, A., & Swartz, E. (1998). *Doing Research in Business and Management: An Introduction to Process and Method*. London: Sage Publications.

Renshaw, S., & Krishnaswamy, G. (2009). Critiquing the Knowledge Management Strategies of Non-Profit Organisations in Australia. *World Academy of Science. Engineering and Technology*, *49*, 456–464.

Robertson, J. (2004). *Intranets and Knowledge Sharing*. Retrieved from http://www.kmtalk.net/article.php?story=20041130051759653

Ruggles, R., & Holtshouse, D. (1999). *The Knowledge Advantage*. TJ International Ltd.

Ryu, S., Ho, S. H., & Han, I. (2003). Knowledge sharing behavior of physicians in hospitals. *Expert Systems with Applications*, *25*(1), 113–122. doi:10.1016/S0957-4174(03)00011-3

Sanchez, R. (2001). *Knowledge Management and Organizational Competence*. Oxford University Press Inc.

Skyrme, D. J. (2004). *The 3Cs of Knowledge Sharing*. Retrieved from http://www.kmtalk.net/article.php?story=2004113004318603

Soriyan, H. A., & Heeks, R. (2004). *A Profile of Nigeria's Software Industry*. Retrieved from http://www.sed.manchester.ac.uk/idpm/research/publications/wp/di/documents/di_wp21.pdf

Soriyan, H. A., Mursu, A., & Korpela, M. (2000). Information System development methodologies: Gender issues in a developing economy. In *Women, Work and Computerization*. Kluwer Academic. doi:10.1007/978-0-387-35509-2_18

Stecking, L. (2000, August). Geteiltes Wissen ist doppeltes Wissen. *Management Berater*.

Stein, E. W., & Zwass, V. (1995). Actualising Organisational Memory with Information Systems. *Information Systems Research*, *6*(2), 85–117. doi:10.1287/isre.6.2.85

Tech, G. (2005). *Questionnaire Design*. Retrieved from http://www.cc.gatech.edu/classes/cs6751_97_winter/Topics/quest-design/

Thurow, L. (2004). Help Wanted: A Chief Knowledge Officer. *Fast Company*, *78*, 91.

Tiwana, A. (2001). *The knowledge management toolkit: Practical techniques for building knowledge management system*. Upper Saddle River, NJ: Prentice Hall, Inc.

Treacy, M., & Wiersema, F. (1993, January-February). Customer Intimacy and Other Value Disciplines. *Harvard Business Review*.

Truch, A., Higgs, M., Bartram, D., & Brown, A. (2002). *Knowledge sharing and personality*. Paper presented at Henley Knowledge Management Forum. New York. NY.

TVU. (2008). *Dissertation Guide: Primary Data Collection Methods*. Retrieved from http://brent.tvu.ac.uk/dissguide/hm1u3/hm1u3fra.htm

United Nations Statistics. (2008). *Environment Statistics Country Snapshot: Nigeria*. Retrieved from http://unstats.un.org/unsd/environment/envpdf/Country_Snapshots_Sep%202009/Nigeria.pdf

Van den Hooff, B., & De Ridder, J. A. (2004). Knowledge Sharing in Context - The Influence of Organisational Commitment, Communication Climate and CMC use on Knowledge Sharing. *Journal of Knowledge Management, 8*(6), 117–130. doi:10.1108/13673270410567675

Watch, E. (2009). *Nigerian Economy*. Retrieved from http://www.economywatch.com/world_economy/nigeria/

Wiig, K. (1997). Knowledge Management: Where Did it Come from and Where Would it Go?. *Journal of Expert Systems with Application*.

William, M. K. (2006). *Introduction to Evaluation*. Retrieved from http://www.socialresearchmethods.net/kb/intreval.htm

Wong, K. Y. (2005). Critical Success Factors for Implementing Knowledge Management in Small and Medium Enterprises. *Industrial Management & Data Systems, 105*(3), 261–279. doi:10.1108/02635570510590101

Yin, R. K. (2003). *Case Study Research, Design and Methods* (3rd ed.). Thousand Oaks, CA: Sage Publications.

Young, T. (2008). *Knowledge Management: For Services, Operations and Manufacturing*. Chandos Publishing.

Zand, D. (1997). *The Leadership Triad: Knowledge, Trust and Power*. Oxford University Press.

ADDITIONAL READING

Hailey, J., & James, R. (2002). Learning Leaders: The Key to Learning Organisations. *Development in Practice, 12*(3/4).

Heeks, R. (2002) 'Failure, success and improvisation of information systems projects in developing countries' Development Informatics Working Paper 11. Manchester: Institute for Development Policy and Management, University of Manchester. (available at http://idpm.man.ac.uk/wp/di/index.html)

Malhotra, Y. (2001) 'Organizational controls as enablers and constraints in successful knowledge management systems implementation' in Yogesh Malhotra (ed.) Knowledge Management and Business Model Innovation. Hershey, PA, USA: Idea Group Publishing. (Available at www.km-network.com)

Marchand, D. (1998) 'Competing with Intellectual Capital' in Georg von Krogh, Johan Roos and Dirk Kleine (Eds.) Knowing in Firms: Understanding, Managing and Measuring Knowledge. London: Sage

KEY TERMS AND DEFINITIONS

Explicit Knowledge: Ruggles and Holtshouse (1999) describe explicit knowledge as knowledge that is put into a formal language including grammatical statements and mathematical expressions. Explicit knowledge can be stored in a database and can also be processed by a computer. It can also be electronically transmitted. Explicit knowledge can also be easily shared and documented; and can be expressed easily in document form.

Knowledge Management: Organizational objectives and it involves sharing of data, so as to enhance competency in an organization (McAdam & McCreedy 2000).

Reverse Mentoring: A technique used in organisations to improve the skills and capability of the older employees who otherwise as because of generational gap find it difficult coping with today's technology. This is done by using younger and technology savvy employees to mentor the older ones. This technique also makes employees to derive job satisfaction and also increase employee retention rate within the organisation.

Tacit Knowledge: Ruggles and Holtshouse (1999) describe tacit knowledge as one that is stored in the heads of people. Gamble and Black-well (2001) also stressed the fact that this type of knowledge is a context-specific knowledge which is hard to record, articulate and formalize. They further go to suggest that tacit knowledge includes individual beliefs, images and technical skills.

Section 5
Globalization and Education

Chapter 18
The Global School in the Local Classroom:
ICT for Cross-Cultural Communication

Jenna Copper
Slippery Rock Area High School, USA

ABSTRACT

This chapter was written to highlight the value for cross-cultural communication practices in schools with the support of innovative Information and Communication Technology (ICT). A detailed theoretical foundation was provided to justify the inclusion of global perspectives in the classroom through cross-cultural communication, which is made possible with ICT. This chapter details the perceptions of 80 pre-K to 12 teachers via a survey study, which shaped the author's suggestions for practical ICT cross-cultural communication opportunities in the classroom. Implementation strategies include classroom-to-classroom and classroom-to-world cross-cultural communication opportunities. This chapter suggests practical solutions supported by solid theoretical justifications for utilizing ICT to facilitate cross-cultural communication and improving student global awareness.

INTRODUCTION

Despite being the most technologically connected generation, members of Generation Z, those born from the late 1990s to the present, are constantly characterized as being the most *dis*connected. Ironically, the label is a result of their technologically connected world. Generation Z members have a permanent audience to advertise themselves at all times of the day. They literally have the world at their fingertips through their cell phones, computer screens, video games, and more, but generally speaking, they maintain a global presence of self-interest. Instead of exploring the vast perspectives available through the Internet, most members of Generation Z would rather project their often singular perspectives on everyone else. Although the criticism is easily justified to a degree, perhaps the blame should not be placed on the members of Generation Z but rather on the system that supports these singular perspectives. Maybe these students need to *learn* to embrace multiple perspectives.

DOI: 10.4018/978-1-4666-6162-2.ch018

Copyright © 2014, IGI Global. Copying or distributing in print or electronic forms without written permission of IGI Global is prohibited.

The responsibility then seems to fall on the teachers who facilitate such thinking in their classrooms every day. In fact, the standards movement charges teachers with the responsibility to emphasize and improve higher-order thinking skills, a seemingly difficult task. Unfortunately, in the United States, for example, teachers' burdens are far reaching. Standardized tests, score accountability, prescribed curriculums, and packed class schedules make it difficult for teachers to create lessons that foster these valuable multiple perspectives. Nevertheless, the technological savvy teacher can use those same technological crutches to create a "Web" within the Web of perspectives that not only engage students but also motivate them to celebrate differences. According to Pirie (1997), "…it is the teacher's job to help the Web become as full and intricately articulated as possible, and to help students reflect on the existence of the Web and the principles upon which it is woven" (p. 22). The Web that Pirie (1997) discusses includes all of the experiences that the student can encounter when studying content if given the opportunity. These new cultural perspectives challenge students to break out of this egocentric routine thinking and experience novel contexts thereby improving their critical thinking skill sets. Global education is the link that ties students' lives to the lives of people around the world in meaningful ways (Osler & Vincent, 2002).

Introducing students to global perspectives has never been easier thanks to the ease of cross-cultural communication. Since millennials already possess the technical skills to communicate globally, why not teach them to expose the perspectives that already exist on the other side of their computer screen? This study was conducted to discover the relevance, priority, and potential of global education in the United States. Although theoretical support exists, the current practices to establish cross-cultural connections and employ global strategies are relatively fragmented and underdeveloped. Therefore, this chapter reports on the perspectives and current practices of cross-

cultural communication to foster global perspectives from a survey study involving 80 educators across the United States. Additionally, it provides practical suggestions and solutions for utilizing cross-cultural communication to improve students' global awareness.

BACKGROUND

Global education is just one buzz word in the educational world that refers to an overarching concept called global awareness; other such names include multicultural education, multiethnic education, culturally relevant education, peach education, citizenship education, and international education (Kist, 2013; Cushner & Mahon, 2009; Osler & Vincent, 2002). Following the guide of Kist (2013), the definition of global education in accordance with the National Council of the Social Studies was used for this study:

The term global education is used by the National Council for the Social Studies (n.d.) to described strategies for: gaining knowledge of world cultures; understanding the historical, geographic, economic, political, cultural, and environment relationships among world regions and peoples; examining the nature of cultural differences and national or regional conflicts and problems; and acting to influence public policy and private behavior on behalf of international understanding, tolerance and empathy. (National Council for the Social Studies, n.d.)

Almost 20 years before, Tye and Kniep (1991) defined global education in a similar manner explaining,

Global education involves learning about those problems and issues which cut across national boundaries and about the interconnectedness of systems—cultural, ecological, economic, political, and technological. Global education involves

learning to understand and appreciate our neighbors with different cultural backgrounds from ours; to see the world through the eyes and minds of others; and to realize that all people of the world need and want much the same things. (p. 47)

These definitions highlight the importance of discovering, analyzing, accepting, and even celebrating cultural differences.

With the emphasis on critical thinking skills, it is no wonder that global education is championed by researchers as a method to improve these valuable skills (Common Core State Standards Initiative, 2010; National Assessment of Educational Progress, 2009). Additionally, in the ever-increasing global marketplace, students need to develop the skills necessary to compete, adjust, and thrive in the real world upon graduation (Merryfield, 2001). According to Shah and Young (2008), "Global learning is essential for the future of both individuals and society. It puts learning in a global context, fostering: critical and creative thinking; self-awareness and open-mindedness towards difference; understanding of global issues and power relationships; and optimism and action for a better world" (p. 15). Discussing multiple perspectives in accordance with Attachment Theory by theorists, Mary Ainsworth and John Bowlby, Morrell and Morrell (2012), describe the importance for multiple perspectives to enhance students' attachments to their own culture in an effort to build cultural awareness. In this model, it is clear that this type of education satisfies an attachment that many students have between their academic and social worlds. Therefore, Morrell and Morrell (2012) conclude, "Ideally, through this type of learning and reading, students will develop mutual recognition of and appreciation for one another inside the classroom and toward others beyond the classroom" (p. 15).

It follows that the responsibility to foster this type of education falls on the teachers. Butler and Cuenca (2009) discuss the importance of critical cultural consciousness for students but ultimately for teachers who create lessons, select curriculum, and project opinions. Using this standard, Butler and Cuenca (2009) write, "Critical cultural consciousness leads teachers to be attentive to incomplete accounts of culture in the curriculum; reflectively questioning and internally deliberating the ways in which perspective and voices are absent or marginalized in cultural depictions" (p. 16).

As a result, many professional organizations have adopted standards pertaining to the objectives consistent with global education. Developing 12 standards with the help of thousands of practicing English educators, the International Reading Association (IRA) and National Council of Teachers of English (NCTE) (1999) expressed the importance of teaching all students through cultural and ethnic studies in an effort to establish cultural sensitivity and appreciation. The ninth standard reads, "students develop an understanding of and respect for diversity in language use, patterns, and dialects across cultures, ethnic groups, geographic regions, and social roles" (IRA & NCTE, 1999, p. 29). Specifically, this standard points to the study of global perspectives through multicultural and multiethnic text in form of primary and secondary sources. While this type of study seems to require traditional teaching strategies, technology certainly has a place in this endeavor.

GLOBAL PERSPECTIVES

Information and Communication Technology for Cross Cultural Communication

The implementation of technology as a way to meet these standards is both helpful and in some cases necessary. In his national bestseller, *The World Is Flat*, Friedman (2005) famously explained that in our technological age the world is getting flatter meaning, "The global competitive playing field was being leveled" (p. 8). The Internet provides a limitless domain for cross-cultural interaction, that is any form of communication with individuals from a different culture. As a result, several organizations and models for the inclusion of information and communication technology (ICT) include global education as a standard or priority. The International Society for Technology in Education includes, "Students use digital media and environments to communicate and work collaboratively, including at a distance, to support individual learning and contribute to the learning of others…c. Develop cultural understanding and global awareness by engaging with learners of other cultures" (p. 1). Additionally, the National Education Technology Plan 2010 recommends in their goals for technological education reform, "All learners will have engaging and empowering learning experiences both in and out of school that prepare them to be active, creative, knowledgeable, and ethical participants in our globally networked society" (United States Department of Education, Office of Educational Technology, p. xvi).

Combing these objectives, teachers can utilize the conveniences of our digital world to bring global perspectives to students in local settings through cross-cultural communication. Cross-cultural communication falls underneath the broader term, intercultural communication, "which generally focuses on communication between people of different national cultures" (Gundykunst, 2003, p. vii). More specifically, according to Gore (2013), "cross-cultural communication describes the ability to successfully form, foster, and improve relationships with members of a culture different from one's own" (p. 61). In this sense, communication is not limited to one form but rather it examines verbal, nonverbal, and written communication in different contexts, such as in-person and telecommunication (Gore, 2013).

Problems

While technology can make this process easier, communicating meaningful information has barriers, such as physical, emotional, perceptual,

cultural, language, and general (Gore, 2013). Thanks to the Internet, geographic barriers are no longer a physical problem. Despite the fact that communication is easily managed through the Internet, the message still requires social consciousness so that those messages are not misconstrued (Gore, 2013).

Communication of the message is one of those barriers that can be problematic for teachers. Appleman (2009) reports that it is common for teachers, unfamiliar with the cultural background of many multicultural authors, for example, to feel uneasy when attempting to cover multiple perspectives. Nevertheless, Appleman (2009) believes that this hesitation only furthers the argument for teaching multiple perspectives. Armed with a plan, teachers can effectively break down the walls of the local classroom and introduce cross-cultural communication practices that improve global perspectives.

Developing that plan poses, yet another challenge. Namely, the time it takes to develop such a plan. In *Prisoners of Time*, a report commissioned by the federal government, the National Education Commission on Time and Learning, NECTL, (1994) found that the time restraints consistent with the six-hour a day, 180-day school year create an environment of limited teacher preparation time.

Survey Study of ICT Current Trends for Cross-Cultural Communication

Current trends in education suggest that educators should empower their students to develop global perspectives. Therefore, a study was conducted by the author to determine the place of global education in current pre-k to secondary curriculums and the current successful trends at accomplishing this task[1]. A survey research design was selected to obtain data for this study, because the researcher was interested in data from a number of participants. The researcher selected both structured and unstructured response choices for the participants. For all questions, the participants were asked to indicate a response from a single-option list. A comment box was added to most questions to allow for open-ended, unstructured responses. Eighty teachers currently practicing in a pre-k to 12 setting participated in this study, and teachers from all grades were represented.

The results were fascinating. To begin with, 60% of respondents indicated that their students do not possess the ability empathize with views and cultures different from their own, thereby leading all 80 respondents to answer that teaching global perspectives is important. Consistent with the literature, 79 participants indicated that teaching global perspectives would improve students' critical thinking skill sets (Merryfield, 2001; Morrell & Morell, 2012; Shah and Young, 2008). Many participants commented that they bring global perspectives through the form of research assignments, be it elementary or high school levels. For example, one participant explained, "In the music classroom, I have my students study specific countries of Africa and how those countries directly impacted the music of America. After studying the historical aspect of those countries, we discuss their music and learn different rhythmical patterns to play on buckets. The unit on African bucket drumming allows students to get a better perspective on other cultures, but also allows them to see how that music, being older than America's music, directly impacted what American music is today."

When addressing ICT to lead to cross-cultural communication as a way to introduce global perspectives, the respondents provided fascinating details. Only approximately 39% of respondents currently use ICT to foster cross-cultural communications. One respondent reported, "I use Skype in my classroom to communicate with students from Costa Rica. The students with whom they are Skyping are learning English just as my students are learning to speak Spanish." Two respondents reported using email to communicate with people across the globe. One respondent described a project in which his/her students write emails to soldiers who are stationed overseas, and the other described an "adoption compassion" program in which students write emails back and forth with their "compassion partner."

These numbers may lead a reader to believe that technology access is a problem for the implementation of ICT for global education. Surprisingly, the results indicated a different trend. A substantial 75% of respondents explained that they have access to technology that makes cross-cultural communication possible. So, why are they not utilizing it for this purpose? As one respondent put it, "I need ideas! I don't have time to figure it out on my own." Consistent with the trend of busy days and lack of time for preparation and planning, this respondent summarizes the response of 94% of respondents who agreed that they need ideas for implementation to make cross-cultural communication through ICT a reality.

Classroom-to-Classroom Cultural Connections

Collaborations with classrooms all over the world are possible with the aid of the Internet. Whereas most students do not have the means and time to interact with people from other cultures via travels to faraway lands, the same students have the opportunity to establish these free-of-charge connections virtually. The use of videoconferencing and online discussion forums makes cross-cultural communication a reality.

For the teacher, it may appear a daunting task to establish a connection with a classroom somewhere else in the world, especially when the teacher does not have any personal connections. Nonetheless, classroom-to-classroom connections can be made as quickly as an Internet search. The global community ePals, accessed at www.epals.com, is a valuable resource for teachers to make these classroom-to-classroom connections. This Website not only provides teachers with resources for establishing global and cultural connections, but it serves as an educational community for the purpose of finding classroom connections (ePals, 2013). Teachers from all over the world advertise their classrooms to make these connections. For example, the "advertisement" includes information about the location of the classroom, the background of the classroom, the number of students, the age of students, and potential connections. The Website is updated with these posts daily, so there is no shortage of potential connections. In addition, the ePals Website includes a quick link to contact the teacher. All communication can be done via email communication; therefore, the time it takes for the teacher to establish this connection is minimal. Once a connection is established, there are a number of communication opportunities to open the doors to new cultural perspectives.

Videoconferencing is a collaborative tool that can visually connect students to their outside world. This tool provides verbal and visual communication in real time through the use of the Internet and Webcam. Video conferencing equipment can be expensive and it may not be available in every school district; however, Skype is a free program that can be downloaded and utilized for video conferencing on Mac or PC. The only requirement is a Webcam, which may be included on your desktop or laptop or it can be purchased rather inexpensively. In this mode, students can hold discussions with their partner classroom about cultural and global topics to learn about differences in cultures. There are some limitations with this form of communication. Accessing or manipulating the video conferencing material could cause a roadblock to get started. Additionally, the real-time necessity to facilitate the discussion may make it difficult to find meeting times with classrooms in different time zones.

There are several asynchronous modes of communication to provide those same cross-cultural connections. Email is the obvious and in many cases preferred mode of communication between adults, so why not update the traditional PenPal program with a twist of technology? Email makes facilitating and observing these interactions trouble-free, and as a bonus, it prepares the students to use a job-ready, real-world tool. The students simply need a classroom or a personal email account to write and respond to their classmates across the world.

To expand the communication, teachers can create a discussion board for which all students from all classes can communicate. A popular site for creating free discussion forums is ProBoards, which can be accessed at www.proboards.com. ProBoards is a secure site that the teacher can manage to create editable board to prompt class discussion. Consistent with the benefit of "email pals," Jewell (2006) explains, "…discussion board answers tend to be more eloquent and better supported than answers given orally in class. Students are inclined to be more careful with their written language than with their oral language." In fact, this form of communication may be the most appropriate to form respectful communication between students unfamiliar with other cultures. Still, establishing parameters is essential to make this a worthwhile experience (Suler, 2004). Table 1 can be used to make the discussion board communication valuable and fair.

Making a direct classroom connection is an effective way to bring cultural perspectives to the classroom. It also gives students a novel experience for several reasons. First, students will develop relationships with people from a completely different culture. These relationships can even be supported by their social media habits. Additionally, students will learn to work with information and communication technology. These interactions are certainly not the only means for brining global perspectives to the classroom, in fact, they can be supplemented or even replaced by classroom-to-world cultural connections.

Classroom-to-World Cultural Connections

According to Clarke and Whitney (2009), "It is important that students see themselves in a larger world beyond the walls of the classroom" (p. 534). Visualizing these experiences, students are encour-

Table 1. Discussion board rubric

	Beginning 1 points	Capable 2 points	Accomplished 3 points	Exemplary 4 points
Initial Comments	Initial comments were posted but did not address the assignment.	Initial comments address some of the assignment requirements. Comments are not well organized and show limited knowledge and evaluation of the topic.	Initial comments address most, but not all, of the assignment. Comments are reasonably organized and demonstrate adequate familiarity and analysis of the content.	Initial comments thoroughly address all parts of the assignment. The comments are clearly and concisely stated, demonstrating that the content was appropriately reviewed and synthesized.
Message Quality	Postings are not substantial, limited to "I agree" types of replies.	Only one substantial message was posted.	Multiple postings including some substantial content were posted, however, a limited number include errors or need additional supporting detail.	Multiple postings are made offering substantial, well written contributions-opinions, observations, questions, experiences, critiques, suggestions, etc.
Response	Questions/comments posed to you were not addressed.	Several questions/comments posed to you were not addressed.	The majority of questions/comments posed to you were addressed.	All questions/comments posed to you were appropriately addressed.
Contribution/ Duration	Participation was not continuous throughout the discussion period (one day only). Replies were only posted for 1 global classmate.	Postings were submitted on at least two different days during the discussion period (11:xx PM and 12:xx AM the next day does not qualify). Replies were posted for at least two global classmates.	Postings were submitted on three or more days during the discussion period but may not reflect participation from start to finish. Replies were posted for at least two global classmates.	Postings are evenly distributed throughout the discussion period reflecting participation from start to finish. Multiple replies were posted for at least three global classmates or more.
Netiquette	Postings are not appropriate--poor grammar/structure, inappropriate slang/abbreviations, etc.	Postings include inappropriate references and may include several errors in grammar/structure.	Postings are reasonably appropriate, but contain a few errors.	Postings are appropriate, using proper language, cordiality, grammar, punctuation, etc.

aged to see the value of perspectives different than their own. In today's world, the Internet provides an extensive archive of current event articles that one easily can connect to a theme or topic discussed in class (Kist, 2013). Using any search engine, such as Bing or Google the "News" link in the header of the Webpage provides hundreds, thousands, or more "hits" on the searched topic. From here, the searcher can type in a keyword to generate a list of news articles related to that topic. These current views provide students with an insightful look at people from all over the world. Reviewing different sources on similar topics can serve as a mechanism for comparing and contrasting different cultural values. Table 2 offers an example of

questions that would be appropriate for comparing and contrasting texts.

As a follow up to the multiple perspectives analysis, Clarke and Whitney (2009) suggest using socially charged activities to encourage students to make a difference in their community or the larger surrounding area. For example, students can research a topic's representation in the editorial section of these online sites and correspond with the editor using email or a comment section if available to express opposing views or ask for representation of an opposing view (Clarke and Whitney, 2009).

In his book, *The Global School*, Kist (2013) describes a Website called Global Voices (http://

Table 2. Questions for comparison

1.	What stances are present in each work? How are these themes similar or different?
2.	What universal belief(s) and idea(s) are expressed in both works?
3.	Who is the audience for each story? How does the audience contribute to the author's purpose in both works?
4.	Identify specific clues that explain the author's purpose in each of the works.
5.	Identify a phrase from each work that contributes to the style of the work. Explain why those phrases indicate the author's style.
6.	Describe the differences between the author's style (direct, down-to-earth, descriptive, poetic, etc.) in both works.

www.globalvociesonline.org), which includes RSS feeds with links to global stories from countries all over the world. Using this Website, students can subscribe to a country's Global Voice's RSS feed as required reading for the class (Kist 2013). Additionally, this project can include a blog assignment so that students can share their reflections on their global reading with the global world (Kist, 2013). Much like the discussion board, students can comment on other students' blogs and receive comments on their own posts. A quick Internet search yields many options for educational blogging sponsor sites. A popular and secure educational blogging Website is Kidblog (http://www.kidblog.org). According to their Website, "Kidblog provides teachers with the tools to help students safely navigate the digital – and increasingly social – online landscape. Kidblog allows students to exercise digital citizenship within a secure, private classroom blogging space" (http://www.kidblog.com).

FUTURE RESEARCH DIRECTIONS

The nature of the global landscape is one of continual and constant change; as a result, research on topics should keep up with the advances in technol-ogy. Technological classroom supports change at such a fast rate that teachers and researchers need to stay up-to-date on the potential to incorporate new technology and strategies supported by those technologies. Action research should be completed frequently to adequately portray new and improved information and communication technology for use in the global classroom.

With these applications of information and communication technology, teachers and students' perceptions of global education and education in general should be studied. Similarly, teachers' and students' perceptions of these cross-cultural communication experiences should be analyzed to report on the success of the strategy in fostering acceptance and appreciation for differing perspectives.

Finally, as a follow up to the survey study discussed in this chapter, future research should explore the participants' response to cross-cultural communication implementation ideas. The likelihood that those participants would, in fact, use cross-cultural communication ideas given these recommendations would be important to further the case for cross-cultural communication in the classroom.

CONCLUSION

Even though it might be impossible for students to travel the globe in person, the ever-expanding information and communication technological advances of this generation have made it possible for students to explore the world in the digital realm. Cross-cultural communication information and communication technology has made global perspectives available to these students in all new ways. This chapter included a theoretical explanation to justify global education, specifically cross-cultural communication in today's global world while providing practical applications and strategies for educators seeking support through the use of specific 21st century skills. Additionally, it demonstrated the call of global education from national councils and partnerships whose standards include global education objectives. Cross-cultural communication is a viable tool for educators who want to tear down the walls of a culturally divided classroom, expand their students' global experiences, and meet the needs of 21st century learners.

REFERENCES

Appleman, D. (2009). *Critical encounters in high school English: Teaching literary theory to adolescents*. New York: Teachers College Press.

Butler, B. M., & Cuenca, A. (2009). Culturally responsible teaching: A pedagogical approach for the social studies classroom. In W. B. Russell III (Ed.), *The International Society for the Social Studies Annual Conference Proceedings*. Orlando, FL: The International Society for the Social Studies.

Clarke, L., & Whitney, E. (2009). Walking in their shoes: Using multiple perspectives texts as a bridge to critical literacy. *The Reading Teacher*, *62*(6), 530–534. doi:10.1598/RT.62.6.7

Common Core Standards Initiative. (2010). *Common core state standards for English language arts & literacy in history/social studies, science, and technical subjects*. Pennsylvania Department of Education.

Cushner, K., & Mahon, J. (2009). Developing the intercultural competence of educators and their students: Creating the blueprints. In D. K. Deardoff (Ed.), *The SAGE handbook of intercultural competence*. Thousand Oaks, CA: SAGE.

ePals. (2013). *Epals global community*. Retrieved from http://www.epals.com/#!/global-community/

Friedman, T. L. (2005). *The world is flat: A brief history of the twenty-first century*. New York: Farrar, Straus, & Giroux.

Global Voices Online. (2013). *Global Voices*. Retrieved from http://globalvoicesonline.org/

Gore, V. (2013). The importance of cross-cultural communication. *The IUP Journal of Soft Skills*, *7*(1), 59–65.

Gundykunst, W. B. (2003). Forward. In W. B. Gundykunst (Ed.), *Cross cultural and intercultural communication* (pp. vii–ix). Thousand Oaks, CA: Sage.

International Reading Association and National Council of Teachers of English. (1996). Standards for the English language arts. [International Reading Association and National Council of Teachers of English.]. *Urbana (Caracas, Venezuela)* IL.

Jewell, V. (2006). Continuing the classroom community: Suggestions for using online discussion boards. *National Council of Teachers of English, 94*(4), 98-87.

Kidblog. (2012). *Why kidblog*. Retrieved from http://kidblog.org/why-kidblog/

Kist, W. (2013). *The global school: Connecting classrooms and students around the world*. Bloomington, IN: Solution Tree Press.

Merryfield, M. (2001). Moving the center of global education. In W. Stanley (Ed.), *Critical Issues in Social Studies Research for the 21st Century*. Greenwich, CT: Information Age Publishing.

Morell, E., & Morrell, J. (2012). Multicultural readings of multicultural literature and the promotion of social awareness in ELA classrooms. *New England Reading Association Journal*, *47*(2), 10–16.

National Assessment of Educational Progress. (2009). *The nation's report card: Grade 12 reading and mathematics 2009 national and pilot state results*. Arlington, VA: United Stated Department of Education.

National Council for the Social Studies. (n.d.). *What are global and international education?* Retrieved from www.socialstudies.org/positions/global/whatisglobaled

National Education Commission on Time and Learning. (1994). *Prisoners of time*. Arlington, VA: United States Department of Education.

Osler, A., & Vincent, K. (n.d.). *Citizenship and the challenge of global education*. Oak Hill, VA: Trentham Books Limited.

Pirie, B. (1997). *Reshaping High School English*. Urbana, IL: National Council of Teachers of English.

ProBoards. (2013). *Free forum*. Retrieved from http://www.proboards.com/

Shah, H., & Young, H. (2008). Global learning in schools, and the implications for policy. *Educational Review*, *21*(1), 15–22.

Suler, J. (2004). Extending the classroom into cyberspace: The discussion board. *Cyberpsychology & Behavior*, (7): 397–403.

Tye, K. A., & Kniep, W. M. (1991). Global education around the world. *Educational Leadership*, 47–49.

United States Department of Education, Office of Educational Technology. (2010). *Transforming American education: Learning powered by technology*. Washington, DC: Author. Retrieved from http://www.ed.gov/sites/default/files/netp2010.pdf

ADDITIONAL READING

Brown, J. S., & Cooper, J. E. (2011). Toward a conceptual framework of culturally relevant pedagogy: An overview of conceptual and theoretical literature. *Teaching Education*, *38*(1), 65–84.

Elmer, D. (2012). *Cross cultural connections: Stepping out and fitting in around the world*. Downers Grove, IL: InterVarsity.

Feast, V., Collyer-Braham, S., & Bretag, T. (2011). Global experience: The development and preliminary evaluation of a programme designed to enhance students' global engagement. *Innovations in Education and Teaching International*, *48*(3), 239–250. doi:10.1080/14703297.2011.593701

Gorski, P. (2005). *Multicultural Education and the Internet: Intersections and Integrations*. Boston: McGraw-Hill.

Kist, W. (2010). *The socially networked classroom: teaching in the new media age*. Thousand Oaks, CA: Corwin.

Lindsay, J., & Davis, V. A. (2013). *Flattening classrooms, engaging minds: Move to global collaboration one step at a time*. Boston: Pearson.

Marshall, H. (2007). Global education in perspective: Fostering a global dimension in an english secondary school. *Cambridge Journal of Education*, *37*(3), 355–374. doi:10.1080/03057640701546672

Marzano, R. J., & Heflebower, T. (2012). *Teaching & Assessing 21st Century Skills*. Bloomington: In Marzano Research Laboratory.

Merryfield, M. M. (1997). *Preparing teachers to teach global perspectives: A handbook for teacher educators*. Thousand Oaks, CA: Corwin Press.

Mundy, K., & Manion, C. (2008). Global education in canadian elementary schools: An exploratory study. *Canadian Journal of Education*, *31*(4), 941–974.

Naiditch, F. (2013). A media literature approach to developing literacy education. *Journal of Media Literacy Education*, *5*(1), 337–348.

Ndemanu, M. T. (2012). The contribution of email exchange to second language acquisition: A case of cross-cultural communication between africa and north america. *Reading Matrix: An International Online Journal*, *12*(1), 1–11.

Nussbaum-Beach, S., & Hall, L. R. (2012). *The connected educator: Learning and leading in a digital age*. Bloomington, IN: Solution Tree.

Parisi, L., & Crosby, B. (2012). *Making connections with blogging: Authentic learning for today's classrooms*. Eugene, OR: International Society for Technology in Education.

Peters, L. (2009). *Global education: Using technology to bring the world to your students*. Eugene, OR: International Society for Technology in Education.

Peterson, C. (2004). Making interactivity count: Best practices in video conferencing. *Journal of Interactive Learning Research*, *15*(1), 63–74.

Richardson, W., & Mancabelli, R. (2011). *Personal learning networks: Using the power of connections to transform education*. Bloomington, IN: Solution Tree.

Schweisfurth, M. (2006). Education for global citizenship: Teacher agency and curricular structure in ontario schools. *Educational Review*, *58*(1), 41–50. doi:10.1080/00131910500352648

Stringer, D. M., & Cassidy, P. A. (2009). *52 activities for improving cross-cultural communication*. Boston: Intercultural.

Suárez-Orozco, M. M. (2007). *Learning in the global era: International perspectives on globalization and education*. Berkeley: University of California.

Taras, V., Caprar, D. V., Rottig, D., Sarala, R. M., Zakaravia, N., Zhao, F., & Huang, V. Z. (2013). A global classroom? Evaluating the effectiveness of global virtual collaboration as a teaching tool in management education. *Academy of Management Learning & Education*, *12*(3), 414–435. doi:10.5465/amle.2012.0195

Tomei, L. A. (2001). *The technology façade: Overcoming barriers to effective instructional technology*. Boston: Allyn and Bacon.

Van Reken, R.E., & Rushmore, S. (2009). Thinking globally when teaching locally. *Kappa Delta Pi*, 60-68.

Yeung, A. S. Brown. E.L., & Lee, C. (2012). Communication and language: Surmounting barriers to cross-cultural understanding. Charlotte, NC: Information Age Pub.

Zhao, Y. (2012). *World class learners: Educating creative and entrepreneurial students*. Thousand Oaks: Corwin.

KEY TERMS AND DEFINITIONS

Blog: An Internet Website consisting of posts, usually listed in reverse chronological order.

Critical Thinking: The mental process involved in studying, interpreting, analyzing, and evaluating information to reach a conclusion.

Cross-Cultural Communication: Communication in any form that involves an exchange between people of different cultures.

Global Education: Education that prepares students for understanding world cultures and interacting in a global environment.

Global Perspectives: Perspectives that represent values and cultures of people from all over the world.

Information and Communication Technology: Any electronic tool that facilitates communication or gives access to content.

Video Conferencing: A conference facilitated with the use of telecommunication technologies for parties in different physical locations.

ENDNOTES

[1] This study was a qualitative participatory action research (PAR) survey design. The researcher used a convenience sampling to select participants. Potential participants were contacted for this study using several social media outlets. From this sampling, 80 respondents consented to participate in the survey from summer and fall of 2013. The respondents answered an online survey created by the researcher for the purpose of this study. The survey can be accessed and completed via a hyperlink; although, the results to the survey are protected by a username and password only known to the researcher. Therefore, the researcher was the only party that viewed the results to protect the identities of the participants and the integrity of this study. This study was limited to teachers who currently hold full-time teaching positions in the United States, thus generalizability may be somewhat limited. Also, because the term Global Education has a variety of meanings, the researcher specifically aligned the definition of Global Education to the National Council for the Social Studies. Consequently, this standard may not be representative of all schools.

Chapter 19
Globalization and its Challenges for Teacher Education in Nigeria

A. O. K. Noah
Lagos State University, Nigeria

Adesoji A. Oni
University of Lagos, Nigeria

Simeon A. Dosunmu
Lagos State University, Nigeria

ABSTRACT

The phenomenon of globalization is defined variously, but in general, it is defined as the establishment of a global market for goods and capital, leading to what could be described as a multiplicity of linkages and interconnections between places, events, ideas, issues, and things, irrespective of whether they are directly related or not. Globalization on the other hand cannot be a reality in any nation if its educational system is not implicitly or explicitly geared towards achieving meaningful and desirable change for that society. However, since education and indeed the (educator) teacher constitute the most viable instruments by which an emerging nation can catch up with the developed countries, globalization will therefore be a mirage if teacher education is not geared towards producing teachers who are globalization friendly, teachers who are not allergic to globalization. In view of the above, this chapter examines the concept of globalization side by side with the current goals of teacher education in Nigeria.

INTRODUCTION

Nigeria recognizes the pivotal role of education as the fountain head of national development thus the National Policy on Education (NPE) (FRN 2004) provides that Nigeria's philosophy of education, is based on the belief among others that:

- Education is an instrument for national development
- Education fosters the worth and development of the individual for the development of the society.
- There is the need for functional education for the promotion of a progressive united

DOI: 10.4018/978-1-4666-6162-2.ch019

Copyright © 2014, IGI Global. Copying or distributing in print or electronic forms without written permission of IGI Global is prohibited.

Nigeria, to this end, school programmes need to be relevant.

The NPE further reiterates the importance of education to National development on page 8 that;

Education shall continue to be highly rated in the national development plans because education is the most important instrument of change; any fundamental change in the intellectual and social outlook of any society has to be preceded by educational revolution.

Based on the statement above, there is the consciousness or belief in the tremendous import of education as the catalyst for national development in Nigeria.

Education is dispensed by teachers and thus, if education occupies a central role in national development, then teacher education is at the epicenter of national development. Again, the national policy on education does not lose sight of this. It provides that no education system can rise above the quality of its teachers that is why all over the world much prominence is given to the teacher because of his peculiar role in national development. The quality of any education system according to Kalusi (2001) depends on the availability and competence of the teaching corps. The teacher factor in any educational programme is regarded as most crucial because what he knows can make a world of difference and what he does not know can be an irreparable loss to the development of the potentialities and abilities of society's younger generation.

One could see from the ongoing discussion that teachers are the hubs of any educational system. They are the determinants of quality. Therefore no matter how grandiose, innovative and imaginative the plans and programmes, the desired objectives may not be achieved without the right number of adequately educated and trained, dedicated and loyal, motivated and disciplined; committed and happy teachers serving at all levels of the educational system. However, the transi-

tion of the world from one of separate units into a globally integrated whole requires a new vision of the teacher's role and pedagogical preparation. In other words, one conspicuous phenomenon of our times which has become a common target of pursuit by both "developed" and "developing" nations is globalization.

Globalization as a phenomenon cannot be a reality in any nation if its educational system is not implicitly or explicitly geared towards globalization. Invariably, globalization will always be a mirage if teacher education is not geared towards producing teachers who are globalization friendly, teachers who are not allergic to globalization. More so, the teachers serve as the think- tank of any nation and since education has been globalized, with no nation as an island of its own, the world has come together through technology whereby each nation is now inter connected with ease. Education, according to Amale (2003) is now international or intercultural. The teacher now stands as the midwife between the new era of globalization and the people. For the teacher to therefore deliver the expecting global baby in any given society, he must be adequately equipped to do so.

In view of the above, this paper shall examine the concept of globalization side by side with the current goals of teacher education in Nigeria. This is with the view to determine whether teacher education goals are consistent or otherwise with the phenomenon of globalization. The paper will also identify the constraints of globalization in the current teacher education programme in Nigeria and suggest possible way forward with some counselling implications.

PERSPECTIVES ON GLOBALIZATION

Globalization is a trend that is engulfing the whole world. It has become the political, media and academic buzzword of the early 21st century. Writers, scholars and professionals are pointing to it as the panacea to many world problems. Globalization has been defined by Ohiorhenuan (1998) as the broadening and deepening linkages of national colonies into a worldwide market for goods, services and especially capital. In his definition, he saw the driver of globalization as technology. He identified the main trigger of the process as changes in economic policy across the world and the information and telecommunications' revolutions. The face of globalization has been quickened by what he called supranational policy regimes such as the world trade organization, the global environment facility, and the re alignment of the international financial institutions (Adeboye, 2002).

Malcolm (1995) defined globalization as a social process in which the constraints of geography on social and cultural arrangements recede and in which people become increasingly aware that they are receding. It is a phenomenon that represents the emerging worldwide interdependence of individuals and countries, which is characterized by various economic, political, cultural, and social realities. Similarly, Robinson (1999) described globalization as a highly dynamic process of growing interdependence among nation states, with implication that issues are becoming global rather than national and that they demand global rather than national attention.

It can be argued however, that globalization is not something entirely new as it is all about connectivity. Even pre-colonial period also showed some elements of globalization. In pre-colonial period there was worldwide trade. International trade had always been a link between civilizations. In fact colonial period was also the period of struggle between orthodoxy and change but there are qualitative differences between pre-colonial, colonial and postcolonial connectivity. In pre-colonial period there were free exchanges of trade and cultural values. No country enjoyed hegemony, as there was no direction in terms of any

power (Mondial, 2006). Hegemonic relationship started with the colonial period and in globalized world, which now happens to be unipolar where relationship of connectivity is totally hegemonic. It is globalization on the terms and conditions set by USA and the military – industrial combine within USA. There is one more difference between colonial and postcolonial globalized world – the revolution in information technology. The hegemonic relationship and information technology are defining elements of today's globalization process.

It can therefore be explained that globalization facilitates worldwide connections, which may be described as a process of complex connectivity between state(s) as well as people(s). And as a process, globalization eliminates geographical distances and territorial barriers.

It can also be observed that the globalization trend has not only witnessed rapid changes in the beginning of early 90's but has posed a serious challenge to all academic programmes in various institutions of learning both in the 21st century and beyond. These innovations are in various dimensions; firstly on technological angles the on-line, e-mail, off-line and others have reflected a positive trend towards decentralization of technological services and operations. Secondly, the position of technological highway has become an enabler to academic works in achieving high level of productivity and efficiency through information processing, dissemination and information acquisitions, all these have assisted substantially to fill the gaps created in the past which would have been impossible without the adoption of computer technology.

Globalization has facilitated linkages among various users through information processing and quality service delivery in order to reduce the artificial barriers orchestrated by researchers in diverse interest areas. In some advanced countries of the world such as USA, Japan and where the learners and scholars have not been able to engage in constant touch, which would have involved long distance travels, is now reduced to a global village. (Oni, 2003). The dynamic and technological innovation according to Osunrinde (2001) has already transformed the general aspiration of teachers and researchers to redefine their focuses and change the orientation of academic from what it used to be, to a more challenging fact-finding mission by making use of technological approach as a genuine way to achieve the lofty objective of our society. In view of these new strategies, the perception has changed from the old to the new by meeting the expectations of the new era. Hence, the use of new facilities such as electronic delivery services, mobile phones and Internet to reach out has created some room for sound technological base for investigators and teachers in search of a new direction associated with positive changes. Since teacher education is at the epicenter of national development, it therefore becomes necessary for teacher education to be relevant to this global trend, so that it will not lose focus in order to be more relevant to global demand.

GOALS OF TEACHER EDUCATION IN NIGERIA

The question that may be asked is: Can the objectives of teacher education in Nigeria be achieved if teacher education is not geared towards producing teachers who are globalization friendly? The National Policy on Education identified five goals of teacher education in Nigeria as follows:

1. To produce highly motivated, conscientious and efficient classroom teachers for all levels of our educational system.
2. To encourage further the spirit of enquiry and creativity in teachers.
3. To help teachers to fit into the social life of the community and society at large and to enhance the commitment to national objectives.

4. To provide teachers with the intellectual and professional background adequate for their assignment and to make them adaptable to our changing situation not only in their life and their country but in the wider world.
5. To enhance teachers' commitment to the teaching profession.

The question that may be asked is "can these objectives be achieved if the educational system is not geared towards achieving desirable change for Nigerian society?" As earlier pointed out, to achieve these goals, teachers are the main determinants of quality in education. If they are apathetic, uncommitted, uninspired, lazy, unmotivated, immoral, anti - social and most especially uninformed, the whole nation is doomed. If they are ignorant in their disciplines and thereby import wrong information, they are not only useless but also dangerous. In other words, there is the need for teacher education to be reviewed to take cognizance of the demanding competition posed by globalization.

TEACHER EDUCATION AND THE CHALLENGES OF GLOBALIZATION IN NIGERIA

The National Policy on Education with its emphasis on science, technical and vocational education was aimed at satisfying the philosophical, economic, sociological and psychological needs of the citizens in a democracy. The wealth of a society according to Bagudo (2002) determines to a large extent the development of the society and for an individual to meet up with the demands of his/her society; he/she needs some skills.

To survive in a globalized world, every Nigerian needs some basic survival skills, which include the ability to reason, the ability to re-adjust one's own term to cultural flux and the ability to control and spend one's uniqueness while participating harmoniously in the society.

Nigeria therefore needs the mastery of specific and identifiable skills in order to participate effectively and bargain boldly in world summits and conferences. Without appreciable skills in science and technology, agriculture and specific economic sectors, a country is poor and powerless, has no voice and may continue to look unto other nations for survival. Consequently, Nigeria has adopted education as an instrument par excellence for achieving national development; education should be seen as the most important change agent in the intellectual and social outlook of any society. The teacher to this end is a builder of a nation, responsible for training the minds of the young ones in the society. It is believed therefore that a functional teacher education in Nigeria, like any developing country can help its citizens explore the networking of our global village. This is achievable through a systematic mobilization of our national resources, through a modernized cadre of scientific and technological manpower.

Nigeria, according to Jimba (2003) is currently described paradoxically as a nation experiencing a downward decay from developing to under-developing and among the poorest nations of the world, despite her abundant human and material resources. Aptly, the country has all it takes to be a great nation, yet her human resources capital is weak. Thus, Nigeria's system of higher education especially should be able to make prospective engineers and technicians problem-solving, creative and innovative, which in turn may change our disadvantaged position in globalization to a vintage one. After all, the West and Japan used their own background resources and environments through liberalizing education to reach their enviable stages of development.

Teacher education must therefore equip teachers at all levels to be capable of self-learning. This will make them not only consumers of information but rather creators, originators and inventors of information. "The belief is that the more we are able to reflect on prescribed goals is to that extent that we are not likely to be exploited, manipulated economically, socially and even culturally" (Oni, Adetoro & Sule; 2011) Teacher education at this level serves as links between unpredictable world in which man lives and the tools to cope with the numerous challenges created by globalization.

In addition, teacher education has a virile role of protecting local studies and local cultures that are inevitably threatened by mega culture and globalization. Through self-knowledge, teachers are able to evaluate and assess critically what to teach and how to teach it. It has also been observed that education has become globalized. No nation is an island of its own. Through technology the world has come together. Each nation is inter-connected with ease. Education is now international or inter cultural. The teacher now stands as the midwife between the new era of globalization and the people. For the teacher to deliver the expecting global baby in any given society he/she must be equipped enough to do so.

It could also be observed that the political democratization process sweeping through the world, which has resulted in both economic and educational change, a tremendous challenge that has been posed to teacher education, particularly in the developing world. It is now accepted that education, particularly for the developing countries of the world, is not the prerequisite but also the prime determinant of economic and technological development as well as political stability and national survival. It is also known that if education unlocks the door to modernization, it is as a result of teachers' actions and commitment. Therefore, it is a national suicide for any developing nation, in this age of science and high technology, either by accident or by design to have its best brain design and build its roads and bridges, cure its sick, formulate and interpret its laws, while its poorest brains teach its youth. The results, as being witnessed in parts of Africa, are roads that wash away after the first rains, bridges that collapse after a few years of use, taps without water, electricity that is most erratic, telephones that are perpetually out of order, hospitals that kill as much as they cure and incongruous laws, purchased and teleguided justice. Clearly, these results are not true of all Africa nations but their elements exist in several African countries and other underdeveloped nations.

Indeed, there cannot be effective and environment engineers without good teachers. There cannot be efficient, dedicated and humane doctors without effective, dedicated, responsible and humane teachers. There cannot be judges without upright, dependable and incorruptible teachers. There cannot even be a strong, effective, efficient and loyal army to defend and protect our territorial integrity without loyal and patriotic teachers. Given this scenario, teacher education curriculum should be revised and enriched with appropriate and current ICT curricular content, sufficient to make teachers knowledgeable enough to teach relevant ideas that will make their students skillful, productive and equipped to cater for the needs of their society and beyond.

Similarly, it can be argued that of all advances in globalization in contemporary times, information and communication technology has had the most serious impact on how we see the world and how we live in it. It has permeated virtually all aspects of human endeavour, thus according to Ojo (2006) we now have e-governance, e-library e-education, etc. ICT is revolutionizing the world of scholarship. In the developed world for instance, someone cannot access books in the library without being computer literate; one becomes an academic vegetable if the person is computer non-compliant. The term "literate" according to Ojo (2006) is assuming a new meaning, in the context of information and communication technology. A literate person, it should be noted,

is a person who can demonstrate some knowledge and competence. This used to be ability to "read and write." But it has long been replaced by more demanding requirement. It is in this context that it can be explained that any individual who cannot use the computer at the basic level, for instance, to browse and check mails or to browse for relevant information, is a 21st century illiterate.

CONCLUSION

We all have to admit the simple fact that the threat of globalization and rapid scientific and technological changes in our society also call for alertness and improvement in the kind of training our present day teachers were given while in the school. Since we also believe that the future of a nation depends considerably on the quality of the educational system which in turn depends on the quality of its teachers and since globalization is an unavoidable international phenomenon in which Nigeria must participate, the country's teacher education programmes must be quantitatively sound to enable the entire educational system cope with the challenges of globalization.

The rapidly changing social and technological events in our globe, the EARTH, are also global in perspective. To a greater extent, all countries of the world are experiencing economic recession, the forgoing of new political alliances and the impact of the advances in science and technology. The challenges these survival and transcendence task pose to mankind are for restructuring and reactivating the socio economic, political, and cultural values arrangement with the committal of the most cherished of our human and material resources, not the least of which is the development of human resource capital through education.

Teacher education is crucial to these restructuring, renewal or reactivating processes and for this reason the global perspective for resolutions of issues must not be lost sight of in our search for solutions. Thus, if teacher education is to gain authority through a shared vision and commitment, it is necessary to include the multicultural dimension. Teachers, now and in the future, must become more aware of the peoples, cultures and events around the world that affect our lives daily.

This paper shows that teacher education is becoming restructured in many places throughout the world. It shows that we all have a similar vision in and commitment towards preparing excellent teachers to meet the demands of the future in our rapidly changing multicultural world. Through this bringing together of ideas, issues and trends and innovations in teacher education, perhaps we will encourage the expansion of existing networks and creation of new networks among teacher educators worldwide.

Recommendations

Going by the submission in this paper there is need for more and regular teachers' seminars and workshops in which teachers would be counseled to develop positive attitudes towards the use of ICT. The usefulness and advantages should be adequately communicated at such fora.

Teachers should be trained on the job and encouraged to go for short term intensive training programmes on ICT through private sponsorship and scholarship awards.

The government should provide opportunity for in – service training with some additional incentives like allowances to motivate the teachers to accept such innovations in the art of teaching. If the goals of the universal Basic Education (UBE) in Nigeria were to be achieved the teacher education programmes have to be enriched with ICT training, and government should adequately fund such training as well as providing a computer set

for each teacher. Hence, right from the period of training, each teacher should be encouraged to purchase a personal computer, which would enhance easy access to relevant and current information in the world at large.

REFERENCES

Adeboye, T. (2002). Globalization: How should Nigeria respond? (NISER Occasional paper 2). Ibadan, Nigeria: Nigerian Institute of Social and Economic Research (NISER).

Amale, S. (2003). Teacher Education in Globalization: An Appraisal of the Nigerian Situation. In Globalization & Education in Nigeria (pp. 62-73). Philosophy of Education Association of Nigeria.

Bagudo, A. A. (2002). Globalization: A challenge to Nigeria's Education System. *Nigerian Journal of Educational Philosophy*, *9*(1), 78–86.

Federal Republic of Nigeria. (2004). *National Policy on Education* (3rd ed.). Abuja: NERDC.

Jinba, D. N. (2003). Teacher Education and Globalization: Some critical challenges. In Globalization and Education in Nigeria (pp. 74-80). Philosophy of Education Association of Nigeria.

Kalusi, J. I. (2001). Teachers' quality in Nigeria. *Nigerian Journal of Educational Philosophy*, *8*(2), 62–72.

Malcolm, W. (1995). *Globalization*. London: Routledge.

Mondial, S. R. (2006). Cultural Globalization and Globalization of Culture – Source observations. *The Oriental Anthropologist*, *6*(2), 297–306.

Ohiorhenuan, J. F. E. (1998). *The south in the era of globalization*. South – Issues in Globalization.

Ojo, M. O. (2006). *Repositioning Teacher Education for National Development*. Paper presented at the 2005 Annual Conference of the Institute of Education. Benin, Nigeria.

Oni, A. A. (2003). Globalization: A menace to African values and education? *Zimbabwe Journal of Educational Research, 15*(1), 51–61.

Oni, A. A., Adetoro, J. A., & Sule, A. A. (2011). Quality Entrant and Capacity Building: Model for Rebranding Teacher Education in Nigeria. In K. Adeyemi, & B. Awe (Eds.), *Rebranding Nigerian Educational System* (pp. 91–107). School of Education, National Open University of Nigeria.

Osunrinde, A. (2001). Globalization: In search of viable direction to our academic growth. *Nigerian Journal of Emotional Psychology, 3*, 84–87.

Robinson, P. P. (1999). *The phenomenon of Globalization and the African Response*. Paper presented at the 3rd Annual Conference of Fulbright Alumni Association of Nigeria. Nzukka, Nigeria.

KEY TERMS AND DEFINITIONS

Challenges: A general term referring to things that are imbued with a sense of difficulty and victory.

Education: The process of receiving or giving systematic instruction, especially at a school or university. What really distinguishes Education is its emphasis on *development*.

Globalization: "Globalization" means the emergence of supranational institutions whose decisions shape and constrain the policy options of any particular nation-state. For others, it is the overwhelming or superseding impact of global economic processes, including processes of production, consumption trade, capital flow and monetary interdependence.

Teacher Education: Refers to the policies and procedures designed to equip teachers with the knowledge, attitudes, behaviours and skills they require to perform their tasks effectively in the school and classroom.

Chapter 20
Challenges and Prospects of Information Communication Technology (ICT) in Teaching Technical Education towards Globalisation

Oladiran Stephen Olabiyi
University of Lagos, Nigeria

ABSTRACT

The relevance of Information and Communication Technologies (ICTs) in the field of Technical Vocational Education and Training (TVET) cannot be overemphasised in the knowledge-based and globalised society. The world of works is in as continuous a state of change as ICT itself, thus posing more challenges to the workers in the 21st century and the institutions responsible for their preparation. Therefore, this chapter discusses the challenges and prospects of ICT in teaching TVE towards globalisation. The chapter points out clearly the meaning, philosophy, and objectives of TVET, concept and types of ICT, the need for effective utilisation of ICTs and its role in TVET, the challenges and solutions to the effective utilisation of ICTs in TVET, and the prospect of using ICT in teaching TVET. The chapter concludes by suggesting solutions for proper planning, management, and effective utilisation of ICTs resources in TVET.

INTRODUCTION

A nation that is aspiring for greatness, self-sufficiency, political and economic emancipation cannot afford running away from effective technical vocational education and training (TVET) because of the importance of technical vocational education and training (TVET) to national development. For

the reason that, knowledge and skills in TVET are very essential to productivity and national development of any nation, Mulemwa (2002) pointed out that, the fast changing applications of technology and the global reliance on its processes and products in all areas of human endeavour have made TVET invaluable that any society or country without it, risk being alienated from the

DOI: 10.4018/978-1-4666-6162-2.ch020

Copyright © 2014, IGI Global. Copying or distributing in print or electronic forms without written permission of IGI Global is prohibited.

global village. TVET has become such a critical factor of economic and social development that life without it can no longer be contemplated. In addition to that, through TVET, nation develops its manpower in such areas as agriculture, forestry, health, engineering, architecture, and business, among others.

The globalisation and the rapid rate of technological changes on work places have informed the recommendation by United Nation Educational, Scientific and Cultural Organization (UNESCO) and International Labour Organization (ILO) (2002) that all technical and vocational education system in the 21st century should be geared towards lifelong learning, this requires that schools in addition to academic skills inculcate workplace skills in order to increase students' flexibility and job mobility which will make them adaptable to present and envisage changes. In Nigeria, there has been emphasis in recent times on improving TVE in tertiary institutions basically for combating unemployment and poverty, as well as improvement of the economic performance globally.

Successive Nigerian government recognises the potentials of information communication technology (ICT) in the school system. This is evidenced in the educational reform policies aimed at integrating the use of ICT in schools. According to Federal Government of Nigeria (FGN, 2000), the necessity for a national Information Technology (IT) policy became more obvious after the participation of the Nigerian delegation to the first African Development Forum on the Challenge to Africa of Globalisation in the Information Age held in Addis Ababa in October 1999. As a result, a national workshop on the National Information and Communication Infrastructure was held in Abuja in March 2000. The outcome was the production of a master plan for the development of national ICT programme (ICT, 2000). Some of the strategies of human resources development stated in the ICT policy are; Making the use of IT mandatory at all levels of educational institutions through adequate financial provision for

tools and resources; and developing relevant IT curricula for the primary, secondary and tertiary institutions. One of the objectives of these strategies is to restructure the educational systems at all levels to respond effectively to the challenges and imagined impact of the information age, and with these obvious challenges, TVET programmes have future prospects.

TECHNICAL VOCATIONAL EDUCATION AND TRAINING IN NIGERIA

Educational attainment is recognised as one of the fundamental indicators of development of a nation. The world cannot think of development of a country without Technical and Vocational Education and Training (TVET). Olaitan, Igbo, Nwachukwu, Onyemachi and Ekong (1999) said that the task of technical education is the transmission of ideas, skills, values of work and environment and what individual can do with his or her life. TVET systems are therefore expected to produce a new breed of competent workforce who can compete and excel in a rapidly changing environment and improve the country's economy in globalised world. TVET makes the single largest contribution in developing human resources in this age of technology. TVET according to United Nation Educational, Scientific and Cultural Organization (UNESCO) (1999) comprise formal, non-formal and informal learning for the world of works. Young people, women and men learn and acquire knowledge and skills from basic to advanced levels across a wide range of institutional and work settings and in diverse socio-economic contexts.

In view of Thomson (2002) TVET is an instructional programme which include general studies, practical training for the development of skills required by the chosen occupation and related theory, the proportion of these components vary considerably depending on the program (vocational agric, vocational business, vocational home economics and vocational technical), but emphasis is usually on practical training. By implication, vocational education develops in individuals psychomotor, cognitive and affective skills, so that they can take their rightful place in the society. Technical vocational education according Federal Republic of Nigeria (NPE, 2004) is explained as a comprehensive term referring to those aspect of the educational process involving, in addition to general education, the study of technologies and related science, and the acquisition of practical skills, attitudes, understanding and knowledge relating to occupations in various sectors of economic and social life. TVE is further understood to be: an integral part of general education; a means of preparing for occupational fields and for effective participation in the world of work; an aspect of lifelong learning and preparation for responsible citizenship; an instrument for promoting environmentally sound sustainable development; a method of facilitating poverty alleviation (FRN, 2004). The goal of TVET is to prepare graduates for recipients that are classified above the skilled crafts but below the scientific or engineering professions.

Technical vocational education and training (TVET) therefore, is the process of teaching individuals the systematic skills, knowledge and attitude that are involved in the production of specific products or services. It incorporate the total learning experiences offered in educational ideas and abilities to make matured judgments and be in a position to create goods and services in the area of business education, industrial technical education, computer education, home economics education, agricultural education and fine and applied arts education. In a nutshell, TVET prepares human resources for the ever changing world of work. In that, for effective participation in the world of work the 'study of technologies and related sciences' as reflected in the definition, is of paramount significance that can be realised with adequate ICT arrangement in TVET institutions.

Practical skills can now be delivered virtually via a well organised ICT set up; gone are the days where practical skills are taught using hands-on learning only. Programmed instruction in form of software and interactive video made it easy for practical skills to be taught using ICTs. As such, the necessitate for ICTs in TVET remains a great challenge, considering the impact ICTs make in the world of work that 'needs a knowledgeable workers skilled in information technologies (Rojewski, 2009). By implication, the use of ICTs in the training, up-grading and re-training of workers is of paramount significance and an essential aspect of teaching's cultural toolkit in the twenty first century, affording new and transformative models of development (Leach, 2005).

PHILOSOPHY AND OBJECTIVE OF TECHNICAL VOCATIONAL EDUCATION AND TRAINING

A philosophy is an expression of feelings, beliefs, attitudes or impressions relative to a given experience. In more general term, a school or programme's philosophy is the values, attitudes, principles, and laws that govern the lives and acts of people within that group. Specifically, the philosophy of the technical vocational education programs held by school determines the direction it wants training to take. The philosophy of TVET is basically to enhance human dignity and enthrone work and labour by making individuals acquire and/or develop enough saleable and employable skills, competencies, attitudes as well as knowledge to enable them gain and maintain basic employment or self-reliance for a comfortable living. The Nigerian dream of building a truly egalitarian society can only be achieved through the effective use of TVET. It offers life-long education to all types of learners and enables them realise and develop their self-potentials maximally. Even special and adult education relies heavily on vocational education.

Technical Vocational Education and Training (TVET) is one of a recognised and effective process by which quality, up-to-date, information literate and knowledgeable workers are prepared, trained or retrained worldwide. TVET needs to adopt or develop well-defined philosophical principles that will guide, support, or create practice in changing workplaces. In order to meet the needs of the place of work of today and the future, TVET educators must be aware of the philosophies that promote both technical-vocational needs and personal development. Technical vocational educators must select and adapt appropriate philosophical views that will guide practice in terms of purpose. TVET educators must be more than transmitters of knowledge; they should be like master painters or craftsperson, professionals engaged in their art or craft and using their experience and creativity to design and make a quality work. Okorie (2001) advocates the following as the philosophical concepts that apply to vocational and technical education:

The occupational choice of individuals should be based on the orientation (interest, aptitude, ability etc.) of the individual; all honorable and honest occupations are worthy of considerations in making the decision about life's work; each individual should have the opportunity to select an occupation in harmony with his orientation and the opportunities for employment in that occupation; the worth of an individual to society grows out of his contribution of skills, knowledge and applied productive capacity to tasks that need to be completed, rather than out of artificial "status connotations" attached to some glamorous jobs; resources for education must be provided to develop all human resources; otherwise, some individuals may possibly menace other resources; and allocation of resources must reflect the needs of people. Priorities must be adjusted to provide resources in direct proportion to the cost of the investment required.

Technical Vocational Education and Training programmes offers a challenging, engaging, effective and relevant curriculum that includes the acquisition of high levels of technical knowledge coupled with employability skills and a firm academic foundation that will prepare students to be successful in the real world of work. Specifically, it is believe that: Technical vocational trainers share joint responsibility with their colleagues to ensure that the academic skills of their students are strong and sufficient to assure their success not only in the career/technical program, but also in the total school experience; technical TVET students should be motivate to assume a high level of responsibility and accountability for developing leadership and other specific skills and knowledge needed for their individual goals; technical vocational teachers should integrate technical, academic and work-place knowledge skills that are essential in developing the individual potential needed to compete in a technological and global society favorably; TVET teachers have to meet the needs of students by addressing various levels of ability, cultural and economic backgrounds, and different career goals; the ultimate goal is to provide opportunities for students to discover individual potential, creativity, and talent as a basis for continuous lifelong learning in a technological and global society.

Objectives on the other hand are concrete and specific targets of achievement. Objectives are embodied in educational aims and at any given point we can in theory tell whether the objectives are achieved or not. An objective provides the framework for determining what should be achieved through education. Today, in spite of the various ideas spelt out in the national policies which should be achieved through education, the objectives of education have become imprecise because of different value system held by different groups and individual in the society. The objectives of technical vocational education and training (TVET) according FRN (2004) are to: provide trained manpower in the applied sciences, technology and business particularly at craft, advanced craft and technical level; provide the technical knowledge and vocational skills necessary for agriculture, commercial and economic development, and give training and impart the necessary skills to individual who shall be self-reliant economically.

Therefore, TVET can be seen as a form of learning designed, tailored and targeted at preparing individuals for gainful employment as semi-skilled or skilled worker or technicians or sub-professional in recognised occupations in new and emerging occupations or to prepare individual for enrolment in advanced technical education programme. The aim of TVET is to prepare people for self-employment and to be a medium of evolution for people to the world of work; by making individual to have a sense of belonging in their communities. Consequently, TVET is seen as an instrument for reducing extreme poverty (Hollander & Mar, 2009). These distinctive features of TVET make ICTs application a mandatory component that aids a sustainable and globally recognised workforce. ICTs according to Muhammad, Babawuro, Noraffandy and Al-Muzammil (2011) facilitate the development and strengthening of TVET around the world by enhancing networking and knowledge sharing opportunities. The implication is for TVET institutions to further deploy and strengthen their commitment toward training and producing ICT-capable graduates that will meet up with the challenges of virtual workplaces. Thus, knowledge in the exploitation of ICTs is critical to the present day workers. One of the possible means of acclimatizing TVET to develop human resources for the ever dynamic world of work is to focus its investment in the integration of ICTs in the curriculum implementation process (teaching and learning).

MEANING AND TYPES OF INFORMATION COMMUNICATION TECHNOLOGY AND TVET

In this era of globalisation, one of the major concepts that cut across all human endeavors is information communication technology (ICT). Government world over has realised the importance of ICT in all facets of human growth and development. To this direction many governments have developed plans, in the late 1990s, to intensify their investments regarding ICT usage in education (Ping, Swe, Hew, Wong & Shanti, 2003; Pelgrum, 2001). In Nigeria, using information technologies in the field of education also started in the 1980s with the establishment of Specialisation Committee on Computer Training in Secondary Education by the Federal Ministry Education (FME). According to United Nation Educational, Scientific and Cultural Organisation (UNESCO, 2002) educational systems around the world are under increasing pressure to use the new information and communication technologies to teach students the knowledge and skills they need in the 21st century.

Information and Communication Technologies (ICTs) are keys in the provision of TVET. Around the world, gaining employment increasingly depends on a person's ability to effectively and efficiently use ICTs. ICTs facilitate the implementation of TVET, the provision of learning content, and communication between teachers and learners. ICTs need to be harnessed with the purpose of providing more widespread access to TVET. The relevance of Information and Communication Technologies (ICTs) in the field of Technical Vocational Education and Training (TVET) cannot be exhausted by studies available in the knowledge based society. The world of work is in continuous change as ICT itself, thus posing more challenges to the workers in the 21st century and the institutions responsible for their preparation. Information Communication Technology (ICT) in the view of Adewoyin (2009) is the new communication and computing technology used for creating, storing, selecting, changing, developing, receiving and displaying many kind of information. According to Adewoyin ICT is classified into three groups namely: (1) those that process information e.g. computer (2) those that disseminate information e.g. communication i.e. electromagnetic devices and system and (3) those for presentation of information e.g. multimedia.

The term, ICTs refer to diverse set of technological tools and resources used to communicate, and to create, disseminate, store, and manage information. According to Tinio (2002) these technologies include: broadcasting technologies (radio and television), video, digital versatile disk (DVD), telephone (both fixed line and mobile phones), satellite systems, computer and network hardware and software; as well as the equipment and services associated with these technologies, such as videoconferencing and electronics mail. Obi (2005) in her view describe ICT as a technological tools and resources used to communicate, create, organise, disseminate, store, retrieve and manage information. In this study ICT does not only mean computers, it has to do with technological tools. These technological tools according to Chika (2008) include computers, the Internet, broadcasting technologies (radio and television) and telephone. Effective application of ICTs eases the expansion and reinforcement of TVET by enhancing networking and knowledge sharing opportunities. Furthermore, ICTs in TVET has the capability to make available practical learning experiences that are needed to the instantaneous work situations. Despite the fact that, the need for ICTs in education and TVET is a global phenomenon, but it is most needed and should be used in developing economies where poverty, conflicts and health are still issues that are not yet resolved (Assaf, 2009). Hence, Nigeria and Africa in general cannot be an exception.

PLACE OF INFORMATION COMMUNICATION TECHNOLOGY (ICT) IN TEACHING AND LEARNING TVET

Teaching in classroom and workshop is no longer conceptualised in the narrow sense as merely a matter of the teacher addressing a class. In more comprehensive approach, it is the outcome or aggregate of a number of inter-related activities. Information communication technology (ICT) is basic and indispensable in the teaching and learning of TVET and in fact, in all facets of human resources development. ICT has become a veritable tool being used to solve TVET related problems ranging from design of article to sale of products in many parts of the world. The inter-relationship between TVET and ICT development and advancement of humans shows the importance of TVET in life due to its relevance in technology world. (Maliki, Ngban, & Ibu, 2009). For TVET to reap the full benefits of ICT in learning, it is essential that students and teachers are able to effectively use these new tools for learning.

TVET institutions need to provide ICT tools for teaching and learning. In this context, UNESCO (2002) noted that, TVET institutions need to develop strategies and plans to enhance the teaching-learning process within TVE programmes and assure that all TVET students are well prepared to use the new tools for learning. It deemed necessary that trainers in TVET institutions in Nigeria use ICT effectively for teaching in order to train trainees to meet the challenges of an information society once they graduate. Chika (2008) in her research finding shows that the quality of learning and teaching can be significantly enhanced when ICT is approached and utilised as an intellectual muti-tool. Teaching is an attempt to assist someone to acquire skills, attitudes, ideas, appreciation and change behaviour. Olaitan and Agusiobo (1981) defined teaching as an attempt to bring about desirable changes in human learning, abilities, and behavoiur. The aim of teaching, therefore, is to influence learners to make those desirable changes in their behaviour that contribute to better livings. Teaching in recent times has been defined by Ogwo and Oranu (2006) as the science and art of assisting students to learn.

The science in teaching entails use of the acquired knowledge from natural and behavioural sciences in order to appreciate the circumstances and personality of a learner while the art aspect of teaching involves the use of creative and demonstrative skills in aiding the delivery of instruction, teaching in recent times entail more than enough use of scientific and humanistic derivatives to facilitate learning. In most cases teaching is considered effective when learning is deemed to have taken place. Technically, teaching involves assisting the learner to develop an insight into a problem or to form an association between a response and stimulus. Learning on the other way is a process of gaining knowledge or acquiring skills or having understanding a new thing and have a better way of carrying it out. In view of the significance of TVET program and it place in the national development. Learning in vocational and technology subjects is the processes by which some activities enable the learner acquire experiences that tend to influence (changes) his/her future behaviour; provided that the characteristics of the change in behaviour cannot be explained on the basis of native response tendencies, maturation, or temporary states of the learner. Learning is the active process that leads to a change within an individual due to the acquisition of skills, knowledge, and/or attitudes. TVET teachers/instructors should possess relevant ICT skills that will aid effective instructional delivery in TVET institutions.

It is important for every teacher to know that the learning style of different students may not be the same; what motivates them may be different, their understanding level may not be the same. ICT facilities can take care of this. (Awotua-Efebo, 1999) though computer cannot solve all the problem of education but ICT can make teaching

that is tailored towards individual students' needs more practical. For instance, Computer Assisted Instruction (CAI) as defined by Ukoha and Eneogwe, (1996) is a learning process whereby a learner interacts with and is directed by computer through a course of study or learning task aimed at achieving specific instructional objectives (skill development). The efficiency of CAI in TVET according to Ukoha and Eneogwe are hinged on the three levels of interactions possible between a learner and the computer. The levels are (1) drill and practice (2) tutorial and (3) dialogue. Through CAI learners may work independently by interacting with the computer. By this, learner at a particular time in skill development may be at different levels. Fundamentally, a computer in a CAI session, instructs learners by displaying symbols, or pictures on the screen, learners respond by typing their responses on the tele-typewriter key-board.

ICTs facilitate the implementation of TVET, the provision of learning content, and communication between teachers and learners. ICTs need to be harnessed with the purpose of providing more widespread access to TVET. The application of ICT offers multiple learning pathways and widespread access to TVET, breaking down barriers for learning and teaching connected to distance and location, so vocational educators can easily have opportunities to update and upgrade their knowledge and skills. (Reschedule, Aktaruzzaman & Che Kum, 2011). UNESCO (2006), reports that the use of ICT in education and training has been a priority in most European countries during the last decade, but progress has been uneven. Most schools in most countries, however, are in the early phase of ICT adoption, characterised by patchy uncoordinated provision and use, some enhancement of the learning process, some development of e-learning, but no profound improvement in learning and teaching.

Around the world, gaining employment increasingly depends on a person's ability to effectively and efficiently use ICTs. ICT has brought unprecedented changes and transformation to TVET and information services, document delivery, interlibrary loan, Audio visual services and customer relations can be provided more efficiently and effectively using ICT, as they offer convenient time, place, cost effectiveness, faster and most-up-to-date dissemination and end users involvement in the library and information services process. The impact of ICT characterised on information services by changes in format, contents and method of production and delivery of information products. Emergence of Internet as the largest repository of information and knowledge, changed role of TVET trainers and trainees, new tools for dissemination of information and shift from physical to virtual services environment and extinction of some conventional information services and emergence of new and innovational Web based.

ROLE OF INFORMATION COMMUNICATION TECHNOLOGY (ICT) IN TEACHING TVET

Concerns for teaching-learning process constitute one of the elements in the combined efforts to update education to the need of the society. ICT is aimed at interaction process among teacher, media, and learner, upon which all others are dependent. All our educational planning, educational management and curriculum development have in the end justify themselves by the effectiveness of learning outcome. The effectiveness of the teaching-learning process has to meet the needs of both the individual and society. Literature is replete with function ICT perform in TVET institutions. Suen and Szabo (1998) identified function of computer for teaching and personal purposes. Cavas, Cavas, Karaoglan, and Kisla (2009) categorised use of ICT into instructional and managerial purposes, while Mumcu and Usluel (2010) identified instructional, managerial and personal purposes of ICT usage by TVET

teachers. Within this context, TVET teachers in technical vocational institutions like any other teachers can use ICT for instructional, managerial and personal purposes.

Uses of ICT for Instructional purpose according to Odogwu, Jimoh, Olabiyi and Yewande (2012) involves such activities like preparation for courses, searching the Internet for course contents, making presentation in the class, carrying out laboratories experiments, preparation of electronic mail for sending course materials and lesson contents to students, preparation of Internet/Web-based devices for students to access and study course material online, video conferencing, use of wiki for students to collaborate on a group work, compile data and share results of research, use of mobile learning, blogs, blended learning and social networking tools such as twitter, yahoo, facebook, myspace among others. Managerial purpose involves use of ICT for preparation and storage of official correspondence, organising students' grades and reports, and preparation of examination. While, personal purpose involves preparation of letters to friends, chatting with friends, sending e-mail to friends, preparation and storage of personal information and files and surfing through the Internet for fun. Making the use of ICT has become mandatory for teaching at all levels of educational institutions and particularly, for TVET programmes.

Three rationales according to International Institute for Technologies Education (UNESCO, 2000) are important in the reasoning about integration of ICTs in the curriculum: the social rationale, the vocational and the pedagogical rationale. All students need to master ICT literacy to become full-fledged members of society (the social rationale). Because of the emergence of new jobs and the change in existing jobs due to ICTs, the curriculum of vocational education programs is affected (the vocational rationale). While the potential of ICTs as a medium for teaching and learning is recognised by many (the pedagogical rationale), the implementation is often problematic, resulting in the fact that relatively few students worldwide are offered the opportunity to learn with the help of ICTs. To effectively integrate ICTs into education, practices teachers need to develop competencies which will help them to integrate domain knowledge, appropriate pedagogy and knowledge about ICTs.

CHALLENGES OF INFORMATION COMMUNICATION TECHNOLOGY (ICT) IN TEACHING TVET

Pearson (2009) viewed challenges as difficulties in a job or undertaking that is stimulating for one engaged in it. Something that, by its nature or character, serves as a call to battle, a tasking activity or a special effort is a challenge. Challenges in using ICTs in teaching TVET cannot completely be avoided, but can be managed; and if well handled, for the effective functioning of TVET programmes, there will be qualified teachers and workers for industries and commerce. The biggest challenges to TVET are to keep quality and effectiveness with many constraints while the enrollment of students in TVET should be increased quickly to meet needs of multi-skilled labor forces for the economic industrialisation and modernisation. Current indicator shows that most TVET graduates are unemployed because of lack of practical skill in their institutions. This is resulted from theory focused teaching of instructors instead of practical emphasis training, so filling the skill gap of teachers is what is so important in achieving strategy. While the uses of ICTs are expanding rapidly, major challenges are faced in terms of capacity development, access, connectivity, and localisation, customisation and content development. (Roslyn & Terry, 2011)

David and John (2012) in their study carried out in Kenya on the challenges of using information communication technology (ICT) in school administration in Kenya identified that lack of electricity connection from the Mains power sup-

ply to some of the institutions has posed major challenge to ICT use in school administration, which has resulted to the use of diesel generators to provide electricity to power the computers. This manner of sourcing power was highly inconveniencing because it was mostly used at night. Consequently, few teachers and administrators were able to utilise the technology, leading to low frequency of ICT use. Equally, studies done in the United Kingdom, the Netherlands, Malaysia and South Africa corroborate the fact that school require facilitation with appropriate computer facilities and related infrastructure in order for optimize the application of ICT in their teaching and administrative engagements (Mentz & Mentz, 2003 and Tearle, 2004).

The challenges related to financing the cost of ICT, one of the greatest challenges in ICT use in TVE is balancing educational goals with economic realities. ICTs in education programmes require large capital investments and developing countries need to be prudent in making decisions about what models of ICT use will be introduced and to be conscious of maintaining economies of scale. Ultimately it is an issue of whether the value added of ICT use offsets the cost, relative to the cost of alternatives. Another challenge is in the area of technical support specialists whether provided by in-school staff or external service providers, or both, technical support specialists are essential to the continued viability of ICT use in schools. While the technical support requirements of institution depends ultimately on what and how technology is deployed and used, general competencies that are required would be in the installation, operation, and maintenance of technical equipment (including software), network administration, and network security. Without on-site technical support, much time and money may be lost due to technical breakdowns.

One of the greatest challenges for TVET teachers in making teaching of TVE effective in today's schools as explained by Olaitan (2010) is the clear usage of technology in teaching. The present classroom is an open one and learners are more exposed to learning information than before through ICT. Some of the information obtained through ICT may not be relevant to what teacher is teaching but may be of interest to the learners, while those that are of relevance to learning situation may not be of interest to the learners who have uncontrolled access to information through Internet. For example, learners may visit Internet to browse for source of making money or business rather than getting information for completing an assignment given by the teacher. There is a general believe in the mind of the learners that all information obtained from the Internet is as good if not better than the one given by TVET teacher because it is electronically supplied; hence, electronic information are never accessed for relevance by learners for any assignment. The challenges to TVET teachers in this direction are complex and require effective management. For example, the TVE teachers must master the subject matter he want to teach, methodology of teaching it and how to teach trainees better ways of making use of information from the Internet.

The most pressing challenges to the effective integration of ICTs in TVET according to Kotsik (2009) includes; content and curriculum; appropriateness and efficacy; quality and branding of ICT-mediated learning; stakeholders' resistance; lack of appropriate software; the digital divide; the cognitive and copy right issues. Albirini (2006) found lack of teacher competency, and access to computers by teachers in schools as a main obstacle to their acceptance or rejection, As such, serious work needs to be done to curtail the worseness of the situation, considering the fact that the fast changing world of work never awaits anybody. This situation also poses a great challenge to stakeholders, policy makers, and curriculum implementers, among others. Louw, Brow, Mulle and Soudien (2009) in their study instructional technologies in social science instruction in south Africa; teachers reported some factors that constraint their use of ICTs, the major ones include; inadequate technol-

ogy (network connection), pedagogical issues, (for example, plagiarism), lack of time to develop or adapt ICT materials, and integrating into courses.

Presently, it has been observed that many TVE teachers though have access to the Internet but lack training and skills for obtaining and using relevant information from the Internet. Many teachers have substituted Internet information for textbook reading and writing, hence, they are reducing daily in impact and critical thinking. It is an effective management of learning tricks and administration that are required for helping the technical vocational teachers cope effectively with modern teaching requirement. The proper policy development and its subsequent implementation of ICT with economic and social activities can make a quantum shift in status of Nigeria economy. Nigerian cannot participate in the global ICT revolution, if they are not connected, there is no point in discussing our ICT potential if we do not build the highway to connect it; Rural dwellers will suffer from the digital divide, being left further in terms of access to markets, education, social and health services. The difficulty of the teaching/learning activities, lack of ICT skills of teachers, inappropriate instructional materials to meet the objectives of teaching and learning, inadequate motivational techniques to increase the interest to learn. Updating of these skills will improve the quality of the present TVET.

SOLUTIONS TO CHALLENGES FACED IN INFORMATION COMMUNICATION TECHNOLOGY IN TVET

Dada (2001) suggested that government should ensure adequate funding through fiscal budgeting and budget implementation so that technical institutions can be relevant to the technology world in terms of ICT utilisation for effective instructional delivery. Adewoyin (2006) revealed that teachers' ICT readiness and competences need to be assessed so as to improve students' learning level. To ensure that TVET programmes are relevant to the society, teachers in technical institutions must use these new technologies that are continually changing the ways people live, work, and learn to teach. Therefore, TVET teachers/instructors should keep pace with changing technology in order to assure their roles still relevant to produce tomorrows' teachers.

However, there are various techniques which can be applied for improving teaching of TVET through ICT. This includes adequate training for teachers on how to use ICT resources for teaching, giving students' assignment which must be done using ICT resources, repairing damaged computer system and maintaining them, back up, supply of electricity and that incentive for professional development should be provided for TVET teachers. Governmental, Non- governmental and private organisations should be encouraged to support ICT application which will in turn encourage the TVET teachers to use ICT resources always in classroom teaching and workshop practical projects. This suggestion is in agreement with the finding of Mouza (2002) who stated that opportunities for exploration of ICT resources given pre-service teachers will not only make them aware of the available software but also how the ICT resources might be adopted to support curricular objectives. ICT resources should be adapted to the teaching in classroom so as to enhance effective learning of the subject.

In the view of Adewoyin (2006) Teacher professional development in ICT should have followings: Skills with particular applications; integration into existing curricula; curricular changes related to the use of IT (including changes in instructional design); changes in teacher role and underpinning educational theories. Ideally, these should be addressed in pre-service teacher training and built on and enhanced in-service. In some countries, like Singapore, Malaysia, and the United Kingdom, teaching accreditation requirements include training in ICT use. ICTs are swiftly

evolving technologies, however, and so even the most ICT fluent teachers need to continuously upgrade their skills and keep abreast of the latest developments and best practices. The country needs to produce a large number of ICT professionals. Specifically, policy statements endorse the need for widespread introduction of ICT training in public and private educational institutions as a prerequisite for producing skilled ICT manpower. The Internet facilities should be widely available in most places of Nigeria. Internet is one of the main technologies which can help to use the ICT efficiently. To get benefit from ICT the educational policy make must ensure the availability of Internet in every Institution both micro and macro level.

PROSPECTS OF USING INFORMATION COMMUNICATION TECHNOLOGY (ICT) IN TEACHING TVET

However great and obvious are the challenges of ICT in teaching and learning, TVET programmes have present and future prospects. Prospect as described by Encarta (2009) is a mental picture of something that is expected or awaited. The possibilities or chances for future success especially based on present work and plan is prospect. Therefore, in Nigeria TVE institutions, prospect is a cognitive content held as true promise and hope about the future of the system. This can only be achieved through effective provision of ICT. ICTs are one of the key tools in the provision of TVET. David and John (2012) observed that educational institutions are increasingly becoming complex multidimensional organisations requiring tremendous input in terms of human, financial and physical resources. Such school working environments are bound to overwhelm the abilities of today's teacher and administrator if they are not aided in the performance of their school administrative duties. These developments demand therefore that educational institutions modernize their tools of conducting business to enhance the effectiveness of management and leadership.

The goal set by UNESCO (2000) in the context of ICT use in TVET is to overview the existing international experience in the field, to determine the most important issues and outline strategic directions of the policy development creating step by step an international expert network. The Institute is intended to focus on the most relevant and global aspects of ICT use in TVET by reviewing national policy, assisting in educational curriculum modernisation, assessing the results of programmes earlier introduced by all UNESCO divisions. At the same time special consideration is to be given and individual and innovative approach is going to be invented regarding specifics of using ICTs for technical and vocational education and training of excluded and most vulnerable groups as well as people with disabilities.

Furthermore UNESCO plans that policy research carried out and recommendations made will contribute to the development of appropriate and modern training programs aimed at raising ICT-competence and developing professional skills of technical vocational teachers with a global recognition. Modern living requires that everyone (all citizens) have more adequate understanding of Technology and the World-of-Work. Technological problems and changes affect the economic and social status of all people. Technology has changed the world-of-work through innovation and design, and science has changed society through inquiry and discovery. These developments call for a much more manipulative, academic, and technically competent individual, having experiences and a broader understanding as to how ICTs affects them in this complex era in which we all live, work, and play - career and technical and technology education offer valuable foundations for the thousands who will make their livelihood in this ever changing society.

The incorporation of ICT into the day-to-day functions of educational institutions has marked impact on every aspect of management struc-

ture and dynamics. It means the study on ICT introduction in the schools would not have been comprehensive if the social and technical aspects were not considered in their entirety explaining the reason for the adoption of the socio-technical approach in the study based on the open systems theory as espoused by Kast and Rosenzweig (2002). These days another significant uses of ICT is in the area of manufacturing. ICTs according to John (1987) are use in designing and making products, keeping track of inventory, and in dozens of other jobs. ICTs are contributing to all of the manufacturing jobs. It also helped in introducing new manufacturing methods. One of these is just-in-time (JIT) manufacturing. With JIT, materials are delivered to the factory as they are needed. Warehouse space is not required. Fewer workers are needed to organize and keep track of materials. Because JIT requires precise planning, every stage of the operation is linked by computer John added.

UTILIZATION OF INFORMATION COMMUNICATION TECHNOLOGY (ICT) FOR TEACHING TVET

A quality TVET programme plays an essential role in promoting country's economic growth and contributing to poverty reduction as well as ensuring the social and economical inclusion of marginalised communities. UNESCO (2003) views TVET as the master key to poverty alleviation and social cohesion and as central to the promotion of sustainable development. Around the world, gaining employment increasingly depends on a person's ability to effectively and efficiently use ICTs. ICTs also simplify and accelerate information and knowledge sharing about TVET, so that best practices and lessons learned can easily be disseminated. ICTs facilitate the administration of education and training, the provision of learning content, and communication between learners and between teachers and learners. ICT supports holistic learning, collaborative grouping, problem-oriented activities and integrated thematic units. Teachers wishing to teach in this way will be both more efficient and effective if they employ ICT to reach their goals (Dellit, 2002). ICTs are widely used in woodworking construction and manufacturing. For instance, computers control the cutting of logs into lumber (plank), ICT are used to control the inventory of materials in a furniture factory. ICTs are also used in ways that are not so easy to see.

For example, the computer is use to design floor and roof trusses. This speeds up house design and construction. Without the ICT, it would take designer and drafter up to a week or more to design the kitchen cabinets for a custom-built home. With a computer, the same job can be done in less than one hour. ICT increases someone ability to do intelligent work. Olabiyi, Jimoh, and Akanni, (2011) stress further that CAD enables a person to work problems quickly-with greater accuracy. The computer extends human brainpower just as a table saw extends human muscle power. CAD/CAM systems are changing the way in which homes and furniture are designed, drawn, and built. CAD is the abbreviation for computer-aided design. (CAM is the abbreviation for computer-aided manufacturing.) CAD is a means of using a computer to produce a design. The cutting and pasting is done electronically.

The main advantage of CAD as stated by John (1987) is that it eliminates repetition. Once a design is created, it rarely has to be completely redrawn. The computer stores all the information. Every design can be kept in file and is always accessible. New designs are created by selecting elements from existing designs and putting them together. The computer allows designers to set up a file of frequently needed design elements, parts, and symbols. This is simply referred to as up and plug them into the drawing. Using CAD, drafter can create a drawing using elements in the computer's storage unit. The efficient use of CAD systems depends on the programmes (software)

that are available. For example, an architect will use programmes dealing with designing homes, rooms, floor plans, and cabinets. A building contractor will use programmes involving bidding and scheduling. He or she may also use programmes for office functions such as payroll. CAM is the other part of the CAD/CAM system. CAM systems take the design from the CAD system. Using computers, numerical control machines, and robots, they produce the product in the factory. CAD can be applied in design needs other than basic drawing. Families of items, such as types of fasteners, can be drawn and stored in the computer. When a new part must be created, the basic drawing is called up, copied, and adapted to the new design analysis. When an architect needs to know if a structure will be strong enough, a model of the structure is created using the computer. The computer analyses the structure in terms of the forces that will act upon it and suggests any needed changes.

Combining with non-drafting software, CAD can be used to prepare such things as bills of materials. The computers carries out calculations and helps transit orders, with database software, CAD can keep track of large inventories of items. Types of wood materials and where they were used in a particular building can all be kept on file and called up as needed later on, such as for repairs. Computer programmes: Computers are used in every step of building houses and furniture. Here are a few examples of available programmes. These programmes are very useful to the architect and builder. A programme entitled energy performance design system (EPDS) allows the architect and builder to check energy saving. He or she can check various ideas for walls, floors, ceilings, windows, doors, siding, and roofing. The programme helps the user to identify those kinds that save most energy. The builder can tell home buyer exactly how much the heating and cooling bill will be at current energy costs. A programme on truss design can be used by manufacturers of truss systems for floors and roofs. This programme develops various truss designs. It makes cutting list for the design. It does structural analysis. With a plotter attachment, it produces drawing and stock-cutting lists. A programme on cabinet designs can be used to build kitchen cabinets and fixtures for stores. This programme is useful for custom woodworking shops. Information (called in-put) must be fed into the computer.

This information includes the size of the area and the woods to be used. It also includes the kinds of doors and drawers. In less than one hour, drawing and stock-cutting list are produced. Computers programmes for furniture manufacturing are available. These programmes include furniture design; programmes for numerically controlled machines are also available. These days another significant uses of ICT is in the area of manufacturing. ICTs are use in designing and making products, keeping track of inventory, and in dozens of other jobs. ICTs are contributing to all of the manufacturing jobs. It also helped in introducing new manufacturing methods. One of these is just-in-time (JIT) manufacturing. With JIT, materials are delivered to the factory as they are needed. Warehouse space is not required. Fewer workers are needed to organize and keep track of materials. Because JIT requires precise planning, every stage of the operation is linked by computer. Mobolaji (2004) view ICT development in terms of what it does to promote institutional efficiency – i.e. enhancing public sector (that is government) and private sector delivery of service; and increasing private-sector profit; human development of the individual citizen – improving access to food, shelter, clothing, water, health, education, employment, among others., of man, woman and child; young and old, literate and non-literate, urban and rural, etc. The challenge then is to encourage decision makers, teachers and the citizenry at large that ICT in general improves ordinary lives if properly deployed, and that it is not just an esoteric notion embarked upon to titillate city dwellers who merely wish to imitate Western apparatuses and systems rather than provide more basic necessities of life.

In his study, Tas (2010) concluded in his analysis on the topic ICT for development: A case study that; ICT education is a must for the ever growing and ever changing global economy. Only in five years time regardless of the industry or the position, most jobs will require at least basic IT levels. That is why IT education has significant importance in development and welfare of people and communities. Regardless of the educational specialisation, training and professional development courses, the integration of ICTs has now become basic requirement and the area that needs special investment. It infers that ICTs are globally recognised tools that needs to be fully integrated in all educational fields especially TVET, considering the nature and sophisticated the field of TVET to the economic, industrial and human resources development, in public or private sector. However, all challenges identified from the literature reviewed have been duly acknowledged, their impact on the effective ICTs integration into TVET could be properly addressed through adequate planning, and management of ICT resources. Application of ICT in teaching in both science and technology, according to Odumosu and Keshiro (2000) is seen as how it is applied in learning aids, simulation, modeling, Internet service, lesson presentation, AutoCAD, ArchiCAD, giving drill and practice and computer assisted instruction (CAI). In addition Adewoyin (2006) ICT can be applied in producing smart draw, semantic, GIF construction, video tape, relay chart, tool book, graphic design, animation, text. All these are often applied in teaching.

The technology is ever changing. Depending on the future demand, government should take appropriate action to introduce ICT in school level. Research should be done for improving the present situation of education. ICT tools should be provided to each TVET institution. Teachers should give their attention to use ICT in their teaching learning process. Students also should use Internet for collecting necessary information for their education. Government should provide enough budgets to ensure the requirement of ICT tools and machineries for each classroom. Government should formulate proper policy to train up the teachers for their respective field as well as in ICT. TVET should be free from political factors; teachers' motivation is a critical factor in ICT adoption. Policies in this area should include measures raising the confidence levels of the teachers (by giving appropriate in-service and initial teacher training on ICT and also by rewarding them for the use of ICT.

SUMMARY

TVET has been variously defined by different scholars. In a nutshell it is seen as the process of teaching individuals the systematic skills, knowledge and attitude involved in the production of specific products or services. ICT refer to diverse set of technological tools and resources used to communicate, and to create, disseminate, store, and manage information. TVET teachers should possess relevant ICT skills that will aid effective instructional delivery. The philosophy of TVET is basically to enhance human dignity and enthrone work and labour by making individuals acquire and/or develop enough saleable and employable skills, competencies, attitudes as well as knowledge to enable them gain and maintain basic employment or self-reliance for a comfortable living. Among the objectives of TVET are; provide trained manpower in the applied sciences, technology and business particularly at craft, advanced craft and technical level; provide the technical knowledge and vocational skills necessary for agriculture, commercial and economic development.

While the uses of ICTs are expanding rapidly, it is faced with challenges. Challenges are difficulties in a job or undertaking that is stimulating for one engaged in it. Something that, by its nature or character, serves as a call to battle, a tasking activ-

ity or a special effort is a challenge some of these challenges are in terms of capacity development, access, connectivity, and localisation, customisation and content development, financial problems, lack of training among teachers and administrators, short in supply in number and therefore not accessible to teachers and administrators among others. There are prospects in using ICT in TVET. Prospects are the possibilities or chances for future success especially based on present work and plan.

ICT are widely utilised in industries for example, in woodworking construction and manufacturing. Computers control the cutting of logs into lumber (plank), ICT are used to control the inventory of materials in factory, Instructional usage of ICT involve for such activities like preparation for courses, searching the Internet for course contents, making presentation in the class, carrying out laboratories experiments, preparation of electronic mail for sending course materials and lesson contents to students. Managerial purpose involves use of ICT for preparation and storage of official correspondence, organizing students' grades and reports, and preparation of examination. While, personal purpose involves preparation of letters to friends, chatting with friends, sending e-mail to friends. Despite huge efforts to position ICT as central tenets of TVET, the fact remains that many make only limited formal academic of computer technology, while this is usually attributed to a variety of operational deficits on part of students, faculty, and universities.

REFERENCES

Adewoyin, J. A. (2006). The Place of Information and Communication Technology in Designing and Utilizing Instructional Materials. In *Proceeding on a One Day Train the Trainer Open Workshop on Understanding New Technologies in Instructional Media Materials Utilization*. Academic Press.

Albirini, A. (2006). Teachers' attitude toward information and communication technologies: The case of Syrian EFL teachers. *Computers & Education*, *47*(4), 373–398. doi:10.1016/j.compedu.2004.10.013

Amadi, Orikpe, & Osine. (1998). *Effective Technical Vocational Education Training Design*. Human Resources Development Press Inc.

Amoor, S. S. (2011). The Challenges of Vocational and Technical Education Programme in Nigerian Universities. *Journal of Research on Computing in Education*, *3*, 479–495.

Assaf, B. (2009). *Immerse approach to ICT in TVET*. Retrieved from http://www.ipac.kacst.edu.sa

Awotua-Efebo, E. B. (2002). *Effective Teaching Principle and Practice*. Para Graphic Publishers.

Basu, C. K., & Majumdar, S. (2009). The role of ICTs and TVET in rural development and poverty alleviation. In R. Maclean & D. Wilson (Eds.), International handbook of education for the changing world of work (pp. 1923-1934). Springer Science + Business Media BV.

Calfery, C. C., & Alton, V. F. (1982). *Vocational Education: Concepts and Operations* (2nd ed.). Wadsworth Publishing Company Inc.

Cameron, R., & O'Hanlon-Rose, T.Cameron & O'Hanlon-Rose. (2011). Global Skills and Mobility Challenges and Possibilities for VET: A cross-border Cross-sectoral case Study. *International Journal of Training Research*, *9*(1-2), 134–151. doi:10.5172/ijtr.9.1-2.134

Cavas, B., Cavas, P., Karaoglan, B., & Kisla, T. (2009). *A study on science teachers' attitudes toward information and communication technologies in education*. Retrieved May 10, 2012 from http://www.tojet.net/articles/v8i2/822.pdf

Danko, A. I. (2006). *Entrepreneurship Education for Vocational and Technical Education Students* (2nd ed.). Academic Press.

David, K. M., & John, M. B. (2012). The challenges of using information communication technology (ICT) in school administration in Kenya. *Journal of Research on computing in Education*, *3*, 479-495.

Dellit, J. (2002). Using ICT for quality in teaching-learning evaluation processes. In *UNESCO Using ICT for quality teaching, learning and effective management*. Retrieved May 10, 2012 from http://www. unesdoc.unesco.org/images/0012/001285/128513eo.pdf

Encarta. (2009). *Prospect*. World English Dictionary (North America Ed.). Retrieved January, 2010, from http://encarta.msu.com/

Federal Government of Nigeria (FGN). (2000). *Nigerian national policy for information and communication technology*. Retrieved May 10, 2012 from http://www.www.uneca.org/aisi/nici/.../it%20policy%20for%20nigeria.pdf

Federal Ministry of Education. (2000). *Technical and Vocational Education Development in Nigeria in the 21ˢᵗ century with the blue-print for the decade 2001-2010*. Federal Ministry of Education.

Federal Ministry of Education (FME). (1988). *Report on national policy on computer education*. Lagos: Author.

Federal Republic of Nigeria. (2004). *National Policy on Education* (4th ed.). Lagos: NERDC Press.

Gaudron, J.-P., & Vignoli, E. (2002). Assessing computer anxiety with the interaction model of anxiety: Development and validation of the computer anxiety trait subscale. *Computers in Human Behavior*, *18*(3), 315–325. doi:10.1016/S0747-5632(01)00039-5

Handler, M. G. (1993). Preparing new teachers to use computer technology: Perceptions and suggestions for teacher educators. *Computers & Education*, *20*(2), 147–156. doi:10.1016/0360-1315(93)90082-T

Hollander, A., & Mar, N. Y. (2009). Towards achieving TVET for All. In R. Maclean, & D. Wilson (Eds.), *International handbook of education for the changing world of work. Springer Science + Business Media BV*. doi:10.1007/978-1-4020-5281-1_3

Isman, A., Yaratan, H., & Caner, H. (2007). *How technology is integrated into Science Education in a Developing Country: North Cyprus Case*. Retrieved May 10, 2012 from http://www.tojet.net/volumes/v6I3.pdf

Joseph, W. A., & Ralph, O. S. (1977). *Course construction in industrial arts, vocational and technical* (4th ed.). American Technical Publisher, Inc.

Kotsik, B. (2009). ICT application in TVET. In R. Maclean, & D. Wilson (Eds.), *International handbook of education for the changing world of work. Springer Science + Business Media BV*. doi:10.1007/978-1-4020-5281-1_127

Kotsik, B., & Rosenueng. (2009). ICT application in TVET. In R. Maclean & D. Wilson (Eds.), *International handbook of education for the changing world of work*. Springer Science + Business Media BV.

Leach, J. (2005). Do new information and communication technologies have a role to play in achieving quality professional development for teachers in the globe south? *Curriculum Journal*, *16*(3), 293–329. doi:10.1080/09585170500256495

Louw, J., Brown, C., Muller, J., & Soudien, C. (2009). Instructional technologies in social science in South Africa. *Comput. Educ., 53*, 234 242.

Maliki, A. E., Ngban, A. N., & Ibu, J. E. (2009). *Analysis of students' performance in junior secondary school mathematics examination in Bayelsa State of Nigeria*. Retrieved may 10, 2012 from http://www.krepublishers.com/.../HCS-03-2-149-09-Index.pdf

Massoud, S. L. (1991). Computer attitudes and computer knowledge of adult students. *Journal of Educational Computing Research, 7*(3), 269–291. doi:10.2190/HRRV-8EQV-U2TQ-C69G

Mobolaji, E. A. (2004). *Some Issues in ICT for Nigerian Development*. Retrieved from http://www.nigerianmuse.com/projects/TelecomProject/InterConnectivity_Aluko.ppt

Muhammad, S. S., Babawuro, S., Noraffandy, Y., & Al-Muzammil, Y. (2011). Effective integration of information and communication technologies (ICTs) in technical and vocational education and training (TVET) toward knowledge management in the changing world of work. *African Journal of Business Management, 5*(16), 6668–6673.

Mumcu, F. K., & Usluel, Y. K. (2010). *ICT in vocational and technical schools: Teachers' instructional, managerial and personal use matters*. Retrieved May 10, 2012 from http://www.tojet.net/volumes/v9i1.pdf

Mumeu, F. K., & Ushel, Y. K. (2011). ICT in vocational and technical school teachers: Instructional, managerial and personal use matters. *The Turkish Online Journal of Educational Technology, 9*(1), 98–106.

Muniandy, V., & Lateh, H. (2010). ICT implementation among Malaysian schools: GIS, obstacles and opportunities. *Procedia: Social and Behavioral Sciences, 2*(2), 2846–2850. doi:10.1016/j.sbspro.2010.03.426

Odogwu, H. N., Jimoh, J. A., Olabiyi, O. S., & Yewande, R. O. (2012). Usage of ICT for instructional, managerial and personal purposes by science, technology and mathematics lecturers in the colleges of education in South-West Nigeria. In *Proceedings towards Effective Teaching and Meaningful Learning in Mathematics, Science and Technology*. University of South Africa.

Odu, O. K. (2011). Philosophical and Sociological overview of vocational and technical education in Nigeria. *American-Eurasian Journal of Scientific Research, 6*(1), 52–57.

Odumosu, A. I. O., & Keshinro, O. (2000). *Effective Science Teaching and Improvisation in the Classroom*. Lagos: Obaroh & Ogbinaka Publishers.

Ogwo, B. A., & Oranu, R. N. (2006). *Methodology in Formal and Non-formal Technical/vocational Education*. University of Nigeria Press, Ltd.

Okorie, J.U. (2001). *Vocational Industrial Education*. Bauchi: League of Researchers in Nigeria.

Olabiyi, O. S., Jimoh, J. A., & Akanni, W. A. (2011). Utilisation of Information Communication Technology by Vocational Technical Education Teachers for Effective Instructional Delivery. *International Journal of Research in Education, 3*(3).

Olaitan, S. O., & Agusiobo, O. N. (1981). *Principles of Practice Teaching*. Toronto, Canada: John Wiley and Sons.

Olaitan, S. O., Nwachukwu, C. E., Igbo, C. A., Onyemachi, G. A., & Ekong, A. O. (1999). *Curriculum Development and Management in Vocational and Technical Education*. Onitsha. Cape Publishers.

Olsson, L. (2006). Implementing use of ICT in teacher education. In *International Federation for Information Processing, Education for the 21st century impact of ICT and Digital Resources*. Boston: Springer. doi:10.1007/978-0-387-34731-8_49

Pearson Education Limited. (2007). *Longman Dictionary of Contemporary English-The living Dictionary*. London: First Impression.

Rashedul, H. S., Aktaruzzaman, & Che, K. C. (2011). Factors influencing use of ICT in Technical and Vocational Education to make teaching-learning effective & efficient: Case study of Polytechnic institutions in Bangladesh. *International Journal of Basic and Applied Science, 11*(3).

Sahin, I., & Thompson, A. (2006). Using Rogers' theory to interpret instructional computer use by COE faculty. *Journal of Research on Technology in Education, 39*(1), 81–104. doi:10.1080/15391523.2006.10782474

Smith, B., Caputi, P., & Rawstorne, P. (2000). Differentiating computer experience and attitudes toward computers: An empirical investigation. *Computers in Human Behavior, 16*(1), 59–81. doi:10.1016/S0747-5632(99)00052-7

Szabo, M., & Suen, C. (1998). *A study of the impact of a school district computer technology program on adoption of educational technology*. Retrieved April 18, 2012 from http://www.quasar.ualberta.ca/edmedia/Suenszabo.html

Tas, E. M. (2010). ICT education for development- a case study. *Procedia: Social and Behavioral Sciences, 3*, 507–512.

Technical and Vocational Education and Training (UNEVOC). (2003). *New Project on ICT Use in Technical and Vocational Education*. UNESCO.

Tella, A. (2011). *Availability and use of ICT in southwestern Nigeria colleges of education*. Retrieved May 10, 2012 from http://www.ajol.info/index.php/afrrev/issue/view/8653

Thompson, J. F. (2002). *Foundation of Vocational Education*. New York: Prentice-Hall Inc.

Tinio, V. L. (2002). *ICT in education*. Retrieved may 10, 2012 from http://www.saigontre.com/FDFiles/ICT_in_Education.PDF

UNESCO. (2002). *Revised Recommendation concerning Technical and Vocational Education (2001)*. Paris: UNESCO.

UNESCO. (2005). *United Nations and Culture of Peace: Manifesto, 2005*. UNESCO.

UNESCO. (2008). *Toward Information Literacy Indicators*. Paris: UNESCO.

United Nation Educational Scientific and Cultural Organization. (2002). *Information and Communication Technology in Teacher Education*. Retrieved May 10, 2012 from http://www.unesdoc.org/images/0012/001295/129533epdf

Usun, S. (2009). Information and Communication Technologies (ICT) in Teacher Education (ITE) programs in the world and turkey (a comparative view). *Procedia: Social and Behavioral Sciences, 1*, 331–334. doi:10.1016/j.sbspro.2009.01.062

Visscher, A. J. (1988). The computer as an administrative tool. *Journal of Research on Computing in Education, 24*(1), 146–296.

Walter, E. C. (1993). *Management Development through Training*. Addison-Wesley Publishing Company, Inc.

Wang, T. (2009). Rethinking Teaching with Information and Communication Technologies (ICTs) in Architectural Education. *Teaching and Teacher Education., 25*, 1132-1140.

KEY TERMS AND DEFINITIONS

Challenges: Something that, by its nature or character, serves as a call to battle, a tasking activity or a special effort is a challenge.

Globalisation: The trend toward increased economic, cultural, and social connectedness between individuals, businesses, and public organisations across international borders.

Information and Communication Technologies (ICTs): Diverse set of technological tools and resources used to communicate, and to create, disseminate, store, and manage information.

Prospects: A mental picture of something that is expected or awaited. The possibilities or chances for future success especially based on present work and plan.

Teaching: An attempt to help people acquire some skills, attitude, knowledge, ideas or appreciation. In other words, the teacher's task is to create or influence desirable changes in behavior in his or her students.

Technical and Vocational Education (TVE): Effective process by which quality, up-to-date, information literate and knowledgeable construction workers are prepared, trained or retrained worldwide.

Training: Acquisition of knowledge (facts, theory, concepts) attitudes (values, styles, beliefs) and skills (how-to-do-it) to enable individual perform their specific tasks or current jobs to the required level of competence.

Chapter 21
M–Health Technology as a Transforming Force for Population Health

Florence F. Folami
Millikin University, USA

ABSTRACT

Information and communication technologies in health practices are known as mobile health. Mobile health (m-Health) is the use of portable electronic devices for mobile voice or data communication over a cellular or other wireless network of base stations to provide health information. Evidence suggests that the use of m-health offers new opportunities for population health. However, resistance to m-health among health professionals is considered to be a main barrier. Evidence shows that m-Health technology would grant patients the long-term support needed during treatment without jeopardizing patient autonomy. The practice of m-health requires a rethinking of the existing frames of reference and adoption of new frames of reference in health practice. This chapter is a descriptive study in which a quantitative technique was used to collect data. The study shows the potential scale and impact of m-health in accelerating the rate of patient education. Healthcare providers can maximize the benefits of electronic tools by educating themselves to better understand the potential uses, challenges, and benefits.

INTRODUCTION

M-health is broadly defined by the World Health Organization as the use of information and communication technology for health (World Health Organization, 2011). Mobile health now often called m-Health is the use of portable electronic devices for mobile voice or data communication over a cellular or other wireless network of base stations to provide health information (Kahn, Yang & Kahn, 2010). M-health is an emerging discipline focusing on the use of information and communication technology to deliver health services (Steinbrook, 2009). A number of different terms and terminologies have been used with this discipline. For example, the terms such as telehealth, telemedicine, and health informatics have been used interchangeably.

Research efforts have been focused on the impacts of m-health technology on population

DOI: 10.4018/978-1-4666-6162-2.ch021

Copyright © 2014, IGI Global. Copying or distributing in print or electronic forms without written permission of IGI Global is prohibited.

health (TPR Media, 2012; Terry, 2008). Steinbrook (2009) explained in his paper on health care and the American recovery and reinvestment act that there is significant increase in the numbers of Internet users as well as mobile. M-health initiatives have evolved to improve access to services and efficiency within the health of people with little or no access to quality health care. Cell phone is one of the components of m-Health technology and have been of the fastest growing industries (TPR Media, 2012).

According to TPR Media (2012), most people have portable phones, and/or cell phones in their respective homes. These devices are connecting people in convenient ways as their cost declines with the expand use. While the Internet services require ground infrastructure, connection junctures, and heavy equipment, mobile technology provide an additional benefit of wireless and hands-free technology that can be maximized in developing health care systems.

Population health is define as the health outcomes of a group of individuals, including the distribution of such outcomes within the group and the field of population health includes health outcomes, patterns of health determinants, and policies and interventions that link these two (Friedman, Parrish & Ross, 2013). There are a variety of ways in which m-Health can potentially be used to improve population health (World Health Organization, 2011). Health is a national and international priority. While the U.S. spends more per capita on healthcare than any other developed country (Kaiser Family Foundation, 2007), it has far from the best health outcomes (World Health Organization, 2011). Effective implementation of m-Health can strategically add a new level of solution to current challenges facing healthcare.

The recent proliferation of wireless and mobile technologies provides the opportunity to connect information in the real-world via these technologies to produce continuous streams of data on an individual's behavior. M-Health has the potential to be a transformative force for population health

by changing when, where, and how healthcare is provided (Coyle, 2012). Mobile phones, particularly smart phones and other mobile computing devices, are becoming increasing globally, which enhances the potential to assess and improve health programs. The purpose of this study is to explore the impact of m-health technology adoption on population health transformation. This study will answer the following two questions; 1) Can m-health accelerate the rate of patient education? and 2) Does m-health technology has the potential to transform the delivery of health messages?

REVIEW OF THE LITERATURE

A systematic review of the literature was conducted using an appropriate search approach and inclusion criteria of population health and the use of social media delivering health messages. Some key areas of focus include (1) m-health and patient compliance and (2) m-health and dissemination of health information among population.

M-Health and Patient Compliance

In a systematic review of text messaging as an intervention for disease prevention and management, the authors stated that there was evidence for short-term effects on behavior changes or clinical outcomes related to disease prevention and management, such as smoking cessation, self-monitoring of blood glucose levels, weight loss and decrease in hemoglobin A1C (Patrick, Griswold & Intille, 2008). They also suggested that the use of m-health interventions has the capacity to interact with the individual with much greater frequency, and in the context of the behavior, at a convenient time for the patient.

The use of m-health provides the potential to deliver health behavior interventions tailored to a person's baseline characteristics, such as disease, demographic, as well as frequently changing behaviors and environmental contexts. A review of randomized clinical trials showed that reminder systems, apart from mailed postcard reminders, improved patient adherence (Glynn, Murphy, Smith, Schroeder & Fahey, 2010). There is potential to improve adherence by direct reminders to patients via voice calling or short message service (SMS). Likewise, wireless technology utilizing phone networks can be used. A 2007 pilot study in South Africa demonstrated that patient compliance jumped to over 90%, in areas previously recording 22-60% compliance, when using a mobile device known as SIMpill (Barclay, 2009). SIMpill is a medication container that interacts with an assigned mobile phone to remind the patient when he or she has not taken the next dosage. Repeated or missed dosages are brought to the attention of health care workers, who then follow-up with the patient and arrange for an in-person visit.

M-Health and Dissemination of Health Information among Population

Primary prevention is the key to the reduction of disability and disease, and mHealth technology provides an effective channel to fulfill this. M-health has great potential to enhance primary prevention. More than any other modern technology, mobile phones are used throughout the world. Innovative applications of mobile technology to existing health care delivery and monitoring systems offer great promise for improving the quality of life. Information may be distributed through text message services, voice calling, or e-mail as a method of delivering care (Barrigan, Poropatich & Casscells, 2010). As mobile phones become one of the first technologies to reverse the digital divide, care must be taken to ensure that information being received is accurate and interpreted correctly; otherwise, there exists a risk of acting upon misleading or false information.

Messaging can connect people to the appropriate services and also act as a search engine to seek care, potentially increasing the health of population. Social networking can also be effective in health promotion, such as in encouraging healthy behaviors through carefully crafted messages disseminated via text messaging. Project Masiluleke in South Africa, for example, sends a million text messages per day to encourage people to be tested and treated for HIV/AIDS. Messages are sent in local languages, directing recipients to the National AIDS Helpline, which provides information about testing services and locations (Barrigan, Poropatich & Casscells, 2010). Messages can target tobacco use prevention, smoking cessation, improved dietary choices, avoidance of risky sex behavior, and violence and injury prevention. A potential downside, though, is that poorly designed or implemented messaging risks antagonizing, desensitizing, or confusing the public.

There is evidence that m-health can truly transform population health by increasing compliance and adherence to treatment (Kahn, Yang & Kahn, 2010). M-Health could potentially provide the greatest impact. By beginning to develop m-health solutions to improve poulation health, technology can be maximized as a preventive measure that would reduce the burden of advanced illness. Mobile phone has come to assume a significance importance in societies with various age using mobiles in their own way to suit their individual needs (TPR Media, 2012).

M-Health Technology can contribute to the evidence base for the use of mobile technology to improve clinical outcomes and public health measure. With technology becoming ever more global, and with growing access to technology among the world's youth, significant potential exists for m-health to have a real impact on health outcomes (Kahn, Yang & Kahn, 2010). Mobile penetration in developing countries, where wireless technologies have jumped the wired computer infrastructure, have produced considerable excitement in the global health community with the prospects of reaching and following individuals who were previously unreachable (Terry, 2008; Kossaraju, Barrigan, Poropatich & Casscells, 2010).

Since 2005, scattered case studies and anecdotal examples documented in the literature on the use of text messaging for health, mobile diagnostic and decision support, disease surveillance and control, and mobile phones to address emergencies and chronic illness have emerged. A comprehensive wireless industry report divides this list into 101 explicit health-related activities, highlighting many of the opportunities becoming available within the health sector to maximize increased access to the technology (Wireless Healthcare, 2005). Within the context of such documentation, there is very little evidence on the health outcomes related to the direct application of mobile phones to support health objectives (Steinbrook, 2009; Terry, 2008).

Application of Transformative Theory

Transformation theory, like other types of theory, seeks to transmit new knowledge, skills, and ways of thinking (Kitchenham, 2008). Transformative learning allows participants to engage in knowledge construction, acting with the facilitators to apply new information and broaden existing schemes of meaning (Dirkx, 1998). This paper dwells on some of the specific challenges that the health care professional faced while developing m-health and how the challenges are addressed with a particular reference to the transformative health. Healthcare often presents a disorienting dilemma in the form of a education.

Changes in health status and the desire for health open up adults to learning. Yet, healthcare often stops prompting transformation at this point (Greenberg, 2001). Information given to patients is often didactic and either explanatory or prescriptive. Patients are often given information about their condition through brief oral instruction or written information. Short visits allow for little discussion with the provider about causes, treatments, options, and the influence of behaviors. The lack of dialogue and time for critical reflection means that most healthcares cannot be transformative. Innovative applications of mobile technology to existing health care delivery and monitoring systems offer great promise for improving health of population. Information may be distributed through text message services, voice calling, or e-mail as a method of delivering care (Barrigan, Poropatich & Casscells, 2010). Glynn, Murphy, Smith, Schroeder, and Fahey (2010) proposed that the components of mHealth technology would grant patients the long-term support needed during treatment, without jeopardizing patient autonomy. Mobile networks cover more than 90% of the world's population, and the proportion of mobile phone users already outweighs those without one (World Health Organization, 2011).

RESEARCH METHOD

This study is a descriptive study in which quantitative techniques was used to collect data. The study population constitutes all users of mobile phones in a prenatal clinic of a hospital in Midwestern, Illinois. A total of 225 respondents were randomly sampled for the study. The data for this study were collected at the individual level using mainly structured questionnaire with closed ended questions where respondents were given options to select the applicable response, semi structured and open ended questions.

This is a researcher-developed instrument. A panel of nursing staff and faculty members in nursing and public health provided a content assessment and feedback to determine clarity and validity of questions. These faculty members are recognized leaders in the fields of nursing and public health. Field-testing occurred with the demographic instrument. The field test took place with 20 patients from two different prenatal clinic in Illinois. They felt that the questionnaire was comprehensive and easy to complete.

Table 1. Characteristics of respondents

Variable Age (in yrs.)	Frequency	Percentage
Below 20	165	73.30
21-25	41	18.20
26-30	14	6.20
31 and above	5	2.30

The questionnaires were self administered and were distributed during their visit for prenatal care. Respondents voluntarily participated in the study. The questionnaire began with the socio demographic characteristics of respondents.

RESULTS

Table 1 and Table 2 are summaries of the characteristics of the respondents involved in the study. As can be seen most (73.30%) of the respondents were below 20 years and the mean age of respondents was 23 years. This shows that usage of mobile phone is widely used. As such, there is opportunity for increased exposure, as well as more private exposure. World Health Organization (2011) found that a total of 10 hours and 45 minutes of exposure are packed into 7.5 hours of use. That is, about 30 percent of adolescents' media time is spent using more than one medium simultaneously. This phenomenon seemed to have been enabled best practices that will transform health to be shared.

On the question reasons for using mobile phone, 67.3% indicated that they used mobile phones to contact friends they do not usually meet, 55.2%

Table 2. Martial status

Single	91	40.44
Married	132	58.66
Divorced	2	0.80

use the phone to consult in times of difficulties while 84.4% of the respondents used it in accessing information 43.6% used the mobile phone for business. About 68.8% of the respondents utilize the call service of the service providers while 17.6% claimed they often used the mobile phone for the short message service and 10.4% of the respondents often use the Multimedia Message Service while 28% of the respondents use the chatting regularly.

On the question how often they use their phones, 60% of the respondents use their mobile phone multiple times in a day, 12% used it ones to five times in a week while 28% use their phones once a day. About 95% of the responded indicated that mobile phones are important to society while 5% of them thought otherwise. On the other hand, 98.7% of the responded specified that, the use of mobile phone is important in transforming and sustaining health while 1.3% however disagreed. The positive impacts mentioned by the respondents include improving relationships, representing 84.8%, access to information 63.2%, improving societal ties 80.4% and enhancing communication was the most cited positive impacts of mobile phone on society and this was indicated by 94% by the respondents.

FINDINGS

It is evidenced that the findings of this study answered the two research questions: Can m-health accelerate the rate of patient education? and 2) Does m-health technology has the potential to transform the delivery of health messages? Most of the participant (98.7%) agreed that the use of mobile phone is important in transforming and sustaining health while 1.3% however disagreed. The positive impacts mentioned by the respondents include improving relationships, access to information, and enhancing communication. It showed that methods of communication are changing and m-health can improve healthcare service delivery and health outcomes. M-Health has great potential to promote healthy lifestyles, improve decisions by health professionals as well as patients. World Health Organization also claimed that m-health enhance healthcare quality by improving access to medical and health information and facilitating instantaneous communication in places where this was not previously (Fox, 2012). M-Health can be used as a basic healthcare delivery method. Due to recent advances in technology and greater attention to problems associated with quality and efficiency of health care delivery, m-health is a new opportunities to transform health care delivery.

The findings showed that m-health must be monitored and measured on an ongoing basis to determine efficacy. Health care providers need effective ways to encourage their patients to make healthy lifestyle choices. The amount of information, encouragement, and support that can be conveyed to individuals during consultations or through traditional media such as leaflets is limited, but mobile technologies such as mobile phones and portable computers have the potential to transform the delivery of health messages (Glynn, Murphy, Smith, Schroeder & Fahey, 2010). The findings also showed that m-health has a significant influence in improving population health and can also enhance strategic thinking and guidance to transform population health.

SUMMARY, CONCLUSION, AND RECOMMENDATIONS

A gap in the literature existed in the study of impact of m-health in transforming population health. The limitations associated with this study must be acknowledged and provide the basis for future research. Since this study only utilized the patients at one hospital, it would be useful to examine other patients in different hospital across the nation. Specific recommendations include replication of the study in different hospital to further understand the impact of m-health in transforming population

health. Replication of the study with multi-ethnic participants would assist to evaluate the cultural influences on m-health. More in depth study on the impact of m-health in transforming population health and also range of factors needed to be considered while developing m-health.

The main purpose of this study is to explore how m-health technology adoption is positively associated with quick transfer of information enhance transformation of population health. Health care providers should share their insights into providing sustainable m-Health technology that will transform health of population. M-Health can improve the provision of care and levels of knowledge. The widespread use of mobile phones is one reason why mHealth technology can be a key factor of improving population health. It is believed in this study that the bare knowledge of m-health would not change the traditional health practices. Transformation of attitudes with perceptions and behaviors coupled with new knowledge and skills would lead to a new way of access to care. This study showed the potential scale and impact of m-health in transforming population health. M-health could accelerate the rate of patient education. Today's nursing leaders can maximize the benefits of electronic tools by educating themselves and their staff, and working with others in their organizations, particularly those with expertise in healthcare informatics, to better understand the potential uses, challenges, and benefits. But they must be proactive in harnessing this opportunity.

REFERENCES

Barclay, E. (2009). Text Messages could hasten tuberculosis drug compliance. *Lancet, 373*(9657), 15–16. doi:10.1016/S0140-6736(08)61938-8 PMID:19125443

Centers for Disease Control and Prevention. (2010). *Chronic diseases and health promotion.* Retrieved from www.cdc.gov/chronicdisease/overview/index.htm

Centers for Disease Control and Prevention. (2011). *Rising health care costs are unsustainable.* Retrieved from www.cdc.gov/workplacehealth-promotion/businesscase/reasons/rising.html

Coyle, S. (2012). Conquering the fear of technology. *Advance for Nurses.* Retrieved from http://nursing.advanceweb.com/Features/Articles/Conguering-the-Fear-of-Technologv.aspx·

Daniel, J., Friedman, R., Gibson, P., & David, A. (2013). Electronic health records and US Public Health: Current realities and future Promise. *American Journal of Public Health, 103*(9), 1560–1567. doi:10.2105/AJPH.2013.301220 PMID:23865646

Fox, S. (2012). *Pew Internet: Health. In Pew Internet & American Life Project.* Retrieved from www.pewinternet.org/Commentary/2011/November/Pew-Internet-Health.aspx

Glynn, L., Murphy, A., Smith, S., Schroeder, K., & Fahey, T. (2010). Interventions used to improve control of blood pressure in patients with hypertension. *Cochrane Database System, 3,* CD005182. PMID:20238338

Kahn, J., Yang, J., & Kahn, J. (2010). Mobile health needs and opportunities in developing countries. *Health Affairs, 29*(2), 254–261. doi:10.1377/hlthaff.2009.0965 PMID:20348069

Lenhart, A. (2009). *Teens and mobile phones over the past five years: Pew Internet looks back.* Washington, DC: Pew Internet.

Media, T. P. R. (2012). UbiCare communication solutions for healthcare. *What's your EQ? A look at healthcare's Facebook® engagement.* Retrieved from https://ubicare.com/engaqement

Nielsen Mobile. (2008). *Critical mass: The worldwide state of the mobile web.* Retrieved from http://nl.nielsen.com/site/documents/nielenmobile.pdf

Patrick, K., Griswold, W., Raab, F., & Intille, S. S. (2008). Health and the mobile phone. *American Journal of Preventive Medicine, 35*(2), 177–181. doi:10.1016/j.amepre.2008.05.001 PMID:18550322

Steinbrook, R. (2009). Health care and the American recovery and reinvestment act. *The New England Journal of Medicine, 360*(11), 1057–1060. doi:10.1056/NEJMp0900665 PMID:19224738

Terry, M. (2008). Text messaging in healthcare: The elephant knocking at the door. *Telemedicine Journal and e-Health, 14*(6), 520–524. doi:10.1089/tmj.2008.8495 PMID:18729749

World Health Organization. (2011). mHealth: New horizons for health through mobile technology: Second global survey on e-Health. WHO Press.

KEY TERMS AND DEFINITIONS

Evidence Based: A descriptor that is used to describe medically-related reference resources.

Mhealth: M-Health is the use of portable electronic devices for mobile voice or data communication over a cellular or other wireless network of base stations to provide health information.

Peer Pressure: Influence that a peer group, observers or individual exerts that encourages others to change their attitudes, values, or behaviors to conform the group norms.

Population Health: Population health is define as the health outcomes of a group of individuals, including the distribution of such outcomes within the group and the field of population health includes health outcomes, patterns of health determinants, and policies and interventions that link these two.

Technology: Technology can also be defined as the scientific methods and materials used to achieve industrial objectives.

Chapter 22
Influence of Globalisation on Teaching and Learning:
What is the Stance of Information Literacy in Nigerian Tertiary Institutions?

A. O. Issa
University of Ilorin, Nigeria

K. N. Igwe
Akanu Ibiam Federal Polytechnic, Nigeria

ABSTRACT

This chapter examines the influence of globalization on teaching and learning and the poor state of Information Literacy skills (IL) of students owing to the neglect of IL programmes in Nigerian tertiary institutions. Conceptualizing IL and situating it within the framework of the Nigerian higher institutions, the chapter discusses the implementation of IL programmes in these institutions and the likely attendant challenges. It concludes on the poor state of IL skills of students, which is due to the lack of implementation of IL programmes in higher institutions of learning in Nigeria. It recommends, among others, that administrators and planners of tertiary education in Nigeria should begin to see IL as more of an academic issue, rather than being a library thing, and urges regulatory agencies of these institutions to become more responsible in embracing contemporary issues like the IL programmes.

INTRODUCTION

Globalisation is a multifaceted and multidimensional concept. It involves unhindered flow of information resources as well as sophistications in e-teaching, e-learning and other e-based educational services across geographical borders. Globalisation has led to the emergence of open source tools, open access resources, online information resources, open educational resources, learning management systems, plagiarism detection systems, and many e-learning platforms on the online environment. These e-based resources are being published every second by formal and informal organisations, government agencies, non-governmental organisations, research and

DOI: 10.4018/978-1-4666-6162-2.ch022

Copyright © 2014, IGI Global. Copying or distributing in print or electronic forms without written permission of IGI Global is prohibited.

development institutions, establishments, associations and individuals, thus leading to the present data smog, information gamut and knowledge explosions, across the globe. This is attributed to the Internet, and its services such as the World Wide Web, the social media and other emerging digital gadgets, which are instruments of globalisation. These developments are encouraging the establishment of e-libraries, digital institutional repositories, e-archives, and other domains of e-resources, by tertiary institutions (universities, polytechnics and colleges of education), and other organisations and individuals, that are either legally or illegally operating in the society.

Thus, the proliferation of these resources is posing challenges to stakeholders in the tertiary educational system, especially students, in terms of utilisation. Students may be familiar with the Internet, search engines and social media platforms for searching information and interacting online, as they are seen as digital natives. However, they may not be aware of techniques of identifying real scholarly works, methods of evaluating online resources and application of critical thinking skills, knowledge of synthesizing information and developing new ideas as well as knowledge of adhering and applying ethical principles in the course of using the resources. Therefore, they need the skills on how to identify, access, critically evaluate and synthesize information, create new knowledge and communicate same in ethical and acceptable pattern for the benefit of all in the society. Information literacy (IL) competencies come in as the enabling factors, but the question is: where does IL stand in Nigerian tertiary institutions in this era of globalization of teaching and learning?

TEACHING AND LEARNING IN THE GLOBALISATION ERA

Globalization era is characterized by flow of data, information and knowledge mainly via the online environment. Data smug, information glut

and knowledge explosions are manifesting in the teaching and learning system across the globe. Also, communication, collaboration and sharing of information by individuals across countries, regions and continents are now carried out with ease due to ICT availability and accessibility; pointing to the fact that teaching and learning in this era via the information superhighway and other digital gadgets are feasible in spite of geographical barriers, if properly articulated and implemented.

The era of globalization has redefined open and distance education as practiced and executed by some institutions of higher learning. Many reputable and accredited universities and other categories of such institutions all over are now providing e-learning and online educational opportunities to qualified individuals ranging from certificate, diploma, bachelor, masters to doctoral programmes. While most of these programmes are accessible from all corners of the globe, and are 100% online, others require some degree of residency. These online programmes are facilitated with learning management systems, plagiarism detection systems, and Web portals, majority of which are open source programmes, freely available online for tertiary institutions. Students of such online programmes are expected to posses certain skills, among which are excellent knowledge of English language rules, communication skills, ICT knowledge and skills as well as information literacy competencies. Even students of conventional tertiary institutions are also expected to posses the above-stated skills because both categories of students are faced with the same volume of online information resources.

The open access movements started in 2002 with the aim of projecting, promoting and facilitating free flow of information resources and knowledge assets of man, coinciding with the conceptualization of open educational resources (OER) by UNESCO. These are key features redefining and reshaping teaching and learning in the globalization era. In 2001, the Massachusetts Institute of Technology (MIT) introduced Open Course Ware (OCW), a free and open digital publication of educational materials organised as courses. The UNESCO organised a conference in 2002, where the term, open educational resources was coined, and defined as 'the open provision of educational resources, enabled by information and communications technologies, for consultation, use and adaption by a community of users for non-commercial purposes' (Hodgkinson-Williams, Willmers, & Gray, 2009; McNally, 2012; Cobo, 2013). OER are also seen as teaching, learning, and research resources that reside in the public domain or have been released under the intellectual property right license that permits their free use or re-purposing by others. It includes full courses, course materials, modules, textbooks, streaming videos, tests, software, and any other tools, materials, or techniques used to support access to knowledge (Atkins, Brown & Hammond, 2007).

They are digitized materials offered freely and openly for educators, students, and self-learners to use and reuse for teaching, learning and research and include learning content, software tools to develop, use, and distribute content, and implementation resources such as open licenses (OECD, 2007). Thus, the emergence of OER aims at addressing challenges of access to teaching and learning resources, not only for open and distance learning (ODL) but also for conventional face-to- face educational systems, characterized by inadequate information resources, especially in Nigeria. However, there have been a lot of concerns about OER in terms of content quality, reliability, authenticity, efficiency and cost-effectiveness, thus requiring effective techniques of applying IL competencies for finding, evaluating, synthesizing and using the resources ethically and responsibly.

With these features of teaching and learning in the globalization era, possession of IL skills by students becomes paramount, calling for articulated attention in Nigeria. This call affects all stakeholders in the business of education such as governments, ministries of education, lecturers, librarians, and educational administrators and planners mainly in universities, polytechnics, colleges of education, colleges of agriculture, vocational and innovation enterprise institutions, for the benefit of students who are regarded as leaders of tomorrow.

CONCEPT OF INFORMATION LITERACY

The concept of information literacy was first introduced in 1974 by Paul Zurkowski, the then president of the United States Information Industry Association, in a proposal submitted to the National Commission on Libraries and Information Science (NCLIS). As a contemporary concept, it took its root from the library instruction, library-use education, user education in libraries, use of library, and bibliographic instruction as the case may be. It is a term that metamorphosed from the then afore-mentioned practices by librarians for facilitating access to user services and the use of information materials by the library users. The emergence and acceptability of IL by stakeholders in the educational sector in the era of globalization is to address the key skills required for training graduates with IL competencies, thereby having all it takes for lifelong learning opportunities and ability to surmount challenges associated with either in working environments or entrepreneurial development.

In this era of globalization, IL is much more than mastering basic library use skills because libraries could no longer claim monopoly of information provision for academic activities, rather sophistications in Internet and other associated components are resulting to too much information thereby requiring certain skills for result-oriented and ethical utilisation. IL is about developing information and technology competencies that foster lifelong learning. Information literate students should be able to find, evaluate, and use information effectively to discover new knowledge, solve problems, make decisions, and become more informed members of the society (University of Colorado, n.d).

According to the Association of College and Research Libraries (ACRL, 2000), IL is a set of abilities enabling individuals to "recognize when information is needed, and be able to locate, evaluate, and use effectively the needed information." It refers to the aggregate of skills, abilities and competencies, which information users need to possess for the determination of their information needs, development of information searching strategies, accessing and retrieving, evaluation and utilization of information resources in all formats in line with ethical and legal issues surrounding use of information. The Middle States Commission on Higher Education (2003) gave an elaborate definition of IL as:

An intellectual framework for identifying, finding, understanding, evaluating and using information. It includes determining the nature and extent of needed information; accessing information effectively and efficiently; evaluating critically information and its sources; incorporating selected information in learner's knowledge base and value system; using information effectively to accomplish a specific purpose; understanding the economic, legal and social issues surrounding the use of information and information technology; and observing laws, regulations, and institutional policies related to the access and use of information.

An individual, who is information literate, can:

- Determine the extent of information needed;
- Access the needed information effectively and efficiently;
- Evaluate information and its sources critically;
- Incorporate selected information into their knowledge base;

- Use information effectively to accomplish a specific purpose; and
- Understand the economic, legal, and social issues surrounding the use of information, and access and use information ethically and legally.

In other words, information literate students from tertiary institutions should be able posses the following:

- Information needs identification skills;
- Information accessibility skills;
- Information evaluation and critical thinking skills;
- Knowledge of synthesizing information; and
- Knowledge of principles of information ethics and their application in the course of information utilisation. Such ethical principles are plagiarism, intellectual property, copyright and fair-use policies, online bullying, and the likes.

Gaining IL skills multiplies opportunities for students' self-directed learning as they become engaged in using a wide variety of information sources to expand their knowledge, ask informed questions, and sharpen their critical thinking abilities for the future. Information literate students necessarily develop some ICT skills, which are interwoven with and support IL, because it augments their competency in evaluating, managing, and using information effectively and efficiently (Van't Hof, Sluijs, Asamoah-Hassan & Agyen-Gyasi, 2010). The information literate students are individuals prepared for lifelong learning. That is why IL is for all disciplines, for all learning environments and for all levels of education, especially higher education institutions that are producing prospective managers and administration of the economy.

INFORMATION LITERACY PROGRAMMES IN NIGERIAN HIGHER EDUCATION INSTITUTIONS

There are justifiable facts to prove that IL is a key ingredient missing at all levels of education in Nigeria, especially the tertiary level. Empirical studies have shown that students of Nigerian higher education institutions (HEIs) have poor IL skills (Issa, Amusan & Daura, 2009; Nwalo & Oyedum, 2011; Adeyomoye, 2012; Igwe & Esimokha, 2012; Babalola, 2012; Ilogho & Nkiko, 2014). This is attributed to the neglect of IL instructions in the curriculum of tertiary institutions in Nigeria (Ojedokun, 2007), thus, IL programmes are neither embedded in the curricula of these HEIs nor provided as a standalone compulsory course for all students. In addition, librarians in these tertiary institutions still rely on teaching traditional use of library or library-use education to students (Ogunmodede & Emeaghara, 2010; Ottong & Ntui, 2010; Baro & Zuokemefa, 2011; Aliyu, 2011; Okoye, 2013), without aligning it with the demands of comprehensive IL competencies in the present globalization era.

Use of library or library-use education course tends to limit students to knowledge of information resources and services in the institution's library alone, which was inadequate enough to meet the contemporary IL skills requirements of students for their academic pursuits and lifelong learning in the present era (Dulle, cited in Ojedokun & Lumande, 2005; Kaur, Sohal & Walia, 2009). Meanwhile, to consider a library orientation or user education a course engendering IL skills is misleading, as such only focused on the ways of locating information or the instrumental aspects of retrieval in libraries. They do not cover the broader contextual elements and the higher-level analytical skills necessary to effectively mine and utilize information in a manner, which will withstand scrutiny (Behrens, 1990), as addressed in IL programmes. This implies that equating IL programme with teaching students how to use a library is as short-sighted as assuming that driving a car simply requires that a person knows how to step on the gas pedal (Badke, 2010). Some individuals still think that IL is about using the library and finding information, however it is not only that (Coonan, 2011; Martin, 2013), but much wider than the acquisition of traditional information skills.

If comprehensive IL programmes are solution to poor IL skills of students and by extension, ill-equipped graduates of Nigerian HEIs without lifelong learning capabilities as well as competencies to function productively in present knowledge-driven organisations, then there is an urgent need for a paradigm shift. Therefore, what does it take to implement holistic IL programmes and what are the likely challenges?

IMPLEMENTATION OF INFORMATION LITERACY PROGRAMMES IN HEIS IN NIGERIA

Information Literacy Programmes are policies, standards and strategies formulated and executed by HEIs, either through or in collaboration with librarians, for the delivery of IL instructions and inculcation of IL skills in students. The programmes encompass library user education, information skills training and education, and those areas of personal, transferable or 'key' skills relating to the use and manipulation of information in the context of learning, teaching and research in higher education (Streatfield & Markless, 2008), mostly as it affects online information resources that are accessible to all in the educational sector.

Implementation of IL programmes in HEIs involve developing IL competencies course; incorporating IL across the university curricula; developing IL teaching methods; collaboration of librarians, faculty and administrators; budgeting for the acquisition of information resources and equipment; personnel training and development; as well as monitoring and evaluating the

IL programme regularly (ACRL, 2000; CAUL, 2001). Essentially, a successfully implemented IL programme will:

- Focus on a conceptual understanding of the research process;
- Lead students to use academic resources of high caliber;
- Focus on class-specific research skills;
- Enable students to produce better researched papers;
- Develop more efficient information seeking and retrieval habits;
- Encourage students to evaluate information systematically;
- Provide a mechanism to address plagiarism and other un-ethical academic practices;
- Contribute to student success and student retention; and
- Provide the basis for lifelong learning. (Brock University, n.d)

In the context of Nigeria, for result-driven IL programmes to be implemented, the following are expected to be carried out:

- Formulation of IL policy in the institutions that will guide the implementation of IL programmes. Such policy should stipulate, include and encompass the following:
  - Clear mission, goals and objectives in line with that of the institutions and reflects the roles of user groups. It should also include expected IL competencies of students, standards, performance indicators, learning outcomes, and methods of delivery. System of periodic assessment and evaluation of the programmes based on established benchmarks will also form part of it.
  - Creation of IL framework or preferably adoption/adaptation of existing models like IL Competency

Standards of Association of College and Research Libraries (ACRL), of the American Library Association (ALA); Society of College, National and University Libraries (SCONUL) UK; Australian and New Zealand Institute of Information Literacy (ANIIL) and Council of Australian University Librarians (CAUL), to suit the information environment in Nigeria.

  - Planning for resources, which include human, financial, infrastructural, learning and information resources for the implementation and sustenance of the programme. The human resources are mainly librarians (who are key IL instructors), lecturers, and instructors, and they need to collaborate for result-oriented programme. Designation of subject and liaison librarians for various faculties/colleges of the institutions should be better for such programme. Then, institutional administrators are to ensure adequate budgetary provision and allocations for the programme.

  - Integration of IL programmes in the curriculum of the institutions, either as standalone courses or embedded in the courses of various departments. Also, involved is reviewing existing library-use education course content to reflect expected up-to-date IL skills and learning outcomes and then changing the course title to IL Instruction/Programme (ILP), which is the contemporary nomenclature globally. The course should have at least two-credit units and made compulsory for all undergraduates in the first semester of their first year of study and second semester in the third year of their study. Also provisions for the course should be made for postgraduate students.

  ○ Creation of interactive Website, (preferably hosted by the institution's library) where IL content, tutorials, competencies and assessment mechanism will be uploaded; there by allowing for comments from users regarding IL.

- Creation of a Centre for IL in the various institutions and the appointment of a director to coordinate and lead an IL committee for holistic implementation. Such director should be a librarian with strong interest and passion for IL delivery.

CHALLENGES TO IMPLEMENTATION OF INFORMATION LITERACY PROGRAMMES IN NIGERIAN HEIS

There are various factors that could impede the implementation of holistic IL programmes in Nigerian tertiary institutions. Although academic departments are always very supportive of the idea of enhancing students' IL skills, they are reluctant to fully embed these competencies into the curriculum. Thus, if high-level information handling skills are crucial to the academic mission, and if IL is fundamental to learning in all contexts, why does IL not form a significant element in the academic curriculum of tertiary institutions (Coonan, 2011) especially in Nigeria? There is:

- Lack of understanding of IL by administrators and lecturers;
- Confusion of IL with ICT competency; and
- Students' misconceptions that they know how to search the Internet, especially Google, and therefore they believe they are information literate (Coonan, 2011).

In addition, Badke (2010) went further stating that IL has been rendered "invisible" within the academia by a number of causes:

Because it is misunderstood, academic administrators have not put it on their institutions' agendas, the literature of information literacy remains in the library silo, there is a false belief that information literacy is acquired only by experience, there is a false assumption that technological ability is the same as information literacy, faculty culture makes information literacy less significant than other education pursuits, faculty have a limited perception of the ability of librarians, and accrediting bodies have not yet advanced information literacy to a viable position in higher education.

The confusion and misunderstanding of IL with IT competency is an issue that has been addressed well and clearly in the literature of library and information science. Information technology skills are 'increasingly interwoven' with IL, but that ILs 'have broader implications for the individual, the educational system, and for society' and that IL abilities 'may use technologies but are ultimately independent of them' (ACRL, 2000). According to Bruce (cited in Coonan, 2011) the distinction between IL and IT literacy is "the difference between the intellectual capabilities involved in using information, and the capabilities required for using technologies that deliver or contain 'information'.

Other factors affecting IL programmes in Nigerian tertiary institutions are:

- Attitude of administrators of tertiary institutions towards library services, of which IL programmes are central to users' service delivery and level of satisfaction in this globalization era.

- Institutional administration's level of knowledge of the essence, importance, academic and lifelong impact of IL on students.
- Perceptions of academic staff, such as lecturers, instructors, head of departments, deans of faculties and directors, about library services such as IL.
- State of teaching and learning resources in Nigerian universities.
- Factors associated with librarians in tertiary institutions, who should be the key IL instructors and main facilitators of IL programmes. Some of the factors include level of their IL competencies, their perceptions about IL programmes, their attitudes towards sharing knowledge and ideas about IL, and the total number of available professional librarians in an institution that can comfortably deliver IL programmes with expected outcomes.

CONCLUSION AND RECOMMENDATIONS

There is no doubt that IL has taken a centre stage in all affairs of man in the universe. Nations are progressing to knowledge economies and IL competencies are required by the citizens of nations to remain active players, and Nigeria cannot afford to be left out. Its higher educational institutions should put machinery in place for the production of information literate and lifelong learning citizens. As emerging technologies continue to develop, thereby moving globalization to a greater level, with continuous explosions of online resources, especially many that are vanity press publications, the essence of IL programmes and the need for its holistic implementation continues to arise, thus, calling for the urgent attention of administrators and planners of tertiary education system in Nigeria.

It is thus recommended that administrators of tertiary institutions should see IL as an academic issue, and not a library thing. The regulatory agencies such as National Universities Commission, National Board for Technical Education, and National Commission for Colleges of Education should rise up to their responsibilities and embrace contemporary issues like IL programmes that are calling for urgent implementation in their various institutions.

Librarians in various tertiary institutions are expected to know that a key responsibility for them in the nearest future will be delivery and implementation of IL programmes. It may likely not only be for students alone, but also faculty and other stakeholders in the academic community. They are therefore expected to fortify themselves with contemporary IL competencies and issues. In addition, they should continuously attend workshops and seminars to enhance their skills, and implement same to sensitize their academic community on the essence, benefits and other issues associated with IL.

REFERENCES

Adeyomoye, J. I. (2012). Information literacy competence among students in Nigerian private universities: A case study of Caleb University Imota, Lagos, Nigeria. *Library Progress International*, *32*(2), 185–193.

Aliyu, U. F. (2011). Influence of library instruction course on students access and utilization of library resources in Abubakar Tafawa Balewa University Bauchi, Nigeria. *Journal of Research in Education and Society*, *2*(3), 96–102.

Association of College and Research Libraries. (2000). *Information literacy competency standards for higher education*. Chicago: ACRL. Retrieved from www.acrl.org/ala.mgrps/divs/acrl/stndards/standards.pdf

Atkins, D. E., Brown, J. S., & Hammond, A. L. (2007). *A review of the open educational resources (OER) movement: Achievements, challenges, and new opportunities* (Report to the William and Flora Hewlett Foundation). Retrieved from http://www.hewlett.org/uploads/files/ReviewoftheO-ERMovement.pdf

Babalola, Y. T. (2012). Awareness and incidence of plagiarism among undergraduates in a Nigerian private university. *African Journal of Library. Archival and Information Science*, *22*(1), 53–60.

Badke, W. (2010). Why information literacy is invisible. *Communications in Information Literacy*, *4*(2), 129–141.

Baro, E. E., & Zuokemefa, T. (2011). Information literacy programmes in Nigeria: A survey of 36 university libraries. *New Library World*, *112*(11 & 12), 549–565. doi:10.1108/03074801111190428

Behrens, S. J. (1990). Literacy and the evolution towards information literacy: An exploratory study. *South African Journal of Library and Information Science*, *58*(4), 355–365.

Brock University. (n.d.). *James A. Gibson Library – Information literacy/library research skills policy*. Retrieved from http://www.brocku.ca/library/about-us-lib/policies/literacy-research-document

Cobo, C. (2013). Exploration of open educational resources in Non-English speaking communities. *International Review of Research in Open and Distance Learning*, *14*(2), 107–128.

Coonan, E. (2011). *A new curriculum for information literacy: transitional, transferable and transformational*. Cambridge University. Retrieved from www.cambridge.academia.edu

Council of Australian University Librarians (CAUL). (2001). *Information literacy standards*. Retrieved from http://www.caul.edu.au/caul-doc/InfoLitStandards2001.doc

Hodgkinson-Williams, C., Willmers, M., & Gray, E. (2009). *International environmental scan of the use of ICTs for teaching and learning in higher education*. Centre of Educational Technology, University of Cape Town. Retrieved from http://www.cet.uct.ac.za/files/file/OS%20PositionPaper3%20_%20%20Final%20typeset.pdf

Igwe, K. N., & Esimokha, G. A. (2012). A survey of the information literacy skills of students in Federal Polytechnic Offa, Kwara State, Nigeria. *The Information Technologist: An International Journal of Information and Communication Technology*, *9*(2), 9–19.

Ilogho, J. E., & Nkiko, C. (2014). Information literacy and search skills of students in five private universities in Ogun State, Nigeria. *Library Philosophy and Practice (ejournal)*. Retrieved from http://digitalcommon.unl.edu/libphilprac/1040

Issa, A. O., Amusan, B., & Daura, U. D. (2009). Effects of information literacy skills on the use of e-library resources among students of University of Ilorin, Kwara State, Nigeria. *Library Philosophy and Practice*. Retrieved from http://www.unlib.unl.edu/LPP/issa-amusan-daura

Kaur, P., Sohal, M. K., & Walia, P. K. (2009). *Information literacy curriculum for undergraduate students*. Paper Presented at the International Conference of Academic Libraries. Delhi, India.

Martins, J. L. (2013). *Learning from recent British information literacy models: A report to ACRL's information literacy competency standards for higher education task force*. Retrieved from www.mavdisk.mnsu.edu/martij2/acrl.pdf

McNally, M. B. (2012). *Democratizing access to knowledge: Find out what open educational resources (OER) have to offer*. Faculty of Information and Media Studies Presentations, University of Western Ontario. Retrieved from http://ir.lib.uwo.ca/fimspres/13

Middle States Commission on Higher Education. (2003). *Developing research and communication skills: Guidelines for information literacy in the curriculum*. Philadelphia, PA: Author Publishers Inc.

Nwalo, K. I. N., & Oyedum, G. U. (2011). Relationship of information literacy to undergraduate students use of university libraries. *Library Progress International, 31*(2), 347–362.

Ogunmodede, T. A., & Emeaghara, E. N. (2010). The effects of library use education as a course on library patronage: A case study of LAUTECH library, Ogbomosho, Nigeria. *Library Philosophy and Practice*. Retrieved 30/6/2011 from http://www.unlib.unl.edu/LPP/ogunmodede_emeaghara

Ojedokun, A. A. (2007). *Information literacy for tertiary education students in Africa*. Ibadan: Third World Information Services.

Ojedokun, A. A., & Lumande, E. (2005). The integration of information literacy skills into a credit-earning programme at the University of Botswana. *African Journal of Library. Archives and Information Science, 4*(1), 41–48.

Okoye, M. O. (2013). User education in federal university libraries: A study of trends and developments in Nigeria. *Library Philosophy and Practice (e-journal)*. Retrieved from http://digitalcommons.unl.edu/libphilprac/942

Organization for Economic Co-Operation and Development (OECD). (2007). *Giving knowledge for free: The emergence of open educational resources*. Paris: Centre for Educational Research and Innovation, OECD.

Ottong, E. J., & Ntui, A. I. (2010). Repositioning information literacy for learning society: Strategy and prospects for lifelong education in the South-South sub region of Nigeria. *Global Review of Library and Information Science, 6*, 41–45.

Streatfield, D., & Markless, S. (2008). Evaluating the impact of information literacy in higher education: Progress and prospects. *Libri, 58*(2), 102–109. doi:10.1515/libr.2008.012

University of Colorado–Colorado Springs. (n.d.). *Kraemer Family Library and Information Literacy Program*. Retrieved from http://www.uccs.edu/library/services/infolit.html

Van't Hof, S., Sluijs, J., Asamoah-Hassan, H., & Agyen-Gyasi, K. (2010). *Information literacy training in an African context: Case study of IL course development at KNUST in Kumasi, Ghana*. Amsterdam: KIT.

KEY TERMS AND DEFINITIONS

Information Ethics: A set of principles such as plagiarism, copyright, fair use policy, intellectual property, censorship, intellectual freedom, citation and referencing styles, acknowledgement of sources, respect for the ideas of people, appropriate and responsible use of the Internet devoid of cyber-bullying and cybercrimes, cyber-ethics and the likes which information users should have knowledge of and adhere to in course of using information resources.

Information Literacy Instructors: Professionally trained individuals, especially librarians that are shouldered with the responsibility of delivering information literacy programmes in tertiary institutions for the inculcation of IL skills in students and other members of the university.

Information Literacy Models: Frameworks formulated by organisations and institutions to serve as guide for the implementation of information literacy programmes. Examples are Information Literacy Competency Standards for Higher Education by ACRL, SCONUL and ANZIL Frameworks.

Information Literacy Programmes: Policies, standards and strategies formulated and implemented by universities, either through or in collaboration with librarians, for the delivery of information literacy instructions, inculcation of information literacy competencies in students and evaluation of the programmes in line with the learning outcomes.

Information Synthesis: A set of evaluation abilities and critical thinking skills for organising and integrating information resources from different sources with strict adherence to information ethics thereby constructing ideas and creating new knowledge.

Chapter 23

Re–Branding Community Organizations for the Actualization of Development Goals in the Rural Communities in Nigeria

Oyekunle Oyelami
University of Lagos, Nigeria

ABSTRACT

Community organizations, also known as community-based organizations, are civil society and non-profit social organizations based in the community with the main thrust being benefiting their members and the community at large. Community organizations have their roots in the community members organizing themselves for needs identification and realization of development goals. They are a subset of the wider group of non-profit organizations. Community organizations operate with the locality to ensure the community with sustainable provisions of community-service and action. This chapter highlights some measures for making community organizations more active and alive in the community of operations.

INTRODUCTION TO THE DISCOURSE

The need for community organization for community development in any country the world over with particular reference to the Third World countries like Nigeria cannot be overemphasized. This is because community organizations have been playing significant roles from time immemorial. World Bank (2012) reported that about 80% of the national population in developing countries including Nigeria dwell in rural areas, and that majority of these people relied on local organizations for survival. In other words, well over 60 percent of Nigerians are said to be living and working in the rural communities, engaging in either farming or non-farming occupations with community organizations offering a lending hand (World Bank, 2012).

DOI: 10.4018/978-1-4666-6162-2.ch023

Copyright © 2014, IGI Global. Copying or distributing in print or electronic forms without written permission of IGI Global is prohibited.

Rural communities and her citizens realized that they have to provide their basic needs through self-help and participatory mechanism by forming themselves into organizations. Many communities have bought this idea of self-participation through organizations in development and have on their own with marginal government support and assistance provided such amenities as access roads, bridges, community schools, community centres, hospitals and electricity to make life worth living in the rural settings (Oyelami, 2007).

Community organization involves the rural people in the whole process of rural development activities, from the early stage of problem identification to the stage of designing, implementing and evaluating of the community projects. It therefore entails that participatory development in community organization is a situation, whereby the beneficiaries are involved in planning, implementing, evaluating and sharing the benefits of the project (Osuji, 1993). Community organizations are therefore organizations set up by the community members themselves to facilitate and enhance speedy growth and development of the community. The major aim of forming community organization is to better the lots of the memberships and the community at large, in terms of providing for the basic needs for all in the community.

As a result of the successes of community organizations towards participatory and community development efforts, there is, therefore, the need for a reviewed thinking on how the community organizations particularly in the rural areas should be re-branded in the face of contemporary realities of development strive in Nigeria. This write-up, in essence, discusses such concepts as: community, community organization, features of community organization, roles of community organization, typologies of community organizations and how community organizations can be re-packaged to meet the contemporary challenges particularly in the rural areas of Nigeria.

COMMUNITY: THE DEFINING FEATURES

Community has been defined variously by different scholars, according to their own perception of what it entails, hence the concept is said to be nebulous. Some see community in the perspective of geography as human settlement; others define it in terms of goal, some as legal entity and others as solidarity, while other scholars see community as just a place of habitation. To this end, in the words of Osuji (2002), community refers to a group of people inhabiting a limited area, who have a sense of belonging together, and who through their organized relationship share and carry out activities in pursuit of their common interest. Osuji (2002) further maintained that a community is a group of people occupying or living in a geographical area, with common historical, political, economic and cultural ties and having feeling of belonging to one another and committed to specific goals. Anyanwu (1999) in his own view saw community as a social group, occupying a more or less defined geographical area and based on the feelings of what of its members have for one another. Hence, Osuji (2002) sum-up the definitions of community thus:

Community is a consciously identified population with common needs and interest, it may occupy a common physical space, engage in common activities, and have some forms of organization that provide or differentiation of functions, making it adaptive to its environment as a means of meeting common needs. Its components include individuals, groups, families and organizations within its population and the institution it forms to meet its needs. (p. 21)

In the same vein, Okafor, Onocha and Oyedeji (1987) described community as a group of mutually dependent people, living in a more or less compact continuous geographical area, having a sense of belonging, and sharing common values, norms and some common interest and acting collectively in an organized manner to satisfy their main needs through a common set of organizations and institutions. Again, Mitchell (1981) defined community in a more encompassing manner thus: "originally the term community denoted a collectivity of people who occupied a geographical area, people who together engaged in economic and political activities and who essentially constituted a self-governing social unit with some common values and experiencing feelings of belonging to one another."

Finally, community is classified into Gemishaft and Geze-shaft but rural and urban types are commonly used in modern day literatures. But for the purpose of this paper, the writer is interested in the linkage between the rural community and its organizations. The official interpretation of a rural community is that of a settlement of less than 20,000 according to the 2006 Nigeria National Population Census.

The rural community is also conservative in nature, with a high degree of cohesion based on widespread sharing of values, beliefs, attitudes and aims. Anyanwu (2002) argued that such features are common among the African rural communities. In such a rural community, rules of relationship are not formalized. They are mainly based on cultural traditions of the people and based on similarities of social expectations rather than on written codes and contracts that are presently the order of the day in the configurations of modern day communities.

COMMUNITY ORGANIZATION: AN OVERVIEW

The importance of community organizations in respect to rural development and emancipation of its populace cannot be underestimated. The rural people develop structures and organizations,

which do help them to become self-reliant and self-dependent. Such organizations are of people themselves, managed by them and structured in a way so as to avoid undue external dependence. Therefore to foster participation and democratic development, the people establish autonomous grassroots organizations to promote participatory self-reliant development and increase the output and productivity of the masses. Faniran, Odugbemi and Oyesiku (1987) quoting Mabogunje (1980) made the following observations concerning community organizations:

Community organizations are concerned with the improvement of the living standard of the low income population living in rural areas on a self-sustained basis through transforming the socio-spatial structures of their productive activities. Rural development entails and transcends agricultural development, which is concerned with one aspect of the productive life in rural areas. It implies a broad-base re-organization and mobilization of rural masses so as to enhance their capacity to cope effectively with daily tasks of their lives and with changes consequent upon this. (p. 28)

Similarly, Abiona (2002) described community organization as a process where social welfare resource or community resources are developed, maintained, extended and coordinated for the purpose of making them available for the community needs so that they may use them together with other resources toward better and effective satisfaction. Community organization entails the setting up of committees at various levels. Such committees take care of the management of organization and administration of community development at the village level. The main function is to ensure that programmes evoke the enthusiasm of the people, as well as secure active participation of the people in order to improve their welfare (Anyanwu, 1999). Oakley (1991) linked organization community with people's participation to mean a process by which the rural people are able to organize themselves and identity their needs and share in the design, implementation and evaluation that breeds participatory action. Such action according to Oyelami (2007) is self-generated based on access to productive resources and services that are meant to emancipate and strengthen the capacities of the inhabitants. It is also based on initial assistance and support of all to stimulate and sustain the development projects action programmes in the community.

In the same vein, community organization according to UNICEF (2009) is a process whereby the people are actively involved in ensuring that they are actively involved in the planning, implementation and evaluation of programmes that most adequately meet their needs. From the different definitions of community organizations enumerated above, it is a known and recognized fact that success comes from being organized into groups, with the aim of pursuing of common interest.

FEATURES OF COMMUNITY ORGANIZATIONS

Community organizations be it in the urban or rural community are identified with indigenosity, collectivity, participatory and mutual supports. In sum, World Bank (2012) listed the followings as some of the features of community organizations:

1. They are started by the people themselves and not by a government or other outside agency.
2. They are more informal and unofficial.
3. They are more flexible in objectives in their set-up.
4. The leaders and members are mainly the inhabitants who reach decisions in face-to-face relationships.
5. Activities are related to the day-to-day situation and needs of the populace (p. 18).

IMPORTANCE OF COMMUNITY ORGANIZATIONS

Through community organization, people do come together to discuss and plan for the programme that will improve conditions of living within the communities. Also meaningful programmes that will enhance the capacity of the populace are usually achieved through the formation of community organization. The main duty of community organization according to Abiona (2002) is to ensure that such programmes evoke the eagerness of the people, so as to ensure citizens' active participation in projects that are meant to improve the welfare of the people. By such organization people will be involved in working out their own development activities in the community.

Community organization also involves timely inputs of beneficiaries in project's planning and implementation hence their participations are used to promote cooperation and friendly interactions among beneficiaries that will enhance quick complication and sustainability of the projects. According to Paul (1987), the involvements of beneficiaries often lead to a better project design management and implementation for better delivery of such programme(s) that are meant to serve all in the community. In terms of sharing of cost, the beneficiaries share the cost by arriving on cost sharing method and enforcement that will be acceptable to all. When beneficiaries share responsibilities, they become active participants; hence, Paul (1987) argued that such activities will arouse genuine interest in the projects' life cycles.

FORMS OF COMMUNITY ORGANIZATIONS

The differences between and among community organizations particularly in the rural settings notwithstanding, because such rural organizations might comprise more than one type of activities or the other; some often have overlapping roles in the community. Some of the identifiable rural community organizations include:

Village Union

According to Anyanwu (1999), the organization at the village level may consist of a committee of people headed by community leaders and change agent and expanded by the addition of representatives of special interest who help the development agent in supplying the specialist techniques for stimulating local enthusiasm and achievement of purpose(s).

The committees at the village level according to Anyanwu (1999) are usually drawn from:

1. Local farming, industrial, cooperative and trading groups.
2. Representatives of religious, social and youths organizations.
3. Political leaders from the village group.
4. Members of the local government body and
5. Members of the technical services (p. 29).

The committee, it must be mentioned should be in charge of producing proposals for development and acting upon such as soon as it is empowered by the stakeholders to do so. The village unions are set up to socially and economically develop the communities through initiating and executing developmental programmes, such as road construction, building of community schools, markets, bridges and wells, with or without government's intervention. Such project(s) must meet the felt need of the community members (Oyelami, 2010).

Age Grades/Groups

This is another organization commonly found in rural communities especially among the Igbo extractions and the Yoruba extractions in Nigeria. Such organizations comprise of indigenes within the same age-range and peers. Age groups contrib-

ute in the maintenance of community cohesion, promotion of harmony, socialization of the youth, the provision of basic amenities and enhancing the capacity of the community through various awareness creation programmes.

Cooperatives Organizations

The cooperatives organizations are jointly owned by members of the community who acquire shares in order to achieve the status of membership and at the same time be contributors to self and community development. The organizations ensure more rational and equitable means of production and resource allocation. The members provide mutual help and joint liability and mutual responsibility. Through these organizations, economies of members and community can be improved. Also purchase and investments can be made for the common good of the members. For instance, technologies which cannot be acquired by individual farmer acting on his own can be shared by the members of the cooperatives. In case of credit, the members of the cooperative can obtain credit from a revolving fund to make purchase which could otherwise not have been made by individuals (Anyanwu, 1999).

Community Self-Help Organizations

Self-help as an approach has become a catchword for development in the community especially in the provision of basic needs, which are not only for the people but by the people. This implies that the beneficiaries provide the major part of the manpower, material resources and even ideas for the project seen as felt need. Self-help is also called "do-it-yourself approach" because it attempts to use resources that are available locally as optimally as possible, especially in providing basic needs. The approach mainly involves a group of volunteers whose duty includes planning, organization and carrying out the planned activities. To ensure success, members must be able to organize the community which is to benefit from the activities. Self-help groups are usually engaged in activities that set community members into action towards the realization of the fact that community is endowed with human and material resources for the self-reliance of the community.

TRADITIONAL ORGANIZATIONS

African societies have relied on communal actions organized along traditional lines before the advent of the whites and modern organizations. The traditional groupings were more effective in such areas as: conflict resolution, taboos, marriage, law making and enforcement, governance and leaderships. Such traditional organizations perform other roles. These according to Anyanwu (2002) include:

a. **Economic Function:** Savings and credit schemes, production and marketing activities, craft making, building of community facilities.
b. **Social Function:** Self-training and education by the group, settlement of conflicts and maintenance of discipline, coverage of such social risks as old age, illness and death.
c. **Cultural Function:** Educational, festive, sporting and theatrical activities (p. 45 – 47).

RURAL WOMEN'S ORGANIZATION

Women in rural communities form groups to perform certain duties such as the empowerment of the members. They do not have formalized and organized structures. The women's groups are small voluntary village or locality-based groups. They usually emerge out of self groups because of the need to improve the material well-being and that of the community where they reside. Other aims of such organization include: socialization, joint farming and formation of cooperative societies.

RURAL YOUTH ORGANIZATIONS

Youths are of vital component in any development strategy. The youths represent the energy needed for rural emancipation. Youths organizations are meant to improve the qualities of life in the rural population. The organization can provide a sense of belonging, satisfaction as well as meaningful activities such as education, sports and possibly employment, for example rural mobilization campaigns. The organizations are formed by youths for non-political purposes but for certain common interest for example income-generating ventures. In history another form of youths organization is the traditional type. This involves a situation where young people at the village level organize themselves to perform certain tasks which are traditionally assigned to people of certain age.

RE-BRANDING OF COMMUNITY ORGANIZATIONS

Community organization whether at the grass-roots or at the urban centres needed re-branding for optimal performance. This is because of the dynamics of community organizations' roles in this ever challenging and changing world, hence the need to re-direct the focus of the community organizations.

It is expected therefore that, community organizations should:

1. Engage in processes in which they obtain both objective and subjective resources of power which according to Paula (1999) will allow those organizations to use these powers to achieve positive outcomes in community development.
2. Acquisition of more control over decisions, which affect members and community at large. This they can do when they are able to manage resources available to achieve felt-needs in the community.

3. Community organizations needed to encourage new and old members to develop entirely new ideas, products, processes and methods through creative approaches. These will further help to actualize the organization's dreams.

4. Community organizations can be re-branded to assist new generations in the community to understand how existing knowledge and ideas can be used to develop product and introduce new ideas, skills, techniques and methods that will translate ideas and knowledge into action(s).

5. The evolution of modern day community organizations, especially in developing countries have strengthened the view that its "bottom-up" model are more effective in addressing local needs than larger organizations full of "up-bottom" approaches.

IMPLICATIONS OF GLOBALIZATION ON COMMUNITY ORGANIZATION

The term globalization refers to acts and processes of international or global integration arising form the interchange of world views products, ideas such as the formation of community organizations and other aspects of human cultures. The major factors in globalization include: advances in transportation, telecommunications, infrastructure, rise in technologies and prosperity in Internet.

The origin of globalization is subject to controversies among scholars. While some traced it to the modern times, others believed that it came before the European age of discovery and voyages of the new world. In the same manner, some scholars traced its origin to the third millennium. It can however be pointed out that the term globalization has been on increase usage since the mid-1980s and the mid-1990s. In 2000, the International Monetary Fund (IMF) identified four basic aspects of globalizations, and these include: trade and transaction, capital and investment movement,

migration and movement of people and the dissemination of knowledge. Again, environmental challenges such as climate change, cross boundary water, air pollution and over-fishing of the ocean are all linked with globalization.

The implications of globalization on the development, formation and applicability of community organizations include:

•   The compression of the world and the intensification of the consciousness of the world as a whole according to Roland (1992) has a major implication on the re-branding of community organizations because such coming together of the community-based organizations has the potential of strengthening the capacities of such organizations.

•   Globalization possesses the feature by which the people of the world are incorporated into single world society (global village). In this sense, since community organizations comprise of people with similar attributes, globalization therefore will afford individuals and groups to pool resources together to solve identical problems.

•   Globalization is a social link which avails distant localities opportunities of linkage. In this sense, globalization enhances widening, deepening, and speeding up of community organizations' interconnections.

•   Finally, globalization according to Wolf (2004) affords community organizations the extensity, intensity, velocity and impact positively on community development because of its interconnectivity nature.

CONCLUSION

In the developing nations of Africa, community organization has its premises on certain underlying assumptions. These assumptions according to Anyanwu (2002) are related to the need and urgency for change for better living in the community concerns. Community organization thus stems from a response to the challenge of change. It is necessary therefore, that, when any change seems necessary and inevitable, the community members through joint efforts should be ready for it.

REFERENCES

Abiona, K. (2002). *Community organization*. Department of Adult Education, University of Ibadan.

Anyanwu, C. N. (1991). *Introduction to community development*. Lagos: Gabesther Educational Publishers.

Anyanwu, C. N. (1999). *Introduction to community development*. Ibadan: Gabesther Educational Publishers.

Anyanwu, C. N. (2002). *Community education: The African dimension*. Ibadan: Alafas Nigeria Company.

Biddle, W. W., & Biddle, L. J. (1965). *The community development process: The rediscovery of local initiatives*. Holt Rinehart and Winston Inc.

Davis-Case, D. (1989). *Community forestry: Participatory assessment, monitoring and evaluation*. Rome: FAO.

Ekong, E. E. (1989). *An introduction to rural sociology*. Ibadan: Jumak Publication.

Faniran, A., Odugbemi, O. O., & Oyesiku, O. O. (1987). *Rural development in Ogun State*. Department of Geography and Regional Planning.

Igbozurike, M. (1976). *Problem-generating structures in Nigeria's rural development*. Bohuslaningens, AB: Uddevalta.

Mitchell, G. O. (1981). *A new dictionary of sociology*. London: Routledge and Kegan Paul.

Nwene, U. P. (1988). Health care planning for the rural community. In Perspectives on community and rural development in Nigeria. University of Jos, Jos Centre for Development Studies Publication (CDS).

Oakley, P. (1991). *Projects with people*. Geneva: ILO.

Okafor, F. C., & Onokerhoraye, A. G. (1987). *Rural system and planning*. The geography and planning series of study notes.

Okpala, P. N., Onocha, C. O., & Oyedeji, O. A. (1993). *Measurement and evaluation in education*. Jatlu-Uzire: Stirling-Horden Publishers (Nig.)

Osuji, E. E. (1993). *Community participation sponsored workshop*. UNICEF/University of Ibadan Consultancy Unit.

Osuji, E. E. (2002). *Community organization*. Department of Adult Education, University of Ibadan.

Oyelami, O. (2010). Evolution of community development process in Nigeria. In S. Jegede (Ed.), *Adult education series* (Vol. 1). Lagos: Edittext Publishers Ltd.

Paul, S. (1987). *Community participation in development projects: The World Bank experience*. Paper presented at Economic Development Institute Workshop on Community Participation. Washington, DC.

Paula, H. O. (1999). *Community development in action: An eastern Nigerian experiment*. Enugu: Image and Slogans.

Roland, V. C. (1992). *Globalization, knowledge and society*. London: Sage.

United Nations Children Fund. (2009). *Women organizations in sub-Saharan Africa*. Lagos, Nigeria: UNICEF.

United Nations Economic Commission for Africa (UNESCA). (1990). *Manual on typologies and activities of rural organization in agriculture.* Author.

Wolf, M. (2004). *Why globalization works.* New Haven, CT: Yale University Press.

World Bank. (1990). *How the world banks with NGOs.* Washington, DC: World Bank.

World Bank. (2012). *Development in sub-Saharan Africa: Policies for adjustment, revitalization and expansion.* Washington, DC: World Bank.

ADDITIONAL READING

Allen, G. (Ed.). (1987). *Community education: An agenda for educational reform.* Philadelphia: Open University Press.

Anyanwu, C. N. (1981). *Principles and practice of adult education and community development.* Ibadan: Abiprint Publishing Company.

Anyanwu, C. N. (1992). *Community development: The Nigerian perspective.* Ibadan: Gabesther Educational Publishers.

Anyanwu, C. N. (1993). *The human commonwealth for a humane society (Inaugural Lecture Series).* Nigeria: University of Ibadan.

Anyanwu, C. N. (2002). *Community education: The African dimension.* Ibadan: Alafas Nigeria Company.

Egenti, M. N. (2012). *Contemporary fundamental issues in adult education and non-formal education.* Lagos: Pre-Press Professionals.

Ekong, E. E. (1988). *Rural sociology: An introduction and analysis of rural Nigeria.* Ibadan: Jumak Publishers.

Fajonyomi, A. (Ed.). (2011). Adult education and extension services. Dept. of Continuing Education and Extension Services, University of Maiduguri, Nigeria.

Haralambos, M., & Holborn, M. (2008). *Sociology: Themes and perspectives* (7th ed.). Italy: Collins.

Jegede, S. (Ed.). (2010). *Adult education series* (Vol. 1). Lagos: Edittext Publishers Ltd.

Johnson, D. (1991). *Joining together: Group theory and group skills.* New Jersey: Prentice-Hall.

Krammer, R., & Specht, H. (Eds.). (1991). *Readings in community organization practice.* New Jersey: Prentice-Hall.

Nnoli, O. (1980). *Ethnic politics in Nigeria.* Enugu: Fourth Dimension Publisher.

Okoye, P. (1989). *Guidance through groups.* Ibadan: External Studies Series.

Oyelami, O. (2007). *Community participation and school system performance in Oyo and Osun States, Nigeria.* Ph.D Thesis, University of Ibadan, Nigeria.

Paul, S. (1987). Community participation in development projects: The World Bank experience. Washington, DC: Readings in community participation.

KEY TERMS AND DEFINITIONS

Community Development: A process, a method, a technique and an act by which the community members plan and act together for the satisfaction of their felt needs. Community development as a method addresses issues, challenges and possible way out towards enhancing the capacity of the community members. Community development also emphasizes the way in which view(s) to attaining the goals are set and implemented.

Community Organizations: Also called Community Based Organizations (CBOs). Such organizations are formed by the community members with the primary thrust of addressing issues and challenges affecting members and the community at large. They are non-profit organizations formed primarily to enhance the capacity of the community through varieties of programmes such as: awareness creation, mobilization, sensitization. They are often called community or social mobilizers.

Community: The group of people living within a geographical bounded area, who are involved in social interaction and have one or more psychological ties with one another and with the place in which they live. It is also defined as local or urban area in which people grow to perceive common needs (felt needs) and problems, opportunities and treats as well as ability to acquire sense of identity and a common set of objectives. The population of the community may be few as the case of a village or it may be large and diverse as the case of an urban community.

Developmental Goal: Development strive and setting a target is said to be having a direction or directions towards achieving a particular goal in the community. Community needs are multifaceted, hence there is the need to have a direction or have a target goal. Such direction is called development goal.

Re-Branding: An act of changing from the old order to the new one. The dynamic nature of the community posses a challenge of its structures and institutions to go for re-branding from time to time in order to meet the new innovations and changes. Re-branding of community organizations therefore is a key towards capacity building of such organizations, in other to reposition their roles and contributions towards community development.

Rural Community: Citing Jegede (2010), the rural area or community comprises of human settlement with small populations. Also, rural space is dominated by farms, forests, water (river), mountains and or deserts. Rural community is characterized with closeness to nature, and people living there usually share homogeneity. Such problems as low density, poor infrastructure, low business services, poverty, emigration and others are usually associated with rural community.

Related References

To continue our tradition of advancing research in the field of education, we have compiled a list of recommended IGI Global readings. These references will provide additional information and guidance to further enrich your knowledge and assist you with your own research and future publications.

Abrami, P. C., Savage, R. S., Deleveaux, G., Wade, A., Meyer, E., & LeBel, C. (2010). The learning toolkit: The design, development, testing and dissemination of evidence-based educational software. In P. Zemliansky, & D. Wilcox (Eds.), *Design and implementation of educational games: Theoretical and practical perspectives* (pp. 168–188). Hershey, PA: Information Science Reference. doi:10.4018/978-1-61520-781-7.ch012

Ackfeldt, A., & Malhotra, N. (2012). Do managerial strategies influence service behaviours? Insights from a qualitative study. In R. Eid (Ed.), *Successful customer relationship management programs and technologies: Issues and trends* (pp. 174–187). Hershey, PA: Business Science Reference. doi:10.4018/978-1-4666-0288-5.ch013

Adi, A., & Scotte, C. G. (2013). Barriers to emerging technology and social media integration in higher education: Three case studies. In M. Pătruţ, & B. Pătruţ (Eds.), *Social media in higher education: Teaching in web 2.0* (pp. 334–354). Hershey, PA: Information Science Reference. doi:10.4018/978-1-4666-2970-7.ch017

Aldana-Vargas, M. F., Gras-Martí, A., Montoya, J., & Osorio, L. A. (2013). Pedagogical counseling program development through an adapted community of inquiry framework. In Z. Akyol, & D. Garrison (Eds.), *Educational communities of inquiry: Theoretical framework, research and practice* (pp. 350–373). Hershey, PA: Information Science Reference.

Alegre, O. M., & Villar, L. M. (2011). Faculty professional learning: An examination of online development and assessment environments. In G. Vincenti, & J. Braman (Eds.), *Teaching through multi-user virtual environments: Applying dynamic elements to the modern classroom* (pp. 66–93). Hershey, PA: Information Science Reference. doi:10.4018/978-1-60960-783-8.ch119

Alegre, O. M., & Villar, L. M. (2012). Faculty professional learning: An examination of online development and assessment environments. In I. Management Association (Ed.), Organizational learning and knowledge: Concepts, methodologies, tools and applications (pp. 305-331). Hershey, PA: Business Science Reference. doi: doi:10.4018/978-1-60960-783-8.ch119

Alegre-Rosa, O. M., & Villar-Angulo, L. M. (2010). Training of teachers in virtual scenario: An excellence model for quality assurance in formative programmes. In S. Mukerji, & P. Tripathi (Eds.), *Cases on transnational learning and technologically enabled environments* (pp. 190–213). Hershey, PA: Information Science Reference. doi:10.4018/978-1-61520-749-7.ch011

Andegherghis, S. (2012). Technology and traditional teaching. In I. Chen, & D. McPheeters (Eds.), *Cases on educational technology integration in urban schools* (pp. 74–79). Hershey, PA: Information Science Reference.

Anderson, K. H., & Muirhead, W. (2013). Blending storytelling with technology in the professional development of police officers. In H. Yang, & S. Wang (Eds.), *Cases on formal and informal e-learning environments: Opportunities and practices* (pp. 143–165). Hershey, PA: Information Science Reference.

Anderson, S., & Oyarzun, B. (2013). Multi-modal professional development for faculty. In J. Keengwe, & L. Kyei-Blankson (Eds.), *Virtual mentoring for teachers: Online professional development practices* (pp. 43–65). Hershey, PA: Information Science Reference.

Annetta, L. A., Holmes, S., & Cheng, M. (2012). Measuring student perceptions: Designing an evidenced centered activity model for a serious educational game development software. In R. Ferdig, & S. de Freitas (Eds.), *Interdisciplinary advancements in gaming, simulations and virtual environments: Emerging trends* (pp. 165–182). Hershey, PA: Information Science Publishing. doi:10.4018/978-1-4666-0029-4.ch011

Austin, R., & Anderson, J. (2006). Re-schooling and information communication technology: A case study of Ireland. In L. Tan Wee Hin, & R. Subramaniam (Eds.), *Handbook of research on literacy in technology at the K-12 level* (pp. 176–194). Hershey, PA: Information Science Reference. doi:10.4018/978-1-59140-494-1.ch010

Ayling, D., Owen, H., & Flagg, E. (2014). From basic participation to transformation: Immersive virtual professional development. In S. Leone (Ed.), *Synergic integration of formal and informal e-learning environments for adult lifelong learners* (pp. 47–74). Hershey, PA: Information Science Reference. doi:10.4018/978-1-4666-5780-9.ch025

Ayoola, K. A. (2010). An appraisal of a computer-based continuing professional development (CPD) Course for Nigerian English teachers and teacher-trainers. In R. Taiwo (Ed.), *Handbook of research on discourse behavior and digital communication: Language structures and social interaction* (pp. 642–650). Hershey, PA: Information Science Reference. doi:10.4018/978-1-61520-773-2.ch041

Baia, P. (2011). The trend of commitment: Pedagogical quality and adoption. In S. D'Agustino (Ed.), *Adaptation, resistance and access to instructional technologies: Assessing future trends in education* (pp. 273–315). Hershey, PA: Information Science Reference.

Banas, J. R., & Velez-Solic, A. (2013). Designing effective online instructor training and professional development. In J. Keengwe, & L. Kyei-Blankson (Eds.), *Virtual mentoring for teachers: Online professional development practices* (pp. 1–25). Hershey, PA: Information Science Reference.

Banks, W. P., & Van Sickle, T. (2011). Digital partnerships for professional development: Rethinking university–public school collaborations. In M. Bowdon, & R. Carpenter (Eds.), *Higher education, emerging technologies, and community partnerships: Concepts, models and practices* (pp. 153–163). Hershey, PA: Information Science Reference. doi:10.4018/978-1-60960-623-7.ch014

Barbour, M. K., Siko, J., Gross, E., & Waddell, K. (2013). Virtually unprepared: Examining the preparation of K-12 online teachers. In R. Hartshorne, T. Heafner, & T. Petty (Eds.), *Teacher education programs and online learning tools: Innovations in teacher preparation* (pp. 60–81). Hershey, PA: Information Science Reference. doi:10.4018/978-1-4666-4502-8.ch011

Bartlett, J. E. II, & Bartlett, M. E. (2009). Innovative strategies for preparing and developing career and technical education leaders. In V. Wang (Ed.), *Handbook of research on e-learning applications for career and technical education: Technologies for vocational training* (pp. 248–261). Hershey, PA: Information Science Reference. doi:10.4018/978-1-60566-739-3.ch020

Baylen, D. M., & Glacken, J. (2007). Promoting lifelong learning online: A case study of a professional development experience. In Y. Inoue (Ed.), *Online education for lifelong learning* (pp. 229–252). Hershey, PA: Information Science Publishing. doi:10.4018/978-1-59904-319-7.ch011

Beedle, J., & Wang, S. (2013). Roles of a technology leader. In S. Wang, & T. Hartsell (Eds.), *Technology integration and foundations for effective leadership* (pp. 228–241). Hershey, PA: Information Science Reference.

Begg, M., Dewhurst, D., & Ross, M. (2010). Game informed virtual patients: Catalysts for online learning communities and professional development of medical teachers. In J. Lindberg, & A. Olofsson (Eds.), *Online learning communities and teacher professional development: Methods for improved education delivery* (pp. 190–208). Hershey, PA: Information Science Reference. doi:10.4018/978-1-61520-869-2.ch020

Begg, M., Dewhurst, D., & Ross, M. (2010). Game informed virtual patients: Catalysts for online learning communities and professional development of medical teachers. In R. Luppicini, & A. Haghi (Eds.), *Cases on digital technologies in higher education: Issues and challenges* (pp. 304–322). Hershey, PA: Information Science Reference. doi:10.4018/978-1-61520-869-2.ch020

Benton, C. J., White, O. L., & Stratton, S. K. (2014). Collaboration not competition: International education expanding perspectives on learning and workforce articulation. In V. Wang (Ed.), *International education and the next-generation workforce: Competition in the global economy* (pp. 64–82). Hershey, PA: Information Science Reference.

Benus, M. J., Yarker, M. B., Hand, B. M., & Norton-Meier, L. A. (2013). Analysis of discourse practices in elementary science classrooms using argument-based inquiry during whole-class dialogue. In M. Khine, & I. Saleh (Eds.), *Approaches and strategies in next generation science learning* (pp. 224–245). Hershey, PA: Information Science Reference. doi:10.4018/978-1-4666-2809-0.ch012

Betts, K., Kramer, R., & Gaines, L. L. (2013). Online faculty and adjuncts: Strategies for meeting current and future demands of online education through online human touch training and support. In M. Raisinghani (Ed.), *Curriculum, learning, and teaching advancements in online education* (pp. 94–112). Hershey, PA: Information Science Reference. doi:10.4018/978-1-4666-2949-3.ch007

Biesinger, K. D., & Crippen, K. J. (2010). Designing and delivering technology integration to engage students. In J. Yamamoto, J. Leight, S. Winterton, & C. Penny (Eds.), *Technology leadership in teacher education: Integrated solutions and experiences* (pp. 298–313). Hershey, PA: Information Science Reference. doi:10.4018/978-1-61520-899-9.ch016

Bledsoe, C., & Pilgrim, J. (2013). Three instructional models to integrate technology and build 21st century literacy skills. In J. Whittingham, S. Huffman, W. Rickman, & C. Wiedmaier (Eds.), *Technological tools for the literacy classroom* (pp. 243–262). Hershey, PA: Information Science Reference.

Bloom, L., & Dole, S. (2014). Virtual school of the smokies. In S. Mukerji, & P. Tripathi (Eds.), *Handbook of research on transnational higher education* (pp. 674–689). Hershey, PA: Information Science Reference.

Bober, M. J. (2005). Ensuring quality in technology-focused professional development. In C. Howard, J. Boettcher, L. Justice, K. Schenk, P. Rogers, & G. Berg (Eds.), *Encyclopedia of distance learning* (pp. 845–852). Hershey, PA: Information Science Reference. doi:10.4018/978-1-59140-555-9.ch121

Bober, M. J. (2009). Ensuring quality in technology-focused professional development. In P. Rogers, G. Berg, J. Boettcher, C. Howard, L. Justice, & K. Schenk (Eds.), *Encyclopedia of distance learning* (2nd ed., pp. 924–931). Hershey, PA: Information Science Reference. doi:10.4018/978-1-60566-198-8.ch129

Boling, E. C., & Beatty, J. (2012). Overcoming the tensions and challenges of technology integration: How can we best support our teachers? In R. Ronau, C. Rakes, & M. Niess (Eds.), *Educational technology, teacher knowledge, and classroom impact: A research handbook on frameworks and approaches* (pp. 136–156). Hershey, PA: Information Science Publishing.

Bovard, B., Bussmann, S., Parra, J., & Gonzales, C. (2010). Transitioning to e-learning: Teaching the teachers. In I. Association (Ed.), *Web-based education: Concepts, methodologies, tools and applications* (pp. 259–276). Hershey, PA: Information Science Reference.

Bowskill, N. (2009). Informal learning projects and world wide voluntary co-mentoring. In P. Rogers, G. Berg, J. Boettcher, C. Howard, L. Justice, & K. Schenk (Eds.), *Encyclopedia of distance learning* (2nd ed., pp. 1169–1177). Hershey, PA: Information Science Reference. doi:10.4018/978-1-60566-198-8.ch167

Bowskill, N., & McConnell, D. (2010). Collaborative reflection in globally distributed inter-cultural course teams. In G. Berg (Ed.), *Cases on online tutoring, mentoring, and educational services: Practices and applications* (pp. 172–184). Hershey, PA: Information Science Reference.

Bradley, J. B., Rachal, J., & Harper, L. (2013). Online professional development for adults: Utilizing andragogical methods in research and practice. In V. Bryan, & V. Wang (Eds.), *Technology use and research approaches for community education and professional development* (pp. 171–193). Hershey, PA: Information Science Reference.

Braun, P. (2013). Clever health: A study on the adoption and impact of an ehealth initiative in rural Australia. In M. Cruz-Cunha, I. Miranda, & P. Gonçalves (Eds.), *Handbook of research on ICTs and management systems for improving efficiency in healthcare and social care* (pp. 69–87). Hershey, PA: Medical Information Science Reference. doi:10.4018/978-1-4666-3990-4.ch004

Breen, P. (2014). An intramuscular approach to teacher development in international collaborative higher education. In S. Mukerji, & P. Tripathi (Eds.), *Handbook of research on transnational higher education* (pp. 368–390). Hershey, PA: Information Science Reference. doi:10.4018/978-1-4666-5780-9.ch101

Brown, C. A., & Neal, R. E. (2013). Definition and history of online professional development. In J. Keengwe, & L. Kyei-Blankson (Eds.), *Virtual mentoring for teachers: Online professional development practices* (pp. 182–203). Hershey, PA: Information Science Reference.

Brown, C. W., & Peters, K. A. (2013). STEM academic enrichment and professional development programs for K-12 urban students and teachers. In R. Lansiquot (Ed.), *Cases on interdisciplinary research trends in science, technology, engineering, and mathematics: Studies on urban classrooms* (pp. 19–56). Hershey, PA: Information Science Reference. doi:10.4018/978-1-4666-4502-8.ch091

Burgess, M. (2013). Using second life to support student teachers' socio-reflective practice: A mixed-method analysis. In R. Lansiquot (Ed.), *Cases on interdisciplinary research trends in science, technology, engineering, and mathematics: Studies on urban classrooms* (pp. 107–127). Hershey, PA: Information Science Reference.

Burner, K. J. (2012). Web 2.0, the individual, and the organization: Privacy, confidentiality, and compliance. In V. Dennen, & J. Myers (Eds.), *Virtual professional development and informal learning via social networks* (pp. 25–38). Hershey, PA: Information Science Reference. doi:10.4018/978-1-4666-1815-2.ch002

Buzzetto-More, N. (2010). Applications of second life. In H. Song, & T. Kidd (Eds.), *Handbook of research on human performance and instructional technology* (pp. 149–162). Hershey, PA: Information Science Reference.

Bynog, M. (2013). Development of a technology plan. In S. Wang, & T. Hartsell (Eds.), *Technology integration and foundations for effective leadership* (pp. 88–101). Hershey, PA: Information Science Reference.

Calway, B. A., & Murphy, G. A. (2011). A work-integrated learning philosophy and the educational imperatives. In P. Keleher, A. Patil, & R. Harreveld (Eds.), *Work-integrated learning in engineering, built environment and technology: Diversity of practice in practice* (pp. 1–24). Hershey, PA: Information Science Reference. doi:10.4018/978-1-60960-547-6.ch001

Carlén, U., & Lindström, B. (2012). Informed design of educational activities in online learning communities. In A. Olofsson, & J. Lindberg (Eds.), *Informed design of educational technologies in higher education: Enhanced learning and teaching* (pp. 118–134). Hershey, PA: Information Science Reference.

Cassidy, A., Sipos, Y., & Nyrose, S. (2014). Supporting sustainability education and leadership: Strategies for students, faculty, and the planet. In S. Mukerji, & P. Tripathi (Eds.), *Handbook of research on transnational higher education* (pp. 207–231). Hershey, PA: Information Science Reference.

Cavanagh, T. B. (2011). Leveraging online university education to improve K-12 science education: The ScienceMaster case study. In M. Bowdon, & R. Carpenter (Eds.), *Higher education, emerging technologies, and community partnerships: Concepts, models and practices* (pp. 221–233). Hershey, PA: Information Science Reference. doi:10.4018/978-1-60960-623-7.ch020

Chapman, D. L. (2013). Overview of technology plans. In S. Wang, & T. Hartsell (Eds.), *Technology integration and foundations for effective leadership* (pp. 71–87). Hershey, PA: Information Science Reference.

Chapman, D. L., Bynog, M., & Yocom, H. (2013). Assessment, evaluation, and revision of a technology plan. In S. Wang, & T. Hartsell (Eds.), *Technology integration and foundations for effective leadership* (pp. 124–150). Hershey, PA: Information Science Reference.

Chylinski, R., & Hanewald, R. (2009). Creating supportive environments for CALL teacher autonomy. In R. de Cássia Veiga Marriott, & P. Lupion Torres (Eds.), *Handbook of research on e-learning methodologies for language acquisition* (pp. 387–408). Hershey, PA: Information Science Reference.

Chylinski, R., & Hanewald, R. (2011). Creating supportive environments for CALL teacher autonomy. In I. Association (Ed.), *Instructional design: Concepts, methodologies, tools and applications* (pp. 840–860). Hershey, PA: Information Science Reference. doi:10.4018/978-1-60960-503-2.ch403

Clouse, N. K., Williams, S. R., & Evans, R. D. (2011). Developing an online mentoring program for beginning teachers. In S. D'Agustino (Ed.), *Adaptation, resistance and access to instructional technologies: Assessing future trends in education* (pp. 410–428). Hershey, PA: Information Science Reference.

Colomo-Palacios, R., Tovar-Caro, E., García-Crespo, Á., & Gómez-Berbís, J. M. (2012). Identifying technical competences of IT professionals: The case of software engineers. In R. Colomo-Palacios (Ed.), *Professional advancements and management trends in the IT sector* (pp. 1–14). Hershey, PA: Information Science Publishing. doi:10.4018/978-1-4666-0924-2.ch001

Corbeil, M. E., & Corbeil, J. R. (2012). Creating ongoing online support communities through social networks to promote professional learning. In V. Dennen, & J. Myers (Eds.), *Virtual professional development and informal learning via social networks* (pp. 114–133). Hershey, PA: Information Science Reference. doi:10.4018/978-1-4666-1815-2.ch007

Corbitt, B., Holt, D., & Segrave, S. (2008). Strategic design for web-based teaching and learning: Making corporate technology systems work for the learning organization. In L. Tomei (Ed.), *Online and distance learning: Concepts, methodologies, tools, and applications* (pp. 897–904). Hershey, PA: Information Science Reference.

Corbitt, B., Holt, D. M., & Segrave, S. (2008). Strategic design for web-based teaching and learning: Making corporate technology system work for the learning organization. In L. Esnault (Ed.), *Web-based education and pedagogical technologies: Solutions for learning applications* (pp. 280–302). Hershey, PA: IGI Publishing.

Coutinho, C. P. (2010). Challenges for teacher education in the learning society: Case studies of promising practice. In H. Yang, & S. Yuen (Eds.), *Handbook of research on practices and outcomes in e-learning: Issues and trends* (pp. 385–401). Hershey, PA: Information Science Reference.

Cowie, B., Jones, A., & Harlow, A. (2011). Technological infrastructure and implementation environments: The case of laptops for New Zealand teachers. In S. D'Agustino (Ed.), *Adaptation, resistance and access to instructional technologies: Assessing future trends in education* (pp. 40–52). Hershey, PA: Information Science Reference.

Crichton, S. (2007). A great wall of difference: Musings on instructional design in contemporary China. In M. Keppell (Ed.), *Instructional design: Case studies in communities of practice* (pp. 91–105). Hershey, PA: Information Science Publishing. doi:10.4018/978-1-59904-322-7.ch005

Croasdaile, S. (2009). Inter-organizational e-collaboration in education. In N. Kock (Ed.), *E-collaboration: Concepts, methodologies, tools, and applications* (pp. 1157–1170). Hershey, PA: Information Science Reference. doi:10.4018/978-1-60566-652-5.ch086

Croasdaile, S. (2009). Inter-organizational e-collaboration in education. In J. Salmons, & L. Wilson (Eds.), *Handbook of research on electronic collaboration and organizational synergy* (pp. 16–29). Hershey, PA: Information Science Reference.

Csoma, K. (2010). EPICT: Transnational teacher development through blended learning. In S. Mukerji, & P. Tripathi (Eds.), *Cases on technological adaptability and transnational learning: Issues and challenges* (pp. 147–161). Hershey, PA: Information Science Reference. doi:10.4018/978-1-61520-779-4.ch008

Cunningham, C. A., & Harrison, K. (2011). The affordances of second life for education. In G. Vincenti, & J. Braman (Eds.), *Teaching through multi-user virtual environments: Applying dynamic elements to the modern classroom* (pp. 94–119). Hershey, PA: Information Science Reference.

Curwood, J. S. (2014). From collaboration to transformation: Practitioner research for school librarians and classroom teachers. In K. Kennedy, & L. Green (Eds.), *Collaborative models for librarian and teacher partnerships* (pp. 1–11). Hershey, PA: Information Science Reference.

Cuthell, J. P. (2010). Thinking things through: Collaborative online professional development. In J. Lindberg, & A. Olofsson (Eds.), *Online learning communities and teacher professional development: Methods for improved education delivery* (pp. 154–167). Hershey, PA: Information Science Reference.

D'Agustino, S., & King, K. P. (2011). Access and advancement: Teacher transformation and student empowerment through technology mentoring. In S. D'Agustino (Ed.), *Adaptation, resistance and access to instructional technologies: Assessing future trends in education* (pp. 362–380). Hershey, PA: Information Science Reference.

Dana, N. F., Krell, D., & Wolkenhauer, R. (2013). Taking action research in teacher education online: Exploring the possibilities. In R. Hartshorne, T. Heafner, & T. Petty (Eds.), *Teacher education programs and online learning tools: Innovations in teacher preparation* (pp. 357–374). Hershey, PA: Information Science Reference.

Dawson, K., Cavanaugh, C., & Ritzhaupt, A. D. (2013). ARTI: An online tool to support teacher action research for technology integration. In R. Hartshorne, T. Heafner, & T. Petty (Eds.), *Teacher education programs and online learning tools: Innovations in teacher preparation* (pp. 375–391). Hershey, PA: Information Science Reference.

De Simone, C., Marquis, T., & Groen, J. (2013). Optimizing conditions for learning and teaching in K-20 education. In V. Wang (Ed.), *Handbook of research on teaching and learning in K-20 education* (pp. 535–552). Hershey, PA: Information Science Reference. doi:10.4018/978-1-4666-4249-2.ch031

Dennen, V. P., & Jiang, W. (2012). Twitter-based knowledge sharing in professional networks: The organization perspective. In V. Dennen, & J. Myers (Eds.), *Virtual professional development and informal learning via social networks* (pp. 241–255). Hershey, PA: Information Science Reference. doi:10.4018/978-1-4666-1815-2.ch014

Dexter, S. (2002). eTIPS - Educational technology integration and implementation principles. In P. Rogers (Ed.), Designing instruction for technology-enhanced learning (pp. 56-70). Hershey, PA: Idea Group Publishing. doi:10.4018/978-1-930708-28-0.ch003

Dickerson, J., Winslow, J., & Lee, C. Y. (2013). Teacher training and technology: Current uses and future trends. In V. Wang (Ed.), *Handbook of research on technologies for improving the 21st century workforce: Tools for lifelong learning* (pp. 243–256). Hershey, PA: Information Science Publishing.

DiMarco, J. (2006). Cases and interviews. In J. DiMarco (Ed.), *Web portfolio design and applications* (pp. 222–276). Hershey, PA: Idea Group Publishing. doi:10.4018/978-1-59140-854-3.ch012

Doherty, I. (2013). Achieving excellence in teaching: A case study in embedding professional development for teaching within a research-intensive university. In D. Salter (Ed.), *Cases on quality teaching practices in higher education* (pp. 280–290). Hershey, PA: Information Science Reference. doi:10.4018/978-1-4666-3661-3.ch017

Donnelly, R. (2009). Transformative potential of constructivist blended problem-based learning in higher education. In C. Payne (Ed.), *Information technology and constructivism in higher education: Progressive learning frameworks* (pp. 182–202). Hershey, PA: Information Science Reference. doi:10.4018/978-1-60566-654-9.ch012

Donnelly, R. (2010). The nature of complex blends: Transformative problem-based learning and technology in Irish higher education. In Y. Inoue (Ed.), *Cases on online and blended learning technologies in higher education: Concepts and practices* (pp. 1–22). Hershey, PA: Information Science Reference.

Donnelly, R., & O'Farrell, C. (2006). Constructivist e-learning for staff engaged in coninuous professional development. In J. O'Donoghue (Ed.), *Technology supported learning and teaching: A staff perspective* (pp. 160–175). Hershey, PA: Information Science Publishing. doi:10.4018/978-1-59140-962-5.ch010

Downing, K. F., & Holtz, J. K. (2008). Virtual school science. In K. Downing, & J. Holtz (Eds.), *Online science learning: Best practices and technologies* (pp. 30–48). Hershey, PA: Information Science Publishing. doi:10.4018/978-1-59904-986-1.ch003

Ehmann Powers, C., & Hewett, B. L. (2008). Building online training programs for virtual workplaces. In P. Zemliansky, & K. St.Amant (Eds.), *Handbook of research on virtual workplaces and the new nature of business practices* (pp. 257–271). Hershey, PA: Information Science Reference. doi:10.4018/978-1-59904-893-2.ch019

Ellis, J. B., West, T. D., Grimaldi, A., & Root, G. (2013). Ernst & Young leadership and professional development center: Accounting designed for leaders. In R. Carpenter (Ed.), *Cases on higher education spaces: Innovation, collaboration, and technology* (pp. 330–355). Hershey, PA: Information Science Reference.

Falco, J. (2008). Leading the art of the conference: Revolutionizing schooling through interactive videoconferencing. In D. Newman, J. Falco, S. Silverman, & P. Barbanell (Eds.), *Videoconferencing technology in K-12 instruction: Best practices and trends* (pp. 133–143). Hershey, PA: Information Science Reference.

Farmer, L. (2009). Fostering online communities of practice in career and technical education. In V. Wang (Ed.), *Handbook of research on e-learning applications for career and technical education: Technologies for vocational training* (pp. 192–203). Hershey, PA: Information Science Reference. doi:10.4018/978-1-60566-739-3.ch015

Farmer, L. (2010). Lights, camera, action! Via teacher librarian video conferencing. In S. Rummler, & K. Ng (Eds.), *Collaborative technologies and applications for interactive information design: Emerging trends in user experiences* (pp. 179–188). Hershey, PA: Information Science Reference.

Farmer, L. S. (2012). Curriculum development for online learners. In V. Wang, L. Farmer, J. Parker, & P. Golubski (Eds.), *Pedagogical and andragogical teaching and learning with information communication technologies* (pp. 88–104). Hershey, PA: Information Science Publishing.

Farmer, L. S. (2013). Assessment processes for online professional development. In J. Keengwe, & L. Kyei-Blankson (Eds.), *Virtual mentoring for teachers: Online professional development practices* (pp. 161–180). Hershey, PA: Information Science Reference.

Farmer, L. S. (2014). The roles of professional organizations in school library education. In V. Wang (Ed.), *International education and the next-generation workforce: Competition in the global economy* (pp. 170–193). Hershey, PA: Information Science Reference.

Fok, A. W., & Ip, H. H. (2009). An agent-based framework for personalized learning in continuous professional development. In M. Syed (Ed.), *Strategic applications of distance learning technologies* (pp. 96–110). Hershey, PA: Information Science Reference.

Fragaki, M., & Lionarakis, A. (2011). Education for liberation: A transformative polymorphic model for ICT integration in education. In G. Kurubacak, & T. Yuzer (Eds.), *Handbook of research on transformative online education and liberation: Models for social equality* (pp. 198–231). Hershey, PA: Information Science Reference.

Fuller, J. S., & Bachenheimer, B. A. (2013). Using an observation cycle for helping teachers integrate technology. In A. Ritzhaupt, & S. Kumar (Eds.), *Cases on educational technology implementation for facilitating learning* (pp. 69–84). Hershey, PA: Information Science Reference. doi:10.4018/978-1-4666-3676-7.ch004

Gairin-Sallán, J., & Rodriguez-Gómez, D. (2010). Teacher professional development through knowledge management in educational organisations. In J. Lindberg, & A. Olofsson (Eds.), *Online learning communities and teacher professional development: Methods for improved education delivery* (pp. 134–153). Hershey, PA: Information Science Reference.

Gairín-Sallán, J., & Rodríguez-Gómez, D. (2012). Teacher professional development through knowledge management in educational organisations. In I. Management Association (Ed.), *Organizational learning and knowledge: Concepts, methodologies, tools and applications* (pp. 1297-1315). Hershey, PA: Business Science Reference. doi:10.4018/978-1-60960-783-8.ch404

García, K., & Suzuki, R. (2008). The blended learning classroom: An online teacher training program. In M. Lytras, D. Gasevic, P. Ordóñez de Pablos, & W. Huang (Eds.), *Technology enhanced learning: Best practices* (pp. 57–80). Hershey, PA: IGI Publishing. doi:10.4018/978-1-59904-600-6.ch003

Gerbic, P., & Stacey, E. (2009). Conclusion. In E. Stacey, & P. Gerbic (Eds.), *Effective blended learning practices: Evidence-based perspectives in ICT-facilitated education* (pp. 298–311). Hershey, PA: Information Science Reference. doi:10.4018/978-1-60566-296-1.ch016

Gibbons, A. N. (2010). Reflections concerning technology: A case for the philosophy of technology in early childhood teacher education and professional development programs. In S. Blake, & S. Izumi-Taylor (Eds.), *Technology for early childhood education and socialization: Developmental applications and methodologies* (pp. 1–19). Hershey, PA: Information Science Reference.

Gonzales, C., Bussmann, S., Bovard, B., & Parra, J. (2007). Transitioning to e-learning: Teaching the teachers. In R. Sharma, & S. Mishra (Eds.), *Cases on global e-learning practices: Successes and pitfalls* (pp. 52–72). Hershey, PA: Information Science Publishing.

Gormley, P., Bruen, C., & Concannon, F. (2010). Sustainability through staff engagement: Applying a community of practice model to web 2.0 academic development programmes. In R. Donnelly, J. Harvey, & K. O'Rourke (Eds.), *Critical design and effective tools for e-learning in higher education: Theory into practice* (pp. 326–345). Hershey, PA: Information Science Reference. doi:10.4018/978-1-61520-879-1.ch020

Grandgenett, N., Ostler, E., Topp, N., & Goeman, R. (2012). Robotics and problem-based learning in STEM formal educational environments. In B. Barker, G. Nugent, N. Grandgenett, & V. Adamchuk (Eds.), *Robots in K-12 education: A new technology for learning* (pp. 94–119). Hershey, PA: Information Science Reference. doi:10.4018/978-1-4666-0182-6.ch005

Grant, M. R. (2010). Train the trainer: A competency-based model for teaching in virtual environments. In W. Ritke-Jones (Ed.), *Virtual environments for corporate education: Employee learning and solutions* (pp. 124–146). Hershey, PA: Business Science Reference. doi:10.4018/978-1-61520-619-3.ch008

Griffin, P., Care, E., Robertson, P., Crigan, J., Awwal, N., & Pavlovic, M. (2013). Assessment and learning partnerships in an online environment. In E. McKay (Ed.), *ePedagogy in online learning: New developments in web mediated human computer interaction* (pp. 39–54). Hershey, PA: Information Science Reference. doi:10.4018/978-1-4666-3649-1.ch003

Griswold, W. (2013). Transformative learning and educational technology integration in a post-totalitarian context: Professional development among school teachers in rural Siberia, Russia. In E. Jean Francois (Ed.), *Transcultural blended learning and teaching in postsecondary education* (pp. 128–144). Hershey, PA: Information Science Reference.

Gruich, M. R. (2013). Defining professional development for technology. In S. Wang, & T. Hartsell (Eds.), *Technology integration and foundations for effective leadership* (pp. 152–170). Hershey, PA: Information Science Reference.

Guidry, K. R., & Pasquini, L. (2013). Twitter chat as an informal learning tool: A case study using #sachat. In H. Yang, & S. Wang (Eds.), *Cases on formal and informal e-learning environments: Opportunities and practices* (pp. 356–377). Hershey, PA: Information Science Reference.

Gunn, C., & Blake, A. (2009). Blending technology into an academic practice qualification for university teachers. In E. Stacey, & P. Gerbic (Eds.), *Effective blended learning practices: Evidence-based perspectives in ICT-facilitated education* (pp. 259–279). Hershey, PA: Information Science Reference. doi:10.4018/978-1-60566-296-1.ch014

Hanewald, R. (2013). Professional development with and for emerging technologies: A case study with Asian languages and cultural studies teachers in Australia. In J. Keengwe (Ed.), *Pedagogical applications and social effects of mobile technology integration* (pp. 175–192). Hershey, PA: Information Science Reference. doi:10.4018/978-1-4666-2985-1.ch010

Hansen, C. C. (2012). ABCs and PCs: Effective professional development in early childhood education. In I. Chen, & D. McPheeters (Eds.), *Cases on educational technology integration in urban schools* (pp. 230–235). Hershey, PA: Information Science Reference.

Hao, S. (2012). Turn on your mobile devices: Potential and considerations of informal mobile learning. In V. Dennen, & J. Myers (Eds.), *Virtual professional development and informal learning via social networks* (pp. 39–58). Hershey, PA: Information Science Reference. doi:10.4018/978-1-4666-1815-2.ch003

Harteis, C. (2010). Contributions of e-collaborative knowledge construction to professional learning and expertise. In B. Ertl (Ed.), *E-collaborative knowledge construction: Learning from computer-supported and virtual environments* (pp. 91–108). Hershey, PA: Information Science Reference. doi:10.4018/978-1-61520-729-9.ch005

Hartsell, T., Herron, S. S., Fang, H., & Rathod, A. (2011). Improving teachers' self-confidence in learning technology skills and math education through professional development. In I. Association (Ed.), *Instructional design: Concepts, methodologies, tools and applications* (pp. 1487–1503). Hershey, PA: Information Science Reference. doi:10.4018/978-1-60960-503-2.ch609

Hartsell, T., Herron, S. S., Fang, H., & Rathod, A. (2012). Improving teachers' self-confidence in learning technology skills and math education through professional development. In L. Tomei (Ed.), *Advancing education with information communication technologies: Facilitating new trends* (pp. 150–164). Hershey, PA: Information Science Reference.

Hartsell, T., & Wang, S. (2013). Introduction to technology integration and leadership. In S. Wang, & T. Hartsell (Eds.), *Technology integration and foundations for effective leadership* (pp. 1–17). Hershey, PA: Information Science Reference.

Hauge, T. E., & Norenes, S. O. (2010). VideoPaper as a bridging tool in teacher professional development. In J. Lindberg, & A. Olofsson (Eds.), *Online learning communities and teacher professional development: Methods for improved education delivery* (pp. 209–228). Hershey, PA: Information Science Reference.

Haythornthwaite, C., & De Laat, M. (2012). Social network informed design for learning with educational technology. In A. Olofsson, & J. Lindberg (Eds.), *Informed design of educational technologies in higher education: Enhanced learning and teaching* (pp. 352–374). Hershey, PA: Information Science Reference.

Heinrichs, L., Fellander-Tsai, L., & Davies, D. (2013). Clinical virtual worlds: The wider implications for professional development in healthcare. In K. Bredl, & W. Bösche (Eds.), *Serious games and virtual worlds in education, professional development, and healthcare* (pp. 221–240). Hershey, PA: Information Science Reference. doi:10.4018/978-1-4666-3673-6.ch014

Helleve, I. (2010). Theoretical foundations of teachers' professional development. In J. Lindberg, & A. Olofsson (Eds.), *Online learning communities and teacher professional development: Methods for improved education delivery* (pp. 1–19). Hershey, PA: Information Science Reference.

Hemphill, L. S., & McCaw, D. S. (2009). Moodling professional development training that worked. In L. Tan Wee Hin, & R. Subramaniam (Eds.), *Handbook of research on new media literacy at the K-12 level: Issues and challenges* (pp. 808–822). Hershey, PA: Information Science Reference. doi:10.4018/978-1-60566-120-9.ch050

Hensley, M. K. (2010). Teaching new librarians how to teach: A model for building a peer learning program. In E. Pankl, D. Theiss-White, & M. Bushing (Eds.), *Recruitment, development, and retention of information professionals: Trends in human resources and knowledge management* (pp. 179–190). Hershey, PA: Business Science Reference. doi:10.4018/978-1-61520-601-8.ch010

Hernández-Gantes, V. M. (2011). Helping faculty design online courses in higher education. In V. Wang (Ed.), *Encyclopedia of information communication technologies and adult education integration* (pp. 779–794). Hershey, PA: Information Science Reference.

Herrington, J., & Oliver, R. (2006). Professional development for the online teacher: An authentic approach. In T. Herrington, & J. Herrington (Eds.), *Authentic learning environments in higher education* (pp. 283–295). Hershey, PA: Information Science Publishing. doi:10.4018/978-1-59140-594-8.ch020

Hicks, T. (2013). Adding the "digital layer": Examining one teacher's growth as a digital writer through an NWP summer institute and beyond. In K. Pytash, & R. Ferdig (Eds.), *Exploring technology for writing and writing instruction* (pp. 345–357). Hershey, PA: Information Science Reference. doi:10.4018/978-1-4666-4341-3.ch020

Hinson, J. M., & Bordelon Sellers, R. (2004). Professional development recommendations for online courses. In C. Cavanaugh (Ed.), *Development and management of virtual schools: Issues and trends* (pp. 135–157). Hershey, PA: Information Science Publishing.

Hirtle, J., & Smith, S. (2010). When virtual communities click: Transforming teacher practice, transforming teachers. In H. Yang, & S. Yuen (Eds.), *Handbook of research on practices and outcomes in e-learning: Issues and trends* (pp. 182–196). Hershey, PA: Information Science Reference.

Holland, I. E. (2007). Evolution of the Milwaukee public schools portal. In A. Tatnall (Ed.), *Encyclopedia of portal technologies and applications* (pp. 397–401). Hershey, PA: Information Science Reference. doi:10.4018/978-1-59140-989-2.ch067

Holt, J., Unruh, L., & Dougherty, A. M. (2011). Enhancing a rural school-university teacher education partnership through an e-mentoring program for beginning teachers. In M. Bowdon, & R. Carpenter (Eds.), *Higher education, emerging technologies, and community partnerships: Concepts, models and practices* (pp. 212–220). Hershey, PA: Information Science Reference. doi:10.4018/978-1-60960-623-7.ch019

Hood, D. W., & Huang, W. D. (2013). Professional development with graduate teaching assistants (TAs) teaching online. In J. Keengwe, & L. Kyei-Blankson (Eds.), *Virtual mentoring for teachers: Online professional development practices* (pp. 26–42). Hershey, PA: Information Science Reference.

Hu, X. C., & Meyen, E. L. (2013). A comparison of student and instructor preferences for design and pedagogy features in postsecondary online courses. In M. Raisinghani (Ed.), *Curriculum, learning, and teaching advancements in online education* (pp. 213–229). Hershey, PA: Information Science Reference. doi:10.4018/978-1-4666-2949-3.ch015

Hucks, D., & Ragan, M. (2013). Technology expanding horizons in teacher education: Transformative learning experiences. In J. Keengwe (Ed.), *Research perspectives and best practices in educational technology integration* (pp. 61–79). Hershey, PA: Information Science Reference.

Hui, D., & Russell, D. L. (2009). Understanding the effectiveness of collaborative activity in online professional development with innovative educators through intersubjectivity. In L. Tomei (Ed.), *Information communication technologies for enhanced education and learning: Advanced applications and developments* (pp. 283–302). Hershey, PA: Information Science Reference.

Hulme, M., & Hughes, J. (2006). Patchwork e-dialogues in the professional development of new teachers. In J. O'Donoghue (Ed.), *Technology supported learning and teaching: A staff perspective* (pp. 210–223). Hershey, PA: Information Science Publishing. doi:10.4018/978-1-59140-962-5.ch013

Hunt, L., & Sankey, M. (2013). Getting the context right for quality teaching and learning. In D. Salter (Ed.), *Cases on quality teaching practices in higher education* (pp. 261–279). Hershey, PA: Information Science Reference. doi:10.4018/978-1-4666-3661-3.ch016

Hur, J. W., Brush, T., & Bonk, C. (2012). An analysis of teacher knowledge and emotional sharing in a teacher blog community. In V. Dennen, & J. Myers (Eds.), *Virtual professional development and informal learning via social networks* (pp. 219–239). Hershey, PA: Information Science Reference. doi:10.4018/978-1-4666-1815-2.ch013

Hurst, A. (2012). Reflections on personal experiences of staff training and continuing professional development for academic staff in the development of high quality support for disabled students in higher education. In D. Moore, A. Gorra, M. Adams, J. Reaney, & H. Smith (Eds.), *Disabled students in education: Technology, transition, and inclusivity* (pp. 288–304). Hershey, PA: Information Science Reference.

Hyatt, K. J. (2011). Technology: A reflective tool for professional development. In L. Tomei (Ed.), *Online courses and ICT in education: Emerging practices and applications* (pp. 134–142). Hershey, PA: Information Science Reference.

Jackson, T. (2012). Ways to mentor methods' faculty integration of technologies in their courses. In D. Polly, C. Mims, & K. Persichitte (Eds.), *Developing technology-rich teacher education programs: Key issues* (pp. 519–534). Hershey, PA: Information Science Reference. doi:10.4018/978-1-4666-0014-0.ch033

Jamieson-Proctor, R., & Finger, G. (2009). Measuring and evaluating ICT use: Developing an instrument for measuring student ICT use. In L. Tan Wee Hin, & R. Subramaniam (Eds.), *Handbook of research on new media literacy at the K-12 level: Issues and challenges* (pp. 326–339). Hershey, PA: Information Science Reference. doi:10.4018/978-1-60566-120-9.ch021

Jarvis, D. H. (2012). Teaching mathematics teachers online: Strategies for navigating the intersection of andragogy, technology, and reform-based mathematics education. In A. Juan, M. Huertas, S. Trenholm, & C. Steegmann (Eds.), *Teaching mathematics online: Emergent technologies and methodologies* (pp. 187–199). Hershey, PA: Information Science Reference.

Jimoyiannis, A., Gravani, M., & Karagiorgi, Y. (2012). Teacher professional development through virtual campuses: Conceptions of a 'new' model. In H. Yang, & S. Yuen (Eds.), *Handbook of research on practices and outcomes in virtual worlds and environments* (pp. 327–347). Hershey, PA: Information Science Publishing.

Johnson, E. S., & Pitcock, J. (2008). Preparing online instructors: Beyond using the technology. In K. Orvis, & A. Lassiter (Eds.), *Computer-supported collaborative learning: Best practices and principles for instructors* (pp. 89–113). Hershey, PA: Information Science Publishing. doi:10.4018/978-1-59904-753-9.ch005

Johnson, K., & Tashiro, J. (2010). Interprofessional care and health care complexity: Factors shaping human resources effectiveness in health information management. In S. Kabene (Ed.), *Human resources in healthcare, health informatics and healthcare systems* (pp. 250–280). Hershey, PA: Medical Information Science Reference. doi:10.4018/978-1-61520-885-2.ch015

Johnson, K., & Tashiro, J. (2013). Interprofessional care and health care complexity: Factors shaping human resources effectiveness in health information management. In I. Management Association (Ed.), User-driven healthcare: Concepts, methodologies, tools, and applications (pp. 1273-1302). Hershey, PA: Medical Information Science Reference. doi:10.4018/978-1-4666-2770-3.ch064

Johnson, M. L. (2014). Moving from theory to practice: Integrating personal learning networks into a graduate-level student development theory course. In S. Leone (Ed.), *Synergic integration of formal and informal e-learning environments for adult lifelong learners* (pp. 165–177). Hershey, PA: Information Science Reference.

Johnson, V. (2009). Understanding dynamic change and creation of learning organizations. In P. Rogers, G. Berg, J. Boettcher, C. Howard, L. Justice, & K. Schenk (Eds.), *Encyclopedia of distance learning* (2nd ed., pp. 2187–2191). Hershey, PA: Information Science Reference. doi:10.4018/978-1-60566-198-8.ch323

Jones, M. G., & Harris, L. (2012). Using student choice to promote technology integration: The buffet model. In D. Polly, C. Mims, & K. Persichitte (Eds.), *Developing technology-rich teacher education programs: Key issues* (pp. 192–204). Hershey, PA: Information Science Reference. doi:10.4018/978-1-4666-0014-0.ch013

Joyes, G., Fisher, T., Firth, R., & Coyle, D. (2014). The nature of a successful online professional doctorate. In K. Sullivan, P. Czigler, & J. Sullivan Hellgren (Eds.), *Cases on professional distance education degree programs and practices: Successes, challenges, and issues* (pp. 296–330). Hershey, PA: Information Science Reference.

Kelly, D. (2009). Modeling best practices in web-based academic development. In R. Donnelly, & F. McSweeney (Eds.), *Applied e-learning and e-teaching in higher education* (pp. 35–55). Hershey, PA: Information Science Reference. doi:10.4018/978-1-60566-982-3.ch085

Kelly, D. K. (2010). Modeling best practices in web-based academic development. In A. Tatnall (Ed.), *Web technologies: Concepts, methodologies, tools, and applications* (pp. 1578–1595). Hershey, PA: Information Science Reference.

Kelly, R. (2014). Administration: Making a connection with the library's strongest advocate. In K. Kennedy, & L. Green (Eds.), *Collaborative models for librarian and teacher partnerships* (pp. 175–184). Hershey, PA: Information Science Reference.

Kennedy-Clark, S., & Thompson, K. (2013). A MUVEing success: Design strategies for professional development in the use of multi-user virtual environments and educational games in science education. In S. D'Agustino (Ed.), *Immersive environments, augmented realities, and virtual worlds: Assessing future trends in education* (pp. 16–41). Hershey, PA: Information Science Reference. doi:10.4018/978-1-4666-4502-8.ch036

Kent, A. M. (2013). Teacher leadership: Learning and leading. In J. Lewis, A. Green, & D. Surry (Eds.), *Technology as a tool for diversity leadership: Implementation and future implications* (pp. 230–242). Hershey, PA: Information Science Reference.

Keppell, M. J. (2007). Instructional designers on the borderline: Brokering across communities of practice. In M. Keppell (Ed.), *Instructional design: Case studies in communities of practice* (pp. 68–89). Hershey, PA: Information Science Publishing. doi:10.4018/978-1-59904-322-7.ch004

Kidd, T. T., & Keengwe, J. (2012). Technology integration and urban schools: Implications for instructional practices. In L. Tomei (Ed.), *Advancing education with information communication technologies: Facilitating new trends* (pp. 244–256). Hershey, PA: Information Science Reference.

King, K. P. (2008). The transformation model. In C. Van Slyke (Ed.), *Information communication technologies: Concepts, methodologies, tools, and applications* (pp. 1102–1108). Hershey, PA: Information Science Reference. doi:10.4018/978-1-59904-949-6.ch073

King, K. P. (2012). Impact of podcasts as professional learning: Teacher created, student created, and professional development podcasts. In S. Chhabra (Ed.), *ICTs for advancing rural communities and human development: Addressing the digital divide* (pp. 237–250). Hershey, PA: Information Science Reference. doi:10.4018/978-1-4666-0047-8.ch016

Kitchenham, A. (2011). Blending professional development for rural educators an exploratory study. In D. Parsons (Ed.), *Combining e-learning and m-learning: New applications of blended educational resources* (pp. 225–238). Hershey, PA: Information Science Reference. doi:10.4018/978-1-60960-481-3.ch014

Klieger, A., & Oster-Levinz, A. (2010). How online tasks promote teachers' expertise within the technological pedagogical content knowledge (TPACK). In T. Yuzer, & G. Kurubacak (Eds.), *Transformative learning and online education: Aesthetics, dimensions and concepts* (pp. 219–235). Hershey, PA: Information Science Reference. doi:10.4018/978-1-61520-985-9.ch015

Koh, S., Lee, S., Yen, D. C., & Havelka, D. (2005). Information technology professional career development: A progression of skills. In M. Hunter, & F. Tan (Eds.), *Advanced topics in global information management* (Vol. 4, pp. 142–157). Hershey, PA: Idea Group Publishing. doi:10.4018/978-1-59140-468-2.ch009

Kopcha, T., & Valentine, K. D. (2013). A framework for developing robust online professional development materials to support teacher practice under the common core. In D. Polly (Ed.), *Common core mathematics standards and implementing digital technologies* (pp. 319–331). Hershey, PA: Information Science Reference. doi:10.4018/978-1-4666-4086-3.ch021

Koumpis, A. (2010). Culture of services. In A. Koumpis (Ed.), *Service science for socio-economical and information systems advancement: Holistic methodologies* (pp. 312–347). Hershey, PA: Information Science Reference.

Kyei-Blankson, L., & Keengwe, J. (2013). Faculty-faculty interactions in online learning environments. In L. Tomei (Ed.), *Learning tools and teaching approaches through ICT advancements* (pp. 127–135). Hershey, PA: Information Science Reference.

Larson, L., & Vanmetre, S. (2010). Learning together with the interactive white board. In N. Lambropoulos, & M. Romero (Eds.), *Educational social software for context-aware learning: Collaborative methods and human interaction* (pp. 69–78). Hershey, PA: Information Science Reference.

Laurillard, D., & Masterman, E. (2010). TPD as online collaborative learning for innovation in teaching. In J. Lindberg, & A. Olofsson (Eds.), *Online learning communities and teacher professional development: Methods for improved education delivery* (pp. 230–246). Hershey, PA: Information Science Reference.

Lawrence, J., Burton, L., Summers, J., Noble, K., & Gibbings, P. D. (2013). An associate dean's community of practice: Rising to the leadership challenges of engaging distance students using blended models of learning and teaching. In J. Willems, B. Tynan, & R. James (Eds.), *Global challenges and perspectives in blended and distance learning* (pp. 212–222). Hershey, PA: Information Science Reference. doi:10.4018/978-1-4666-3978-2.ch017

Lee, D. M. (2004). Organizational entry and transition from academic study: Examining a critical step in the professional development of young IS workers. In M. Igbaria, & C. Shayo (Eds.), *Strategies for managing IS/IT personnel* (pp. 113–142). Hershey, PA: Idea Group Publishing.

Leh, A. S., & Grafton, L. (2009). Promoting new media literacy in a school district. In L. Tan Wee Hin, & R. Subramaniam (Eds.), *Handbook of research on new media literacy at the K-12 level: Issues and challenges* (pp. 607–619). Hershey, PA: Information Science Reference. doi:10.4018/978-1-60566-120-9.ch038

Lehew, A. J., & Polly, D. (2013). The use of digital resources to support elementary school teachers' implementation of the common core state standards. In D. Polly (Ed.), *Common core mathematics standards and implementing digital technologies* (pp. 332–338). Hershey, PA: Information Science Reference. doi:10.4018/978-1-4666-4086-3.ch022

Leng, J., & Sharrock, W. (2010). Collaborative practices in computer-aided academic research. In I. Portela, & M. Cruz-Cunha (Eds.), *Information communication technology law, protection and access rights: Global approaches and issues* (pp. 249–270). Hershey, PA: Information Science Reference. doi:10.4018/978-1-61520-975-0.ch016

Ley, K., & Gannon-Cook, R. (2010). Marketing a blended university program: An action research case study. In S. Mukerji, & P. Tripathi (Eds.), *Cases on technology enhanced learning through collaborative opportunities* (pp. 73–90). Hershey, PA: Information Science Reference. doi:10.4018/978-1-61520-751-0.ch005

Linton, J., & Stegall, D. (2013). Common core standards for mathematical practice and TPACK: An integrated approach to instruction. In D. Polly (Ed.), *Common core mathematics standards and implementing digital technologies* (pp. 234–249). Hershey, PA: Information Science Reference. doi:10.4018/978-1-4666-4086-3.ch016

Lithgow, C. M., Wolf, J. L., & Berge, Z. L. (2011). Virtual worlds: Corporate early adopters pave the way. In S. Hai-Jew (Ed.), *Virtual immersive and 3D learning spaces: Emerging technologies and trends* (pp. 25–43). Hershey, PA: Information Science Reference.

Lloyd, M., & Duncan-Howell, J. (2010). Changing the metaphor: The potential of online communities in teacher professional development. In J. Lindberg, & A. Olofsson (Eds.), *Online learning communities and teacher professional development: Methods for improved education delivery* (pp. 60–76). Hershey, PA: Information Science Reference.

Lockyer, L., Patterson, J., Rowland, G., & Hearne, D. (2007). ActiveHealth: Enhancing the community of physical and health educators through online technologies. In M. Keppell (Ed.), *Instructional design: Case studies in communities of practice* (pp. 331–348). Hershey, PA: Information Science Publishing. doi:10.4018/978-1-59904-322-7.ch017

Loose, C. (2013). Teachers as researchers and instructional leaders. In V. Wang (Ed.), *Handbook of research on teaching and learning in K-20 education* (pp. 710–725). Hershey, PA: Information Science Reference. doi:10.4018/978-1-4666-4249-2.ch041

Luetkehans, L. M., & Hunt, R. D. (2014). School librarians as significant other: Using online professional learning communities for the development of pre-service teachers. In K. Kennedy, & L. Green (Eds.), *Collaborative models for librarian and teacher partnerships* (pp. 56–66). Hershey, PA: Information Science Reference. doi:10.4018/978-1-4666-5780-9.ch078

Lyublinskaya, I., & Tournaki, N. (2012). The effects of teacher content authoring on TPACK and on student achievement in algebra: Research on instruction with the TI-Nspire™ handheld. In R. Ronau, C. Rakes, & M. Niess (Eds.), *Educational technology, teacher knowledge, and classroom impact: A research handbook on frameworks and approaches* (pp. 295–322). Hershey, PA: Information Science Publishing.

Mackey, J. (2009). Virtual learning and real communities: Online professional development for teachers. In E. Stacey, & P. Gerbic (Eds.), *Effective blended learning practices: Evidence-based perspectives in ICT-facilitated education* (pp. 163–181). Hershey, PA: Information Science Reference. doi:10.4018/978-1-60566-296-1.ch009

Mackey, J., & Mills, A. (2003). An examination of ICT planning maturity in schools: A stage theory perspective. In T. McGill (Ed.), *Current issues in IT education* (pp. 376–395). Hershey, PA: IRM Press.

Manathunga, C., & Donnelly, R. (2009). Opening online academic development programmes to international perspectives and dialogue. In R. Donnelly, & F. McSweeney (Eds.), *Applied e-learning and e-teaching in higher education* (pp. 85–109). Hershey, PA: Information Science Reference.

Marinho, R. (2010). Faculty development in instructional technology in the context of learning styles and institutional barriers. In S. Mukerji, & P. Tripathi (Eds.), *Cases on interactive technology environments and transnational collaboration: Concerns and perspectives* (pp. 1–38). Hershey, PA: Information Science Reference. doi:10.4018/978-1-61520-909-5.ch001

Mark, C. L. (2013). Evaluating and funding the professional development program. In S. Wang, & T. Hartsell (Eds.), *Technology integration and foundations for effective leadership* (pp. 206–226). Hershey, PA: Information Science Reference.

Marshall, J. C. (2013). Measuring and facilitating highly effective inquiry-based teaching and learning in science classrooms. In M. Khine, & I. Saleh (Eds.), *Approaches and strategies in next generation science learning* (pp. 290–306). Hershey, PA: Information Science Reference. doi:10.4018/978-1-4666-2809-0.ch015

Marshall, K. (2008). E-portfolios in teacher education. In G. Putnik, & M. Cruz-Cunha (Eds.), *Encyclopedia of networked and virtual organizations* (pp. 516–523). Hershey, PA: Information Science Reference. doi:10.4018/978-1-59904-885-7.ch068

Martin, M. (2008). Integrating videoconferencing into the classroom: A perspective from Northern Ireland. In D. Newman, J. Falco, S. Silverman, & P. Barbanell (Eds.), *Videoconferencing technology in K-12 instruction: Best practices and trends* (pp. 253–268). Hershey, PA: Information Science Reference.

Maurer, M. J. (2012). Telementoring and virtual professional development: A theoretical perspective from science on the roles of self-efficacy, teacher learning, and professional learning communities. In I. Management Association (Ed.), Organizational learning and knowledge: Concepts, methodologies, tools and applications (pp. 1158-1176). Hershey, PA: Business Science Reference. doi:10.4018/978-1-60960-783-8.ch319

McAnuff-Gumbs, M., & Verbeck, K. (2013). Toward a model of multi-level professional learning communities to guide the training and practice of literacy coaches. In H. Yang, & S. Wang (Eds.), *Cases on online learning communities and beyond: Investigations and applications* (pp. 361–402). Hershey, PA: Information Science Reference.

McCarthy, J. (2012). Connected: Online mentoring in Facebook for final year digital media students. In A. Okada, T. Connolly, & P. Scott (Eds.), *Collaborative learning 2.0: Open educational resources* (pp. 204–221). Hershey, PA: Information Science Reference. doi:10.4018/978-1-4666-0300-4.ch011

McConnell, D. (2005). Networked collaborative e-learning. In E. Li, & T. Du (Eds.), *Advances in electronic business* (Vol. 1, pp. 222–257). Hershey, PA: Idea Group Publishing.

McCormack, V. (2010). Utilizing VoiceThread to increase teacher candidates' reflection and global implications for usage. In J. Yamamoto, J. Kush, R. Lombard, & C. Hertzog (Eds.), *Technology implementation and teacher education: Reflective models* (pp. 108–123). Hershey, PA: Information Science Reference. doi:10.4018/978-1-61520-897-5.ch007

McGrath, E., Lowes, S., McKay, M., Sayres, J., & Lin, P. (2012). Robots underwater! Learning science, engineering and 21st century skills: The evolution of curricula, professional development and research in formal and informal contexts. In B. Barker, G. Nugent, N. Grandgenett, & V. Adamchuk (Eds.), *Robots in K-12 education: A new technology for learning* (pp. 141–167). Hershey, PA: Information Science Reference. doi:10.4018/978-1-4666-0182-6.ch007

McGuigan, A. (2012). Blogospheric learning in a continuing professional development context. In A. Okada, T. Connolly, & P. Scott (Eds.), *Collaborative learning 2.0: Open educational resources* (pp. 222–237). Hershey, PA: Information Science Reference. doi:10.4018/978-1-4666-0300-4.ch012

McIntosh, S. (2005). Expanding the classroom: Using online discussion forums in college and professional development courses. In K. St. Amant, & P. Zemliansky (Eds.), *Internet-based workplace communications: Industry and academic applications* (pp. 68–87). Hershey, PA: Information Science Publishing.

McNair, V., & Marshall, K. (2006). How eportfolios support development in early teacher education. In A. Jafari, & C. Kaufman (Eds.), *Handbook of research on eportfolios* (pp. 474–485). Hershey, PA: Idea Group Publishing. doi:10.4018/978-1-59140-890-1.ch042

McNair, V., & Marshall, K. (2008). How eportfolios support development in early teacher education. In L. Tomei (Ed.), *Online and distance learning: Concepts, methodologies, tools, and applications* (pp. 2130–2137). Hershey, PA: Information Science Reference.

McPherson, M., Baptista Nunes, M., Sandars, J., & Kell, C. (2008). Technology and continuing professional education: The reality beyond the hype. In T. Kidd, & I. Chen (Eds.), *Social information technology: Connecting society and cultural issues* (pp. 296–312). Hershey, PA: Information Science Reference. doi:10.4018/978-1-59904-774-4.ch019

Medina, A. L., Tobin, M. T., Pilonieta, P., Chiappone, L. L., & Blanton, W. E. (2012). Application of computer, digital, and telecommunications technologies to the clinical preparation of teachers. In D. Polly, C. Mims, & K. Persichitte (Eds.), *Developing technology-rich teacher education programs: Key issues* (pp. 480–498). Hershey, PA: Information Science Reference. doi:10.4018/978-1-4666-0014-0.ch031

Meletiou-Mavrotheris, M. (2012). Online communities of practice as vehicles for teacher professional development. In A. Juan, M. Huertas, S. Trenholm, & C. Steegmann (Eds.), *Teaching mathematics online: Emergent technologies and methodologies* (pp. 142–166). Hershey, PA: Information Science Reference.

Meltzer, S. T. (2013). The impact of new technologies on professional development. In V. Bryan, & V. Wang (Eds.), *Technology use and research approaches for community education and professional development* (pp. 40–52). Hershey, PA: Information Science Reference.

Milman, N. B., Hillarious, M., O'Neill, V., & Walker, B. (2013). Going 11 with laptop computers in an independent, co-educational middle and high school. In J. Keengwe (Ed.), *Pedagogical applications and social effects of mobile technology integration* (pp. 156–174). Hershey, PA: Information Science Reference. doi:10.4018/978-1-4666-2985-1.ch009

Moon, B. (2012). Teaching teachers: The biggest educational challenge in sub-Saharan Africa. In R. Hogan (Ed.), *Transnational distance learning and building new markets for universities* (pp. 198–209). Hershey, PA: Information Science Reference. doi:10.4018/978-1-4666-0206-9.ch012

Mørch, A. I., & Andersen, R. (2012). Mutual development: The software engineering context of end-user development. In A. Dwivedi, & S. Clarke (Eds.), *End-user computing, development, and software engineering: New challenges* (pp. 103–125). Hershey, PA: Information Science Reference. doi:10.4018/978-1-4666-0140-6.ch005

Morrow, D., & Bagnall, R. G. (2010). Hybridizing online learning with external interactivity. In F. Wang, J. Fong, & R. Kwan (Eds.), *Handbook of research on hybrid learning models: Advanced tools, technologies, and applications* (pp. 24–41). Hershey, PA: Information Science Reference.

Mountain, L. A. (2008). Videoconferencing: An alternative to traditional professional development in the K-12 setting. In D. Newman, J. Falco, S. Silverman, & P. Barbanell (Eds.), *Videoconferencing technology in K-12 instruction: Best practices and trends* (pp. 213–225). Hershey, PA: Information Science Reference.

Mouzakis, C., & Bourletidis, C. (2010). A blended learning course for teachers' ongoing professional development in Greece. In J. Yamamoto, J. Kush, R. Lombard, & C. Hertzog (Eds.), *Technology implementation and teacher education: Reflective models* (pp. 1–24). Hershey, PA: Information Science Reference. doi:10.4018/978-1-61520-897-5.ch001

Mouzakis, C., Tsaknakis, H., & Tziortzioti, C. (2012). Theoretical rationale for designing a blended learning teachers' professional development program. In P. Anastasiades (Ed.), *Blended learning environments for adults: Evaluations and frameworks* (pp. 274–289). Hershey, PA: Information Science Reference. doi:10.4018/978-1-4666-0939-6.ch014

Murphy, M. G., & Calway, P. B. (2011). Continuing professional development: Work and learning integration for professionals. In P. Keleher, A. Patil, & R. Harreveld (Eds.), *Work-integrated learning in engineering, built environment and technology: Diversity of practice in practice* (pp. 25–51). Hershey, PA: Information Science Reference. doi:10.4018/978-1-60960-547-6.ch002

Mustapha, W. Z. (2012). The art and science of designing and developing an online English language training module for adult learners. In N. Alias, & S. Hashim (Eds.), *Instructional technology research, design and development: Lessons from the field* (pp. 270–286). Hershey, PA: Information Science Reference.

Mutohar, A., & Hughes, J. E. (2013). Toward web 2.0 integration in indonesian education: Challenges and planning strategies. In N. Azab (Ed.), *Cases on web 2.0 in developing countries: Studies on implementation, application, and use* (pp. 198–221). Hershey, PA: Information Science Reference.

Newman, D. L., Clure, G., Deyoe, M. M., & Connor, K. A. (2013). Using technology in a studio approach to learning: Results of a five year study of an innovative mobile teaching tool. In J. Keengwe (Ed.), *Pedagogical applications and social effects of mobile technology integration* (pp. 114–132). Hershey, PA: Information Science Reference. doi:10.4018/978-1-4666-2985-1.ch007

Newman, D. L., Coyle, V. C., & McKenna, L. A. (2013). Changing the face of ELA classrooms: A case study of TPACK professional development. In J. Keengwe (Ed.), *Research perspectives and best practices in educational technology integration* (pp. 270–287). Hershey, PA: Information Science Reference.

Ng, A. W., & Ho, F. (2014). Dynamics of knowledge renewal for professional accountancy under globalization. In P. Ordóñez de Pablos, & R. Tennyson (Eds.), *Strategic approaches for human capital management and development in a turbulent economy* (pp. 264–278). Hershey, PA: Business Science Reference.

Ng, F. F. (2005). Knowledge management in higher education and professional development in the construction industry. In A. Kazi (Ed.), *Knowledge management in the construction industry: A socio-technical perspective* (pp. 150–165). Hershey, PA: Idea Group Publishing.

Ng, F. F. (2008). Knowledge management in higher education and professional development in the construction industry. In M. Jennex (Ed.), *Knowledge management: Concepts, methodologies, tools, and applications* (pp. 2355–2368). Hershey, PA: Information Science Reference.

Nguyen, V., & Szymanski, M. (2013). A state of the art cart: Visual arts and technology integration in teacher education. In J. Keengwe (Ed.), *Research perspectives and best practices in educational technology integration* (pp. 80–104). Hershey, PA: Information Science Reference. doi:10.4018/978-1-4666-4502-8.ch013

Niemitz, M., Slough, S., St. John, K., Leckie, R. M., Peart, L., & Klaus, A. (2010). Integrating K-12 hybrid online learning activities in teacher education programs: Reflections from the school of rock expedition. In J. Yamamoto, J. Kush, R. Lombard, & C. Hertzog (Eds.), *Technology implementation and teacher education: Reflective models* (pp. 25–43). Hershey, PA: Information Science Reference. doi:10.4018/978-1-61520-897-5.ch002

Norris, D. M. (2005). Driving systemic change with e-learning. In C. Howard, J. Boettcher, L. Justice, K. Schenk, P. Rogers, & G. Berg (Eds.), *Encyclopedia of distance learning* (pp. 687–695). Hershey, PA: Information Science Reference. doi:10.4018/978-1-59140-555-9.ch100

Northrup, P. T., & Harrison, W. T. Jr. (2011). Using learning objects for rapid deployment to mobile learning devices for the U.S. coast guard. In I. Association (Ed.), *Instructional design: Concepts, methodologies, tools and applications* (pp. 527–540). Hershey, PA: Information Science Reference. doi:10.4018/978-1-60960-503-2.ch303

Northrup, P. T., Rasmussen, K. L., & Dawson, D. B. (2004). Designing and reusing learning objects to streamline WBI development. In A. Armstrong (Ed.), *Instructional design in the real world: A view from the trenches* (pp. 184–200). Hershey, PA: Information Science Publishing. doi:10.4018/978-1-59140-150-6.ch011

Northrup, P. T., Rasmussen, K. L., & Dawson, D. B. (2008). Designing and reusing learning objects to streamline WBI development. In S. Clarke (Ed.), *End-user computing: Concepts, methodologies, tools, and applications* (pp. 1–1). Hershey, PA: Information Science Reference. doi:10.4018/978-1-59904-945-8.ch037

Oigara, J. N. (2013). Integrating technology in teacher education programs. In J. Keengwe (Ed.), *Research perspectives and best practices in educational technology integration* (pp. 28–43). Hershey, PA: Information Science Reference.

Orrill, C. H., & Polly, D. (2012). Technology integration in mathematics: A model for integrating technology through content development. In D. Polly, C. Mims, & K. Persichitte (Eds.), *Developing technology-rich teacher education programs: Key issues* (pp. 337–356). Hershey, PA: Information Science Reference. doi:10.4018/978-1-4666-0014-0.ch022

Ostashewski, N., & Reid, D. (2013). The networked learning framework: A model for networked professional learning utilizing social networking sites. In J. Keengwe, & L. Kyei-Blankson (Eds.), *Virtual mentoring for teachers: Online professional development practices* (pp. 66–83). Hershey, PA: Information Science Reference.

Ostashewski, N., & Reid, D. (2013). The iPad in the classroom: Three implementation cases highlighting pedagogical activities, integration issues, and teacher professional development strategies. In J. Keengwe (Ed.), *Pedagogical applications and social effects of mobile technology integration* (pp. 25–41). Hershey, PA: Information Science Reference. doi:10.4018/978-1-4666-2985-1.ch002

Pachler, N., Daly, C., & Turvey, A. (2010). Teacher professional development practices: The case of the haringey transformation teachers programme. In J. Lindberg, & A. Olofsson (Eds.), *Online learning communities and teacher professional development: Methods for improved education delivery* (pp. 77–95). Hershey, PA: Information Science Reference.

Parker, D. (2013). Implementing the professional development program. In S. Wang, & T. Hartsell (Eds.), *Technology integration and foundations for effective leadership* (pp. 190–205). Hershey, PA: Information Science Reference.

Payne, A. (2013). Designing a professional development program. In S. Wang, & T. Hartsell (Eds.), *Technology integration and foundations for effective leadership* (pp. 171–189). Hershey, PA: Information Science Reference.

Peacock, S., & Dunlop, G. M. (2006). Developing e-learning provision for healthcare professionals' continuing professional development. In J. O'Donoghue (Ed.), *Technology supported learning and teaching: A staff perspective* (pp. 106–124). Hershey, PA: Information Science Publishing. doi:10.4018/978-1-59140-962-5.ch007

Piecka, D. C., Ruberg, L., Ruckman, C., & Fullwood, D. (2012). NASATalk as a discovery learning space: Self-discovery learning opportunities. In S. Hai-Jew (Ed.), *Constructing self-discovery learning spaces online: Scaffolding and decision making technologies* (pp. 49–71). Hershey, PA: Information Science Reference.

Pilkington, R. (2010). Building practitioner skills in personalised elearning: Messages for professional development. In J. O'Donoghue (Ed.), *Technology-supported environments for personalized learning: Methods and case studies* (pp. 167–184). Hershey, PA: Information Science Reference.

Polly, D. (2011). Preparing teachers to integrate technology effectively: The case of higher-order thinking skills (HOTS). In S. D'Agustino (Ed.), *Adaptation, resistance and access to instructional technologies: Assessing future trends in education* (pp. 395–409). Hershey, PA: Information Science Reference.

Polly, D. (2013). Designing and teaching an online elementary mathematics methods course: Promises, barriers, and implications. In R. Hartshorne, T. Heafner, & T. Petty (Eds.), *Teacher education programs and online learning tools: Innovations in teacher preparation* (pp. 335–356). Hershey, PA: Information Science Reference.

Polly, D., Grant, M. M., & Gikas, J. (2011). Supporting technology integration in higher education: The role of professional development. In D. Surry, R. Gray Jr, & J. Stefurak (Eds.), *Technology integration in higher education: Social and organizational aspects* (pp. 58–71). Hershey, PA: Information Science Reference.

Polly, D., Mims, C., & McCombs, B. (2012). Designing district-wide technology-rich professional development. In I. Chen, & D. McPheeters (Eds.), *Cases on educational technology integration in urban schools* (pp. 236–243). Hershey, PA: Information Science Reference.

Powell, E. (2009). Facilitating reflective teaching: Video-stimulated reflective dialogues as a professional development process. In V. Wang (Ed.), *Handbook of research on e-learning applications for career and technical education: Technologies for vocational training* (pp. 100–111). Hershey, PA: Information Science Reference. doi:10.4018/978-1-60566-739-3.ch008

Prisk, J., & Lee, K. (2012). How to utilize an online community of practice (CoP) to enhance innovation in teaching and learning. In V. Wang (Ed.), *Encyclopedia of e-leadership, counseling and training* (pp. 532–544). Hershey, PA: Information Science Reference.

Prpic, J. K., & Moore, G. (2012). E-portfolios as a quantitative and qualitative means of demonstrating learning outcomes and competencies in engineering. In K. Yusof, N. Azli, A. Kosnin, S. Yusof, & Y. Yusof (Eds.), *Outcome-based science, technology, engineering, and mathematics education: Innovative practices* (pp. 124–154). Hershey, PA: Information Science Reference. doi:10.4018/978-1-4666-1809-1.ch007

Pullman, N., & Streff, K. (2009). Creating a security education, training, and awareness program. In M. Gupta, & R. Sharman (Eds.), *Handbook of research on social and organizational liabilities in information security* (pp. 325–345). Hershey, PA: Information Science Reference.

Quinton, S. (2007). Delivering online expertise, online. In M. Keppell (Ed.), *Instructional design: Case studies in communities of practice* (pp. 193–214). Hershey, PA: Information Science Publishing. doi:10.4018/978-1-59904-322-7.ch010

Reali, A. M., Tancredi, R. M., & Mizukami, M. D. (2012). Online mentoring as a tool for professional development and change of novice and experienced teachers: A Brazilian experience. In V. Dennen, & J. Myers (Eds.), *Virtual professional development and informal learning via social networks* (pp. 203–218). Hershey, PA: Information Science Reference. doi:10.4018/978-1-4666-1815-2.ch012

Redmon, R. J. Jr. (2009). E-mail reflection groups as collaborative action research. In J. Salmons, & L. Wilson (Eds.), *Handbook of research on electronic collaboration and organizational synergy* (pp. 349–361). Hershey, PA: Information Science Reference.

Rice, M. L., & Bain, C. (2013). Planning and implementation of a 21st century classroom project. In A. Benson, J. Moore, & S. Williams van Rooij (Eds.), *Cases on educational technology planning, design, and implementation: A project management perspective* (pp. 76–92). Hershey, PA: Information Science Reference. doi:10.4018/978-1-4666-4237-9.ch005

Richardson, S. L., Barnes, S. L., & Torain, D. S. (2012). Using technology to support algebra teaching and assessment: A teacher development case study. In I. Chen, & D. McPheeters (Eds.), *Cases on educational technology integration in urban schools* (pp. 224–229). Hershey, PA: Information Science Reference.

Rieber, L. P., Francom, G. M., & Jensen, L. J. (2011). Feeling like a first year teacher: Toward becoming a successful online instructor. In D. Surry, R. Gray Jr, & J. Stefurak (Eds.), *Technology integration in higher education: Social and organizational aspects* (pp. 42–57). Hershey, PA: Information Science Reference.

Ring, G., & Foti, S. (2006). Using eportfolios to facilitate professional development among pre-service teachers. In A. Jafari, & C. Kaufman (Eds.), *Handbook of research on eportfolios* (pp. 340–357). Hershey, PA: Idea Group Publishing. doi:10.4018/978-1-59140-890-1.ch031

Riverin, S. (2009). Blended learning and professional development in the K-12 sector. In E. Stacey, & P. Gerbic (Eds.), *Effective blended learning practices: Evidence-based perspectives in ICT-facilitated education* (pp. 182–202). Hershey, PA: Information Science Reference. doi:10.4018/978-1-60566-296-1.ch010

Robertshaw, M. B., Leary, H., Walker, A., Bloxham, K., & Recker, M. (2009). Reciprocal mentoring "in the wild": A retrospective, comparative case study of ICT teacher professional development. In E. Stacey, & P. Gerbic (Eds.), *Effective blended learning practices: evidence-based perspectives in ICT-facilitated education* (pp. 280–297). Hershey, PA: Information Science Reference. doi:10.4018/978-1-60566-296-1.ch015

Robertson, L., & Hardman, W. (2013). More than changing classrooms: Professors' transitions to synchronous e-teaching. In P. Ordóñez de Pablos, & R. Tennyson (Eds.), *Strategic role of tertiary education and technologies for sustainable competitive advantage* (pp. 156–175). Hershey, PA: Information Science Reference.

Rockland, R., Kimmel, H., Carpinelli, J., Hirsch, L. S., & Burr-Alexander, L. (2012). Medical robotics in K-12 education. In B. Barker, G. Nugent, N. Grandgenett, & V. Adamchuk (Eds.), *Robots in K-12 education: A new technology for learning* (pp. 120–140). Hershey, PA: Information Science Reference. doi:10.4018/978-1-4666-0182-6.ch006

Rockland, R., Kimmel, H., Carpinelli, J., Hirsch, L. S., & Burr-Alexander, L. (2014). Medical robotics in K-12 education. In I. Management Association (Ed.), *Robotics: Concepts, methodologies, tools, and applications* (pp. 1096-1115). Hershey, PA: Information Science Reference. doi:10.4018/978-1-4666-4607-0.ch053

Rodesiler, L., & Tripp, L. (2012). It's all about personal connections: Pre-service English teachers' experiences engaging in networked learning. In V. Dennen, & J. Myers (Eds.), *Virtual professional development and informal learning via social networks* (pp. 185–202). Hershey, PA: Information Science Reference. doi:10.4018/978-1-4666-1815-2.ch011

Ronau, R. N., & Rakes, C. R. (2012). A comprehensive framework for teacher knowledge (CFTK): Complexity of individual aspects and their interactions. In R. Ronau, C. Rakes, & M. Niess (Eds.), *Educational technology, teacher knowledge, and classroom impact: A research handbook on frameworks and approaches* (pp. 59–102). Hershey, PA: Information Science Publishing.

Rosen, Y., & Rimor, R. (2013). Teaching and assessing problem solving in online collaborative environment. In R. Hartshorne, T. Heafner, & T. Petty (Eds.), *Teacher education programs and online learning tools: Innovations in teacher preparation* (pp. 82–97). Hershey, PA: Information Science Reference.

Ruberg, L., Calinger, M., & Howard, B. C. (2010). Evaluating educational technologies: Historical milestones. In L. Tomei (Ed.), *ICTs for modern educational and instructional advancement: New approaches to teaching* (pp. 285–297). Hershey, PA: Information Science Reference.

Russell, D. L. (2007). The mediated action of educational reform: An inquiry into colloaboative online professional development. In R. Sharma, & S. Mishra (Eds.), *Cases on global e-learning practices: Successes and pitfalls* (pp. 108–122). Hershey, PA: Information Science Publishing.

Sáenz, J., Aramburu, N., & Rivera, O. (2010). Exploring the links between structural capital, knowledge sharing, innovation capability and business competitiveness: An empirical study. In D. Harorimana (Ed.), *Cultural implications of knowledge sharing, management and transfer: Identifying competitive advantage* (pp. 321–354). Hershey, PA: Information Science Reference.

Sales, G. C. (2009). Preparing teachers to teach online. In P. Rogers, G. Berg, J. Boettcher, C. Howard, L. Justice, & K. Schenk (Eds.), *Encyclopedia of distance learning* (2nd ed., pp. 1665–1672). Hershey, PA: Information Science Reference. doi:10.4018/978-1-60566-198-8.ch244

Sales, G. C. (2011). Preparing teachers to teach online. In I. Association (Ed.), *Instructional design: Concepts, methodologies, tools and applications* (pp. 8–17). Hershey, PA: Information Science Reference. doi:10.4018/978-1-60960-503-2.ch102

Sampson, D. G., & Kallonis, P. (2012). 3D virtual classroom simulations for supporting school teachers' continuing professional development. In J. Jia (Ed.), *Educational stages and interactive learning: From kindergarten to workplace training* (pp. 427–450). Hershey, PA: Information Science Reference. doi:10.4018/978-1-4666-0137-6.ch023

Sari, E., & Lim, C. P. (2012). Online learning community: building the professional capacity of Indonesian teachers. In J. Jia (Ed.), *Educational stages and interactive learning: From kindergarten to workplace training* (pp. 451–467). Hershey, PA: Information Science Reference. doi:10.4018/978-1-4666-0137-6.ch024

Scheckler, R. (2010). Case studies from the inquiry learning forum: Stories reaching beyond the edges. In J. Lindberg, & A. Olofsson (Eds.), *Online learning communities and teacher professional development: Methods for improved education delivery* (pp. 42–59). Hershey, PA: Information Science Reference.

Schifter, C. (2008). "Making teachers better": A brief history of professional development for teachers. In C. Schifter (Ed.), *Infusing technology into the classroom: Continuous practice improvement* (pp. 41–57). Hershey, PA: Information Science Publishing. doi:10.4018/978-1-59904-765-2.ch003

Schifter, C. (2008). Effecting change in the classroom through professional development. In C. Schifter (Ed.), *Infusing technology into the classroom: Continuous practice improvement* (pp. 259–274). Hershey, PA: Information Science Publishing. doi:10.4018/978-1-59904-765-2.ch014

Schifter, C. (2008). Continuous practice improvement. In C. Schifter (Ed.), *Infusing technology into the classroom: Continuous practice improvement* (pp. 58–86). Hershey, PA: Information Science Publishing. doi:10.4018/978-1-59904-765-2.ch004

Schifter, C. (2008). Finger painting to digital painting: First grade. In C. Schifter (Ed.), *Infusing technology into the classroom: Continuous practice improvement* (pp. 109–126). Hershey, PA: Information Science Publishing. doi:10.4018/978-1-59904-765-2.ch006

Schrader, P., Strudler, N., Asay, L., Graves, T., Pennell, S. L., & Stewart, S. (2012). The pathway to Nevada's future: A case of statewide technology integration and professional development. In I. Chen, & D. McPheeters (Eds.), *Cases on educational technology integration in urban schools* (pp. 204–223). Hershey, PA: Information Science Reference.

Scott, D. E., & Scott, S. (2010). Innovations in the use of technology and teacher professional development. In J. Lindberg, & A. Olofsson (Eds.), *Online learning communities and teacher professional development: Methods for improved education delivery* (pp. 169–189). Hershey, PA: Information Science Reference.

Scott, D. E., & Scott, S. (2012). Multi-faceted professional development models designed to enhance teaching and learning within universities. In A. Olofsson, & J. Lindberg (Eds.), *Informed design of educational technologies in higher education: Enhanced learning and teaching* (pp. 412–435). Hershey, PA: Information Science Reference.

Scott, S. (2010). The theory and practice divide in relation to teacher professional development. In J. Lindberg, & A. Olofsson (Eds.), *Online learning communities and teacher professional development: Methods for improved education delivery* (pp. 20–40). Hershey, PA: Information Science Reference.

Semich, G. W., & Gibbons, B. (2011). The professional development school: A building block for training public school faculty on new technologies. In L. Tomei (Ed.), *Online courses and ICT in education: Emerging practices and applications* (pp. 99–108). Hershey, PA: Information Science Reference.

Shambaugh, N. (2013). A professional development school technology integration and research plan. In A. Ritzhaupt, & S. Kumar (Eds.), *Cases on educational technology implementation for facilitating learning* (pp. 45–68). Hershey, PA: Information Science Reference. doi:10.4018/978-1-4666-3676-7.ch003

Sherman, G., & Byers, A. (2011). Electronic portfolios in the professional development of educators. In S. D'Agustino (Ed.), *Adaptation, resistance and access to instructional technologies: Assessing future trends in education* (pp. 429–444). Hershey, PA: Information Science Reference.

Simelane, S. (2010). Professional development programme in the use of educational technology to implement technology-enhanced courses successfully. In S. Mukerji, & P. Tripathi (Eds.), *Cases on technology enhanced learning through collaborative opportunities* (pp. 91–110). Hershey, PA: Information Science Reference. doi:10.4018/978-1-61520-751-0.ch006

Skibba, K. (2013). Adult learning influence on faculty learning cycle: Individual and shared reflections while learning to teach online lead to pedagogical transformations. In J. Keengwe, & L. Kyei-Blankson (Eds.), *Virtual mentoring for teachers: Online professional development practices* (pp. 263–291). Hershey, PA: Information Science Reference.

Skinner, L. B., Witte, M. M., & Witte, J. E. (2010). Challenges and opportunities in career and technical education. In V. Wang (Ed.), *Definitive readings in the history, philosophy, theories and practice of career and technical education* (pp. 197–215). Hershey, PA: Information Science Reference. doi:10.4018/978-1-61520-747-3.ch012

Slabon, W. A., & Richards, R. L. (2012). Story-based professional development: Using a conflict management wiki. In V. Dennen, & J. Myers (Eds.), *Virtual professional development and informal learning via social networks* (pp. 256–275). Hershey, PA: Information Science Reference. doi:10.4018/978-1-4666-1815-2.ch015

Spaulding, D. T. (2008). Virtual field trips: Advantages and disadvantages for educators and recommendation for professional development. In D. Newman, J. Falco, S. Silverman, & P. Barbanell (Eds.), *Videoconferencing technology in K-12 instruction: Best practices and trends* (pp. 191–199). Hershey, PA: Information Science Reference. doi:10.4018/978-1-59904-955-7.ch060

Speaker, R. B., Levitt, G., & Grubaugh, S. (2013). Professional development in a virtual world. In J. Keengwe, & L. Kyei-Blankson (Eds.), *Virtual mentoring for teachers: Online professional development practices* (pp. 122–148). Hershey, PA: Information Science Reference.

Stacey, E., & Gerbic, P. (2009). Introduction to blended learning practices. In E. Stacey, & P. Gerbic (Eds.), *Effective blended learning practices: Evidence-based perspectives in ICT-facilitated education* (pp. 1–19). Hershey, PA: Information Science Reference. doi:10.4018/978-1-60566-296-1.ch001

Stanfill, D. (2012). Standards-based educational technology professional development. In V. Wang (Ed.), *Encyclopedia of e-leadership, counseling and training* (pp. 819–834). Hershey, PA: Information Science Reference.

Steel, C., & Andrews, T. (2012). Re-imagining teaching for technology-enriched learning spaces: An academic development model. In M. Keppell, K. Souter, & M. Riddle (Eds.), *Physical and virtual learning spaces in higher education: Concepts for the modern learning environment* (pp. 242–265). Hershey, PA: Information Science Reference.

Stewart, C., Horarik, S., & Wolodko, K. (2013). Maximising technology usage in research synthesis of higher education professional development research. In J. Willems, B. Tynan, & R. James (Eds.), *Global challenges and perspectives in blended and distance learning* (pp. 1–16). Hershey, PA: Information Science Reference. doi:10.4018/978-1-4666-3978-2.ch001

Stieha, V., & Raider-Roth, M. (2012). Disrupting relationships: A catalyst for growth. In J. Faulkner (Ed.), *Disrupting pedagogies in the knowledge society: Countering conservative norms with creative approaches* (pp. 16–31). Hershey, PA: Information Science Reference.

Stockero, S. L. (2010). Serving rural teachers using synchronous online professional development. In J. Yamamoto, J. Leight, S. Winterton, & C. Penny (Eds.), *Technology leadership in teacher education: Integrated solutions and experiences* (pp. 111–124). Hershey, PA: Information Science Reference. doi:10.4018/978-1-61520-899-9.ch007

Stylianou-Georgiou, A., Vrasidas, C., Christodoulou, N., Zembylas, M., & Landone, E. (2006). Technologies challenging literacy: Hypertext, community building, reflection, and critical literacy. In L. Tan Wee Hin, & R. Subramaniam (Eds.), *Handbook of research on literacy in technology at the K-12 level* (pp. 21–33). Hershey, PA: Information Science Reference. doi:10.4018/978-1-59140-494-1.ch002

Szecsy, E. M. (2011). Building knowledge without borders: Using ICT to develop a binational education research community. In G. Kurubacak, & T. Yuzer (Eds.), *Handbook of research on transformative online education and liberation: Models for social equality* (pp. 67–85). Hershey, PA: Information Science Reference.

Tawfik, A. A., Reiseck, C., & Richter, R. (2013). Project management methods for the implementation of an online faculty development course. In A. Benson, J. Moore, & S. Williams van Rooij (Eds.), *Cases on educational technology planning, design, and implementation: A project management perspective* (pp. 153–167). Hershey, PA: Information Science Reference. doi:10.4018/978-1-4666-4237-9.ch009

Taylor, D. B., Hartshorne, R., Eneman, S., Wilkins, P., & Polly, D. (2012). Lessons learned from the implementation of a technology-focused professional learning community. In D. Polly, C. Mims, & K. Persichitte (Eds.), *Developing technology-rich teacher education programs: Key issues* (pp. 535–550). Hershey, PA: Information Science Reference. doi:10.4018/978-1-4666-0014-0.ch034

Tedford, D. (2010). Perspectives on the influences of social capital upon internet usage of rural Guatemalan teachers. In S. Mukerji, & P. Tripathi (Eds.), *Cases on technological adaptability and transnational learning: Issues and challenges* (pp. 218–243). Hershey, PA: Information Science Reference. doi:10.4018/978-1-61520-779-4.ch012

Terantino, J. M. (2012). An activity theoretical approach to examining virtual professional development and informal learning via social networks. In V. Dennen, & J. Myers (Eds.), *Virtual professional development and informal learning via social networks* (pp. 60–74). Hershey, PA: Information Science Reference. doi:10.4018/978-1-4666-1815-2.ch004

Thompson, T. L., & Kanuka, H. (2009). Establishing communities of practice for effective and sustainable professional development for blended learning. In E. Stacey, & P. Gerbic (Eds.), *Effective blended learning practices: Evidence-based perspectives in ICT-facilitated education* (pp. 144–162). Hershey, PA: Information Science Reference. doi:10.4018/978-1-60566-296-1.ch008

Thornton, J. (2010). Framing pedagogy, diminishing technology: Teachers experience of online learning software. In H. Song, & T. Kidd (Eds.), *Handbook of research on human performance and instructional technology* (pp. 263–283). Hershey, PA: Information Science Reference.

Thornton, K., & Yoong, P. (2010). The application of blended action learning to leadership development: A case study. In P. Yoong (Ed.), *Leadership in the digital enterprise: Issues and challenges* (pp. 163–180). Hershey, PA: Business Science Reference.

Ting, A., & Jones, P. D. (2010). Using free source eportfolios to empower ESL teachers in collaborative peer reflection. In J. Yamamoto, J. Kush, R. Lombard, & C. Hertzog (Eds.), *Technology implementation and teacher education: Reflective models* (pp. 93–107). Hershey, PA: Information Science Reference. doi:10.4018/978-1-61520-897-5.ch006

Tomei, L. A. (2008). The KARPE model revisited – An updated investigation for differentiating teaching and learning with technology in higher education. In L. Tomei (Ed.), *Adapting information and communication technologies for effective education* (pp. 30–40). Hershey, PA: Information Science Reference.

Torrisi-Steele, G. (2005). Toward effective use of multimedia technologies in education. In S. Mishra, & R. Sharma (Eds.), *Interactive multimedia in education and training* (pp. 25–46). Hershey, PA: IGI Publishing.

Torrisi-Steele, G. (2008). Toward effective use of multimedia technologies in education. In M. Syed (Ed.), *Multimedia technologies: Concepts, methodologies, tools, and applications* (pp. 1651–1667). Hershey, PA: Information Science Reference. doi:10.4018/978-1-59904-953-3.ch118

Trujillo, K. M., Wiburg, K., Savic, M., & McKee, K. (2013). Teachers learn how to effectively integrate mobile technology by teaching students using math snacks animations and games. In J. Keengwe (Ed.), *Pedagogical applications and social effects of mobile technology integration* (pp. 98–113). Hershey, PA: Information Science Reference. doi:10.4018/978-1-4666-2985-1.ch006

Tynan, B., & Barnes, C. (2010). Web 2.0 and professional development of academic staff. In M. Lee, & C. McLoughlin (Eds.), *Web 2.0-based e-learning: Applying social informatics for tertiary teaching* (pp. 365–379). Hershey, PA: Information Science Reference. doi:10.4018/978-1-60566-294-7.ch019

Tynan, B., & Barnes, C. (2012). Web 2.0 and professional development of academic staff. In I. Management Association (Ed.), Virtual learning environments: Concepts, methodologies, tools and applications (pp. 94-108). Hershey, PA: Information Science Reference. doi:10.4018/978-1-4666-0011-9.ch107

Uehara, D. L. (2007). Research in the Pacific: Utilizing technology to inform and improve teacher practice. In Y. Inoue (Ed.), *Technology and diversity in higher education: New challenges* (pp. 213–232). Hershey, PA: Information Science Publishing.

Velez-Solic, A., & Banas, J. R. (2013). Professional development for online educators: Problems, predictions, and best practices. In J. Keengwe, & L. Kyei-Blankson (Eds.), *Virtual mentoring for teachers: Online professional development practices* (pp. 204–226). Hershey, PA: Information Science Reference.

Venkatesh, V., Bures, E., Davidson, A., Wade, C. A., Lysenko, L., & Abrami, P. C. (2013). Electronic portfolio encouraging active and reflective learning: A case study in improving academic self-regulation through innovative use of educational technologies. In A. Ritzhaupt, & S. Kumar (Eds.), *Cases on educational technology implementation for facilitating learning* (pp. 341–376). Hershey, PA: Information Science Reference. doi:10.4018/978-1-4666-3676-7.ch019

Watson, C. E., Zaldivar, M., & Summers, T. (2010). ePortfolios for learning, assessment, and professional development. In R. Donnelly, J. Harvey, & K. O'Rourke (Eds.), Critical design and effective tools for e-learning in higher education: Theory into practice (pp. 157-175). Hershey, PA: Information Science Reference. doi:10.4018/978-1-61520-879-1.ch010

Whitehouse, P., McCloskey, E., & Ketelhut, D. J. (2010). Online pedagogy design and development: New models for 21st century online teacher professional development. In J. Lindberg, & A. Olofsson (Eds.), *Online learning communities and teacher professional development: Methods for improved education delivery* (pp. 247–262). Hershey, PA: Information Science Reference.

Williams, I. M., & Olaniran, B. A. (2012). Professional development through web 2.0 collaborative applications. In V. Dennen, & J. Myers (Eds.), *Virtual professional development and informal learning via social networks* (pp. 1–24). Hershey, PA: Information Science Reference. doi:10.4018/978-1-4666-1815-2.ch001

Wilson, A., & Christie, D. (2010). Realising the potential of virtual environments: A challenge for Scottish teachers. In J. Lindberg, & A. Olofsson (Eds.), *Online learning communities and teacher professional development: Methods for improved education delivery* (pp. 96–113). Hershey, PA: Information Science Reference.

Wilson, G. (2009). Case studies of ICT-enhanced blended learning and implications for professional development. In E. Stacey, & P. Gerbic (Eds.), *Effective blended learning practices: Evidence-based perspectives in ICT-facilitated education* (pp. 239–258). Hershey, PA: Information Science Reference. doi:10.4018/978-1-60566-296-1.ch013

Witt, L. A., & Burke, L. A. (2003). Using cognitive ability and personality to select information technology professionals. In M. Mahmood (Ed.), *Advanced topics in end user computing* (Vol. 2, pp. 1–17). Hershey, PA: Idea Group Publishing. doi:10.4018/978-1-59140-065-3.ch001

Wynne, C. W. (2014). Cultivating leaders from within: Transforming workers into leaders. In S. Mukerji, & P. Tripathi (Eds.), *Handbook of research on transnational higher education* (pp. 42–58). Hershey, PA: Information Science Reference.

Yakavenka, H. (2012). Developing professional competencies through international peer learning communities. In V. Dennen, & J. Myers (Eds.), *Virtual professional development and informal learning via social networks* (pp. 134–154). Hershey, PA: Information Science Reference. doi:10.4018/978-1-4666-1815-2.ch008

Yamamoto, J., Linaberger, M., & Forbes, L. S. (2005). Mentoring and technology integration for teachers. In D. Carbonara (Ed.), *Technology literacy applications in learning environments* (pp. 161–170). Hershey, PA: Information Science Publishing. doi:10.4018/978-1-59140-479-8.ch012

Yukawa, J. (2011). Telementoring and project-based learning: An integrated model for 21st century skills. In D. Scigliano (Ed.), *Telementoring in the K-12 classroom: Online communication technologies for learning* (pp. 31–56). Hershey, PA: Information Science Reference.

Zellermayer, M., Mor, N., & Heilweil, I. (2009). The intersection of theory, tools and tasks in a postgraduate learning environment. In C. Payne (Ed.), *Information technology and constructivism in higher education: Progressive learning frameworks* (pp. 319–333). Hershey, PA: Information Science Reference. doi:10.4018/978-1-60566-654-9.ch021

Zuidema, L. A. (2008). Parawork. In P. Zemliansky, & K. St.Amant (Eds.), *Handbook of research on virtual workplaces and the new nature of business practices* (pp. 81–97). Hershey, PA: Information Science Reference. doi:10.4018/978-1-59904-893-2.ch007

Zygouris-Coe, V. I. (2013). A model for online instructor training, support, and professional development. In J. Keengwe, & L. Kyei-Blankson (Eds.), *Virtual mentoring for teachers: Online professional development practices* (pp. 97–121). Hershey, PA: Information Science Reference.

Zygouris-Coe, V. I., & Swan, B. (2010). Challenges of online teacher professional development communities: A statewide case study in the United States. In J. Lindberg, & A. Olofsson (Eds.), *Online learning communities and teacher professional development: Methods for improved education delivery* (pp. 114–133). Hershey, PA: Information Science Reference.

314

Compilation of References

Abanikanda, M. O. (2011). *Integrating Information and Communication Technology (ICT) in Teacher Education.* Higher Education & Globalization.

Abiona, K. (2002). *Community organization.* Department of Adult Education, University of Ibadan.

Aboelmaged, M. G. (2010). Predicting e-procurement adoption in a developing country: An empirical integration of technology acceptance model and theory of planned behaviour. *Industrial Management & Data Systems, 110*(3), 392–414. doi:10.1108/02635571011030042

Abolade, A. O. (2009). Importance of Learning and Instructional Material in Nigerian Educational Industries. *Nigeria Journal of Curriculum Studies, 12*(1), 22–108.

Abroms, L., & Maibach, E. (2008). The effectiveness of mass communication to change public behavior. *Annual Review of Public Health, 29*, 219–234. doi:10.1146/annurev.publhealth.29.020907.090824 PMID:18173391

Abubakar, M. (2003). *Stewardship Report of Professor A.R. Anao: Information and Communication Technology Department, 1999-2004.* University of Benin.

Adeboye, T. (2002). Globalization: How should Nigeria respond? (NISER Occasional paper 2). Ibadan, Nigeria: Nigerian Institute of Social and Economic Research (NISER).

Adeoye, B. F. (2010). The use of ICTs in education: A case study of lecturers from the University of Lagos, Nigeria. *Journal of Educational Review, 3*(4), 429–434.

Adewoyin, J. A. (2006). The Place of Information and Communication Technology in Designing and Utilizing Instructional Materials. In *Proceeding on a One Day Train the Trainer Open Workshop on Understanding New Technologies in Instructional Media Materials Utilization.* Academic Press.

Adeyomoye, J. I. (2012). Information literacy competence among students in Nigerian private universities: A case study of Caleb University Imota, Lagos, Nigeria. *Library Progress International, 32*(2), 185–193.

Adiwas, A., & Iyamu, E.O.S. (2004). Curriculum Implementation in Nigeria. *Journal of Technology Education.*

Aduwa-Ogiegbaen, S. E., & Iyamu, E. O. S. (2005). Using Information and Communication Technology in Secondary Schools in Nigeria: Problems and Prospects. *Journal of Educational Technology & Society, 8*(1), 104–112.

Agba, P. C. (2005). Media Technology and the Enlarging World of Distance Education in Nigeria. *International Journal of Communication, 2*, 21–31.

Agun, I. (1982). Strategies for developing resources centers in Nigerian secondary schools. *Nigeria Educational Forum, 3*(1).

Agyeman, O. T. (2007). *Survey of ICT and education in Africa: Nigeria country report.* Retrieved from www.infodev.org

Ajelabi, A. (2000). *Production and utilization of educational media.* Lagos: Reltel Communication.

Akande, M. O. (2002). *The theory and practice of professional teaching. Lagos.* Ekanag Publishers.

Akpınar, S., & Kaptan, H. (2010). Computer aided school administration system using RFID technology. *Procedia: Social and Behavioral Sciences*, 2(2), 4392–4397. doi:10.1016/j.sbspro.2010.03.699

Akpoghome, T. U., & Idiegbeyan-Ose, J. (2010). The role of digital library in law research. *International Journal of Library and Information Science*, 2(6).

Alavi, M., & Leidner, D. E. (2001). Knowledge management and knowledge management systems. *Management Information Systems Quarterly*, 25(1), 107–137. doi:10.2307/3250961

Albirini, A. (2006). Teachers' attitude toward information and communication technologies: The case of Syrian EFL teachers. *Computers & Education*, 47(4), 373–398. doi:10.1016/j.compedu.2004.10.013

Alexa. (2013). *Top 500 Global Sites*. Retrieved October 5, 2013 from http://www.alexa.com/topsites

Aliyu, U. F. (2011). Influence of library instruction course on students access and utilization of library resources in Abubakar Tafawa Balewa University Bauchi, Nigeria. *Journal of Research in Education and Society*, 2(3), 96–102.

Allen, E., & Seaman, J. (2010). Class differences: Online education in the United States, 2010. *BABSON Survey Research Group, Sloan Consortium*. Retrieved from http://sloanconsortium.org/publications/survey/survey05.asp

Allen, I. E., & Seaman, J. (2013). *Changing course: Ten years of tracking online education in the United States*. Babson Survey Research Group and Quahog Research Group. Retrieved from http://www.onlinelearningsurvey.com/reports/changingcourse.pdf

Allen, V. G. Heitschmidt & Sollenberger. (2007). Grazing systems and strategies. Academic Press.

Allen, I. E., & Seaman, J. (2011). *Going the Distance: Online Education in the United States 2011*. Pearson.

Almogbel, A. N. (2002). *Distance Education in Saudi Arabia: Attitudes and Perceived Contributions of Faculty, Students and Administrators in Technical Collage*. (Unpublished Ph.D. Thesis). University of Pittsburgh, Pittsburgh, PA.

Amadi, Orikpe, & Osine. (1998). *Effective Technical Vocational Education Training Design*. Human Resources Development Press Inc.

Amale, S. (2003). Teacher Education in Globalization: An Appraisal of the Nigerian Situation. In Globalization & Education in Nigeria (pp. 62-73). Philosophy of Education Association of Nigeria.

Amedeker, M. K. (2005). Reforming Ghanaian Teacher Education Towards Preparing an Effective Pre-service Teacher. *Journal of Education for Teaching*, 31(2), 99–110. doi:10.1080/02607470500127194

Amoor, S. S. (2011). The Challenges of Vocational and Technical Education Programme in Nigerian Universities. *Journal of Research on Computing in Education*, 3, 479–495.

Anantatmula, V. S. P. (2004). *Criteria for measuring knowledge management efforts in organizations*. Retrieved from http://proquest.umi.com/pqdweb?index=6&did=765360761&SrchMode=1&sid=2&Fmt=6&VInst=PROD&VType=PQD&RQT=309&VName=PQD&TS=1265786437&clientId=9678

Anao, A. (2003, November 11). Society, knowledge incubation and management. *The Guardian*, p. 75.

Anderson, L. W., & Krathwohl, D. (Eds.). (2001). *A taxonomy for learning, teaching, and assessing: A revision of Bloom's taxonomy of educational objectives*. New York: Longman.

Angline, G. (1995). *Instructional technology: Past present and future* (2nd ed.). Englewood, CO: Libraries Unlimited, Inc.

Animoto. (2014). *Animoto Web Site*. Retrieved January 13, 2014, from http://animoto.com

Anyanwu, C. N. (1991). *Introduction to community development*. Lagos: Gabesther Educational Publishers.

Anyanwu, C. N. (2002). *Community education: The African dimension*. Ibadan: Alafas Nigeria Company.

Appleman, D. (2009). *Critical encounters in high school English: Teaching literary theory to adolescents*. New York: Teachers College Press.

Armstrong, V., Barnesa, S., Sutherland, R., Curran, S., Mills, S., & Thompson, I. (2005). *Collaborative research methodology for investigating teaching and learning: The use of interactive whiteboard technology.* Retrieved from http://smartboards.typepad.com/smartboard/files/article1.pdf

Arneson, P. (2007). *Exploring communication ethics: Interviews with influential scholars in the field.* New York: P. Lang.

Arnett, R. C., Fritz, J. M., & Bell, L. M. (2009). *Communication ethics literacy: Dialogue and difference.* Los Angeles, CA: SAGE Publications.

Ask.com. (2013). *What is instructional media?* Retrieved December 16, 2013 from www.ask.com/question/what-is-instrumental-media

Aşkar, P. (2003). *Uzaktan Eğitim Teknolojileri ve TCMB'de Teknoloji Destekli Bilgisayar Eğitimi Konferansı.* Ankara.

Asogwa, U. D. (2006). *Integration of information and communication (ICT) for quality distance education.* Paper presented on the occasion of 2006 Annual Conference of Institute of Education. Nsukka, Nigeria.

Assaf, B. (2009). *Immerse approach to ICT in TVET.* Retrieved from http://www.ipac.kacst.edu.sa

Association of College and Research Libraries. (2000). *Information literacy competency standards for higher education.* Chicago: ACRL. Retrieved from www.acrl.org/ala.mgrps/divs/acrl/stndards/standards.pdf

Atkins, D. E., Brown, J. S., & Hammond, A. L. (2007). *A review of the open educational resources (OER) movement: Achievements, challenges, and new opportunities* (Report to the William and Flora Hewlett Foundation). Retrieved from http://www.hewlett.org/uploads/files/ReviewoftheOERMovement.pdf

Avery, E., Lariscy, R., Amador, E., Ickowitz, T., Primm, C., & Taylor, A. (2010). Diffusion of social media among public relations practitioners in health departments across various community population sizes. *Journal of Public Relations Research, 22*(3), 336–358. doi:10.1080/10627261003614427

Awotua-Efebo, E. B. (2002). *Effective Teaching Principle and Practice.* Para Graphic Publishers.

Ayoade, J. (2007). Roadmap to solving security and privacy concerns in RFID systems. *Computer Law & Security Report, 23*(6), 555–561. doi:10.1016/j.clsr.2007.09.005

Babalola, Y. T. (2012). Awareness and incidence of plagiarism among undergraduates in a Nigerian private university. *African Journal of Library. Archival and Information Science, 22*(1), 53–60.

Badke, W. (2010). Why information literacy is invisible. *Communications in Information Literacy, 4*(2), 129–141.

Baggett, S.B., & Williams, M. (2012, January-March). Student behaviors and opinions regarding the use of social media, mobile technologies, and library research. *Virginia Libraries*, 19-22.

Bagudo, A. A. (2002). Globalization: A challenge to Nigeria's Education System. *Nigerian Journal of Educational Philosophy, 9*(1), 78–86.

Bahra, N. (2001). *Competitive Knowledge Management.* Palgrave Houndmills. doi:10.1057/9780230554610

Bailey, G. D. (1997). What technology leaders need to know: The essential top 10 concepts for technology integration in the 21st century. *Learning and Leading with Technology, 25*(1), 57–62.

Bain, K. (2004). *What the Best College Teachers Do?* Harvard University Press.

Baird, D. E., & Fisher, M. (2005-2006). Neomillennial user experience design strategies: Utilizing social networking media to support always on learning styles. *Journal of Educational Technology Systems, 34*(1), 5–32. doi:10.2190/6WMW-47L0-M81Q-12G1

Balasubramanian, S., & Manivannan, S. (2010). *Knowledge Management in Software Organisation.* Retrieved from http://www.indianmba.com/Faculty_Coloumn/FC1077/fc1077.html

Ball, S. (2008). *The education debate.* Bristol, UK: Policy Press.

Barclay, E. (2009). Text Messages could hasten tuberculosis drug compliance. *Lancet, 373*(9657), 15–16. doi:10.1016/S0140-6736(08)61938-8 PMID:19125443

Barker, C. (2002). *The role of ICT in Higher Education: ICT as a change agent for education.* Academic Press.

Baro, E. E., & Zuokemefa, T. (2011). Information literacy programmes in Nigeria: A survey of 36 university libraries. *New Library World, 112*(11 & 12), 549–565. doi:10.1108/03074801111190428

Barrett, H. (2009). My Online Portfolio Adventure. *electronicportfolios.org*. Retrieved from http://electronicportfolios.org/myportfolio/versions.html#Overview

Barton, A. (2011). Big pharma wants to 'friend' you. *Globe and Mail, 25.*

Baryamureeba, V. (2007). *ICT as an Engine for Uganda's Economic Growth: The role of and opportunities for Makerere university*. Retrieved from http://www.cit.mak.ac.ug/iccir/downloads/SREC_07/Venansius%20Baryamureeba,_07.pdf

Basu, C. K., & Majumdar, S. (2009). The role of ICTs and TVET in rural development and poverty alleviation. In R. Maclean & D. Wilson (Eds.), International handbook of education for the changing world of work (pp. 1923-1934). Springer Science + Business Media BV.

Baumard, P. (1999). *Tacit Knowledge in Organisations*. Sage Publications Limited.

Beatty, I. (2004). Transforming student learning with classroom communication systems. *Educause Research Bulletin, 3*, 1–13.

Beck, R. J. (2008). *What are learning objects?* University of Wisconsin. Retrieved from http://www.uwm.Edu/Dept/CIE/AOP/LO

Beckman, T. (1998). *Designing Innovative Systems through Reengineering*. Paper presented at the 4th World Congress on Expert Systems. Mexico City, Mexico.

Beckman, T. J. (1999). The Current State of Knowledge Management. In *The Knowledge Management Handbook*. Boca Raton, FL: CRC Press.

Beebe, M. A. (2004). Impact of ICT Revolution on the African Academic Landscape. In *Proceedings of CODESRIA Conference on Electronic Publishing and Dissemination*. Retrieved September 20, 2013 from http://www.codesria.org/Links/conferences/el_publ/beebe.pdf

Beer, V. (2000). *The Web Learning Fieldbook: using the World Wide Web to build workplace learning Environments*. San Francisco, CA: Jossey-Bass.

Behrens, S. J. (1990). Literacy and the evolution towards information literacy: An exploratory study. *South African Journal of Library and Information Science, 58*(4), 355–365.

Beijerse, R. P. (2000). Knowledge Management in Small and Medium-sized companies: Knowledge management for entrepreneurs. *Journal of Knowledge Management, 4*(2), 162–182. doi:10.1108/13673270010372297

Bencisk, A., Lore, V., & Marosi, I. (2009). From Individual Memory to Organisational Memory: Intelligence of Organisations. *World Academy of Science. Engineering and Technology, 56*, 1–6.

Bennett, G., & Glasgow, R. (2009). The delivery of public health interventions via the internet: Actualizing their potential. *Annual Review of Public Health, 30*, 273–292. doi:10.1146/annurev.publhealth.031308.100235 PMID:19296777

Bernard, M. (2000). Constructing user-centered websites: The early design phases of small to medium sites. *Usability News 2*(1).

Berry, J. (2009). Technology support in nursing education: Clickers in the Classroom. *Nursing Education Perspectives, 30*(5), 295–298. doi:10.1043/1536-5026-30.5.295 PMID:19824239

Berson, M. J. (1996). Effectiveness of computer technology in the social studies: A review of the literature. *Journal of Research on Computing in Education, 28*, 486–499.

Beswick, W. (1972). *School resources centers*. London Evans/Methuen Educational.

Bicen, H., & Uzunboylu, H. (2013). The Use of Social Networking Sites in Education: A Case Study of Facebook. *Journal of Universal Computer Science, 19*(5), 658–671.

Biddle, W. W., & Biddle, L. J. (1965). *The community development process: The rediscovery of local initiatives*. Holt Rinehart and Winston Inc.

Biggam, J. (2008). *Succeeding With Your Masters Dissertation: A Step-by-Step Handbook*. The McGraw-Hill Companies.

Black, P., & Atkin, J. M. (Eds.). (1996). *Changing the Subject: Innovations in Science, Mathematics and Technology Education*. London: Routledge.

Bloom, B., Englehart, M., Furst, E., Hill, W., & Krathwohl, D. (1956). Taxonomy of educational objectives: The classification of educational goals. In I. Handbook (Ed.), *Cognitive domain*. New York: Longmans, Green.

Bojinova, E. D., & Oigara, J. N. (2011). Teaching and Learning with Clickers: Are Clickers Good for Students? *Interdisciplinary Journal of E-Learning and Learning Objects, 7*, 169–184.

Bosch, T. E. (2009). Using online social networking for teaching and learning: Facebook use at the University of Cape Town. *Communicatio, 35*(2), 185–200. doi:10.1080/02500160903250648

Boubsil, O., Carabajal, K., & Vidal, M. (2011). Implications of globalization for distance education in the United States. *American Journal of Distance Education, 25*(1), 5–20. doi:10.1080/08923647.2011.544604

Bouie, E. L. (1998). Creating an information rich environment. *Technological Horizons in Education, 26*(2), 78–79.

Boyd, D. M., & Ellison, N. B. (2007). Social network sites: Definition, history, and scholarship. *Journal of Computer-Mediated Communication, 13*(1), 210–230. doi:10.1111/j.1083-6101.2007.00393.x

Bransford, J., Brophy, S., & Williams, S. (2000). When computer technologies meet the learning sciences: Issues and opportunities. *Journal of Applied Developmental Psychology, 21*(1), 59–84. doi:10.1016/S0193-3973(99)00051-9

Bridges, E. M., & Reynolds, L. B. (1968). Teachers' Receptivity to Change. *Administrator's Notebook, 16*(6), 1–4.

Brock University. (n.d.). *James A. Gibson Library – Information literacy/library research skills policy*. Retrieved from http://www.brocku.ca/library/about-us-lib/policies/literacy-research-document

Brothen, T., & Wambach, C. (2001). Effective student use of computerized quizzes. *Teaching of Psychology, 28*(4), 292–294. doi:10.1207/S15328023TOP2804_10

Brown, S., & Mclntyre, D. (1982). Influences upon teachers' attitudes to different types of innovation: A study of Scottish integrated science. *Curriculum Inquiry, 12*(1), 35–51. doi:10.2307/1179745

Bruff, D. (2009). *Teaching with Classroom Response Systems: Creating Active Learning Environments*. San Francisco, CA: Jossey-Bass.

Butler, B. M., & Cuenca, A. (2009). Culturally responsible teaching: A pedagogical approach for the social studies classroom. In W. B. Russell III (Ed.), *The International Society for the Social Studies Annual Conference Proceedings*. Orlando, FL: The International Society for the Social Studies.

Butler, D., & Sellbom, M. (2002). *Barriers to adopting technology for teaching and learning*. Retrieved from http://cmapspublic3.ihmc.us/rid=1KC10V38V-C21P-MV-GG/Barriers%20To%20Technology.pdf

Byrom, E., & Bingham, M. (1999). *Factors influencing the effective use of technology for teaching and learning: Lessons learned from the SEIR*TEC intensive site schools*. Southeast and Islands Regional Technology in Education Consortium (SEIR*TEC).

Cain, J., & Policastri, A. (2011). Using Facebook as an informal learning environment. *American Journal of Pharmaceutical Education, 75*(10), 207. doi:10.5688/ajpe7510207 PMID:22345726

Caldwell, J. E. (2007). Clickers in the large classroom: Current research and best-practice tips. *Life Sciences Education, 6*(1), 9–20. doi:10.1187/cbe.06-12-0205 PMID:17339389

Calfery, C. C., & Alton, V. F. (1982). *Vocational Education: Concepts and Operations* (2nd ed.). Wadsworth Publishing Company Inc.

Cameron, R., & O'Hanlon-Rose, T.Cameron & O'Hanlon-Rose. (2011). Global Skills and Mobility Challenges and Possibilities for VET: A cross-border Cross-sectoral case Study. *International Journal of Training Research, 9*(1-2), 134–151. doi:10.5172/ijtr.9.1-2.134

Cartelli, A., Stanfield, M., Connolly, T., Jimoyiannis, A., Magalhaes, H., & Maillet, K. (2008). Towards the development of a new model for best practice and knowledge construction in virtual campuses. *Journal of Information Technology Education, 7*, 121–134.

Casey, K. (2012). *Risks Your BYOD Policy Must Address*. Information Week.

Cavas, B., Cavas, P., Karaoglan, B., & Kisla, T. (2009). *A study on science teachers' attitudes toward information and communication technologies in education.* Retrieved May 10, 2012 from http://www.tojet.net/articles/v8i2/822.pdf

Centers for Disease Control and Prevention. (2010). *Chronic diseases and health promotion.* Retrieved from www.cdc.gov/chronicdisease/overview/index.htm

Centers for Disease Control and Prevention. (2011). *Rising health care costs are unsustainable.* Retrieved from www.cdc.gov/workplacehealthpromotion/businesscase/reasons/rising.html

Central People's Government of the People's Republic of China. (2010). 国家中长期教育改革和发展规划纲要 *(2010-2020年).* [The National Medium and Long-Term Education Reform and Development Plan (2010-2020)]. Retrieved from http://www.gov.cn/jrzg/2010-07/29/content_1667143.htm

Chan, F. M. (2002). *ICT in Malaysian schools: Policy and strategies.* Retrieved from http://unpan1.un.org/intradoc/groups/public/documents/apcity/unpan011288.pdf

Chauhan, P. (2004). *ICT enabled library and information service journal of winter school on ICT enabled.* Academic Press.

Chen, C. (2007). Analysis of the knolwegde creation Process: An Organisational Change Perspective. *International Journal of Organization Theory and Behavior, 10*(3), 287–313.

Chen, J. C., Whittinghill, D. C., & Kadlowec, J. A. (2010). Classes that click: Fast, rich feedback to enhance students' learning and satisfaction. *Journal of Engineering Education, 99*(2), 158–169. doi:10.1002/j.2168-9830.2010.tb01052.x

Chen, S. J., Hsu, C. L., & Caropreso, E. J. (2006). Cross-cultural collaborative online learning: When the west meets the east. *International Journal of Technology in Teaching and Learning, 2*(1), 17–35.

Chickering, A. W., & Gamson, Z. F. (Eds.). (1991). *Applying the seven principles for good practice in undergraduate education.* San Francisco, CA: Jossey-Bass.

Chi, M. T. H., De Leeuw, N., Chiu, M., & Lavancher, C. (1994). Eliciting self explanations improves understanding. *Cognitive Science, 18,* 439–477.

China Internet Network Information Center. (2012). *CNNIC发布《第29次中国互联网络?展状?统?报告》.* [CNNIC announces the 29th Chinese Internet development report]. Retrieved from http://www.cnnic.net.cn/dtygg/dtgg/201201/t20120116_23667.html

China Internet Network Information Center. (2013). *CNNIC发布《第32次中国互联网络?展状?统?报告》.* [CNNIC announces the 32th Chinese Internet development report]. Retrieved from http://www.cnnic.net.cn/hlwfzyj/hlwxzbg/hlwtjbg/201307/t20130717_40664.htm

Chinnamma, S. (2005). Effects of globalisation on education and culture. In *Proceeding ICDE International Conference.* ICDE.

Chisenga, I. (2004). *ICT in libraries: An overview and general information to ICT in libraries in Africa.* Paper presented at INASO ICT Workshop. Johannesburg, South Africa.

Chou, C. (1998). Developing CLUE: A formative evaluation system for computer networks learning courseware. *Journal of Interactive Learning Research, 10*(2), 179–193.

Chou, C. (2000). Constructing a computer-assisted testing and evaluation system on the world wide web-The Cates experience. *IEEE Transactions on Education, 42*(1), 179–193.

Chou, C., & Lin, H. (1998). The Effect of Navigation Map Types and Cognitive Styles on Learners' Performance in a Computer-networked Hypertext Learning System. *Journal of Educational Multimedia and Hypermedia, 7*(2/3), 151–176.

Chou, C., & Sun, C. T. (1996). Constructing a Cooperative Distant Learning System: The CORAL experience. *Educational Technology Research and Development, 44*(4), 71–84. doi:10.1007/BF02299822

Chou, C., & Tsai, C. C. (2002). Developing web-based curricula: issues and challenges. *Journal of Curriculum Studies, 34*(6), 623–636. doi:10.1080/00220270210141909

Chou, C., & Tsal, H. F. (2001). Developing a networked VRML, learning system for health science education in Taiwan. *International Journal of Educational Development*, *21*(4), 293–303. doi:10.1016/S0738-0593(00)00003-1

Christensen, R. (2002). *Effects of Technology Integration Education on the Attitudes of Teachers and Students*. Retrieved from http://mytechtips.pbworks.com/f/Effects%20 of%20Technology%20Integration%20Education%20 on%20the%20Attitudes%20of%20Teachers%20and%20 Students%20(1).pdf

Chuang, S.-C., & Tsai, C.-C. (2005). Preferences toward the constructivist internet-based learning environments among high school students in Taiwan. *Computers in Human Behavior*, *21*(1), 255–272. doi:10.1016/j. chb.2004.02.015

Churches, A. (2009). Bloom's Digital Taxonomy v3.01. *Educational Origami*. Retrieved from http://edorigami. wikispaces.com/file/view/bloom%27s+Digital+taxono my+v3.01.pdf

CIConsulting. (2012). *2013-2017年中国网络教育行业 投资分析及前景预?报告*. [2013-2017 Chinese network education investment analysis and perspective report]. Retrieved from http://service.ocn.com.cn/rpts/fw/wan-gluojiaoyu.htm

Clarke, L., & Whitney, E. (2009). Walking in their shoes: Using multiple perspectives texts as a bridge to critical literacy. *The Reading Teacher*, *62*(6), 530–534. doi:10.1598/RT.62.6.7

Clark-Wilson, A., Oldknow, A., & Sutherland, R. (2011). *Digital technologies and mathematics education: A report from a working group of the Joint Mathematical Council of the United Kingdom*. London: Joint Mathematical Council.

Classmint. (2014). *Classmint Web Site*. Retrieved January 13, 2014, from http://classmint.com

Clinton, W. J. (1998, January 28). President Clinton's 1998 state of the union address. *The New York Times*, pp. A20-21.

Cobo, C. (2013). Exploration of open educational resources in Non-English speaking communities. *International Review of Research in Open and Distance Learning*, *14*(2), 107–128.

Cochrane, T., & Bateman, R. (2010). Smartphones give youwings: Pedagogical affordances of mobile Web 2.0. *Australasian Journal of Educational Technology*, *26*(1), 1–14.

Cognition and Technology Group at Vanderbilt. (1992). The Jasper experiment: An exploration of issues in learning and instructional design. *Educational Technology Research and Development*, *40*, 65–80. doi:10.1007/ BF02296707

Collins, J., Hammond, M., & Wellington, J. (1997). *Teaching and Learning with Multimedia*. London: Academic Press.

Common Core Standards Initiative. (2010). *Common core state standards for English language arts & literacy in history/social studies, science, and technical subjects*. Pennsylvania Department of Education.

Conklin, J. (1987). Hypertext: An introduction and survey. *Computer*, *20*(9), 17–41. doi:10.1109/MC.1987.1663693

Conrad, D. (2008). Building Knowledge through portfolio learning in prior learning assessment and recognition. *Quarterly Review of Distance Education, 9*(2), 139-150, 219.

Coonan, E. (2011). *A new curriculum for information literacy: transitional, transferable and transformational*. Cambridge University. Retrieved from www.cambridge. academia.edu

Council of Australian University Librarians (CAUL). (2001). *Information literacy standards*. Retrieved from http://www.caul.edu.au/caul-doc/InfoLitStandards2001. doc

Covey, S. (2004). *The eighth habit*. New York, NY: Free Press.

Coyle, S. (2012). Conquering the fear of technology. *Advance for Nurses*. Retrieved from http://nursing.ad-vanceweb.com/Features/Articles/Conguering-the-Fear-of-Technologv.aspx·

Craighead, G. (2009). *High-rise security and fire life safety*. Burlington, MA: Butterworth-Heinemann.

Creswell, J. W. (2008). *Educational research: Planning, conducting, and evaluating quantitative and qualitative research* (3rd ed.). Upper Saddle River, NJ: Pearson Education.

Crozier, W. R., & Hostettler, K. (2003). The influence of shyness on children's test performance. *The British Journal of Educational Psychology*, *73*(3), 317–328. doi:10.1348/000709903322275858 PMID:14672146

Cushner, K., & Mahon, J. (2009). Developing the intercultural competence of educators and their students: Creating the blueprints. In D. K. Deardoff (Ed.), *The SAGE handbook of intercultural competence*. Thousand Oaks, CA: SAGE.

Czerniewicz & Brown. (2006). Paper. In *Proceedings of Scan ICT 20005: Economic commission for Africa: Fourth Meeting of the Committee on Development Information*. Addis Ababa, Ethiopia: Scan ICT.

Dahlman, C., Zeng, D., & Wang, S. (2007). *Enhancing China's Competitiveness through Lifelong Learning*. Retrieved from http://web.worldbank.org/WBSITE/EXTERNAL/WBI/WBIPROGRAMS/KFDLP/0,contentMDK:21387573~menuPK:1727232~pagePK:64156158~piPK:64152884~theSitePK:461198,00.html

Damoense, M. Y. (2003). Online learning for higher education in South Africa. *Australian Journal of Educational Technology*, *19*(1), 25–45.

Daniel, D. B. (2006). *Do teachers still need to teach? Textbook-related pedagogy and student learning preferences*. Paper presented at the Teaching of Psychology Preconference of the Annual Convention of the Association for Psychological Science. New York, NY.

Daniel, J., Friedman, R., Gibson, P., & David, A. (2013). Electronic health records and US Public Health: Current realities and future Promise. *American Journal of Public Health*, *103*(9), 1560–1567. doi:10.2105/AJPH.2013.301220 PMID:23865646

Danko, A. I. (2006). *Entrepreneurship Education for Vocational and Technical Education Students* (2nd ed.). Academic Press.

Davenport, T., & Prusak, L. (1998). *Working Knowledge: How Organizations Manage What They Know*. Harvard Business School Press.

David, K. M., & John, M. B. (2012). The challenges of using information communication technology (ICT) in school administration in Kenya. *Journal of Research on computing in Education, 3*, 479-495.

Davis-Case, D. (1989). *Community forestry: Participatory assessment, monitoring and evaluation*. Rome: FAO.

Dearing, R. (1997). *National Committee of Inquiring into Higher Education*. Retrieved from http://.www.leeds.ac.uk/educol/ncihe/

Dellit, J. (2002). Using ICT for quality in teaching-learning evaluation processes. In *UNESCO Using ICT for quality teaching, learning and effective management*. Retrieved May 10, 2012 from http://www. unesdoc.unesco.org/images/0012/001285/128513eo.pdf

Deng, X., & Kong, L. (2011). 广播电视大学的战略转型. [The strategic transformation of radio and TV universities]. *Distance Education in China, 8*.

Diame, Heller, & Mahmoud. (1991). American and Soviet Children's Attitude towards Computer. *Journal of Educational Computing Research*, *8*(2), 155–185.

Diller, K. R., & Phelps, S. F. (2008). Learning outcomes, portfolios, and rubrics, oh my! Authentic assessment of an information literacy program. *Portal: Libraries and the Academy*, *8*(1), 75–89. doi:10.1353/pla.2008.0000

DiMarco, J. (2007). Web Portfolio Design for Teachers and Professors. In *Proceedings of the 2007 Information resources management Association International Conference*. IGI Global.

DiMarco, J. (2006). *Web Portfolio Design and Applications*. IGI Global.

DiMarco, J. (2012). Implementing a Website Portal using Portfolio Village to evaluate Professional Credentials. In *Technology Integration and Foundations for effective Technology Leadership*. Hershey, PA: Idea Group. doi:10.4018/978-1-4666-2656-0.ch018

DiMarco, J. (2013). *Career Power Skills*. New York: Pearson.

Dockstader, J. (1999). Teachers of the 21st century know the what, why, and how of technology integration. *Technological Horizons in Education*, *26*(6), 73–74.

Draves, W. A. (2000). *Teaching Online*. River Falls, WI: LEARN Books.

Drestke, K. (1981). *Knowledge and the Flow of Information*. MIT Press.

Dubose, C. (2011). The social media revolution. *Radiologic Technology, 83*(2), 112–119. PMID:22106386

Duffy, T. M., & Cunningham, D. J. (1996). Constructivism: Implications for the design and delivery of instruction. In D. H. Jonassen (Ed.), *Handbook of research for educational communications and technology*. New York: Macmillan.

Dunbar, R. (1991). Adapting distance education for Indonesians: Problems with learner heteronomy and a strong oral tradition. *Distance Education, 12*(2), 163–174. doi:10.1080/0158791910120203

Duncan, D. (2005). *Clickers in the classroom: How to enhance science teaching using classroom response systems*. San Francisco, CA: Pearson Education/Addison-Wesley/Benjamin Cummings.

Educause (2006). Seven Things you should know about Facebook. *Educause learning initiative*. Retrieved September 22, 2013 fromhttp://net.educause.edu/ir/library/pdf/ELI7017.pdf

Eftekharzadeh, R. (2008). *Knowledge Management Implementation in Developing Countries: An Experimental Study*. St John's University.

Eisenstein, E. L. (1980). *The Printing Press as an Agent of Change*. Cambridge, UK: Cambridge University Press. doi:10.1017/CBO9781107049963

Ekong, E. E. (1989). *An introduction to rural sociology*. Ibadan: Jumak Publication.

Elizojie, P. O. (1989). The use of A-V and other aids in the teaching of English. In Handbook for junior secondary school language teachers. Lagos: NERDC.

Encarta. (2009). *Prospect*. World English Dictionary (North America Ed.). Retrieved January, 2010, from http://encarta.msu.com/

ePals. (2013). *Epals global community*. Retrieved from http://www.epals.com/#!/global-community/

Ertl, H., & Kai, Y. (2010). The discourse on equality and equity in Chinese higher education. *Chinese Education & Society, 43*(6), 3–14. doi:10.2753/CED1061-1932430600

Erumban, A. A., & Jong, S. B. (2003). *Cross-country differences in ICT adoption - A consequence of culture?* Retrieved from http://som.rug.nl

Esiobu, G. O. (2005). Gender issues in science and technology educational development. In Science and technology education for development, (pp. 137-156). Lagos: NERDC.

Eubanks, V. (2011). *Digital dead end—Fighting for social justice in the information age*. Cambridge, MA: The MIT Press.

F.R.N. (2004). *National Policy on Education* (4th ed.). Lagos: NERDC Press.

Facer, K., Furlong, J., Furlong, R., & Sutherland, R. (2001). *Screenplay: Children and computing in the home*. London: RoutledgeFalmer.

Fadeiye, J.O. (2001). *Social studies for NCE*. Oyo: Immaculate-City Publisher.

Fadzliaton, Z., & Kamarulzaman, I. (2010). *Measuring Malaysia school resource centers standards through IQ-PSS: An online management information system*. Academic Press.

Familoni, O. (2013). *Science education can solve our problems*. The Punch Newspaper.

Fang, B. (2009). From Distraction to Engagement: Wireless Devices in the Classroom. *EDUCAUSE Quarterly, 32*(4), 12–18.

Faniran, J. (2010). Paul's Communication Strategies: A challenge to Agents of Evangelisation in the Third Millennium. In CATHAN: A searchlight on Saint Paul (pp. 162-176). Makurdi: Aboki.

Faniran, A., Odugbemi, O. O., & Oyesiku, O. O. (1987). *Rural development in Ogun State*. Department of Geography and Regional Planning.

Fassinger, P. A. (1995). Professors' and students' perceptions of why students participate in class. *Teaching Sociology, 24*(1), 25–33. doi:10.2307/1318895

Federal Government of Nigeria (FGN). (2000). *Nigerian national policy for information and communication technology.* Retrieved May 10, 2012 from http://www.www. uneca.org/aisi/nici/.../it%20policy%20for%20nigeria.pdf

Federal Ministry of Education (FME). (1988). *Report on national policy on computer education.* Lagos: Author.

Federal Ministry of Education. (2000). *Technical and Vocational Education Development in Nigeria in the 21ˢᵗ century with the blue-print for the decade 2001-2010.* Federal Ministry of Education.

Federal Republic of Nigeria (FRN). (2004). National policy on education (4th Ed.). Lagos: NERDC Press.

Feng, L. (2010). 远程教育资源库?源共享服务研究. [A study of the sharing of information from distance education resource banks]. *Contemporary Distance. Education Research, 2,* 48–52.

Forawi, S. A., & Liang, X. (2005). Science electronic portfolios: Developing and validating the scoring rubric. *Journal of Science Education, 6*(2), 97–99.

Fox, S. (2012). *Pew Internet: Health. In Pew Internet & American Life Project.* Retrieved from www.pewinternet. org/Commentary/2011/November/Pew-Internet-Health. aspx

French, D., Hale, C., Johnson, C., & Farr, G. (Eds.). (1999). Internet Based Learning: An Introduction and Framework for Higher Education and Business. Sterling, VA: stylus.

Friedman, T. L. (2005). *The world is flat: A brief history of the twenty-first century.* New York: Farrar, Straus, & Giroux.

Friend, J. (1989). *Interactive radio instruction developing instructional methods.* Academic Press.

Fuchs, C., & Horak, E. (2006). *Informational capitalism and the digital divide in Africa.* Retrieved from http:// storage02.video.muni.cz/prf/mujlt/storage/1205244869_ sb_s02-fuchs.pdf

Gamble, P. R., & Blackwell, J. (2001). *Knowledge Management: A State of the Art Guide.* Biddles Ltd.

García, M. R., Rey, I. G., Ferreira, P. B., & Puerto, G. D. (2007). *University 2.0 - How well are teachers and students prepared for Web 2.0 best practices.* Paper presented at MICTE 2009. Lisbon, Portugal.

Garrison & Anderson. (2003). [*ˢᵗ century: A framework for research and practice.* Routledge.]. *E-learning, 21.*

Gaudron, J.-P., & Vignoli, E. (2002). Assessing computer anxiety with the interaction model of anxiety: Development and validation of the computer anxiety trait subscale. *Computers in Human Behavior, 18*(3), 315–325. doi:10.1016/S0747-5632(01)00039-5

Gay, L., Mills, G., & Gall, J. (2006). *Educational research: Competencies for analysis and application* (9th ed.). Upper Saddle River, NJ: Prentice Hall.

Genç, Ö. (2004). *Uzaktan Eğitimde Alternatif Yaklaşımlar, Bilişim Teknolojileri Işığında Eğitim Kongresi ve Sergisi.* Bildiriler Kitabı.

Glenn, A. D. (1997). Technology and the continuing education of classroom teachers. *Peabody Journal of Education, 72*(1), 122–128. doi:10.1207/s15327930pje7201_6

Glik, D. (2007). Risk communication for public health emergencies. *Annual Review of Public Health, 28,* 33–54. doi:10.1146/annurev.publhealth.28.021406.144123 PMID:17222081

Global Information Technology Report. (2004). *The Networked Readiness Index Rankings 2005.* Author.

Global Voices Online. (2013). *Global Voices.* Retrieved from http://globalvoicesonline.org/

Glynn, L., Murphy, A., Smith, S., Schroeder, K., & Fahey, T. (2010). Interventions used to improve control of blood pressure in patients with hypertension. *Cochrane Database System, 3,* CD005182. PMID:20238338

Goatman, C. (2011, September 26). *How using social media can help you with your online college classes.* Retrieved from http://soshable.com/how-using-social-media-can-help-you-with-your-online-college-classes

Golder, S. A., Wilkinson, D., & Huberman, B. A. (2007). *Rhythms of social interaction: Messaging within a massive online network.* Paper presented at the 3rd International Conference on Communities and Technologies (CT2007). Academic Press.

Goldsby, D., & Fazal, M. (2001). Web-Based Portfolios for Technology Education: A Personal Case Study. *Journal of Technology and Teacher Education*, *9*(4), 606–607.

Gordon, J. R. (1993). *A Diagnostic Approach to Organisational Behaviour* (4th ed.). Simon & Schuster, Inc.

Gore, V. (2013). The importance of cross-cultural communication. *The IUP Journal of Soft Skills*, *7*(1), 59–65.

Greenberg, G. (2004). The digital convergence: Extending the portfolio. *EDUCAUSE Review*, *39*(4), 28.

Greenhow, C., Robelia, B., & Hughes, J. E. (2009). Learning, teaching, and scholarship in a digital age: Web 2.0 and classroom research: What path should we take now? *Educational Researcher*, *38*(4), 246–259. doi:10.3102/0013189X09336671

Gundykunst, W. B. (2003). Forward. In W. B. Gundykunst (Ed.), *Cross cultural and intercultural communication* (pp. vii–ix). Thousand Oaks, CA: Sage.

Gupter, J. N. D., & Sharma, S. K. (2004). *Creating Knowledge Based Organizations*. Idea Group Inc.

Gurteen, D. (1999). Creating a Knowledge Sharing Culture. *Knowledge Management Magazine*, *2*(5).

Haddad, W. D., & Jurich, S. (n.d.). *ICT for education: Potential and potency*. Retrieved September 20, 2013 from http://cbdd.wsu.edu/edev/Nigeria_ToT/tr510/documents/ICTforeducation_potential.pdf

Haggie, K., & Kingston, J. (2003). Choosing you Knowledge Management Strategy. *Journal of Knowledge Management Practice*.

Handler, M. G. (1993). Preparing new teachers to use computer technology: Perceptions and suggestions for teacher educators. *Computers & Education*, *20*(2), 147–156. doi:10.1016/0360-1315(93)90082-T

Han, J. H., & Finkelstein, A. (2013). Understanding the effects of instructors' pedagogical development with Clicker Assessment and Feedback technologies and the impact on students' engagement and learning in higher education. *Computers & Education*, *65*, 64–76. doi:10.1016/j.compedu.2013.02.002

Harrison, N., & Bergen, C. (2000). Some design strategies for developing an online course. *Educational Technology*, *40*(91), 57–60.

Hedberg, J. G. (2011). Towards a disruptive pedagogy: Changing classroom practice with technologies and digital content. *Educational Media International*, *48*(1), 1–16. doi:10.1080/09523987.2011.549673

Helmi, A. (2002). An analysis on the impetus of online education Curtin University of Technology, Western Australia. *The Internet and Higher Education*, *4*(3-4), 243–253. doi:10.1016/S1096-7516(01)00070-7

Heward, W. L. (1994). Three low-tech strategies for increasing the frequency of active student response during group instruction. In *Behavior analysis in education: Focus on measurably superior instruction*. Pacific Grove, CA: Brooks/Cole.

Hodgkinson-Williams, C., Willmers, M., & Gray, E. (2009). *International environmental scan of the use of ICTs for teaching and learning in higher education*. Centre of Educational Technology, University of Cape Town. Retrieved from http://www.cet.uct.ac.za/files/file/OS%20PositionPaper3%20_%20%20Final%20typeset.pdf

Hoffler, E. (2000). *Equity research*. WR Hambrecht & Co. Retrieved from http://www.wrhambrecht.com/research/coverage/elearning/ir/ir_explore.pdf

Hoffman, E. (2009). Social media and learning environments: Shifting perspectives on the locus of control. *Education*, *15*(2).

Holahan, P. J., Aronson, Z. H., Jurkat, M. P., & Schoorman, F. D. (2004). *Implementing Computer Technology: A multiorganizational test of Klein and Sorra's model*. Academic Press.

Hollander, A., & Mar, N. Y. (2009). Towards achieving TVET for All. In R. Maclean, & D. Wilson (Eds.), *International handbook of education for the changing world of work. Springer Science + Business Media BV*. doi:10.1007/978-1-4020-5281-1_3

Homer, B., Plass, J., & Blake, L. (2008). The effects of video on cognitive load and social presence in multimedia learning. *Computers in Human Behavior*, *24*(3), 786–797. http://doi.org/c45wb6 doi:10.1016/j.chb.2007.02.009

Homme, J., Asay, G., & Morgenstern, B. (2004). Utilisation of an audience response system. *Medical Education, 38*(5), 575. doi:10.1111/j.1365-2929.2004.01888.x PMID:15107128

Honebein, P. C. (1996). Seven goals for the design of constructivist learning environments. In B. G. Wilson (Ed.), *Constructivist learning environments: Case studies in instructional design.* Englewood Cliffs, NJ: Educational Technology Publications.

Hooker, M. (1997). The transformation of higher education. In D. Oblinger, & S. C. Rush (Eds.), *The Learning Revolution.* Bolton, MA: Anker Publishing Company, Inc.

Hron, A., & Friedrich, H. F. (2003). A review of web-based collaborative learning: Factors beyond technology. *Journal of Computer Assisted Learning, 19*(1), 70–79. doi:10.1046/j.0266-4909.2002.00007.x

Huang, W. D., & Nakazawa, K. (2010). An empirical analysis of how learners interact in wiki in a graduate level online course. *Interactive Learning Environments, 18*(3), 233–244. doi:10.1080/10494820.2010.500520

Huang, X., & Jiang, H. (2011). 论开放大学的法律地位及其办?自主权的法律保障. [On judicially safeguarding open universities' legal status and their autonomy]. *Contemporary Distance. Education Research, 2,* 3–8.

Hu, X., & Bian, J. (2010). 信息化进程中教育资源配置的区域性差异研究. [A study of the regional differences in the distribution of educational information and communication technology resources]. *Journal of Distance Education, 3,* 64–68.

Igbozurike, M. (1976). *Problem-generating structures in Nigeria's rural development.* Bohuslaningens, AB: Uddevalta.

Igwe, K. N., & Esimokha, G. A. (2012). A survey of the information literacy skills of students in Federal Polytechnic Offa, Kwara State, Nigeria. *The Information Technologist: An International Journal of Information and Communication Technology, 9*(2), 9–19.

Ijaduola, K. O. (1997). *Psychology of Learning Made Easy. Ijebu-Ode: Lucky Odoni, Nig.* Enterprise.

Ilogho, J. E., & Nkiko, C. (2014). Information literacy and search skills of students in five private universities in Ogun State, Nigeria. *Library Philosophy and Practice (ejournal).* Retrieved from http://digitalcommon.unl.edu/libphilprac/1040

Imhoof, K. (1985). *Interactive radio in the classroom.* Academic Press.

Innis, H. A. (2008). *The bias of communication* (2nd ed.). Toronto, Canada: University of Toronto Press.

International Reading Association and National Council of Teachers of English. (1996). Standards for the English language arts.[International Reading Association and National Council of Teachers of English.]. *Urbana (Caracas, Venezuela),* IL.

Islam, M. S., & Islam, M. N. (2006). Information and Communication Technology in Libraries: A. New Dimension in Librarianship. *Asian Journal of Information Technology, 5*(8), 609–617.

Isman, A., Yaratan, H., & Caner, H. (2007). *How technology is integrated into Science Education in a Developing Country: North Cyprus Case.* Retrieved May 10, 2012 from http://www.tojet.net/volumes/v6I3.pdf

Issa, A. O., Amusan, B., & Daura, U. D. (2009). Effects of information literacy skills on the use of e-library resources among students of University of Ilorin, Kwara State, Nigeria. *Library Philosophy and Practice.* Retrieved from http://www.unlib.unl.edu/LPP/issa-amusan-daura

Ives, B., & Learmonth, G. (1984). The information system as a competitive weapon. *Communications of the ACM, 27*(12), 1193–1201. doi:10.1145/2135.2137

JAMB. (2006/2007). *Joint Admissions and Matriculation Board: Polytechnics, and Colleges of Education and the programs / courses offered.* Retrieved September 20, 2013 from http://www.jambng.com/pce_institution1.php

James, Bangert, & Williams. (1983). Effect of Computer–Based Teaching on Secondary School Students. *Journal of Educational Psychology, 75,* 19–26. doi:10.1037/0022-0663.75.1.19

Jegede, O. J. (2002). Facilitating and sustaining interest through an on-line distance peer-tutoring system in a cooperative learning environment. *Virtual University Gazette,* 35-45.

Jenks, C. (1998). *Core sociological dichotomies*. London: Sage.

Jewell, V. (2006). Continuing the classroom community: Suggestions for using online discussion boards. *National Council of Teachers of English, 94*(4), 98-87.

Jhurree, V. (2005). Technology integration in education in developing countries: Guidelines to policy makers. *International Education Journal, 6*(4), 467–483.

Jinba, D. N. (2003). Teacher Education and Globalization: Some critical challenges. In Globalization and Education in Nigeria (pp. 74-80). Philosophy of Education Association of Nigeria.

JISC. (1950). *Explaining Information System in Higher Education*. Retrieved from http://info.mccuk/Nti/JISC-issues.htm

Johnson, B., & McClure, R. (2004). Validity and Reliability of a Shortened, Revised Version of the Constructivist Learning Environment Survey (CLES). *Learning Environments Research, 7*(1), 65–80. doi:10.1023/B:LERI.0000022279.89075.9f

Johnson, J. P., & Lenartowicz, T. (1998). Culture, freedom and economic growth: Do cultural values explain economic growth? *Journal of World Business, 33*, 332–356. doi:10.1016/S1090-9516(99)80079-0

Jonassen, D. H. (2011). Learning to solve to solve troubleshoot problems. *Performance Improvement, 42*(4), 34–38. doi:10.1002/pfi.4930420408

Jonassen, D. H. (in press). *Problem solving: the enterprise*. Mahwah, NJ. *Lawrence Eribaun Associates*.

Jones, J. (2009). *Research Methodology: Questionnaire Design and Interviewing Skills*. Warwick Manufacturing Group.

Jones, S. G. (1997). The Internet and its social Landscape. In S. G. Jones (Ed.), *Virtual culture: Identity and communication in Cyber Society* (pp. 7–35). London: Sage.

Jorgenson, Ho, & Stiroh. (2007). *A retrospective look at the U.S. productivity growth resurgence*. Retrieved from http://www.newyorkfed.org/research/staff_reports/sr277.pdf

Joseph, A. (2006, April 21). Nigeria places 90th of 115th Countries in IT ratings. *The Punch*, 3.

Joseph, W. A., & Ralph, O. S. (1977). *Course construction in industrial arts, vocational and technical* (4th ed.). American Technical Publisher, Inc.

Jude, W. I., & Dankaro, J T. (2012). ICT resource utilization, availability and accessibility by teacher educators for instructional development in college of education Katsina-Ala. *New Media and Mass Communication, 3*.

Judson, E., & Sawada, D. (2002). Learning from past and present: Electronic response system in college lecture halls. *Journal of Computers in Mathematics and Science Teaching, 21*(2), 167–181.

Jyothi, P., & Venkatesh, D. N. (2006). *Human Resource Management*. Oxford University Press.

Kahn, J., Yang, J., & Kahn, J. (2010). Mobile health needs and opportunities in developing countries. *Health Affairs, 29*(2), 254–261. doi:10.1377/hlthaff.2009.0965 PMID:20348069

Kaleta, R., & Joosten, T. (2007). Student response systems: A university of Wisconsin system study of clickers. *Educause Research Bulletin*, (10), 1-12.

Kalusi, J. I. (2001). Teachers' quality in Nigeria. *Nigerian Journal of Educational Philosophy, 8*(2), 62–72.

Kaplan, B. (2007). *Creating Long-Term Value as Chief Knowledge Officer: Key Attributes, Messages and Ambitions for Success-Seeking CKOs*. KM Review.

Kaplan-Leiserson, E. (2000). *Glossary*. Alexandria, VA: American Society for Training and Development. Retrieved from http://www.learningcircuits.org/glossary.html

Karrer, T. (2007). *Understanding e-learning*. Retrieved from http://www learning circuit.org/2007/0707 karrer.html

Katz, E. H., Dalton, S., & Giaquinta, J. B. (1994). Status risk taking and receptivity of home economics teachers to a state wide curriculum innovation. *Home Economics Research Journal, 22*(4), 401–421. doi:10.1177/0046777494224003

Kaur, P., Sohal, M. K., & Walia, P. K. (2009). *Information literacy curriculum for undergraduate students*. Paper Presented at the International Conference of Academic Libraries. Delhi, India.

Kautto-Koivula, K. (1993). *Degree-Oriented Professional Adult Education in the Work Environment: A Case Study of the Mian Determinants in the management of a Long-term Technology Education Process.* (Unpublished PhD Dissertation). University of Tampere, Tampere, Finland.

Kautto-Koivula, K. (1996). Degree-Oriented Adult Education in the Work Environment. In Professional Growth and Development: Direction, Delivery and Dilemmas. Career Education Books.

Kaya, N. (2004). Sezgilerimiz ve Takıntılarımız. *Sistem Yayıncılık, 2.*

Kearsley, G. (2002). *Online Education: Learning and Teaching in Cyberspace.* Toronto, Canada: Wadsworth.

Keller, C., et al. (2007). *Research-based Practices for Effective Clicker Use.* Paper presented at Physics Education Research Conference. New York, NY.

Kelm, O. R. (2011). Social media: It's what students do. *Business Communication Quarterly, 74*(4), 505–520. doi:10.1177/1080569911423960

Kent, N., & Facer, K. (2004). Different worlds? A comparison of young people's home and school ICT use. *Journal of Computer Assisted Learning, 20*(6), 440–455. doi:10.1111/j.1365-2729.2004.00102.x

Keskin, H. (2005). The relationships between explicit and tacit oriented KM strategy and firm performance. *Journal of American Academy of Business, 7*(1), 169–173.

Kidblog. (2012). *Why kidblog.* Retrieved from http://kidblog.org/why-kidblog/

Kirkwood, A. (2009). E-learning: You don't always get what you hope for. *Technology, Pedagogy and Education, 18*(2), 107–121. doi:10.1080/14759390902992576

Kist, W. (2013). *The global school: Connecting classrooms and students around the world.* Bloomington, IN: Solution Tree Press.

Kling, R., & Jonathan, P. (1993). *How the marriage of management and computing intensifies the struggle for personal privacy.* Retrieved from http://glotta.ntua.gr/IS-Social/KlingInfoCapitalism.html

Knight, J. K., & Wood, W. B. (2005). Teaching more by lecturing less. *Cell Biology Education, 4*(4), 298–310. doi:10.1187/05-06-0082 PMID:16341257

Knowles, M. S. (1980). *The modern practice of adult education: From pedagogy to andragogy. Englewood Cliffs, NJ.* Cambridge: Prentice Hall.

Koçer, H. E. (2001). *Web Tabanlı Uzaktan Eğitim, Yayınlanmış Yüksek lisans Tezi, Selçuk Üniversitesi, Fen bilimleri Enstitüsü*, Konya.

Kotsik, B., & Rosenueng. (2009). ICT application in TVET. In R. Maclean & D. Wilson (Eds.), *International handbook of education for the changing world of work.* Springer Science + Business Media BV.

Kotsik, B. (2009). ICT application in TVET. In R. Maclean, & D. Wilson (Eds.), *International handbook of education for the changing world of work. Springer Science + Business Media BV.* doi:10.1007/978-1-4020-5281-1_127

Kreie, J., & Cronan, T. P. (2000). Making Ethical Decisions: How Companies might influence the Choices one Makes. *Communications of the Association for Computing, 43*(12), 66–71.

Krubu, D., & Osawaru, K. (2011). *The impact of information communication Technology (ICT) in Nigeria library and information services.* Tietpatiala.

Kumar, K. (2008). Virtual design studios: Solving learning problems in developing countries. In S. Hirtz, D. G. Harper & S. Mackenzie (Eds.), *Education for a Digital World: Advice, Guidelines, and Effective Practice From Around the Globe* (pp. 23 – 30). BCC and Commonwealth of Learning. Retrieved from http://creativecommons.org

Lai, K.-W. (2011). Digital technology and the culture of teaching and learning in higher education. *Australasian Journal of Educational Technology, 27*(8), 1263–1275.

Larose, F., David, R., Dirand, J., Karsenti, T., Vincent Grenon, V., Lafrance, S., & Cantin, J. (1999). Information and Communication Technologies in University Teaching and in Teacher Education: Journey in a Major Québec University's Reality. *Electronic Journal of Sociology.* Retrieved September 20, 2013 from http://www.sociology.org/content/vol004.003/francois.html

Latchem. (2005). Article. In *Proceedings of Scan ICT 20005: Economic commission for Africa: Fourth Meeting of the Committee on Development Information*. Addis Ababa. Ethiopia: Scan ICT.

Laudon, K. C., Laudon, J. P., & Brabston, M. E. (2012). *Management information systems: Managing the digital firm* (Vol. 12). Pearson.

Laurilland, D. (2005). *How Can Learning Technologies Improve Learning?* Retrieved from http://www.law.warwick.ac.uk/ltj/3-2j.htm

Lavenne, F., Renard, V., & Tollet, F. (2005). Fiction Between Inner Life and Collective Memory: A Methodological Reflection. *New Acardia Review*, *3*, 1–11.

Lawal, H. S. (2003). Teacher Education and the Professional Growth of the 21st Century Nigeria Teacher. *The African Symposium, 3*(2).

Leach, J. (2005). Do new information and communication technologies have a role to play in achieving quality professional development for teachers in the globe south? *Curriculum Journal*, *16*(3), 293–329. doi:10.1080/09585170500256495

Learsk, M., Lee, C., Milner, T., Norton, M., & Rathod, D. (2008). *Knowledge Management Tools and Techniques: Helping you Access the Right Knowledge at the Right Time*. Improvement and Development Agency for Local Government.

Lei, S., & Govra, K. (2010). College Distance Education Courses: Evaluating Benefits and Cost from Institutional, Faculty and Students'. *Perspectives in Education*, *130*(4), 616–631.

Lenhart, A. (2009). *Teens and mobile phones over the past five years: Pew Internet looks back*. Washington, DC: Pew Internet.

Leonard-Barton, D. (1995). *Wellsprings of Knowledge: Building and Sustaining the Sources of Innovation*. Boston, MA: Harvard Business School Press.

Leslie, S., & Landon, B. (2008). *Social software for learning: What is it, why use it?* The Observatory.

Levesque, C. (1979). *Learning: The paradigm shift*. Paris: UNESCO.

Levin, J. S. (2001). *Globalizing the community college: Strategies for change in the 21st century*. New York: Palgrave Books. doi:10.1057/9780312292836

Li, Y. (2011). 开放大学国际合作模式探究. [An exploration of international cooperation among open universities]. *Distance Education in China, 11.*

Liang, Z., Ran, L., & Wan, S. (2013). 远程教育综合型网络?程开?. [Development of combined network courses in distance education]. *Distance Education in China, 7.*

Liao, J., Tan, G., & Zhu, X. (2008). 我国大学教育国际化的路径?择. [The approach we should adopt in internationalizing our higher education]. *Chinese. Higher Education, 1.*

Li, B. (2011). 我国远程高等教育质量保证活动?行主体研究. [A study of the implementers of Chinese distance higher education quality assurance policies]. *Contemporary Distance. Education Research*, *3*, 30–34.

Liebowitz, J. (2002). Knowledge management and its link to artificial intelligence. *Expert Systems with Applications*, *20*(1), 1–6. doi:10.1016/S0957-4174(00)00044-0

Lin, H. (2007). Knowledge Sharing and Firm Innovation Capability: An Empirical Study. *International Journal of Manpower*, *28*(3/4), 315–332. doi:10.1108/01437720710755272

Liu, C. (2011). 新一轮教育改革与远程开放教育的发展（五）. [New education reform and the development of distance open education (5)]. *Distance Education in China, 3.*

Liu, H., & Zhang, X. (2010). 社会认可:远程教育质量外因分析. [Social recognition: An analysis of external quality factors in distance education]. *Contemporary. Distance Education*, *6*, 22–24.

Li, Y., Chen, H., & Han, Y. (2010). 为什么辍学. [Why do they withdraw from their programs?]. *Open. Education Research*, *4*, 71–75.

Liyanage, C., Elhag, T., Ballal, T., & Li, Q. (2009). Knowledge communication and translation - A knowledge transfer model. *Journal of Knowledge Management*, *13*(3), 118–131. doi:10.1108/13673270910962914

Louw, J., Brown, C., Muller, J., & Soudien, C. (2009). Instructional technologies in social science in South Africa. *Comput. Educ., 53*, 234 242.

Lu, P. (2013, July 1). 高考：今年不再炒状元. [Higher education entry examination: No more fuss about the first place]. People's Daily Overseas Ed., p. 4.

Mac-Ikemenjima, D. (2005). *e-Education in Nigeria: Challenges and Prospects*. Paper presentation at the 8th UN ICT Task Force Meeting. Dublin, Ireland.

Maczewski, M. (2003). *Research Methodologies*. Retrieved from http://webhome.cs.uvic.ca/~mstorey/teaching/infovis/course_notes/researchmethods.pdf

Maduekwe, A. N. (2007). *Principles and Practice of Teaching English as a Secondary Language*. Lagos: Vitamins Educational Books.

Magarick, R. H., & Galbracth, C. (1988). *The teaching of production of materials by computer assisted learning system and interactive video disc technology*. Academic Press.

Ma, H. (2013, September13). *45* [It is estimated that this year over 450,000 will go overseas for education]. (p. 6). People's Daily Overseas Ed.

Malcolm, W. (1995). *Globalization*. London: Routledge.

Malhan, I. V., & Gulati, A. (2003). *Knowledge Management Problems of Developing Countries, with Special Reference to India*. SAGE Publications.

Maliki, A. E., Ngban, A. N., & Ibu, J. E. (2009). *Analysis of students' performance in junior secondary school mathematics examination in Bayelsa State of Nigeria*. Retrieved may 10, 2012 from http://www.krepublishers.com/.../HCS-03-2-149-09-Index.pdf

Manasco, B. (1996). Leading Firms Develop Knowledge Strategies. *Journal of Knowledge Management Practice, 1*(6), 1–29.

Marcus, A., & Gould, E. (2000). Cultural dimensions and global web user-interface design: What? So what? Now what? In *Proceedings of the 6th Conference on Human Factors and the Web* (pp. 1–15). Austin, TX: Academic Press.

Marling, L. (2004). *Knowledge Management: People, Process and Technology*. Retrieved from http://www.cutter.com/content/itjournal/fulltext/2004/12/itj0412b.html

Marriott, N., & Marriott, P. (2003). Student learning style preferences and undergraduate academic performance at two UK universities. *International Journal of Management Education, 3*(1), 4–13.

Martins, J. L. (2013). *Learning from recent British information literacy models: A report to ACRL's information literacy competency standards for higher education task force*. Retrieved from www.mavdisk.mnsu.edu/martij2/acrl.pdf

Masalela, R. K. (2012). *Implementing e-Learning at the University of Botswana: The practioner's perspective*. Retrieved from www.westga.edu/.../Masalela_142.html

Massoud, S. L. (1991). Computer attitudes and computer knowledge of adult students. *Journal of Educational Computing Research, 7*(3), 269–291. doi:10.2190/HRRV-8EQV-U2TQ-C69G

Matrix-Controls. (2009). *Facility booking system (FBS)*. Retrieved from http://www.matrix-controls.com/cms/index.php?page=content/products

Mavers, D. (2005). *ICT Test Bed Evaluation*. Retrieved from http://www.evaluation.icttestbed.org.uk/

Mayer, R. E., Stull, A., DeLeeuw, K., Almeroth, K., Bimber, B., & Chun, D. et al. (2009). Clickers in college classrooms: Fostering learning with questioning methods in large lecture classes. *Contemporary Educational Psychology, 34*(1), 51–57. doi:10.1016/j.cedpsych.2008.04.002

Mc Daniel, E., Melnerney, W., & Armstrong, P. (1993). Computer and School. *Reform Educational Technology Research and Development, 4*(91), 73–78. doi:10.1007/BF02297093

McAdam, R., & McCreedy, S. (2000). A Critique of Knowledge Management: Using a Social Constructionist Model. *New Technology, Work and Employment, 15*(2), 155–168. doi:10.1111/1468-005X.00071

McFarland, F. W. (1984). Information technology changes the way you compete. *Harvard Business Review, 62*(3), 98–103.

McInnerney, J., & Robert, T. S. (2004). Collaborative or cooperative learning. In T. S. Roberts (Ed.), *Online collaborative learning: Theory and practice* (pp. 203–214). Hershey, PA: Information Science Publishing.

McKeachie, W. (1990). Research on college teaching: The historical background. *Journal of Educational Psychology*, *82*(2), 190–200. doi:10.1037/0022-0663.82.2.189

McKellar, H. (2005). *KMWorld's 100 Companies that Matter in Knowledge Management*. Retrieved from http://www.kmworld.com/Articles/Editorial/Feature/KMWorld%27s-100-Companies-That-Matter-in-Knowledge-Management--9611.aspx

McLoughlin, C., & Lee, W. J. M. (2007). *Social software and participatory learning: Pedagogical choices with technology affordances in the web 2.0 era*. Academic Press.

Mcmillan, S. (1996). Literacy and computer literacy: Definitions and comparisons. *Computers & Education*, *27*(3-4), 161–170. doi:10.1016/S0360-1315(96)00026-7

McNally, M. B. (2012). *Democratizing access to knowledge: Find out what open educational resources (OER) have to offer*. Faculty of Information and Media Studies Presentations, University of Western Ontario. Retrieved from http://ir.lib.uwo.ca/fimspres/13

Media Education. (n.d.). Retrieved from http://www.medialiteracyweek.ca/en/101

Media, T. P. R. (2012). UbiCare communication solutions for healthcare. *What's your EQ? A look at healthcare's Facebook® engagement*. Retrieved from https://ubicare.com/engaqement

Mehrabian, A., & Stefl, C. A. (1995). Basic temperament components of loneliness, shyness, and conformity. *Social Behavior and Personality*, *23*(3), 253–264. doi:10.2224/sbp.1995.23.3.253

Mellar, H. (2007). *A study of effective practice in ICT and adult literacy*. Retrieved from http://www.nrdc.org.uk/publications_details.asp?ID=87

Menchik, D. (2004). *Educational equality through technology*. Paper presented at the World Summit on the Information Society and Schooling in Development. New York, NY.

Meridith, L. (2007). *Knowledge Management and Solutions*. Retrieved from http://www.cio.com/article/40343/Knowledge_Management_Definition_and_Solutions?page=2&taxonomyId=3000

Merrill, M. D. (1991). Constructivism and Instructional Design. *Educational Technology*, *3*(5), 45–53.

Merryfield, M. (2001). Moving the center of global education. In W. Stanley (Ed.), *Critical Issues in Social Studies Research for the 21st Century*. Greenwich, CT: Information Age Publishing.

Middle States Commission on Higher Education. (2003). *Developing research and communication skills: Guidelines for information literacy in the curriculum*. Philadelphia, PA: Author Publishers Inc.

Miller, G. S., & Miller, W. W. (1999). Secondary agriculture instructor's opinion and usage of a telecommunications network for distance learning. In *Proceedings of the 53rd Annual AAAE Central Region Research Conference & Seminar in Agricultural Education*. St. Louis, MO: AAAE.

Miller, L., & Olson, J. (1998). Literacy research oriented to features of technology. In D. Reinking, M. Mckenna, L. Labbo, & D. Kieffer (Eds.), *Handbook of Literacy and Technology* (pp. 343–360). Mahwah, NJ: Erlbaum.

Miller, R. G., Ashar, B. H., & Getz, K. J. (2003). Evaluation of an audience response system for the continuing education of health professionals. *The Journal of Continuing Education in the Health Professions*, *23*(2), 109–115. doi:10.1002/chp.1340230208 PMID:12866330

Miniaoui, H., & Kaur, A. (2014). Introducing a Teaching Innovation to Enhance Students' Analytical and Research Skills: A Blended Learning Initiative. In N. Ololube (Ed.), *Advancing Technology and Educational Development through Blended Learning in Emerging Economies* (pp. 21–35). Hershey, PA: Information Science Reference.

Ministry of Education. (2004). *The Regulation on Chinese-Foreign Cooperation in Education in the People's Republic of China*. Retrieved from http://www.moe.edu.cn/publicfiles/business/htmlfiles/moe/moe_621/201005/88508.html

Ministry of Education. (2011a, July 15). 教育部新闻发布会：介绍《国家中长期教育改革和发展规划纲要(2010—2020年)》发布实施一年来?彻落实有关情况. [Ministry of Education news conference: The implementation of the national medium and long-term education reform and development plan (2010-2020) one year after its promulgation]. Retrieved from http://www.moe.edu.cn/sofprogecslive/webcontroller.do?titleSeq=2657&gecsmessage=1

Ministry of Education. (2011b, November 14). 中国教育概况—2010年全国教育事业发展情况. [Chinese Education—2010 Chinese Education Development]. Retrieved from http://www.moe.edu.cn/publicfiles/business/htmlfiles/moe/s5990/201111/126550.html

Ministry of Education. (2012a, March 13). 教育部关于印发《教育信息化十年发展规划(2011-2020年)》的通知. [Ministry of Education Announcement: The 10 Year Development Plan for the Informationalization of Education (2011-2020)]. Retrieved from http://www.moe.gov.cn/publicfiles/business/htmlfiles/moe/s5892/201203/xxgk_133322.html

Ministry of Education. (2012b, September 6). 国新办就中长期教育改革和发展规划纲要颁布实施两年来介绍?展情况. [State Council News Office conference on the implementation of the National Medium and Long-Term Education Reform and Development Plan two years after its promulgation]. Retrieved from http://www.moe.edu.cn/publicfiles/business/htmlfiles/moe/s6819/201209/141694.html

Ministry of Education. (2013a, February 28). 教育信息化工作进展情况. [Development of education informationlization]. Retrieved from http://www.moe.gov.cn/publicfiles/business/htmlfiles/moe/s7204/201302/148023.html

Ministry of Education. (2013b, June 26). 首批中国大学资源共享课上线. [First batch of Chinese open university courses are uploaded]. Retrieved from http://www.moe.edu.cn/publicfiles/business/htmlfiles/moe/s7432/201306/153524.html

Ministry of Education. (2013c, August 16). 2012年全国教育事业发展统?公报. [2012 Chinese Education Development Statistics]. Retrieved from http://www.moe.edu.cn/publicfiles/business/htmlfiles/moe/moe_633/201308/155798.html

Ministry of Education. (2013d, September 5). 教育规划纲要实施三年来中外合作办学发展情况. [Development of Chinese and foreign collaboration in education three years after the National Medium and Long-Term Education Reform and Development Plan]. Retrieved from http://www.moe.gov.cn/publicfiles/business/ htmlfiles/moe/s7598/201309/156992.html

Ministry of Education. (2013e, November 19). 介绍教师?伍建设相关政策. [Recent policies on teacher development]. Retrieved from http://www.moe.edu.cn/publicfiles/business/htmlfiles/moe/s7731/201311/159548.html

Miniwatts Marketing Group. (2012). *Top 50 countries with the highest Internet penetration rate.* Retrieved from http://www.internetworldstats.com/top25.htm

Mitchell, G. O. (1981). *A new dictionary of sociology.* London: Routledge and Kegan Paul.

Mmugenda, O. M. (2006). *University roles in meeting aspirations for ICT and economic development.* Retrieved from http://www.foundation-partnership.org/pubs/leaders/assets/papers/mugendasession4paper.pdf

Mobolaji, E. A. (2004). *Some Issues in ICT for Nigerian Development.* Retrieved from http://www.nigerianmuse.com/projects/TelecomProject/InterConnectivity_Aluko.ppt

Moja, T. (2000). *Nigeria education sector analysis: An analytical synthesis of performance and main issues.* World Bank Report. Retrieved from http://siteresources.worldbank.org/NIGERIAEXTN/Resources/ed_sec_analysis.pdf

Mokobane, S. (2011). The academic engagement of intellectually challenged learners in inclusive schools: A case study. *Cypriot Journal of Educational Sciences, 6*(2), 83–90.

Mondial, S. R. (2006). Cultural Globalization and Globalization of Culture – Source observations. *The Oriental Anthropologist, 6*(2), 297–306.

Moonen, J., & Tulner, H. (2004). *E-Learning and electronic portfolio: Some new insights.* Retrieved from http://www.csun.edu/cod/conf/2004/proceedings/12.htm

Moon, J. A. (1999). *Reflection in learning and professional development: Theory and practice.* Sterling, VA: Kogan Page.

Moore, K. (2002). Professional development through distance learning. *Scholastic Early Childhood Today*, *16*(6), 6–7.

Moore, M. G., & Kearsley, G. (1996). *Distance education: A systems view*. Wadsworth Publishing Company.

Moran, M., Seaman, J., & Tinti-Kane, H. (2011). *Teaching, learning, and sharing: How today's higher education faculty use social media*. Pearson. Retrieved from www.pearsonlearningsolutions.com

Morell, E., & Morrell, J. (2012). Multicultural readings of multicultural literature and the promotion of social awareness in ELA classrooms. *New England Reading Association Journal*, *47*(2), 10–16.

Morrison, J., & Olfman, L. (1998). *Organisational Memory*. Paper presented at 31st HICSS. Maui, HI.

Morrison, G., & Lowther, D. (2010). *Integrating computer technology into the classroom, skills for the 21st century* (4th ed.). Boston, MA: Pearson Education.

Mueller, G. (1980). Visual Contextual Clues and listening comprehension: An experiment. *Modern Language Journal*, *64*, 335–340. doi:10.1111/j.1540-4781.1980.tb05202.x

Muhammad, S. S., Babawuro, S., Noraffandy, Y., & Al-Muzammil, Y. (2011). Effective integration of information and communication technologies (ICTs) in technical and vocational education and training (TVET) toward knowledge management in the changing world of work. *African Journal of Business Management*, *5*(16), 6668–6673.

Mumcu, F. K., & Usluel, Y. K. (2010). *ICT in vocational and technical schools: Teachers' instructional, managerial and personal use matters*. Retrieved May 10, 2012 from http://www.tojet.net/volumes/v9i1.pdf

Mumeu, F. K., & Ushel, Y. K. (2011). ICT in vocational and technical school teachers: Instructional, managerial and personal use matters. *The Turkish Online Journal of Educational Technology*, *9*(1), 98–106.

Muniandy, V., & Lateh, H. (2010). ICT implementation among Malaysian schools: GIS, obstacles and opportunities. *Procedia: Social and Behavioral Sciences*, *2*(2), 2846–2850. doi:10.1016/j.sbspro.2010.03.426

Musaazi, J. C. S. (1982). *The theory and practice of educational administration*. London: Macmillan Nigeria.

Nagy, A. (2005). The impact of e learning. In E. Content (Ed.), *Technologies and perspective for the European Market*. Berlin: Springerverlag.

National Assessment of Educational Progress. (2009). *The nation's report card: Grade 12 reading and mathematics 2009 national and pilot state results*. Arlington, VA: United Stated Department of Education.

National Board for Technical Education (NBTE). (2013). *List of institutions with contact addresses under the purview of NBTE*. Retrieved September 12, 2013 from http://www.nbte.gov.ng/institutions.html

National Commission for Colleges of Education (NCCE). (2013). *Welcome to NCCE*. Retrieved September 12, 2013, from http://ncceonline.org/about-us/

National Council for the Social Studies. (n.d.). *What are global and international education?* Retrieved from www.socialstudies.org/positions/global/whatisglobaled

National Education Commission on Time and Learning. (1994). *Prisoners of time*. Arlington, VA: United States Department of Education.

National Grid for Learning. (n.d.). *Connecting the Learning Society*. Retrieved from http/www.opwn.gov.uk/defee/grid/content.htm

National Institute of Standards and Technology. (n.d.). Adaptive learning systems. *National Institute of Standards and Technology*.

National University Commission (NUC). (2013). *List of Nigerian universities*. Retrieved September 12, 2013, from http://www.nuc.edu.ng/pages/universities.asp

Newby, B. M. Z., Cutright, T., Barrios, C. A., & Xu, Q. (2006). Zosteric acid-an effective antifoulant for reducing fresh water bacterial attachment on coatings. *Journal of Coatings Technology and Research*, *3*(1), 69–76. doi:10.1007/s11998-006-0007-4

Newby, T. J., Stepich, D. A., Lehman, J. D., & Russell, J. D. (2006). *Educational technology for teaching and learning*. Pearson Education, Inc.

Newhouse, C. P. (2002a). *The Impact of ICT on Learning and Teaching*. Perth, Australia: Special Educational Service.

Newhouse, C. P. (2002b). *A Framework to Articulate the Impact of ICT on Learning in Schools*. Perth, Australia: Special Educational Service.

News, B. B. C. (2010). *Nigeria Country Profile*. Retrieved from http://news.bbc.co.uk/1/hi/world/africa/country_profiles/1064557.stm

Nielsen Mobile. (2008). *Critical mass: The worldwide state of the mobile web*. Retrieved from http://nl.nielsen.com/site/documents/nielenmobile.pdf

Nigeria Educational Research and Development Council (NERDC). (2005). *Workship on difficult concepts: Physics group report*. Lagos: NERDC.

Noar, S. (2006). A 10-year retrospective of research in health mass media campaigns: Where do we go from here? *Journal of Health Communication, 11*(1), 21–42. doi:10.1080/10810730500461059 PMID:16546917

Nonaka, I., & Takeuchi, H. (1995). *The Knowledge-Creating Company: How Japanese Companies create the Dynamics of Innovation*. Oxford University Press.

Nonaka, I., & Teece, D. (2001). *Managing Industrial knowledge creation, transfer and utilization*. SAGE Publications Ltd.

Norris, P. (2001). *Digital divide: Civic engagement, information poverty, and the internet worldwide*. Cambridge, UK: Cambridge University Press. doi:10.1017/CBO9781139164887

NRC. (2009). *Assessing the impacts of changes in the information technology R&D ecosystem: Retaining Leadership in an Increasingly Global Environment*. Retrieved from www.nap.edu/catalog/12174.html

NSE. (2010). *The Nigerian Stock Exchange*. Retrieved from http://www.nigerianstockexchange.com/index.jsp

Nwalo, K. I. N., & Oyedum, G. U. (2011). Relationship of information literacy to undergraduate students use of university libraries. *Library Progress International, 31*(2), 347–362.

Nwene, U. P. (1988). Health care planning for the rural community. In Perspectives on community and rural development in Nigeria. University of Jos, Jos Centre for Development Studies Publication (CDS).

O'Reilly. (2005). *What is web 2.0?* Retrieved April 23, 2013 from http://www.oreillynet.com/pub/a/oreilly/tim/news/2005/09/30/what-is-Web-20.html

Oakley, P. (1991). *Projects with people*. Geneva: ILO.

O'Dell, C., & Grayson, C. J. Jr. (1998). *If Only We Knew What We Know*. New York: The Free Press.

Odigie, H. A., & Li-Hua, R. (2009). *Unlocking the Channel of Tacit Knowledge Transfer*. Retrieved from http://motsc.org/unlocking_the_chennel_of_tacit_knowledge_transfer.pdf

Odogwu, H. N., Jimoh, J. A., Olabiyi, O. S., & Yewande, R. O. (2012). Usage of ICT for instructional, managerial and personal purposes by science, technology and mathematics lecturers in the colleges of education in South-West Nigeria. In *Proceedings towards Effective Teaching and Meaningful Learning in Mathematics, Science and Technology*. University of South Africa.

Odumosu, A. I. O., & Keshinro, O. (2000). *Effective Science Teaching and Improvisation in the Classroom*. Lagos: Obaroh & Ogbinaka Publishers.

Odu, O. K. (2011). Philosophical and Sociological overview of vocational and technical education in Nigeria. *American-Eurasian Journal of Scientific Research, 6*(1), 52–57.

Office of Technology Assessment (OTA). (1995). *Teachers and technology: Making the connection*. Washington, DC: U.S. Government Printing Office. Retrieved May 28, 2001, from http://www.wws.princeton.edu/~ota/disk1/1995/9541_n.html

Ogundare, S. E. (2003). *Fundamentals of teaching social studies. Oyo*. Immaculate Publishers.

Ogunmodede, T. A., & Emeaghara, E. N. (2010). The effects of library use education as a course on library patronage: A case study of LAUTECH library, Ogbomosho, Nigeria. *Library Philosophy and Practice*. Retrieved 30/6/2011 from http://www.unlib.unl.edu/LPP/ogunmodede_emeaghara

Ogunsheye, F. A. (2001). *Syllabuses for library use.* Ibadan: University of Ibadan, Abadina Media Resources Centre.

Ogwo, B. A., & Oranu, R. N. (2006). *Methodology in Formal and Non-formal Technical/vocational Education.* University of Nigeria Press, Ltd.

Ohiorhenuan, J. F. E. (1998). *The south in the era of globalization.* South – Issues in Globalization.

Ojedokun, A. A. (2007). *Information literacy for tertiary education students in Africa.* Ibadan: Third World Information Services.

Ojedokun, A. A., & Lumande, E. (2005). The integration of information literacy skills into a credit-earning programme at the University of Botswana. *African Journal of Library. Archives and Information Science, 4*(1), 41–48.

Ojo, M. O. (2006). *Repositioning Teacher Education for National Development.* Paper presented at the 2005 Annual Conference of the Institute of Education. Benin, Nigeria.

Okafor, F. C., & Onokerhoraye, A. G. (1987). *Rural system and planning.* The geography and planning series of study notes.

Okebukola, P. A. O. (2005). *Quality Assurance in Teacher Education: The role of Faculties of Education in Nigerian Universities.* Paper presented at the Annual Meeting of the Committee of Deans of Education in Nigerian Universities. Ilorin, Nigeria.

Oketola, D. (2010). *Nigeria's Software Industry and the Journey Ahead.* Retrieved from http://www.punchng.com/Articl.aspx?theartic=Art2010061412141350

Okonkwo, S. C. (2000). Relationship between some school and teacher variables and students achievement in mathematics. *Journal of Science Association of Nigeria, 35,* 43–49.

Okorie, J.U. (2001). *Vocational Industrial Education.* Bauchi: League of Researchers in Nigeria.

Okoye, M. O. (2013). User education in federal university libraries: A study of trends and developments in Nigeria. *Library Philosophy and Practice (e-journal).* Retrieved from http://digitalcommons.unl.edu/libphilprac/942

Okpala, P. N., Onocha, C. O., & Oyedeji, O. A. (1993). *Measurement and evaluation in education.* Jatlu-Uzire: Stirling-Horden Publishers (Nig.)

Okunoye, A., Innola, E., & Karsten, H. (2002). *Benchmarking Knowledge Management in Developing Countries: Case of Research Organisations in Nigeria.* The Gambia and India: University of Turku.

Olabiyi, O. S., Jimoh, J. A., & Akanni, W. A. (2011). Utilisation of Information Communication Technology by Vocational Technical Education Teachers for Effective Instructional Delivery. *International Journal of Research in Education, 3*(3).

Olaitan, S. O., & Agusiobo, O. N. (1981). *Principles of Practice Teaching.* Toronto, Canada: John Wiley and Sons.

Olaitan, S. O., Nwachukwu, C. E., Igbo, C. A., Onyemachi, G. A., & Ekong, A. O. (1999). *Curriculum Development and Management in Vocational and Technical Education. Onitsha.* Cape Publishers.

Olatokun, W. M. (2007). *Availability, accessibility and use of ICTs by Nigerian women academics.* Retrieved from http://majlis.fsktm.um.edu.my/document.aspx?FileName=564.pdf

Olele, C. N. (2012). Alternative assessment: Emerging trends of classroom assessment in digital era. *Academic Research International, 3*(1), 42–49.

Ololube, N. P. (2005a). Benchmarking the Motivational Competencies of Academically Qualified Teachers and Professionally Qualified Teachers in Nigerian Secondary Schools. *The African Symposium, 5*(3), 17-37.

Ololube, N. P. (2005b). School Effectiveness and Quality Improvement: Quality Teaching in Nigerian Secondary Schools. *The African Symposium, 5*(4), 17-31.

Ololube, N. P. (2006a). Teachers Instructional Material Utilization Competencies in Secondary Schools in Sub-Saharan Africa: Professional and non-professional teachers' perspective. In *Proceedings of the 6th International Educational Technology Conference EMU.* EMU.

Ololube, N. P. (2006b). Appraising the Relationship Between ICT Usage and Integration and the Standard of Teacher Education Programs in a Developing Economy. *International Journal of Education and Development Using ICT, 2*(3), 70–85.

Ololube, N. P. (2007). The Relationship between Funding, ICT, Selection Processes, Administration and Planning and the Standard of Science Teacher Education in Nigeria. *Asia-Pacific Forum on Science Learning and Teaching, 8*(1), 1–29.

Ololube, N. P. (2011). Blended learning in Nigeria: Determining students' readiness and faculty role in advancing technology in a globalized educational development. In A. Kitchenham (Ed.), *Blended learning across disciplines: Models for implementation* (pp. 190–207). Hershey, PA: Information Science Reference. doi:10.4018/978-1-60960-479-0.ch011

Ololube, N. P. (2014). Blended Learning Methods in Introduction to Teaching and Sociology of Education Courses at a University of Education. In N. P. Ololube (Ed.), *Advancing Technology and Educational Development through Blended Learning in Emerging Economies* (pp. 108–127). Hershey, PA: Information Science Reference.

Ololube, N. P., Kpolovie, P. J., Amaele, S., Amanchukwu, R. N., & Briggs, T. (2013). Digital Natives and Digital Immigrants: A study of Information Technology and Information Systems (IT/IS) Usage between Students and Faculty of Nigerian Universities. *International Journal of Information and Communication Technology Education, 9*(3), 42–64. doi:10.4018/jicte.2013070104

Ololube, N. P., Umunadi, K. E., & Kpolovie, P. J. (2014). Barriers to Blended Teaching and Learning in Sub-Saharan Africa: Challenges for the Next Decade and Beyond. In N. P. Ololube (Ed.), *Advancing Technology and Educational Development through Blended Learning in Emerging Economies* (pp. 232–247). Hershey, PA: Information Science Reference.

Olorundare, S. (2010). *Utilization of Information and communication Technology (ICT) in curriculum development, implementation and evaluation.* Paper presented at the 1st International Conference on Higher Education: Collaboration of Education Faculties in West Africa (CEFWA). New York, NY.

Olson, J. (2002). Systemic change / teacher tradition: Legends of reform continue. *Journal of Curriculum Studies, 34*(2), 129–137. doi:10.1080/00220270110085697

Olsson, L. (2006). Implementing use of ICT in teacher education. In *International Federation for Information Processing, Education for the 21st century impact of ICT and Digital Resources.* Boston: Springer. doi:10.1007/978-0-387-34731-8_49

Oni, A. A. (2003). Globalization: A menace to African values and education? *Zimbabwe Journal of Educational Research, 15*(1), 51–61.

Oni, A. A., Adetoro, J. A., & Sule, A. A. (2011). Quality Entrant and Capacity Building: Model for Rebranding Teacher Education in Nigeria. In K. Adeyemi, & B. Awe (Eds.), *Rebranding Nigerian Educational System* (pp. 91–107). School of Education, National Open University of Nigeria.

Open University of China. (n.d.). *The Chinese Language Center.* Retrieved from http://en.crtvu.edu.cn/academics/clc

Oremeji, C. J. (2002). *Strategies in educational administration and supervision.* Port Harcourt: High Class Publishers.

Organization for Economic Co-Operation and Development (OECD). (2007). *Giving knowledge for free: The emergence of open educational resources.* Paris: Centre for Educational Research and Innovation, OECD.

Osler, A., & Vincent, K. (n.d.). *Citizenship and the challenge of global education.* Oak Hill, VA: Trentham Books Limited.

Osokoya, I. O. (1996). *Writing and teaching history: A guide to advanced study.* Ibadan: Lawrel Educational Publishers.

Osuji, E. E. (1993). *Community participation sponsored workshop.* UNICEF/University of Ibadan Consultancy Unit.

Osunde, A. U., & Omoruyi, F. E. O. (2004). An Evaluation of the National Teachers Institute's Manpower Training Program for Teaching Personnel in Mid-western Nigeria. *International Education Journal, 5*(3), 405–409.

Osunrinde, A. (2001). Globalization: In search of viable direction to our academic growth. *Nigerian Journal of Emotional Psychology, 3*, 84–87.

Otte, G., Gold, M., Gorges, B., Smith, M., & Stein, C. (2012). *The CUNY academic commons: Social network as hatchery*. Sloan-C. Retrieved from http://sloanconsortium.org/effective_practices/cuny-academic-commons

Ottong, E. J., & Ntui, A. I. (2010). Repositioning information literacy for learning society: Strategy and prospects for lifelong education in the South-South sub region of Nigeria. *Global Review of Library and Information Science*, *6*, 41–45.

Oxford Economics. (2010). *Nigeria*. ABI/INFORM Global.

Oyelami, O. (2010). Evolution of community development process in Nigeria. In S. Jegede (Ed.), *Adult education series* (Vol. 1). Lagos: Edittext Publishers Ltd.

Pageflip-Flap. (2014). *Pageflip-flap Web Site*. Retrieved January 13, 2014, from http://pageflip-flap.com

Parker, J., Maor, D., & Herrington, J. (2013). Authentic online learning: Aligning learner needs, pedagogy and technology. *Issues in Educational Research*, *23*(2), 227–241.

Passerini, K., & Granger, M. J. (2000). A Developmental Model For Distance Learning Using The Internet. *Computers & Education*, *34*(1), 1–15. doi:10.1016/S0360-1315(99)00024-X

Patrick, K., Griswold, W., Raab, F., & Intille, S. S. (2008). Health and the mobile phone. *American Journal of Preventive Medicine*, *35*(2), 177–181. doi:10.1016/j.amepre.2008.05.001 PMID:18550322

Patton, M. Q. (1990). *Qualitative evaluation and research Methods* (2nd ed.). Newbury Park, CA: Sage Publications.

Paul, S. (1987). *Community participation in development projects: The World Bank experience*. Paper presented at Economic Development Institute Workshop on Community Participation. Washington, DC.

Paula, H. O. (1999). *Community development in action: An eastern Nigerian experiment*. Enugu: Image and Slogans.

Pearson Education Limited. (2007). *Longman Dictionary of Contemporary English-The living Dictionary*. London: First Impression.

Pelgrum, W. J. (2001). Obstacles to the integration of Information Communication Technology (ICT) in education: Results from worldwide educational assessments. *Computers & Education*, *37*, 163–178. doi:10.1016/S0360-1315(01)00045-8

Peng, S. (2011). 论远程教育人员的道德建设. [On enhancing ethical practices of people working in distance education]. *Distance Education in China, 6*.

Pfeffer, J., & Sutton, R. I. (2000). *The Knowing-Doing Gap: How Smart Companies Turn Knowledge into Action*. Academic Press.

Phenomenology. (2013). *Stanford Encyclopedia of Philosophy*. Retrieved April 5, 2013, from http://plato.stanford.edu/entries/phenomenology/

Philip, T. M., & Garcia, A. D. (2013). The importance of still teaching the igeneration: New technologies and the centrality of pedagogy. *Harvard Educational Review*, *83*(2), 300–319.

Pinterest. (2014). *Pinterest Web Site*. Retrieved January 13, 2014, from http://pinterest.com

Pirie, B. (1997). *Reshaping High School English*. Urbana, IL: National Council of Teachers of English.

Plato. (1990). Phaedrus. In *The Rhetorical tradition: Readings from classical times to the present*. Boston: Bedford Books of St. Martin's Press.

Polanyi, M. (1975). Personal Knowledge. In *Meaning*. University of Chicago Press.

Postman, N. (1983). Engaging Students in the Great Conversation. *Phi Delta Kappan*, *64*(5), 310–316.

Postman, N. (1992). *Technopoly: The surrender of culture of Technology*. New York: Alfred A. Knopf.

Prezi. (2014). *Prezi Web Site*. Retrieved January 13, 2014, from http://prezi.com

ProBoards. (2013). *Free forum*. Retrieved from http://www.proboards.com/

Quintas, P., Lefrere, P., & Jones, G. (1997). Knowledge management: A strategic Approach. *Journal of Long Range Planning*, *30*(3), 385–391. doi:10.1016/S0024-6301(97)90252-1

Quizrevolution. (2014). *Quizrevolution Web Site*. Retrieved January 13, 2014, from http://quizrevolution

Rana, H. K. (2009). *Impact of information and communication technology on academic libraries in punjab*. Retrieved from http/www.goarticles.com/cgi-bin/showa/cgi

Rashedul, H. S., Aktaruzzaman, & Che, K. C. (2011). Factors influencing use of ICT in Technical and Vocational Education to make teaching-learning effective & efficient: Case study of Polytechnic institutions in Bangladesh. *International Journal of Basic and Applied Science*, *11*(3).

Raychaudhuri, P., & De, P. (2007). Barriers to trade in higher education services: Empirical evidence from Asia-Pacific countries. *Asia-Pacific Trade and Investment Review*, *3*(2), 67–88.

Recursos Humanos. (2010). Dueling age groups in today's workforce: From Baby Boomers to Generations X and Y. *Universia Knowledge @ Wharton*. Retrieved from http://www.wharton.universia.net/

Reiser, R. (1987). Instructional Technology: A History. In R. Gagne (Ed.), *Instructional Technology: Foundation* (pp. 11–48). Hillsdale, NJ: Lawrence Associates.

Reiser, R. A., & Dempsey, J. V. (2002). *Trends and Issues in Instructional Design and Technology*. Upper Saddle River, NJ: Merrill Prentice Hall.

Relan, A., & Gillani, B. B. (1997). Web-based instruction and the traditional classroom: Similarities and difference. In B. H. Khan (Ed.), *Web-based instruction* (pp. 41–46). Englewood Cliffs, NJ: Educational Technology Publications.

Remenyi, D., Williams, B., Money, A., & Swartz, E. (1998). *Doing Research in Business and Management: An Introduction to Process and Method*. London: Sage Publications.

Renshaw, S., & Krishnaswamy, G. (2009). Critiquing the Knowledge Management Strategies of Non-Profit Organisations in Australia. *World Academy of Science. Engineering and Technology*, *49*, 456–464.

Reynol, J. (2012). The relationship between frequency of Facebook use, participation in Facebook activities, and student engagement. *Computers & Education*, *58*, 162–171. doi:10.1016/j.compedu.2011.08.004

Ribbens, E. (2007). Why I like personal response systems. *Journal of College Science Teaching*, *37*(2), 60–62.

Richardson, V. (1991). How and why teachers change. In S. C. Conely, & B. S. Cooper (Eds.), *The School As a Work Environment, Implications for reform* (pp. 66–78). Boston, MA: Allyn and Bacon.

Richey, R. C. (2008). *Reflection on the 2008 AECT Definitions of the field Tech Trends*. Academic Press.

Riel, M. (2003, September). *Written testimony for the web-based education commission*. Retrieved from http://www.gse.uci.edu/mriel/e-testify/

Robertson, J. (2004). *Intranets and Knowledge Sharing*. Retrieved from http://www.kmtalk.net/article.php?story=20041130051759653

Robinson, P. P. (1999). *The phenomenon of Globalization and the African Response*. Paper presented at the 3rd Annual Conference of Fulbright Alumni Association of Nigeria. Nzukka, Nigeria.

Rogers, E. M. (1983). *The diffusion of innovations* (3rd ed.). New York: The Free Press.

Roland, V. C. (1992). *Globalization, knowledge and society*. London: Sage.

Roschelle, J., Penuel, W. R., & Abrahamson, L. (2004). *Classroom response and communication systems: Research review and theory*. Paper presented at the 2004 Meeting for the American Educational Research Association. San Diego, CA.

Rosenberg, R. (2004). *The Social Impact of Computers* (3rd ed.). London: Elsevier Academic.

Ruggles, R., & Holtshouse, D. (1999). *The Knowledge Advantage*. TJ International Ltd.

Ruhleder, K., & Michael, T. (2000). Reflective collaborative learning on the web: Drawing on the master class. *First Monday*, *5*(5). doi:10.5210/fm.v5i5.742

Ryu, S., Ho, S. H., & Han, I. (2003). Knowledge sharing behavior of physicians in hospitals. *Expert Systems with Applications*, *25*(1), 113–122. doi:10.1016/S0957-4174(03)00011-3

Sahin, I., & Thompson, A. (2006). Using Rogers' theory to interpret instructional computer use by COE faculty. *Journal of Research on Technology in Education, 39*(1), 81–104. doi:10.1080/15391523.2006.10782474

Salmon, T. P., & Stahl, J. N. (2005). Wireless audience response system: Does it make a difference? *Journal of Extension, 43*(3), 26–31.

Sanchez, R. (2001). *Knowledge Management and Organizational Competence.* Oxford University Press Inc.

Sanders, M. (2000). Web-Based Portfolios for Technology Education: A Personal Case Study. *The Journal of Technology Studies.* Retrieved from http://scholar.lib.vt.edu/ejournals/JOTS/Winter-Spring-2000/pdf/sanders.pdf

Saunders, J. (2003). Campusdirect helps Government Employee Continue e-learning. *Technology in Government, 10* (9).

Scarratt, E. (2007). *Citizenship and Media Education: An Introduction.* Retrieved from www.citized.info/pdf/commarticles/Elaine%20Scarratt.doc

Schein, R., Wilson, K., & Keelan, J. (2010). *Literature review on the effectiveness of the use of social media: A report for peel public health.* Academic Press.

SchulzB. (2003). Collaborative learning in an online environment: Will it work for teacher training? In Proceedings of the 14th Annual Society for Information Technology and Teacher Education International Conference (pp. 503-504). Charlottesville, VA: Association for the Advancement of Computers in Education.

Scott, B. G. (2003). *Faculty Attitudes Toward Residential and Distance Learning: A Case Study in Instructional Mode Prefences Among Theological Seminary Faculty.* (Unpublished Ph.D. Thesis). University of North Texas.

Screenleap. (2014). *Screenleap Web Site.* Retrieved January 13, 2014, from http://screenleap.com

Secondlife. (2014). *Secondlife Web Site.* Retrieved January 13, 2014, from http://secondlife.com

Seels, B. B., & Richey, R. C. (1994a). *Instructional technology: The definitions and domains of the field.* Washington, DC: Association for Educational Communications and Technology.

Seels, B. B., & Richey, R. C. (1994b). Redefining the field: A collaborative effort. *TechTrends, 2*(39), 36–38. doi:10.1007/BF02818746

Shah, H., & Young, H. (2008). Global learning in schools, and the implications for policy. *Educational Review, 21*(1), 15–22.

Sharma, P., Singh, M., & Kumar, P. (2009). Approach to ICT in library Training education and technology issuess and challenges. In *Proceedings of ICAL.* ICAL.

Shaw. (2003). *Contextual and mutilated learning in the context of design, learning and (RE) use teaching and learning with technology.* Retrieved from http://www.shawmultimedia.com/edtechOct.B

Silius, K., Kailanto, M., & Tervakari, A.-M. (2011). Evaluating the quality of social media in an educational context. *International Journal of Emerging Technologies in Learning, 6*(3), 21–27.

Singh, N., & Papa, R. (2010). *The Impacts of Globalization in Higher Education.* Retrieved September 30, 2013 from http://cnx.org/content/m34497/1.1/

Sketchfu. (2014). *Sketchfu Web Site.* Retrieved January 13, 2014, from http://sketchfu.com

Skyrme, D. J. (2004). *The 3Cs of Knowledge Sharing.* Retrieved from http://www.kmtalk.net/article.php?story=2004113004318603

Sloan Consortium. (2007). *Making the grade: Online education in the U.S., 2006.* Retrieved April 1, 2013, from http://www.sloan-c.org/publications/survey/index.asp

Smaldino, S. E., Russell, J. D., Heinich, R., & Molenda, M. (2005). *Instructional technology and media for learning* (8th ed.). Upper Saddle River, NJ: Pearson/Prentice Hall.

Smith, B., Caputi, P., & Rawstorne, P. (2000). Differentiating computer experience and attitudes toward computers: An empirical investigation. *Computers in Human Behavior, 16*(1), 59–81. doi:10.1016/S0747-5632(99)00052-7

Smith, D. (1977). College classroom interactions and critical thinking. *Journal of Educational Psychology, 69*(2), 180–190. doi:10.1037/0022-0663.69.2.180

Soriyan, H. A., & Heeks, R. (2004). *A Profile of Nigeria's Software Industry*. Retrieved from http://www.sed.manchester.ac.uk/idpm/research/publications/wp/di/documents/di_wp21.pdf

Soriyan, H. A., Mursu, A., & Korpela, M. (2000). Information System development methodologies: Gender issues in a developing economy. In *Women, Work and Computerization*. Kluwer Academic. doi:10.1007/978-0-387-35509-2_18

St. Clair, R. (2002). Andragogy revisited: Theory for the 21st century. *Cal-Pro Online*. Retrieved from www.calpro-online.org/eric/docs/mr00034.pdf

Starkey, H. (2006). *Designing online tasks for effective discussions*. Retrieved from http://www.cde.london.ac.uk/support/awards/generic2534.htm

Statistics Canada. (2008). *Information and communications technologies (ICTS)*. Retrieved from http://www.statcan.gc.ca/pub/81-004-x/def/4068723-eng.htm

Stecking, L. (2000, August). Geteiltes Wissen ist doppeltes Wissen. *Management Berater*.

Steinbrook, R. (2009). Health care and the American recovery and reinvestment act. *The New England Journal of Medicine*, *360*(11), 1057–1060. doi:10.1056/NEJMp0900665 PMID:19224738

Stein, E. W., & Zwass, V. (1995). Actualising Organisational Memory with Information Systems. *Information Systems Research*, *6*(2), 85–117. doi:10.1287/isre.6.2.85

Streatfield, D., & Markless, S. (2008). Evaluating the impact of information literacy in higher education: Progress and prospects. *Libri*, *58*(2), 102–109. doi:10.1515/libr.2008.012

Stutzman, F. (2006). *An evaluation of identity-sharing behavior in social network communities*. Paper presented at the iDMAa and IMS Code Conference. Oxford, OH.

Suler, J. (2004). Extending the classroom into cyberspace: The discussion board. *Cyberpsychology & Behavior*, (7): 397–403.

Sweller, J. (2010). Element interactivity and intrinsic, extraneous, and germane cognitive load. *Educational Psychology Review*, *22*(2), 123–138. http://doi.org/dmvdm doi:10.1007/s10648-010-9128-5

Szabo, M., & Suen, C. (1998). *A study of the impact of a school district computer technology program on adoption of educational technology*. Retrieved April 18, 2012 from http://www.quasar.ualberta.ca/edmedia/Suenszabo.html

Tapanes, M. A., Smith, G. G., & White, J. A. (2009). Cultural diversity in online learning: A study of the perceived effects of dissonance in levels of individualism/collectivism and tolerance of ambiguity. *The Internet and Higher Education*, *12*(1), 26–34. doi:10.1016/j.iheduc.2008.12.001

Tas, E. M. (2010). ICT education for development-a case study. *Procedia: Social and Behavioral Sciences*, *3*, 507–512.

Tebo, M. G. (2000). First Class Delivery. *ABA Journal*, *86*(87), 1.

Tech, G. (2005). *Questionnaire Design*. Retrieved from http://www.cc.gatech.edu/classes/cs6751_97_winter/Topics/quest-design/

Technical and Vocational Education and Training (UNEVOC). (2003). *New Project on ICT Use in Technical and Vocational Education*. UNESCO.

Tella, A. (2011). *Availability and use of ICT in south-western Nigeria colleges of education*. Retrieved May 10, 2012 from http://www.ajol.info/index.php/afrrev/issue/view/8653

Terry, M. (2008). Text messaging in healthcare: The elephant knocking at the door. *Telemedicine Journal and e-Health*, *14*(6), 520–524. doi:10.1089/tmj.2008.8495 PMID:18729749

Thompson, J. F. (2002). *Foundation of Vocational Education*. New York: Prentice-Hall Inc.

Thurow, L. (2004). Help Wanted: A Chief Knowledge Officer. *Fast Company*, *78*, 91.

Tian, H., Brimmer, D., Lin, J., Tumpey, A., & Reeves, W. (2009). Web usage data as a means of evaluating public health messaging and outreach. *Journal of Medical Internet Research*, *11*(4), e52. doi:10.2196/jmir.1278 PMID:20026451

Tinio, V. L. (2002). *ICT in education*. Retrieved may 10, 2012 from http://www.saigontre.com/FDFiles/ICT_in_Education.PDF

Tiwana, A. (2001). *The knowledge management toolkit: Practical techniques for building knowledge management system*. Upper Saddle River, NJ: Prentice Hall, Inc.

Tomlinson, J. (1997). Cultural globalization and cultural imperialism. In A. Mohammadi (Ed.), *International communication and globalization* (pp. 170–190). London: Sage.

Treacy, M., & Wiersema, F. (1993, January-February). Customer Intimacy and Other Value Disciplines. *Harvard Business Review*.

Troy, B. E., Elizabeth, F., & Kaelin, O. (2009). Clicker satisfaction for students in human development: Differences for class type, prior exposure, and student talkativity. *North American Journal of Psychology*, *11*(3), 19–32.

Truch, A., Higgs, M., Bartram, D., & Brown, A. (2002). *Knowledge sharing and personality*. Paper presented at Henley Knowledge Management Forum. New York. NY.

Tsinakos, A. A. (2003). Asynchronous distance education: Teaching using case based reasoning. *Turkish Online Journal of Distance Education, 4*(3).

TVU. (2008). *Dissertation Guide: Primary Data Collection Methods*. Retrieved from http://brent.tvu.ac.uk/dissguide/hm1u3/hm1u3fra.htm

Tye, K. A., & Kniep, W. M. (1991). Global education around the world. *Educational Leadership*, 47–49.

Umunadi, K. E., & Ololube, N. P. (2014). Blended Learning and Technological Development in Teaching and Learning. In N. P. Ololube (Ed.), *Advancing Technology and Educational Development through Blended Learning in Emerging Economies* (pp. 213–231). Hershey, PA: Information Science Reference.

UNESCO. (2002). *Information and Communication Technologies in Teacher education: A Planning Guide*. Paris: UNESCO.

UNESCO. (2002). *Revised Recommendation concerning Technical and Vocational Education (2001)*. Paris: UNESCO.

UNESCO. (2003). *Manual for Pilot Testing the Use of Indicators to Assess Impact of ICT Use in Education*. Retrieved September 20, 2013 from http://www.unescobkk.org/education/ict/resource

UNESCO. (2005). *United Nations and Culture of Peace: Manifesto, 2005*. UNESCO.

UNESCO. (2005). *United Nations Decade of education for Sustainable development 2005-2014*. Retrieved September 20, 2013 from http://portal.unesco.org/education/en/ev.php-URL_ID=27234&URL_DO=DO_TOPIC&URL_SECTION=201.html

UNESCO. (2008). *Toward Information Literacy Indicators*. Paris: UNESCO.

United Nation Educational Scientific and Cultural Organization. (2002). *Information and Communication Technology in Teacher Education*. Retrieved May 10, 2012 from http://www.unesdoc.org/images/0012/001295/129533epdf

United Nations Children Fund. (2009). *Women organizations in sub-Saharan Africa*. Lagos, Nigeria: UNICEF.

United Nations Development Programme. (2013). *Human Development Report 2013*. Retrieved from http://hdr.undp.org/en/media/HDR_2013_EN_complete.pdf

United Nations Economic Commission for Africa (UNESCA). (1990). *Manual on typologies and activities of rural organization in agriculture*. Author.

United Nations Statistics. (2008). *Environment Statistics Country Snapshot: Nigeria*. Retrieved from http://unstats.un.org/unsd/environment/envpdf/Country_Snapshots_Sep%202009/Nigeria.pdf

United Nations. (2003). *Youth information and communication technologies (ICT)*. Retrieved from http://www.un.org/esa/socdev/unyin/documents/ch12.pdf

United States Department of Education, Office of Educational Technology. (2010). *Transforming American education: Learning powered by technology*. Washington, DC: Author. Retrieved from http://www.ed.gov/sites/default/files/netp2010.pdf

University of Colorado – Colorado Springs. (n.d.). *Kraemer Family Library and Information Literacy Program*. Retrieved from http://www.uccs.edu/library/services/infolit.html

Usta, E. (2007). *Harmanlanmış Öğrenme ve Çevrimiçi Öğrenme Ortamlarının Akademik Başarı ve Doyuma Etkisi*. Gazi Üniversitesi, Eğitim Bilimleri Enstitüsü.

Usun, S. (2009). Information and Communication Technologies (ICT) in Teacher Education (ITE) programs in the world and turkey (a comparative view). *Procedia: Social and Behavioral Sciences*, *1*, 331–334. doi:10.1016/j.sbspro.2009.01.062

Uzunboylu, H., Bicen, H., & Cavus, N. (2011). The efficient virtual learning environment: A case study of web 2.0 tools and windows live spaces. *Computers & Education*, *56*(3), 720–726. doi:10.1016/j.compedu.2010.10.014

Van den Hooff, B., & De Ridder, J. A. (2004). Knowledge Sharing in Context - The Influence of Organisational Commitment, Communication Climate and CMC use on Knowledge Sharing. *Journal of Knowledge Management*, *8*(6), 117–130. doi:10.1108/13673270410567675

Van't Hof, S., Sluijs, J., Asamoah-Hassan, H., & Agyen-Gyasi, K. (2010). *Information literacy training in an African context: Case study of IL course development at KNUST in Kumasi, Ghana*. Amsterdam: KIT.

Vance, K., Howe, W., & Dellavalle, P. (2009). Social internet sites as a source of public health information. *Dermatologic Clinics*, *27*(2), 133–136. doi:10.1016/j.det.2008.11.010 PMID:19254656

Vanhorn, S., Pearson, J. C., & Child, J. T. (2008). The Online Communication Course: The Challenges. *Qualitative Research Reports in Communication*, *9*(1), 29–36. doi:10.1080/17459430802400332

Visscher, A. J. (1988). The computer as an administrative tool. *Journal of Research on Computing in Education*, *24*(1), 146–296.

Voki. (2014). *Voki Web Site*. Retrieved January 13, 2014, from http://voki.com

Vygotsky, L. S. (1978). *Mind in society*. Cambridge, MA: Harvard.

Walker, A. (2012). *What Is Boko Haram?* (United States Institute of Peace Special Report). Washington, DC: US Institute of Peace. Retrieved from http://www.xtome.org/docs/groups/boko-haram/SR308.pdf

Walsh. K. (2012). *Flipped class workshop in a book*. Retrieved from http://www.knewton.com/flip

Walter, E. C. (1993). *Management Development through Training*. Addison-Wesley Publishing Company, Inc.

Wang, L. (2011). 开放教育资源的社会化分析. [A socialization analysis of open education resources]. *Distance Education in China, 7*.

Wang, S., & Ma, Z. (2008). Supervisory and optimal control of building HVAC systems: A review. *HVAC&R Research, 14*(1), 3-32.

Wang, S., & Wang, H. (2012). Organizational schemata of e-portfolios for fostering higher-order thinking. *Information Systems Frontiers*, *14*(2), 395–407. doi:10.1007/s10796-010-9262-0

Wang, Y. (2010). 进步与发展之路:开放远程教育与信息通讯技术在中国的应用. [Progress and development: The application of open distance education and information and communication technology in China]. *Open. Education Research*, *16*(3), 56–61.

Watch, E. (2009). *Nigerian Economy*. Retrieved from http://www.economywatch.com/world_economy/nigeria/

Wei, S. (2011). 网络高等教育学生毕?时?预?研究. [A study of graduation time of students in network higher education]. *Distance Education in China, 10*.

Wertsch, J. (1991). *Voices of the mind: a socio cultural approach to mediated action*. London: Harvester.

Wiig, K. (1997). Knowledge Management: Where Did it Come from and Where Would it Go?. *Journal of Expert Systems with Application*.

William, M. K. (2006). *Introduction to Evaluation*. Retrieved from http://www.socialresearchmethods.net/kb/intreval.htm

Wolf, M. (2004). *Why globalization works*. New Haven, CT: Yale University Press.

Wong, K. Y. (2005). Critical Success Factors for Implementing Knowledge Management in Small and Medium Enterprises. *Industrial Management & Data Systems*, *105*(3), 261–279. doi:10.1108/02635570510590101

Woodhead, N. (1991). *Hypertext and Hypermedia: Theory and Application*. Winslow, UK: Sigma Press.

World Bank. (1990). *How the world banks with NGOs*. Washington, DC: World Bank.

World Bank. (2012). *China 2030: building a modern, harmonious, and creative high-income society*. Retrieved from http://wwwwds.worldbank.org/external/default/WDSContentServer/WDSP/IB/2012/02/28/000356161_20120228001303/Rendered/PDF/671790WP0P12750 0China020300complete.pdf

World Bank. (2012). *Development in sub-Saharan Africa: Policies for adjustment, revitalization and expansion*. Washington, DC: World Bank.

World Health Organization. (2011). mHealth: New horizons for health through mobile technology: Second global survey on e-Health. WHO Press.

Xing, X. (2010). 对开放教育学生惰学现象的思考. [Thoughts on the phenomenon of open education students' lack of interest in learning]. *Contemporary. Distance Education, 4*, 22–24.

Xiong, Y., Xie, B., & Wu, Y. (2010). 中国远程教育发展环境的SWOT分析.[An SWOT analysis of the Chinese distance education environment]. *Contemporary Distance Education, 6*, 18–21.

Yelland, N. (2001). *Teaching and learning with ICT for numeracy in the early childhood and the primary years of schooling*. Canberra, Australia: Department of Education, Training and Youth Affairs.

Yin, R. K. (2003). *Case Study Research, Design and Methods* (3rd ed.). Thousand Oaks, CA: Sage Publications.

Young, T. (2008). *Knowledge Management: For Services, Operations and Manufacturing*. Chandos Publishing.

Youtube. (2014). *Youtube Web Site*. Retrieved January 13, 2014, from http://youtube.com

Yuan, G. (2012, September 6). *Responses to questions at the Ministry of Education news conference*. Retrieved from http://www.moe.gov.cn/sofprogecslive/webcontroller.do?titleSeq=4305&gecsmessage=1

Yusuf, M. O. (2005). Information and Communication Technologies and Education: Analyzing the Nigerian National Policy for Information Technology. *International Education Journal, 6*(3), 316–321.

Zand, D. (1997). *The Leadership Triad: Knowledge, Trust and Power*. Oxford University Press.

Zhang, W. (2011). 我国开放大学的地位、理念和办学策略的探讨. [Positions, concepts and strategies of Chinese open universities]. *Distance Education in China, 6*.

Zhou, J. (2007). 现代远程教育—实现我国高等教育公平的砝码. [Contemporary distance education, a means to realize equity in Chinese higher education]. *Contemporary. Distance Education, 113*, 9–13.

Zilberberg, M. (2011). The clinical research enterprise: time to change course? *Journal of the American Medical Association, 305*(6), 604–605. doi:10.1001/jama.2011.104 PMID:21304086

Zwass, V. (2003). Electronic commerce and organizational innovation: Aspects and opportunities. *International Journal of Electronic Commerce, 7*(3), 7–38.

About the Contributors

Blessing F. Adeoye, PhD, is a Senior Lecturer in the Department of Science and Technology Education, Faculty of Education, University of Lagos, Nigeria. He obtained a Bachelor of Architecture in May 1990 at Southern University, Baton Rouge, LA; Master of Science (Technology Education) in June 1995 at Eastern Illinois University, Charleston, Illinois, and Doctor of Philosophy, Human Resource Education/Educational Technology at the University of Illinois in 2004. His areas of specialization and interests include integration of technology in the classroom, relationship between culture and technology, usability of e-learning system, and use of research to improve the quality of teaching and learning in schools. His most recent work has been in the area of educational technology, relationship between the use of technology and culture, e-learning, and using of social networking tools to support teaching and learning. He is an active member of numerous national and international organizations and has published extensively in both local and international journals.

Lawrence Tomei is Associate Provost for Academic Affairs and a Professor in Education at Robert Morris University. Born in Akron, Ohio, he earned a BSBA from the University of Akron (1972) and entered the US Air Force, serving until his retirement as a Lieutenant Colonel in 1994. Dr. Tomei completed his MPA and MEd at the University of Oklahoma (1975, 1978) and EdD from USC (1983). His articles and books on instructional technology include *Professional Portfolios for Teachers* (1999), *Teaching Digitally: Integrating Technology into the Classroom* (2001), *Technology Facade* (2002), *Challenges of Teaching with Technology across the Curriculum* (2003), and *Taxonomy for the Technology Domain* (2005).

* * *

Ayotunde Adebayo has over 25 years experience in manpower development. He is versed in using and optimizing computing tools in training sessions. He is a Certified Customer Service Strategy Consultant with focus on organizational development and use of Action Learning. He has trained extensively on IT, biometrics, due diligence, HR Best practices, performance management, governance, marketing, leadership, sales, strategy, and business management, and has attended workshops in several countries in Europe and Africa/Middle East. He has published several articles in business and academic journals. Ayotunde has a PhD and also lectures at the University of Lagos.

Stephen Oyeyemi Adenle is Senior Lecturer with the University of Lagos, Nigeria, and heads the Technological Education Unit of the Department of Science and Technology Education, University of Lagos. He has taught in different institutions of learning. He is a member of Nigerian Association of

Teachers of Technology (NATT), Science Teachers Association of Nigeria (STAN), Nigeria Vocational Association (NVA), and Educational Research Network for West and Central Africa (ERNWACA).

Egbe Adewole-Odeshi holds a Master's degree in Information Science from University of Ibadan. She is presently a Librarian 2 at Centre for Learning Resources (Covenant University Library).She is a Certified Librarian of the Librarians Registration Council of Nigeria (LRCN) and a member of the Nigeria Library Association (NLA). Her research interests include Web 2.0, e-resources, e-learning, the use of ICT in libraries, and many more.

J. O. Akinyemi is a lecturer at the Department of Epidemiology and Medical Statistics, University of Ibadan. He holds a Bachelor of Technology in Computer Science with a MSc and PhD in Medical Statistics. With expertise in study designs, data management, demographic techniques, and statistical analysis, he plays active roles in many multidisciplinary research projects. He is a member of the International Union for the Scientific Study of Population (IUSSP) among other professional organizations.

Abubakar Sadiq Bappah was born in Gombe, Gombe state of Nigeria on 25/11/1968 and is currently an Associate Professor of Technical and Engineering Education at the Faculty of Technology Education, Abubakar Tafawa Balewa University Bauchi, Nigeria. He holds a Bachelor Degree in Technical Education and an MEng and PhD in Electrical Engineering. He is a member Institute of Electrical Electronics Engineers (MIEEE) and Nigerian Association of Teachers of Technology (MNATT) as national vice president (North-East). His research interests include innovation strategies, system modeling and simulation, and technical, engineering education, and training. Dr. Bappah is happily married with children.

Anyikwa Egbichi Blessing is a lecturer in the Department of Adult Education at the University of Lagos, Nigeria. A lecturer in the Literacy and Non-Formal Unit and a Coordinator of the Adult Literacy Centre. She holds a bachelor degree in Adult Education from the University of Ibadan, a Master's degree in Adult and Non-Formal Education, and PhD in Adult Teaching Methodology and Literacy Education from the University of Lagos, Nigeria. She lectures and supervises research theses at the undergraduate and postgraduate levels. She is married with children.

Michele T. Cole, JD, PhD, Professor of Nonprofit Management at Robert Morris University, Moon Township, PA. Dr. Cole earned an AB in English Literature from Wheeling Jesuit University, a JD from Duquesne University, and a PhD in Public Administration with a concentration in Nonprofit Management from The University of Pittsburgh. Her research interests include enhancing online instruction and e-learning, capacity building in the nonprofit sector, legal issues in personnel management, and the application of technology to learning strategies.

Jenna Copper is an English teacher at Slippery Rock Area High School. She received her Bachelor of Arts degree in English Literature and Master of Education degree in English from Slippery Rock University of Pennsylvania. She completed her PhD in Instructional Management and Leadership from Robert Morris University. She is the creator of the Literary Theory Implementation (LTI) Model, a model designed to introduce multiple perspectives to students. She presented her model and training program at the Society for Information Technology and Teacher Education International Conference. Additionally, she has published articles and lesson plans based on her research in teaching multiple perspectives and applying ICT to education.

John DiMarco, PhD, is an Associate Professor of Communications at St. John's University in New York City. He is a speaker and writer who has authored four textbooks, published a host of academic chapters, and written articles for business and career publications including *Business News Daily*, socialhire.com, expertbeacon.com, and *T&D Magazine*. Dr. DiMarco contributes his expertise to the media and has been quoted in articles on foxbusinessnews.com, thestreet.com, and *Newsday*. He is the founder of portfoliovillage.com.

Simeon Dosunmu is a rare gem of academic excellence. He is a Senior Lecturer in Sociology of Education in the Department of Educational Foundations and Counselling Psychology, Faculty of Education, Lagos State University, Ojo. He currently serves as one of the Editors of the *Nigerian Journal of Sociology of Education*. He is a professionally Registered Teacher of the Federal Republic of Nigeria. He has published and co-authored books and articles locally and internationally.

Daniel Ekhareafo Ofomegbe hails from Ojah in Akoko-Edo Local Government Area of Edo State. He holds BA and MA degrees in Mass Communication from the Delta State University, Abraka and University of Nigeria, Nsukka, and a PhD in Mass Communication in view awaiting defence at the University of Uyo. His areas of interest include media studies, political communication, development communication, and communication research. He has published a number of articles both in local and international journals and co-authored two books: *Research Methods in Mass Communication* and *Dimensions of Community and Media Relations*. Currently, he teaches media courses at the department of Theatre Arts and Mass Communication, University of Benin.

Matthew D. Fazio (Doctoral Candidate, Duquesne University) is an adjunct professor at Robert Morris University and Point Park University. After attaining a Bachelor of Arts degree in English Studies from Robert Morris University and a Master of Arts degree in English Literature from Slippery Rock University, Fazio continued his education for a Doctor of Philosophy degree in Rhetoric at Duquesne University. His areas of research overlap his teaching experience including media ecology, existential phenomenology, and ethics.

Florence Folami is an associate professor at Millikin University, Decatur, Illinois and also a Lactation Consultant for St. Mary's Hospital, Decatur, Illinois. She is the founder and the coordinator of the breastfeeding support group, Decatur, Illinois. She is the president of board of directors of Family Advocacy of Champaign County in Champaign, Illinois. She also serves on other boards of organizations locally and globally. She holds PhD degrees in Public Health.

MaryEbele Idahosa hails from Benin, Oredo local Government Area of Edo State, Nigeria. She was educated at St. Bridig's Girls Grammar School, Asaba; OND Federal Polytechnic, Oko; BSc University of Benin; MLIS Nnamdi Azikiwe University Akwa, Nigeria. She is presently working in Benson Idahosa University Benin City as a graduate assistant in the university library. She has published some articles journal articles.

Jerome Idiegbeyan-Ose is presently Senior Librarian and head of Technical Services Section at Covenant University Library Nigeria; he has over 10 years of academic library working experience, a Certified Librarian of Nigeria (CLN), and is a member of the Nigerian Library Association. He has written some articles in both local and international journals; his research interests are ICTs application in libraries, information needs of users, digital library, and education. He co-authored a book chapter recently, titled "Librarian without Building in an E-Learning Environment: Needed Skills, Challenges, and Solutions," published by IGI Global.

Kingsley Nwadiuto Igwe is Lecturer in the Department of Library and Information Sciences, Akanu Ibiam Federal Polytechnic Unwana, Afikpo, Ebonyi State, Nigeria. He was formerly a lecturer at Federal Polytechnic Offa, Kwara State, and holds BLIS and MLIS degrees from Abia State University, Uturu, Nigeria. He has served as a college teacher, a college librarian, and with many years of experience spanning practice, teaching, and research, as well as many scholarly publications in national and international journals, academic conferences, chapter contributions in reputable books, and coauthored books to his credit. He has interests in the areas of knowledge management, e-learning, ICT in libraries and information centres, online and open educational resources, and open access model of scholarly communication, with deep concern on the state of as well as neglect of information literacy in Nigeria. He is Associate Editor, *Journal of SCIT* as well as *Middlebelt Journal of Library and Information Science*. He was an Adjunct Lecturer on Information Literacy Instruction at Metropolitan College of Operations Research and Management Sciences Offa, Nigeria.

Abdulwahab Olanrewaju Issa is Senior Lecturer and Head, Department of Library and Information Science, and Sub-Dean (Professional), Post Graduate School, University of Ilorin, Ilorin, Nigeria. With over two decades of experience, he holds DLS, BLS, MLS, and PhD degrees from Ahmadu Bello University, Zaria and University of Ibadan, Nigeria, respectively. He also holds a Postgraduate Diploma in Education from the National Teachers Institute, Kaduna, and Diploma in Desktop Publishing from Federal Polytechnic Offa, Nigeria. He started teaching at the Ahmadu Bello University, Zaria Library School in 1992 as Graduate Assistant and became Assistant Lecturer by 1996. He joined the Federal Polytechnic Offa Library School in 2000 (served as Head of Department: 2000-2004; Director, Centre for Continuing Education: 2004-2009; and left as Chief Lecturer in 2010); he taught at the Tai Solarin University of Education Ijagun, Ijebu Ode, Ogun State, and is currently appointed Adjunct Senior Lecturer at the Kwara State University Malete and registered with the Librarians Registration Council of Nigeria (2005) and Teachers Registration Council of Nigeria (2007). He was Vice-Chairman (2004-2006) and Chairman (2010-2012) of Kwara State Chapter of the Nigerian Library Association. He is at present the Editor-in-Chief of *Middlebelt Journal of Library and Information Science*.

Xiaobin Li is an associate professor at the Department of Graduate and Undergraduate Studies, Faculty of Education, Brock University in St. Catharines, Ontario, Canada. He received his BA in English from Anqing Teachers' College in China, MA in English from Fudan University in China, MEd in Educational Administration from Lakehead University in Canada, and PhD in Educational Administration from Ontario Institute for Studies in Education of the University of Toronto in Canada. His research interests include Chinese education, international education, information and communication technology in education, education finance, educational law, and quantitative methods in research.

Olumuyiwa Noah has a PhD in Sociology of Education from the University of Jos Nigeria. He teaches Political Economy of Education and Sociology of the Curriculum at the Lagos State University. Between 1998 and 2005, he was the Provost of Adeniran Ogunsanya College of Education, where he emphasized the legal aspects of business education. He is a member of the Lagos State Research and Development Council.

Bamidele O. Ogunlade obtained his BSc Ed in Auto-Mechanics/Metalwork, and MEd (Educational Technology) from the University of Ado-Ekiti (now Ekiti State University, Ado-Ekiti). He is currently working on his PhD, and he has researched and published both in national and international journals. He is a member of Nigeria Association for Educational Media and Technology (NAEMT).

Oladiran Stephen Olabiyi had his secondary education at Fiditi Grammar School, Fiditi, where he sat for West African Examination Council O/L. He holds Nigerian certificate in Education (Technical) in Woodwork/Technical Drawing from St. Andrew's College of Education, Oyo, now Emmanuel Alayande College of Education in 1993. He also attended Federal University of Technology, Minna, where he obtained a Bachelor degree in Woodwork Technology Education (BTech Ed Hons) in 1999. He is a product of University of Nigeria, Nsukka Enugu State, where he obtained his Master's degree and Doctor of Philosophy (MEd and PhD) in Industrial Technical Education in 2005 and 2009, respectively. He is currently teaching in University of Lagos, Faculty of Education, Department of Science and Technology Education. He is the author of numerous books, has published refereed articles, and national and international journals. He is a member of different professional associations, some of which include Nigeria Association of Teachers Technology (NATT), Nigeria Association of Engineering Craftsman (NAEC), International Research and Development Institute, and Nigeria Vocational Association (NVA). He is an editorial member of NATT. He is happily married, and the union is blessed with children.

Nwachukwu Prince Ololube, PhD, is a Senior Lecturer in the Department of Educational Foundations and Management, Faculty of Education, University of Education, Port Harcourt, Nigeria. He holds a PhD in Education and Teacher Education with focus in Educational Management and Planning/ Curriculum Studies from the University of Helsinki, Finland. He also holds a post-graduate diploma in Human Resources Management, a Masters of Education in Educational Management and Planning, and a Bachelors of Science in Political Science. His research focuses on institutional management and leadership, education effectiveness, instructional effectiveness and quality improvement, ICT in education, adult and non-formal education, and research methodologies. Dr. Ololube has published 5 books, presented at various international conferences, and contributed chapters to a number of books and encyclopedias. In all, he has authored and co-authored more than 70 publications. His professional contributions include Editor-in-Chief, *International Journal of Scientific Research in Education* (IJSRE), Editor, *International Journal of Educational Research* (IJER), Managing Editor, *International Journal of Educational Foundations and Management* (IJEFM), Editorial Board Member, *The International Journal of Economics, Education and Development* (IJEED), International Editorial Review Board Member, *International Journal of Information and Communications Technology Education* (IJICTE), and Editorial Board Member, *Journal of Information Systems Education* (JISE).

Adesoji Oni is a senior lecturer in the Department of Educational Foundations, Faculty of Education, University of Lagos, Nigeria. He specializes in Sociology of Education. His areas of research focus include social problems in education, social change in education, social deviances/social disorganizations in education with particular focus on students' secret cult in Nigeria. He has published widely in these areas.

Adekunle Olusola Otunla is a Research Fellow at the Institute of Education, University of Ibadan, Nigeria. He holds a Bachelor of Education in Educational Technology, MEd and PhD degrees in Educational Technology. His areas of research activity cover communication media and technology/ICT integration, design and development of multimedia courseware for teaching and learning in higher education, as well as Vocational and Technology Education and Training (VTET).

Oyekunle Oyelami (PhD) holds a BEd (Hons) Political Science, MEd and PhD in Community Development from the University of Ibadan, Nigeria. He lectures at the University of Lagos, Akoka, Nigeria, in the Department of Adult Education. His areas of specialization are community development, social welfare, and social work. He has published widely in learned journals in his areas of specialization in both local and international journals. He is an active member of NNCAE and Community Development Association.

Daniel J. Shelley, PhD, University Professor of Education at Robert Morris University, Moon Township, PA. Dr. Shelley earned his BS in Elementary Education from Penn State University in 1971. He completed a Master's Degree in Social Science with an emphasis in American History at Penn State in 1972. He earned his PhD in Education at the University of Pittsburgh in 1986. Dr. Shelley is also a certified Elementary Principal and a Curriculum Program Specialist. His research interests include enhancing pre-service teacher's skills and expertise in applying educational technology to their teaching along with online and blended learning.

Louis B. Swartz, JD, Professor of Legal Studies at Robert Morris University, Moon Township, PA. Mr. Swartz teaches Legal Environment of Business and The Constitution and Current Legal Issues at the undergraduate level and Legal Issues of Executive Management in the MBA program. He received his Bachelor's degree from the University of Wisconsin in Madison, Wisconsin (1966) and his Juris Doctorate from Duquesne University in Pittsburgh, PA (1969). He is the Coordinator of the Robert Morris University Pre-Law Advisory Program and a member of the Northeast Association of Pre-Law Advisers (NAPLA). His research interests include online education, legal studies, and business law.

Oroboh Ambrose Uchenunu holds a BA Theatre Arts, University of Calabar, MA Theatre Arts, University of Ibadan in Nigeria; MA and PhD Film Studies at the University of Nottingham, and Diplomas in Film and Television Productions and C&G Teacher Training at New College Nottingham in the United Kingdom. Currently, he teaches film and electronic media at the University of Benin, Benin City. He has published essays from his doctoral thesis, which studies the history of the decline of cinema in Nigeria. He has been a member of college of screener for Africa Movie Academy Awards (AMAA) for four years in a row. He is fascinated with the study of feminism of late and has delivered numerous talks in that regard in conferences spanning Nigeria, the United States, and the United Kingdom. He is from Ibrede (Isoko speaking) in Ndokwa-East LG of Delta State.

Jennifer N. L. Ughelu is a PhD researcher at the University of Lagos, and a part-time Lecturer at the Federal College of Education, Akoka, Lagos, Nigeria. She is a member of Nigerian Association of Educational Media Technology (NAEMT).

Zhonggen Yu (于中根), male, PhD, associate professor/post-doctor in Hohai University, Zhejiang Yuexiu University of Foreign Languages, a post-doctor in Post-Doctoral Research Station of Psychology, School of Psychology, Nanjing Normal University, and Tongda College of Nanjing University of Posts and Telecommunications. Born in May, 1973, he is interested in use of technologies in education and applied linguistics. He obtained both a Master's degree in Law and a Master's degree in Foreign Languages Linguistics and Applied Linguistics, coupled with a PhD degree in English Linguistics.

Index

A

B

C

D

E

F

G

CPSIA information can be obtained
at www.ICGtesting.com
Printed in the USA
BVOW03*0653120517

482889BV00013B/39/P